THE PAKISTAN MILITARY IN POLITICS

THE PAKISTAN MILITARY IN POLITICS

Origins, Evolution, Consequences

Ishtiaq Ahmed

AMARYLLIS

AMARYLLIS

This edition first published 2013
Second impression 2013

AMARYLLIS

An imprint of Manjul Publishing House Pvt. Ltd.
7/32, Ansari Road, Daryaganj,
New Delhi 110 002
Email: amaryllis@amaryllis.co.in
Website: amaryllis.co.in

Registered Office:
10, Nishat Colony, Bhopal 462 003

ISBN: **978-93-81506-29-5**

Printed and Bound in India by
Gopsons Papers Ltd.

Indian edition - For sale only in India

Contents

Preface

In December 2008, I met General Pervez Musharraf at the Chief of Army Staff (COAS) House in Rawalpindi. The meeting was arranged by a mutual friend, Colonel (Retd.) Aslam Cheema. Musharraf had only recently stepped down as president of Pakistan. We had a very pleasant conversation for about an hour. The bottom line, in his review of the situation, was that as long as the Pakistan military was strong the existence and integrity of Pakistan were assured. Some would question that thesis keeping in mind what happened in the former East Pakistan in 1971, when it broke away after a bitter and bloody civil war. Musharraf was probably thinking of the Pakistan that survived in the western wing, where the real strength of the Pakistan military has always resided.

It is, however, doubtful if the strong military imperative must necessarily translate into a culture of militarisation of state and society. That is exactly what has happened. Since at least the 1980s, radical political Islam has been at the forefront of Pakistan's external and internal politics. A visitor to Pakistan cannot but notice that Islamist rhetoric has profoundly affected society, creating a 'mind-set' that is violence prone. Terrorism is salient and wrecks lives continually in contemporary Pakistan. Government offices and buildings, with armed guards posted all-round, are a common sight. However, such measures are not confined to government offices. In early March 2011, I visited Karachi, Lahore, and Islamabad and found security guards armed with automatic firearms posted at superior hotels, private firms, and businesses. Similar scenes can be seen in the Indian capital, New Delhi, but the security arrangements are subdued and there is no official patronage of a culture of militarisation.

In Pakistan, the feeling that Pakistan is a 'fortress of Islam' has been cultivated as part of the national identity. Why? This question becomes all the more intriguing and perplexing when Pakistani census claims that, at least since 1971, Muslims constitute a solid and overwhelming majority of at least ninety-six percent. Such a compact majority—if ideological rhetoric about Muslim nationalism and Islamic Ummah is to be believed—should have ensured cultural and religious cohesiveness, social peace, and solidarity. That, however, is not the case. Who then poses the existentialist threat to Pakistan?

Looking around for possible candidates that could harbour nefarious intentions and designs on Pakistan, one must first discount some typical bogeys. For example, one does not find a Communist insurgency in Pakistan comparable to the Naxalite movement in present-day India. Neither is there a separatist movement comparable to the Spanish Euskadi Ta Askatasuna (ETA) or the militant factions of the Irish Republican Army (IRA) that some years ago were able to strike targets on a recurring basis all over Spain and the United Kingdom, respectively. There is a bleeding insurgency going on in Balochistan at present but the Baloch guerrillas have kept their ambit of activities confined to their province thus far.

In psycho-ideological terms, however, the Pakistan nation has been fed, since the early twenty-first century, on propaganda that a grand conspiracy hatched by Hanud-Yahud-Ansara (Hindus, Jews, and Christians) exists. In a nutshell, the argument is that since Pakistan is the only Islamic nation that possesses nuclear bombs, it is on the hit-list of all those forces hell-bent on reducing Muslims to subjugation and slavery, and thus subverting the triumph of Islam in all the nooks and corners of the world. Such an idea is extremely tempting to anyone who believes in the eternal conflict between Dar-ul-Islam and Dar-ul-Harb.

Indeed, conspiracies against Pakistan may exist, but it can also be a self-fulfilling prophecy. What cannot be denied, however, is that most, if not all, acts of violence and terrorism that spill blood in Pakistan are home-grown. Home-grown terrorism, in turn, comprises different factions and groups with anti-minority, anti-women, and patently sectarian and sub-sectarian agendas. Since at least December 2003, when an assassination attempt was made on General Pervez Musharraf, Pakistani officials and government installations and buildings, including those of the armed forces, have been the objects of vicious terrorist attacks by home-grown extremist organisations on the grounds that by joining the Bush administration's so-called 'war on terror', the Pakistani rulers have betrayed global jihad.

Home-grown terrorists cannot possible hit targets all over society without some help and assistance from rogue elements within the security and military forces, both serving and retired. Therefore, defeating the real or imaginary conspiracy against Pakistan requires that home-grown terrorist cells and networks are uprooted and destroyed.

It is possible that if Pakistan can successfully deal with terrorism at home, and learns to behave responsibly in the regional and international domains, the perceived international detractors of Pakistan can be persuaded to change their attitude towards it. After all, Pakistan is a nuclear power and it is never going to be easy to treat it unfairly if it is willing to adhere to the rules of the game, which apply under international law in regard to relations between states. On the other hand, the constant violation of the rules of the game by a state is a sure recipe for conspiracies to be plotted against it by those who feel threatened by it. It is, of course, not as simple as that but more or less this is how states behave in the international arena. There are very few permanent friends and permanent enemies in the international system of states.

Pakistan's geostrategic location has, in the past, been appreciated narrowly in military and security terms by both the Pakistani power elite and the major powers and superpowers. In this study, the military and security aspect is dealt with at great length. However, one can change the focus to more lucrative ends as well. The twenty-first century is being celebrated as the Asian Century. Actually, the Asian Century began to gestate in the 1960s and, ironically, Pakistan was one of the earliest beneficiaries. In the first half of the 1960s, its economy performed so well that it won admirers in several Southeast Asian countries which studied its industrial planning and later became engines of economic growth.

It all started, however, farther away in East Asia. Japan, ravaged and destroyed during the Second World War, rose from the ashes to become the paragon power-horse of industrial and economic development in the early 1960s. From the 1970s onwards, several Southeast Asian countries embarked upon a transformation that earned them the title of 'Asian Tigers'. China followed suit in the 1980s, and it is now the second largest power of the world. India jumped onto the bandwagon of economic development in the 1990s and has been performing impressively. It seems that the movement of economic growth and development in Asia is following a westerly direction;

now, it is Pakistan's turn to benefit from it.

Pakistan's ideal geographical location qualifies it to partake in the new opportunities that are currently available. Nations have to seize the moment that history, or rather the historical moment, offers—that moment seems to be now for Pakistan. Pakistan's cultural and religious links with West Asia and Central Asia can be enviable assets, especially with regard to the emerging Central Asian republics where the situation is of a virgin nature. Pakistan's professionals, semi-skilled and unskilled workers can be interesting for many markets in Central Asia. Admittedly, the situation in Afghanistan is currently bad, and Iran and Saudi Arabia are hurdles to the normalisation of politics in the Persian Gulf, but that is not necessarily the situation in Central Asia. Therefore Pakistan need not wait for some ideal or optimal situation to come about. It can decide to opt out of ideological politics in favour of enlightened pragmatism. For such transformation to succeed, a lot needs to be done within Pakistan. In this inquiry, those problematic aspects are identified and analysed in an historical perspective. This study covers the events till the end of December 2011.

One thing needs to be noted with regard to the references from newspapers: I have referred to their online editions. They are easily accessible in the archives maintained by the newspapers on the Internet.

Ishtiaq Ahmed
Sollentuna (Greater Stockholm)
24 February 2012

1

The Fortress of Islam: A Metaphor for a Garrison State

This study seeks to solve the following puzzle: in 1947, the Pakistan military was poorly armed and lacked the infrastructure and training needed to function as an effective branch of the state. It was not directly involved in politics. Over time, not only has it become a middle-range power possessing nuclear weapons, it has also become the most powerful institution in the country with de facto veto powers over politics. How and why did this happen and what were its consequences? The clues are to be found in a unique mix of real and imagined existentialist threats to Pakistan, and the nature of international politics in which the emerging bipolar rivalry between the United States of America and the former Union of Soviet Socialist Republics was exploited by the Pakistani rulers – civil and military – to market Pakistan as a frontline state against the latter in the hope that the former would supply them with the weapons needed to offset the advantage India enjoyed over it in terms of size, resources, and other such factors. Internally, incompetent politicians and their factionalism generated conflict and instability while the civil servants, and later the military, came to represent stability. Additionally, a lack of clarity on national identity drove Pakistan towards a search for an Islamic identity that should also be democratic. However, over time, this acquired more and more dogmatic features and fundamentalist overtones. The convergence of such external and internal factors created the metaphor of Pakistan being a fortress of Islam.

I first heard the phrase 'fortress of Islam', in relation to Pakistan, at the end of 2001 or early 2002 when more than a million Indian and Pakistani troops were amassed on their mutual international border as well as the Line of Control (LoC) in the divided Jammu and Kashmir state. This unprecedented mobilisation had been provoked because some militants, allegedly linked to Pakistan, attempted a daring attack on the Indian Parliament while it was in session. The terrorists failed to enter Parliament House but six policemen, one civilian, and five raiders were killed in the shootout. The Indian government was furious, and the Indian media and political parties reacted with great revulsion to the atrocity and called for revenge. Another war between the two major South Asian nations seemed imminent. All-out war between the two nuclear powers would have rendered large parts of the subcontinent uninhabitable for thousands of years. Bill Clinton observed that, in case of a nuclear war between the two rivals, India could wipe out 120 million of Pakistan's 170 million population but not before 500 million of its own citizens were annihilated (Jha 2009).

Dressed in full military attire, with all his medals pinned on smartly, General Pervez Musharraf addressed the Pakistani nation on national television. He assured the people that their armed forces were fully prepared to face any threat or aggression from India. In doing so, he used the expression 'Pakistan Islam ka qila hai' (Pakistan is the fortress of Islam). That struck me as peculiar since Musharraf generally avoided Islamist jargon but, on that occasion, took recourse to what the Islamists and ultra-nationalists had been cultivating for a long time: that Pakistan represented a superior military tradition, historically and contemporaneously, though as far as the latter part of the claim was concerned it was quite unwarranted given the history of India–Pakistan armed encounters. Had war broken out, it would have been the fifth military confrontation between the two countries since August 1947 – when both gained independence as a result of the partition of British India. From its very inception, Pakistan has been beset by the question of security: India has been identified, historically, as the villain of the piece, and Afghanistan its sidekick if ruled by hostile forces demanding a redrawing of the Afghanistan–Pakistan border. Indeed, the feeling of being beleaguered is imperative in order to construct a strong and formidable fortress – a garrison; the Pakistani establishment staked its dominant position in Pakistani society by prioritising security and defence.

Now, the metaphor 'for tress of Islam' carries multi-layered connotations in both Urdu and English. Musharraf had most likely used it to underline the Pakistan military's role as the core element in the composition of a fortress.

A qila, or fortress, includes not only the armed soldiers but also those who live inside it and perform multifarious civilian tasks and functions and thus constitute a viable community. It is, ipso facto, a garrison community, vigilant and armed to defend and assert its independence, to thwart aggression, and to carry out punitive actions against enemies. Simultaneously, a garrison is also an outpost of a state, kingdom, or empire. Historically, garrison towns were set up by empires to guard their frontiers. In fact, empires themselves represented proto-garrison states (Yong 2005); during the Cold War, garrison states emerged as part of the global contest between the United States and the Soviet Union.

Pakistan became a beneficiary of the Cold War military contest between the two rival superpowers, the United States and the Soviet Union, by aligning militarily with the former. The initiative to solicit the United States' help came from the Pakistani power elite, both civil and military. Initially, the Americans were not keen as the focus was then on Western Europe, and the United States was involved in building an alliance in that theatre. It was consummated with the establishment of the North Atlantic Treaty Organization (NATO). However, relentless lobbying by Pakistan finally convinced the Americans to co-opt Pakistan into their worldwide strategy to contain the spread of Soviet communism. The fact that Indian Prime Minister Jawaharlal Nehru decided not to align with either of the superpowers (Ganguly 2010: 1–2) inadvertently helped Pakistan's case for co-optation by the United States in its policy of containing communism. It began with a first consignment of armament in 1951, followed by formal military alliances in 1954 and 1959. During the 1960s, that alliance became more or less dormant as mistrust and misgivings emerged between the two sides.

Consequently, Pakistan sought to develop a strategic understanding with China, which in turn had strained relations with India. Later, further diversification of dependence was attempted by Pakistan – on Saudi Arabia. The three donors represented very different ideologies: the United States as the leader of the capitalist-liberal world, China as the challenger to Soviet domination within the Communist movement, and Saudi Arabia as the leader of Islamic fundamentalism. The Communist takeover of power in Afghanistan in 1978, the capturing of power by the Shiite Ayatollahs in Iran, and the arrival of the Red Army in Afghanistan vigorously revived the Pakistan–US alliance. This time around, a very prominent Saudi and a significant, though less visible, Chinese partnership was informally added to that alliance. While the United States and China were in it because of an overriding anti-Soviet agenda, the United States joined forces with Saudi Arabia to contain the spread of Iranian millenarian Islam as well. All three donors could realise their objectives via Pakistan. This created a situation that the Pakistani power elite tried to exploit to its advantage: to what extent it succeeded in that endeavour will be assessed in the course of this investigation.

Suffice it to say that at least from the 1980s onwards, hawkish Pakistani military officers began to nurture a vision of Pakistan that went beyond the confines of the territorial nation-state. Along with hard-core Islamists, the hawks began to imagine Pakistan as a great, expansive, regional power extending to Western and Central Asia and a liberated Kashmir free from Indian occupation. More ambitious projections of such an ambition were about Pakistan serving as the launch pad for a worldwide jihad (holy war) to restore the caliphate that once represented Muslim power in world politics but had been in decline since at least the nineteenth century. That caliphate had been abolished in 1924 by the Turkish reformer Mustafa Kemal Ataturk. It is important to note that such pan-Islamist ambitions began to be nurtured in a world order that no longer permitted military expansion and empire-building.

Pan-Islamism was, therefore, incongruent with the post-Second World War world order based on the presumption of the legal equality of all states. Territorial ambiguity was to be eliminated and replaced by states with clear demarcation of their boundaries. In reality, however, the international system lacked a chain of command comparable to the structure of power and authority within states. Rather, the international system represented global and regional asymmetries of power. The two superpowers – the United States and the Soviet Union – and several major powers, middle-range powers, small states, and banana republics presented scope for manoeuvre and re-adjustment. Such an international system was anarchic, notwithstanding the presumptions of a stable world order.

The worldwide Islamist revival in the wake of the Afghan jihad rendered Pakistan a key player in the imagination of those Muslims seeking the creation of an Islamic super-state in southern, central, and portions of western, Asia as preparatory to the resurrection of the universal caliphate. Consequently, a possible connotation of the metaphor about the fortress of Islam could be that not only did such forces aspire that Pakistan should be an independent sovereign state, both militarily vigilant and strong, but also a champion ready to take on any threats faced by the universal Muslim Ummah. Whether this was sheer bluster on the part of Musharraf, or delusion on the part of the wider Islamist and ultra-nationalist lobbies in Pakistan, or a serious assertion of the role they wanted to ascribe to Pakistan in regional and world politics is beside the point. In political terms, such imagination ascribed a deeper ideological connotation to the 'fortress of Islam'.

That trend has grown over time and acquired virtually pathological dimensions. With few exceptions, contemporary Pakistani talk shows churn out such images as variations on the 'fortress' theme many times a day. Right-wing political parties and leaders, as well as journalists, revel in peddling such images. Pakistani textbooks are replete with the glorification of Muslims who defeated Hindus in the past, as well as the celebration of spectacular successes supposedly won by Pakistan over India on the battlefield since 1947. At the core is the emphasis on maintaining a powerful military. Such militaristic imagery has, over time, earned Pakistan the reputation of being the epicentre of international terrorism, a rogue state, and similar sensational descriptions. That such grand visions of military greatness were imagined while Pakistan largely remained an underdeveloped and poor nation, nowhere near the take-off stage of economic transformation as an industrial and military power that could sustain regional or worldwide jihad, was indicative of the profound hold that an idealised past could exercise to generate delusions of grandeur.

Pakistani Analysts

Ayesha Jalal (1990), Hasan-Askari Rizvi (2000, 2003), Husain Haqqani (2005), Hassan Abbas (2005), Ahmed Rashid (2009), Zahid Hussain (2008), and Shuja Nawaz (2008) have produced empirically rich studies on the rise of the military as the most powerful institution in Pakistan. In reality, it is the very large Pakistan Army that calls the shots; the air force and the navy are much smaller forces. Such militarism has been accompanied by the appropriation of a substantial chunk of the meagre scarce resources of the poor and underdeveloped country by its armed forces. Thus, for example, a twelve percent hike in expenditure on defence has been included in the budget for

2011–12. Raja Muhammad Khan has argued that despite the increase, it is a decline in military spending from 2.6 percent for 2010–11 to 2.4 percent of the Gross Domestic Product (GDP). He argues that while threats to Pakistan's existence continue to be posed by India, which has constantly been modernizing its armed forces and greatly increasing spending on them – $34 billion as compared to Pakistan's $5.57 billion – Pakistan's economy cannot sustain an arms race and therefore must instead focus on maintaining a credible deterrent (meaning nuclear weapons and missile technology) (Khan 2011). Ahmad Faruqui (2003) has made a similar recommend at ion, emphasising a smaller but better trained and equipped army.

It is to be noted that in March 2011, the Stockholm International Peace Research Institute (SIPRI) described India as the largest importer of arms in the international market (SIPRI, 14 March 2011). From the Pakistani point of view, it meant a heightened threat from India; hence the emphasis on security remaining paramount and so also the increasing expenditure it entails. However, defence spending needs to be put into perspective by relating it to spending on health and education. In 2009, Pakistan spent 23.1 percent on defence, and only 1.3 percent on health and 7.8 percent on education. In comparison, India spent 18.6 percent on defence, 3.4 percent on health, and 12.7 percent on education. Most developed countries maintain a balance between defence and development or welfare spending; many developing countries are able to do the same (Visual Economics 2010). However, this is not true of Pakistan and India – though the latter has a much bigger economic base to support its defence expenditure. Both are guilty of gross neglect of the basic social and economic rights of their citizens. However, while the Indian economy has been performing impressively for several years, this is not true for Pakistan. In the third annual report, released by the Lahore-based Institute of Public Policy on 1 June 2010, it was noted that the Pakistan economy was in a terrible shape. The authors noted: 'Of prime concern is the near total breakdown in the delivery of basic public services like power, gas and water' (IPP's Third Annual Report 2010: 3). The ruling class pays little or no taxes, especially the powerful landowners, while enjoying luxury, privileges, and perks (ibid.). It is the urban middle and lower-middle classes that have to cope with no respite from the soaring heat during the summers; it is industry that remains at a standstill during the frequent load-shedding, thus exacerbating the abject poverty, illiteracy, and disease afflicting huge portions of the population.

Mazhar Aziz's (2008) point of departure in explaining the domination of the Pakistan military is institutional theory and the concomitant path-dependency it entails. The argument is that if civil institutions are not firmly anchored in the polity, the state apparatus represented by the military and civil bureaucracy come to dominate the political system. Such domination means the military manages the civil affairs of the state as well. As a result, civil institutions suffer diminution of authority and fail to entrench. Once that happens, a path is established that the polity later follows.

Ayesha Siddiqa has propounded a political economy basis to explain the domination of the military. She developed a framework, deriving from Hamza Alavi's notion of a post-colonial state, in which she has demonstrated that the political economy of the military's so-called institutional interests in actual practice means control by senior military officers over vast economic and financial sources through ownership of agricultural land, real estate, businesses, and industrial enterprises. Such control over the economy means that even when the military is not directly in power, the higher officer class is able to wield enormous influence in Pakistani politics. Thus, the higher military officers' interests become institutional interests and are conflated with the interests of the nation. She has estimated that the legally acquired assets of the generals vary from ₹150 to 400 million; indirect economic power would be much greater. She has asserted that their active involvement in the development of real estate has made them the new land barons of Pakistan (2007: 174–205).

The Post-Colonial State Hypothesis

In his essay, 'The State in Post-Colonial Societies: Pakistan and Bangladesh' (1972) – premised on the neo-Marxist dependency school of political economy that identified a global structure of capitalism centred on the United States, with the underdeveloped nations of Asia, Africa, and Latin America as the periphery – Hamza Alavi sought to explain the peculiar balance of power between the classes and the post-colonial state. Classic Marxist theory of the state is premised on the assumption that the state is merely an instrument of exploitation in the hands of the ruling class. However, during crises, the state could assume relative autonomy vis-à-vis the classes and mediate their interests. In contrast, Alavi asserted that the relative autonomy of the state was a constant in post-colonial states such as Pakistan. Arguing thus, he observed that Pakistan represented a continuation of the colonial imbalance between state and society, the former being more developed than the latter. Additionally, the political party that demanded, and won, Pakistan was essentially a one-man show with the founder of Pakistan, Mohammad Ali Jinnah, enjoying supreme powers. After his death, the Muslim League quickly disintegrated and, therefore, could not establish civilian hegemony. As a result, the civil service and the military – two institutions established by British colonialism in India – became the institutions that constituted an oligarchy that came to dominate both politics and economics. Because of his structuralist framework, Alavi, in passing, noted that the domination of the oligarchy began at the very onset – although he does not provide empirical evidence to support it. In any case, Alavi argued that the oligarchy enjoyed relative autonomy vis-à-vis the metropolitan neo-colonialist bourgeoisie (Western capitalism centred on the United States) and the two indigenous exploitative classes, consisting of the Pakistani bourgeoisie and the landowners. Such autonomy enabled the oligarchy to mediate between their interests, which no longer conflicted but were complementary: all three classes exploited and appropriated the surplus produced by the labour of the Pakistani workers and peasants. Further, he argued that the two indigenous classes – the Pakistani bourgeoisie and the landowners – were 'underdeveloped'. In doing so, he contrasted the bourgeoisie in the West, which led the struggle for democracy, with the bourgeoisie of a post-colonial state such as Pakistan, which needs the state to restrict democracy in order to grow and expand. As regards the landowning class, there is no historical record of it leading the struggle for democracy anywhere and, therefore, Alavi must be thinking essentially about the Pakistani bourgeoisie in relation to democracy. Proceeding further, the author makes useful distinctions between right-wing conservative generals, radical left and right-wing elements, and hawks. Each category of military personnel was linked to different classes and class fractions. He noted that the radicals had mostly been of the right-wing persuasion. The hawks represented those elements that were interested in maintaining and guarding the interests of the army (ibid., 67–69).

Alavi hinted at, but did not develop and work out, the political implications and ramifications of a post-colonial oligarchy's relative autonomy in relation to international capitalism during the Cold War. Also, the significance of the Cold War during that period did not receive much attention from him. Moreover, a problem with the dependency perspective, subscribed to by Alavi, was that it assumed a rather fixed structure of exploitation of the periphery by the centre.

Such a perspective, therefore, depreciated and thus obfuscated the ideological and military competition that was going on during the Cold War. Equally, it did not take into account the anarchic nature of international relations. Pakistan came to play an important role in that competition. Its importance lay not in providing a surplus to imperialism but in being of vital geostrategic importance to the Cold War. Moreover, even as a post-colonial state, Pakistan's location in South Asia, far away from the United States, enabled it to enjoy considerable autonomy, when compared to Latin American countries that were in the backyard, so to say, of the United States. In the overall dynamics of the Cold War, and the variability in the international system, a scope for diversification of dependence and concomitant alliance-building existed – which the Pakistani state took advantage of, though such room for manoeuvre did not detract from its post-colonial dependency vis-à-vis the United States and, later, other major players as well.

Towards a Theoretical Framework

Samuel Edward Finer's famous *The Man on Horseback: The Military in Politics*, published originally in 1962 and revised in 1976, drew attention to the fact that military coups were taking place in states that were neither liberal democracies nor communist, but were autocracies and oligarchies. Many states in Asia, Africa, and Latin America fitted that description. The military took over the reins of power in such countries because it possessed superior organisation and armaments. It could ensure stability and security, if not democratic freedom. So, according to Finer, military takeovers are facilitated when, instead of democracy, autocratic and oligarchic regimes exist. This makes a great deal of sense as Pakistan has failed to develop into a modern democracy. Not only that, but radicalism, extremism, and terrorism have undermined Pakistan's chances of becoming a credible moderate Muslim state.

All such outcomes were poorly anticipated by the Western development theory of the 1960s. On the contrary, the military was conceived of as a modernising force in countries deficient in a strong middle class. Samuel Huntington, an influential proponent of such a view, asserted that in poor, resource-deficient societies lacking a strong middle class and entrepreneurial skills, the men in uniform could become the agents of economic and social development as well as of political stability and institution-building (Huntington 1962: 32–5). However, he made the incisive observation: 'Prolonged military participation in politics inevitably means the military reflect the divisions, stresses, and weaknesses of politics' (ibid., 36). Huntington never addressed the deeper ideological and cultural roots of military power and prestige. On the other hand, the connection that Finer made between autocracy and the rise of the military opens avenues for probing the deeper historical, cultural, structural, and ideological factors of Pakistani autocracy.

The National Security State

The National Security State Doctrine was established by the US National Security Act of 1947, during Harry Truman's presidency, as the beginning of an assault on the New Deal state his predecessor had established, as well as a worldwide offensive to contain the spread of communism and Soviet influence. Jack Nelson-Pallmeyer identified seven characteristics of the national security state as it evolved internationally with US assistance:

1. The military is the highest authority. It claims the role of the guardian of national interest and extends its influence over political, economic, and military affairs.
2. A national security state views democracy with suspicion. Even if a façade of democracy is maintained formally, real powers reside with the military.
3. The military wields substantial political and economic power.
4. Such a state is obsessed with enemies, both external as well as internal.
5. Enemies are described as cunning and ruthless. Therefore, all means to crush them are considered legitimate.
6. The national security state restricts public debate and limits popular participation through secrecy or intimidation.
7. It expects the church to mobilise its financial, ideological, and

> theological resources to support the national security state (Nelson-Pallmeyer 1993: 35–40).

Nelson-Pallmeyer asserted that while the United States justified its invasion of Iraq in 1991 as punishment for Saddam Hussain's invasion of Kuwait – because he had disturbed the regional and international peace – it itself was, simultaneously, deeply involved in subversive warfare in Central America, which made the economies of that region crumble and caused widespread misery and poverty. Even in the United States, poverty has been aggravated while enormous wealth concentrated in fewer hands than before (ibid., 18–32).

The Garrison State Concept

It seems Nelson-Pallmeyer was not familiar with an almost identical concept – of the garrison state – advanced by Harold Lasswell in the late 1930s, which the latter further developed in the backdrop of the rising tide in Nazi Germany. The advantage with the garrison state concept is that Lasswell vividly depicted the social and cultural characteristics of the specialists on violence – the military – who dominate society. Thus, it furnishes an opportunity to probe the role of religious-cultural traditions as well. In this regard, it is worth recalling that Max Weber had made a very incisive observation that the warrior class came to dominate Muslim societies at a very early stage, with the result that the erstwhile trader's value system that the Prophet Muhammad (PBUH) represented was eclipsed and receded into the background (Weber 1993: 262–3). Moreover, the garrison state concept links up with the indigenous historical roots of the Pakistani garrison state from the pre-colonial and colonial periods. In other words, the domination of the Pakistan military cannot be explained merely as an effect of the Cold War; rather, it is a peculiar evolution of historical and contemporaneous internal and external factors, as well as religious-cultural and social dimensions.

Pre-Colonial Garrison Towns

In the ancient and medieval periods, when states were not yet established in the formal sense of fixed territorial entities, large kingdoms and empires were sustained garrison towns playing a central role in that decentralised structure of power. The Roman Empire was maintained over a number of centuries because of the strong garrison towns that represented Roman power in distant lands far removed from Rome. Ultimately, those garrison towns sought to reproduce the supremacy of Rome over the subject people in the lands conquered by the Roman armies. In the conquest of northern India by the Turco–Afghans during the eleventh to thirteenth centuries, garrison towns manned by Muslim–Turkish horse-troops, many of them slaves, played a pivotal role. The troops were small in number and represented a monetised type of economy and wealth transactions, whereas the vast peasantry that surrounded the garrison towns lived a separate, detached life subsisting on a natural economy. Few of the latter had converted to Islam at that time; their conversion to Islam picked up pace sometime from the sixteenth century onwards (Wink 1997). The garrison towns 'became the fulcrum of both the sedentary world of nomadic, mobile wealth and expansion' (ibid., 212). The garrison towns were not necessarily located on the frontiers; rather, they were the embattled arena in which 'fusion of settled society and frontier ultimately took place' (ibid.).

Garrisons continued to be part of the Mughal Empire as well as of the Indian British Empire. In the contemporary period, garrison outposts and towns continue to be found in India and Pakistan. Their main function has been to keep centrifugal tendencies in the outlying provinces and regions in check – in particular, to curb separatism and secessionism. Such places represent urban paraphernalia, with its trappings of modernity and centrism that clash with the power and influence of the traditional tribal and clan chiefs. Pakistan inherited several garrison forts in Baluchistan and the North-West Frontier Province (NWFP) from the British Raj. Their numbers have grown, as have some new ones been established in Sindh as well.

The British Indian Empire: A Garrison State

Unlike most historians and political scientists who emphasise the role of civilian institutions in the sustenance of the British Indian Empire, Tan Tai Yong has argued that British rule in India was mediated through a garrison state. The British were fully aware of the fact that they ruled India through force, and could hold on to it for the same reason (Yong 2005: 23). Therefore, they needed to maintain a strong and formidable British Indian Army. Recruited locally, but mainly under the command of British officers, the British Indian Army comprised select castes belonging to specific regions (ibid., 57–97). Moreover, from the second half of the nineteenth century, the fear of a Russian advance into India began to haunt British strategic planning. Because of its geographical location, the Punjab in north-western India became the natural frontline province from which the British partook in the Great Game against perceived Russian threats (ibid., 69). Consequently, a strong but dependent army, with a large Punjabi component, was raised. It was sent to serve in foreign lands and took part in both the First and Second World Wars.

The political linchpins of British rule in the Punjab were the Punjabi landlords, the vast majority of whom were Muslims. They were staunch supporters of the Raj. Pakistan inherited a large portion of that army and, indeed, the powerful Muslim landlord class of Punjab that had been loyal to British rule until almost the end of the colonial era (ibid., 240–80). That garrison state began to weaken as the two competing nationalist movements – led by the Indian National Congress (INC) and by the Muslim League – could not agree on a power sharing formula to keep India united. Not only did it culminate in the division of India, but also in a bloody partition of the Punjab. Participation of demobilised Punjabi soldiers in the communal rioting was a conspicuous feature of the violence and bloodshed that took place in the Punjab. Nevertheless,'the rump of the civil-military regime, especially in western Punjab, was quickly restored to constitute the mainstay of the new state of Pakistan' (ibid., 308). Tan Tai Yong went on to remark:

> The story of the militarization of colonial Punjab can therefore be crucial in explaining the character of post-colonial state of Pakistan. While the 'interplay of domestic, regional and international factors' in the post-1947 period may have facilitated the dominance of the bureaucracy and the military in the evolving structure of the Pakistani state, it can be suggested that the rise of a Punjabi-controlled military-bureaucratic oligarchy which was organized and powerful enough to wrest control of, and dominate, the post-independence state of Pakistan stemmed from developments in colonial Punjab during the first half of the twentieth century. (Ibid., 308–309).

The bottom line of Yong's argument is that the structure of power that devolved upon Pakistan was such that the colonial garrison state could continue in

Pakistan, albeit in the context of regional and international conditions. This is interesting because the idea of making Pakistan a garrison state, ready to serve external patrons, predates the creation of Pakistan itself. Mohammad Ali Jinnah and his close associates began to solicit US interest in Pakistan, as a garrison state, before it actually came into being.

Harold Lasswell's Garrison State

As a political science concept, the garrison state was propounded by the American political scientist Harold Lasswell in 1937. Formulated in the context of the Sino–Japanese war, it was premised on the basic assumption that technological changes within the military alter the relationship between military institutions and the larger civilian societies. In 1942, he further refined it as the rise of Nazism and fascism posed a great threat to Western democracy. Lasswell made the controversial assertion that the garrison state would emerge in modern industrial societies where the specialists on violence would capture the leadership, thus establishing the supremacy of the military over the state and society (Stanley 1997: 22–23). Lasswell (1997: 59) wrote:

> The military men who dominate a modern technical society will be very different from the officers of history and tradition. It is probable that the specialists on violence will include in their training a large degree of expertness in many of the skills that we have traditionally accepted as part of modern civilian management.

Further, he argued that an officer corps, recruited from a broad social base rather than the traditional narrow social base of ruling or aristocratic families, would dominate the garrison state. The aim would be to create a large and competent military force dominated by a corps of officers that could provide a broad range of societal services besides security. The garrison state would strive to manage the economy and production in order to provide employment and other services, but the aim would not be to create an active citizenry but rather its opposite: an obedient and docile population indoctrinated to believe in the inevitability of war and the need to maintain the garrison state. To carry out concerted propaganda and indoctrination in the 'socialisation of danger', technology would be put to full use (ibid., 64–6). As the garrison state would grow stronger and more firmly entrenched:

> Decisions will be more dictatorial than democratic, and institutional practices long connected with modern democracy will disappear. This means that instrumental democracy will be in abeyance, although the symbols of mystic 'democracy' will doubtless continue. Instrumental democracy is found wherever authority and control are widely dispersed among the members of a state. Mystic 'democracy' is not, strictly speaking, democracy at all, because it may be found where authority and control are highly concentrated yet where part of the established practice is to speak in the name of the people as a whole. Thus, any dictatorship may celebrate its 'democracy' and speak with contempt of such 'mechanical' devices such as majority rule at elections or in legislatures (ibid., 66–7).

The main hypothesis advanced was that 'societies which are faced with a chronic threat of modern war are likely to become garrison states' (ibid., 22). Further, that 'the presence of continued crises radically alters the structure of societies' (ibid., 32). In short, 'A culture under constant threat of war would presumably develop a significant level of fear, which would, in turn, serve as a spur toward the consolidation of technical enterprise' (ibid., 26).

Security, Threat, and Threat Perception

All states maintain armies and weapons to defend themselves against aggression or to launch offensive actions on enemies. According to the Realism paradigm, it is in the very nature of the beast, so to say, because, in the international arena, the Hobbesian state of nature still prevails and states and their governments have to be prepared for conflict (Morgenthau 1948; Waltz 1979). Machiavelli had, of course, used the realism argument to justify all the acts of the Prince that made the State strong, including the use of lies, deceit, and force to crush internal opposition. He had advocated the influential thesis that nations preserved their freedom if they maintained strong and powerful armies – which has served as a cornerstone of state-building projects in the modern period. However, at what point does realism become perverted into cynicism, so that deception and manipulation simply become instruments to preserve a regime rather than to advance the interests of the nation – this was not clearly identified by him. Suffice it to say, he was not an advocate of perpetual manipulation and force as guarantors of the well-being of the nation and state. He relativised the notion of power to suggest that, through education and reform, people can be groomed to become responsible citizens so that a republic based on the rule of law can be established. His emphasis on a strong army, however, remained an essential part of his theory of the modern state (Machiavelli 1982). Sometimes, the perceived threat to their existence from external and internal sources is acute and overwhelming, and security becomes a paramount concern of the state.

Security, it may be noted, is an aspect of threat perception. Scholars draw a distinction between the terms 'threat' and 'threat perception' (Walt 1987). Whereas the former simply means the possibility of trouble or danger, the latter refers to how trouble or danger is sensed or felt. Pervaiz Iqbal Cheema has written: 'Perceptions can deviate from reality as a result of incorrect information or misinformation or factual distortion or because of the incumbent force of preconceived ideas and the professional bias of the perceiver' (1990: 68). One can develop this argument further and say that the threat perception can be exaggerated or underplayed because those authoritatively defining and describing it can use their vantage position to manipulate the facts to serve their vested interests. Thus, for example, an exaggeration of the threat to national security can be used to justify heavier spending on defence or on the maintenance of a very large fighting force. At the bottom of all descriptions of threats to national security and survival, by the military, is the claim that the state has scarce resources at its disposal.

Pakistan and US Containment of Soviet Communism

The garrison state that Lasswell feared could emerge in the United States never happened. Democratic institutions survived, notwithstanding the scourge of witch-hunting of suspected leftist intellectuals and public figures during the McCarthy era which lasted from the end of the 1940s to the end of the 1950s. In 1962, Lasswell re-examined the garrison state hypothesis, in light of the fact that total war through nuclear weapons was a distinct possibility. He recognised that while the world was not 'moving soon into a world relatively free of the chronic threat of serious coercion, a policy that favoured enhancing human dignity and thus "civilianism" in opposition to "militarism" could help in maintaining effective institutions of free society' (Lasswell 1997: 106–7). In other words, Lasswell wanted public policy to strengthen civilian hold over the state to obviate the garrison state emerging in the US.

However, the fear that the military could acquire excessive power and influence was even expressed by President Dwight D. Eisenhower, a hero of the Second World War. He warned against the rise of the military-industrial complex in the US, which was linked to the obsession that the Soviet Union would launch a nuclear attack. On 17 January 1961, Eisenhower succinctly observed:

> This conjunction of an immense military establishment and a large arms industry is new in the American experience. The total influence, economic, political and even spiritual, is felt in every city, every State house, and every office of the Federal government… In the councils of government, we must guard against the acquisition of unwarranted influence, whether sought or unsought, by the military-industrial complex. The potential for the disastrous rise of misplaced power exists and will persist. We must never let the weight of this combination endanger our liberties or democratic processes. We should take nothing for granted. Only an alert and knowledgeable citizenry can compel the proper meshing of the huge industrial and military machinery of defence with our peaceful methods and goals, so that security and liberty may prosper together.

Significant in such a description was the possibility that the arms industry could manipulate information and distort the threat scenarios to serve its own sectional interests. In other words, Eisenhower feared it would 'turn the US into a garrison state, with an economy dominated by military spending and civil liberties eroded' (Schwartz 2005). Ironically, such a realisation did not dissuade Eisenhower from actively pursuing a policy of containment of Soviet power through the establishment of military bases worldwide. In order to realise such an objective, he sought military alliances with other nations (Kux 2001: 51). Thus, the Eisenhower administration followed an active policy of garrison-building all over the world.

In the 1970s, such obsession reached new heights as authoritarian regimes headed by military strongmen and civilian dictators were co-opted into the containment of communism strategy. As a result, the United States was constantly engaged in armed conflicts and wars in many regions of the world. Wars in Indo–China were the most gruesome manifestation of such a policy. Subverting democratically-elected governments perceived to be inimical to US interests became part of such a policy. The classic case was Chile, in 1973, when an elected government under the leftist president, Salvador Allende, was overthrown in a bloody military coup masterminded by the Central Intelligence Agency (CIA). The system of military bases survived the end of the Cold War and the collapse of the Soviet Union, as other threats appeared on the horizon, especially from radical Islam and China.

Garrison States in Post-Colonial Contexts

The leaders of Pakistan began to seek US help even before the state was founded, marketing it as a geostrategically against Soviet Communism. That policy was pursued relentlessly when the country came into being. Initially, the United States was not keen to co-opt Pakistan since building NATO remained its main priority. However, by 1951, there was a change in the US perception of Pakistan's usefulness; when Eisenhower became president, Pakistan became one of the chief beneficiaries of the worldwide garrison-building strategy that the new administration had adopted – garrison states emerged in Asia and Africa in the 1950s and 1960s (LaPorte 1969: 842). Besides Pakistan, garrison states were supported by the United States in Israel, Turkey, Taiwan, South Korea, and Indonesia. The Soviet Union promoted garrison states in Eastern Europe, the Middle East, and in Southeast and East Asia. After the Cold War, things began to change. Turkey, Taiwan, Indonesia, and South Korea made the gradual transition to democracy, but retained a strong military organisation. In the case of Israel, notwithstanding regular elections, Israel has behaved like a garrison state because of its wars with the Arab states, the Arab populations' hostility to its existence, and resistance towards it in the occupied territories (Stanley 1997: 35; Stanley and Segal 1997: 132). Israel's policy of occupation and illegal appropriation of Palestinian land has necessitated the establishment of border controls, entry and exit checkpoints, and high walls to separate Jews from Arabs. Thus, Israel is a very visible garrison state, notwithstanding its regular elections and democracy that clearly privileges Jews over non-Jews.

More importantly, Pakistan and India attained independence in mid-August 1947 through a partition of the British Indian Empire. However, India became a democracy that, over time, has only deepened (Oldenburg 2010). Lieutenant General Kuldip Singh Khajuria, Major General Afsir Karim, and Brigadier Vijai K. Nair of the Indian Army, and Commodore C. Uday Bhaskar of the Indian Navy, told me that the supremacy of the Indian Parliament and the right of the elected government to make political decisions has never been challenged in India. Commodore Bhaskar has succinctly surmised his ideas in an article in the Pakistani weekly, *The Friday Times* (Bhaskar 2008). It is to be noted that India's woes, about external threats, are not confined to Pakistan – against whom it has fought several wars – but also with the much stronger China.

Brigadier (Retd.) A.R. Siddiqi, in the preface of his book, *The Military in Pakistan: Image and Reality*, has described the Pakistani state in terms that are strikingly similar to Lasswell's. He has written:

> Since there is no other institution to rival the military in organization and discipline, above all, in its control of the instruments of violence, its image grows apace, and presently reaches a point of predominance and power where it becomes an object of mass reverence or fear. A sort of [sic] prussianism is born to produce an army with a nation in place of a nation with an army. The national identity and interest is progressively subordinated to the growing power of the military image (1996: ii).

The erstwhile Muslim League elite did express a commitment to democracy. For the most part, it was going to be Muslim democracy, also called spiritual democracy or Islamic democracy. What such rhetoric implied was that democracy was to be qualified by Islamic prerequisites. In other words, Pakistan was not to be the usual type of secular democracy. In my book, *The Concept of an Islamic State: An Analysis of the Ideological Controversy in Pakistan* (1987), I demonstrated that, notwithstanding an imagination that furnished an inexhaustible scope for playing with words and flirting with logic and common sense, Islamic qualifications to democracy defeated the purpose of democracy. Contemporary democracy assumes the equality of all citizens irrespective of differences based on birth, race, ethnicity, religion, and gender. The Pakistani modernist rulers, who held power from 1947 to 1977, failed to provide an alternative to the Islamic state: on the contrary, more and more dogmatic features were added to the Pakistani national identity until, in 1977, General Mohammad Zia-ul-Haq set aside the charade of democracy and went about constructing Pakistan as the fortress of Islam, braced with not only military but also repressive legal and cultural measures.

Consequently, contemporary Pakistan bears the hallmarks of not only a fortress state, but also a society with garrisons studded all over it to ward off various assaults: political, ideological, sectarian, military, and so on. In such circumstances, it is not surprising that the military has become the most powerful institution. It exercises de facto veto powers over both internal and external policies. According to one estimate, in 2008 Pakistan had: 650,000 Active Military Personnel; 528,000 Active Military Reserve; and 302,000 Active Paramilitary Units (Global Fire Power, 2011). An earlier estimate by Ayesha Siddiqa gave a breakdown of 550,000 military personnel; 45,000 air force personnel; 25,000 navy personnel (Siddiqa 2007: 59). The Pakistan Armed Forces have been an attractive avenue for educated young men; those who join it become part of a fraternity that is powerful and privileged. Over the years, recruitment has been democratized so that representation from the middle and lower-middle classes has increased though, in ethnic terms, the Punjabis are still preponderant (Nawaz 2008). Until the beginning of the 1990s, seventy-five percent of the army continued to be recruited from the Punjab and the NWFP. Moreover, recruitment continued to take place from the same narrow regional base: the districts of Rawalpindi, Jhelum, and Campbellpur (now known as Attock), now reconstituted to include Chakwal, Khushab, and Mianwali in Punjab; and, two districts from NWFP, Kohat and Mardan. Together, they represented only nine percent of the male population of Pakistan (Cohen 1998: 44). Shuja Nawaz, however, has asserted that noteworthy changes are underway. He has written:

> Based on separate GHQ (army headquarters) data for soldiers and officers, Punjab shows an overall decline in recruitment of soldiers from 63.86 percent in 1991 to 43.33 in 2005, with Central Punjab outpacing Northern Punjab, the traditional recruitment ground, by 7,500 to 5000 recruits in 2005. Southern Punjab has 1,800 recruits. Recruitment from the NWFP and FATA (Federally Administered Tribal Areas) increased from 20.91 to 22.43 percent, Sindh rose from 8.85 to 23.02 percent – with rural Sindh accounting for the majority of the recruits (5,095 to 2,500 in 2005) – in Balochistan, it rose from 0.49 to 1.52 percent in 2005 with 200 urban to 300 rural recruits in 2005, and in Azad Kashmir

> and the Northern Areas, recruitment rose from 5.86 to 9.70 percent.
>
> Looking at the officers commissioned into service during the period 1970–89 in comparison with 1990–2006, we also see a change in the relative share of different parts of the country. The Punjab rose marginally from 66.46 to 66.93 percent, but within the Punjab there are notable changes in the home districts of the officers, shifting to the more populous and emerging urban centres of Central and even Southern Punjab. This is in line with urbanization trends nationwide. These bigger cities and towns are also the traditional strongholds of the growing Islamist parties and conservatism, associated with the petit bourgeoisie (2008: 571).

Nawaz described them as 'Zia bharti' or 'Zia recruitment', during the period when General Mohammad Zia-ul-Haq was Pakistan's military dictator (1977–88). He has suggested that the men recruited during this period would be in commanding positions in the twenty-first century (ibid., 572). Despite the changes that are underway, the largely Punjabi-Pukhtun military has been viewed with suspicion and fear in the provinces that are poorly represented in it – particularly so in Balochistan where the military, in response to having to crush several uprisings and resistance movements, has responded by building garrison outposts and bases. That trend started soon after the princely state of Kalat was annexed in 1948. During the first military government of Ayub Khan, garrisons began to be built on a larger scale – a trend that has continued.

However, on the whole, the expansion of Pakistan's armed forces has been in response to India constantly upgrading its armed forces, thus aggravating Pakistan's sense of insecurity. For example, in 2008 India had 1,325,000 Active Military Personnel; 1,155,000 Active Military Reserve; and 1,293,300 Active Paramilitary Units (Global Fire Power, 2011). India has currently surpassed even China in its military spending.

International relations scholars, such as Barry Buzan, have argued that as rival or enemy states improve their armed might, they compel each other into an arms race. As a result, better and more lethal weapons are acquired, and consequently the destructive capacities of such states increase. However, improvement in destructive capacity does not decrease the sense of insecurity; rather, it diminishes it so that the rival or enemy states strive to obtain even better and more destructive armament (Buzan 1991). Acquisition of weapons of mass destruction, such as nuclear weapons, is the ultimate heightener of insecurity. It is, therefore, a vicious circle that acquires a life of its own.

From the Horse's Mouth

The Pakistan military does not deny its power but asserts that Pakistan's integrity and survival is gravely threatened by its next-door neighbour, India (Khan 2006; Khan 1973: 1–4; Khan 1988: 8–17 and 135–40). The former head of the Inter-Services Intelligence (ISI), Lieutenant General (Retd.) Asad Durrani, described Pakistan as a 'national security state'. The same assessment was made by the former COAS, General Mirza Aslam Beg, Lieutenant General (Retd.) Ashraf Qazi (also former head of the ISI), and Brigadier (Retd.) Yasub Ali Dogar, the ISI director of Afghan Affairs (1991–92).

Their standpoint was that Pakistan had to ensure its survival in the face of a constant threat posed to its security by India. All three pointed out that the latter is much bigger in terms of population and territory; it initiated nuclear weapons testing in 1974; it spends enormous amounts of money on buying arms, and possesses one of the largest militaries in the world; and has been at war with Pakistan on several occasions, with the 1971 war resulting in the break-up of Pakistan. Consequently, Pakistan must maintain a credible defence against Indian designs. With regard to its dependence on the United States, former COAS General Jehangir Karamat, Lieutenant General (Retd.) Asad Durrani, Lieutenant General (Retd.) Nishat Ahmed, Major General (Retd.) Mahmud Ali Durrani, Major General (Retd.) Sarfraz Iqbal, Brigadier (Retd.) Dogar, and Colonel (Retd.) Aslam Cheema told me that Pakistan cooperates with the Americans only to the extent that its own interests are served. However, General Aslam Beg and Lieutenant General (Retd.) Hamid Gul (also former head of the ISI) were of the view that it has not been in Pakistan's interest to support the US-led 'war on terror'. Referring to China as an all-weather friend is part of the mainstream military standpoint; dependence on Saudi Arabia arouses less enthusiasm among the liberal and secular sections of the higher officers' cadre. Lieutenant General Javed Ashraf Qazi and Major Agha Humayun Amin frankly criticized General Muhammad Zia-ul-Haq for introducing fundamentalist ideas into the Pakistan Army and thus, negatively, affecting its professionalism.

Most of them discounted the argument that the creation of a powerful military necessarily resulted in military domination over civil institutions. Rather, they blamed inept and corrupt politicians for creating dangerous law and order situations that have necessitated military intervention. Conspiracies hatched by regional nationalists and secessionists, hell-bent on breaking up the country, also figured in the interviews. Almost invariably, the officers said that they were not opposed to democracy, and readily conceded that military interventions were not good for the country and, more importantly, adversely affected the professionalism of the military. In short, they described their praetorian role as not one of their choosing but of necessity. Pakistani columnist Shahid Siddiqui has succinctly captured this line of reasoning in the first speech of the four coup-makers: Ayub Khan, Yahya Khan, Zia ul Haq, and Musharraf. According to Shahid Siddiqui, the generals suggested:

> [t]hat the country is on the verge of destruction, condemn the politicians and the toppled government, pat the people on the back, lionize the army, describing the takeover as something 'unpleasant', emphasize publicly the 'reluctance' with which they had to take the action, suggest that the action is taken in the interest of the greater interest national interest, claim that the country has been saved by this action and promise greener pastures for the masses. (Quoted in Waseem 2009: 201).

One can wonder whether Siddiqui was being sarcastic or simply stating the considered opinion of the generals who took over the reins of power. Both interpretations contain a grain of truth. It is to be noted, however, that there is an absence of any reference to the external threat posed by India in the legitimisation of military takeovers. The takeovers have essentially been driven by internal developments, though the fact that the military had become more powerful facilitated the takeovers and, in the process, established a precedent that tempted the generals to assert themselves with greater confidence in relation to the politicians.

A Dissenting View From Inside

There is a countervailing standpoint within the armed forces on the 'India-as-external-threat' thesis, as well as on the military taking charge of Pakistan to save it from predatory politicians or hostile secessionists. Air Marshal (Retd.)

Asghar Khan, who is generally celebrated as the man who organized and trained the Pakistan Air Force, has taken the view that the four wars with India were the result of Pakistani adventurism; they lacked a clear objective and, therefore, caused more harm than good to Pakistan (Khan 2005: 235–46). Asghar Khan has also disputed that the military interventions and dominant role the Pakistan Army acquired were the result of either lack of good political leadership or vile plots to break-up Pakistan. He has identified politicians whose activities have harmed the cause of civil rule and democracy but has maintained that such things happened because the military was willing to go along with their negative politics (Khan 2008: 11–13). It may be added that such views are not uncommon; privately and anonymously, military officers critique the generals for developing political ambitions.

The Post-Colonial Garrison State Theory Recapitulated

It can be argued that if a state is beset by the fear of foreign aggression, it can acquire the characteristics of a garrison state. This is possible in an industrially-backward society, as it is in an industrially-advanced society, because a garrison state is essentially driven by the perception of threats and an ability to arm itself against them. This pre-condition, for the emergence of a garrison state, is amply fulfilled in the case of Pakistan.

Fear of foreign aggression and internal subversion, concomitant with a weak base for democracy and an opportunity for a sufficiently large number of specialists on violence to acquire armament and training, furnish the basis for garrison building to post-colonial states.

If such a state can solicit the support of a powerful patron state, or states, willing to strengthen its economic and military power, the problem of underdevelopment can be circumvented and it can acquire characteristics of a garrison state by building up its military capabilities.

However, foreign economic and military aid also means that the donor state gains influence over the post-colonial state. Carrot and stick tactics are usually employed to extract compliance from the recipient post-colonial state.

Given the anarchical nature of international politics, room for manoeuvre exists even for a dependent post-colonial state. The latter can resist donor pressure through the diversification of dependence, although the donors enjoy an advantage over the latter. Pakistan's longest and deepest dependence has been on the United States; China and Saudi Arabia are the two other main donors.

In addition to the fear of foreign aggression, historical and cultural factors can help generate an ideology of the garrison state. The core elements of such an ideology will be a damning narrative about the enemy, a victimhood self-identity, and an imperative to maintain a strong and powerful military.

Moreover, for an ideological state such as Pakistan, the question of national identity contains dimensions that refer to higher purposes and the aims and objectives of such a state. Political Islam, in its various incantations and manifestations, furnishes ideational and ideological inspiration from which state ideology can be derived.

Pakistan can continue as a post-colonial garrison state as long as the donors are willing to provide it with the required resources, and it can convince or coerce its population that the struggle for sur vival necessitates prioritisation of the allocation of scarce resources to security and defence.

2

British, American, and Soviet Attitudes Towards the Pakistan Scheme

Great Britain

The demand for Pakistan emerged in the aftermath of the 1937 provincial elections in which the All-India Muslim League (AIML) suffered a heavy defeat despite its claim of representing the Muslim community of India. On the other hand, the Indian National Congress won 711 out of a total of 1,585 general seats. Congress formed ministries first in six, and later eight, provinces. In the strategic north-western zone of the subcontinent, it was the regional Muslim-dominated parties that won most of the reserved seats for Muslims. There is some evidence that an agreement existed between the provincial Congress and Muslim League in the United Provinces of northern India to form a coalition government, but Congress reneged on this after the Muslim League was routed. In reaction, the Muslim League set out on a separatist course that culminated in the partition of India (Jalal 1985; Seervai 1989; Wolpert 1984). In 1939, the Second World War broke out and the British committed India to the war without consulting the Indian leaders. The Congress ordered its ministries to resign in protest, and began to agitate for immediate self-rule. The British interpreted Congress' lack of support as betrayal in their hour of need. The Muslim League, after some hesitation, decided to support the war effort.

Muslim League Demands Separate Muslim States

On 23 March 1940, the Muslim League formally demanded the creation of separate Muslim state/states in the Muslim-majority zones of north-western and north-eastern India. The Muslim League had been encouraged to demand a separate state by Viceroy Linlithgow who had conveyed the message through Sir Muhammad Zafrulla Khan, a prominent leader of the pro-British Ahmadiyya community. The idea was to pressurize the assertive Congress leaders, who were refusing to cooperate in the war effort in spite of forming the government in eight provinces (Khan 1987: 29–30). However, the British were under pressure from the Americans to take measures to transfer power to Indian hands. Prime Minister Winston Churchill sent Sir Stafford Cripps to India, in March 1942, to probe the possibility of a transfer of power to the Indians but within the framework of a dominion. The Cripps Mission alluded obliquely to the establishment of a separate Muslim dominion, but did not guarantee it. Both the Congress and the Muslim League rejected its recommendations as it did not satisfy their basic demands: the former wanting independence in a united India, and the latter separate statehood (Mansergh and Lumby 1970: 745–51).

In August 1942, Gandhi launched the Quit-India movement. Gandhi calculated that the British were weak and beleaguered, and that a popular uprising would spontaneously break out which would force the British to leave. It proved to be a delusion. The Congress did not enjoy such overwhelming support and the regional leaders, especially in key provinces such as Punjab from where a substantial portion of the colonial Indian Army was recruited, were solidly behind the war effort. On the national level, the Muslim League was supporting the British. Viceroy Lord Linlithgow cracked down forcefully and, within weeks, the Congress leadership was behind bars. Volatile and defiant sections of the public were intimidated into submission through public floggings and other severe punishments. The Quit India movement earned the Congress party the unmitigated contempt of the British while the Muslim League and its leader, Mohammad Ali Jinnah, began to be recognised as an important ally (French 1997: 149–72, 198; Sarila 2005: 135–9; Talbot 1996: 134).

Viceroy Lord Wavell

Field Marshal Lord Wavell became the viceroy of India on 20 October 1943. Although his predecessor, Linlithgow, had successfully suppressed the movement launched by Gandhi, Wavell was convinced that India could not be ruled for very long. The Muslim League's popularity had increased dramatically while the Congress leaders remained in incarceration. Wavell organised a conference at Simla, in June 1945, to probe the terms for the transfer of power to Indian hands. Congress leaders were released from jail, a few days earlier, where they had been kept since their arrests at the time of the Quit India movement in August 1942. Jinnah insisted that the Muslim League alone could nominate Muslim delegates to the conference; Wavell conceded to this. The Simla Conference ended in failure but, in practical terms, Jinnah emerged as the sole spokesman of the Muslims (Jalal 1985). Provincial elections were announced for early 1946. In December 1945, Wavell prepared a top secret document, the Breakdown Plan, for a quick withdrawal in case the law and order situation got out of hand. The plan recommended that if the Muslims insisted then India should be partitioned to create a Muslim-majority Pakistan. However, large non-Muslim populations could not be compelled to remain in Pakistan. Therefore, the provinces of Bengal and Punjab should be partitioned so that non-Muslim majority areas would be excluded from Pakistan and instead given to India. Wavell believed that such a radical division of India, which would result in a much smaller Pakistan, would dissuade Jinnah from insisting on the partition of India (Mansergh and Moon 1976: 700–701). He also proposed an international border between the two states (ibid., 912). The Radcliffe Award of 17 August 1947, which fixed the international India–Pakistan boundary, was almost a ditto copy of the border demarcated by Wavell. Such recommendations remained top secret, shared only by a select number of officials in London and Delhi.

February 1946 Provincial Elections

Meanwhile, Jinnah continued his relentless campaign to garner support for the Pakistan scheme. In order to muster support from the Muslim voters, Jinnah sought the support of the ulema (clerics) as they already had access to existing networks – through the mosques and religious ceremonies and activities. From 1944 onwards, the ulema and pirs (spiritual guides and teachers) were mobilised to support the demand for Pakistan. Pakistan was projected as an Islamic utopia where social justice and piety would prevail in accordance with the lofty vision of true Islam. Consequently, the Muslim League exploited Islamic sentiments, slogans, and heroic themes to rouse the masses during their public meetings and mass contact campaigns. This has been stated clearly in the fortnightly confidential report, of 2 February 1946, sent to Viceroy Wavell by the Punjab Governor Sir Bertrand Glancy:

> The ML [Muslim League] orators are becoming increasingly fanatical in their speeches. Maulvis [clerics] and Pirs [spiritual masters] and students travel all round the Province and preach that those who fail to vote for the League candidates will cease to be Muslims; their marriages will no longer be valid and they will be entirely excommunicated.... It is not easy to foresee what the results of the elections will be. But there seems little doubt the Muslim League, thanks to the ruthless methods by which they have pursued their campaign of 'Islam in danger' will considerably increase the number of their seats and unionist representatives will correspondingly decline (Carter 2006, 171).

Similar practices were prevalent in the campaigns in the NWFP (now Khyber-Pakhtunkhwa). Erland Jansson noted in his doctoral dissertation, *India, Pakistan or Pakhtunistan?*:

> The Pir of Manki Sharif...founded an organisation of his own, the Anjuman-us-asfia. The organisation promised to support the Muslim League on condition that Shariat would be enforced in Pakistan. To this Jinnah agreed. As a result the Pir of Manki Sharif declared jehad to achieve Pakistan and ordered the members of his anjuman to support the League in the 1946 elections (p. 166).

In this regard, Jinnah's letter of November 1945 to Pir Manki Sharif is quite revealing. He wrote:

> It is needless to emphasize that the Constituent Assembly which would be predominantly Muslim in its composition would be able to enact laws for Muslims, not inconsistent with the Shariat laws and the Muslim will no longer be obliged to abide by the Un-Islamic laws (Constituent Assembly of Pakistan Debates, Volume 5, 1949, p. 46).

The Muslim League swept the polls. It won 440 out of 495 seats reserved for Muslims. The Indian National Congress won most of the general seats, 905 out of 1585 seats. Earlier, in July 1945, the Labour Party had come to power in the UK. Prime Minister Clement Attlee was not averse to a quick transfer of power to the Indians, but he wanted India to remain in the British Commonwealth, preferably undivided.

British Military's Perspective on India and Pakistan

The position of the British military establishment, in May 1946, was that Britain should maintain effective control over India and that India should remain united, even if substantive self-government was granted to it. It would mean that, for many years to come, Britain would share responsibility with the Indian leadership for the defence and security of a united India. The key to the realisation of such an objective would be a strong and united Indian Army. Thus, on 11 May 1946, Field Marshal Sir Claude Auchinleck prepared a top secret note on 'The Strategic Implications of the Inclusion of "Pakistan" in the British Commonwealth'. In a long and detailed study of the pros and cons of partitioning India and thus creating Pakistan – either as one unit in the north-west of the subcontinent, or as two with the second part in the north-east zone – he concluded that it would not serve British interests in the Indian Ocean because it would be a weak state in military and economic terms whereas a stronger India, estranged from Britain, could move closer to the Soviet Union. In the end of his report he summed up his position:

> If we desire to maintain our power to move freely by sea and air in the Indian Ocean area, which I consider essential to the continued existence of the British Commonwealth, we can do so only by keeping in [it] being a United India which will be a willing member of that Commonwealth, ready to share its defence to the limit of her resources (ibid., 806).

This view was not necessarily shared by his peers. General Mayne underlined the section 'which I consider essential…to the British Commonwealth' and wrote 'I do not' in the margin (ibid.). General Officer Commander-in-Chief of the Eastern Command, Lieutenant General Sir Francis Tuker, took up cudgels on behalf of Pakistan. He was convinced that Hinduism was a superstitious creed and that the caste system prevented the establishment of national solidarity among the Hindus. Therefore, unless a buffer was created, the oppressed Indian masses would find the communist ideology's strong emphasis on equality and social emancipation an allurement they would not be able to withstand (Tuker 1951: 537–54). Proceeding from such a pessimistic view of Hindu India, Tuker opined:

> There was much therefore to be said for the introduction of a new Muslim power supported by the science of Britain. If such a power could be produced and if we could orient the Muslim strip from North Africa through Islamia Desertia, Persia, Afghanistan to the Himalayas, upon a Muslim power in Northern India, then it had some chance of halting the filtration of Russia towards the Persian Gulf. These Islamic countries, even including Turkey, were not a very great strength in themselves. But with a northern Indian Islamic state of several millions it would be reasonable to expect that Russia would not care to provoke them too far (ibid., 26–27).

The Cabinet Mission Plan

The July 1945 British election proved a major upset as Winston Churchill's Conservative Party was comprehensively defeated, and Labour's Clement Attlee became prime minister. He despatched three cabinet ministers, in early 1946, to probe the preconditions for a transfer of power. As they conducted extensive discussions and negotiations for a transfer of power, preferably to a united India, they found Congress unwilling to make any concessions on its goal of a united India with a strong centre, while the Muslim League held fast to its demand for a separate Pakistan. Moreover, Jinnah demanded a 50:50 representation in government, even though the Muslims constituted roughly one-fourth of the total Indian population (Moore 1983: 556–7). Consequently, on 16 May 1946, the Cabinet Mission announced its own scheme. It rejected Pakistan's demand as impractical but recognised Muslim concerns:

> This decision does not however blind us to the very real Muslim apprehensions that their culture and political and social life might become submerged in a purely unitary India, in which the Hindus with their greatly superior numbers must be a dominating element (Mansergh and Moon 1977: 586).

The solution offered by the Cabinet Mission Plan included, among other things, the establishment of a union of India embracing British India and the princely states, which would deal with foreign affairs, defence, and communications. The federal government would have powers to raise finances for those three areas of government activity. Three sections or groups would be constituted by the provinces. Group A would include the Hindu-majority provinces of Madras, Bombay, United Provinces, Bihar, Central Provinces, and Orissa. Group B would include the Muslim-majority provinces of the north-west: Punjab, North-West Frontier Province (now Khyber-Pakhtunkhwa), and Sind (Sindh). Group C would include the Muslim majority provinces of the north-east: Bengal and Assam. Moreover:

> The constitutions of the Union and of the Groups should contain a provision whereby any Province could, by a majority vote of its Legislative Assembly, call for reconsideration of the terms of the constitution after an initial period of 10 years and at 10 years intervals thereafter' (ibid.).

In a resolution passed on 24 May 1946, Congress stated that it was not agreeable to the proposals since it believed that an independent India 'must necessarily have a strong central authority capable of representing the nation with power and dignity in the councils of the world' (ibid., 679–80). For its part, the Muslim League passed a resolution on 6 June 1946 in which it regretted that the demand for Pakistan had not been fully conceded but, nevertheless, accepted the Cabinet Mission's proposals because the idea of Pakistan was inherent in them 'by virtue of the compulsory grouping of the six Muslim Provinces in Sections B and C' (ibid., 837).

On 16 June 1946, the Cabinet Mission proposed the formation of an interim government. On 25 June, the Congress party's Working Committee rejected the proposal to form an interim government but accepted the constitutional proposals and suggested that it would put its own interpretation on the Cabinet Mission Plan. The same day, the Muslim League accepted the proposals for an interim government but rejected the idea that the Congress could place its own interpretation on the British plan (ibid., 1032–49). On 10 July, in a press conference in Bombay, Nehru stated that Congress would not be bound by any agreements when it entered the Constituent Assembly (Mansergh and Moon 1979: 25). The Muslim League, in a statement on 29 July, declared itself greatly perturbed by Nehru's remarks, on the grounds that it made the future status of the minorities in India uncertain. Some days later, the League took the decision to withdraw its support for the Cabinet

Mission Plan and threatened to resort to direct action to achieve Pakistan (ibid., 135–9). It fixed 16 August as the date for the direct action.

Interim Government and Communal Riots

To the great surprise of the Muslim League, Wavell invited Jawaharlal Nehru to form an interim government. On 13 August, Nehru wrote to Jinnah inviting his co-operation in the formation of a provisional national government. However, the direct-action call resulted in exceptionally barbaric communal rioting in the port city of Calcutta. While the initial attacks were carried out by Muslim hoodlums, there was a fierce retaliation by the Hindus a few days later which resulted in a bloodbath that claimed 2000–4000 lives, some 100,000 were rendered homeless as shanty towns and other poor localities were torched and pillaged (ibid., 239–40; 293–304).

However, the Interim government took office on 24 August; Jawaharlal Nehru was its vice-president while the viceroy remained its chief executive. The government renewed its efforts to convince the Muslim League to join it. The League made its joining the cabinet conditional on the recognition of its status as the sole representative of the Indian Muslims. This was agreed, and the League took the decision to join the cabinet on 15 October. However, mutual suspicion and animosity among the members of the interim government proved to be too strong. The Congress and Muslim League ministers worked at cross-purposes. In the absence of a power-sharing formula being agreed upon at the centre, the partition of India became a very distinct possibility.

Also, the Calcutta killings proved to be a contagion; communal riots broke out in many parts of India. In Bombay, Muslims and Hindus clashed; the resulting deaths were in the hundreds on both sides. In Noakhali, East Bengal, Muslims attacked Hindus and killed about 400. The Hindus retaliated – on 27 September, and then again on 25 October which continued into the first week of November – with barbaric revenge attacks on the Muslims in Bihar. According to some observers, it was the Hindu workers who had escaped the Muslim fury in Calcutta, and returned to Bihar, who wreaked havoc on the Muslims. The governor of Bihar, Sir H. Dow, pointed out that the Congress government in Bihar did little to stop the carnage (Mansergh and Moon 1980: 38–9). As many as 5000 people were slaughtered in Bihar, almost entirely Muslims (ibid., 188). Smaller riots followed in the northern

Indian province of United Provinces. In December 1946, bloody rioting targeting the Hindu–Sikh minority took place in the NWFP. In early March 1947, bloody rioting took place in a number of cities in Punjab. Some 2000 to 5000 people were killed (Ahmed 2012: 127–193).

20 February 1947 Statement and Mountbatten as Last Viceroy

On 20 February 1947, Attlee announced the intention of His Majesty's Government to definitely transfer power to the Indians by June 1948. Attlee chose a cousin of the king, Lord Louis Mountbatten, as the last viceroy to India – to oversee and manage the transfer of power. The bloodbath that had taken place in the Punjab had deeply antagonized the Sikhs (Mansergh and Moon 1980: 965–69). Since the passing of the Lahore Resolution in March 1940, the Sikhs had insisted that if India was divided on a religious basis, the Punjab should also be so divided so that areas where the Hindus and Sikhs were in a majority would be separated from the Muslim-majority parts of the Punjab. The Congress party supported this Sikh demand in a resolution dated 8 March 1947 (Ahmed 2012: 139).

Mountbatten took over power on 24 March 1947, and started protracted parleys with Indian leaders of all communities over the transfer of power. He had been specifically tasked to ensure that, united or divided, India remained in the British Commonwealth. One of Jinnah's confidants, the Nawab of Bhopal, sent a telegram to Mountbatten in which he suggested that, if Pakistan was granted, Jinnah could be persuaded 'to remain within the Commonwealth' (Mansergh and Moon 1981: 36). However, the viceroy tried to convince Jinnah not to demand the division of India because a united India would be a strong and powerful nation whereas Pakistan would be economically and militarily weak. Jinnah remained unimpressed. Rather, he insisted that a separate Pakistan would seek membership of the Commonwealth, which should not be denied to it. In the Viceroy's Personal Report No. 5 dated 1 May 1947, Mountbatten noted that Jinnah told him:

> All the Muslims have been loyal to the British from the beginning. We supplied a high proportion of the Army which fought in both wars. None of our leaders has ever had to go to prison for disloyalty. Not one member of the Muslim League was present in the Constituent Assembly

> when the resolution for an Independent Sovereign Republic was passed [passed on 22 January 1947]. Not one of us had done anything to deserve expulsion from the Commonwealth. And what about the other dominions – Australia and New Zealand – will the other Dominions agree to us being thrown out against our will? Is there anything in the Statute of Westminster which allows you to kick out parts of the Commonwealth because a neighbouring State which used to be a member wants to leave? I asked Mr Churchill and Sir Stafford Cripps for their views when I was in London. Mr Churchill has assured me that the British people would never stand for our being expelled. Sir Stafford Cripps informed me that he could not answer how the legislation would be framed and whether we should be given the opportunity of deciding whether to stay in on our own (ibid., 541).

The viceroy replied to Jinnah that, although he agreed with him emotionally, if only one part – Pakistan – remained in the Commonwealth, and on that basis retained British officers and received British help, it would create an odd situation if it went to war with the other part that had opted out of the Commonwealth. Therefore, Mountbatten warned him to be prepared for Pakistan's request to join the Commonwealth to be refused if India did not join it. To this, Jinnah reportedly retorted that he would rely on the power of appeal to the Commonwealth, over the heads of His Majesty's Government; he was confident that he would receive support from the British people (ibid.).

On the other hand, Mountbatten noted that, within the Congress party, 'violent discussion is going on to this effect....As they now realise Jinnah's game and are beginning to be very frightened by its consequences on the rest of India' (ibid., 542). Yet, the viceroy believed that, in order to convince the Congress leaders to remain in the Commonwealth, it was necessary to emphasise that Pakistan wanted to remain in it, and to remain outside would not be beneficial for India (ibid.).

Support for Pakistan from Heads of the British Armed Forces

At this stage, there was a dramatic change in the attitude of the British military on partition and the creation of Pakistan. Thus, senior military and civil officers – RAF Marshal Lord Tedder (in the chair), Admiral Sir

John H.D. Cunningham, Field Marshal Viscount Montgomery of Alamein, Lieutenant General Sir Leslie C. Hollis, Minister of Defence, A.V. Alexander, Chief of the Viceroy Staff, Lord Ismay, and Major General R.E. Laycock – in a memorandum prepared at the meeting of the Chiefs of Staff Committee in London on 12 May 1947, strongly supported the assumption that it would be good for Britain if Pakistan remained in the Commonwealth. The committee discussed the final proposals for the partition of India, which was presumed to be the basis of the political settlement. It was expected that Pakistan would comprise Sindh, Baluchistan, the NWFP, Western Punjab, Assam, and possibly a part of Bengal. It was noted:

> It was feasible that Jinnah…might well announce a Moslem application to remain within the Commonwealth. A number of Princes might do the same thing. On the other hand, Hindustan might well stick to the declared intention of Congress to be a free Sovereign State, although there were signs that some Congress leaders had doubts of their ability to continue without some British advisers and administration (ibid., 788).

Montgomery asserted that 'it would be a tremendous asset if Pakistan, particularly North West, remained within the Commonwealth. The bases, airfields and ports in North West India would be invaluable to Commonwealth defence' (ibid., 791). After considerable deliberation, the Chiefs of Staff agreed that their views should be submitted to the prime minister. They agreed:

> From the strategic point of view there were overwhelming arguments in favour of Western Pakistan remaining within the Commonwealth, namely, that we should obtain important strategic facilities, the port of Karachi, air bases and the support of the Moslem manpower in the future; be able to ensure the continued integrity of Afghanistan; and be able to increase our prestige and improve our position throughout the Muslim world.…There was therefore everything to gain by admitting Western Pakistan into the Commonwealth. A refusal of an application to this end would amount to ejecting loyal people from the British Commonwealth, and would probably lose us all chances of ever getting strategic facilities anywhere in India, and at the same time shatter our reputation in the rest of the Moslem world. From a military point of view, such a result would be catastrophic (ibid., 791–2).

Thus, top military and civil officials had begun to be convinced of the merit of Pakistan, on its own, remaining in the Commonwealth. Pakistan's help would be required, given its proximity to the Persian Gulf, in the protection of British interests in the important oilfields located in the Gulf.

Pressure on Congress to Agree to India Remaining in the Commonwealth

Meanwhile, Mountbatten continued to work on keeping the whole of India in the Commonwealth. He exerted intense pressure on the Congress leaders; most came around to the view that membership would be beneficial to them. In the minutes of the twenty-seventh Viceroy Staff Meeting dated 7 May 1947, it was stated that Sardar Patel had been won over and that Nehru, too, would agree (ibid., 659). The Congress' left wing, led by Jawaharlal Nehru, had initially resisted India becoming a dominion in the Commonwealth as they wanted complete independence.

In an undated report – presumably early May – of the minutes of the viceroy's twenty-ninth Staff Meeting, it was recorded: 'HIS EXCELLENCY THE VICEROY said that he considered it most desirable that, if Dominion status was to be granted to India before June 1948, the grant should take place during 1947' (ibid., 702–3). He stated the real advantage of keeping India in the Commonwealth in the following words:

> From the point of view of Empire defence an India within the Commonwealth filled in the whole framework of world strategy; a neutral India would leave a gap which would complicate the problem enormously; a hostile India would mean that Australia and New Zealand were virtually cut off (ibid., 704).

Mountbatten appears to have calculated that if the Congress party agreed to India remaining in the Commonwealth, it was in British interests to transfer power quickly so that it would become a fait accompli and thus obviate further wavering by the Indian leaders. It was clear, by the middle of May 1947, that both India and Pakistan would remain in the Commonwealth.

The Partition Plan of 3 June 1947

The announcement of a Partition Plan, on 3 June 1947, was the most important step towards the creation of Pakistan. It drastically expedited the transfer of power from June 1948, as had been announced on 20 February 1947 by Attlee, to mid-August 1947 – that is, in less than eleven weeks. It envisaged a Pakistan comprising two separate geographical entities, East and West Pakistan, where the Muslims were in a majority. Moreover, the Partition Plan stipulated that the legislative assemblies of Bengal and Punjab would vote on partitioning their provinces; it prescribed a procedure that required the members of the Bengal and Punjab assemblies, elected in the 1946 provincial elections, to be divided into two blocs – East and West Bengal, and East and West Punjab – on a notional basis of contiguous Muslim and non-Muslim districts, deriving from the census of 1941. If a simple majority of either part voted in favour of the partition of their province, this would be implemented (Mansergh and Moon 1982: 89–94).

On 20 June, the Muslim-majority eastern bloc voted by 106–35 votes against the partitioning of Bengal, while the non-Muslim majority western bloc voted in favour of partition by a division of 58–21 (Chatterji 1999: 168–194). The Punjab Assembly voted on 23 June: the Muslim-majority western bloc voted by 99–27 against partitioning Punjab, whereas the non-Muslim-majority eastern bloc voted by 50:22 in favour of it. During 21–31 July, territorial claims by the conflicting parties were presented before the Bengal and Punjab boundary commissions. The fundamental principle identified, to determine the distribution of territory, was contiguous Muslim and non-Muslim majority areas. However, it was qualified by considerations of 'other factors' which were left undefined. The arguments put forth were based on zero-sum tactics that nullified any consensus on the distribution of territory. Even the judges nominated by the two sides made partisan recommendations (Ahmed 1999: 149–53). Therefore, the chairman of the Boundary Commission, Sir Cyril Radcliffe, prepared an award which, although ready on 13 August, was not made public until 17 August – that is, after India and Pakistan had become independent! It created considerable bitterness on both sides. In Pakistan, particularly, it was assailed as a conspiracy hatched by Nehru and Mountbatten to compel Radcliffe to award Muslim-majority areas to India.

The United States

Prior to the Second World War, the United States took only cursory interest in the politics of the subcontinent. That changed once war broke out. From 1940 onwards, it began to keenly follow developments in India and started advising Winston Churchill to grant self-rule to the Indians. When the Muslim League passed the Lahore Resolution, demanding the partition of India, it went largely unnoticed in the United States.

The Atlantic Charter

On 12 August 1941, US President Franklin D. Roosevelt and British Prime Minister Winston Churchill, and their staffs, met in utmost secrecy on a warship in the Atlantic Ocean to discuss general strategy vis-à-vis the Axis Powers during the war. The meeting resulted in the two leaders signing the Atlantic Charter, the precursor to the United Nations Charter. The Atlantic Charter publicly denounced Nazi Germany and the use of force and aggression. Furthermore, it stated that sovereignty should be restored to people who had been deprived of it. Churchill interpreted the reference to the restoration of sovereign rights to people in a limited sense, to those countries that had been forcibly annexed during the Second World War. Roosevelt considered it a general principle for decolonisation. In order to mislead the American president, Churchill lied to Roosevelt and told him that seventy-five percent of the Indian Army comprised Muslim soldiers (French 1997: 136–9). He portrayed the Congress party as a cover for Brahminic priesthood and its beastly caste system, as well as Japanese sympathisers in a secret alliance with the Nazis (ibid., 139–64). Although such information dampened US pressure for a while, the United States kept the pressure on. Towards the end of the Second World War, thousands of American soldiers were stationed in north-eastern India but, on the whole, much of Roosevelt's contemporaneous information was derived from some diplomats and visiting US media reporters.

A Vision of Collective Security

The British had been engaged in the Great Game with, first, Czarist Russia and, later, the Soviet Union for more than a century. In that long period, the

British establishment had acquired deep suspicions about Russian intentions which, following the Bolshevik Revolution, had transformed into veritable anathema.

Yalta Conference

Such a pessimistic viewpoint was not shared by Roosevelt. Thus, for example on 11–14 February 1945, when Roosevelt, Churchill, and Stalin met at Yalta to discuss the post-war reorganisation of Europe, Roosevelt was convinced that if Stalin was conceded a legitimate role in Eastern Europe, the latter would be amenable to working with the West in the interest of world peace and democracy. The Soviet Union accepted Roosevelt's invitation to join the United Nations (Ray 2004: 10). The Soviet Union also committed itself to entering the war against Japan, ninety days after the defeat of Nazi Germany, and to the holding of elections in Poland which, at that time, was under a pro-Soviet regime. On that occasion, while speaking in the House of Commons, Churchill remarked:

> The impression I brought back from Crimea, and from all other contacts, is that Marshal Stalin and the Soviet leaders, wish to live in honourable friendship and equity with the western democracies. I also feel that their word is their bond. I know of no government which stands to its obligations, even in its own despite, more steadily than the Russian Soviet government (ibid., 35).

However, in March 1946, Churchill dramatically altered his stand when he made the famous 'Iron Curtain' speech in which he denounced the Soviet Union as the greatest peril to post-war peace. In the British security paradigm, the containment of the Soviet Union was paramount to its position on South Asia. Therefore, the Pakistani scheme began to receive British support towards the end of their rule, when it was realised that the Indian Army could not be kept united and that the Muslim League and Muslim officers in the armed forces wanted a separate state. Such a state was considered to be more amenable to being co-opted into a military alliance than an India under the leadership of Nehru.

Realism Replaces Liberal Idealism in US Foreign Policy

Roosevelt died on 12 April 1945, soon after being elected president for the third time. His successor, Vice-President Harry Truman, was deeply sceptical about Stalin's peaceful intentions. Powerful right-wing Republicans ensured that the president took a hard-line against the Soviet Union. Aswini Ray calls it an intellectual coup that replaced liberal idealism based on international cooperation with hard-core realism rooted in the inevitability of war and conflict between states (2004: 3–5). Such a significant change was manifest in the unfriendly and rude attitude Truman adopted when he received Soviet Foreign Minister Molotov in Washington on 23 April 1945, and was supported by Republican Senator Arthur H. Vandenberg, who was opposed to the concord that was announced at Yalta (Horowitz 1967: 37). The hawks were hoping that the Soviet Union would react by boycotting the San Francisco Conference – which had been called for by Roosevelt, before his death, to formally launch the United Nations. The Soviet Union attended the conference in a constructive manner, and accepted the essentially liberal framework for world peace that the United States had proposed (ibid., 38; Ray 2004: 16).

The Truman administration continued to provoke the Soviet Union. Moreover, in accordance with the pledge given at Yalta to Roosevelt by Stalin, the Soviets began to prepare to enter the war against Japan in the Far East, ninety days after the defeat of Germany. Before that could happen, in August, the United States dropped atom bombs on Japan. These two blasts claimed 400,000 Japanese lives; the Japanese surrendered. The explosion of the atom bombs greatly aggravated the Soviet sense of insecurity. The Soviets had paid a staggering price in lives during the war – at least twenty million Soviet citizens were killed and its villages and towns had been ravaged in a manner hitherto unknown; her industries were in ruins, and food production was greatly reduced. At that point in time, it hardly had the means to embark upon an arms race with the United States. On the other hand, the latter had greatly increased its national wealth through the production of armament. In any event, notwithstanding transformative change in US perceptions about the Soviet Union under Truman, there was no change in policy towards the freedom struggle in South Asia. Consequently, pressure on the British government for an early transfer of power in a united India remained undiminished.

Muslim League Leaders Woo Americans

Jinnah and other Muslim League leaders were acutely aware of the United States' rise as the leader of the Western world. Consequently, the lack of US interest in, and support for, Pakistan was a cause for concern for them. M.A.H. Ispahani, later the first Pakistani ambassador to the United States, after a visit to the United States in November 1946, wrote to Jinnah emphasising the importance of cultivating the Americans. He said, 'I have learnt that sweet words and first impressions count a lot with Americans' (Kux 2001: 260). Earlier, Jinnah had appeared on the cover of *Time* magazine; his rise in politics had been described as 'a story of lust for power, a story that twists and turns like a bullock-cart track in the hills' (ibid.). Such negative profiling by the US administration and media did not deter the Muslim League. On 27 December 1946, Liaquat Ali Khan wrote to the US Charge d'Affaires to India, George Merell, that the massacre of Muslims in Bihar could result in chaos and tempt the USSR to move into the subcontinent (Sarila 2005: 259). Such a tactic failed to make an impact. On 4 April 1947, the US undersecretary of state, Dean Acheson, sent a telegram to the American embassy in London, in which he wrote, 'Our political and economic interest in that part of the world would best be served by the continued integrity of India' (quoted in Sarila 2005: 263).

On 1 May 1947, Jinnah told Raymond Hare of the US State Department that the 'establishment of Pakistan is essential to prevent "Hindu Imperialism" from spreading into Middle East; Muslim countries would stand together against possible Russian aggression and would look to us for assistance' (quoted in Kux 2001: 13). Still, the United States remained unenthusiastic about gaining Pakistan as an ally at the expense of India (Sarila 2005: 311). Unlike the British whose obsession with a perceived Russian thrust for warm waters southwards had resulted in the Great Game between them for more than a century, the American concerns in Asia were driven largely by concerns of a communist takeover in China where their nationalist allies, the Kuomintang, had for quite some time been facing defeat. A united India with a large army was considered important to contain the Chinese in Asia (Kux 2001: 15–16. Nevertheless, once India and Pakistan emerged as separate states, the United States exchanged messages of goodwill with both (ibid., 7–16).

The Soviet Union

The Soviet Union's policy on the colonial question was premised in Vladimir Lenin's famous tract, Imperialism, the Highest Stage of Capitalism (1917). In it, he argued that Karl Marx's dialectical understanding of the role of British colonialism in India, as both the destroyer of the old order and the harbinger of the new, modern, capitalist one, had become obsolete. European colonial powers were exploiting the cheap labour and raw materials of the colonies through direct investment in the colonies, while obstructing indigenous enterprise and investment. Consequently, the Soviet Union became a supporter of decolonisation. However, Soviet support before the end of the Second World War, against various European colonialisms, was more in terms of spreading Marxist literature and encouraging the formation of Communist parties in the colonies. The exception was China where it originally advised the communists to subsume their struggle under the nationalists, but later supported them when the communists and nationalists clashed.

The Indian Freedom Struggle

Some Indians – Hindus, Muslims, and Sikhs – visited the Soviet Union shortly after the Russian Revolution and came back greatly impressed. Among the early arrivals from India were a large number of Muslims who left India during the Hijrat movement of 1920 (Reitz 1995) that evolved when the Khilafat movement (1919–24) failed to convince the British not to dismember the Ottoman Empire (Qureshi 1999). Some returned to India, committed to an overthrow of colonial rule and feudalism. Notwithstanding severe repression, some sections of the population were radicalised; the communists organised a number of strikes among industrial workers and peasant agitations. The British response was to initiate conspiracy cases against them (Antonova, Bongard-Levin, and Kotovsky 1979: 176–93) and to mete out harsh punishments including the death sentence and long prison terms; some were sent to the Andaman Islands for life.

The Soviet Union encouraged the Indian communists to join the freedom movement against colonial rule. However, conflict between the Communist and Congress leaders, over the aims of the freedom movement and the strategy needed to realise freedom from colonial rule, made them difficult partners.

Moreover, in the late 1930s, the Soviet politburo took a radical leftist line on India and supported a militant class struggle as against Gandhi's non-violent movement. Stalin believed that the aim of the Gandhian strategy was 'to keep the people disarmed and to retard progress' (Sarila 2005: 309–10). The Soviet leader was worried about a united India becoming a vast base for the British military after independence. Further complications arose when the Indian Communists joined hands with the British once the Soviet Union was attacked by Germany. Suddenly, Indian Communist propaganda which, hitherto, had described the war as an imperialist conflict began to portray it as a people's war. Many Communists took up jobs in the colonial administration and became allies of the government. That created further tension between the Congress and the Communist Party of India (CPI), because the former remained opposed to the war effort (Antonova, Bongard-Levin, and Kotovsky 1979: 224–9).

The Pakistan Scheme

The attitude of the Soviet leaders towards the Pakistan scheme was confused and ambivalent. On the one hand, they considered it a reflection of British divide-and-rule policy. On the other hand, the CPI began to portray the demand for Pakistan as a progressive movement of the oppressed Muslim minority for liberation from the stranglehold of Hindu moneylenders and capitalists. It was a contradiction of the Soviet state's official position on nations that rejected religion as a basis for claiming the status of a nation. Anyhow, the CPI stand – that the Muslims of India were a nation – was formulated in 1944 by a leading theorist of the party, Dr G. Adhikari (1944). The CPI enjoined its Muslim cadres to join the Muslim League and help it acquire a more class-based political approach instead of only a religious one. Muslim communists took a leading part in the 1945–46 Muslim League election campaign. In the key province of Punjab, communist orators such as C.R. Aslam and Abdullah Malik addressed public gatherings along with Muslim clerics, projecting Pakistan as a socialist paradise where Islamic socialist justice would prevail (interviews with Pakistani communists). Such overtures, however, did not receive a friendly response from the Muslim League leaders who looked upon them with great suspicion. Nevertheless, the Soviet academician, Yuri Zhukov, who visited India in March 1947, returned with the belief that the creation of Pakistan would not harm Soviet interests in the subcontinent.

3

The Colonial Roots of the Pakistan Army

In the late eighteenth century, the English East India Company (EEIC) started recruiting soldiers of Indian stock into their army. As a result, the Bengal, Bombay, and Madras armies came into being. Recruitment of Punjabis into the Bengal Army, especially Sikhs, had begun but their numbers were small until 1857 (Yong 2005: 38). The loyalty of the Bengal Army (consisting not only of Bengalis but also Northern Indians from Bihar and the United Provinces or UP) was subverted in 1857 when a mutiny erupted amongst the Indian sipahis (soldiers, hence sepoys).

The mutiny has been hallowed as the First War of Independence in nationalist Indian and Pakistani writings. It was triggered by a combination of accumulated grievances against the racist attitude of the British officers as well as an immediate reaction to the introduction of a newly introduced cartridge, reportedly laced with cow and pig fat, to be used in the new Enfield rifle. It had to be chewed open before the gunpowder could be poured into the rifle. High-caste Hindu, as well as Muslim, sepoys found such a procedure revolting since the rules of purity, as prescribed by their religions, were being violated. Most of the sepoys who took part in the uprising had been recruited from Bengal, the United Provinces (Uttar Pradesh), and Bihar. Such units were also posted in the Punjab, and there were mutinies in some places in that province too (Yong 2005: 44–49).

The rebels proclaimed the Mughal Emperor, Bahadur Shah Zafar, their sovereign. Some Hindu princes and princesses, who had previously accepted the Company's paramountcy, also joined the uprising because they were adversely affected by the Doctrine of Lapse – which gave the East India Company's government the right to annex princely states if there was no natural heir and one was not adopted in good time. Other disgruntled forces that joined the movement were the warlords and religious figures. The descendants of Shah Waliullah issued a fatwa, calling it a jihad. The followers of Syed Ahmed Shaheed Barelvi, known as Wahabis, also participated in the battles that ensued against the British (Allen 2006). However, most princes, both Hindu and Muslim, kept away or even sided with the British while the participation of the common people was isolated, sporadic, and spontaneous.

To defeat the rebels, the British mobilised former Sikh soldiers of the deceased Maharaja Ranjit Singh, as well as Sikh princes and large contingents of Muslim soldiers from north-western India provided by Muslim tribal and clan leaders from the Punjab and the Trans-Frontier Areas. Taking part in warfare as mercenaries, was an established tradition in these regions. Ironically, just a few years earlier, the British had used soldiers from Bengal, Bihar, and UP to defeat the Sikh armies, which had resulted in the Punjab being annexed in 1849. Afterwards, those Punjabi notables who had sided with the British were rewarded with titles and land grants in the Punjab and the settled areas known as the Trans-Frontier Areas – which, in 1905, were named the North-West Frontier Province. Thus, a structure of loyal landlords was consolidated.

In any case, the 1857 uprising lacked effective leadership and clear objectives. Initially, the rebels killed many Englishmen including their families; but, the counterattack by the British was even bloodier and vengeance was wreaked without any sense of proportion or mercy. The British were later to allege that a grand conspiracy had been hatched by the Muslims, with Bahadur Shah Zafar at the centre of the plot, to establish an Islamic state in India. The facts, however, suggested that such a role was thrust upon him by the mutineers and he himself wanted to avoid confrontation with the East India Company (Dalrymple 2006: 439–43). The British were particularly repressive towards the Muslim rebels and inflicted extreme punishments on them, while the collaborators from among them were rewarded. Jawaharlal Nehru observed succinctly: '…the heavy hand of the British fell more on the Moslems than on the Hindus' (1955: 460).

Indian soldiers from miscellaneous regional backgrounds continued to serve in the army. There were also purely British units, which were not part of the Indian Army but were part of the British Army. With regard to the Indian Army, the colonial government's most significant policy decision was to exclude the rebellious castes and tribes of northern India and Bengal, who had been at the helm of the mutiny, from recruitment opportunities. Instead, emphasis was shifted to the Punjab. Given the geographical contiguity of the Punjab to the Pushto-speaking regions in the north-west, beyond which lay Central Asia, it became the nodal point from which the British launched activities purporting to expand British influence in Afghanistan and the khanates in Central Asia. Consequently, in the Great Game that had already begun in the early nineteenth century between Britain and Czarist Russia to dominate and bring the peoples of Central Asia under their spheres of influence, Punjab's key role was keenly appreciated by the British (Yong 2005: 67–69).

Establishment of the Indian Army

In 1895, the existing military structures were reorganised into the Indian Army. It absorbed the armies of the Bengal, Bombay, and Madras presidencies, as well as the growing body of soldiers from north-western India. Thenceforth, preference was given to Punjabis in the Indian Army. The Indian Army served as the linchpin upon which British power and authority rested (Haq 1993: 1–22; Riza 1989: 75; Yong 2005: 68). A so-called 'martial races theory' was adopted, which justified restrictive selection of Muslims, Hindus, and Sikhs from specific castes and regions in the Punjab – which meant developing a firm structure of dependence, among the Punjabis, on the Raj as well as bonds of loyalty among the upper-crust of Punjabi society. While Rajputs from all the three religious communities were recruited from across the province, special emphasis was given to three regional caste groups: the Khalsa Sikhs of the Jat (Jatt in Punjabi) caste from central Punjab, especially those of the Majha region around Amritsar; Muslim tribes of northern Punjab, such as the Awans, Ghakkars, Janjuas, and Tiwanas (the latter two being Rajputs), especially those from the Salt Range tract comprising the districts of Rawalpindi, Jhelum, and Shahpur; and smaller numbers of Hindu Jats of Rothak and Hissar from south-eastern Punjab (present-day Haryana), and some Dogras from Kangra (Yong 2005: 70–8).

These three major groups faced acute economic hardship in their districts – overpopulation and land fragmentation in the Majha, scarce and poor-quality land in the rain-fed broken hills of the Salt Range, and recurring famines in the south-eastern districts. Moreover, historical enmity existed between the Sikhs and the Muslims of the Salt Range because the Sikh ruler of the kingdom of Lahore in central Punjab, Maharaja Ranjit Singh, had inflicted defeat on the elders of the latter and curtailed their powers. These three groups did not share strong fraternal bonds and were recruited in different companies and regiments, but under the overall unified command of British officers (ibid., 78–90).

Besides such careful selection, based on 'class' and 'military districts', the British evolved a sophisticated system of rewarding those connected to the army. Regular pay and allowances, pensions, and other economic benefits were available to the soldiers as well as those who helped recruit them. The development, in the late nineteenth century, of one of the largest irrigation systems in the world, in western Punjab, had resulted in a network of irrigation canals, barrages, and dams being built to provide irrigation water to the agricultural areas known as 'canal colonies'. The beneficiaries of the land allotments were the peasantry, mainly from the overpopulated, land-fragmented East Punjab, as well as personnel from the Indian Army (Ali 1989). Others to benefit were tribal and clan leaders, village headmen, zaildars, sufedposhs, and so on who helped recruit men for the army. Titles such as Khan Bahadur, Rai Bahadur, Nawab, and even Sir were conferred on them. Simultaneously, the government maintained the threat of cancellation and confiscation of titles and land grants if their bearers did not cooperate in supplying soldiers to the Indian Army and in containing trouble in their areas.

Moreover, through the Land Alienation Act of 1901, the British made sure that its rural support base in the Punjab was safeguarded against moneylenders and the rising urban entrepreneurs. The extent of Punjabi involvement in the Indian Army can be gauged from the fact that out of a total of 683,149 combatant troops recruited in India between August 1914 and November 1918, about 60 percent were Punjabis (Yong 2005: 70–98). It is no wonder that, at the beginning of the twentieth century, Punjab was celebrated as the 'sword arm of the Raj'. The Indian Army was deployed in war theatres in Europe and the Middle East during the First World War. Initially, the Indian Army was exclusively comprised British officers but, in 1917, it was decided that Indians should also be included in the officer corps. The first Indians were commissioned in 1919.

Muslims in the Indian Army

Notwithstanding a large Muslim presence in the Indian Army, suspicion and wariness existed in the military establishment about them (Khan 2006: 49). As mentioned earlier, prejudice had persisted since 1857 that Muslims played the major role in the mutiny of 1857. Before the First World War, there were purely Muslim battalions – that was to change later. Indian Muslims were extremely worried about Turkey joining the war, in alliance with Germany and against Britain. When that happened, it became clear that Indian Muslims would be fighting fellow Muslims. At the time, the Ottoman Sultan was considered the leader of the worldwide Sunni Muslim communities. However, the British were able to procure fatwas (religious decrees) from mainstream Barelvi–Sunni ulema (clerics) and pirs (spiritual divines) to the effect that since the Ottomans were not from the Prophet's Quraish tribe they could not be the caliphs of the Muslims and claim the Sunni Muslims' allegiance. Therefore, according to the clerics and spiritual divines, Turkey's participation in the war was not an Islamic war (Alavi 2002; Qureshi 1999: 76). Such a fatwa was important as the Barelvi school had a stronghold in Punjab and the NWFP from where a very large number of soldiers were recruited into the Indian Army.

Classic Sunni political theory restricted the right to the caliphate to the Quraish tribe, while Shia theory narrowed down the leadership exclusively to the Imam: with Ali as the first Imam, and then his direct descendants through his marriage to the daughter of the Prophet, Fatima. The centrality of the caliphate, to Islamic power, diminished over the centuries after the later caliphs lost control over their vast empire that had come into being through conquest during ad 632–750. In 1258, the Mongols laid waste to Baghdad and, with it, ended the line of caliphs in the Arab heartland that traced their descent from the Quraish. In the thirteenth century, the Syrian, Ibn Taymiyyah, began to argue that the spiritual leadership of the Muslim community resided in the custodians of the Islamic faith, the ulema, and therefore rejected the centrality of the caliph to Islamic power. Ibn Khuldun went even further and made the Quraish descent to the caliphate a purely historical fact and not a religious one. However, in 1774, the caliphate theory was revived, albeit in a modified manner. The precondition of Quraish descent was waived to enable the Ottoman Sultan to claim equal status in his negotiations with Czarina

Katherine, who claimed to represent the Orthodox Christians (Ahmed 1987: 56–60; Faruki 1971: 142–51). In the twentieth century, the Ottoman Sultan symbolised the façade of Islamic power and suzerainty in a world increasingly dominated by the Christian powers of the West.

Despite the *fatwas*, some minor mutinies occurred among Muslim soldiers reluctant to fight fellow Turks – the Ottoman Sultan had entered the war on Germany's side – the most notable took place in Singapore in February 1915, when some Muslim soldiers killed some British officers (Qureshi 1999: 78–79). At the same time, ironically, resentment towards Ottoman rule over the Middle East had been growing among the Arabs – something the British made full use of to instigate the Arab revolt of 1916. In any event, at the start of the First World War, the British had obtained a fatwa against the Ottomans, clearing the way for the Indian Muslims to fight against the Turks during the First World War.

When the War ended, British policy changed: purely Muslim units were not established because Muslim soldiers were deemed susceptible to pan-Islamic appeals. Besides the religious factor, which particularly affected the loyalties of the Muslim troops, a general feeling of alienation was prevalent among the Indian personnel. The future founder of Pakistan, Mohammad Ali Jinnah, who was already a leading voice in Indian politics, began to advocate the 'Indianization of the army'. By that, he meant that there was a need for a greater representation of Indians in the officer corps. He also demanded that a military academy, on the model of Sandhurst, should be established in India. His argument was that such inclusive measures would generate loyalty to the King-Emperor and enhance the Indian sense of participation in the functioning of the Indian Empire. In this connection, he delivered four speeches between March 1924 and March 1928, reiterating the need for more Indian officers (ibid., 240–77). In 1931, he pointed out that out of 3000 officers, only 70 to 71 were Indians (Jafar, Rehman and Jafar 1977: 240). His efforts, and that of other members of the Indian Legislative Council, resulted in more Indians being granted the King's Commission. The Dehra Dun Military Academy was established in 1932. At the start of the Second World War, there were 333 Indian officers, as against 3031 British officers (Amin 1999: 61).

The Punjab Unionist Party and Army Recruitment

The Punjab Unionist Party was founded in 1923. Although predominantly Muslim in composition, its first leader, Sir Fazl-i-Hussain (d. 1936), managed to mobilise landowning interests across the religious divides and establish a stable inter-communal political order. His successor, Sir Sikander Hayat Khan (d. 1942), and Sir Chhottu Ram (d. 1945), the leader of the Hindu Jats of eastern Punjab, continued to work in alliance with the Sikh Khalsa Nationalist Party led by Sir Sunder Singh Majithia and Sir Joginder Singh. The Unionists and their Sikh allies were British loyalists who provided political stability and, notwithstanding some radical influence on sections of the Sikhs, the Punjab remained the most loyal as well as the most favoured province of the British. When the Second World War broke out, Sir Sikander declared that half a million men from the Punjab would be recruited into the army (Ahmed 2012: 61). Altogether, 2.5 million men served in the Indian Army during the War (Marston 2009: 471), resulting in a further increase of Indian officers, but few were promoted to senior positions. Thus, for example, as late as 1946 only one Indian, K.M. Cariappa, had been promoted to the rank of full brigadier and four to temporary brigadiers (Riza 1989: 100). Some became colonels, but most retired as majors and captains.

It is noteworthy, thirty-six percent of the men in the Indian Army were recruited from the Punjab. The actual number of combatants from the Punjab increased though, in absolute numbers, the share of the Punjab went down to one-third of the Indian Army. The martial race theory was practically abandoned and the doors were opened to a wider pool of people from all over India, as well as from castes and tribes in the Punjab that hitherto had not been included among the martial races (Haq 1993: 80). In spite of such significant changes, the martial castes and tribes continued to be the major component of the Punjabis in the armed forces. During the Second World War, the Indian Army fought not only in Europe, Africa, and the Middle East, but also in Southeast Asia.

No Muslim state was involved in the Second World War, but misgivings against the Muslims remained steadfast among the policy makers. Even as late as 1947, there were no exclusively Muslim units whereas there were purely Hindu and Sikh ones (Mansergh and Moon 1981: 35). According to Noor-ul-Haq, before 1939, the Muslim and Hindu components of the Indian Army were about thirty-eight percent each. After 1942, the Muslim percentage declined to about thirty-two percent while, by the end of 1945, the Hindu percentage had increased to about forty-seven percent (Haq 1993: 83). The figures that Haq has given apply to India as a whole. He does not mention the situation in the Punjab, where it was reversed. The Sikh intake declined because of the spread of Communist influence in central Punjab, while that of the Muslims quadrupled. The percentage of the total male population enrolled in the Indian Army, especially from the western districts of Rawalpindi, Attock, and Jhelum, reached fifteen percent (Yong 2005: 290–91). The regional emphasis on recruitment assumed a pronounced western province complexion. 'By 1943, Punjabi Muslims and Pathans accounted for twenty-five percent of the annual intake into the army, while the Sikhs and Hindu Jats accounted for roughly seven and five percent respectively' (ibid., 291).

With regard to the command structure, there was a significant increase in the number of Indian officers during the Second World War, but as noted already, they held middle level and lower positions. By 1946–47, almost eighty percent of the officers were Indians, mostly Hindu (Cohen 1998: 6). Except for the establishment of the Indian National Army (INA) by the Japanese, from among the Indian soldiers and officers that they had captured, the Indian Army as a whole remained loyal to the King-Emperor (Hamid 1986: 15–22). There was, however, an abortive uprising of Indian naval ratings in February 1946 (Haq 1993: 132–37).

Dividing the Armed Forces

As mentioned earlier, the British establishment believed, almost until the time of the partition, that the Indian Army should not be divided even if India was partitioned (Nath 2009: 514). However, as soon as Mountbatten became viceroy on 24 March 1947, he began to consider the possibility of the division of the Indian armed forces if India was partitioned. He probed this with the commander-in-chief, Field Marshal Auchinleck, on 28 March during one of his earliest meetings with top British civil and military officials. Auchinleck expressed the view that it would take 'from five to ten years satisfactorily to divide the Indian Army' (Mansergh and Moon 1981: 35). However, the Muslim League refused and insisted that Pakistan would need its separate military. When Mountbatten again took up this issue, conveying the Muslim

League's complaint to Auchinleck, that Muslims were underrepresented in the Indian Army, the latter dismissed it as incorrect and stated that the proportion of Muslims in the army was twenty-nine percent – though it had dropped from thirty-seven percent before the War because the number of Madrasis had risen from a mere three to twenty percent. He reiterated that dividing the army would be a very difficult task and would take a long time to complete (ibid., 223–5).

However, Mountbatten had become increasingly convinced that India would be partitioned as the chances of agreement between the Congress and Muslim League, or between the Muslim League and the Sikhs in the Punjab, had begun to fade away as they assumed uncompromising positions. Moreover, as, from the second half of May, rioting in the Punjab was again on the rise, Auchinleck was compelled to consider the division of the armed forces once more. On 27 May, he submitted a detailed note in which he elaborated the very serious practical difficulties in managing such a division. He wrote that there were no 'Muslim' units or 'Hindu' units in the navy and air force. All units were religiously mixed. However, in the army, there were certain fighting units (battalions and regiments) that consisted of, 'as far as rank and file are concerned, wholly of Hindus or wholly of Muslims, but this does not apply to their officers. British, Muslim, and all other classes of Indian Officers are completely mixed throughout the army without any regard to their race or religion' (ibid., 1005). He strongly emphasised that till such time that the process of dividing them was not completed, it must be 'centrally controlled until it is completed, unless there is to be a complete administrative breakdown and a consequent disintegration of the Armed Forces' (ibid., 1005–6).

3 June 1947 Partition Plan

The long-standing arguments to effect a smooth partition of the armed forces became irrelevant after the British government announced the Partition Plan on 3 June 1947 – which dramatically moved forward the date for the transfer of power from June 1948 to mid-August 1947. A day before the public announcement of the Partition Plan, a conference paper entitled, 'The Administrative Consequences of Partition', redrafted on Mountbatten's instructions and detailing different aspects for effecting the colonial state's division of assets, was discussed. A Partition Committee, headed by the Viceroy a nd comprising senior civil and military officers and representatives of the main political parties, was to oversee the partition process. With regard to the military, it stipulated that a Defence Committee for the division of the Indian Armed Forces would be set up by the commander-in-chief, who would also establish sub-committees as deemed necessary. The Defence Committee was to report directly to the Partition Committee (Mansergh and Moon 1982: 56). From 12–26 June 1947, its members, besides the viceroy, were Liaquat Ali Khan and Abdur Rab Nishtar of the Muslim League, and Sardar Vallabhbhai Patel and Dr Rajendra Prasad of the Congress party. On 27 June, its name was changed to the Partition Council, and Mohammad Ali Jinnah replaced Abdur Rab Nishtar.

Committee for the Reconstitution of the Indian Armed Forces

On 15 June, Field Marshal Auchinleck elaborated the committee he had set up for the reconstitution of the Indian Armed Forces and the sub-committees. The Armed Forces Reconstitution Committee was to be assisted by the Navy Sub-Committee, Army Sub-Committee, and Air Force Sub-Committee. Senior British and Indian officers were included in the main committee and sub-committees (ibid., 410–13). The Indian personnel of the three branches were to be given a choice to opt for either India or Pakistan, subject to acceptance by the governments of the two dominions (ibid., 412).

On 16 June, Mountbatten met with some of his senior advisers, including V.P. Menon, and informed them that 'Auchinleck was now satisfied that the division of the Indian Armed Forces could be carried out without vitally impairing their efficiency, provided that there was goodwill and trust, and provided that political pressure was not applied to hurry the process unduly' (ibid., 419–20). So, a fundamental change had taken place in the commander-in-chief's views on the division of the armed forces; he now argued that instead of five-ten years, as he had previously argued, the task could be accomplished in a few weeks.

On 20 June, Mountbatten met Liaquat Ali Khan who, among other things pertaining to the armed forces, informed him that 'he and Mr Jinnah were resolved that they would not take over the reins of Government in Pakistan unless they had an Army on the spot, and under their control' (ibid., 534).

Moreover, Liaquat expressed the view that, 'it would help to steady matters if British troops were to remain while the Indian Army was under process of transition' (ibid.). A twist to the division of the armed forces occurred when Jinnah told Mountbatten, on 23 June, that 'the Muslims no longer had faith in Field Marshal Auchinleck and they would much prefer to see someone else in his place' (ibid., 582). Mountbatten disagreed strongly and replied that 'there was no more reliable or respected officer in India than Field Marshal Auchinleck' (ibid.). Apparently, Mountbatten did not convey Jinnah's opinion to Auchinleck because we will learn that, in the days ahead, Auchinleck's position turned out to be sympathetic to Pakistan – on the grounds that a proper and fair distribution of the joint assets of the armed forces was not allowed by India.

Also, on 23 June, the Field Marshal submitted a note to Mountbatten in which he argued that while the original date of transfer of power was June 1948, but as the date had been drastically brought forward, a complete nationalisation of the armies of India and Pakistan would not be possible and that British officers would be needed by both for some time (ibid., 583–4). On 24 June, Field Marshal Viscount Montgomery met Jinnah and Nehru separately in Delhi. Jinnah wanted the withdrawal of British troops only after 15 August, as trouble was expected; both wanted some British officers to serve in the armed forces of their respective countries (ibid., 607–8).

In a meeting of the Partition Committee on 26 June, which Liaquat Ali Khan, Sardar Patel, Dr Rajendra Prashad, Abdur Rab Nishtar, Lord Ismay, Sir E. Mieville, Mohamad Ali (Chaudhry Muhammad Ali), A.H. Patel, and Osman Ali (Secretariat) attended, non-members such as Sardar Baldev Singh and Field Marshal Auchinleck were also present. Auchinleck informed them that while the division of the armed forces would take place before partition, nationalisation would have to wait and that British officers would be needed during the transition (ibid., 652–3). Moreover, until the division was completed, administrative control for the whole army would remain with a joint headquarters under the commander-in-chief (ibid., 654). He also informed them that a reasonable principle for the division 'would be to move units composed predominantly of Muslims to Pakistan and the rest to India respectively' (ibid.).

Auchinleck only learnt about Montgomery's meeting with Jinnah and Nehru informally and hoped to receive formal confirmation. On 26 June, he made it clear, in a brief note, that Jinnah should not expect British troops to be used to curb communal disturbances. They were to be used strictly in 'protecting British life' (ibid., 660–61). Meanwhile, in a meeting of the Chiefs of Staff in London on the same day, the opinion was expressed that both India and Pakistan would be well-advised to retain British troops for at least two to three years, during which period both states could organise themselves better to ward off foreign aggression (ibid., 665–71).

A detailed note, dated 27 June, prepared by H.M. Patel – a bureaucrat nominated to the Partition Council by the Congress party – on the instruction of Mountbatten took up different problems relating to the division of the armed forces, and also discussed the terms of reference of the Armed Forces Reconstitution Committee. Most centrally, it was to make proposals for the division of the Royal Indian Navy, Royal Indian Army, and the Royal Indian Air Force. It stated, 'For the successful division of the Armed Forces, the services of a number of British officers now serving will be required' (ibid., 699).

Troop Composition in early July 1947

On 1 July 1947, the Indian Army comprised 373,570 Indians: 154,780 or 41.4 percent Hindus; 135,268 or 36.2 percent Muslims; 35,390 or 9.5 percent Sikhs; 16,382 or 4.4 percent Christians and others; and 31,750 or 8.5 percent Gurkhas (Husain 1999). Thus, of the 2.5 million who had been mobilised during the Second World War, most had been demobilised and sent home while some were sill stationed abroad. In addition, much smaller numbers were also serving in the navy and air force in July 1947. British troops in India, at that time, consisted of only six battalions (Mansergh and Moon 1982: 976).

On 8 July, Nehru informed Mountbatten that 'a British Commander-in-Chief and a number of British senior commanders are being asked to stay on' (Mansergh and Moon 1983: 14). With regard to Pakistan,

Jinnah told Mountbatten that 'the C-in-C of Pakistan and several of the senior officers retained will similarly be British' (ibid., 21). On 9 July, Mountbatten informed the governor of the Punjab, Sir Evan Jenkins, that:

> The Commander-in-Chief has asked me urgently to impress on all governors that, in order to carry out the proposed reconstitution of the

> Armed Forces, it is necessary that as many troops as possible should be released from their duties in aid of the civil power so that they can be concentrated in their normal locations (ibid., 34–5).

At a meeting on 10 July, it was decided that, on 15 August 1947, the Army Headquarters of each Dominion would become responsible for operational control of 'all Indian formations and units within their respective territories.... The present Armed Forces Headquarters will continue to exist and will become Supreme Headquarters' (ibid., 75). Moreover, with effect from 15 August, 'British formations will come under command of the Major General British Troops in India, who will be responsible directly to the Supreme Commander' (ibid.). In a meeting between Mountbatten and Auchinleck on 15 July, the latter noted that Sardar Baldev Singh, who was defence member of the Interim Government at that time, had spoken ill of British officers and 'had become quite intolerable recently and was dictated by his inane desire to do down Pakistan at all costs during the partition of the Armed Forces; whereas the British officers were anxious to see ordinary fair play' (ibid., 165–6).

The India Independence Act of 18 July 1947 referred, only briefly, to provisions being made for the 'division of the Indian armed forces of His Majesty between the new Dominions, and for the command and governance of those forces until the division is completed' (ibid., 242). While such moves were under way in India, opinion in London continued to be that the two dominions, as members of the British Commonwealth, should continue to be linked to Britain through defence and security arrangements. On 24 July, secretary of state for India and Burma, the Earl of Listowel, conveyed these ideas to Prime Minister Attlee. While, on the one hand, Britain would ensure that British troops remained in the subcontinent to thwart the invasion of these two dominions, on the other hand, India and Pakistan would provide access to strategic airfields, as well as the cooperation of their armed forces, in case of British interests being threatened in a war.

However, mutual help was to be freely decided by the two dominions; even if they did not join the war, they were to provide bases and other facilities (ibid., 314–21). The Earl of Listowel did not dwell on another possibility – what would happen if India and Pakistan went to war against each other. Since both would be members of the Commonwealth, the role of the former paramount power would become very difficult to define. Therefore, he did not express an opinion on such a situation. Earlier, Mountbatten had exerted great pressure on both to join the Commonwealth and had succeeded.

In a letter dated 26 July to Mountbatten, Jawaharlal Nehru opposed the appointment of Chaudhri Muhammad Ali as financial adviser for military finance to the commander-in-chief because he had opted for Pakistan. Nehru wanted someone else as the financial adviser on India to the commander-in-chief, or possibly a joint Military Finance and Accounting Organization under Chaudhri Muhammad Ali or a British officer. Nehru complained that the commander-in-chief's attitude was not in line with the position that Congress had developed. As supreme commander, for a short transitional period, he would not 'be free to carry out administration in accordance with his own ideas' (ibid., 366).

The point Nehru was making was that Auchinleck would have to abide by the policies the Indian government would make during that period. Mountbatten reported at the 65th Staff Meeting, on 28 July, that the Indian position had been explained to the commander-in-chief – that Chaudhri Muhammad Ali was not acceptable to India – and that he understood it and would make the required changes. More importantly, it was clarified that, apart from some minor clashes between the two dominions in which British officers in the employ of the two dominions may play a role, they would not do so if it escalated into a war between them (ibid., 374).

The chief of general staff in India, Lieutenant-General Arthur Smith prepared a top secret document dated 29 July that was 'not to be divulged to Indians' (ibid., 394), and which was only to be shared by the highest level of British officers that were going to serve with India and Pakistan; when they left, all copies of it were to be destroyed. It stated that, after 14 August, British troops could not be used to save Indian lives in communal disturbances in either India or Pakistan. They could, however, be used in a communal disturbance to protect British lives (ibid., 395).

A personal report of the Viceroy dated 1 August mentioned, among other things, the formula upon which the division of the armed forces would take place:

> I should explain that we have been working on the basis of communal proportions in dividing the fighting services, the smaller partner by far

> being, of course, Pakistan. In the case of the Army this was the obvious method of dividing the actual soldiers since there was no shortage of equipment, and it worked out at a rough proportion of 70:30. In the case of the Navy it worked out at about 60:40, but as India [sic] have a far bigger coastline with more harbours and a far greater proportion of the trade to guard, the actual ships were divided in the proportion of 70:30. When it came to the Air the communal proportions worked out at 80:20. As there were ten squadrons to divide (2 transports and 8 fighters) the India representatives claimed 8. The Armed Forces Reconstitution Committee recommended that on the [sic] analogy of the naval partition the proportions should be 70:30, since Pakistan had the North-West Frontier to guard (ibid., 446).

Such a decision did not please the Indian representatives in the Armed Forces Reconstitution Committee, noted Mountbatten. Previously, they had turned down Mountbatten's suggestion that India should send air squadrons to help Pakistan if there was trouble with the tribes in the NWFP. However, they agreed that if Pakistan was invaded by Afghanistan or any other foreign power they would consider lending their squadrons to Pakistan. However, 'They now took the line that even to give Pakistan one of the squadrons to which they [India] would be entitled would be equivalent to giving them India's facilities to use them against the tribes' (ibid., 447). Moreover, Sardar Patel infuriated Jinnah and Liaquat by referring to the tribes of the NWFP as 'our people'; more significantly, he suggested that Auchinleck and his senior commanders 'are becoming pro-Pakistan, whereas in fact they are, of course, merely trying to be fair' asserted Mountbatten (ibid.).

With specific regard to the Pakistan Army, Mountbatten wrote on 8 August that General Messervy – who was going to be the commander-in-chief of the Pakistan Army – had informed him that after Pakistan became independent, there would be only thirty-five battalions left at the disposal of Pakistan, instead of the current sixty-seven, including five British battalions. This would create a dangerous situation on the North-West Frontier border. Therefore, 'up to 10,000 demobilized Punjabi Mussalmen and Pathan infantrymen should be re-enlisted for the Regular Army as soon as possible', wrote Messervy (ibid., 600). He also suggested that Pakistan should declare that there was no question of altering the border with Afghanistan, now or in the future.

4

The First Kashmir War, 1947–48

Pakistan and India became independent on 14 and 15 August 1947, respectively. However, the Radcliffe Award, which fixed the international border between them, was publicly announced afterwards on 17 August 1947. The Pakistan that emerged was 'moth-eaten', as its founder, Mohammad Ali Jinnah, had famously exclaimed, in exasperation, when he realised after the announcement of the 3 June 1947 Partition Plan that the Muslim-majority provinces of Bengal and Punjab may not be awarded to Pakistan as a whole. By the last week of that month, it was certain that Bengal and Punjab would be divided. In Bengal, Radcliffe gave away some Muslim majority districts or portions to India but, simultaneously, placed the Chittagong Hill Tracts – which was predominantly comprised of Buddhist and Animist tribes – in Pakistan, even when they and their leaders wanted to be in India (Banu 1991: 240).

The award on Punjab was even more controversial. It was ready by 13 August but made public on 17 August, i.e. after Pakistan and India had become independent. It pleased neither India nor Pakistan, though both accepted it as legally binding (Ahmed 2012: 273–76). Pakistan developed an acute sense of injustice because Gurdaspur district, which had a very slight Muslim majority (fifty-one percent), was split. Three of the four tahsils – a revenue and administrative unit smaller than a district – which were mainly located on the eastern bank of the river Ravi, were given to India. Such a decision was attributed to a purported conspiracy, hatched by Mountbatten and Nehru, to provide India with a dirt road to the Kashmir Valley via the Pathankot tahsil of the Gurdaspur district. Moreover, some portions of Lahore district, that had Sikh majorities, were taken away and given to East Punjab to make the border between Lahore on the Pakistani side and Amritsar on the Indian side more or less equidistant. The final border was almost a ditto copy of Viceroy Lord Wavell's top secret Demarcation Plan of February 1946, which was an auxiliary to the Demarcation Plan of February 1946; the latter had been prepared by Viceroy Wavell as part of the Breakdown Plan of December 1945. Wavell had argued that Amritsar, a non-Muslim majority district of the Lahore division and a sacred city for the Sikhs, would remain in India. Therefore, the adjoining Muslim-majority tahsils to the left of Amritsar – Batala and Gurdaspur – and the whole of the non-Muslim majority Ferozepore district on the right of Amritsar, including its abutting Muslim-majority tahsils of Ferozepore and Zira, would remain in India. Thus, Amritsar would not protrude into Pakistani territory and so face permanent insecurity and an existentialist risk (Mansergh and Moon 1976: 912).

On the other hand, the Sikhs were denied Nankana Sahib, the birthplace of the founder of their religion, Guru Nanak. Additionally, Sikh and Hindu claims on Lahore, Lyallpur, Montgomery, and many other districts of Lahore division, on the basis of overwhelming property ownership, were also rejected (Ahmed 1999: 153–4). Wrangling about the division of territory was greatly exacerbated by the fact that the partition process proved to be a very bloody affair. It resulted in the biggest forced migration of people in modern history: an estimated fourteen–eighteen million crossed the India–Pakistan border. It was also the first experiment in ethnic, or rather religious, cleansing in the Punjab – almost no Hindu or Sikh was left in the Pakistani West Punjab. Equally, in East Punjab, the Muslims were nearly wiped out except for in the tiny princely state of Malerkotla. Anywhere between a million and two million people perished in the partition of India, of which 500,000 to 1,000,000 were the Hindus, Muslims, and Sikhs of the Punjab. At least 90,000 women were abducted, many were raped, and some were never recovered (Ahmed 2012 xxxvi–xxxviii).

The international border in the Punjab was drawn frightfully close to Lahore, the designated capital of the Pakistani West Punjab and arguably the most important city of Pakistan in 1947. Other major towns, such as Sialkot, were also not far from the border. In case of a successful advance by the Indian Army in the Pakistani Punjab, West Pakistan could easily be split into two. On the opposite side, in East Punjab, Amritsar and Ferozepore were equally close to the border, and Jullundhar and Hoshiarpur were not very far. However, India had vast space at its disposal, to furnish it with strategic depth. Its key cities of Delhi, Bombay, and Madras were safely removed from the border.

Moreover, there was 1000 miles of Indian territory between East and West Pakistan. Pakistan's worries did not stop at its border with India. On the western border, Pakistan inherited the Durand Line which divided the Pakhtun tribes of India and Afghanistan. Pakistan wanted the status quo to be maintained; something the Afghans were opposed to. Therefore, Afghanistan expressed its displeasure by opposing Pakistan's membership of the UN. Afghanistan, however, had amicable relations with India. From a military and defence point of view, Pakistan was in an exceptionally vulnerable situation at the time of its birth. Earlier, during the 1946 provincial elections, the Frontier Congress, which was supported by the Khudai Khidmatgars of Abdul Ghaffar Khan, won 30 seats including 19 Muslim seats, while the Muslim League secured 17 seats (Ahmed 1998: 184). Yet, after a referendum that allowed only two options: the province could either join India or Pakistan, the province was allotted to Pakistan. The Frontier Congress wanted a third option, namely the creation of an independent state of Pakhtunistan. As this demand was overruled by the British, the Frontier Congress boycotted the referendum. Thus, out of a total electorate of 572,798 only 292,118 cast their votes. Votes cast for Pakistan were 289,244 and for India 2874. This meant that 50.5 percent votes were cast for Pakistan (Jansson 1981: 222).

Balochistan, the largest area in West Pakistan in terms of area but the most sparsely populated, became part of Pakistan in a different manner. British Balochistan acceded to Pakistan in 1947 through the decision of the Shahi Jirga – a consultative assembly whose members were nominated by the government. The Khan of Kalat, however, declared himself independent on 11 August 1947 – until, under the threat of military action, the state of Kalat 'acceded' to Pakistan at the end of March 1948. On 1 April 1948, the Pakistan Army was sent into Kalat. The Khan had already signed the accession bill on 27 March, but his younger brother, Prince Abdul Karim, declared a revolt against Pakistan. Although some skirmishes took place, the rebels were finally defeated (Harrison 1981: 22–23). Sindh, in southern West Pakistan, was the only province that was awarded to Pakistan without any change in its boundaries.

Under the circumstances, while being a South Asian state, Pakistan could claim geographical and cultural linkages beyond South Asia. West

Pakistan was geographically and culturally linked to central and west Asia. East Pakistan was located on the border with Southeast Asia. Communist movements were prevalent in many parts of Southeast Asia; in China, the Communists were emerging as powerful competitors for power against the nationalists. Given such a sui generis location, Pakistan was in a position to serve as an outpost for military action to other regions.

Weak and Poorly-Equipped Armed Forces

However, such potential for worldwide military assignments was only hypothetical in 1947. Pakistan was to receive assets from the British Indian Army in the proportion of 64:36; India was to receive the greater share since it was larger in terms of territory and population – in roughly the same proportion. Consequently, Pakistan received six armoured divisions while India received fourteen. Pakistan was given eight artillery regiments while forty were given to India; eight infantry regiments were awarded to Pakistan, and twenty-one to India. Moreover, there was an acute dearth of officers and technically trained personnel in Pakistan (Cohen 1998: 7). Viceroy Mountbatten had established the Joint Defence Council (JDC) comprising himself, the defence ministers of India and Pakistan, and Field Marshal Claude Auckinleck – who, on 15 August 1947, was appointed supreme commander of both the Indian and Pakistani armies. The JDC had been tasked to complete its work of dividing the armed forces and military assets by the end of March 1948 (Cheema 2003: 18). However, according to Pervaiz Iqbal Cheema, the JDC could not work properly because the Indians did not cooperate and exerted immense pressure on Governor-General Mountbatten – Mountbatten served as governor-general of India after independence – to abolish the JDC, which he did. Cheema has remarked:

> Auchinleck had predicted that Pakistan would not get its share of military assets, and that proved to be the case. Pakistan's Foreign Minister later informed the UN Security Council that the Indians as well as Lord Mountbatten had failed to honour their pledges to deliver Pakistan its proper share, and 'out of 165000 tons of ordnance stores due to Pakistan only 4703 tons were delivered by 31st March 1948'. That meant that only 3 percent of the total allocated stores were delivered. Not a single one

> out of 249 allocated tanks was delivered and whatever Pakistan received in terms of ammunition or other items of military stories was either damaged or unserviceable or obsolete. Moreover, India inherited all the ordnance factories, as these were situated in areas that formed part of India, and Pakistan was deprived of the compensation that would enable it to build its own (ibid.).

Robert B. Osborn, who has written a doctoral dissertation on Auchinleck's position on the partition of India and his role in dividing the Indian Army, has succinctly captured the field marshal's state of mind in the following words:

> For Auchinleck the decision to partition the Indian Army was his worst nightmare come true. The traditions of nearly two hundred years were to be abandoned, and the Army in which he had achieved adulthood was finally to die, and to die by his own hand.…Auchinleck himself continued to require some justifying reason for perpetrating what must have been a crime, or at least a tragedy, to his conscience. He found such justification in a growing determination that if partition must be accomplished then it must be done so as fairly as possible (1994: 110).

This ambition could not be sustained because of many reasons. Since Jinnah had left Delhi, he could not influence what was happening in India any longer. This problem was compounded by the fact that Mountbatten was not the governor-general of both India and Pakistan – which further weakened Pakistan's ability to be represented in Delhi. Auchinleck had found Jinnah's abrupt departure to Karachi especially dangerous as Pakistan no longer had a leader of stature present in Delhi – where the supreme commander had his office – to represent it while negotiations were taking place. The field marshal expressed this in the following words:

> Pakistan representation…has undoubtedly suffered from the fact that her Government is in Karachi and not in Delhi and this has resulted on more than one occasion in my having to suggest or present the case for Pakistan, which is undesirable as it has undoubtedly increased the already strong and carefully fostered conviction of members of the Indian Cabinet and their subordinate officials that I and the officers of Supreme Commander's Headquarters are biased in favour of Pakistan (quoted in Osborn 1994: 173).

Nevertheless, Auchinleck continued to insist on a fair division of the colonial Indian Army's joint assets, only to face increasingly hostility from India. The Indian government began a concerted campaign to demand that he be removed from the position of supreme commander. By 26 September 1947, Mountbatten gave in to such pressure and wrote to the field marshal that the Indian government wanted his removal. He told him that the Pakistan government would oppose that, but only to draw capital out of the situation. He informed Auchinleck that, 'It is only a while ago that they were pressing for your removal on the grounds of your anti-Moslem sentiments' (ibid., 186). Mountbatten was referring to what Jinnah had stated some months earlier about the Muslim League having no faith in the field marshal. It is clear that Mountbatten was no longer interested in defending the field marshal. Jinnah had rebuffed Mountbatten by denying him the position of governor-general of Pakistan as well. Such a rebuff, in all probability, prejudiced Mountbatten against Pakistan though the truth is that, at least until 1 August, he tried to get Pakistan its fair share.

Auchinleck informed Mountbatten and other British officials, in early October, that he had decided to leave Delhi by 30 November and to close his office on 31 December 1947. He also informed Jinnah. On 16 October, when the JDC met, Jinnah objected to the decision, asserting that the task of dividing the assets had not been completed and, therefore, such a decision was unacceptable. Mountbatten countered by stating that most of the assets had been divided and whatever was left to be sorted out could be done by the commanders-in-chief of the two armies (both were Englishmen). On 21 October, the Indian government publicly endorsed the early closure of the Supreme Commander Headquarters. Thereafter, some legal quibbling followed about whether the JDC could also be dissolved before April 1948 (ibid., 187–98). The British government had already been won over by Mountbatten's argument, to the idea of winding up the Supreme Commander Headquarters. The JDC also lost its relevance in the subsequent months. In any case, by 7 November 1947, movement of all armoured and artillery regiments had been completed in both directions. Similarly, all infantry units from India to Pakistan, and all except one from Pakistan to India, had also been completed (Amin 1999: 78). However, with regard to equipment and military hardware, Pakistan did not receive its due share of the military assets, as Cheema has noted.

Getting Started

Although some industrialisation had been taking place in British India since the beginning of the twentieth century, this was in areas that remained in India. The level of education in Pakistan was extremely low, and overall social development poor. Pakistani society comprised of rich landlords, a small intelligentsia, and millions of peasants, artisans, and other poor. A substantial middle-class was conspicuous by its absence. Pakistan's exchequer was nearly empty when it began its journey as an independent state. In the regard, it is important to mention the famous fast-unto-death that Mahatma Gandhi undertook to force the Indian government to give Pakistan its due share of Rs 550 million from a common kitty bequeathed by the colonial state. The argument that Nehru and Home Minister Patel pleaded, for withholding the cash, was that Pakistan would buy arms to sustain its ongoing covert military activities in Kashmir. However, they had to give in to Gandhi's pressure (Ahmed 2010).

In any case, lack of capital and infrastructure created a basis for soliciting foreign help and aid – to finance Pakistan's modernisation and development (Burki 1991: 111). However, attention to modernisation and development was eclipsed by security concerns immediately after Pakistan came into being. The India Independence Act of 15 June 1947 had left the status of the princely states contentious. On the one hand, they were free to decide their future and could, in principle, remain independent but were expected to negotiate their relationships with the two successor states of India and Pakistan. Most of the princely states that were surrounded by Indian territory sought merger with India. The same happened in Pakistan. The princely states of Bahawalpur, Khairpur, Makran, Lasbela, Chitral, Dir, Swat, Amb, and Phulra sought merger with Pakistan (Gankovsky and Gordon-Polonskaya 1972: 97–98). On the other hand, there were some cases where annexation by India and Pakistan was controversial, and in some cases involved military action. Thus, for example, Kalat state in Baluchistan declared independence on 11 August 1947 but was coerced into acceding to Pakistan at the end of March 1948. Hyderabad state, ruled by a Muslim but with a population that was eighty-nine percent Hindu and totally surrounded by Indian territory, declared itself independent but was militarily annexed by India in September 1948. Junagarh and Manavadar, two small states on the Kathiawar Peninsula, were ruled by Muslims but their populations were overwhelmingly Hindu. Their rulers decided to join Pakistan even though their states lay well within Indian territory. Pakistan accepted such a procedure; India did not (Fyzee 1991: 331). Uprisings took place in the two states and, in October–November 1947, Indian troops moved in. In January 1948, Pakistan raised the question of the annexation of these states by India at the UN Security Council (UNSC). A plebiscite, arranged by India, indicated that the people of these states wanted to join India. The government of Pakistan, however, refused to recognise the validity of the plebiscite (Gankovsky and Gordon-Polonskaya 1972: 165). But, none of these issues embittered relations between India and Pakistan more than the dispute over the princely state of Jammu and Kashmir – more on that below.

The most pressing problem that Pakistan faced immediately upon attaining independence was the influx of millions of refugees, especially in West Pakistan and specifically in West Punjab. Uprooted, devastated, and traumatised, the refugees needed food, shelter, and medical attention. The relief camps that were established proved woefully inadequate and it took a long time for the refugees to be rehabilitated. Amid such egregious difficulties, the Kashmir conflict erupted and, for more than a year, military hostilities continued between Pakistan and India over the possession of Kashmir.

The First Kashmir War

The princely state of Jammu and Kashmir was purchased from the British by Gulab Singh Dogra, a Rajput Hindu ruler of Jammu, who paid Rs 7.5 million for the annexation of the Kashmir Valley and other adjoining territories – previously a part of the Sikh kingdom of Punjab under Ranjit Singh. The total area of the undivided pre-Partition Jammu and Kashmir state, in 1947, was 85,783.096 sq miles. There was an overall Muslim majority of seventy-eight percent. Technically, the lapse of paramountcy on British withdrawal meant that the princely states could declare themselves independent. However, they were expected to join either India or Pakistan. On the other hand, the legal right to sign the Accession Bill was vested in the ruler, who was expected to take the wishes of his people into consideration. The Maharaja wanted to retain his princely state's independence and therefore did not seek merger with either India or Pakistan. He even negotiated a standstill agreement with

Pakistan, from where much of the food items and other essential supplies were traditionally acquired by his government. He had also offered a standstill agreement to India, but no response had been received from it (Teng 1990: 33). As mentioned earlier, the Radcliffe award had provided a dirt road, to India, to Kashmir via Pathankot in the Punjab. Such vague guidelines left it entirely to the discretion of the rulers – to choose their relationships with India and Pakistan. Both Congress and the Muslim League had begun to vie with each other over Kashmir. The National Conference, led by Sheikh Abdullah from the Kashmir Valley, was allied to the Congress while the Muslim Conference of Chowdhary Ghulam Abbas from Jammu was pro-Pakistan. However, the influx of tribesmen from Pakistan made the Maharaja change his mind.

Major General (Retd.) Shahid Hamid, private secretary to Auchinleck, has asserted that Ram Chandra Kak, a Kashmiri Brahmin and the premier of Kashmir, advised Maharaja Hari Singh to join Pakistan, warning him that the Muslims of Kashmir would rebel if he acceded to India; he, however, started encashing his assets in Kashmir and transferring the money to India and the United Kingdom. Moreover, he secretly began negotiating the terms of accession to India, which would maintain the independence of his princely state. But then, his Muslim subjects of Poonch rebelled, and the Kashmir army sent to quell the rebels joined them instead (Hamid 1986: 272–5). Hamid made this observation:

> As long as there was hope that wise counsel would prevail and the Maharajah would respect the wishes of his people [to join Pakistan], the tribesmen were held back from entering Kashmir. Once it was known that Hari Singh was likely to accede to India, they could not be held back any more and started infiltrating Kashmir (ibid., 275).

Hamid does not provide conclusive proof that the Maharaja was indeed thinking of acceding to India. To say that it was 'known that Hari Singh was likely to accede to India' is, at most, a strong suspicion. Meanwhile, the communal riots that were raging in Punjab quickly spread to Kashmir. In the Poonch region, on 24 August, an uprising started in reaction to firing on a political meeting being held in a village in that district by the Kashmir State Force. The rebels massacred many Hindus and Sikhs. Nearly 60,000 demobilized ex-servicemen joined the rebellion; they began to harass the

Kashmir forces and disrupted traffic on the roads and bridges. Most of the Muslim members of the Kashmir army deserted and joined the rebels (Amin 1999: 88). Anti-Muslim riots, in turn, broke out on a large scale in Jammu. Jammu's Muslims were killed in the thousands, and more than half a million fled to Pakistan.

The key figure in the raid on Kashmir, Akbar Khan, has provided detailed information on the whole Kashmir project in his book, *Raiders in Kashmir* (1992). He has argued that, without Kashmir, Pakistan would always be vulnerable to Indian attack if India placed its troops on the western border of Kashmir from where it could easily threaten Pakistan's security between Lahore and Rawalpindi. Moreover, West Pakistan's agricultural economy was dependent on the rivers entering its territory from Kashmir. Mian Iftikharuddin, Rehabilitation and Refugee Minister in the Pakistani Punjab government, was tasked, by the Muslim League leaders, to contact the Kashmiri leaders with a view to convincing them to accede to Pakistan. While some money would be made available to them, the action had to be unofficial and no Pakistani troops or officers were to take an active part in it. As Director of Weapons and Equipment at GHQ, Akbar Khan knew that there was a serious shortage of arms and ammunition as most of it still lay in India. Weapons of the Pakistan Army could not be used without the permission of the Commander-in-Chief, General Messer vy. So, exploiting a previous precedent, Akbar Khan had 4000 rifles issued to the Punjab police (ibid., 20).

Akbar developed an overall plan that included a number of entry points into Kashmir, and other details about how to launch and coordinate the whole operation. He gave it to Iftikharuddin who took it to Lahore where a conference was held in the office of Sardar Shaukat Hayat – who was also a minister in the Punjab government. Akbar Khan has complained that his plan was not considered and the one by Shaukat Hayat adopted instead (ibid., 18–22). Besides, Prime Minister Liaquat Ali Khan, the others present were Finance Minister Ghulam Mohammad, Mian Iftikharuddin, Zaman Kiyani (formerly an officer in Subhash Chandra Bose's Indian National Army), Khurshid Anwar (a commander of the Muslim League National Guards), Sardar Shaukat Hayat, and Akbar Khan himself. He has described the attitude of the people present as enthusiastic but 'there was no serious discussion of the problems involved' (ibid., 23). The whole operation lacked effective central control.

Shaukat Hayat and Khurshid Anwar mistrusted each other and were not going to cooperate with each other. At that stage, although Akbar Khan had no responsibility for the Kashmir project, he took Brigadier Sher Khan, who was head of intelligence, into confidence; the latter provided him with information and assistance. A number of other officers from the army and air force also helped with clothing, ammunition, and some weapons and ammunition. Meanwhile, India had begun to complain that Pakistan was violating the standstill agreement with Kashmir by applying economic pressure on it to accede to Pakistan. The economic pressure included an economic blockade on essential supplies of kerosene, petrol, foodstuffs, and salt. Moreover, India complained that Pakistan had tampered with the railway service between Jammu and Sialkot. Meanwhile, even the pro-India Sheikh Abdullah had been criticising the Maharaja for not doing anything to assuage the fears of the Kashmiri Muslims who were afraid that the violence against Muslims in East Punjab could also spread to Kashmir. Akbar Khan then made a startling remark:

> As even Sheikh Abdullah was putting the blame on the Maharajah, it seems that the latter could not bring himself to accede to India, and he was unable to find any excuse for inviting Indian assistance, But, then, suddenly at this stage, the whole situation was radically altered by the entry of Frontier tribesmen into Kashmir on the 23rd of October. This event was of such significance that it led to the accession of the State to India within four days (ibid., 27).

Apparently, Akbar Khan was not informed about the entry of the tribesmen; Khurshid Anwar was the person who gathered the laskhar (army). A telegram was sent from the Pakistan GHQ to the commander-in-chief of India informing him that 5000 tribesmen had attacked and captured Muzaffarabad and Domel. The tribal attack was a roaring success, according to Akbar Khan, but it meant that India was bound to respond to it. He has written, 'In Delhi, on the third day of the attack, the Indian Service Chiefs were ordered, in expectation of the Maharajah's appeal for help, to prepare troops to Kashmir.…Next morning when the tribesmen captured Baramula, 35 miles from Srinagar, the Maharajah decided he was going to have no more nonsense' (ibid., 28–9). The Maharaja fled, totally traumatized, to Jammu. He reportedly instructed his ADC that 'if in the morning Mr V.P. Menon did not return from India with help, it would mean that everything was lost and in that case the ADC was to shoot him in his sleep!' (ibid., 29).

Hari Singh requested help from India on 24 October. India dispatched V.P. Menon to Srinagar, who told the Maharaja that Indian troops would be sent only if he acceded to India. The Maharaja, according to India, signed the accession bill on 26 October 1947. On 27 October, as Commander-in-Chief General Messervy was on leave, Gover nor-General Mohammad Ali Jinnah ordered the acting Commander-in-Chief, General Gracey, to attack Kashmir. However, the supreme commander of both the armies, Field Marshal Auchinleck, overruled it and threatened to withdraw all British officers – which madc Jinnah change his mind (Amin 1999: 91). Akbar Khan has claimed that, many years later, he learnt that Jinnah had ordered an attack upon Jammu on the 27th but Gracey refused to comply without first seeking permission from Auchinleck, who refused it (Akbar 1992: 33–34). He explains other reasons that Gracey may have given: More likely, that General Gracey had persuaded the Quaid-e-Azam to withdraw his orders after giving him his reasons which might have been, for instance, that the Pakistan army was still being organised, that a neutral Boundary Force under another General still existed in the Punjab, and the British government would most probably withdraw all British officers from the army in case of a war between two Dominions (Khan 1992: 34).

About the time when Indian troops entered Kashmir territory, Akbar Khan wrote:

> The tribesmen had reached here [Baramula which was only 35 miles from Srinagar] on the 26th. Until then Kashmir had not acceded to India and Indian troops had not been flown in. The State troops thoroughly demoralized, had retreated in disorder. Only 35 miles remained of level road and virtually no resistance. The tribesmen had barely two hour journey left – and before them lay Srinagar, trembling, seemingly at their mercy. But the tribesmen had not moved forward that day, nor the next day. When at last they had advanced on the 28th, they had encountered the Indian troops that a hundred aircraft had been bringing in since the previous day (ibid., 39).

The tribesmen indulged in looting, plundering, and rape (Cloughley 2000: 14). Akbar Khan has not mentioned these incidents. In a moment of exuberance, he claimed that the Indian armed forces were only twice the strength of the Pakistan ones and that, in the past, smaller armies have successfully defeated larger ones. Moreover, he boasted that: 'Had they [the Indians] gone into East Pakistan, they would have exposed East Punjab against which, they feared, we could open the flood gates of 200,000 armed tribesmen and this was a paralysing thought' (Khan 1992: 35). Presumably, he was assuming that the tribesmen's notoriety for cruelty and barbarism would deter India from attempting to gain the upper hand against Pakistan. He does not consider an Indian counter-move into West Punjab, in the event that its troops were on the verge of losing Kashmir to the Pakistani tribesmen and irregular and regular forces. Carrying on with the narrative, he stated that a liberation committee was formed; Liaquat Ali Khan informed the committee that the fighting had to go on for the next three months so that Pakistan's political objective could be achieved through negotiations and other means. Akbar did not explain the political objective. In any event, he saw the tribal lashkar for the first time on 29 October at Muzaffarabad (later capital of Pakistani Azad Kashmir) and was ecstatic. He has noted:

> And then suddenly the scene changed as if by the lifting of a curtain. The tribesmen were on their way to Sri Nagar. The spectacle before us was like a page out of old history. Memory flashed back many, many centuries. This, one felt, is what it might have been like when our forefathers had poured in through the mountain passes of the Frontier (ibid., 37).

Thereafter, the author goes into the details of what followed – more tribesmen poured into Kashmir. However, they soon began to fall back, instead of advancing, as the Indians struck back. The tribesmen's skills at sniper shooting and other guerrilla tactics did not prove useful in the plains of the valley. Nor did Pakistan fully support them by trying to capture Jammu, asserts Akbar Khan. By 5 November, the major portion of the tribal lashkar had withdrawn from Kashmir. Meanwhile, the Indians kept bringing in more forces and skirmishes continued through the winter. In the middle of February 1948, Akbar Khan was relieved, on his request (ibid., 53–80).

Sir George Cunningham, an old NWFP-hand who served as governor of the NWFP till the beginning of 1946 and then returned to Britain, was invited, on 4 July 1947, to return and assume that office again by the colonial government. Jinnah had requested his services but Cunningham was reluctant; he obliged when Mountbatten supported Jinnah's request, and took the oath of office on 15 August. At that time, there was some unease about the NWFP government being headed by the pro-Congress Dr Khan Sahib. On 23 August 1947, Jinnah amended the 1935 Government of India Act to legalise the dismissal of the government of Dr Khan Sahib and, instead, a Muslim League-led government under Abdul Qayyum Khan was appointed. Cunningham was uneasy about the constitutional propriety of such a decision but went along (Norval 1968: 130). The change of government resulted in attacks on the Hindu and Sikh minorities who were forced to flee to India. News of the atrocities against Muslims in East Punjab had incensed the Pakhtun tribesmen and they wanted to kill or drive the non-Muslims out of NWFP. Cunningham was opposed to the invasion of Kashmir by tribesmen but they had already entered Kashmir through Punjab. On 25 October, Colonel Iskandar Mirza (later president of Pakistan) arrived from Lahore and gave him the following background to the invasion:

> He told me all the underground history of the present campaign against Kashmir, and brought apologies from Liaquat Ali for not letting me know anything about it sooner. Liaquat had meant to come here last week and tell me about it personally but was prevented by his illness, which seems to be fairly serious heart trouble. Apparently Jinnah himself heard of what was going on about fifteen days ago, but said 'Don't tell me anything about it. My conscience must be clear'. Iskandar is positive that Hari Singh means to join India as soon as his new road from Pathankot is made, which might be within three months. He has got a lot of Sikhs and Dogras into Poonch and Jammu, and has been trying to shove Muslims into Pakistan in accordance with the general Indian strategy. It was decided apparently a month ago that the Poonchis should revolt and should be helped. Abdul Qayyum was in it from the beginning. British Officers were kept out simply not to embarrass them (ibid., 140–41).

Cunningham goes on to say that more and more tribesmen were pouring into Kashmir, but Indians troops began to land in Srinagar on 27 October. He flew to Lahore the next day to attend a conference where senior generals such as Gracey and Auchinleck were also present, as well as Jinnah, Liaquat, and other Muslim League leaders. Jinnah made a case for the right of intervention, asserting that Hari Singh's accession to India was fraudulent –

Cunningham claimed he could not understand how it was fraudulent (ibid., 142–3). Jinnah wanted to send regular Pakistani troops into Kashmir but let himself be persuaded, by Gracey, that since Pakistan was weak it was not in its interest to send in soldiers and risk an escalating war with India. Jinnah then talked to Gracey and Mudie (governor of Punjab), urging them to actively support the struggle to save the lives of Kashmiri Muslims.

In any case, by November, the tribesmen had begun to return from Kashmir, laden with loot. In an interview in Noida, outside Delhi, granted to me on 10 November 2010, Lieutenant General (Retd.) Kudip Singh Khajuria told me that he was then a young lad living in Srinagar. Not only did the tribal lashkars loot and pillage property, but they also carried away young Sikh girls in large numbers who were later sold off in the tribal areas or to brothels. Cunningham regretted that the Pakistan government was permitting this and was so demoralised that he wrote: 'I could have found half a dozen excellent grounds for resigning in the last two weeks or so, but I feel that we may be able to get the thing gradually under control again and that one must try to see it through' (ibid., 147). According to an estimate he made on 7 November, some 7000 tribesmen were in Kashmir at that time, not far from Srinagar. However, they then made contact with the Indian troops outside Srinagar and suffered heavy casualties. He noted that, because of the excesses of the tribesmen, 'many Muslims of Kashmir would have voted to adhere to India and not to Pakistan if a plebiscite had been held then' (ibid., 148). Moreover, Cunningham thought that 'the time for obtaining India's agreement to a plebiscite ended when the tribes were in ascendant in the vale of Kashmir; even the Chief Minister [Qayyum Khan] told him that those who were organising the Kashmir operations 'were fed up with our tribesmen' (ibid.).

Major (Retd.) Agha Humayun Amin has referred to three principal parties that were involved in the whole invasion affair. Of the three, 'One side was the Muslim League leaders like Shaukat Hayat (an ex-major), Iftikharuddin and Khurshid Anwar who had been ordered by Mr Jinnah to do something to help the Kashmiri Muslims...' (Amin 1999: 89). Amin also noted, 'It may be noted that Mr Jinnah had ordered General Gracey the British Acting Commander-in-Chief...to attack Kashmir' (ibid., 91). Ayesha Jalal has observed:

> One has perforce to conclude that the government of Pakistan with the connivance of the Frontier ministry was actively promoting the sentiments that had encouraged the tribesmen to invade Kashmir. Admittedly, the Pakistani leadership refrained from officially committing the army in Kashmir. But they did so because of the severe shortage of arms and ammunition, not because this was the preferred course of action. If they had been in a position to do so, the Muslim League leaders, with Jinnah's blessings, would have thrown in the army behind the tribal effort.... The Commander-in-Chief of the Azad forces was a Pakistani army officer, Colonel Mohammad Akbar, who went under the pseudonym of 'General Tariq' [legendary conqueror of Spain in the eighth century] and was known to be in close contact with Qayyum Khan and through him with Jinnah and the League leaders in Karachi. (1990: 58–9)

Official War between India and Pakistan

Governor-General Jinnah promoted Gracey to commander-in-chief in February, as General Messervy retired. By then, Pakistan had procured some armaments from Britain. This time, Jinnah was able to convince Gracey to commit Pakistani regular troops to the war. Officially, the first Pakistani formation entered the fighting in the latter half of April 1948. The two sides fought each other in appalling conditions and in difficult terrain. However, by May, the Indians had started to gain the upper hand (Cloughley 2000: 20). The Indians did not hesitate to use air power and artillery, and drove the Pakistani forces out of some major locations that they had captured earlier. On the other hand, Pakistan was successful in capturing the northern areas – Gilgit and its adjoining areas – but, as 1948 progressed, the Indians started winning back some of the locations; the Pakistanis also achieved success in some theatres. Given the vast area of the state, the war remained a collection of several battles while the political leaderships negotiated the terms for a ceasefire. Shaukat Riza has observed, 'On 30 December [1948] both sides saw the wisdom of ceasefire' (Riza 1989: 297).

The UN Security Council

While hostilities were underway, political moves had also been going on.

On 1 January 1948, the Indian government took the Kashmir dispute to the United Nations. It alleged that regular Pakistani troops were fighting in Kashmir and that they should be expelled. That, of course, was true, though Pakistan initially denied any direct involvement. On 25 March 1948, Sheikh Abdullah became the prime minister of Jammu and Kashmir. Such formalities apart, it was not certain that, following the communal rioting that had taken place in different parts of the state, Sheikh Abdullah commanded the support of the Kashmiri Muslims. He needed express guarantees from the Indian government to convince his essentially Muslim constituency that joining India was better for them than becoming a part of Muslim Pakistan. These guarantees, principally, required recognition of Kashmir's autonomy (Navlakha 1991: 2953).

India assured the UN that the accession of Kashmir was only provisional and that the ultimate status of Kashmir was to be determined through a free and universal plebiscite. However, both India and Pakistan took the position that the Kashmiris could choose to join either India or Pakistan. The idea of a separate Kashmiri state was overruled by both. The Security Council Resolution on the Kashmir problem, which laid down the terms for the settlement, was passed on 21 April 1948. It prescribed that a plebiscite would be held under UN supervision once peace had been established. Pakistan was to see to it that the tribesmen and Pakistani nationals vacated the territories of the state before the plebiscite was held. Thereafter, the Indian government was to withdraw its own troops gradually, in stages, until only a minimum number required for the maintenance of law and order remained (Jain 2007a: 7–8; Haque 1992: 74; Subrahmanyam 1990: 142–46).

Article B.7 of the resolution stated: 'The Government of India should undertake that there will be established in Jammu and Kashmir a Plebiscite Administration to hold a plebiscite as soon as possible on the question of accession of the State to India or Pakistan'. A UN Commission composed of Czechoslovakia, Argentina, Belgium, Colombia, and the United States was set up to look into the Kashmir problem. The resolution recognised India's legal presence in Kashmir, resulting from the signing of the Accession Bill. However, armed clashes between India and Pakistan continued and their troops remained in the state.

Finally, a ceasefire was arranged by the United Nations which came into effect on 1 January 1949. By that time, less than one-third of the Kashmir state had come under Pakistani control. In July 1949, agreement was reached on the cease-fire line (later known as the Line of Control [LoC]) and United Nations observers were stationed on both sides of it to monitor it. In subsequent years, Pakistan was to reiterate its demand for a plebiscite while India was to overrule it on the plea that Pakistani forces were occupying parts of the state and, therefore, the holding of an impartial plebiscite was out of the question (Choudhary 1991: 40–42).

It seems that the Pakistani objective of pushing the international border as far into Kashmir as possible succeeded in that western Kashmir came into Pakistani possession. Pakistan was, of course, hoping to acquire the rest through the auspices of the United Nations; India, instead, demanded that Pakistan must withdraw from those areas under its control. Pakistan-administered Kashmir was named Azad Kashmir. Such posturing was to characterise the two countries' standpoints in the years ahead. India later asserted that the accession had been confirmed by a vote of the Kashmir Assembly in 1954 and, therefore, it had become permanent and irrevocable. An Article 370 was incorporated into the Indian constitution recognising Kashmir's special status within the Indian union. Pakistan asserted that since the Kashmiri subjects living in Azad Kashmir had not voted for accession it was not valid (Ahmed 1998: 144–6).

Military Image Building

In terms of the garrison state's image building, the most important aspect of the Kashmir War of 1947–48 was the legend of a brave Pakistani fighting force that militarily annexed one-third of Kashmir. Valiant Muslim fighters fought a much bigger enemy and won many a laurel on the battlefield. Such claims were accepted by the people as there was a long tradition of singing praises to the warriors of Islam. The poet Iqbal had portrayed such sentiments in his inimitable style many years earlier when he wrote about the past glory of Muslim soldiers:

> *Yeh ghazi ye terey pur israr banday*
> These warriors, these mysterious creatures of thine, Oh, God
>
> *Jinhen tu ne bakhsha hai zauq-e-khudai*
> Whom thou hast blessed with the passion of lording it over.

> *Shahadat hai maqsood-o-matloob-i-momin*
> The aim of the true Muslim is martyrdom
>
> *Na mal-ghanimat na kishwar kushai*
> neither war booty nor conquest
>
> (Siddiqi 1996: 2)

This was not exactly true of the tribal elements who looted, plundered, and raped their way into the Kashmir Valley. It is also quite extraordinary that just when millions of people were moving across the India–Pakistan border with the gigantic attendant problems of relocation and resettlement on the one hand, and at the same time the Pakistani establishment had to consolidate the authority of the state over a vast region, they were willing on the other hand, to risk a conflict with India that, in the worst of circumstances, would have meant a war that may not have been confined to the disputed state of Jammu and Kashmir. It was such risk-taking that Air Marshal Asghar Khan must have had in mind when he described the Kashmir war as a misadventure. In any case, a romance between the Pakistan military and the Pakistani nation, especially the Punjabis, took root by design as the military, deliberately, exuded such a belief which was fully supported by the government and media.

The blame for the failure to capture the whole of Kashmir was laid at the door of the British officers, on both sides, who allegedly conspired with Mountbatten to deprive Pakistan of its rightful claim to the Muslim-majority state of Jammu and Kashmir. In particular, the ire was reserved for Auchinleck and Gracey (Amin 1999: 91). Considering that Jinnah promoted Gracey to commander-in-chief of the Pakistan Armed Forces in February, a good three months after he allegedly refused to attack India, the accusation makes no sense; it seems to be an afterthought. Within the army, the hawks, with Akbar Khan as their spokesman, began a whispering campaign against Prime Minister Liaquat Ali Khan for having agreed to the ceasefire. In any case, the Kashmir dispute became the focal point of Pakistan's foreign policy. That it was built into the vagaries of the transfer of power, and had caused a war between India and Pakistan, meant that it helped the military build a strong case for not only a formidable defence capability but also the belief that it alone could force India to resolve the Kashmir dispute. India and Pakistan both suffered some 1500 fatalities each, while those injured were even more (US Library of Congress).

UN Initiatives

In any event, the Indian government had begun to doubt the wisdom of taking the Kashmir dispute to the Security Council. Intelligence reports were warning that Sheikh Abdullah's popularity was declining and, therefore, the support of the Muslim majority in a plebiscite could no longer be taken for granted. A number of experts were appointed, by the Security Council, to advise on the steps needed to resolve the Kashmir dispute. The first was General McNaughton of Canada who prescribed demilitarisation on both sides of Kashmir – which the Indians rejected out of hand, and Pakistan accepted with minor changes (Schaffer 2009: 28). He was followed by Sir Owen Dixon of Australia who realised that Indian intransigence made it impossible to hold a free and fair plebiscite covering the entire state. He then suggested that the plebiscite should be held only in the Kashmir Valley, while other parts should be divided on an ethnic basis between the two rivals. US policy on Kashmir was formulated by Assistant Secretaries George McGhee and John Hickerson. Both concluded that the resolution of the Kashmir dispute was vital for the establishment of peace in South Asia. They held India's intransigence responsible for the lack of progress on settling the dispute. They also noted that India was determined not to hold an overall plebiscite (ibid., 29). On 30 March 1951, the UNSC adopted Resolution 91, which called upon India and Pakistan to accept arbitration to be carried 'out by an arbitrator, or a panel of arbitrators, to be appointed by the President of the International Court of Justice after consultation with the parties'.

July 1951 Indian Military Exercises

India had carried out military exercises in 1950, which Pakistan perceived as threatening. However, it was not until July 1951 that large-scale Indian military exercises along the border with Pakistan began to be interpreted, by Pakistan's leaders, as demonstrations of Indian designs against Pakistan. Suddenly, some 200,000 Indian troops faced about 70,000 Pakistani soldiers along the Punjab border. There were two Indian destroyers in the Gulf of Kutch, south of Pakistan's first capital, Karachi. India also deployed three brigades near the border of East Pakistan (Cloughley 2000: 31). Both sides began to move their troops closer to the border. These movements were observed and reported by foreign correspondents, including those of the *Manchester Guardian*, the *Daily Telegraph*, and the *Times*. These British newspapers, along with the US newspapers the *New York Observer* and the *New York Herald Tribune*, condemned India's actions (ibid., 31).

During this period, Nehru and Liaquat were engaged in brisk correspondence. Liaquat offered a peace plan that Nehru rejected. Brian Cloughley summed up India's attitude in the following words: 'It seemed that India simply did not want to withdraw its troops, did not want to hold a plebiscite in Kashmir (to which it had agreed), and was not prepared to renounce the use of force or declare it would not attack Pakistan' (ibid.) As India began to gain international recognition as a leader in the developing world, it became increasingly averse to offers by other statesmen to proffer their good offices to resolve the Kashmir dispute (ibid., 32).

Both sides now assumed quite different positions in international politics. While Pakistan embarked on a concerted effort to win economic and military aid from the US, India evolved a strategy that projected it as a neutral power. After 1954, Pakistan entered into a treaty of cooperation with the US on military matters, and joined South East Asian Treaty Organization (SEATO) and (CENTO), while India assumed a leading role in the Non-Aligned Movement. Both states became adversaries in the international tug of war between the US and the Soviet Union.

5

Wooing the Americans, and Civil–Military Relations

Mountbatten had noted that Pakistan would always feel insecure vis-à-vis India; and, the moth-eaten Pakistan that emerged on 14 August 1947 greatly accentuated that sense of vulnerability because of the ultimate division of Bengal and Punjab. As noted already, offers to rent out Pakistan's services and facilities to the West pre-dated the creation of Pakistan. Margaret Bourke-White of *Life* magazine covered the partition of India and published photographs and comments on what happened during those days. She interviewed Jinnah in September 1947. He told her that Islam was democratic and Pakistan would be a democracy, but she doubted the reasonableness of such a claim given the remnants of feudalism in Pakistan as well as the totalitarianism and extremism in the Islamic heritage (Bourke-White 1949: 92). More importantly, Jinnah had offered to make Pakistan a frontline state in the West's strategy to contain Soviet communism. He told her:

> America needs Pakistan more than Pakistan needs America...Pakistan is the pivot of the world, as we are placed...the frontier on which the future position of the world revolves....Russia is not so very far away.... If Russia walks in the whole world is menaced (ibid., 92–3).

Bourke-White made the following remarks:

> In the weeks to come I was to hear the Quaid-i-Azam's thesis echoed by government officials throughout Pakistan. 'Surely America will build our army' they would say to me. 'Surely America will give us loans to keep Russia from walking in'. But when I asked whether there were any

> signs of Russian infiltration, they would reply almost sadly, as though sorry not to be able to make more of the argument. 'No, Russia has shown no signs of being interested in Pakistan.'
>
> This hope of tapping the US Treasury was voiced so persistently that one wonders whether the purpose was to bolster the world against Bolshevism or to bolster Pakistan's own uncertain position as a new political entity. Actually, I think it was more nearly related to the even more significant bankruptcy of ideas in the new Muslim state – a nation drawing its spurious warmth from the embers of an antique religious fanaticism, fanned into a new blaze.
>
> Jinnah's most frequently used technique, during the struggle for his new nation, had been the playing of opponent against opponent. Evidently, this technique was now to be extended into foreign policy (ibid., 93).

Bourke-White's observations are amply corroborated by the minutes of a cabinet meeting on 7 September 1947. Jinnah told the ministers, 'Pakistan [is] a democracy and communism [does] not flourish in the soil of Islam. It [is] clear therefore that our interests [lie] more with the two great democratic countries, namely the United Kingdom and the US, rather than with Russia' (Kux 2001: 20). Jinnah also alluded to the Great Game logic when he asserted, 'The safety of the North Western Frontier [is] of world concern and not merely an internal matter for Pakistan alone' (ibid.). He asserted that the Russians were behind Afghanistan's demand for Pakhtunistan. Such tactics were meant to make the Americans appreciate Pakistan's geostrategic importance in any strategy purporting to contain Soviet influence, not only in South Asia but also in the Middle East and Southeast Asia.

The United States remained uninterested. The US policy of containment, at that time, was focused on Europe where the Soviet Union had begun flexing its muscles to assert its sphere of influence in eastern and central Europe. The United States combated it through the Marshall Plan, which provided much-needed economic aid, not only to war-ravaged Britain and France but also to the main enemy during the Second World War, Germany. Truman announced the Truman Doctrine, which was the beginning of a crusade against totalitarianism (Horowitz 1967: 67–8). The Soviet Union and its allies were practically excluded from benefiting from it because the plan was perceived as one that was aimed at preventing the industrialisation of Eastern Europe and, instead, of rendering them merely as producers of agricultural goods (ibid., 70–4). Also, a Soviet request for a US loan of US$6 billion was rejected. As the Cold War gained momentum, the United States consummated its diplomatic and economic offensive by consolidating its sphere of influence in Europe through a military pact, the NATO, in 1949.

However, the orbit of the Cold War could not have been confined to Europe. Events in eastern Asia dragged the emerging superpowers towards that region. The bloody civil war between Chinese communists and nationalists entered a decisive phase. The former were winning and the nationalists, who had received help from the United States, were fast losing. On 21 September 1949, Mao Zedong declared the Chinese People's Republic; the nationalist leader, Chiang Kai-shek, was forced to flee to Taiwan (Young 1993: 107–8). In Korea, the communists were being drawn into a conflict with the pro-Western forces in the south of the peninsula. Both the United States and the Soviet Union were being forced to supply weapons to their allies far beyond Europe (ibid., 112–3). Amid all this, South Asia was, by comparison, still peaceful and without any serious ideological conflict.

As far as Pakistan was concerned, South Asia, in 1947, was peripheral to the US foreign policy objective of containing Soviet influence and power. Thus, when Pakistan requested military material and assistance to the tune of some US$2 billion for five years – $170,000,000 for the army, $75,000,000 for the air force, and $60,000,000 for the navy – it was rejected out of hand. Instead, on 17 December 1947, Pakistan received a mere $10 million relief grant, which was 0.5 percent of what it had requested. Dejected, the Pakistani foreign minister, Sir Muhammad Zafrulla Khan, expressed his disappointment in the following words: 'well-known friendship of Pakistan toward the US and Pakistan's obvious antipathy to the Russian ideology would seem to justify serious consideration by the US government of the defence requirements of Pakistan' (Kux 2001. 21).

Such utterances did not make much of an impact on the US. It continued to look upon India as the rightful product of a prolonged freedom struggle, while Pakistan was deemed a product of negative politics based on communal differences and atavistic passions. The US imposed an informal arms embargo on India and Pakistan when war broke out between them in 1948 (Jain 2007a: 297–8). President Harry Truman urged the two governments to work together in the interest of peace and to move forward with their social and political progress (Kux 2001: 30).

Pakistan, however, persisted in its efforts to cultivate the Americans, inviting even lower-ranking officials to important functions and parties. Jinnah and his sister, Fatima, even tried to convince the Americans to rent his house in Karachi but, to their disappointment, the Americans rented a smaller and cheaper place as Pakistan was not an important station for them at that time (ibid., 25). Thus, for the first year and a half after Pakistan came into being, its leaders kept up their charm offensive on the Americans. A dip in that relationship occurred in mid-1949 when Truman invited the Indian prime minister, Jawaharlal Nehru, to visit the US but a similar invitation was not extended to his Pakistani counterpart, Liaquat Ali Khan.

Meanwhile, the Soviet Union exploded nuclear devices in August 1949; the self-fulfilling prophecy of a communist threat had become real. The emerging communist superpower was no longer seeking cooperation and help from the US. Both began to confront each other in ideological and political propaganda and were involved in ongoing violent conflicts, as in East Asia. Such posturing from both sides accentuated tensions worldwide. For the Pakistanis, nothing would have made a greater impact on the Americans than to make them believe that the Soviet Union was seeking good relations with Pakistan. This was achieved by Pakistani diplomats when they got the Soviet Union to invite the Pakistani prime minister on a friendly visit. It is to be noted that the two countries had not as yet established embassies in each other's capitals. The Pakistani ambassador to the US, Ispahani, described such a move as 'a masterpiece in strategy' (Kux 2001: 32).

It certainly had the anticipated effect on the United States, which became aware of the need to balance the invitation to Nehru with a similar gesture to Pakistan. US Assistant Secretary of State McGhee travelled to Karachi in December 1949 to personally extend an invitation to Liaquat to visit the United States. Liaquat did not visit the Soviet Union – the reasons for that are not very clear but apparently both sides lost interest when it became known that the Pakistani prime minister was prioritising the visit to the United States.

Liaquat's visit was scheduled for May 1950. In the meanwhile, US–Soviet relations had worsened and a military conflict between their ideological protégés in Korea was imminent. The US State Department proffered a brief to Truman highlighting US–Pakistan relations and policy implications. It was observed that Liaquat was pro-West, but could not openly profess such a preference because of misgivings about western imperialism in Pakistan. It was pointed out that Pakistan had received very little economic or military aid. It was also noted that US policy on Palestine had been seen as pro-Israel in Pakistan and resulted in demonstrations. Most importantly, it was stated:

> 'The entire South Asian region is of relatively secondary importance to the United States from a military point of view,' although Pakistan may have value in the event of a war with the Soviet Union as a place from which U.S. aircraft could operate. 'However, this should not be openly stressed since it negates our oft-expressed interest in helping the region for economic reasons' (ibid., 34).

Liaquat visited the US in May 1950. In response to a question from a reporter about how large a standing army Pakistan wanted to have, he said it depended on Washington's intentions: 'If your country will guarantee our territorial integrity, I will not keep any army at all' (ibid., 35). During the same trip, Pakistan supported the US position on Korea, but when a tangible request to send troops as part of the UN contingent was made, Liaquat found a way out by saying that 'as long as Pakistan felt threatened by India, he could not commit his country's limited security resources for other causes' (ibid., 38). During his three-week long trip, Liaquat made a positive impression on the Americans. McGee found him to be 'a man we could do business with'. In contrast, he had found Nehru, who had visited earlier in October 1949, 'vague and shifty'. The Americans also disapproved of his neutralist foreign policy (ibid., 35–6).

In any event, in spite of the positive impressions, Liaquat was unable to make any breakthrough in getting the US to provide Pakistan with the economic and military aid it wanted. US foreign policy continued to give greater priority to India, while acknowledging the importance of Pakistan as well. Thus, on 25 January 1951, President Truman approved a study which stressed that:

> The loss of India to the Communist orbit would mean that for all practical purposes all of Asia will have been lost; this would constitute a serious threat to the security position of the United States. The loss of China, the immediate threat to Indochina and balance of Southeast Asia, the invasion of Tibet, and the reverses in Korea have greatly increased the significance to the United States of the political strategic

> manpower and resource potential of the countries of South Asia and made it more important that this potential be marshalled on the side of the United States. India, especially, and Pakistan as well, possess leaders having great prestige throughout the whole of Asia; the future support of these countries diplomatically and in the United Nations is of great importance; India in particular has certain strategic materials of importance to our national defense…' (Jain 2007b: 15).

A former governor of the NWFP, Sir Olaf Caroe, who was generally considered to be hostile to the Congress party during the freedom struggle, took up cudgels on behalf of Pakistan in 1951 – as a state central to Western interests in the Middle East. He wrote: 'India is no longer an obvious base for Middle East defence: it stands on the fringe of the defence periphery. Pakistan on the other hand lies well within the grouping of South-Western Asia.' (Caroe 1951: 180) Caroe was particularly convinced about the role of air power in future struggles, and of Pakistan being vital for providing air bases to the West. Olaf's view, however, was not the official policy of Britain.

A tilt, apparently towards Pakistan and away from India, took place at a conference of US ambassadors in Sri Lanka during 26 February–2 March 1951. In it, Nehru's neutral line in international politics was seen, with dismay, as a hegemonic move and it was suggested that the United States should actively oppose Nehru's efforts and expose the fallacious basis of Indian foreign policy because it ignored the dangers posed by international communism. It was agreed, at that conference, that the US should deal firmly with Nehru but cultivate Pakistan as a friendly country. Pakistan's geostrategic location, close to the Gulf oil fields, was also recognised as significant for the Western allies to take advantage of. It was also observed that the Persian–Iraq sector could not be defended without help from Pakistan. It was urged that Pakistan should be given territorial guarantees against aggression. Consequently, it was recommended that the US and Britain should quickly build up its armed forces. This, however, did not receive support from the British foreign office as it was feared that both India and Afghanistan would be alienated (Jalal 1990: 125–6).

General Ayub Khan Cultivates the Americans

Pakistan's first Muslim commander-in-chief, General Mohammad Ayub

Khan, an unabashed pro-American, embarked upon a relentless effort to try to convince the US to co-opt Pakistan in its strategy to contain the Soviet Union (Cheema 1990: 146–8). In the autumn of 1951, a Pakistan mission arrived in Washington to seek arms but, since Pakistan had not sent troops to Korea, the Americans were not forthcoming with any major commitment. The foiling of a pro-Soviet military coup in Pakistan by Ayub Khan, earlier in March 1951, had gained him admirers in the US administration; his personal charm also seemed to have had a contagious influence on the US administration. In late 1951, Henry Byroade, who was more sympathetic to the Pakistani overtures, became the US regional assistant secretary. He began to believe that a 'defense arrangement extending from Turkey to Pakistan – a geographical arch of Muslim, but mainly non-Arab states – bolstered by small amounts of military assistance from the US, would help stabilize the region and make it less vulnerable to Soviet inroads' (Kux 2001: 47).

Within US domestic politics, the McCarthy era saw a major onslaught on political freedom. An arch right-wing politician, Senator Joseph McCarthy of the Republican Party embarked upon a vicious campaign, with the connivance of the intelligence and security communities, to purge America of people who were allegedly engaged in 'un-American activities'. His witch-hunt searched for real and imaginary communists and leftists in all walks of life, and particularly targeted entertainment professionals in Hollywood. Hundreds of screenwriters, actors, directors, musicians, and others were blacklisted and denied employment in the field because of their political beliefs or associations, real or suspected (Buhle and Wagner, 2003). As the Cold War began to gather storm with menacing intensity, the newly-independent countries were pressured to take sides. The polarisation that followed led more and more governments to fear war. A burgeoning arms industry, in collaboration with other sections of big business, began to set the agenda for US foreign policy – through a power elite that existed in the State Department as well as in the US Congress and the Pentagon (Ray 2004: 18–34).

The Eisenhower Presidency

Dwight D. Eisenhower, supreme commander of the Allied forces during the Second World War and an American war hero, was elected president of the United States in 1953 on the ticket of the Republican Party. Eisenhower was very mindful of preserving liberty at home, but advocated building security pacts worldwide to contain the Soviet bloc (Cheema 1990: 145). As noted already, while he was wary about the growing power of the arms industry and warned about its adverse impact on the liberal freedoms of the American nation, Eisenhower backed a policy of establishing military bases all over the world to contain the Soviet Union. His secretary of state, John Foster Dulles, was also convinced about the need to contain 'Godless Communism'. Looking at the Asian continent, they were attracted to Pakistan's geostrategic significance as the arenas of tension and future conflicts had expanded well beyond Europe. Both Eisenhower and Dulles found Pakistan amenable to their worldview. In May 1953, Dulles visited India and Pakistan. In their meetings with him, the Pakistani leaders 'stressed their allegiance to the anticommunist cause and emphasized Pakistan's desire to join the free world's defence team' (Kux 2001: 55).

General Ayub gave a strategic assessment of Pakistan's situation to the US secretary of state, fashioned on the classic Great Game doctrine, and highlighted 'the possibility of a massive Soviet invasion through the warm waters of the Arabian Sea. The proposed reform was an expanded Pakistani army properly equipped for the task of blocking the Soviets' (ibid., 55). He spoke enthusiastically of the Pakistan government's willingness to cooperate with the supply of manpower and bases (ibid., 55). In order to allay US concerns about the impact on India, Ayub Khan argued, 'If Pakistan were strengthened by US economic and military aid, it would result in India dropping its present intransigent attitude [on Kashmir]' (ibid., 55). Upon his return to Washington, Dulles gave a very favourable impression of Pakistan. He claimed to have been impressed by the 'martial and religious qualities of the Pakistanis' (ibid., 56). In contrast, he found India's Prime Minister Nehru to be an 'utterly impractical statesman' (ibid., 56). Thereafter, a process was set in motion which culminated in Pakistan being described as the United States' 'most allied ally in Asia' (ibid., 70).

In his autobiography, *Unlikely Beginnings: A Soldier's Life* (2003), Major General (Retd.) Abu Bakr Osman Mitha wrote that all officers of the rank of lieutenant colonel, and the General Headquarters (GHQ), were asked to give their opinion as to whether Pakistan should accept military aid. About his response he wrote:

> I recommended that we should not because accepting aid would prevent us from developing our own arms industry and then we would be at the mercy of the Americans. As a country we would develop a beggar mentality. However, the authorities decided otherwise and a United States Military Aid and Advisory Group (USMAAG) commanded by a boor called Col. Brown arrived and was located at the GHQ (Mitha 2003: 165).

Defence Agreement and Military Pacts

The cumulative effect of such interactions and overtures was that a US–Pakistan Mutual Defense Agreement was eventually signed on 19 May 1954. It was laid down that the US would provide Pakistan with 'equipment, materials and services or other assistance' consistent with the Charter of the United Nations. In this regard, Clause 2 of Article 1 is particularly interesting. It reads:

> The Government of Pakistan will use this assistance exclusively to maintain its internal security, its legitimate self-defence, or to permit it to participate in the defence of the area, or in United Nations collective security arrangements and measures, and Pakistan will not undertake any act of aggression against any other nation. The Government of Pakistan will not, without prior agreement of the Government of the US, devote such assistance to purposes other than those for which it was furnished (Jain 2007a: 303).

In this bilateral agreement, there was no explicit mention either of the defence agreement being a part of the overall anti-communist military strategy of the US or that the material and equipment Pakistan would receive should not be used in a war against India. However, Vice President Richard Nixon was of the view that arming Pakistan should be used to marginalise Nehru (Kux 2001: 62). The Indian prime minister's active participation in the Non-Alignment Movement (NAM) clearly irked the conservative sections of the US power elite. On the other hand, the US wanted to keep military aid to Pakistan at a modest level, somewhere between US$29 million and US$30 million, because South Asia continued to be considered peripheral to the containment of the Soviet Union. This was very different from the expectations of the Pakistanis, who expressed deep disappointment. Professor Robert McMahon noted:

> A gaping chasm existed between the free-flowing dollars that Pakistani military officers and bureaucrats conjured up as their just reward for open alignment with the West and the modest dollar figures contemplated by Washington planners (ibid., 67).

Nevertheless, Pakistan continued with its relentless lobbying that Pakistan was willing to play an important role in containing Soviet influence not only in South Asia but also in the Middle East as well as in South East Asia. In the autumn of 1954, a high-powered Pakistani team consisting of Prime Minister Mohammad Ali Bogra, General Ayub Khan, and Chaudhri Muhammad Ali visited the United States. They persisted that Pakistan needed more than just $30 million in assistance.

On that occasion, Dulles retorted that he 'thought Pakistan had undertaken its anti-communism stand because it was right, not just to make itself eligible for certain sums of dollar aid' (ibid., 68). To the Pakistanis, such sermonising did not mean much and they kept insisting on a sharp increase in economic and military aid, until their strategy finally prevailed when Bogra met Eisenhower. The net gain for Pakistan was a secret aide-memoire that provided a steep increase in economic aid as well as a total defence programme costing, altogether, US$171 million. It was to equip four army infantry and 1.5 armoured divisions, provide aircraft for six air force squadrons, and supply twelve vessels for the navy (ibid., 69).

This breakthrough was celebrated by the Pakistani establishment with great gusto. They expressed their gratitude by Pakistan joining the SEATO in September 1954 – their claim to membership deriving from the fact that East Pakistan was in proximity to South East Asia even though Pakistan had a rather poor military presence in that part of the country. Pakistan followed up on the policy of participating in US-sponsored military pacts by joining the Baghdad Pact in 1955, and its successor, the CENTO, in 1959. Washington only became a formal member of the SEATO. From the Pakistani point of view, such membership was incontrovertible evidence of its willingness to play the role of a frontline state against the Soviet Union. As a Muslim nation with declared commitment to containing the spread of communism in three geographical regions – South Asia, South East Asia, and the Middle East – Pakistan gained a rather unique reputation as America's 'most allied ally in Asia', noted Ayub Khan (2006: 151). That meant that processes were set in motion to establish routine connections and networks between the Pakistani and US military and security establishments.

However, the US remained mindful of the need to cultivate the Indians as well. By 1955, the US had provided seventeen C-119G aircraft to India under a programme of some $33 million in military aid, and also approved the sale of British radar equipment. The US hoped that these moves would help dissuade India from buying sixty Soviet light bombers (Nawaz 2008: 131). While this did not please Pakistan, the US remained steadfast in cultivating India as well in its larger policy of bracing India as a democratic alternative to both Soviet and Chinese communism.

It is worth noting that these crucial foreign policy decisions, to align with the West, were taken by the Pakistan government without proper debate in Parliament. When there was a debate in 1954, the opposition, mainly from East Pakistan, strongly opposed such moves (Ray 2004: 81). Thus from the very beginning, such matters were determined by a narrow power elite; the politicians were reduced to second fiddle while the civil servants and military formed the 'bureaucratic-military oligarchy' – a description made famous by Hamza Alavi (1972).

Inter-Services Intelligence

The ISI was established in 1948 with a view to representing all three services – the army, navy, and air force – in a single organization. It was the brainchild of Major General R. Cawthome, an Australian who was then deputy chief of staff in the Pakistan Army. Apparently, there had been a lack of coordination between the intelligence agencies of the three services during the Kashmir War. The ISI was to prevent the recurrence of such lapses in information and intelligence. It was tasked to collect, analyse, and assess external intelligence, both military and non-military. Initially, it had no role in the collection of internal intelligence, except in NWFP and Pakistan-administer Azad Kashmir. Later, it was to acquire a greater role in the domestic arena, but gained international recognition during the so-called Afghan jihad – which it conducted in close cooperation with the American spy agency, the CIA (Ahmed 2010).

The Special Services Group (SSG)

The US helped Pakistan build a very special elite commando force, the SSG. Lieutenant Colonel Ghulam Jilani Khan has presented an exhaustive account of the history, evolution, composition, and tasks undertaken by the SSG in a 479-page *SSG: Tarikh key Ayeney Mein* [The SSG in the Mirror of History] (2004). While it has been written with great passion, the author has had to essentially rely on interviews with people who had served in it because its charter remains classified. The SSG was initiated as an elite group in 1953–4, with the support of the US military, but became fully operational in 1956 – with its headquarters at Cherat, near Peshawar, and another facility at Attock Fort. Essentially, it came into being to facilitate the US war strategy against the Soviet Union. In case of a Soviet advance into Pakistan or neighbouring Afghanistan and other territories, the SSG was to assist in launching a guerrilla resistance. Its first commanding officer was Mitha. He has presented some fascinating details of the interaction between US and Pakistani military personnel; Americans were sent to Cherat and Attock Fort, while Pakistanis were sent to the US for training.

The selection process was very rigorous and few Pakistanis managed to qualify to be admitted to the SSG. In those days, there was no relaxation during Ramazan and food was served to those who chose not to fast. Also, the prevailing traditions among the senior officers were very much those that characterised the British military, trained at Sandhurst and at similar institutions in the colonies. Interaction between the Americans and Pakistanis resulted in some friendships and bonding, but Brigadier Mitha was wary of the close relations because he suspected that most of the Americans worked for the CIA (Mitha 2003: 209). Moreover, the Americans tended to act in a superior way and looked down on their Pakistani counterparts. It appeared as though they felt that they deserved to be treated specially, which was resented by the Pakistani officers (ibid., 209–214). In other words, while both sides lived together and intermixed, they also maintained their separate identities and were suspicious of each other.

The Eisenhower–Dulles Doctrine

The Eisenhower–Dulles Doctrine was propounded in 1957 to contain Soviet influence in the Middle East. It was formulated in the background to the Suez crisis of 1956. A tripartite force, consisting of French, British, and Israeli troops, committing aggression on Egypt did not receive US support. On the contrary, the US forced Israel out of the Sinai. However, that policy was not consolidated in seeking a closer understanding with Nasser, whose radical nationalism became suspect in the eyes of the anti-communist crusader, John Foster Dulles. Instead, the Americans decided to co-opt Saudi Arabia as their main ally in the region. The latter was a major producer of oil; US policy, since the time of Franklin Roosevelt, had been to protect it, and thus US interest in its oil. Moreover, the Americans believed that Saudi Arabia enjoyed a special status among Muslims because Islam originated there and the holiest Muslim sites were located on its soil. CIA Director Allen Dulles, and his brother, John Foster Dulles, sought to build an alliance with the Saudi Wahabis against Nasser. The measures taken included the secret strengthening of the Egyptian fundamentalist Muslim Brotherhood against Nasser (Dreyfuss 2005: 120–25). Moreover, in 1962, the Muslim World League was founded with US connivance. Centred on the holy city of Makkah, it included well-known figures of the radical-right political Islam, including the chief ideologue of Islamism in Pakistan, Abul Ala Maududi. It established a network that sought to advance the Islamist agenda all over the Muslim world (ibid., 131–35). However, a 1956 US study on the Middle East cast doubts about Pakistan's usefulness in the Middle East. By 1957, Eisenhower and Dulles had come around to the view that India's neutralism was not against American interests. On the contrary, doubts began to be expressed about close alignment with Pakistan. Eisenhower called the military agreement with Pakistan 'perhaps the worst kind of a plan and decision we could have made. It was a terrible error, but we now seem hopelessly involved in it' (Kux 1992: 84). The Americans were not convinced that Pakistan's anti-communism commitment was the prime reason for it seeking an alliance with them. A US intelligence report made the following remark:

> Pakistan's main reason for devoting more than a quarter of its budget to defense, and seeking additional US arms is not to protect the country against a Soviet and Communist Chinese attack, for which Pakistani resources will never be sufficient, nor to maintain internal security, for which the present military establishment is excessive. Its chief purpose is to bolster Pakistan's position vis-à-vis India (Jain 2007a: 33).

The Military and Internal Politics

The two external concerns of Pakistan – conflict with India and help from the United States – proceeded more or less on the basis of consensus between the politicians and the civil and military bureaucracies. Pakistan also valued its membership of the British Commonwealth, and continued cooperation on the military level as well (Sohail 1991).

The Rawalpindi Conspiracy Case of 1951

From the outset, some ultra-nationalist Muslim officers resented the British officers holding superior positions in the military. Such resentment, coupled with a belief that Prime Minister Liaquat Ali Khan had not risen to the occasion and backed the Kashmir war whole-heartedly, began to give shape to a plot to overthrow the government and establish a patriotic regime. However, intelligence about the conspiracy reached the government. In early March 1951, Prime Minister Liaquat Ali Khan announced that his government had uncovered a plot to overthrow the government involving some officers of the armed forces and some leading members of the Pakistan Communist Party. It was alleged that the conspirators intended to 'create commotion in the country by violent means and to subvert the loyalty of the Pakistan defence forces' (quoted in Gankovsky and Gordon-Polonskaya 1972: 175).

The central character of the case was Major General Akbar Khan, who had played a prominent role in the Kashmir War of 1948. According to Asghar Khan, a large reception had been arranged on 14 August 1947 on the lawns of the governor-general's House in Karachi. Some of the officers had been invited to take part. When Akbar Khan, reportedly, complained to Jinnah about the British holding senior posts in the country's armed forces, Jinnah retorted: 'Never forget that you are the servants of the state. You do not make policy. It is we, the people's representatives, who decide how the country is to be run. Your job is only to obey the decisions of your civilian masters' (2005: 3). Ayesha Jalal has drawn attention to the fact that the very strong urge, among Pakistani officers, for quick promotions served as a 'cold sore for Britain's post-war strategic designs. It was not only a main factor hastening the departure of some 400 to 435 British officers in the Pakistan army, but a major barrier to pulling it firmly behind Britain's policing efforts in the Near and Far East' (Jalal 1990: 117). The British tried, unsuccessfully, to delay that from happening; they, instead, tried to secure promotions to key positions of officers with reliable pro-Western sympathies. Ayub Khan's promotion, in January 1951, as Pakistan's first Pakistani commander-in-chief was based on his pro-Western orientation. Apparently, such officers were amenable to a partition of Kashmir along the ceasefire line (ibid., 118–19).

In contrast, Akbar Khan, the 'hero' of the Kashmir war, was frustrated by Pakistan's acceptance of the ceasefire, which he believed had benefited India. Akbar was known to express his feelings against the government, including the prime minister, in very strong language. Having collected a number of like-minded army and air force officers, and some leaders of the Communist Party, he entered into a conspiracy to plan the overthrow of the government. The plan, allegedly, was that Liaquat Ali Khan and Governor-General Khawaja Nazimuddin would be arrested. Then, the governor-general would be forced to dismiss the government. Akbar Khan would form the government and order general elections, which had not been held in Pakistan since independence. The new government would allow the Communist Party to participate in the political process; the communists' activities had been severely restricted as Prime Minister Liaquat dealt with them with a heavy hand.

Apparently, the Central Government was aware of the disgruntled Young Turks for half a year. It was a time when 'British, American and Pakistani intelligence began their joint operations against pro-Soviet propaganda, both within and outside the armed force' (ibid., 120). Anyhow, the conspiracy, if it was at all serious, was exposed and the plotters arrested. The courts sentenced the civilians to four years in prison and a fine of ₹500 each. The military officers received various sentences, ranging from three to seven years. General Akbar Khan was sentenced to twelve years of exile from public life (Gankovsky and Gordon Polonskaya 1972: 175 6).

Assassination of Prime Minister Liaquat Ali Khan

On 16 October 1951, Liaquat Ali Khan was assassinated by an Afghan, Said Akbar, who shot the prime minister dead during a public meeting in Rawalpindi. The assassin was shot dead by a police officer. Was it the misdeed of a single person or a conspiracy involving others? As the assassin was shot at the scene, the case was not satisfactorily investigated and details remained inconclusive. At any rate, with Liaquat gone, no other leader of national stature was around to lead the nation. Thenceforth, senior civil servants began to dominate the political scene. As a first indication, the rather weak but affable Bengali leader, Khawaja Nazimuddin, who was serving as the governor-general at the time, was made prime minister; a senior bureaucrat, Malik Ghulam Mohammad, who was serving as the finance minister became the governor-general. As Pakistan had not adopted a new constitution, the government machinery was still largely based on the 1935 Act which reposed real powers in the governor-general (Ahmed 1998: 172).

The Anti-Ahmadiyya Riots of 1953

While the Rawalpindi conspiracy case was an example of military officers aspiring to take over power, an entirely different situation arose in 1953 when they were ordered to intervene and establish law and order – when the ulema launched the Khatam-e-Nabuwat (finality of the prophethood of Muhammad [pbuh]) movement in 1953. The roots of the conflict went back to the early twentieth century when Mirza Ghulam Ahmad (1835–1908), born at Qadian in the Punjab, began to claim that he was a prophet who received revelations from God. Mirza also claimed to be carrying the attributes of Jesus and of the Hindu god, Krishna. He rejected jihad against the British. Such claims were unacceptable to the Sunni and Shia ulema, who denounced him as an imposter. After his death, the Ahmadiyya movement went through a period of internal rift. A minority, called the Lahori party, broke away asserting that Mirza was not a prophet but a mujadid (reviver of Islam), while the majority, known as the Rabwah party, clung to the belief that he was a prophet (Court of Inquiry 1954: 187–200).

In 1912, his son, Mirza Bashiruddin Mahmud Ahmad, made a statement to the effect that those Muslims who had not converted to Ahmadiyyat were outside the pale of Islam (Jones 1989: 200; Court of Inquiry 1954: 1999). In reaction, the ulema denounced the Ahmadis as heretics. During the colonial period, the Ahmadis received government protection and patronage. Although opposed to jihad, they were serving in large numbers in the Indian Army. In some of the Ahmadiyya writings, it was suggested that if British rule ended they would succeed as the new power in India (Court of Inquiry 1954: 196). Moreover, their literature was full of sycophancy towards the colonial authorities. In any event, they were able to win some converts in Punjab. Nevertheless, some prominent Ahmadis, among whom Sir Muhammad Zafrulla Khan was the most well-known, played a leading role in the struggle for the creation of Pakistan. Jinnah reposed complete trust in him – to plead the Muslim League's claims to territory in the division of Punjab before the Punjab Boundary Commission. Jinnah later rewarded him with the position of Pakistan's first foreign minister. Ironically, when Jinnah died, Foreign Minister Zafrulla did not take part in the funeral prayers, as was the standard practice of the Ahmadis (ibid., 199).

The *Khatam-e-Nabuwat* movement was revived by the ulema, who feared that the Ahmadis were conspiring to capture the state. The spiritual head of the Ahmadis, Mirza Bashiruddin Mahmud Ahmad, made an inflammatory speech in Quetta, 'in which he openly advocated the conversion of the population of the Province [Baluchistan] and the use of that Province as a base for further operations' (ibid., 261). Such statements incited a reaction from the mainstream ulema who called for direct action (mass agitation) against the Ahmadis. The ulema also demanded that since Pakistan was an Islamic state, only Muslims could hold key positions in the state. Therefore, it was asserted that since Ahmadis held beliefs that were irreconcilable with Islam, they should be removed from key positions. Consequently, in March 1953, a violent agitation broke out in the Punjab. Direct action quickly degenerated into violent attacks on Ahmadis; many were killed and the looting of their property was widespread. Prime Minister Khawaja Nazimuddin imposed martial law in the Punjab, and the agitation was crushed. The military acted swiftly and firmly.

A Court of Inquiry headed by two judges of the Lahore High Court, Justice Muhammad Munir and Justice Rustum Kayani, was set up to enquire into the causes of the disturbances and rioting. The Munir Report, as it came to be known, carried out a lengthy examination of the ideological basis of the ulema's agitation. In the extended question and answer sessions with the spokespersons of the different Sunni sub-sects, and the Shias, the judges noted that not only did the ulema want the Ahmadis to be declared non-Muslims – and therefore removed from key posts – but they also believed that those Ahmadis who had not inherited their beliefs from their parents and had voluntarily converted to that faith were guilty of apostasy and should be punished with death (ibid., 218–20). In the section dealing with 'Responsibility for the Disturbances', the Inquiry blamed not only the ulema and other anti-Ahmadiyya movements such as the Ahrar for fomenting the riots, but noted that Ahmadi propaganda and attitudes had played an important role in precipitating the crisis. It was pointed out that many prominent Muslim Leaguers, whose party was in power in the Punjab, were actively involved in the anti-Ahmadiyya disturbances (ibid., 237–262).

The report also suggests that the anti-Ahmadiyya controversy was exploited by the Punjab chief minister, Mian Mumtaz Daultana, to bring down the central government of Prime Minister Khawaja Nazimuddin; both belonged to the Muslim League (ibid., 262–286). The military acted with great firmness. At that time, the Ahmadi component was quite substantial in the officer corps. Lieutenant General Azam Khan, who was made chief martial law administrator in the Punjab, ordered stern action. Rioters were fired upon and, within a few days, law and order had been established. Some of the ringleaders were tried under martial law and sentenced to death; those sentences were later commuted to an overall clemency and they were released.

Constitution Making

Internal squabbles and intrigues amongst the Muslim Leaguers greatly weakened the party and undermined its prestige. Liaquat evaded elections, primarily because he had no constituency from which to ensure his election – that fear and diffidence became an excuse for his lesser successors to also postpone general elections. Equally, the Pakistan Constituent Assembly's members had been elected in 1946, even though the Muslim League never attended its sessions to frame a constitution for a united India. Many of them were now members of the Pakistan Constituent Assembly, which was to frame a constitution for Pakistan. In an address to the members of the Pakistan Constituent Assembly on 11 August 1947 – three days before Pakistan achieved independence as a separate state for the Muslim nation of India – the founder of Pakistan, Mohammad Ali Jinnah, made a speech in which he observed:

> You are free; you are free to go to your temples, you are free to go to your mosques or to any other place of worship in this State of Pakistan. You may belong to any religion or caste or creed – that has nothing to do with the business of the State.... We are starting with this fundamental

> principle that we are all citizens and equal citizens of one State.... I think we should keep that in front of us as our ideal and you will find that in due course Hindus would cease to be Hindus and Muslims would cease to be Muslims, not in the religious sense, because that is the personal faith of each individual, but in the political sense as citizens of the State (Speeches of Mr Jinnah 1976: 403–4).

Jinnah's speech generated endless controversy as it negated the confessional basis on which the demand for Pakistan was made. The question in everyone's mind was: if Pakistan was going to be a secular state, then what was the justification for demanding a separate state for Muslims? Jinnah, a non-practising Shia himself, had been a liberal constitutionalist committed to keeping India united before he began to champion a separate state for Muslims in a predominantly Sunni environment. Once he took up the cause of separate Muslim nationhood, he increasingly employed religious criteria for justifying that. By the early 1940s, he had realised that Pakistan could be brought into being only if the ulema were mobilised to win the broad sympathies of the Muslim masses. Accordingly, the Muslim League allied itself with the largest group among the religious leaders – that of mainstream Sunnis belonging to the Barelvi school who controlled thousands of mosques and Sufi shrines. From around 1944 onwards, Islamic slogans and emotional appeals in favour of Pakistan became the standard practice of the Muslim League election campaign. Such a strategy paid rich dividends when elections were held in 1946.

The Shia minority was wary of a Muslim state that might be based on Sunni principles coming into being. Similarly, the Ahmadiyya sect, considered to be heretics by both the Sunni and Shia ulema, was also reluctant to support the demand for a separate Muslim state because of fear of persecution. To all such doubters, Jinnah assured that Pakistan would not be a sectarian state. Consequently, in addition to the various sections of the Sunni majority, the Shia minority and the Ahmadiyya also supported the demand for Pakistan. Moreover, when Pakistan came into being, Hindu and Christian minorities were also residing in its territories, especially in East Pakistan where they constituted twenty-three percent of the population.

Given the diverse sectarian and religious composition of Pakistan, Jinnah was probably proposing that Muslim nationalism, which had served as the basis for claiming separate statehood, should be supplanted by an inclusive concept of Pakistani nationalism. If one reads the text carefully, there can be no doubt that he was advocating the privatisation of religion. Current definitions of secularism emphasize the following: the state must guarantee individual and corporate freedom of religion, deal with the individual as a citizen irrespective of his religion, and it must not constitutionally privilege a particular religion nor seek either to promote or interfere with religion (Ahmed 1987: 36).

After Jinnah's death on 11 September 1948, the succeeding governments suppressed that speech. It was deleted from government compilations of Jinnah's speeches. In any event, Pakistani left-wing liberals and Marxists continued to invoke that speech in defence of a secular-democratic Pakistan while right-wing liberals, conservatives, and Islamists described it as a statement in favour of an ideal Islamic state which, they believed, practised religious tolerance during the pre-colonial era. Jinnah's immediate successors, however, were keen to find a synthesis between his secular-liberal vision for Pakistan and the fact of Muslim nationalism. Consequently, on 7 March 1949, the prime minster moved the Objectives Resolution, which proclaimed that sovereignty belonged to God; the members of parliament, it was suggested, had merely been delegated functions of law-making in accordance with the law of God (Constituent Assembly Debates, vol. V: 1949: 1–2). The ulema interpreted this as recognition of the supremacy of the Sharia (dogmatic Islamic law). The prime minister and his modern, educated colleagues explained that it did not mean a theocracy or a rejection of democracy and minority rights; rather, democracy and minority rights were to be sublimated in accordance with Islamic precepts (ibid., 1–49). Besides the novel Islamic features of Pakistani democracy, the Constituent Assembly also had to find a formula that would make Pakistan a federation with a distribution of powers acceptable to the various nationalities of Pakistan. From the very beginning, the Bengalis, who alone constituted a majority of the total Pakistani population, as well as the smaller nationalities of Baloch, Pakhtuns, and Sindhis developed grievances over what they alleged was Punjabi domination (Gankovsky and Gordon-Polonskaya 1972).

Outside parliament, the ulema under the leadership of the Jamaat-e-Islami's Abul Ala Maududi had begun to campaign for an Islamic constitution (Ahmed 2009: 159–60). The 1952 Basic Principles Committee recommended a board of experts who were to ascertain whether a law made by the legislature was commensurate with Islam. Also, it was proposed that approval by the Muslim members of the legislature was to be decisive for law making.

It recommended a bicameral national parliament with parity of representation between the units of East and West Pakistan, though the East Pakistan population alone constituted a majority. In 1955, the West Pakistani provinces of NWFP, Punjab, Sindh, and the Balochistan territories were amalgamated to constitute a single West Pakistan province amid strong opposition from Bengali, Baloch, Pakhtun, and Sindhi nationalist leaders (Gankovsky and Gordon-Polonskaya 1972).

Bureaucrats Consolidate Their Hold over the Political Process

The utter incompetence and patent mediocrity of the Pakistani politicians largely paved the way for senior bureaucrats to consolidate their hold over the political system. Prime Minister Nazimuddin proved incompetent in dealing with a food and economic crisis that hit Pakistan; his government's worries were aggravated by a balance of payment crisis as well as budgetary difficulties (Callard 1957: 22). People all over Pakistan began to display considerable restlessness. On 17 April 1953, Governor-General Ghulam Mohammad dismissed Nazimuddin. His choice of prime minister was even more arbitrary. He summoned Pakistan's ambassador to the United States, Mohammad Ali Bogra, also a Bengali like Nazimuddin, to Pakistan and made him prime minister. The only apparent qualification Bogra had for the job, besides his Bengali ethnicity, was his reputation as a devout pro-American diplomat. In the provincial elections held in East Bengal in March 1954, a united front of a number of parties opposed to West Pakistani domination won 223 out of a total of 237 seats reserved for Muslims (Gankovsky and Gordon-Polonskaya 1972: 201). The landslide victory of those opposed to a strong and overbearing central government created panic in Karachi.

The Central Government reacted by alleging that the Jugtu Front, as the alliance was called, had conspired with the Pakistan Communist Party to undo the unity of Pakistan The Jugtu Front government was dismissed, and a ban imposed on the Communist Party in July 1954. Major General Iskander Mirza, an army officer who had changed career and become a civil servant, was made governor of East Bengal (Callard 1957: 24). Nevertheless, infighting between different factions of the central elite continued. Prompting by a number of disgruntled members of parliament helped Bogra develop enough confidence to challenge the indomitable Ghulam Mohammad. With the help of the members of parliament, the 1935 Act was amended to preclude the governor-general from acting except under advice of his prime minister.

The governor-general struck pre-emptively. He ordered Bogra and some other ministers, as well as Ayub Khan, who had gone to the US to return. According to Ayub Khan, Ghulam Mohammad offered him the powers to produce a constitution in three months, which he refused. Many ups and downs and palace intrigues followed. Finally, on 24 October 1954, the Pakistan Constituent Assembly was dissolved by Ghulam Mohammad on the grounds that it had become unrepresentative and had failed to produce a constitution. A pliable Pakistan Supreme Court, headed by Justice Muhammad Munir, provided him with a legal cover to dissolve the Constituent Assembly under the so-called Doctrine of Necessity. There was, however, a dissenting note, written by Justice A.R. Cornelius, who pleaded for the sovereignty of the parliament (Nawaz 2008: 126). Ghulam Mohammad again invited Ayub to join the 'cabinet of talents'. This time he agreed and became defence minister (Khan 2006: 68–70). It is worth noting that Ayub's term as commander-in-chief was to be completed in 1954.

Ayub agreed to join the cabinet only if he could retain the post of commander-in-chief. He also secured an extension to his term as commander-in-chief. Ghulam Mohammad, however, had to pull back because of bad health in 1955 and Iskander Mirza, became governor-general. Both Mirza and Ayub Khan were stoutly pro-American – the former actually outdid the latter in his manifest preference for Pakistan becoming a protégé of the United States. The US was taking a keen interest in the developments taking place in Pakistan. Admiral Arthur W. Radford, who visited Pakistan during that period, was basically pleased that the military was in a robust position. He wrote that 'Pakistan was a potential ally of great importance, and…from a military point of view, they have a trained armed force which no other friendly power can match, not even the Turks' (quoted in Nawaz 2008: 125).

1956 Constitution

Amid the bad news, the country also had some basis to celebrate. The new Constituent Assembly worked under the leadership of Prime Minister Chaudhri

Muhammad Ali – also previously a bureaucrat in the financial services – who had replaced Bogra. The Constituent Assembly worked to give the nation a constitution that was promulgated on 23 March 1956 – exactly sixteen years after the Lahore Resolution of 1940 when the demand for Pakistan had been made by the Muslim League. And so, Pakistan ceased to be a British dominion. The 1956 Constitution declared Pakistan an 'Islamic Republic'. It provided for a parliamentary form of government with a popularly elected prime minister as head of the government, and a president – elected by the members of the national and provincial legislature – as head of state. A bicameral legislature, based on the principle of parity, was laid down. Both Bengali and Urdu were to be the national languages of Pakistan. Fundamental rights were guaranteed for all citizens of Pakistan. However, some specific Islamic provisions were included. Thus, for example, the president of Pakistan would be a Muslim. All existing laws were to be brought in consonance with the Quran and Sunnah (practices of the Prophet Muhammad [pbuh]), and no law would be made that was repugnant to Islam. The president would set up an organisation for Islamic research and instruction in advanced studies to assist in the reconstruction of Muslim society on a truly Islamic basis (Constitution of the Islamic Republic of Pakistan 1956).

Amid much fanfare, Iskander Mirza became the president while Chaudhri Muhammad Ali remained prime minister but only for a short while. He was followed, as prime minister, for short spurts of time by Huseyn Shaheed Suhrawardy, Ibrahim Ismail Chundrigar, and Firoz Khan Noon. The situation in the provinces was equally pathetic. Quite simply, political instability in Pakistan was ubiquitous and endemic.

Provincial Grievances and Attempt to Secede by Kalat

Grievances had begun to emerge among the Bengali, Baloch, Pakhtun, and Sindhi politicians almost immediately after Pakistan came into being. The irony was that although, during the negotiations with the Congress leaders, the Muslim League had championed a loose federation, once Pakistan came into being, the external as well as internal situation of Pakistan was such that it could only be ruled with the help of a strong centre. Historically, the locus of power in Pakistan was centred on the Punjab – from where the armed forces were mainly recruited. In the powerful civil service, the

Urdu-speaking migrants were well-represented, followed by the Punjabis and some Pakhtuns. At any rate, separatist tendencies were to be found in all the provinces and nationalities that felt alienated from the perceived alliance in the centre between the Punjabis and Urdu-speakers. Nothing expressed this more dramatically than the alleged attempt, by the Khan of Kalat, to exploit the deteriorating situation in Pakistan to make another bid to secede in 1958. Such developments were, according to Ayub Khan, breeding great consternation among the armed forces:

> The army could not remain unaffected by the conditions around it, nor was it conceivable that officers and men would not react to all the political chicanery, intrigue, corruption, and inefficiency that was manifest in every sphere of life. They had their relatives, they read newspapers, and some had contacts. Being a patriotic and national army, it was bound to respond to the thinking of the people of the country. (Khan 2006: 75)

6
The First Military Takeover

The assassination of Liaquat Ali Khan, in 1951, set in motion the internal slide of Pakistani politics. From 1951 onwards, when US military aid began to arrive, the military establishment became the most powerful entity in the country and enhanced its clout over the decision-making process, especially pertaining to defence and foreign policy (Siddiqa 2007: 71). From such a point of advantage, it could appropriate more than one-fourth of the annual budget, as the US intelligence report has indicated.

The Coup Set in Motion

In any event, a scuffle took place between the government and the oppositional members of the East Pakistan Legislative Assembly on 21 September 1958. It was followed, two days later, by a hand-to-hand fight between them. Chairs, microphones, tables, and rods were deployed. The deputy speaker, Shahid Ali, was badly injured and later died from his injuries. Earlier, in May 1958, Dr Khan Sahib of the Republican Party had been assassinated in Lahore. Pakistani political scientist Khalid bin Sayeed portrayed the situation in the following words:

> Pakistan was very much like Hobbes' state of nature where every politician or provincial group fought against every other group. It was a ceaseless and ruthless struggle for power. Most of the leaders thought of themselves, their families, or at best their provincial groups and did not give a second thought to Pakistan. Pakistan needed a desperate remedy for its malady (quoted in Rizvi 2009: 84).

Such developments sufficed to set the coup in motion. At 8 p.m., on 7 October 1958, Mirza abrogated the Constitution, proclaimed martial law throughout Pakistan, dismissed the central and provincial governments – the National and Provincial Assemblies – and appointed Ayub as the chief martial law administrator (ibid., p. 86). Ayub, in turn, with Mirza's approval, imposed martial law throughout the country from midnight 7–8 October.

Ayub claimed that the coup had been carried out without much planning or preparation; only some military units were moved into key positions in the capital, Karachi. In spite of such a token stationing of troops in the capital, Ayub stated that the military always has a basic plan and strategy to deal with such situations; all the commanders had been informed about the coup, and duties had been allotted to deal with situations as they arose. The military did not expect much resistance because 'The people were completely fed up with the state of affairs and desperately wanted a change. And they had great respect for the army' (Khan 2006: 90). This was largely true. There were no public displays of dissatisfaction or anger. In fact, the people were visibly relieved. Apparently, some generals who were opposed to the army getting involved in politics were told that the country needed 'shaking up' (Nawaz 2008: 145).

The First Coup D'état

Hasan-Askari Rizvi has asserted that Ayub Khan had been weighing up the possibility of such an intervention from, at least, 1957 when he visited East Pakistan. Major General Umrao Khan (General Officer Commanding, East Pakistan) arranged for him to meet a cross section of political leaders who expressed their dissatisfaction with the existing sordid situation. In response, Ayub is reported to have said, 'if the people want me, I shall not shirk my duty' (Rizvi 2009: 82). The second hint, that he was thinking along such lines, was a reply he reportedly gave to journalists who asked him how he hoped to defend Pakistan against external aggression when the internal situation was so depressing. He reportedly said, 'Do not worry about the defence of the country. That is my business. Attend to your leaders who are wrecking the country. Do not talk of external dangers. The real danger is within the country. Cannot you see it?' (ibid., 82–3).

External Stimuli

The entirely internal motivations and compulsions of the coup are doubted by some researchers. Shuja Nawaz has asserted that President Iskander Mirza and General Ayub had been thinking of a military takeover for quite some time, and had been sharing their views with the Americans (Nawaz 2008: 139). The reason was also external. In the Middle East, Arab nationalism was on the rise following the Suez Crisis of 1956. Gamal Abdul Nasser of Egypt had introduced a trend of left-leaning radicalism in the Arab world; the bloody coup by the Iraqi Army, against the pro-Western Hashemite kingdom in 1958 was an alarming manifestation of that trend. In Pakistan, students and workers had taken to the streets in the second half of 1958. Elections were due in 1959 but, given the experience of 1954 in East Pakistan, the pro-Western power elite was worried about a similar turnout all over Pakistan. The Muslim League was in tatters; regional parties and separatist movements were in ferment. Yet, it seems, the Americans were not entirely convinced that a military takeover was the best bet for their interests. They preferred the retention of a civilian facade (Jalal 1991: 273–76).

Ayub justified the military coup of 7 October 1958 in the following words:

> The army could not remain unaffected by the conditions around it; nor was it conceivable that officers and men would not react to all political chicancry, intrigue, corruption, and inefficiency manifest in every sphere of life....A well-organized, trained, and disciplined army would find it extremely distasteful to be turned into an instrument for securing political power. But as conditions were, the army alone could act as a coercive force and restore normalcy' (Khan 2006: 75).

With the few exceptions of leftist newspapers such as the *Pakistan Times* and the *Imroze* of Lahore, and some Bengali dailies of East Pakistan, the Pakistani press was positively inclined towards the military takeover. The US and British press wrote approving editorials in favour of the coup, and the influential *Dawn* of Karachi came out strongly a few days after the coup, in support of it in an editorial entitled 'A Sane Revolution':

> There have been many revolutions in the world...but this revolution of ours has been of a different sort. A complete change of both system and regime has been brought about without any strife or bitterness,

> and without disorganizing the normal lives of citizens…this unique feat will perhaps stand out in history as a shining testimony to the wisdom, humanity and large-hearted patriotism of the architects of the new order (quoted in Ray 2004: 105).

Mirza's Exit On 27 October, 1958

However, soon after the coup had been successfully staged, Mirza became suspicious of Ayub – after troops moved into key positions around President's House and other government buildings. Ayub has noted that on his return from East Pakistan – where he had addressed a large public gathering – his officers informed him that Mirza had been trying to test their loyalty to him as the president. Mirza, allegedly, ordered Air Commodore Rabb to arrest some top commanders who were close to Ayub, such as General Yahya Khan, General Sher Bahadur, and General Hamid. Rabb, instead, requested a meeting with Mirza and demanded that he put such an order down in writing. In the meanwhile, when Ayub returned from East Pakistan and learnt about Mirza's intentions, he consulted legal experts who advised him and his close associates that, after the imposition of martial law and the dissolution of the government and parliament, the office of president had become redundant.

A few days later, Ayub was told by his commanders that Mirza had become unbearable because, allegedly, he had approached some persons to enter into a deal with him. Ayub asserted that, additionally, a feeling was growing among the people that Mirza represented the past; that link had to be severed to allow the revolution to give a new start to Pakistan. After some further prevarication, he decided to send General Burki, General Azam, and General Khalid Shaikh to Mirza – to convey to him that he must step down. Mirza, realizing that he was in an impossible situation, was despatched to England (Rizvi: 90–4).

The *Dawn* sang praises of this new development in the following words:

> This step, taken in the best interests of the country, eliminates the likelihood of divided counsels at the highest level of authority.… There is little doubt now that the initiative and the driving force which arrested the rot that was eating into the vitals of Pakistan, due to the misbehaviour of politicians, was primarily his.… President Ayub Khan

> has spoken of the fear of God and sought to instil that wholesome fear into the minds of the people...it is very heartening that President Ayub himself attaches so much importance to these larger spiritual values as is evident from his frequent references to God (quoted in Ray 2004: 105).

Jinnah's sister and, ironically, later the joint candidate of the Combined Opposition Parties against Ayub in the 1964–65 presidential election, Fatima Jinnah, expressed very similar sentiments:

> A new era has begun under General Ayub Khan and the Armed Forces have undertaken to root out the administrative malaise and anti-social practices, to create a sense of confidence, security and stability and eventually to bring the country back to a state of normalcy. I hope and pray that God may bring wisdom and strength to achieve their objective (quoted in Ziring 1971: 10).

Asghar Khan is of the view that the US was positively inclined to the change even when:

> Iskander Mirza at the time was even closer than Ayub Khan to the United States. Indeed Mirza's pro-Americanism often embarrassed the Americans. He believed to a greater degree than Ayub Khan that Pakistan's destiny was linked with the West and felt and behaved like a staunch ally of the United States. Iskander Mirza did not draw a line between the interests of the United States and those of Pakistan. Any facility or information required by the United States was, if he could help it, made available to them. Ayub Khan, though more discreet in his outward behaviour, had the same belief. Insofar as Ayub Khan's takeover reflected a neater arrangement, Washington probably preferred Ayub Khan to his predecessor and he soon began to enjoy the full confidence and increased support of the United States (2005: 17–18).

Martial Law

It is not difficult to appreciate that the transition from an inept, corrupt, faction-ridden, unrepresentative civilian government to military rule, through martial law, achieved without a single bullet being fired, was widely supported by the larger society. The military moved into the major cities and towns, but Ayub Khan decided to exercise authority through the civil administration. A Presidential Cabinet was set up. It included three generals and a number of civilians, including Zulfikar Ali Bhutto – later the nemesis of his downfall. The army, naval, and air force chiefs became deputy martial law administrators, while Ayub became president and chief martial law administrator. He also promoted himself to field marshal. However, civil servants were accommodated in the overall administration at all levels. It was decided that until such time that a new constitution was adopted, the abrogated constitution would be adhered to, subject to martial law regulations and ordinances. The Supreme Court, High courts, and lower courts continued to function, though fundamental rights were suspended (Rizvi 2009: 88–91). The most important step, taken by Ayub, was the appointment of a number of expert committees to investigate and recommend policy on different political, educational, and legal matters. Troops were withdrawn by the second week of November 1958 as the new government felt that the civil administration was functioning effectively, albeit under the overall command of the military.

After consolidating power, the government tried to build up public support. The government undertook a number of measures to weed out corruption, within the state as well as in the larger society. Altogether, 1662 government officials were punished through dismissal, compulsory retirement, reduction in rank, and other lesser punishments. With regard to the rampant factionalism and corruption among politicians, a number of individuals were tried under the Public Office (Disqualification) Order (PODO) and The Elective Bodies (Disqualification) Order (EBDO), and disqualified from holding public office for a period not exceeding fifteen years. Such cases were tried in special tribunals of not less than two persons, one of whom had to be a judge of the supreme or high court. At least 1600 individuals were tried and excluded from holding public office (Rizvi 2009: 100–102). Also, efforts were made to weed out black marketeers and hoarders: some were arrested and punished.

Reforms–I

In his political autobiography, *Friends not Masters* (2006), Ayub revealed that he had begun to reflect on what needed to be done to set things right in Pakistan by October 1954, when he had broken journey in London on his way to the United States. The core idea he developed was that Pakistan could evolve as a cohesive nation only 'if as a start a constitution is evolved that will suit the genius of the people and be based on the circumstances confronting them, so that they are set on the path of unity, team work and creative progress' (2006: 210). He began by comparing and contrasting the ethno-racial composition of East and West Pakistan, concluding that the former were descendants of the ancient races of India and had a long history of being a subjugated people – a fact that made them suspicious, exclusive, and aggressive. On the other hand, the latter were, as a result of invasions and conquests, a mixture of many races who spoke different languages, but who, thus, enjoyed a 'fusion of ideas, outlooks and cultures' (ibid., 210). Ayub did not put on paper that the latter were better rulers, but that inference is quite justified. However, ostensibly, the purpose of comparing the two was to argue for a framework that encouraged cooperation between the East and West Pakistanis. Therefore, he supported parity between them, and for the western units to be amalgamated into one province.

With regard to the political system, Ayub made the following observation:

> It would be appropriate to reiterate the fact that our eventual aim must be to develop democracy in Pakistan, but a type that suits the genius of our people. Our people are mostly uneducated and our politicians not so scrupulous. The people are capable of doing great things, but they can also be easily misled. Unfettered democracy can, therefore, prove dangerous, especially nowadays when Communism from within and without is so quick to make use of weaknesses. We, therefore, have to have a controlled democracy with checks and counter-checks (ibid., 212).

Such an approach was reminiscent of Lasswell's observations that the specialists on violence would emphasize their role as custodians of national interest and a political system that sought to control people. Ayub invoked the perceived danger posed by communism, from within and without, to justify a democracy that was properly controlled by the state.

Reforms–II

In the light of such reflections, the military embarked on an ambitious programme of comprehensive reforms covering economic, educational, constitutional, and legal matters. Between 1958 and 1962, using his special powers under martial law, Ayub initiated a number of reforms. He identified the landlord class as being responsible for holding Pakistan back in both socioeconomic and political terms. Land reforms introduced by him imposed a ceiling of 500 acres of irrigated land, and 1000 acres of un-irrigated land, for a single holding in West Pakistan. The government claimed that some two million acres were surrendered by the landlords and distributed among the peasants. In East Pakistan, where radical land reforms had already taken place earlier, the ceiling was in fact raised drastically, from 33 to 120 acres for self-cultivated land (Khan 2006: 110). The different approaches seem to have been motivated by the need to promote a strong upper middle class of farmers, rather than a vast peasantry owning small fragmented holdings. Such measures set the Green Revolution, which greatly increased food production as well as commercial crops such as cotton, in motion (Ziring 1971: 87). Land was allotted to military officers in the development schemes that resulted from the building of barrages on the river Indus – which accentuated the anti-military and anti-Punjabi feelings in Sindh. The One-Unit scheme, which had amalgamated the different provinces and regions into a consolidated West Pakistan, with Lahore as the capital, was blamed for enabling Punjabis to acquire agricultural land in Sindh.

Economic and Industrial Policies

Ayub also adopted an industrial policy that offered generous tax incentives to industrial entrepreneurs and exporters. Bonus vouchers facilitated access to foreign exchange for imports of industrial machinery and raw materials. Tax concessions were offered for investment in less-developed areas (Nyrop 1984: 46). These measures had important consequences in bringing industry to Punjab, and gave rise to a new class of small industrialists. Hitherto, it was mainly Karachi that had benefited from investment by the non-Punjabi entrepreneurs belonging to the ethnic minorities, such as the Memons, Ismailis, and Bohras. The diversification of industrialisation benefited Ayub's family and relatives. The overall thrust of the economic reforms was modernisation and development within a capitalist framework – light consumer industries based on an import substitution strategy. Such measures were very successful and, within a few years, Pakistan was being celebrated as a model of capitalist transformation (Ziring 1971: 86–88).

Harvard scholar and World Bank adviser Gustav Papanek pointed out that the average consumer's lot improved in the 1960s, but the concentration of wealth in a few hands – notoriously known as the twenty-two-families – began to be discussed in Pakistani politics and by scholars. The argument that a trickle-down effect would follow did not register well with the people. 'Amid the squalor and wretched poverty of the Pakistani masses a new elite now flaunted its prowess and privilege', noted Lawrence Ziring (1971: 89).

Reforming Muslim Family Law

The Marriage and Family Laws Commission was originally formed in 1954 under the chairmanship of Justice Mian Abdur Rashid. However, its recommendations were not implemented by the civilian governments. Through the Muslim Family Laws Ordinance of 1961, the military government adopted many of its recommendations. The Ordinance lay down that marriages and divorces should be registered with the local government entity known as the Union Council. Second marriages and divorces also needed to be referred to the Union Council. In the case of a second marriage, permission from the first wife had to be obtained and the applicant had to convince the council that he was in a financially sound position to provide for a second wife. The divorce process also first required submission to an Arbitration Council, which had to try to reconcile the couple. Moreover, the minimum age of marriage for girls was fixed at sixteen years. Another important reform was that grandsons could now inherit from their grandfathers, even if their father had died. Previously, according to Sunni law, the grandfather's property went to the siblings of the deceased son; the latter's children were given no share of the property that would have been given to him were he alive (Rizvi 2000: 103).

Some clerics opposed the ordinance but the government stood its ground. Many years later, when the Ayub regime weakened, opposition to the Muslim Family Laws Ordinance was revived by the right-wing political forces. However, notwithstanding the vicissitudes that followed later in Pakistani politics, the Muslim Family Laws Ordinance has survived all subsequent governments that have come to power in Pakistan, including the openly Islamist one of General Muhammad Zia-ul-Haq (r. 1977–88).

Basic Democracies

Of all the reforms, the most crucial one was of the political system – called Basic Democracies. As noted already, Ayub Khan did not believe that parliamentary democracy was suitable for Pakistan. His concept was that the people should elect their representatives locally, who would then constitute an electoral college that would elect the chief executive. Consequently, 80,000 directly elected Basic Democrats – 40,000 from each wing of the country – constituted the lowest level of a tiered system of decision-making. The lowest unit was the union council. Each union council comprised ten directly elected members and five appointed members, all called Basic Democrats. Union councils were responsible for local community development and the maintenance of law and order. The next levels consisted of the sub-district, district, and divisional tiers – each assigned a number of developmental and educational functions (Khan 2006: 232–35). The system formed a sort of pyramid, with the union councils at the bottom and the divisional councils at the top. The most important were the union councils; the most important members were the 80,000 elected Basic Democrats assigned the central role of electing the president. In 1960, they voted to confirm Ayub Khan as president (Nyrop 1984: 46–7).

The 1962 Constitution

Pakistan received its second constitution from Ayub Khan. It was to embody his vision of a political system that suited the genius of the Pakistani people – a concept that he emphasised very strongly. In doing so, he developed his position on the relationship between religion and state or, rather, Islam and Pakistan. He admitted that neither the Quran nor the examples of the Prophet and his successors sufficed to serve as the basis of a proper constitution, but believed that they could serve as guidance for good and responsible government. He attacked the ulema who had opposed the creation of Pakistan on the basis that it would be a secular-national state, alleging that what they wanted, instead, was to institute a system that would ensure their central authority in running the state. While critiquing the ulema and their dogmatism, he also regretted that the modern, educated elite were alienated from their Islamic roots. He asserted that the Islamic system of government did not approve of kingship or hereditary rule. According to Ayub Khan:

> The community as a whole must have the right to choose its leader and the right to remove him. Another feature of Islamic history which found general acceptance was that the leader, once he is chosen by the community, should have sufficient power to coordinate, supervise, and control the activities of the government. Delegation of authority was permissible but central control must remain in the hands of the chosen leader who should provide unified direction to the country and its administration (2006: 229).

He then debunked the parliamentary system as divisive, and one that had brought the country to the verge of collapse because of the shifting majorities in parliament and the consequent fall of governments. He further wrote 'We have suffered enough in the past on account of it and could ill afford to repeat the same mistake. The alternative form, and the one which seemed to meet our requirements, was the Presidential form of government' (ibid., 230).

Consequently, the 1962 constitution was a presidential one, with the president elected indirectly by the electoral college of 80,000 directly elected Basic Democrats. Initially, Pakistan was only declared 'The Republic of Pakistan', which provoked angry protests from the ulema and other conservative sections of society. The first amendment re-introduced the epithet 'Islamic' and so, once again, Pakistan became 'The Islamic Republic of Pakistan'. The president was to be a Muslim, and an Advisory Council of Islamic Ideology and the Islamic Research Institute were established to advise the government in bringing all legislation in conformity with the Quran and Sunnah. Ayub Khan sought to retain certain aspects of his dominant authority, which had ended after the constitution was promulgated in 1962. The president exercised substantive powers to issue ordinances, the right of appeal to referendum, protection from impeachment, control over the budget, and special emergency powers including the power to suspend civil rights. On the other hand, fundamental rights were made justiciable. The courts continued their traditional function of protecting the rights of individual citizens. However, it was laid down that the courts could not nullify their previous progressive legislation on land reforms and family laws. In late 1962, political parties were legalized again (Nyrop 1984: 48–9). Ayub Khan combined fragments of the old Muslim League, and created the Convention Muslim League as the official government party.

Samuel P. Huntington showered lavish praise on Ayub's reforms. In particular, he considered the system of Basic Democracies and the strong presidency as the two core elements that connected the whole country to a strong president at the centre. That Ayub also accepted the system of political parties and created one of his own, the Convention Muslim League, completed the framework needed for political modernisation and institution-building – necessary for a developing nation that was, as yet, not properly groomed in managing the pulls and pushes of the usual western type of democracy (1968: 252–55).

The 1965 Presidential Election

The first test of the new system was the presidential election of January 1965. Four political parties joined to form the Combined Opposition Parties (COP) – the Council Muslim League, strongest in Punjab and Karachi; the Awami League, strongest in East Pakistan; the National Awami Party, strongest in the NWFP, where it stood for dissolution of the One Unit Plan; and the fundamentalist Jamaat-e-Islami. The COP nominated Fatima Jinnah – sister of the Quaid-i-Azam, and known as Madar-e-Millat (the Mother of the Nation) – as their presidential candidate. Miss Jinnah had been persuaded, by the opposition, to challenge Ayub Khan who they accused of converting Pakistan into a dictatorship. The nine-point programme, put forward by the COP, emphasised the restoration of parliamentary democracy. There was an irony involved in the selection of a woman as the candidate. The arch-fundamentalist Jamaat-e-Islami (JI), which stood for an Islamic type of government and had always opposed women's participation in public life, had to reverse its stand on the matter. I remember listening to the leader of the JI at an election rally and public meeting in Lahore when he argued that just as Islam ordinarily forbade pork but allowed it when life was threatened and no halal (permitted) food was available, similarly a woman should not take part in politics under normal circumstances but could in extraordinary circumstances.

The election resulted in a victory for Ayub Khan: he won 63.3 percent of the Electoral College vote. His majority was larger in West Pakistan (73.6 percent) than in East Pakistan (53.1 percent). The opposition made some complaints about rigging but, by and large, it was clear that the election was fair. The people of Pakistan seemed to have endorsed Ayub Khan's policies even though the mass of the people had not benefited, in a substantial way, from the economic developments that were underway (Nyrop 1984: 49).

US–Pakistan Interaction

Irrespective of what the Americans may have wanted to happen in Pakistan, Washington had not raised any serious objections to the military coup once it had taken place. Rather, they expressed the hope that Pakistan would soon return to democracy. The coup was largely a product of the internal developments in Pakistani politics, which paved the way for the military to take charge of the country in a direct and comprehensive sense. It inevitably gave impetus to its praetorian role in a garrison state. As noted already, the garrison state was being consolidated through a military alliance between Pakistan and the US, formalised in 1954; it was followed by Pakistan joining SEATO, the Baghdad Pact, and later CENTO. Regular linkages between the Pentagon and GHQ Rawalpindi had already been established. At the level of the officers, regular interaction had begun to take place – training of the SSG and joint exercises being major forms of it.

The US–Pakistan Agreement of 5 March 1959

As noted in the last chapter, the Americans had begun to doubt Pakistan's usefulness to their anti-Soviet strategy in the Middle East. However, Pakistan's geostrategic importance continued to be the main attraction for the United States to enhance its cooperation with it. It seems that the Pentagon and the Eisenhower administration remained convinced that they had enough leverage on Pakistan to make it serve US interests, if and when needed. Consequently, economic and military cooperation was further deepened through the US–Pakistan agreement of 5 March 1959 – of which Article 1 was probably the most important:

> The Government of Pakistan is determined to resist aggression. In case of aggression against Pakistan, the Government of the United States of America, in accordance with the Constitution of the United States, will

> take such appropriate action, including the use of armed forces, as may be mutually agreed upon and as is envisaged in the Joint Resolution to Promote Peace and Stability in the Middle East, in order to assist the Government of Pakistan at its request (Jain 2007a: 33).

No clause or article in the main text referred to India. The Americans, nevertheless, chose not to be caught on the back foot and, therefore, a few weeks later, on 6 May, Secretary of Defense Neil H. McElroy, in a hearing before the Senate Committee for Foreign Relations, made it clear that such an agreement should not be construed to include military aid or intervention in case of an India–Pakistan war. He stated:

> So the Pakistan military assistance program is geared to preparing Pakistan to defend against aggression from the north and is not in relationship to any possibility of conflict with India.... This defense, of course, is not against India. This is allocated to Pakistan for defense against Russia and China (ibid., 35).

Such a statement was also meant to placate the Indians. Notwithstanding the change of guard, from Democratic to Republican leadership, US foreign policy remained steadfast in its estimation that India, and not Pakistan, was the most important country in South Asia; in the overall contest with the Soviet Union and China, it was important that India remained a western type of democracy. Not surprisingly, the Indian prime minister issued a statement in the Indian Parliament on 13 March 1959, in which he informed the members:

> We have been assured by the US authorities that their latest bilateral agreement with Pakistan has no effect other than the extension of the Eisenhower Doctrine to cover Pakistan and that the Eisenhower Doctrine restricts the use of United States armed forces to cases of armed aggression from any country controlled by international communism. We have been specifically assured by the US authorities that this Agreement cannot be used against India. We have also been assured by the United States authorities that there are no secret clauses.... (Jain 2007b: 26).

The Eisenhower Doctrine, it may be recalled, was purported to support Middle Eastern nations against the spread of communism and Soviet influence. Pakistan had been insisting on its usefulness in playing a central role – through its army – in the Middle East on behalf of the West, long before the Eisenhower Doctrine was formulated or announced. Meanwhile, an incident took place that greatly angered the Soviet leaders vis-à-vis Pakistan. On 1 May 1960, the Soviet Union shot down an American U-2 reconnaissance aircraft that had taken off from Peshawar in northern Pakistan. Earlier, in July 1959, a 'communication facility' had been granted to the US at Badaber, near Peshawar, which was staffed by personnel of the US Air Force (Jain 2007a: 309). From it, the Americans could monitor developments in the Middle East as well as the Soviet Union. The U-2 pilot, Gary Powers, was captured and the Soviet Union issued a stern warning to Pakistan, threatening it with severe punishment if it allowed further such flights from its territory. While further U-2 flights were stopped, the Pakistan Air Force and US and British pilots continued to fly another aircraft – the RB-57F – which had an altitude capability of 82,000 feet. These flights were confined to the border areas along the Soviet Union and China, and continued for many years (Singleton 2010). East Pakistan could, at most, serve as a servicing base for SEATO operations in case of war in Southeast Asia.

Ayub Khan continued to appeal to the United States for greater help and assistance. Writing in the mouthpiece of the US foreign policy establishment's, *Foreign Affairs*, in July 1960, he thanked the Americans for their 'magnanimous aid' and went on to say:

> Moreover, in the context of present-day world politics Pakistan has openly and unequivocally cast its lot with the West, and unlike several other countries around us, we have shut ourselves off almost completely from the possibility of any major assistance from the Communist bloc. We do not believe in hunting with the hound and running with the hare (Jain 2007a: 35–6).

Simultaneously, Pakistan's US ambassador, Aziz Ahmed, wrote in the *Annals of the American Academy of Political and Social Sciences* in July 1960:

> Pakistan is...the most allied of America's Asian allies in that it is signatory to more mutual assistance arrangements with which the United States is associated than any other Asian country. Strategically, it occupies a position of unusual interest...a bridge between the Middle East and Southeast Asia. West Pakistan, furthermore, has a common

> border with China and is very close to the Soviet Union's southern frontiers....(ibid., 36).

Ayub Khan's, and Aziz Ahmed's, articles were published soon after Pakistan decided not to join the NAM. That decision, in itself, was significant because it carried major foreign policy implications and demonstrated a clear break with the option of neutrality that had existed in Pakistan for a while. In 1955, Pakistan had been one of twenty-nine countries, mostly former colonies in Africa and Asia, that had convened a meeting at Bandung, in Indonesia, to discuss common concerns and to develop joint policies in international relations; their core concern was a commitment to maintaining national independence and territorial integrity, and to oppose imperialism, colonialism, and other forms of domination by the big powers. However, by the time the First NAM Summit Conference was held in Cairo, from 5–12 June 1961, Pakistan had moved decisively away from neutrality in the Cold War. The intellectual and ideological leadership of NAM rested with left-of-centre statesmen, such as Jawaharlal Nehru, Ahmed Soekarno, Gamal Abdul Nasser, and Joseph Tito. Thus, when the preconditions for membership of NAM were discussed and formulated, it was laid down that members should not be part of a military pact sponsored by any great power – an allusion to the United States and the Soviet Union. Since Pakistan had entered into a military pact with the United States in 1954, and joined US-backed regional military alliances, NAM was no longer a forum that was relevant for the ascendant civil-military oligarchy that was now entrenched in Pakistan. In fact, the Pakistani leaders tried to contrast their loyalty to the West with India's non-committal approach. This point was stressed by Ayub Khan in an address to the US Congress in 1961. He proudly announced that 'Pakistan was the only country in the continent where the United States armed forces could land at any moment for the defence of the 'free world' (Bhutto 1969: 1).

The Sino–India War and Pakistani Concerns

During the 1950s, while Pakistan had appropriated the designation of 'the most allied ally in Asia' for itself, India had been providing leadership to the NAM. However, in October–November 1962, a border clash occurred between India and the People's Republic of China – the two most populous nations in the world – thus exposing the weak and fragile nature of the alliance that had supposedly been formed against the great powers. Nehru had supported the communist regime's triumph over the nationalists, and advocated that China should be admitted to the United Nations. In the early years, after both states became independent, slogans like 'Hindi-Chini Bhai Bhai' (Indians and Chinese are brothers) were in circulation but such manifestations did not suffice to prevent the emergence of a serious border conflict between the two most populous nations of Asia. The origin of the conflict lay in a dispute over demarcation of the international border between China and India; both states inherited the historical ambiguities of areas of control over the preceding hundred or more years, particularly about Tibet – a principality which traditionally recognized Chinese suzerainty.

When Chinese Premier Zhou En-Lai visited India in April 1960, Hindu ultra-nationalists protested against alleged Chinese imperialism and opposed any territorial concessions. He met a cross section of Indian leaders, but was lectured by everyone on the righteousness of the Indian position. While the whole atmosphere was charged with hardcore Indian nationalism, there was also a hope that an agreement would be reached between Zhou and Nehru. The Chinese proposals reiterated their earlier position – that, while Aksai Chin remained with China in the eastern areas, India could retain its existing positions. The McMahon Line, more or less, was proposed as the boundary to be converted into the international border, but India refused to accept such an arrangement (Maxwell 1970: 158–70).

This was followed by the Indian leaders, especially on the Right, resorting to irresponsible bluster about war. The Indian military also began to advocate an aggressive posture vis-à-vis China. Jingoism gained the upper hand as India wrested the tiny colony of Goa away from the Portuguese in December 1961. Projected as a war of liberation, it was a rather easy success because of the very weak Portuguese presence in Goa. Somehow, such successes began to be confused with similar possibilities in the event that India decided to drive the Chinese out of areas that it had, allegedly, been occupying. Indian troops began to be despatched to the border areas in the north. Over the months, although the Chinese and Indian troops clashed a number of times, their skirmishes remained local and of little military importance. Both sides began to build-up their military presence along the disputed border. A bigger border clash was in the offing and, on 20 October, the Chinese attacked in real strength.

As the Indians were poorly clothed, trained, and armed to fight at such great heights and in such extreme – cold – weather conditions, they quickly suffered reverses. On 29 October, the American ambassador called on Nehru and offered military equipment, which Nehru accepted immediately although, some weeks earlier, he had dismissed the idea of accepting American military aid. In fact, it was Nehru who wrote to President Kennedy requesting US military intervention (Maxwell 1970: 435). Military aid began to arrive in India from France, Britain, and the United States within a few days. However, nothing helped and India was defeated. While fleeing, the Indians surrendered some 2000 square miles of disputed territory. This put the Chinese in control of 15,000 square miles in the Kashmir region. Reverses in the northeast were even more dramatic and, had the Chinese wanted, they could have continued gaining control over more territory. However, on 21 November, they decided on a unilateral ceasefire and withdrew to behind the McMahon Line – vacating the entire area that they had captured (Khan 2006: 154–55). The Chinese move rendered US intervention unnecessary. However, the Indian right-wing opposition called on the government to keep fighting until all the occupied land was liberated. Such proclamations carried no value as India had been roundly defeated.

A historian of the Sino–Indian war of 1962, Neville Maxwell, noted that even though the Cold War was still raging, both the superpowers had reached some sort of understanding that India had to be propped up against China. The Indian leadership decided to work with the US in Asia (Maxwell 1970: 434), which resulted in US and British military aid worth $120 million to India. The aid was to equip six Indian divisions for mountain warfare. At the same time, India decided to increase its strength from eleven to twenty-two divisions (Khan 2006: 155). India accepted this help but insisted that it would remain steadfast to its non-aligned foreign policy. On the other hand, the US and Britain pressed India to settle its dispute with Pakistan. Here, the Indian position was diametrically opposed to the one it had taken vis-à-vis China – it wanted Pakistan to accept the status quo. At any rate, US arms and military aid continued to be given to India, despite Pakistan's protests. Also, India sharply increased its spending on the modernisation and expansion of its armed forces. Ayub Khan, expressing his frustration at the way India was managing to hoodwink the world, wrote:

> India currently presents three faces to the world: one to the West, simulating a resolve to fight China in order to secure maximum of western arms assistance; a second to the Soviet Union, stressing her resolve, nevertheless, to remain 'non-aligned'; and a third to China, seeking a peaceful settlement of the dispute by peace overtures through neutral emissaries (ibid., 156).

In military terms, India was probably at its weakest while the war was going on with China. Pakistan could have taken advantage of it but Ayub Khan did not do so. Within the Pakistani power elite, hawks, such as Foreign Minister Zulfikar Ali Bhutto, were in favour of exploiting the opportunity by attacking India (Aijazuddin 2002: 21). Subsequently, the missed opportunity was falsely magnified by the hawkish elements of the power elite (Schofield 2007: 42). The Sino–Indian border war set an arms race in motion. While India began to arm, primarily for a future military threat from China but at the same time concerned about Pakistan's military ambitions, Pakistan felt that a better armed and stronger India was a greater threat than previously. The Chinese obviously considered the two superpowers to be a threat to its existence. In South Asia, the border issue also resulted in increasing Chinese interest in courting Pakistan – a gesture that the latter reciprocated with enthusiasm and considerable exaggeration.

Kennedy's Letter to Ayub

Kennedy wrote to Ayub on 28 October 1962 – while the Sino–India, border war was at its height – requesting that the latter write to Nehru, assuring him that Pakistan did not have any intention of attacking India during its conflict with China. Ayub wrote a long letter to Kennedy on 5 November 1962, in which he complained that India had posed a major military threat to Pakistan for fifteen years, and that eighty percent of its armed forces were amassed on its western front with Pakistan. He argued that Pakistan's vital economic interests were linked to Kashmir. Because of the Indian threat, Pakistan had been forced to keep itself, constantly, in a state of mobilization. He then went on to demonstrate that India was an unreliable and dangerous neighbour and a deceptive player in international politics. He pointed out the Indian military invasions of Junagarh, Hyderabad, Kashmir, and Goa, and told Kennedy that the Chinese operations were, in his estimation, of a limited nature and would not lead to a bigger war (Khan 2006: 162–5).

The US and Britain took various initiatives to encourage India and Pakistan to reach a settlement of the Kashmir dispute but nothing came of these efforts. However, just before his death in May 1964, Nehru sent the Kashmiri leader, Sheikh Abdullah, to Pakistan to probe the possibility of resolving the conflict. Apparently, Nehru had come round to the belief that, in the event of any future conflict with China, India needed to secure its western border. For that to happen, the Kashmir problem had to be resolved. Sheikh Abdullah was received with great warmth, and he addressed public meetings and met Kashmiri and Pakistani leaders. However, his visit was cut short on 27 May 1964 by the news that Nehru had died (Gauhar 1998: 257). Abdullah flew back to Delhi where, after a while, he was again put into detention. The change of guard in Delhi brought more hawkish elements into power. No further Indian gesture, akin to the one made by Nehru, followed.

Improvement in Pakistan–China Relations

Meanwhile, Pakistan and China had begun to develop more than a friendly neighbourly relationship. The initial contacts had begun in the 1950s; Chinese Premier Zhou En-Lai's visit to Pakistan in 1956 had received a very warm and ostentatious welcome. While remaining an ally of the US, Pakistan had, since the mid-1950s, been trying to improve relations with China. This was not received sympathetically in Washington; the suspicion that Pakistan's commitment to fighting communism was merely a tactic to secure Western arms was strengthened. Consequently, the US viewed the early overtures with some reservation. But, after the split between the Soviet Union and China in the early 1960s, the United States was not particularly concerned vis-à-vis Pakistan's friendly overtures to China and vice versa. The Sino–Indian war of 1962 brought China and Pakistan even closer and, in 1963, they reached an agreement on the demarcation of their international border. Pakistan conceded some territory to the Chinese, from the area of Kashmir under its control. Both agreed to the building of a road connecting China's Muslim-majority Xingjian province with Pakistan's northern region. A trade agreement was also signed. Pakistan's Foreign Minister, Zulfikar Ali Bhutto, was the main architect of this policy of developing a closer understanding with China (Bhutto 1969).

On the Indian side, the rapid expansion of the armed forces and the acquisition of modern military hardware had generated greater confidence. India had been spending much larger sums of money on its armed forces than Pakistan though, in percentage terms, Pakistan was spending more. The Soviet Union, in particular, greatly expanded military aid and sales to India. Its deteriorating relations with China apparently made it come to the same conclusion as its superpower rival: that India had to be made militarily strong so that the debacle of 1962 could not be repeated.

India–Pakistan Relations

India had offered a 'No War Pact' to Pakistan in 1950, but it had been rejected by Pakistan because the Kashmir dispute was not being settled in accordance with the pledges India had made in the UN Security Council – to hold a plebiscite to ascertain the wishes of the Kashmir, people. Subsequently, the offer of a no-war-pact was repeated many times but, each time, it was turned down by Pakistan as it was suspected that it was a crafty move engineered at making the ceasefire line into the international border – which was unacceptable to Pakistan (Bhutto 1966: 40). Nevertheless, in November 1959, Ayub offered India a 'joint defence pact' which Nehru rejected with the caustic remark, 'defence against whom' (Tahir-Kheli 1997: 34). In any event, the Kashmir problem continued to dog India–Pakistan relations and, as usual, the UN was the venue where much of sabre rattling took place.

The Indus Waters Treaty

The ideological and identity aspects of the Kashmir dispute are well-known – for India, retention of Kashmir is considered essential to its secular identity while, for Pakistan, its acquisition is necessary to complete the division of India on a religious basis. However, apart from such identity clashes and emotional traumas, the deeper reasons for claiming Kashmir are economic and military. It is quite intriguing that neither side has clearly staked its claims on such bases. The fact is that the Kashmir dispute is basically a hydro-political problem that carries profound economic and military implications and ramifications. Both India and Pakistan have to feed huge populations; this pressure is constantly increasing because of rapid population growth.

Both have invested heavily in the agricultural sector, which forms a major portion of their economies. The most developed regions of Indian agricultural production, and almost the whole Pakistani agricultural sector, are dependent on the waters from the rivers that originate in the mountains of Kashmir or the adjacent Himalayan range. These rivers meander into the territories of both the states. Consequently, the state that controls the upper riparian enjoys a strategic advantage because it can divert the flow of water, or even deny it, to the other. This advantage is enjoyed by India (Malik 2005).

Surprisingly, although tensions and hostility between India and Pakistan over Kashmir had remained high, both sides realised that they could not afford to postpone an agreement on water sharing until the final status of Kashmir was settled. Consequently, under the auspices of the World Bank, a treaty was signed by them in 1960 whereby the waters of the three eastern rivers – Ravi, Sutlej, and Beas – were awarded to India, while Pakistan was allocated the waters from the western rivers of Indus, Jhelum, and Chenab. Nehru and Ayub Khan signed the Indus Waters Treaty in Karachi on 19 September 1960. The treaty also allowed Pakistan to construct a system of replacement canals to convey water from the western rivers into those areas in West Pakistan that had previously depended on water from the eastern rivers for their irrigation supplies (text given in Kux 2006: 67–8).

In subsequent years, Pakistan built – with funding from international donors – the Mangla and Tarbela dams and several other similar facilities on the waters of the Indus, Jhelum, and Chenab. Similarly, India built dams and barrages on the Ravi, Sutlej, and Beas. The treaty also prescribed a mechanism for resolving any conflicts that may arise over its interpretation.

7
The 1965 War

While Pakistan and India continued to dispute the status of Jammu and Kashmir in international forums, they assumed positions that made a negotiated settlement impossible. In 1963, India took further steps to integrate Kashmir into India – in the wake of Pakistan giving away some territory, from the Kashmir territory under its control, to China. Tension between India and Pakistan continued to grow in 1964 and 1965. George Singleton, who was posted as a senior officer with the Communications Group at the US Embassy in Karachi, recalled that Foreign Minister Bhutto wanted to use the RB-57F reconnaissance aircraft to fly over Kashmir and India to gather intelligence. He wrote:

> Mr Bhutto tried hard to get the RB-57Fs flown over Kashmir and India to gather intelligence. But the professional and honourable air chief marshal Asghar Khan refused Bhutto's bullying and did his job with the US to stay focused on our joint mission of intelligence gathering of and from the USSR and China. One thing I knew of first hand was that foreign minister Bhutto also tried, again unsuccessfully, to pressure the UK air adviser to the British High Commissioner in Pakistan, the US air attaché, and my boss to fly intelligence gathering missions, which Bhutto wanted over Kashmir and India. Again, Mr Bhutto met absolute rebuffs and turndowns. Kashmir and India were not the mission of our Cold War-focused intelligence programme (2010).

In March 1965, India and Pakistan were drawn into a border skirmish in the remote marshy region known as the Rann of Kutch – on the border between Pakistan's Sindh and India's Gujarat provinces. Initially, it involved skirmishes between the border police of both nations but, soon afterwards, their armed forces were drawn into it. While their armies fought each other, the chiefs of the two air forces, Air Marshal Arjun Singh of India and Air Marshal Asghar Khan of Pakistan, who had served together during the British period, informally decided not to commit their aircraft to the conflict (Khan 2005: xii). Apparently, the Pakistanis outclassed their Indian counterparts in the battles that took place (Khan 1993: 163–6). However, in contravention of their agreements with the US, Pakistan used the Patton tanks it had received as part of the military aid purportedly given for a future conflict with communist states (Husain 2010: 209). Moreover, there were no major gains to be made in such terrain. A ceasefire was agreed on, by both sides, on 30 June. The showdown attracted the international media, and Pakistan's success was mentioned in a number of despatches by Western correspondents. Such an outcome greatly boosted the image of the Pakistan Army among the people. Brian Cloughley has summed up the impact of the Rann of Kutch operation on Pakistan in the following words:

> The significance of the Rann of Kutch affair was the false sense of optimism and superiority engendered with the Pakistan army concerning its ability to fight a war against India. The tiny affair was a Pakistani victory, but it created a mistaken euphoria for which payment was made in short order (Cloughley 2000: 61).

The direct fallout of the perceived success in the Rann of Kutch was that those forces in the Pakistani establishment who favoured active policy on the Kashmir dispute were greatly encouraged to challenge Indian intransigence on Kashmir. The mood had turned jingoistic and militaristic. In India, too, warmongers benefited. It redeployed six divisions – 125,000 troops – to its western front with Pakistan in mid-1965 (ibid., 65–6).

Operation Gibraltar

After Sheikh Abdullah's visit to Pakistan in 1964, Ayub Khan tasked the Foreign Office with preparing a plan, in consultation with GHQ, to 'defreeze' the Kashmir dispute. It set secretive meetings of high ranking officers belonging to the foreign ministry, the intelligence agencies, and GHQ in motion. The pivot around which the Kashmir situation was constantly reviewed was Foreign

Secretary Aziz Ahmed. He was convinced that if Pakistan sent its soldiers into Indian-administered Kashmir, a spontaneous uprising of the Kashmiris would follow. The assumption seems to have been that a fear of China would prevent India from provoking all-out war (Gauhar 1998: 318–21).

In December 1964, a plan was prepared by the Foreign Office and the ISI, and submitted to Ayub Khan, to send infiltrators into Kashmir. He and his advisers were sceptical about it but, after he won the 1965 election, discussed it again. Training in tank warfare in hilly tracts, began to take place in complete secrecy. At a meeting held in February 1965, the commander-in-chief, General Musa, and his senior aides, Foreign Minister Bhutto and Aziz Ahmed, were present. The air force and naval chiefs were not invited! ISI Deputy Director T.S. Jan explained the details of the plan. Ayub reportedly chided those responsible for it because it exceeded their brief. Altaf Gauhar, who was information secretary, has written that Ayub said:

> If there are no more comments, let me ask: Who authorised the Foreign Office and the ISI to draw up such a plan? It is not their job. All I asked them was to keep the situation in Kashmir under review. They can't force a campaign of military action on the Government (ibid., 320–21).

Ayub was also shown another plan, called 'Operation Gibraltar', prepared by General Akhtar Hussain Malik. General Musa, Bhutto, and some other senior military brass were present. Ayub reportedly directed that the main objective of the campaign should be to capture Akhnur, which had great strategic importance. Ayub's plan received a favourable response from those present (Gauhar 1998: 322).

Grand Slam

Capturing Akhnur was also Malik's objective, but it was a part of the larger undertaking planned in Operation Gibraltar. Malik was reluctant to dash for Akhnur, arguing that a lot more resources and men would be needed to accomplish such an objective. This was accepted, and Ayub sanctioned additional funds. Thus, Operation Grand Slam was born. There is considerable confusion as to whether or not this meant that Operation Gibraltar was to be abandoned and, instead, Operation Grand Slam implemented directly. Shuja Nawaz remarked:

> The second part of the plan, Grand Slam, had been given the edge by Ayub Khan who had suggested that Akhnur, a key choking point on the only land route between India and Kashmir, be made the target of the attack by Akhtar Malik's troops. Akhtar Malik, while reluctant to fully tie himself down to that objective, acceded to the request in his meeting with Ayub and others. But, in his operational instructions to his commanders, he kept the option open once he had broken through the Indian defences (2008: 208).

Air Marshal Asghar Khan, who had kept the air force out of the Rann of Kutch conflict, was retired in July 1965. On the other hand, Bhutto had been re-appointed as foreign minister and, day earlier, had written to Ayub that India was in no position to risk a war with Pakistan and that Pakistan 'enjoyed relative superiority' in terms of quality and equipment (Gauhar 1998: 322). Bhutto assured Ayub that 'the risk of India unleashing a war on Pakistan, in retaliation of raids in Kashmir, was negligible and could certainly be contained by Pakistan's diplomatic skills and military superiority' (ibid., 323). However, General Musa remained unconvinced. He was rather alone because Bhutto had won many in the GHQ over to his point of view. Altogether, five groups, named after five legendary Islamic generals, were tasked with Operation Gibraltar. A subsidiary force, named Nusrat (which was incidentally Bhutto's wife name), was added to them. Altogether, some 4000 Mujahideen (Islamic warriors) were infiltrated into Indian-administered Kashmir on 28 July – although the Indians claimed that the number was 30,000.

Contrary to what the Kashmir cell had been telling GHQ and the other authorities, the Indians had taken effective measures to silence the Kashmiri leaders. Most of those who had taken critical positions on Indian efforts to integrate Kashmir into India were under detention.

Very few of the men, sent by Pakistan, spoke Kashmiri. As they had no idea of the conversion rates, they faced problems when converting weights and measures into the metric system, which was used in Kashmir, and when using Indian currency (Nawaz 2008: 208). When they came into contact with the local villagers, the latter informed the Indian forces about their movements. 'By 16 August the Indians had neutralised the infiltrators and started retaliatory operations by occupying two important posts in Uri Sector', noted Gauhar (1998: 323–5). It was only in Jammu that they received some help, and the Pakistan flag was hoisted in a few places (Khan 2007: 91).

Gohar Ayub Khan has asserted that the operation had been badly planned by Akhtar Malik. The Indians, having moved their troops quickly, closed the infiltrators' entry points and then began to hunt them down, killing some and capturing others. 'Major General Akhtar Hussain Malik had not properly planned the exit routes for the Mujahideen' (2007: 91). The Indians followed up with a major operation to separate Uri from Poonch. On 28 August, they captured Haji Pir Pass, which put the Pakistanis in a critical situation. General Musa reportedly rushed to Bhutto's house and told him that the Pakistani forces were now at the mercy of the Indians. He also talked to Malik, who was in dire straits, and insisted that Grand Slam be launched immediately, otherwise everything would be lost (Gauhar 1998: 326). Musa urged Bhutto to obtain Ayub's approval, to launch Operation Grand Slam, forthwith. Gauhar has noted the serious implication such a decision would, however, entail:

> The problem was that Grand Slam would require the Pakistani forces to move across a small section of the international frontier between Sialkot and Jammu....It was obvious that Bhutto and Aziz Ahmad were now in a hopeless situation; they knew that Gibraltar had collapsed and their whole plan had come apart, Akhnur looked like the proverbial last throw of a gambler but there was no other way to retrieve the situation. Perhaps the Indians would not notice the minor transgression of the international boundary. Bhutto decided that it was a gamble worth taking (ibid., 326).

Apparently, just as such frantic exchanges of opinions were taking place, the Chinese ambassador arrived to be briefed. He shared China's experience of guerrilla warfare with Bhutto, including the elaborate training and planning required to merge with the rural people and to conduct guerrilla warfare in cooperation with them. He did not respond to Bhutto when asked his advice whether the fight should be expanded beyond the international border.

Brigadier Yasub Ali Dogar has explained that, from the Pakistani military point of view, the international border was not crossed; rather, it was the 'working boundary' that was crossed. The working boundary was the pre-Partition border between Punjab and the Jammu and Kashmir state, and was not a product of the ceasefire line of the 1947–48 war. The Pakistanis advanced from that point where the pre-partition border and the ceasefire line met, and therefore were convinced that the international border was not breached. India, however, did not recognise the working boundary; it considered it to be the international border because the Maharaja had signed a bill of accession to India in October 1947. Crossing the border, from any point, was deemed to be a violation of the international border by the Indians. Major General Afsir Karim, a retired Muslim officer of the Indian Army, told me in an extended interview that the Pakistanis had tangled themselves in the finer points of international law while themselves being guilty of violating it through the despatch of infiltrators into Kashmir – infiltrators who were alienated from the native Kashmiri population.

Ayub Khan Leaves for Swat

Ayub Khan went to Swat soon after Gibraltar was launched! Bhutto visited him and returned with a directive – 'Political aim for struggle in Kashmir' – signed by Ayub, on 29 August 1965. In it, Ayub Khan had reiterated that action should be taken to 'defreeze the Kashmir problem, weaken Indian resolve, and bring her to the conference table without provoking a general war' (Gauhar 1998: 328). Ayub had emphasised that preparation must, nevertheless, be made for any Indian move on the international border. He favoured quick, hard blows. 'Hindu morale would not stand more than a couple of hard blows at the right time, and place. Such opportunities should, therefore, be sought and exploited' (ibid.). Altaf Gauhar has concluded that such reflections were indicative of the fact that he did not know that Gibraltar had foundered completely. The information secretary, otherwise sympathetic to Ayub, deplores his absence from Islamabad at that critical juncture, and remarks:

> Having given the go-ahead to Gibraltar he removed himself to Swat hoping to keep the Indians in ignorance of the scope and purpose of the operation. He did not realise at that time that he would become the victim of his own stratagem. His absence from the capital gave Bhutto and Aziz Ahmed the freedom to take control of Gibraltar, not only in the context of Foreign Affairs, but also in the field of military planning and manoeuvres (ibid., 328–9).

Even General Musa was not informed about the real situation. The forces in the field were sending dubious and exaggerated messages of brilliant advances (ibid., 328). Gauhar also wondered why Akhnur was not given priority – had they succeeded, it would have disconnected the five Indian divisions in Kashmir from India. With Gibraltar ending in failure, the Indians had begun to move towards Muzaffarabad, the capital of Pakistani Azad Kashmir.

Operation Grand Slam was finally launched on 31 August. It met with strong resistance, halting in one place and advancing inexplicably slowly in another. It was in shambles by 2 September when in the afternoon, General Akhtar Malik was ordered to hand over command to General Yahya Khan (ibid., 330). The assumption that the Indians were in an extremely exposed position in Akhnur, and had insufficient forces, was erroneous according to Gauhar. The Indians had built up their strength. Referring to some details from the battle, Gauhar has argued that General Malik was not leading the battle in a coherent manner, and that the command headquarters in the field was being shifted with the result that the operation was running into problems. He has cited General Musa, who remarked, 'There was no proper articulation of command and grouping of forces' (ibid., 330–1). When Grand Slam did not materialise, the picture looked gloomy in spite of Pakistan capturing some Indian posts. Finally, the truth came out:

> Ayub summoned Bhutto and Musa and demanded the truth. Musa admitted, at last, that Gibraltar had been a complete failure and Grand Slam was frozen in its tracks. After some discussion it was decided that the time had come to cut the losses and wind up the operation. Hopefully, the Indians would get the message and avoid any further escalation. General Malik, had by now lost all credibility with the high command. His enthusiasm had got the better of his judgement and he had launched Gibraltar, a guerrilla operation, for which he had neither the right type of manpower nor any support among the villagers of Kashmir. The task of winding up the operation was entrusted to General Yahya Khan, who was hitting the bottle because he had been given a marginal role in Gibraltar (ibid., 332).

The news about the change in command spread quickly in Pakistan; the newspapers had been in a triumphant mood and greatly exaggerated, to the Pakistani public, false claims of victories and advances (ibid., 331). According to Altaf Gauhar:

> Independent newspapers were vying with the official media in projecting the exploits of their heroes in Kashmir. Radio Pakistan, which normally inspired only boredom and scepticism, became compulsive listening. General Malik, following in the footsteps of the great Muslim hero, Tariq, who burnt his boats before he conquered Spain, was being poised to inflict a crushing blow on the enemy. Why had he been relieved of command at such a critical moment? Few people knew that GHQ had been feeding the press with highly exaggerated stories of imaginary victories against fictitious foes. Within the government there was no arrangement to check or verify these stories. Whether it was an advanced form of camouflage, self-delusion, or prevarication by common consent to boost one another's morale and prospects, conscience had certainly yielded place to wilful fabrication (ibid., 331–2).

The more familiar version, and the one popular with retired military officers, has been that General Malik had nearly captured Akhnur when General Musa relieved him of his charge, and Yahya Khan failed to consolidate that crucial gain. The director of military operations, General Gul Hassan Khan, who was one of the key players in the Kashmir cell – established in 1964 – casts doubt on the wisdom of relieving Malik. He has asserted that the change in command, and the inordinate delay in launching Operation Grand Slam, was a major factor: 'Had he [Malik] been permitted to attack on 26 or 27 August, I am convinced we would have obtained our objective in not more than three days.' (Khan 1993: 187).

Brian Cloughley has expressed a somewhat similar opinion, arguing that Malik produced a good plan, notwithstanding the confusion about the ultimate objective of the whole campaign (2000: 75). Bhutto reportedly held the same view, 'Had General Akhtar Malik not been stopped in the Chamb-Jaurian Sector, the Indian forces in Kashmir would have suffered serious reverses, but Ayub Khan wanted to make his favourite, General Yahya Khan, a hero' (quoted in Abbas 2005: 51). In any case, the change in command on 2 September meant that twenty-four hours were lost in the process – which the Indians took advantage of and regrouped. Fierce fighting followed on the 4th and 5th and Pakistan made some advances but, on the 6th, the Indians opened the front at Lahore and Sialkot.

Such a point of view has been refuted by Altaf Gauhar who has admitted that certain aspects of Gibraltar and Grand Slam are still shrouded in mystery. I quote him at length:

> Much would be made of the decision to relieve General Akhtar Malik of command of Grand Slam. The prevailing view in the GHQ was that Ayub lost his nerve. Just when the Pakistani forces were poised to capture Akhnur and inflict a crushing defeat on India, Ayub decided to call off the operation because he did not want to provoke a general war with India. Later, Bhutto would contribute to this belief to malign Ayub. The truth is that General Malik was a broken man because he knew better than anyone else that his mission had failed. He met the Information Secretary [that is Altaf Gauhar] in Rawalpindi on 4 September and burst into tears. 'I don't know what to say to my children' was all he could manage to mumble. He did not say a word against anyone. The change in command was used by GHQ and the Foreign Office as a cover to hide their own incompetence and indiscretions. Both Bhutto and Musa had been guilty of grave errors of judgement, which they tried to conceal in a culpable and deceitful manner, and they relied on the Grand Slam myth to exonerate themselves from blame (ibid., 334).

In December 2008, I met General Akhtar Malik's son, Major (Retd.) Saeed Akhtar Malik, in Islamabad. He gave me a printed copy of the letter his father wrote to his younger brother, Major General [later Lieutenant General] Abdul Ali Malik, in which he claimed that everybody was on board about his plan. The letter, dated 23 November 1967, was posted from Ankara where General Akhtar Malik was serving as Pakistan's permanent military deputy. Excerpts from it are reproduced below:

a. The de facto command changed the very first day of the ops (that is the military operations) after the fall of Chamb.... This was a betrayal of many dimensions.
b. I reasoned and then pleaded with Yahya that if it was the credit he was looking for, he should take the overall command but let me go up to Akhnur as his subordinate, but he refused....
c. At no time was I assigned any reason for being removed from command by Ayub, Musa or Yahya. They were all sheepish at best. I think the reasons will be given when I am no more.

d. Not informing pro-Pak Kashmiri elements before launching Gibraltar was a command decision and it was mine. The aim of the op [operation] was to defreeze the Kashmir issue, raise it from moribund state, and bring it to the notice of the world. To achieve this aim the first phase of the op was vital, that is, to effect undetected infiltration of thousands across the CFL [the ceasefire line]. I was not willing to compromise this in any event. And the whole op could be stillborn by just one double agent.

e. Haji Pir did not cause me much anxiety. Because impending Grand Slam Indian concentration in Haji Pir could only help us after Akhnur, and they would have to pull out troops from there to counter the new threats and surrender their gains, and maybe more, in the process. Actually it was only after the fall of Akhnur that we would have encashed the full value of Gibraltar, but that was not to be!

f. Bhutto kept on insisting that his sources had assured him that India would not attack if we do not violate the international border. I however was certain that Gibraltar would lead to war and told GHQ so. I needed no op intelligence to come to this conclusion. It was simple common sense. If I get you by your throat, it will be silly for me to expect that you will kiss me for it. Because I was certain that war would follow, my first choice as objective for Grand Slam was Jammu. From there we could have exploited our success either toward Samba or Kashmir proper as the situation demanded. In any case whether it was Jammu or Akhnur, if we had taken the objective, I do not see how the Indians could have attacked Sialkot before clearing out either of these towns.

g. I have given serious consideration to writing a book, but given up the idea. The book would be truth. And truth and the popular reaction to it would be good for my ego. But in the long run it would be an unpatriotic act. It will destroy the morale of the army, lower its prestige among the people, be banned in Pakistan, and become a textbook for the Indians. I have little doubt that the Indians will never forgive us the slight of 65 and will avenge it at the first opportunity. I am certain they will hit us in E. Pakistan and we will need all we have to save the situation.…And yes, Ayub was fully involved in the enterprise. As a matter of fact it was his idea.…

Although Shuja Nawaz is generally sympathetic to Akhtar Malik's assertions, he has noted that the idea of capturing Jammu was Malik's 'secret weapon', which he did not share with anyone. Had Jammu been captured, India's land link with Kashmir would have been severed. Such a move would have been a brilliant tactical success; but, Shuja Nawaz has also mentioned a number of countermoves the Indians had been planning, in case of a limited war in Kashmir (Nawaz 2008: 209–14). Major Agha Humayun Amin, however, believes that Pakistan had a good chance of achieving a fait accompli in Kashmir had they dashed for Akhnur and captured it.

The September War

The belief that India would not retaliate and stab Pakistan's soft belly – Lahore and Sialkot – proved to be a colossal miscalculation. The Indian cabinet had, in 1949, already prepared a plan to win Akhnur back in the event of a Pakistani advance on it, as well as to attack Lahore and Sialkot. It read:

> ...In the event of such actions Indian troops in Kashmir would seek to contain the opposing forces while the main Indian field army made a determined and rapid advance towards Lahore and Sialkot, with a possible diversionary action towards Rawalpindi or Karachi to prevent a concentration of Pakistan forces in the major operational theatre in the West Punjab. The primary aim of this strategy was to inflict a decisive defeat on Pakistan's field army at the earliest possible time and, along with possible occupation of Lahore, to compel the Pakistan government to seek peace (Cloughley 2000: 82).

On 6 September 1965, at 05:30 hours, the Indian forces began their movement towards Lahore. Pakistani intelligence, including the ISI – which years later gained great importance in Pakistani politics – failed miserably to notice and report that the SSG commandos, who had infiltrated into India, had failed to interrupt the Indian advance. In any case, at that time, the Pakistani soldiers should have been ready and vigilant to stop an Indian advance on Lahore. But, the soldiers of some of the infantry battalions were, in fact, busy doing their morning physical training exercises as the advancing Indian troops reached Lahore. It was the PAF that first detected an unusual movement of Indian troops outside Lahore and reported it to the GHQ. The military high command, it seemed, was convinced that India would not cross the international border under any circumstance. In any case, when the news was finally relayed, the Pakistanis put up a stiff resistance at Lahore. At the same time, the Indians did not make full use of the element of surprise to gain a strategic advantage over Lahore. Gauhar has described the reaction of the Pakistani leaders in the following words:

> When India attacked Pakistan the most surprised person was Ayub Khan. His surprise was shared by the Commander-in-Chief of the Pakistan army. Both of them had assumed that with the winding down of Grand Slam the Indians would relax, but they did not realise that the Indian military intelligence services were perhaps as tardy as their Pakistani counterparts. Bhutto and Aziz Ahmed were temporarily halted in their tracks. All their forecasts and assurances about Indian military intentions based, as they claimed at the time, on unimpeachable sources had proved utterly fallacious. They could not even claim that they had not received any warming of the coming Indian attack (Gauhar 1998: 335).

Gauhar has given several examples of public statements made by the Indian government and its leaders that left no doubt that India would take military action. Also, he has mentioned that the Pakistan High Commissioner to India, Arshad Hussain, sent a cipher message to the Pakistan Foreign Office, through the Turkish embassy in Delhi, on 4 September 1965 that India was going to attack on 6 September. He has alleged that 'Bhutto and Aziz Ahmed decided to suppress the message because they thought that Arshad Hussain, known for his nervous temperament, had panicked as usual' (ibid., 336).

Seventeen days of fierce battles between the Indian and Pakistani armed forces followed – on land, in the air, and at sea. Field Marshal Ayub Khan addressed the nation, first in English and then in Urdu, and declared that Pakistan was at war with India as India had invaded Pakistan. He invited all the political leaders for consultations; nobody could come from East Pakistan as flights between the two wings – which would have had to over-fly India – were suspended. All the leaders, reportedly, pledged their support.

Khem Karan, an Indian hamlet not far from Lahore, was captured by Pakistani troops and the Pakistan leadership began to feel confident of more successes. Radio Pakistan's news bulletins churned out stories of spectacular successes. The press backed up such a propaganda barrage with detailed stories and pictures of knocked out Indian tanks, shot-down aircraft, and other equipment.

Aziz Ahmed even demanded 'propaganda leaflets to be printed in the millions for the air force to drop them over Amritsar to reassure the Sikhs that Pakistan had come to liberate them from Hindu domination' (ibid., 339). Once again, the frontier tribesmen were brought in. According to Gauhar:

> Large bands of tribesmen from the NWFP were invited by GHQ to proceed toward the Lahore border to provide support to the men on the front. The tribesmen looted whatever shops came their way along the route to the front but the administration treated these incidents as part of the customary exuberance of tribesmen in pursuit of their foe. The tribesmen were to become a serious nuisance to General Hamid because he could not find them any hilly terrain along the Punjab border where they could hide and display their traditional skills. They refused to expose themselves to air attacks in an area where clouds of dust were their only cover. General Hamid had to forcibly repatriate them to their tribal sanctuaries (ibid., 340).

I myself saw a dog fight between Indian and Pakistan fighter aircraft over Lahore. People came out into the streets and onto the rooftops to see the combat. One of the aircraft was shot down; it nosedived, with a plume of white smoke forming its tail. The next day, the wreckage of an Indian Gnat fighter was displayed in all the newspapers, generating unprecedented euphoria. On the whole, the myth of Pakistani/Muslim bravery and Indian/Hindu cowardice became household currency. Amid all this, there were long queues of the city's rich and influential decamping from Lahore in their fancy cars in search of safe havens in the western regions away from the India–Pakistan border. Rumours were spread that spies and fifth columnists were in Pakistan, on sabotage missions, resulting in vigilantes beating up people simply on suspicion. There was also an ugly angle to all this as people from the minority communities were hounded by mobs for allegedly sending signals to India. The same happened in India where Muslims, in particular, were hounded on charges of spying for Pakistan.

UN Security Council

Bhutto and Aziz Ahmed were banking on UN intervention in case the war did not proceed according to their script, which was based on the ludicrous assumption that India would not counter-attack in the Punjab. The UN Security Council went into action, unanimously passing resolutions on 4 and 6 September calling for an immediate ceasefire. This was indicative of the fact that, from its point of view, the war had already begun before India crossed the border and attacked Pakistan on the Lahore front. Ayub told the UN Secretary General, U Thant, who visited Pakistan, that the 'UN would be laying the foundations of another war' if it did not resolve the Kashmir dispute (ibid., 340). The King of Saudi Arabia offered financial help, and Indonesia sent submarines and surface ships, but by then the ceasefire had taken place. The French agreed to provide thirty aircraft, of which ten were to be delivered immediately. However, it remained doubtful whether Turkey would supply any ammunition, notwithstanding the CENTO agreement. While CENTO did not take a formal stand, SEATO announced, soon after the war started, that 'Indo–Pakistani hostilities were outside its jurisdiction' (Ziring 1971: 62). On 9 September, Ayub informed his ministers that any advance by Pakistan would be heavily resisted by the Indians (ibid.).

US–Pakistan Communications

Some months before the Kashmir adventure, Foreign Minister Bhutto said, at a press conference on 28 March 1965 in Karachi, that the US was rushing military assistance to India, a country hostile to Pakistan. This meant that the whole idea of a Pakistan–US alliance had been shattered. However, he had thanked the US for its generous economic and military aid and explained that moving close to China 'has not been at the cost of the United States' (Jain 2007a: 51). Just prior to the Mujahideen being sent into Indian-administered Kashmir, Ayub Khan had written to President Johnson asking him to use his good offices to deter India 'from involving the subcontinent in a war' (ibid., 51). In an address to the Pakistani nation on 1 August, Ayub Khan informed the people that Pakistan had tried, unsuccessfully, to reason with the US in the hope that it would appreciate the danger that military assistance to India posed to Pakistan (ibid., 52).

Such pleas did not impress the Americans. They knew about the Pakistani infiltrators going into Indian-administered Kashmir, and about the escalating level of conflict. On 29 August, just before the September war started, Johnson expressed great concern over the flare-up between the two countries and remarked, 'Our longstanding and our very consistent stance has always been that the Kashmir issue must, and should be, solved by peaceful means' (ibid., 53).

On 8 September, the State Department announced an embargo on military supplies to both India and Pakistan. The US Ambassador to Pakistan, Walter P. McConaughy, met Bhutto on 9 September and told him that the Congress [US Congress] had decided to stop all military aid to Pakistan and India but that it was 'not a punitive action; it was meant only to lend support to the UN Secretary General's efforts to attain peace' (Gauhar 1998: 341). Bhutto retorted that Pakistan was a friend and ally, fighting for its survival, while the United Nations was letting it down in its hour of need as its cities were being bombed. Gauhar described the next stage in the tense conversation in the following words:

> McConaughy asked him whether this had not been foreseen: 'It was a fateful decision you took to plan and organise the Mujahid operation.' Bhutto flatly denied that Pakistan had been involved in any such operation but conceded that the Mujahids had the support of Pakistan. Bhutto claimed: 'It is India that has committed aggression and we are fighting for our honour' (ibid.,).

The Pakistan Government's Mounting Difficulties

Within the first few days, the war was not going Pakistan's way. Gauhar reveals something quite astounding – it was not until 10 September that the top officials of the relevant ministries, including Gauhar, met with a representative of GHQ to decide to examine the question of Pakistan's political objectives in the war with India. Apparently, this question was not addressed when Gibraltar was planned! 'Aziz Ahmed could no longer explain why the country had been pushed into the war', notes Gauhar (ibid., 342). Nobody had been assigned the task of examining the question of 'the duration and length of the present conflict with India and how Pakistan's defence needs could be met' (ibid).

Air Marshal (Retd.) Asghar Khan, who had retired soon after the Rann of Kutch combat, was sent to Beijing by Ayub Khan on the fourth day of the war to request military assistance, particularly aircraft – but that they should be sent via Indonesia. The reason was that Ayub Khan did not want to upset the Americans. The Chinese found this request quite strange but agreed to it. The Chinese were also requested to move their troops to the Ladakh–Tibet border. The Chinese told Asghar Khan that although such a move could have international repercussions they would consider it. Zhou Enlai even offered to meet Ayub, but the latter evaded him till after the war. In any event, the Chinese sent the aircraft and other equipment via Indonesia. Asghar Khan also visited Indonesia, where he found President Soekarno eager to help (Khan 2005: 235–40). He also visited Iran and Turkey with requests for military assistance.

Pakistan's difficulties continued to mount. An offensive launched in the Khem Karan sector came to a halt when the Indians breached the Madhupur Canal and inundated the area (Husain 2010: 228). Another version is that Pakistani tanks proved to be too heavy and the banks of the canal gave way under their weight. The result was that the Pakistani tanks got bogged down. This had a shattering effect on the Pakistani war strategy: 'The Khem Karan counter-offensive ran aground on 11 September and with that collapsed Pakistan's entire military strategy. For Pakistan the war was over' (Gauhar 1998: 343). In interviews conducted in Delhi in November 2010 with two Indian officers, Lieutenant General Kuldip Singh Khajuria and Brigadier Vijai Nair, who fought against Pakistan in the 1965 war, I was told that Pakistani tanks became sitting ducks as they were bogged down in muddy water and could not move. According to them, the Pakistanis abandoned their tanks in panic. One explanation for this, according to them, could be religious as being burnt to death was considered the wrong way to die. At any rate, after a few days of full-scale war, Pakistan began to face an acute shortage of weaponry, spare parts, and ammunition. Gauhar portrayed the predicament in the following words:

> The Army and Air Force were now experiencing acute shortage of spare parts, ammunition and petroleum, and desperate efforts were being made to secure additional supplies from friendly countries. On the evening of 11 September, Nazir Ahmed told that neither Turkey nor Iran were

> willing to provide armour-piercing ammunition. Ayub was mortified.... Since major tank battles were developing on the Sialkot front the Pakistan Army desperately needed armour-piercing ammunition (ibid., 344).

The Chinese Card

At this juncture, the Pakistani leadership realised that the Western powers, especially the United States, was not willing to help Pakistan. There was even some mention of sanctions being imposed on Pakistan. Altaf Gauhar has claimed that, to counter it, he advised Ayub Khan not to go for a ceasefire without resolving the Kashmir dispute, and that the Chinese card would have to be used to force the Indians to resolve it. The Chinese, for their part, issued warnings and threats to India and made statements supporting Pakistan's stand on Kashmir. An ultimatum was also issued to the Indians to dismantle military activity on the Chinese side of the border, return Chinese livestock, and return kidnapped Chinese civilians. On 7 September, China condemned India's aggression and warned that India was wrong to believe that, as it had the backing of the Americans and Soviets, it could bully its neighbours with impunity (ibid., 347).

The Indians turned to the USA, Britain, and USSR for help against the Chinese. The British prime minister, Harold Wilson, issued a statement that if China intervened, Britain and the United States would assist India (ibid., 348). However, the situation in Pakistan was such that a prolonged war made no sense; defence stores and supplies were low. Ayub was told, by the chiefs of the army and air force, to request American assistance. The BBC reported that, at a press conference on 15 September, Ayub Khan urged the US president, Lyndon Johnson, to intervene directly (ibid., 349). The Indian Prime Minister responded by issuing a statement warning Pakistan to keep its 'hands off Jammu and Kashmir', and that Indian defence operations would continue unabated (ibid., 350).

The American reaction was markedly different. On 17 September, the US representative, Goldberg, informed the UN Security Council that:

> We have suspended arms shipments to both countries, since we want, in support of the Security Council resolutions calling for a cease fire, to help bring an end to this conflict and not to escalate it....We deplore the

> use of arms supplied by us in this conflict in contravention of solemn agreements (Jain 2007a: 309).

The reference to US arms being used in contravention of agreements was surely directed at Pakistan since it relied heavily on US armament. It had already violated that rule during the Rann of Kutch skirmishes when it used the Patton tanks (Husain 2010: 209).

Ayub's Secret Visit to China

On the night of 19–20 September, Ayub and Bhutto paid a closely guarded visit to Beijing and met with Zhou Enlai. Apparently, the Chinese urged Pakistan to fight on, and not give up the struggle even if some Pakistani cities were lost. Numerous examples of Chinese experiences of guerrilla warfare were given. The Chinese assured Pakistan of their unconditional support in the event that Pakistan decided to fight a prolonged guerrilla war. Neither Ayub nor Bhutto was prepared for anything of the sort. Gauhar tells us:

> Ayub had never foreseen the possibility of the Indians surviving a couple of hard blows, and Bhutto had never envisaged a long drawn out people's war. Above all, the Army and Air Force were totally against any further prolongation of the conflict.
>
> General Musa was demoralised by the lack of ammunition and spare parts, and Air Marshal Nur Khan by the high attrition rate which was daily reducing the number of operational aircraft available to him (Gauhar 1998: 353).

Ayub was extremely worried about the Indians capturing Lahore. Bhutto contacted the Chinese ambassador who urged him to fight on. Altaf Hussain, editor of the English-daily, *Dawn*, believed that the Chinese threat of 7 September had created jitters in Washington DC. This inference was a flight of fantasy. According to the information secretary, Air Marshal Nur Khan's 'face dissolved into a convulsion to register the disagreement' with the *Dawn* editor (ibid., 355).

The next few days were busy with discussions on the UN draft resolution urging ceasefire. On 22 September, both countries ceased fire. Apparently, the US and USSR had cooperated in making both sides agree to this. The Indian side had lost 3000 men on the battlefield, while the Pakistanis suffered 3800 battlefield deaths (US Library of Congress). Soviet Prime Minister Kosygin invited Ayub Khan and Shastri to Tashkent to meet and try to resolve their differences.

Veteran career diplomat Sultan Muhammad Khan has confirmed that after its only armoured division got bogged down during the Khem Karan offensive, the war had ended as far as Pakistan was concerned. He was part of the Pakistani delegation that accompanied Bhutto to the Security Council meeting, where the ceasefire was accepted by Pakistan. He presents a damning image of Bhutto exploiting the difficult situation in which Ayub Khan had been placed, by waxing eloquently, during the discussion, on the Kashmiri right to self-determination and asserting that Pakistan would 'continue to wage this struggle for a thousand years if necessary' (Khan 1997: 147). However, after making hyperbolic statements, Bhutto went out and apparently talked to Ayub Khan who was on the phone. On his return to the discussion, with tears in his eyes, he announced that the president of Pakistan had instructed him to accept the ceasefire (ibid., 146–7). However, Sultan has claimed that as the Pakistani delegation was returning from the meeting, Bhutto was laughing and saying that while Ayub Khan would be furious, the people would put garlands around his neck (ibid., 147). Sultan Muhammad Khan has noted:

> What can one think of a performance like this? Was it cheap, theatrical or a calculated drama staged by a politician wanting to cash in on the gullibility of an unsophisticated home audience? Bhutto had come to the Security Council with instructions (which he had himself advocated) to accept the cease-fire resolution. By staging a drama about a phone call Bhutto was distancing himself from Ayub; he did the same after Tashkent Agreement and promised to reveal the secret one day, but of course nothing was ever revealed (because there was no secret) (ibid., 147–8).

Major General Syed Wajahat Husain Comments on the War

Major General Syed Wajahat Husain, who took part in the military encounters from 12–17 September, has expressed amazement at Ayub Khan's statement to a gathering of officers on 24 September:

'Gentlemen – the first lesson we have learnt from this war is that any action taken in Kashmir will lead India to cross the international border' (2010: 230). Wajahat Hussain went on to say, 'This had been apparent even to a layman from the beginning' (ibid.), and asserted that, a couple of years before his death, Ayub Khan admitted that 'his biggest mistake was getting involved in the war, qualifying further that he was ill advised by Foreign Minister Bhutto and his hawkish associates' (ibid., 232). Wajahat Husain has made a scathing attack on the hawks, including Akhtar Malik, Z.A. Bhutto, and Gul Hassan Khan, and asserted that the Americans had always made it crystal clear that the US would stop the supply of spares and equipment in case of hostilities with India – this had been laid down, unambiguously, in the 1954 agreement (2010: 209).

Air Marshal Nur Khan's Revelations

Years later, the strongest indictment of the 1965 war came from Air Marshal Nur Khan who had headed the Pakistan Air Force during the war. The *Dawn* of Karachi published an interview he gave to its special correspondent on 5 September 2005, i.e. the eve of the fortieth anniversary of the 1965 war. He stated that before Pakistan embarked upon the Kashmir adventure, rumours were rife about an impending operation but the army had not shared its plans with the other forces. He took over from Air Marshal Asghar Khan on 29 July 1965 but his predecessor did not brief him about any plan – simply because he himself was not informed about it. So, Nur Khan called on the then commander-in-chief, General Musa Khan, who admitted that something was afoot. On hearing this, Nur Khan's immediate reaction was that it would mean war but Musa told him not to worry because the Indians would not retaliate. He directed Nur Khan to talk to General Akhtar Malik, the man in-charge of Operation Gibraltar, for further details. General Malik told him that the plan was to send some 800,000 infiltrators into the occupied territories, to expel the Indian troops with the help of the local population. The whole operation was designed in such a way, he was told by Akhtar Malik, that the Indians would not be able to retaliate. Consequently, the air force did not need to get into war-time mode (Khan 2005: 1). Nur Khan was shocked when, on further inquiry, he learnt that, except for a small coterie of top generals, very few in the armed forces knew about Operation Gibraltar. That made him wonder how professionals like Musa and Malik could be so naïve and irresponsible. Even the Lahore garrison commander had not been taken into confidence. Equally, the governor of West Pakistan, Malik Amir Mohammad Khan of Kalabagh, did not know what was afoot and had gone to Murree on his vacation.

Nur Khan has stated that although his first instinct was to resign and go home, he recognised that such a rash move would further undermine the nation's interests. Therefore, he decided to remain at his post. The Pakistan Air Force performed miraculously well on the first day of the main war, which started on 6 September. Nur Khan has given full credit for that to Asghar Khan, who had been given charge of the PAF in 1957 – to prepare it to be a dedicated fighting machine, and who had trained his airmen on the best available US-made fighters, bombers, and transport planes. Those who flew those machines, and those who maintained them on the ground, worked as a team; each member of the PAF performed beyond the call of duty to realise this miracle (ibid., 2). With regard to the performance of the military, Nur Khan has remarked:

> The performance of the Army did not match that of the PAF mainly because the leadership was not as professional. They had planned the 'Operation Gibraltar' for self-glory rather than in the national interest. It was a wrong war. And they misled the nation with a big lie that India rather than Pakistan had provoked the war and that we were the victims of Indian aggression (ibid.).

Furthermore, on the second day of the war, when Ayub Khan wanted to know how the army was faring, Musa informed him that the army had run out of ammunition. That shocked General Ayub so much that it might even have triggered his heart ailment, which overtook him a couple of years later. Nur Khan has described the 1965 war as 'an unnecessary war', and said that Ayub Khan should have held his senior generals accountable for the debacle and resigned himself. He has further observed:

> This would have held the hands of the adventurers who followed Gen Ayub. Since the 1965 war was based on a big lie and was presented to the nation as a great victory, the Army came to believe its own fiction

> and has used since, Ayub as its role model and therefore has continued to fight unwanted wars – the 1971 war and the Kargil fiasco in 1999.... In each of the subsequent wars we have committed the same mistakes that we committed in 1965 (ibid., 3).

Military Image Building

In so far as the Pakistan military is concerned, the 1965 war was a massive exercise in image building – even when the expedition was a failure. The images of Pakistanis inflicting defeat on India – in the air, on land, and on sea – proved so enticing that the hard facts of Pakistan's failure in achieving its objectives of liberating Kashmir, or in forcing India to make major concessions on it, were totally eclipsed. This in itself was no mean achievement; Altaf Gauhar, as information secretary, most certainly played a central role in recording failure as success in the popular mind.

In July 2009, I visited Washington DC to interview American experts on the US–Pakistan relationship. Most of them, to my very great surprise, told me that the myth of Muslim soldiers being far superior to Hindus was one of the arguments that the erstwhile Pakistani officers used to tell the Americans when they were courting the United States to co-opt Pakistan in the anti-Soviet alliance. The fantastic 1:10 Muslim–Hindu ratio suggesting that one Muslim soldier was worth 10 Hindu soldiers, was the usual figure mentioned (Fair, Andersen, Harrison, Weinbaum). In some ways, then, the Pakistan military was the victim of a delusion of its own making.

Nevertheless, the 1965 war was fought by 'gentleman officers', many of whom – from both sides of the border – had been trained at the same military academies and socialised on a regular basis. Gohar Ayub Khan has recounted one story:

> A Hawker Hunter of the Indian Air Force was shot down by ground fire. The pilot was the son of General Cariappa who had been a good friend of Father's. My mother and Akhtar went to see the young Cariappa in the CMH hospital in Rawalpindi, where he was recovering from the back injury he had sustained while ejecting from his damaged aircraft. General Cariappa was informed of his son's well-being and on 22 January 1966, twenty-seven year old Flight Lieutenant K.C. Cariappa was repatriated to India (2007: 99–100).

Brigadier (Retd.) A.R. Siddiqi, who was in the public relations office of the Pakistan Army, has remarked:

> After ten years of American arms aid, Pakistan's armed forces had been itching to prove their mettle in action. There is nothing more trying for a well equipped army than to have remained out of action over so many years. With vivid accounts of military manoeuvres and limited border skirmishes, the Pakistani PR had already created the image of a super force (1996: 77).

Tashkent and the Fall of Ayub Khan

The ceasefire was not popular with sections of the Pakistani population. In the popular perception, the United States' arms embargo was a betrayal by a country with which Pakistan was closely allied. Some rioting took place in Karachi; the US consulate was subjected to stone-throwing by angry students. However, the prospect that Pakistan would be able to compel India to agree to a resolution of the Kashmir dispute at Tashkent – after all, it had supposedly agreed to the ceasefire from a position of strength and not weakness – was generally accepted. The Americans supported the Soviet initiative of inviting Ayub Khan and Shastri to Tashkent. Secretary of State Dean Rusk candidly explained why:

> We encouraged the Russians to go ahead with the Tashkent idea, because we felt we had nothing to lose. If they succeeded in bringing about any détente at Tashkent, then there would be more peace in the subcontinent and we would gain from that fact. If the Russians failed at Tashkent, at least the Russians would have the experience of some of the frustration that we had for twenty years in trying to sort out things between India and Pakistan (quoted in Kux 2001: 165).

The atmosphere at Tashkent was tense, but the two leaders managed to reach an understanding that formally brought the bellicose mood on both sides to an end. The Tashkent Declaration was announced on 10 January 1966. Both sides agreed to pull their troops back, no later than 22 February 1966, to the positions they held prior to 5 August 1965; they were to desist from interfering in each other's internal affairs; hostile propaganda against each other was to be discouraged; normal diplomatic relations were to be restored; trade between them was to be restored, and so on. With regard to Kashmir, the only mention it received was that the dispute was discussed and both sides set forth their positions (text given in Kux 2006: 73–5). That night, Shastri succumbed to a massive heart attack. Reportedly, when Bhutto was told by an aide that 'the bastard had died', he said, 'Which one?'

During the Tashkent Summit, Bhutto made his displeasure known with histrionic finesse. The photographs show him uptight and angry. Within forty-eight hours of the Tashkent Declaration, angry students came out in the streets all over Pakistan; rioting was extensive in Lahore, where the jingoistic mood was at its height. Public transport vehicles, shops, private cars, and many other things were torched. Veiled women and children, who claimed to be the dependents of the men killed in the war, walked down Lahore's Mall Road shouting, 'Give us back our husbands, fathers, and brothers' (Ziring 1971: 68). Other slogans were about 'Kashmir being sold to Hindus'.

The West Pakistani leadership, consisting of people like Chaudhri Muhammad Ali, Sardar Shaukat Hayat Khan, and Maulana Maududi, vehemently assailed the Tashkent Declaration. East Pakistani leaders, such as Sheikh Mujibur Rahman and Maulana Bhashani, refrained from criticising it (ibid., 75). The protests and demonstrations continued for several weeks. A rumour began to circulate of a split between Ayub and Bhutto, which culminated in Bhutto's resignation as foreign minister in the summer of that year. Other difficulties compounded Ayub Khan's worries. The upward economic development achieved during the preceding years received severe jolts as the bill for making war was shifted to the people. The prices of essential commodities began to rise, while employment opportunities shrank. In East Pakistan, the Awami League leader, Sheikh Mujibur Rahman, was reported to have expressed views that were inimical to Pakistani unity, and was also accused of being involved in a conspiracy, with the Indians, to break up Pakistan.

However, Ayub Khan had still not grasped the full implications of the harm that was coming his way. Rather, on the advice of his advisers and sycophants, he announced month-long celebrations – October 1968 – to celebrate the tenth anniversary of his military coup. The lavish spending on the celebrations fell flat as people accused the government of wasteful expenditure. Students began to agitate on a regular basis. Government repression failed to quell the protests that had now broken out all over Pakistan. Universities were closed, but that did not prevent the students and others from joining the demonstrations. Bhutto encouraged the students to protest. Air Marshal (Retd.) Asghar Khan also announced that he would join the agitation to protest against corruption, nepotism, bribery, and incompetence (ibid., 89–100). In particular, the people and the political opposition began to accuse Ayub Khan of abusing his power to benefit his relatives and sons with illicit economic gains.

Towards the end of January 1969, the Pakistan Army moved into the major urban centres, such as Karachi, Lahore, Peshawar, Dacca, and Khulna, where some of the worst agitation had taken place. By that time, thousands of individuals had been arrested and hundreds had died as a result of police brutality, including incidents of shooting. However, the protests continued unabated. On 21 February, Ayub Khan announced that he was not going to be a candidate in the next presidential election in early 1970. This surprise announcement, however, failed to placate the opposition. A number of political parties, that had formed the Democratic Action Committee, met him at the end of February. After deliberations that lasted four days, Ayub capitulated and agreed to dispense with the system of Basic Democracies. Direct elections, based on universal adult franchise, were to be the basis of elections in future. The parliamentary system was to be revived. Bhutto did not join the parleys with Ayub Khan but demanded that the president should resign and a caretaker government be formed – which should then hold fresh elections based on a federal constitution that guaranteed the autonomy of East Pakistan as well as of the West Pakistani provinces of Balochistan, Punjab, NWFP, and Sindh; the West Pakistan Province would be abolished.

As the protests were not subsiding, and the politicians were railed against him, the military realised that Ayub would have to go. It was considered expedient to abandon him in the larger strategic interest of the military as an institution (LaPorte 1969). This message was conveyed to him by the top military brass. Ayub Khan stepped down and Yahya Khan took over on 25 March 1969. Yahya re-imposed martial law throughout the country. The 1962 constitution was abrogated, the national and provincial legislatures were dissolved, and a ban put on all political parties.

United States and Ayub Khan

Ayub Khan had visited Washington in December 1965, when the Americans let him know that they did not look upon, with favour, too close a relationship with China. Ayub Khan assured them that the alliance with the US remained his top priority and would not be compromised under any circumstance. When Ayub dropped Bhutto as foreign minister, the Americans were pleased. However, Ayub did not achieve much success with regard to the removal of the ban on the sale of arms to Pakistan. Anyhow, the Johnson administration decided that the 'United States would sell spare parts for previously supplied US equipment but would not provide financial credits or grant military assistance. The door remained closed against the export of tanks, fighters and bomber aircraft, and artillery to Pakistan' (Kux 2001: 173).

On the other hand, while reiterating the strategic alliance with the United States, Pakistan decided not to renew the Badaber military base as President Johnson had requested. On 19 July 1968, Ayub Khan wrote to Johnson: 'I concede this facility is valuable to your country but by its very nature, it lays us open to the hostility and retaliation of powerful neighbours [the Soviet Union]' (Jain 2007a: 73). However, he noted, in his diary on 19 October 1968, that Pakistan could not afford to alienate the Americans completely. As Pakistan's economic dependence on them was considerable, it was decided that Pakistan should show flexibility and not demand immediate compliance – dismantling the military base did not have to start until 1 January 1969 and they had a year to complete it.

8
Alienation Between East and West Pakistan

The relationship between the Bengali Muslim majority and the Punjabi-dominated establishment, comprising civil servants, centrist politicians, and the military, began to sour rather soon after Pakistan came into being. The reasons were a mix of cultural, economic, and political grievances – some inherited from the past and the others a product of the omissions and commissions of the politicians and civil–military oligarchy that had evolved in Pakistan.

Ayub Khan's Impression of East Pakistan

In January 1948, Ayub Khan was posted to East Pakistan as general officer commanding. Acknowledging that he was not the least excited by it, he wrote: 'All we had in East Pakistan at the time of Independence were two infantry battalions' (2006: 38). Both had Hindu and Sikh companies that were transferred to India. He went on: 'We had very poor accommodation: at Headquarters there was no table, no chair, no stationery – we had virtually nothing at all; not even maps of East Pakistan.' He noted that, at the time of independence, there was only one Bengali officer in the superior civil services, so officers from West Pakistan were posted to East Pakistan – a move that was resented by the Bengalis. Suhrawardy, in particular, exploited the East Pakistanis' perceived sense of domination by the West Pakistanis (ibid., 41).

With regard to the recruitment of Bengalis to the army, he asserted that they completely lacked education. He brought this to the notice of Chief Minister Khawaja Nazimuddin and others, but they were reluctant to establish elite schools as the people would object as most Bengalis did not even have access to government schools. Also, he claimed that Bengalis lacked 'manpower with qualities of leadership' (ibid., 42). The Army Selection Board that visited East Pakistan every sixth months would find one or two boys, but they tended to be non-Bengalis from refugee families. He then goes on to repeat that the Bengalis resented the presence of the West Pakistani officers and developed grievances based on minor cultural sensitivities. The West Pakistani officers worked hard, and were generally up to the mark, but they were easily irritated by the inefficiencies of the East Pakistanis. He observed, 'It was a peculiar phenomenon that while an average East Pakistani in Dacca thought the West Pakistan officials were a manifestation of some kind of colonialism, the West Pakistanis were the most unwilling and unhappy instruments of that imaginary "domination"' (ibid., 43).

Military and the Law and Order Situation

Even more interesting, to note in Ayub Khan's narrative on East Pakistan, is the fact that the military had to be deployed to establish law and order on a number of occasions. The first such incident took place on 13 July 1948 when the 60,000-strong police force, that Ayub Khan considered an assortment of heterogeneous elements, mutinied. He learnt that the police had armed themselves and were surrounding Government House in Dacca. At that time, both he and the inspector general of police, Zakir Hussain, were touring Mymensingh. Ayub has claimed that he tried to pacify the latter while simultaneously dealing with the police who had taken up defensive positions. The battalion commander was told, by Ayub, to give them a warning and to prevent them from doing anything reckless. Ayub has stated that 'whenever an appeal was made to them, they would start abusing the army. We were left with no option but to take action. I told the Battalion Commander to take military action against the mutineers, using as little force as possible' (ibid., 44). In the military action that followed, a couple of policemen including the ringleader were killed and ten or twelve were injured. On the whole, Ayub Khan found the Bengali leaders to be troublemakers, and those in power incompetent.

However, Ayub has claimed that before he left for West Pakistan, in November 1949, a basic military organisation had been put in place in East Pakistan. He has noted:

> I was able to build up an adequate Ansar (civil armed guards) force. In this I received great support from Aziz Ahmed who was then Chief Secretary of the provincial government. He felt that such a force would bring discipline to the masses and persuaded the provincial government to spare resources for it. The East Bengal Regiment also came into existence in my time. It was the first time that people from this part had been enlisted in a combat unit. I was also able to establish the East Pakistan Rifles, a police force, and initiate a system of giving all police officers battle-training. It did the force immense amount of good and they developed tremendous confidence and pride in themselves (ibid., 46–7).

A civil servant, Hasan Zaheer, who served in East Pakistan during 1956–62, formed a more benign opinion about the people of East Pakistan. He asserted that while tensions did exist between East and West Pakistan, there was a strong feeling of Pakistani nationalism in the day-to-day interactions between East and West Pakistanis. He stated, 'Even the prosperous Hindu middle classes were part of mainstream community life. Generally, they co-operated with the administration, and played a leading role in social, educational and charitable projects' (Zaheer 1995: xiv).

Bengali Grievances

The Bengali sense of grievance, however, was more diverse than the impression Ayub Khan had gathered. He does not mention the controversy that erupted, while he was in East Pakistan, over the national language. From the Bengali point of view, it symbolised cultural domination by West Pakistan [Punjabis and Urdu-speakers essentially]. It is worth noting that the Bengali Muslims, as a whole, had been attracted to the idea of separate Muslim states in the Indian subcontinent much earlier than the Muslims of West Pakistan. Although the former constituted 55.4 percent of the total population of Pakistan, the capital, Karachi, was in West Pakistan and the power elite that ruled from there was constituted of Punjabis and non-Bengali migrants. In East Bengal, only a minuscule Urdu-speaking aristocracy – remnants of both the Mughal and British periods – and some Urdu-speaking Muslims who had migrated to East Bengal from Bihar in 1947, spoke Urdu. Moreover, Bengali was a highly developed language that had been in official usage in Bengal for a long time.

Yet, in February 1948, Prime Minister Liaquat Ali Khan stated, in the Constituent Assembly, that Urdu would be the sole national language of Pakistan. This was supported by Khawaja Nazimuddin, a scion of the Urdu-speaking family of the Nawab of Dacca, who was chief minister of the Muslim League government of East Bengal.Governor-General Mohammad Ali Jinnah reiterated the same when he delivered a public speech in Dacca in March 1948. Jinnah's speech provoked angry student demonstrations. The language question was the first manifestation of the brittle and precarious nature of Muslim nationalism that had brought Muslims together behind the Muslim League's demand for Pakistan (Ahmed 1998: 220–21; Alam 1995: 40–3: Chowdhury 2009: 12).

On 23 June 1949, Huseyn Shaheed Suhrawardy, Maulana Abdul Hamid Khan Bhashani, and Shamsul Haq founded the East Pakistan Awami Muslim League. In 1955, 'Muslim' was dropped from its name and it became the East Pakistan Awami League. Sheikh Mujibur Rahman, who would later lead the Bengali nationalist movement that culminated in the breakup of Pakistan in 1971, was one of the younger stalwarts of the party. The Awami League became one of the main platforms for Bengali nationalism and regional aspirations to aggregate on and be ventilated from. The Muslim League government in East Pakistan abolished the zamindari system in 1951 and carried out a radical land reform – a measure that largely affected the Hindu absentee landlords who had fled to India (Baxter 1997: 16).

Land distribution to benefit the peasants provided relief, but it was not something that placated the urban Bengali middle class that felt alienated from the power centre in West Pakistan. A change of government at the Centre, after the assassination of Liaquat Ali Khan in October 1951, resulted in Khawaja Nazimuddin stepping down as governor-general – to become prime minister. Despite his East Bengali origin and support base, in 1952 he reiterated his earlier stand – in support of Liaquat and Jinnah – that Urdu would be the sole national language of Pakistan. This resulted in a second round of riots in East Bengal (Jackson 1975: 16–17).

Two years later, in the provincial elections held in East Pakistan on 8 March 1954, the Bengalis expressed their dissatisfaction with West Pakistani domination. The United Front – consisting of Bengali parties such as the Awami League, the Krishak Sramik Party, and the Nizam-i-Islam Party – won 223 out of the 237 Muslim seats, while the ruling Muslim League secured only 10 seats. A United Front government was formed on 3 April 1954, creating panic in West Pakistan. A damage limiting exercise was undertaken; on 19 April 1954, the Constituent Assembly of Pakistan passed a resolution recognising both Urdu and Bengali as the national languages, but stipulated that English would be the official language for another twenty years. However, this was followed by punitive measures. On 30 May, the Central Government dissolved the East Pakistan Assembly and the government was dismissed, ostensibly for advocating secession (Gankovsky and Gordon-Polonskaya 1972: 204–5). At the time, the Bengalis were in no position to challenge the power of the Muslim League government.

Parity

The fact that the population of East Bengal (East Pakistan) alone constituted a majority meant that, in a democracy based on universal adult franchise, the Bengalis would enjoy an advantage over the nationalities of West Pakistan. In 1947, the population of East Bengal included at least twenty-three percent Hindus. Such a large proportion of Hindus, coupled with the overall majority of Bengalis, were from the very beginning viewed with concern and dismay by the power elite of West Pakistan, who wanted to assert an Islamic identity of the Pakistani polity. It had become a core concern of constitution-making from at least the adoption of the Objectives Resolution on 7 March 1949. One way of rendering the Bengali majority a minority would be to place the Hindus on a separate electoral role.

That suited the West Pakistani establishment but, at that stage of political development in Pakistan, the power elite were not convinced about the need to make Pakistan a full-fledged Islamic state. On the other hand, for the Bengali Muslims, their majority status could only be translated into parliamentary advantage if the Bengali Hindus were not excluded from the general category of voters (Jackson 1975: 16). Given such a clash of interests between the East and West Pakistani politicians, another round of negotiations took place between them. The East Bengalis realised that as the state power – the civil bureaucracy and especially the army – was essentially West Pakistani, they would have to compromise. After considerable give-and-take, the principle of parity between East and West was agreed on as the basis for representation in the national assembly. The 1956 constitution represented such a compromise.

Economic Disparity

Parity in representation did not translate into parity in economic development. As noted already, the top positions in the bureaucracy and army remained in the hands of the West Pakistanis. Feroz Ahmed has asserted that a process of internal colonisation took place over the years. He has marshalled an array of statistics to establish that, in 1947, the GDP of East Pakistan exceeded that of West Pakistan, mainly because Pakistan's main export item – raw jute – was produced in East Pakistan. However, by 1969, West Pakistan's GDP was greater than East Pakistan's. The following table, based on a study by Gustav Papanek, illustrates the uneven development that took place (cited in Ahmed 1973: 421):

Gross Domestic Product in 1959–1960: Constant Prices (million rupees)		
	East Pakistan	**West Pakistan**
1949–50	13,130	11,830
1954–55	14,320	14,310
1959–60	15,550	16,790
1964–65	18,014	21,788
1968–69	20,670	27,744

Ahmed has asserted that during this period, resources transferred from East to West Pakistan amounted to ₹31,120 million (calculated in terms of official rate, US$1 = ₹4.76; current market rate US$1 = ₹83.85). Industrialisation in Pakistan began with the investment of capital in the cotton textile industries that were based in West Pakistan and the jute mills in East Pakistan. However, whereas the textile mills were owned by West Pakistanis, the jute mills were not owned by the Bengalis. Rather, it was the West Pakistan-based bourgeoisie who owned the jute mills. In the early years, seventy percent of Pakistan's export earnings were derived from the export of raw and processed jute, and to some extent even tea. According to Ahmed, such earnings were used for the industrialisation of West Pakistan. The pattern of economic development was based on the assumption that the East Pakistanis would consume a significant portion of West Pakistani products – mainly textiles (ibid., 425).

Foreign aid played the single most important role in Pakistan's economic growth. By 1969, the US had provided $3 billion in grants and loans (mainly loans in the later years) which helped finance the development of privately-owned light consumer industries. The bourgeoisie that benefited from it was mainly West Pakistani. Such lopsided developments generated disparities:

> By the end of the notorious 'decade of development' (1958–1969), West Pakistan's GDP exceeded that of East Pakistan by 34 percent, the official disparity in per capita income had become 62 percent, and the real difference in the average standard of living had widened 126 percent (ibid., 428).

The result was that the Bengali peasants, workers, and the middle class were all alienated from a share in the economic growth that was taking place; thence the origins of a nationalist movement that increasingly sought to offset their domination by West Pakistan. It was under these circumstances that the Awami League, led by Sheikh Mujibur Rahman, emerged as the main representative of Bengali separatism. The fact that, during the 1965 war, East Pakistan had been virtually defenceless against an Indian invasion – the only deterrent the Central Government could invoke was a Chinese threat to India not to attack East Pakistan – was vociferously criticised by Mujib and the other Bengali nationalists. The idea that East Pakistan must be self-sufficient began to be put forth and became a rallying point for the regionalism that would later develop into separatism and secessionism. Several other Bengali radical-nationalists, such as the peasant leader Maulana Bhashani, also demanded greater autonomy for East Pakistan.

In 1966, at a political conference, Sheikh Mujibur Rahman put forward a six-point programme for East Pakistani autonomy (The Bangladesh Papers n.d.: 23–33). The conference was not held in Dacca, but in Lahore, which created an even greater sensation. The six-points – see below – were transformative in terms of the relationship that had hitherto existed, and they envisaged a loose federation or, rather, a confederation:

1. Pakistan should be a true federation based on the 1940 Lahore Resolution.
2. The federal government should deal with only two subjects, viz.

defence and foreign affairs, and all other residuary subjects should be vested in the federating states.

3. There should be two separate but freely convertible currencies, or one currency may be maintained if flight of capital from East to West Pakistan is stopped through constitutional provisions.
4. The powers of taxation and revenue collection should be vested in the federating units.
5. There should be two separate accounts for the foreign exchange earnings of the two wings, indigenous products would move freely between the two wings, and the units should be empowered to directly establish trade and commercial relations with foreign countries.
6. A separate militia or paramilitary force should be set up for the defence of East Pakistan.

There was a sharp contrast in the reception to the points. In East Pakistan, the support base of the Awami League began to expand rapidly. All sections of society were attracted to it; the East Bengal Hindus, who had begun to distance themselves from politics, were again animated into political activism. The reaction in Pakistan, especially of the Ayub regime, was hysterical. On 8 May 1966, Sheikh Mujib was arrested under the Defence of Pakistan Rules. His arrest provoked a mass upsurge throughout East Pakistan. In December 1967, and again in January 1968, the government accused him and his associates of nurturing secessionist ambitions. On 17 June 1968, he was moved from Dacca Central Jail to Kurmitola Cantonment, and charged with conspiring to make Bangladesh independent with the help of India.

The Agartala Case

In early 1968, the government claimed to have uncovered a plot involving some forty-six East Pakistanis. Thirty-five were later charged; eleven were pardoned when they promised to assist the prosecution. Among the charged were Sheikh Mujibur Rahman, three Bengali civil servants, and twenty-four junior Bengali officers from the armed forces. The government case was that the plotters had met with Indian officials in Agartala, on the Indian side of the Bengal border, on 12 July 1967 to discuss a plan to launch an armed revolt with Indian help, which would result in the establishment of an independent state of East Bengal (Ziring 1971: 90–91). It was also alleged that

Mujib had been in contact with Indian officials from as early as September 1964. Allegedly, he had received money from them in August 1965, which he distributed among the conspirators. The trial, which dragged on for months into the beginning of 1969, helped foster Mujib's image as a Bengali martyr in East Pakistan. In spite of the government calling 251 witnesses, the state prosecutors were unable to substantiate the charges in a winning manner.

Things came to a head when one of the accused was shot dead on the grounds that he was trying to escape. His funeral, the next day, triggered large-scale rioting. Meanwhile, there were student protests in both the East and the West, and politicians from both parts of the country joined ranks against the government. They demanded an end to the Agartala Conspiracy case and a release of all the accused. Ayub Khan, now completely beleaguered, had to give in. He had already declared his intention not to contest the next election, but the Agartala fiasco further exposed his government's weakness (ibid., 92–3). This weakness became even more apparent when Mujib had to be released from detention, and received a hero's welcome in Dacca.

The Yahya Regime and the 1970 Election

After months of agitation that rocked West and East Pakistan, Ayub Khan stepped down on 25 March and General Yahya Khan took over the reins of power. Apparently, the top commanders had pressured Ayub Khan to step down. Martial law was imposed throughout the country. Initially Yahya Khan did not claim to be the president of Pakistan but, a few days later, he assumed that office as well. With regard to East Pakistan, Admiral S.M. Ahsan was appointed as governor, and Lieutenant General Sahibzada Yaqub Khan as martial law administrator. The government succeeded in establishing law and order rather easily even though the administration in East Pakistan was run by pro-Awami League students for almost a week before Yahya Khan took over. A new government was formed with the help of a coterie of close confidantes from the civilian and military top brass. Yahya Khan made clear the caretaker role of his government, when he addressed the people the next day – 26 March:

> My sole aim in imposing Martial Law is to protect life, liberty and property of the people....Fellow countrymen, I wish to make it absolutely clear to you that I have no intention other than the creation of conditions conducive to the establishment of a constitutional government. It is my

> firm belief that a sound and clean administration is a pre-requisite for sane and constructive political life and for the smooth transfer of power to the representatives of the people elected freely and impartially on the basis of adult franchise (quoted in Hamoodur Rehman Commission Report 2001: 67).

By the end of July 1969, the government was claiming that law and order had been established and that the next objective was to restore democracy. Hence, he embarked on consultations with leaders from both East and West Pakistan. He appointed a team to draft a new constitutional formula. On 28 November 1969, he addressed the Pakistani nation informing them that consensus could not be obtained on the future constitution of Pakistan. Therefore, he was going to propound a Legal Framework Order (LFO) that would serve as the basis for elections and, subsequently, for the transfer of power to the elected representatives of the people. On 30 March 1970, the LFO was ready. Two fundamental changes were wrought by it: (1) it dissolved the One Unit in West Pakistan; and, (2) the principle of parity was replaced by the norm of one man one vote. Both these reforms strengthened the legitimate position of East Pakistan. As it emerged as the most populous province in the country, it was entitled to more seats in the national parliament by virtue of its more than fifty-five percent proportion of the total Pakistan population. With regard to the unicameral Pakistan National Assembly, it was decided that the National Assembly should consist of 313 seats, including thirteen seats reserved for women. Women could contest the elections from general seats as well. The distribution of seats was to be as follows:

	General seats	Reserved seats
East Pakistan	162	7
Punjab	82	3
Sindh	27	1
NWFP	18	1
Balochistan	4	1
Centrally Administered Tribal Areas	7	

Some further preconditions for the restoration of democracy were also elaborated on. Among them, the most important was that the Constituent Assembly would stand dissolved if it failed to frame a constitution in 120 days. A number of Directive Principles of State Policy, that the future constitution of Pakistan could not violate, were announced. These were: upholding an Islamic way of life; observation of Islamic moral standards; and, teaching of the Quran and Sunnah to Muslims. Moreover, Pakistan was to be a federation, known as the Islamic Republic of Pakistan. It was also laid down that the constitution must uphold Islamic ideology, as well as democratic values. Moreover, all the citizens of Pakistan were to enjoy fundamental human rights; the judiciary was to be independent from the executive, and provincial autonomy was to be protected. The LFO authorised the President to reject any constitution framed by the constituent assembly if the document did not fulfil the above-mentioned preconditions. He also enjoyed the power to interpret and amend the constitution, and his decision could not be challenged in a court of law (Story of Pakistan 2010).

Thus, the LFO was purported to virtually serve as an interim constitution. A major flaw of the LFO was that it did not specify the extent of provincial autonomy that could legitimately be claimed. Such ambiguity, on a crucial issue, would prove problematic when the election results came out. In any event, political activity had already been allowed from 1 January 1970 – which resulted in the election campaign getting underway even before the LFO was announced. The different political parties issued their election manifestos. The Awami League put forth the Six Points as its main plank in seeking a mandate from the electorate, to effect radical decentralisation of powers and maximum autonomy to the provinces. It has been suggested that the military government must have been fully aware of the wide gap between its own notion of federation and regional autonomy, and the one the Awami League stood for. Mujib, however, conducted the election campaign fully aware of the fact that the six points, and the LFO, were not easily commensurable.

The procedure adopted to monitor the election campaign was that the speeches of the political leaders were first to be vetted at the provincial headquarters of the martial law administrators and then sent to the headquarters of the chief martial law administrator, General Yahya Khan. Anything objectionable could lead to action being taken against the violation of the LFO. The government did not, at any point, object to the six-point programme as incompatible with the LFO, although Mujib was quite openly critical of it. Thus, in a meeting at Naogaon on 25 October, he categorically stated that 'he and his party condemned the Legal Framework Order but at the same time decided to participate in the elections as they regarded the elections as a referendum on regional autonomy on the basis of the Six-Point Programme' (quoted in Khan 1973: 35). It could be that the intelligence agencies' assessment did not portend a landslide victory that would qualify the Awami League to, alone, form the government. The intelligence agencies expected the Awami League to win, at most sixty percent East Pakistan seats (Hamoodur Rehman Commission Report 2001: 74).

The elections were scheduled for October 1970, but floods in September forced the government to postpone the elections to 7 and 17 December, for the national and provincial assemblies, respectively. Although Mujib objected to the postponement, the government did not budge from its decision. In November, a cyclone that caused enormous devastation, struck East Pakistan. Some 500,000 people lost their lives. The administration in East Pakistan, largely manned by West Pakistani civilian and military officers in the upper echelons, was blamed for incompetence and apathy. Hardly any West Pakistani political leaders expressed sympathy for the Bengalis, and no senior member of the military government paid a visit to East Pakistan. Such behaviour was exploited by the Awami League to whip up more hatred against West Pakistan (ibid., 74).

Such a strategy paid ample dividend as the Awami League won 160 out of the 162 general seats. Thus, it obtained a massive landslide victory that procured a majority in the National Assembly for itself. It could form the government all by itself. All the seats it won were from East Pakistan. The stunned West Pakistani establishment panicked. This was particularly true of the martial law administration in East Pakistan which had a very large component of West Pakistani officers. On the other hand, the Bengali civilian and military officers felt encouraged to assert themselves.

In West Pakistan, Z.A. Bhutto's Pakistan People's Party emerged as the main victor though the number of seats it won was less dramatic: 84 out of the 138 West Pakistani seats. It won majorities in the provinces of Punjab and Sindh. Although Bhutto congratulated the Awami League on its fantastic victory, and said that he respected the majority, he added the rider that 'both Punjab and Sind are centres of power. We may or may not be able to form a government at the Centres but the keys of the Punjab Assembly are in my pocket...' (Cloughley 2000: 162). He went on to say that in the other pocket were 'the keys of the Sind Assembly and...no central government can run without our co-operation. If the People's Party does not support it, no government will be able to work, nor will the Constitution be framed...' (ibid.).

Such a statement had no support in parliamentary theory or practice, and was simply a negative stance expressing Bhutto's ambition for power. This was to become the Pakistan People's Party (PPP) main line of argument, as it joined ranks with the military in the next few months to obstruct the Awami League from forming the government at the centre.

Yahya-Mujib-Bhutto Parleys

For several weeks after the elections, the military regime made no announcement about the National Assembly being called into session. Such inaction only accentuated the Awami League's suspicion and fear – that the establishment was unwilling to let it assume power in accordance with the conventional procedures that apply in parliamentary democracy. On 3 January 1971, the Awami League called a mammoth public meeting in Dacca. Mujib made the elected members take an oath pledging their loyalty to the six points. By that time, Z.A. Bhutto and his PPP had taken a tougher position than the other West Pakistani parties against the six points. Yahya Khan finally met Mujib on 7 January in Dacca.

The Hamoodur Rehman Report notes that in the parleys that took place, Mujib endeavoured to placate West Pakistani fears about the six points being some sort of sinister move aimed at bringing about the virtual secession of East Pakistan from the Pakistan federation. Mujib then asked Yahya to tell him what objections the general had to the six points – to which Yahya replied that he had none but that 'Mujib would have to carry with him the West Pakistani leaders' (Hamoodur Rehman Commission Report 2001: 77). On hearing that, Mujib requested Yahya to summon the National Assembly on 15 February so that he could demonstrate that 'I will not only obtain a simple majority but a two-third majority' (ibid.). This indicates that Mujib was confident that he would receive support from the West Pakistani leaders as well. Admiral Ahsan, who accompanied Yahya, has recorded that, when

Yahya told Mujib that the Awami League could abuse its majority votes, Mujib replied:

> No, I am a democrat and the majority leader of all Pakistan. I cannot ignore the interests of West Pakistan. I am not only responsible to the people of East and West Pakistan but also to world opinion. I shall do everything on democratic principles. To begin with I hope you will arrive 3 or 4 days before the Assembly session. I will show you our draft constitution. If you find objections I will accommodate your wishes (ibid., 78).

Apparently, Mujib even suggested that his party had decided to elect Yahya Khan as the president of Pakistan because he had played a crucial role in the restoration of democracy. Yahya, however, told him that he was a simple soldier and would rather return to the barracks. However, he advised Mujib to work closely with the PPP because it was the largest party from West Pakistan in the National Assembly. Mujib assured him that he would do that, and also try to win the support of other West Pakistani leaders. Their discussions ended on an amicable note. Next day, at Dacca Airport before leaving for West Pakistan, Yahya Khan referred to Mujib as his future prime minister. On 17 January, he and some other generals visited Bhutto at his estate in Larkana, Sindh. The generals were later to allege, in their testimony before the Hamoodur Rehman Commission, that Bhutto was 'conspiring to do Mujib out of the fruit of his favourable election result' (ibid., 79). Bhutto denied that in his testimony. At any rate, Bhutto is said to have requested that time be given to him to parley with Mujib; otherwise, 'Mujib bent upon his Six-Point programme and supported by a clear majority, would surely be able to go through with the Constitution which meant the end of one Pakistan' (ibid.). He also wanted time to prepare public opinion that would allow him to go as far as possible in accommodating the six points.

Bhutto, and some of his party members, then went to Dacca again and met Mujib on 27 January 1971. As the Commission did not have access to the Awami League leaders, it reported the PPP version of the discussions between the two leaders and their advisers. Bhutto claimed that Mujib was rather inflexible on the six points. Although he understood Bhutto's plea that the people of West Pakistan had to be convinced that the six points would not threaten the unity of Pakistan, he was unwilling to postpone the calling of the National Assembly into session to later than 15 February. Bhutto returned to West Pakistan disappointed. He met Yahya Khan on 11 February and reported the result of the discussions with the Awami League to him. Bhutto proposed that the National Assembly should meet at the end of March at the earliest. He claimed that Yahya seemed to agree, but was surprised when the latter then announced 3 March as the date for the National Assembly to meet. In the meantime, agitation was mounting in East Pakistan vis-à-vis the delay in the government-formation process.

On 15 February, Bhutto called a press conference in Peshawar where he declared that 'his party would not participate in the National Assembly session on 3 March, unless their point of view would be heard and, if found to be reasonable, accepted by the Awami League' (ibid., 80). Bhutto was to later deny, in the testimony before the Commission, that he or his party had threatened to boycott the National Assembly session – all he and his party wanted was 'an assurance that there would be reciprocity from the Awami League for adjustment in the Six Points' (ibid.). In any case, on 21 February, a convention of the PPP took 'an oath to abide by the party decision not to attend the Assembly on the 3 March' (ibid.). Finally, on 28 February, Bhutto addressed a mammoth meeting in Lahore where he declared that his party would not attend the session on 3 March. Apparently Yahya and his advisers had decided to postpone the Assembly meeting on 22 February, but did not convey this to Mujib until the 28th – the same day that Bhutto addressed the crowds in Lahore. At that meeting, he threatened the other parties that 'if any of their members decided to go, they should do so on a one-way ticket as they would not be allowed to return to West Pakistan, that their legs would be broken', and that 'the country would be set ablaze from Khyber to Karachi' (ibid.).

I am witness to that meeting. Actually, Bhutto was at his theatrical best on the occasion. He held up the hands of one of his own senior members, Mian Mahmud Ali Kasuri, and told the crowd that not only would legs, but also hands, be broken. Therefore, it was a warning to even his own members who might have held a more conciliatory stand on the six points. The next day, Bhutto addressed the students of Punjab University in their New Campus Auditorium. The bottom line of his address was that the six points would result in the breakup of Pakistan. Such performances meant that the impasse between the Awami League, the Yahya government, and

Bhutto became public and anchored in the popular mind in West Pakistan.

The Commission noted that a close associate of Yahya Khan's, General Umar, ostensibly secretary of the National Security Council, had been engaged in distributing funds in pursuance of Yahya's 'own political plan' during the election campaign (ibid.). After the elections, he had been busy trying to persuade some West Pakistani politicians not to attend the National Assembly or to demand its postponement. The military government, however, wanted to convey the impression, to the public, that the postponement that Yahya announced on 1 March was something that he had been forced to accept by the attitude of the West Wing politicians and not something he himself wanted. In other words, the Yahya regime had its own secretive agenda which coincided with the stand that Bhutto had taken. The Commission overruled that Yahya and Bhutto were necessarily acting in concert (ibid., 81).

On the other hand, the PPP had alleged that Yahya and Mujib were collaborating – the evidence given was that Yahya had stated that he did not find anything objectionable in the Six Points, had called Mujib his prime minister, and had accepted the invitation of the Awami League to continue as president. The Commission remarked: 'General Yahya collaborating with Mr Bhutto or with Shaikh Mujibur Rahman much less with any minor party, he was playing one party against the other' (ibid.). The net result was that instead of reaching a power-sharing formula, conflicts emerged; it all culminated in the disintegration of Pakistan. The delay in calling the newly-elected National Assembly into session resulted in massive protests in East Pakistan. On 2 March, the army was instructed to restore order but, within forty-eight hours, it was told to go back to the barracks.

From early March, the law and order situation had begun to deteriorate rapidly. Awami League activists and the criminal underworld started attacking all non-Bengalis. They received help and assistance from disgruntled Bengali soldiers of the East Pakistan Rifles (EPR) and the East Bengal Regiment (EBR). The Urdu-speaking Biharis, who stood out as a separate ethnic group in the population, were easier to attack than the West Pakistanis who were living in protected areas. As a result, scores of deaths and incidents of injury took place. Those West Pakistanis who could, began to send their families back to West Pakistan. It was clear that there was widespread demoralization among them, and they were increasingly isolated from the local population. Major General Hakim Arshad Qureshi has alleged that the Awami League had even used highhanded tactics during the election campaign and later, which became part of its tactics to intimidate all opposition. He has narrated how, in August 1970 – that is before the elections were held – he travelled in East Pakistan, with an escort, to take over command of a battalion at Saidpur-Rangpur-Dinajpur; however, his second-in-command was not pleased because it was dangerous to do so (Qureshi 2002: 5).

Once the National Assembly session scheduled for 3 March was postponed, attacks on West Pakistanis became more frequent. Thus, Lieutenant Abbas of the 29th Cavalry, who had gone with an escort of Bengali soldiers to buy fresh vegetables, was attacked by Bengali militants and killed. The Bengali members of the escort were sent back unharmed, though their weapons were 'taken' by the militants (2002: 16 17). I interviewed a witness to the events in Chittagong during those early days of March 1971. Juned Chowdhury belongs to a prominent East Pakistani family of Assamese origin. His father, Matin Chowdhury, was a leading member of the Muslim League and a close associate of Jinnah. He told me that:

> Bengali militants began to attack Biharis in Chittagong after it became know that the Assembly was not meeting on 3 March. Those who took part in the assaults were a mixture of Awami League cadres and local criminals. They operated in connivance with low-ranking officials who had turned against West Pakistani domination and considered the Biharis a fifth column since they were Urdu-speaking. Quite a few gruesome murders of Biharis had taken place already before the military action that began on 25 March. On the other hand, the Biharis identified themselves with West Pakistan and when the Pakistan military began its crackdown they lent support to the soldiers in the hunt for Bengalis.

The Pakistan Army remained passive till 25 March. During that time, the situation in East Pakistan turned from bad to worse. In its report, the Hamoodur Rehman Commission wondered why the military had not tried to quell the agitation at that early stage and had, instead, been ordered to return to its barracks. The findings suggested that the martial law government in East Pakistan was restrained from taking any action by the central government. The governor, Admiral Ahsan, told the Commission that he had made desperate efforts to persuade the president to visit East Pakistan but without success. Both Admiral Ahsan and General Yaqub Ali Khan were convinced that only a political solution could save the country. Ahsan telephoned Rawalpindi several times to talk to Yahya Khan but was told that he was in Karachi. Such persistence, on his part, resulted in him being informed that he had been relieved. Accordingly, he handed power over to General Yaqub on 4 March and left Dacca. General Yaqub, however, adopted the same line, advising a search for a political solution. In practical terms, it meant that a provisional provincial government should be formed, headed by Mujib or his nominee. When his advice was rejected, Yaqub too resigned – via telephone – on the evening of 4 March; the resignation was accepted, by a signal, on 5 March. He handed power over to Lieutenant General Tikka Khan, who arrived on 7 March to take over from him (Hamoodur Rehman Commission Report 2001: 82–3).

The Commission was of the opinion that there was not enough solid evidence to suggest that Rawalpindi had categorically restrained the East Pakistan government from taking action. Both Admiral Ahsan and General Yaqub could have taken stern action but got cold feet. However, it was not overruled that the:

> Authorities in Rawalpindi also had some part to play in this curious inaction. For, although General Yahya concluded that General Yaqub had developed cold feet and, therefore, sent General Tikka Khan to replace him, the latter also followed the same policy up to the 25th March 1971, after which of course an all out military action was launched (ibid., 83).

General Yaqub wanted additional troops as he thought the existing strength was inadequate as half were Bengalis. During that period, two more divisions were airlifted. General Yahya claimed that, in his opinion, there was no point in convening the assembly if the PPP was going to boycott its proceedings. The Commission has gone into further details about what could have been done and concludes that, after announcing the postponement of the assembly session, Yahya should have taken steps to meet Mujib at the earliest but did not do so. On the other hand, the Commission has also noted that, in the first week of February, Yahya had invited Mujib to visit him in Rawalpindi but the latter refused to do so. That, too, was a provocation. Yahya Khan responded by sending a strongly-worded telegram, expressing his anger at Mujib's refusal of his invitation (ibid., 84). The East Pakistan governor and chief minister kept urging Yahya to visit Dacca and meet Mujib but, even as late as

4 March, he refused. Anyhow, the new date for convening the National Assembly had been announced. Mujib put forth four conditions for his attending it:

1. Martial law should be immediately withdrawn
2. Military personnel should be ordered to their barracks forthwith
3. The loss of life that had been incurred since the troubles began should be investigated
4. Power should be transferred to the elected representatives of the people (before the National Assembly session was held)

Yahya and West Pakistani Politicians Converge on Dacca

Yahya arrived in Dacca on 15 March; other West Pakistani leaders followed suit. Yahya met the party leaders one by one, instead of all together. The Hamoodur Rehman Report has recorded, 'In any case Sheikh Mujibur Rahman himself and Mr Z.A. Bhutto never, except for one occasion, met each other or the President at the same time' (ibid., 85). The negotiations took place in the backdrop of a rapidly deteriorating law and order situation. Mujib issued a directive, dated 7 March, that instructed East Pakistanis to defy the writ of the martial law government: strikes, refusal to pay taxes, closure of all educational institutions, and other such measures were to be taken to defy the authority of the West Pakistani-run state machinery. Yahya and Mujib met to resolve the deadlock. Mujib demanded the immediate lifting of martial law and that the National Assembly should start functioning. Yahya agreed, subject to the concurrence of the West Pakistani leaders, especially Bhutto. Bhutto reached Dacca on 21 March, where he was accorded a hostile reception by agitators at Dacca Airport. Bhutto and Mujib met Yahya together on 22 March, and then alone. Bhutto reported that although Mujib had been clamouring for the National Assembly to meet in two separate blocs, when they met, Mujib wanted the National Assembly to be adjourned sine die.

At that stage, Yahya and his aides – Justice A.R. Cornelius (law adviser); M.M. Ahmad (economic adviser); General Pirzada (principal staff officer); and another officer, Colonel Hassan – separately met with the PPP and Awami League. The president also talked to other West Pakistan leaders who were more accommodating of Mujib and the Awami League than the PPP were. Wali Khan, of the West Pakistan's National Awami Party, claimed that Mujib showed him a letter in which Yahya offered:

> Mujibur Rahman a solution which would more than satisfy him, one that would be in excess of the Six Points. One is left wondering what such a solution could be short of complete secession. General Yahya of course categorically denies having sent any such letter and in the nature of things we have not seen such a document. We have no reason to doubt the Khan's [Wali Khan's] word but in the absence of the evidence of Mujibur Rahman and the document itself, we cannot possibly reach a finding that such a letter exists or that the paper shown to the Khan was a genuine one (ibid., 88).

The Report has noted that, during 23 and 24 March, the position of the Awami League's leaders hardened and become uncompromising. For the first time, they publicly began using the expression 'confederation of Pakistan'. The general secretary of the Awami League, Tajuddin Ahmed, declared that there was nothing left to negotiate and that the Awami League had made its position clear. On Pakistan Day, 23 March, instead of Pakistan flags, a profusion of Bangladesh flags were hoisted all over East Pakistan; the exceptions were the Bihari strongholds of Saidpur and Parbatipur (Qureshi 2002: 29).

It is clear that negotiations between the three entities were crucial for the resolution of the political impasse that had occurred. It was not a constitutional deadlock because, according to parliamentary constitutional theory and practice, the Awami League was entitled to form the Central Government on the basis of its incontrovertible majority in the Pakistan National Assembly. However, that was unacceptable to the military establishment and the leader of the largest party (the PPP) in West Pakistan, Z.A. Bhutto. The Awami League's uncompromising stand, towards the end, only made matters worse. In any case, Bhutto met Yahya on 24 and 25 March to discuss the stand taken by the Awami League. What transpired at that meeting has not been reported.

Responsibility for Failure of the Parleys

The Commission made a most intriguing revelation: the decision not to hand over power, and the use of a military crackdown codenamed 'Operation Blitz', had been prepared way ahead; and, 'the negotiations which were carried on from the middle of March up to this date were no more than a camouflage, it being all along the intention of General Yahya Khan and his military advisers to cow down the Awami League with a heavy hand' (Hamoodur Rehman Commission Report 2001: 89). Meanwhile, the troop build-up took place.

The Commission has not provided background into the history of Operation Blitz, but subsequent research has shown that it was formulated well before the 1970 elections and an 'operation directive was signed and issued by Yaqub Khan on 11 December 1970, within four days of the National Assembly elections' (Nawaz 2008: 264). By early March, General Yaqub had realised that such an operation would be counterproductive and had recommended the search for a political solution, but that was unacceptable to the military high command. Yahya and his coterie of advisers stuck to the original plan, based on denying the Awami League the right to form the government at the centre.

In any case, with regard to the responsibility of the Awami League for precipitating the crisis, the Commission noted that 'we have reason to believe that the Awami League itself intended to take action at 3 a.m. on the morning of the 26 March 1971' (Hamoodur Rehman Commission Report 2001: 89). Moreover, 'Dacca was by now a city in which it was impossible for anybody at least for any Pakistani of consequence and more specially those associated with the government of Pakistan to move without armed escort' (ibid.). It has also been recorded that the military government had failed to develop effective intelligence gathering because 'it was difficult to have a sufficient number of local agents from whom information could be gathered' (ibid.). In other words, by that time, the West Pakistanis' alienation and isolation from the local society was nearly complete.

With regard to Bhutto's role, the Commission noted that this needed to be assessed in three main contexts: He demanded that the National Assembly session scheduled for 3 March be postponed; he insisted that a grand coalition comprising the Awami League and the PPP should form the government at the national level; and, following the election results, he began to speak of a two-majority theory. The Commission members were of the opinion that, during the election campaign, the PPP did not make the six points an issue. Therefore, once the elections had taken place and the Awami League had won a majority, Bhutto's insistence that the Awami League should enter into a compromise or make concession on the six points was not consistent with any democratic or parliamentary practice. Similarly, the PPP's stand, that no constitution could be made without its concurrence, was not justified in constitutional terms.

The PPP had won a majority of only two provinces of West Pakistan – Punjab and Sindh. The Awami League enjoyed an overall majority in parliament, and it was likely to expand its support with the help of other West Pakistani leaders. Therefore, Bhutto's insistence on consensus on the constitution was not justified because what he meant, on the basis of the so-called two-majority theory, was consensus between the Awami League and the PPP. The Commission found his standpoint to be incompatible with the principles of parliamentary democracy. Moreover, even after visiting East Pakistan after the elections, he failed to assess the degree of resentment such demands were causing in East Pakistan (ibid., 94–96). The Commission concluded that Yahya Khan, Sheikh Mujibur Rahman, Z.A. Bhutto, and their advisers were all responsible, in different ways, for the worsening of the situation in East Pakistan. The Report does not identify who, among them, bore ultimate responsibility.

Air Marshal (Retd.) Asghar Khan travelled to Dacca while the negotiations were underway and spoke to Mujib. Mujib was convinced that Yahya had decided, before he went to Dacca for the negotiations, not to hand power over to the Awami League. He lamented that the patriotism and loyalty of the Bengalis was never acknowledged by the West Pakistani leaders. Asghar Khan has provided details about Bhutto's alleged complicity in precipitating the crisis that broke up Pakistan (Khan 2005: 31–42).

It can be argued that since Yahya Khan held the reins of power, and thus enjoyed the ultimate prerogative to make crucial decisions, his role must be treated as decisive. If it is true that the negotiations after 15 March were a camouflage, and the military had decided to carry out a military action, then a conspiracy existed already. It is also clear that Bhutto obstructed a peaceful resolution of the problem. Whether Bhutto was privy to the military plan to order a crackdown on the Awami League and the Mukti Bahini remains a matter of conjecture. It cannot be discounted that he was because, just as the military had decided not to hand power over to the Awami League, so too Bhutto was determined not to sit in the opposition. The provocations of the Awami League, on 24–25 March, provided the excuse the military needed to implement the pre-meditated crackdown.

9

Civil War and Pakistan–India War of 1971

By the time the army crackdown was let loose, Pakistan had managed to assemble around 45,000 West Pakistani fighting troops in East Pakistan. These included a brigade stationed in Dacca, as well as a group of the elite SSG commandos (Nawaz 2008: 267). Lieutenant General Tikka Khan was given a directive, operative till 10 April 1971, to achieve the following:

1. Disarming of the East Bengal Regiment Battalions, the East Pakistan Rifles, and the Police
2. Security of the cantonments
3. Security of the Chittagong Naval Base
4. Control of airfields including those at Lalmunirhat and Ishurd
5. Security of towns (Khan 1973: 71)

Operation Searchlight

There was nothing peculiar about such a brief as the objectives were formulated in typical military fashion. No mention was made of arresting the Awami League leaders, or rebels in general. However, the first action taken, understandably, was to arrest Mujib from his home at 10:30 p.m. Some resistance was put up by his supporters, which was easily suppressed. Other prominent leaders either went underground or escaped the border into West Bengal. Bhutto was in Dacca when the military action, codenamed Operation Searchlight, started on the night of 25–26 March. He would most certainly have heard the explosions, tank fire, and gunshots from his room in the hotel where he was staying. The next day, he famously remarked, 'Thank God, Pakistan has been saved.' This statement has subsequently appeared, with minor variations, in several publications (Khan 2005: 42; Nawaz 2008: 268; Qureshi 2002: 23). It is impossible to interpret such a proclamation in any way other than as an endorsement of military action. Whether it was inspired by patriotic passions or a Machiavellian calculation is a moot point. Many months later, Bhutto was still defending the military action because he claimed that it was a necessary pre-emptive action to stall the Awami League from declaring East Pakistan's independence the next day. He wrote in September 1971:

> A number of places were ablaze and we saw the demolition of the office of the newspaper The People. This local English daily had indulged in crude and unrestrained provocation against the Army and West Pakistan. With the horizon ablaze, my thoughts turned to the past and to the future. I wondered what was in store for us. Here, in front of my eyes, I saw the death and destruction of our own people (quoted in Nawaz 2008: 268).

Military action received support not only from the PPP but also from the West Pakistani power elite, including the capitalist class, and the right-wing Pakistani press including the Urdu-language newspapers *Nawa-i-Waqt* and *Jang* and the English-language *Dawn*. In particular, the *Nawa-i-Waqt* stressed 'the usual West Pakistan bogies of Hindu influence, anti-Islamic forces, and the promotion of the Bengali language, and urged they should be strongly curbed' (Alam 1995: 326). The Indian involvement was greatly exaggerated at that stage. In any case, as soon as Mujib was arrested, army tanks and infantry units moved in on the Dacca University campus. The shelling and firing that took place targeted Jagannath Hall and Jagannath Hostel, Iqbal Hall and Iqbal Hall Hostel, Hindu temples in Ramna ground, and other Hindu strongholds (Ali 2007: 247–8). Some resistance was offered but the firepower of the army was overwhelming. Some 500–700 people were killed. Pro-Awami League newspaper officers were raided, and more killings took place. The next day, Mujib was flown to West Pakistan as a prisoner.

The same day, a Bengali officer – Major Ziaur Rahman – announced the independence of Bangladesh. The position he took was that East Pakistan had ceased to exist. He swore allegiance to Sheikh Mujibur Rahman and exhorted other Bengalis to do the same. Accordingly, the Bengali armed forces personnel who heeded his call were not revolting but were fighting a war of liberation against an army of occupation. On 17 April, a government-in-exile was announced that, Bangladeshi sources have claimed, was based within the country in a part of Kushtia district. It also established branches in Delhi and Kolkata. Most of the Bengali civil servants and military personnel declared their allegiance to Bangladesh. Consequently, according to their point of view, a liberation struggle had begun. A retired colonel, Osmany, was declared in charge of the liberation forces, which consisted of two elements: the Niyamita Bahini (a liberation force constituted by members of the armed forces) and the Mukti Bahini (a liberation force consisting of armed civilians). Later, both came to be known as the Mukti Bahini (interview: Iftekhar Ahmed Chowdhury). Thousands of Bengalis crossed the border into West Bengal for safety. In the refugee camps that were set up for them, many were recruited into the Mukti Bahini. They were armed and trained and sent back to fight the Pakistani forces.

Accounts of the war, and the atrocities that followed, differ dramatically. Major General Hakim Arshad Qureshi has alleged that thousands of pro-Pakistan Bengalis, Biharis, and West Pakistanis were massacred by the Mukti Bahini in the early stages of the conflict (Qureshi 2002: 33). Major General A.O. Mitha, who took part in the military operations till 9 April, described how, during a visit to the Chittagong sector, one wounded Bengali officer admitted his guilt but without remorse:

> As I was walking down the ward, a Bengali officer who was wounded and under guard called out to me. I stopped and went to him, and he said that all he wanted to tell me was that he and his men had stripped women from West Pakistan, and after raping them, had made them dance in the nude; having done this, he was quite happy to die (Mitha 2003: 341).

Meanwhile, Yahya relieved Tikka Khan of his position as commander of Eastern Command although he remained martial law administrator and governor of East Pakistan. Instead, A.A.K. Niazi was promoted, over other generals, and sent to East Pakistan to take over the position of Commander Eastern Command from Tikka. He took over on 10 April. Niazi wrote:

> On the night between 25/26 March 1971, General Tikka struck. Peaceful night was turned into a time of wailing, crying, and burning. General

> Tikka let loose everything at his disposal as if raiding an enemy, not dealing with his own misguided and misled people. The military action was a display of stark cruelty, more merciless than the massacres at Bukhara and Baghdad by Changez Khan and Halaku Khan, or at Jallianwala Bagh by the British General Dyer.

General Tikka, instead of carrying out the task given him, i.e., to disarm the Bengali units and persons and to take into custody the Bengali leaders, resorted to a scorched earth policy. His orders to his troops were: 'I want the land (sic) and not the people'...Major General Rao Farman [Ali] had written in his table diary, 'Green land of East Pakistan will be painted in red' (Niazi 1999: 45–6).

Some other commanders were also changed. Later, during Niazi's stint as commander Eastern Command, he recommended that Brigadier Arbab be 'removed from command on charges of looting and theft. He was found guilty in the court of inquiry carried out against him and was sent back to West Pakistan to be court-martialled' (ibid., 50). On the whole, Niazi lamented that he had a small and inadequately armed number of troops at his disposal. The humid weather and topography did not suit his West Pakistani troops, who got ill rather easily. Yet, by the end of May 1971, the 'rebel resistance had been broken with heavy losses to both men and material. The rebels were demoralized. They were forced to take shelter in inaccessible areas or were licking their wounds in sanctuaries provided by the Indians on Indian soil' (ibid., 62).

He noted that the Pakistan Army captured thousands of rifles and other weapons left behind by the rebels. He then requested permission to enter Indian territory, in pursuit of the rebels, but that was not given. Also, by June, 'we had achieved a great moral, political and tactical victory under most unfavourable conditions and that too in a very short time' (ibid., 65). He has referred to Major General Khushwant Singh of the Indian Army who apparently confirmed his strategy:

> Yahya had valid reasons for crossing International borders in the eastern wing in pursuit of guerrillas as well as to overrun their bases in India about the end of May 1971, and of the opportunity to enlarge the conflict into a full-fledged war by hitting India also in the West. That was India's worst hour, its reserve formations were in the hinterland, it

> had serious shortfalls of war material and soldiers and civilians were not mentally attuned to immediate war. If Yahya had struck at that time, he could have gained profitable objectives both in the Western and Eastern theatres before the onset of the monsoons (ibid., 67–8).

Pakistan–China Consultations

Yahya Khan despatched senior diplomat Sultan Muhammad Khan to Beijing to solicit Chinese support for the military action. Premier Zhou Enlai told Sultan that Yahya Khan should find a political solution to the East Pakistan crisis. Also, while China supported the unity of Pakistan and was willing to help Pakistan raise two new army divisions, such support did not entail Chinese military intervention in East Pakistan on behalf of the military regime. Sultan remarked: 'it is also relevant to point out once and for all that China, during these or subsequent talks, never held out any possibility of coming to Pakistan's aid with her military forces' (Khan 2006: 308).

This assertion is indeed important because, while the Chinese wanted to express solidarity with Pakistan, they were not willing to commitment themselves militarily in a conflict against a political party that enjoyed the overwhelming support of the people of East Pakistan. Moreover, military intervention in East Pakistan, in the event that India entered the war, would have provoked a strong reaction from the Soviet Union; also, the Americans were unlikely to let that happen with impunity if it meant that China and India would be involved in a war. Such calculations, it seems, never entered the calculus of a Pakistani defence strategy; rather, faith in China deterring India continued to be something that, at least officially, the Pakistan government wanted to encourage.

US–Pakistan Communications

In 1970, a Republican administration headed by Richard Nixon was in office in Washington DC. The Americans had begun to think in terms of cultivating the Chinese; Secretary of State Henry Kissinger was to play the key role in the first negotiations. The US, however, wanted such overtures to remain a secret, and Pakistan was chosen as the conduit for the initial contacts. Some other governments, such as that of Romania, were also involved in setting the ball rolling. As a reward to Pakistan, the US offered a one-time exception to their embargo on an arms package for sale to Pakistan, but without tanks – because that would have upset India. Also, food aid and economic aid was offered to Pakistan (Aijazuddin 2002: 91–104). Nixon told Yahya Khan that 'there was strong feeling in this country favouring India, but this Administration would keep its word with Pakistan' (ibid., 109). In reply, having assured the Americans that Pakistan would not embarrass the United States, Yahya also pleaded for greater economic aid to Pakistan. With regard to the assurance he gave about not embarrassing the Nixon Administration, Yahya was surely alluding to the fact that Pakistan had used US weapons in both the Rann of Kutch and during the war with India in 1965 – in contravention of the US position that such US weapons were not to be used in a conflict with India, especially one initiated by Pakistan. In any case, the news that Pakistan was going to get US arms elicited a strong reaction from India. Both Yahya Khan and Indira Gandhi were in the US to attend the twenty-fifth anniversary of the founding of the UN. Nixon invited them, and other leaders, to a dinner but Indira Gandhi declined the invitation (ibid., 111). In any event, on 25 October 1970, US interest in secretly meeting the Chinese was discussed during a conversation between Nixon, Kissinger, and Yahya Khan; Yahya promised to convey this to the Chinese. Accordingly, Yahya spoke to Zhou Enlai, who responded positively, and that set the ball rolling.

From late March 1971 onwards, the situation in Pakistan had started deteriorating. The US expressed concern about Pakistan's security and hoped that Yahya Khan would succeed in restoring normality. China made similar statements, but accused India of harbouring nefarious designs to harm Pakistan. Pakistan, on the other hand, conveyed messages between the US and China, and so the thaw quickly began to take place. Secretary of State Henry Kissinger camouflaged his visit to China by giving the impression that it was a general visit to South Asia. The first stop was India. Kissinger met Indira Gandhi on 7 July 1971. Mrs Gandhi expressed her concerns about Chinese influence in East Pakistan and her own desire not to use force in the ongoing civil war in East Pakistan. Kissinger, on the other hand, expressed an understanding for India's concerns over the refugees who had poured into India from East Pakistan. He also said that the US–India relationship had to be stable, and it should not be jeopardised periodically because of a regional dispute. A strong India was in the US's interest, emphasised Kissinger (ibid., 157–8).

On 9 July, Kissinger arrived in Pakistan and told the Pakistanis that the chances of war with India were 'two in three'. But, he found Yahya and his advisers convinced that India was not planning for war – but, if they were to start a war with Pakistan, they were convinced that 'they [Pakistanis] could win' (Kux 2001: 191). How that would be possible without air support, and amid the hostility of the local population, was something that the military did not seem to have been discouraged by in assuming an unrealistic position on a war with India in East Pakistan. When Kissinger returned to the US and briefed the National Security Council, he was of the opinion that India was bent on a war with Pakistan and that Yahya 'lacked the imagination to solve the political problems in time to prevent an Indian assault' (ibid., 193). He recommended that the US should prepare for an 'evolution that would lead to eventual independence for East Pakistan' (ibid.). Interestingly enough, in subsequent discussions, President Nixon expressed the opinion that India should be discouraged from using the 'refugee issue' to break up Pakistan, but breaking up Pakistan 'is what he might do if he were in New Delhi' (ibid., 196). However, when the military government put Mujib on trial for sedition, instead of opening negotiations with him, the Americans were quite exasperated.

Indo-Soviet Peace Treaty

The Awami League, Mukti Bahini, and other such forces were able to sustain an armed resistance movement from their bases in India. All along, the Indians planned their moves with great care. While training camps had been established to train the Bengali freedom fighters, their activities were thoroughly monitored and supervised. Leadership positions were maintained with moderate Awami League figures, and radicals and extremists were marginalised. From July onwards, New Delhi assumed direct responsibility for the training and arming of the expanding fighting force as more and more refugees arrived and young men joined the Mukti Bahini (Sisson and Rose 1991: 143). The Indian leadership, no doubt, had been preparing for war with Pakistan. In response to Yahya Khan's accusation, that if India made any attempt to seize any part of East Pakistan he would declare war, the Indian foreign minister, Sardar Swaran Singh, made a speech on 21 July in the Upper House of the Indian Parliament – the Rajya Sabha – in which he asserted that:

> Pakistan has been trying for some time to mislead the world into thinking that the situation in Bangla Desh is a matter between Pakistan and India whereas in fact it is a matter between the military rulers of West Pakistan and the people of Bangla Desh. It is the Pakistan regime's own actions, and the brutalities committed by the Pakistan Army in Bangla Desh, that have landed Pakistan in a morass in Bangla Desh. Only a settlement with the already elected representatives of the people of Bangladesh will enable the military rulers of Pakistan to extricate themselves from this morass (Deora 1995: 102).

Meanwhile, the Indian leadership had been taking necessary measures to ensure that, in case of a war with Pakistan, China would not intervene with impunity. Consequently, on 9 August 1971, an Indo–Soviet Treaty of Friendship and Co-operation was signed. Article IX stated:

> Each High Contracting Party undertakes to abstain from providing any assistance to any third country that engages in armed conflict with the other Party. In the event of either being subjected to an attack or a threat thereof, the High C ontracting Parties shall immediately enter into mutual consultations in order to remove such threat and to take appropriate effective measures to ensure peace and the security of their countries.

The treaty was for twenty years. Having secured a counterweight against possible Chinese intervention, Indira Gandhi intensified diplomatic activities to muster support for India's position on East Pakistan. Alleged human rights violations by the Pakistan Army in East Pakistan became one of the main arguments to prepare the world for an Indian intervention. It culminated with Mrs Gandhi proceeding, on 25 October, on a worldwide tour to personally explain, to world leaders, that the situation in East Pakistan was very bad and that Pakistan was doing nothing to find a political resolution to the civil war. In November, Z.A. Bhutto was sent to China to solicit help in case of war, but he did not receive much encouragement (Khan 2006: 346–7). Foreign Secretary Sultan Muhammad Khan was despatched to some western capitals to present the Pakistani point of view – that the conflict in East Pakistan was an internal problem, and India had no right to train and arm Bengali rebels to carry out terrorist activities inside East Pakistan. Further, that an Indian intervention would result in all-out war (ibid., 349–54).

War with India

The conflict in East Pakistan became increasingly unmanageable over the months that followed. Yahya Khan was under great pressure from the international community to take the necessary measures to placate the East Pakistanis. On 31 August, Yahya appointed an East Pakistani, Abdul Motelib Malik, as governor of East Pakistan while Tikka Khan continued as the martial law administrator. According to Niazi, the Indians raided East Pakistan several times, at battalion and brigade levels, from late August till November. The full-fledged attack on East Pakistan by the Indian Army, from all directions, was launched on the night of 20–21 November (Ali 2007: 271; Niazi 1999: 119). This news was suppressed by the Yahya regime; people in West Pakistan knew nothing about it. Niazi has claimed that, despite being outnumbered by a ratio of 1:10, Pakistan repulsed the invaders. On 3 December, Pakistan attacked India from its stronghold of West Pakistan. Thus, the third war between India and Pakistan was now fought on all fronts. Niazi has also claimed that, by that time, some 4000 fatalities and the same number of injuries had been sustained in East Pakistan. Also, that he contacted chief of general staff, Lieutenant General Gul Hassan Khan in Rawalpindi, to discuss the Indian invasion but the latter had gone to Lahore to celebrate Eid. Similarly, COAS General Hamid was not available. Niazi has remarked:

> I learnt later that both he and the President had left for Sialkot, ostensibly to visit troops but actually for a partridge shoot – no C-in-C visits Muslim troops on an Eid day. The callous attitude of the three senior most officers of the Army shows that they were not interested in the affairs of East Pakistan or the integrity of Pakistan. Like Nero, they played while Dhaka burned (1999: 123).

Nevertheless, Niazi stated his men put up a brave fight despite all the odds against them in East Pakistan. The Indian attack got bogged down and they suffered heavy casualties (ibid., 126). Niazi has referred to a number of secret signals from GHQ praising the bravery and perseverance of his men – most probably to claim that he and his troops were doing their job properly and with success. He also takes issue with the Indian invasion of 21 November not being taken to the Security Council as that could have resulted in a ceasefire before defeat at the hands of the Indians. Moreover, he has stated that he and his men wanted more time, and were not in favour of hostilities being started by Pakistan on the West Pakistan border with India. They wanted that to happen after the period October–March (ibid., 131).

Niazi goes on to prove that the high command was not interested in saving East Pakistan, in spite of his men fighting fearlessly. On 5 December, Niazi has claimed, he received a message from GHQ to the effect that he should keep the maximum number of Indian troops engaged in East Pakistan, and was told that Chinese activities were expected very soon. He goes on to deplore the fact that such assurances were totally misleading as no contact had been made with the Chinese. On 6 December, he sent a signal to GHQ expressing his resolve to fight to the last man. This, he has noted, was approved by his superiors (ibid., 135). The details of the battles fought on several fronts all over East Pakistan, as given by Niazi, show his men fighting with great bravery and intelligence, and the Indians not making much headway in spite of their vastly superior forces including their air force. However, he has alleged that a totally misleading message was sent to GHQ, from the Governor House, stating that although Niazi and his men were fighting bravely, the enemy was advancing and the Pakistani defence was collapsing (ibid., 176).

Niazi's claims, however, have been called into question by other Pakistani military officers. Brigadier (Retd.) A.R. Siddiqi, the chief of the Inter-Services Public Relations (ISPR) and press adviser to Yahya Khan, had access to the key senior-most officers – including, of course, Yahya and his coterie of generals – who called all the shots. Siddiqi has scathingly criticised Niazi for advocating extremist measures against the East Pakistanis, including condoning rape and other indignities against Bengali women – activities the GOC Jessore, Major General Mohammad Hussain Ansari, did not approve of. Siddiqi has noted:

> Niazi...openly encouraged the jawans in their unsoldierly, inhuman, and carnal indulgences. 'What is your score, Shera (Tiger)?' he would ask the jawans with a satanic glint in his eyes. The score referred to

> the number of women the soldiers might have molested. Niazi argued brazenly in support of the rape cases. 'You cannot expect a man to live, fight and die in East Pakistan and go to Jhelum [one of the major recruiting districts in West Pakistan] for sex, would you?' As for the killings – he believed that only the miscreants were killed. The soldiers were under orders not to show any mercy to subversive, anti-state elements, Bengalis or non-Bengalis (2009: 167).

Siddiqi visited East Pakistan several times during the ongoing conflict, and noted that the Biharis took a very active part in the armed raids on the Bengalis. They, and some Bengalis who were Islamists, sided with the military. The number of people killed during the military action has been estimated from a mere 26,000 presented by the Pakistan military (Hamdoodur Rahman Commission Report 2001: 513) to three million by Bangladeshi sources. Both are highly exaggerated figures: downwards and upwards. In any case, it is impossible for an army that was increasingly confined to its cantonments to have liquidated three million human beings in less than nine months. I have interviewed many top Bengali civil servants and public figures, of a neutral bent of mind, on this topic. I was told that the origin of the story about the three million dead was to be found in a statement of Mujib's in which he had confused a 'million' for the South Asian 'lakh' or 'lac' which means 100,000. This is not surprising because Mujib's command over the English language was far from enviable. The official position on the death toll – as per the other major political party of contemporary Bangladesh, the Bangladesh National Party – is 300,000.

Pakistan launches Operation Chengiz Khan from West Pakistan

On 3 December 1971, the Yahya regime decided to open the front on the West Pakistan border. 'Operation Chengiz Khan' – a bizarre name for the military of an Islamic nation to use considering the havoc wreaked upon the Muslim powers in both Central and South Asia by the notorious Mongol conqueror Genghis/Chengiz Khan in 1162–1227 – began with the PAF mounting simultaneous attacks on airfields in a number of places in East Punjab and Indian-administered Kashmir. At the same time, land operations were launched but to no avail. The Indians rapidly moved into East Pakistan and headed towards Dacca. It appeared that Yahya Khan's objective, in opening the front in West Pakistan, was to hasten a ceasefire. The Pakistan Army surrendered in Dacca on 16 December. The ceremony was shown on Indian and international television channels. Some 93,000 Pakistanis became prisoners-of-war (PoW), including civilians. Pakistan had been roundly defeated and its eastern wing seceded to become Bangladesh.

Yahya Khan was bitter that the Americans and the Chinese had not come to his rescue. Brian Cloughley has observed that 'Any action on the part of China would have concentrated the Indian mind on the northern borders, and greatly assisted Pakistan. But China sat on the fence, in spite of making belligerent statements' (Cloughley 2000: 237). Nixon made a gesture by sending an aircraft carrier into the Bay of Bengal, but it was purportedly to 'scare off an attack on West Pakistan' according to Kissinger (ibid.). China had been granted membership of the United Nations on 25 October 1971; its representative attended the UN, including a meeting of the Security Council, on 23 November 1971. This was possible because the United States and China had established a rapport, and the former no longer opposed China's right to represent the Chinese people. Kissinger solicited Chinese cooperation in achieving the limited aim of discouraging India from launching a counter-attack on West Pakistan (Aijazuddin 2007: 367–86). The US also took an initiative, on 4 December 1971, to start proceedings in the Security Council for a resolution calling upon both India and Pakistan to agree to a ceasefire. Once again, it sought Chinese help which was given. Although China outwardly maintained its support for the unity of Pakistan, it was disillusioned by Pakistan's failure to seek a political solution to the conflict in East Pakistan. In other words, a breakup of Pakistan seemed to have been accepted by all the major powers. The loss of life on the battlefield, for both India and Pakistan, has not been clearly established but it seems it far exceeded the fatalities suffered during the two earlier wars. The trauma of defeat, and the breakup of Pakistan, greatly undermined the prestige of the Pakistan military, whose public relations office had been spreading fictitious stories of spectacular victories over the Indians – identical to the propaganda offensive during the 1965 war.

In any event, following the surrender at Dacca on 16 December, it took Yahya and the high command, on Nixon's advice, another two days to agree to the unilateral ceasefire offered by Indira Gandhi (Siddiqi 2009: 212). There were two pressing issues that the government had to attend to forthwith. The first was the growing resentment, among the officers, about the great military debacle. The officers were up in arms at Kharian cantonment. Elsewhere, too, the mood was charged with indignation. Yahya's most trustworthy comrade, General Hamid, addressed the officers at Ayub Hall in Rawalpindi on 20 December and tried to argue that the government had tried to find a 'political solution'. But, this was rejected by the audience who shouted 'shame, shame' and liberally used expletives. Hamid ostensibly broke down and left but, according to Brigadier Siddiqi, it was all feigned. He had come to gauge if Yahya and the junta could continue. As the men left, Radio Pakistan announced that Yahya had resigned. A number of names were considered for his successor. General Gul Hassan Khan and Air Marshal Rahim Khan favoured Z.A. Bhutto being called upon to take over power (ibid., 213–4).

Interview with Lieutenant General (Retd.) Javed Ashraf Qazi

'It is generally believed that the 1970 election was fair and free. Nothing can be further from the truth. I was a young major posted in East Pakistan during those fateful days. During the election campaign Awami League goondas (roughnecks) terrorized all those who did not support them. They beat up people and threatened them with dire consequences if they opposed Sheikh Mujib and his close associates. I remember hearing Mujib addressing an election rally. He was a fiery demagogue who knew how to inflame public opinion. He told the thousands of people who had gathered that he just been to Islamabad. Each road and building in that city smelled of jute. It was the exploitation of East Pakistan that had provided the money for building that fancy capital of Pakistan. He told them that East Pakistan will never be a colony of West Pakistan. Awami League goondas attacked West Pakistanis and killed many innocent people. We reacted to a reign of terror let loose by the Awami League.'

Interview with Brigadier (Retd.) Yasub Ali Dogar

Brigadier (Retd.) Yasub Ali Dogar was serving as a captain in East Pakistan in 1971, and became a POW when Dacca surrendered on 16 December 1971. I requested him to write down his responses to a number of questions of mine on the events in the former East Pakistan. The following is the entire script he sent me by email on 27 April 2010: 'I would like to state that my family had a long association of stay in East Pakistan: 1962–1968. My father Major (Late) Mahbub Ali was the first Pakistani principal of Adamjee Public School/College in Dacca Cantt. It was considered then as the most prestigious higher secondary school in East Pakistan, an equivalent of Aitchison College. I was myself a student of Dacca College from November 1962–April 1964, thereafter I joined the Dacca University and was selected for PMA Kakul from there in November 1964. Ex-President of Bangladesh Mr Iajuddin Ahmed was Head of Soil Science Department and I have the honour of being his student for a few months.

'Till 2 December 1971, I was manning SSG posts in Chittagong Hill tracts bordering Pakistan-India-Burma border triangle. On 2 December my company The Jangju Company, 2 Commando Battalion (SSG) was airlifted to Dacca for further employment in the Northern Sector. On 3rd morning at mid-day we were airlifted in PIA aircrafts to Saidpur for operations in Thakargaon-Rangpur Sector. This was perhaps the last PIA flight in East Pakistan because the same evening with the declaration of all out war all PIA flights ceased to operate. I remained in this sector till cessation of hostilities on 16 December 1971.

'The overall environment had been deteriorating since the mega-cyclone killing over a 100,000 people in December 1970. There was a feeling in East Pakistan that the West-Pakistani leadership under General Yahya Khan and his cronies did not provide adequate response to the requirements of the cyclone affected population of East-Pakistan. The political environment was absolutely hostile to all non-Bengalis in general and the army in particular. It got accentuated to the highest level since the beginning of March when rumours of the declaration of an independent Bangladesh became very imminent. Maximum killings of Biharis and other non Bengalis took place during this period.

'I was a Platoon Commander (Captain) in Jangju Company of 2 Commando Battalion (SSG) in the Chittagong Hill Tracts. Till 2 December my responsibilities were to ensure that there is no incursion or infiltration of any hostile elements (Indians or Muktis) in my area of responsibility. On outbreak of all out war I was part of 34 Brigade Headquarter at Rangpur in the north carrying out various tasks given by the Brigade Headquarter having moved there on 3 December 1971.

'In my area Indians had moved in strength on 11/12 of November. We were under full-fledged attack by an Indian Battalion on 22nd of November, which we were able to beat back. So, I am very clear as far as international borders were breached, it is the Indians who breached it first. Pakistanis were only responding, in fact two of our F86 Sabre jets had been shot down over Jessore in November much before the break out of war on 3 December 1971.

'The Agartala Conspiracy Case was discovered in 1966–1967. Till March 1971 Indians were subverting the intelligentsia, students, officers and soldiers belonging to East Pakistan. From March 1971 onwards they were providing full support to the Mukti Bahini including recognition of Mr Taj-ud-Din Ahmed's government in exile. They finally crossed the borders in Nov 1971. My feeling is that they had realized that Pakistan Army had stabilized the situation inside East Pakistan to a large extent and now a long drawn guerrilla war would be required to cause sufficient attrition to Pakistan Army to get a political solution of their choice. Meanwhile, the number of refugees was causing India a large financial drain on their resources. It was imperative that such a state of affairs could not be tolerated for long and India had to find a solution quickly.

'The Ansar were basically a second line force on the pattern of "Qaumi Razakars" in West Pakistan. Some joined Mukti Bahini while some were made use of by the Pakistan Army; they were of little use for both sides. I did not get a chance to operate with Al Badr; therefore, I will say what I have heard from others. They were well motivated and by and large acted as good auxiliary to the army. It seems that they had their own political agenda besides helping the army. However I do not subscribe to the view that they carried out large scale massacres. Being Bengalis they had no reason to do so. The effectiveness of the Mukti Bahini was largely depended on their background, training and motivation. Old EBR regiment/EPR cadres were excellently led by ex-Pakistan Army officers. The bulk was recruited from refugee camps, given a few days training and infiltrated for operations inside. Theirs was generally a lacklustre performance. Some independent Bahinis such as the "Tiger Siddiqi" and "Mujib Bahini" were slightly better organized and armed. 'From 11 November to 3 December it was a matter of confusion for Pakistani high command. Some thought Indians are trying to gain a chunk of territory which could be handed over to the Bangladesh government in exile to operate from there. Others thought that Indians would move in as deep as possible till such time their casualties are of acceptable level to them. I subscribe to the view that if the all out war had not been declared on 3 December the Indians would have remained at the periphery and not moved deep inside East Pakistan. It would have also given sufficient time to find a political solution if the military/ political leadership sincerely wanted to fine one.

'Basically cut off from the rest of Pakistan with no local support in the population and depleted of arms and ammunition against over-whelming odds there was no other choice. They could have fought for a few more days, gotten some more casualties with the same result. The heavy handed army action had totally antagonized the Bengalis. General Niazi in his statement before the Hamoodur Rehman Commission had reportedly castigated the doctrine that the defence of East Pakistan lies in the West. Throughout the war we were waiting for that final offensive which would have forced the Indian troops to recoil backwards to face the deep intrusion coming in from West Pakistan. With regard to human rights violations, yes, I feel that the performance of Pak Army leaves much to be desired on all counts.

'The treatment of the Indian Army differed from place to place. I and some fellow officers tried to dig a tunnel to attempt escape but the Indians uncovered that plot. We were put in solitary confinement where the hygienic conditions were appalling. We were placed on half rations for thirty days while undergoing detention in cells; the food given initially was almost unpalatable. We therefore decided to go on hunger strike. This created a commotion and the conditions were relaxed. I had terrible mosquito bites all over my body. I complained to an Indian doctor, Major Bannerjee who immediately ordered that I should be given proper treatment and provided proper facilities to sleep comfortably. On the whole, Indian Bihari units were harsh in their treatment of Pakistanis. Goan Christians and Sikhs were friendly but it is to Major Bannerjee that I owe most gratitude for treating me humanely.'

Interview with Colonel (Retd.) Riaz Jafri

Colonel Riaz Jafri was among the 195 POWs in Indian custody that the Bangladeshi government wanted to put on trial for war crimes. He has had the following to say about that episode:

'I was a Lieutenant Colonel and posted as General Staff Officer (Grade One) in the Civil Affairs wing of the Martial Law Headquarters, Zone B, Dacca, East Pakistan. I was the senior-most principal staff officer to (late) Major General Rao Farman Ali Khan who was the Martial Law Administrator (Civil Affairs). I landed there on 30 June 1971.

'The military had no particular plan to target Hindus. However, in quite a few cases, entire families of Hindu, as well as Muslim, Bengalis were forcefully taken to India where their young men were trained as saboteurs and sent on subversive missions to East Pakistan. We did not use excessive force against the insurgents – this was only propaganda by India and the Awami League. During my very early days in office, I happened to come across a small English textbook for the kindergarten class. I was astonished to read, in one of its opening pages, "Ram [Hindu; also name of a Hindu god] is a good boy. Rahim (Muslim name; also a designation of God according to Islam) is a bad boy". A quick scan of the book showed it to be full of such mind-poisoning phrases that presented Hindus positively and Muslims negatively. The book was printed by a publishing house of Calcutta. On enquiring from the principal of Adamjee High School, Dacca Cantonment, I was told that the book was approved by the Provincial Text Book Board and had been in use for the last two decades or more! The other element against Pakistan was the Bengali government servants – who were eager to get quick rises and promotions in a newly-born country with a vacuum at the top. The third element comprised of intellectuals, professors, and lawyers – mostly Hindus.

'Gopal Sharma (a Hindu Brahmin), a member of the Mukti Bahini cadre, was under detention when he developed gangrene in an arm wound. I got the wound dressed, castigated him severely, and let him off saying that he was a stupid person simply playing into the hands of the Indians. My lower staff didn't much like my freeing a sworn enemy, but imagine their astonishment when Gopal came back after about a week and asked for a rifle. "What for?", I asked. "Sir, tonight some Muktis [his old gang mates] will attack the grain silo at Manak Ganj and I want to defend the building." I sent some men with him and, sure enough, the Muktis did appear during the night. Thereafter, Gopal was a welcome buddy of the subedar – junior commissioned officer – who had shown the most resentment on his release.

'The Indian intervention had started before my arrival – immediately after 25 March 1971. However, on 21 November 1971, the Indians launched a full-fledged attack with tanks and artillery. On 3 December, after the war was declared in the West, the Indian Air Force also started bombing and strafing our locations in East Pakistan.

'I didn't have the heart to go to Paltan Maidan to witness the humiliation of the surrender on 16 December, but watched it on TV. The Indians allowed us to keep our arms for three days as there were not enough Indian troops to guarantee our safety and afford protection against the Mukti Bahinis who had gone wild with jubilation and could do anything under such intoxication.

'I had the misfortune of becoming a POW and was kept at Camp 61, Gwalior, India, along with other sixty-three officers, seven of us Lieutenant Colonels. The Indians treated us properly and according to the Geneva Convention. The officers were lodged in an Officers' Mess; the colonels were kept two to a reasonably well-furnished room with attached bathroom. We, the colonels, started digging a tunnel from one of the bathroom floors, but it was detected after some time when almost complete. Thereafter, we were shifted to an army barrack, huddled up on charpoys six inches apart, and with only one deep-trench open latrine under the sky to serve as a toilet for nearly eighty-three officers and other ranks.

'When, around December 1973, repatriation started, I, along with four other officers, was taken to Camp 88, Agra – where the infamous 195 POWs were being collected, from the various camps, for trial for the purported war crimes committed by them in East Pakistan. I was one of those included in the list of 195, and always wondered at my being included among them. My guess is that we were targeted because we had some important assignment or we were connected to important people in Pakistan. At the Simla Conference, the demand for the trial of the "war criminals" was dropped. Consequently, we 195 were repatriated in April 1974. I was on the last but one train that arrived at the Attari/Wagah border on 28 April 1974.

'There is no doubt that we handled the situation badly and wrongly. We could have won over the Bengalis by giving them due respect and a proper say in the affairs of Pakistan.'

Colonel (Retd.) Nadir Ali

An interview with Colonel (Retd.) Nadir Ali, who was posted in East Pakistan at that time, was published in the online weekly magazine, Viewpoint, in 2010.

His evidence indicates a definite anti-Hindu policy of the martial law authorities in the former East Pakistan. Here, excerpts from it are presented below:

'During the fateful months preceding the dismemberment of Pakistan, I served as a young Captain, meantime promoted to the rank of the Major, in Dhaka [as it has been renamed post-secession] as well as Chittagong. In my position as second-in-command and later as commander, I served with 3 Commando Battalion.

'My first action was in mid-April 1971. "It is Mujibur Rahman's home district. It is a hard area. Kill as many Bastards as you can and make sure there is no Hindu left alive," I was ordered. "Sir, I do not kill unarmed civilians who do not fire at me," I replied. "Kill the Hindus. It is an order for everyone. Don't show me your commando finesse!"...

'Thousands were killed and millions rendered homeless. Over nine million went as refugees to India. An order was given to kill the Hindus. I received the same order many times and was reminded of it. The West Pakistani soldiery considered that Kosher. The Hamoodur Rehman Commission Report mentions this order. Of the ninety three lakh (9.3 million) refugees in India, ninety lakh were Hindus. That gave us, world-wide, a bad press and morally destroyed us. Military defeat was easy due to feckless military leader ship. Only couple of battalions in the north offered some resistance. For example, the unit of Major Akram, who was awarded highest military medal, Nishan-e-Haider, resisted and he lost his life....

'With federal capital in Islamabad, dominated by West Pakistani civil servants and what they called a Punjabi Army, East Pakistanis felt like subjects of a colony. They never liked it ever since 1947. In early sixties, my fellow Bengali officers called each other general, a rank they would have in an independent East Pakistan. We all took it in good humour. But 1971 was not a joke. Every single Bengali felt oppressed

'General Tikka was branded as "Butcher of Bengal". He hardly commanded for two weeks. Even during those two weeks, the real command was in the hands of General Mitha, his second-in-command. General Mitha literally knew every inch of Bengal. He personally took charge of every operation till General Niazi reached at the helm. At this juncture, General Mitha returned to GHQ. General Tikka, as governor, was a good administrator and made sure that all services ran. Trains, ferries, postal services, telephone lines were functioning and offices were open.' (Ali 2010)

10

The Rise and Fall of Zulfikar Ali Bhutto

Zulfikar Ali Bhutto came to power in Pakistan once the old order had been badly bruised. His meteoric rise to power had been possible because of his espousal of egalitarianism in the form of Islamic socialism: that message went to the heart of the downtrodden and they, in turn, celebrated him as their champion. A scion of the big landowning class of Sindh, his charisma, demagogic skills, and radiant intelligence were compromised by his vindictive and combative personality. His Sindhi ethnicity worked against him in the context of the power equation in Pakistan – there was no worthwhile Sindhi representation in the Pakistani state structure, especially in the military. After the loss of East Pakistan, Punjab's position as the dominant province greatly increased as it also became the majority province ethnically. Thus, the population breakdown was as follows:

Punjab	58% (including the roughly 9.83% Seraiki-speaking areas of southern Punjab)
Sindh	21.6%
NWFP	16.7%
Balochistan	2.4%
Tribal areas	1.3%

Ethnic composition of the military:

<table>
<tr><td>Punjabi</td><td>70%</td></tr>
<tr><td>Pakhtun</td><td>20%</td></tr>
<tr><td>Mohajirs</td><td rowspan="4">10%</td></tr>
<tr><td>Sindhis</td></tr>
<tr><td>Balochis</td></tr>
<tr><td>Kashmiris</td></tr>
<tr><td colspan="2">Source: Shafqat 1997: 171.</td></tr>
</table>

The ethnic composition of the officers corps, according to two estimates – based on interviews:

Ethnicity	First estimate	Second estimate
Punjabis	70%	68%
Pakhtuns	15%	15%
Muhajirs	10%	10%
Balochis and Sindhis	5%	7%
Source: Shafqat 1997: 173.		

Bhutto began his stint in power in a rather unorthodox manner: not only as president but also as supreme commander, chief martial law administrator, foreign minister, interior minister, and inter-provincial co-ordination minister (Taseer 1979: 132). More than 90,000 Pakistani POWs were in Indian custody, including 20,000 women and children. The Indians had captured 5795.64 square miles of Pakistani territory on the western front, while Pakistan had succeeded in capturing merely 110.35 square miles of Indian territory (Nawaz 2008: 329).

Nationalisation of Heavy Industry

On 2 January 1972, Bhutto's government nationalised all the major industries, including iron and steel, heavy engineering, petrochemicals, cement, and the public utilities. Public speeches, and television addresses to the people, were full of populist rhetoric demonizing the capitalists and industrialists as exploiters, tax evaders, and much worse. The anti-industrialist campaign was consummated with the announcement, on 10 February 1972, of a new labour policy:

1. 20 percent representation was to be given to workers in a factory's administration.
2. The workers' share in the annual profits of a production unit was raised from 2.5 to 4 percent; later, it was increased to 5 percent.
3. Any party to a labour dispute could take its complaint or case to the labour court for redress.
4. The court was to give a decision within 30 days; previously it was 60 days.
5. A worker fired from his job had to be informed about the reasons for his dismissal in writing.
6. An old-age pension was announced, and it was made obligatory for factory-owners to support the education of one child of each worker up to matriculation.
7. Regarding medical treatment, the two-percent deduction from the worker's wages was stopped. Instead, the owners' share, to such a fund, was increased from 4 to 6 percent.
8. Registration of trade unions was made much easier. As a result, their number increased dramatically (Ahmed and Amjad 1984: 92–93).

Such measures inadvertently infused revolutionary fervour among radical leftists. Consequently, spontaneous as well as planned industrial agitation began to take place all over Pakistan. The tactics of gherao – surrounding and detaining owners and managers of industrial enterprises – and kabza – taking over control – were common practices amongst radical trade unionists in neighbouring India. Pakistani leftists seemed to have taken their cue from their counterparts in India. But, such tactics exceeded the limits that Bhutto had in mind. The government adopted a stern tone and warned the radical socialists and trade union activists that disruptive activities would not be tolerated. The government also made it clear that any future manifestation of street power would be met with the might of the state (Mahmud 1987: 19–22). That threat was translated into practice: when the gherao and kabza methods created unrest in industrial areas all over Pakistan, Bhutto ordered strong action against the growing insurgency. The police and paramilitary forces used considerable force and repression to crush the resistance – although, earlier, when he had ordered the military to take action, General Gul Hassan had refused to comply (Khan 1993:362). In any event, by the end of 1972, the workers' resistance had been dealt severe blows and it quietly petered out during the next year.

Land Reforms

On 1 March 1972, Bhutto's much-awaited land reforms were introduced under Martial Law Regulation No. 115. The rhetoric concomitant with the speech included a tirade against Ayub Khan's land reforms, which Bhutto alleged had buttressed feudalism through various concessions and exceptions to the landed elite. Under his scheme, the ceiling was lowered to 150 acres of irrigated, and 300 acres of un-irrigated, land. Excess land was confiscated without any compensation. However, instead of the ceiling applying to the family, it applied to individual ownership – which Bhutto justified on the basis that ownership, in Islam, resided with the individual! This was a major disappointment for his socialist followers. Moreover, in a balancing political act purportedly not to alienate the landed classes, Bhutto began to welcome the big landowners into his party. Such overtures disillusioned the leftists in the party who, over time, were increasingly sidelined; many left the PPP.

In 1977, another land reform was announced. The ceiling was lowered to 100 acres of irrigated, and 200 acres of un-irrigated, land. However, compensation was introduced at the rate of ₹30 per Produce Index Unit for land acquired by the state (Saeed 2010: 3–4). On the whole, the tenancy provisions formally improved the legal status of the tenant-cultivators, but no effective mechanisms were put in place to enforce them. The reforms failed to alter the rural power structure because the limits were fixed in terms of individual, and not family, holdings. Moreover, by transferring land to relatives outside the immediate family, and even retainers and servants, the landowners continued to maintain their power and influence. The 1977 reforms were abandoned after Bhutto was ousted from power by the military.

Trimming the Wings of the Military

Military defeat at the hands of India had put the Pakistani generals on the back foot. The new government let Pakistan's state television air the complete ceremony of the surrender of the Pakistan Army in Dacca on 16 December 1971. This evoked an angry response from the military, and even people in general were greatly perturbed by the bizarre spectacle. More significantly, differences between Bhutto and the army chief, General Gul Hassan Khan, developed rather quickly. Gul Hassan complained that Bhutto and his associates interfered in his work and kept a tab on his activities. As already noted, Gul Hassan refused to use the military against the workers in Karachi. Further tensions between the two men developed when Bhutto's military adviser, Major General (Retd.) Akbar Khan – the hero of the Kashmir war who was later dismissed for masterminding the Rawalpindi Conspiracy – ordered the movement of artillery guns to help the civil authorities of Nowshera, in the NWFP, quell a police mutiny. Gul Hassan overruled the order. A mutiny in Punjab also found the Bhutto government and military chief giving contradictory orders to the army (Khan 1993: 350–64). Gul Hassan has claimed that it was his refusal to kowtow to Bhutto's whimsical and irregular demands and orders that resulted in his being retired on 3 March. Bhutto, simultaneously, retired Air Marshal Rahim Khan: both men had been instrumental in bringing him to power some months earlier. What surprised many was that he chose General Tikka Khan, of East Pakistan fame, to replace Gul Hassan. When the Italian journalist Oriana Fallaci questioned Bhutto about his choice of Tikka Khan, he reportedly said:

> Tikka Khan was a soldier doing a soldier's job [in East Pakistan]. He went to East Pakistan with precise orders and came back by precise orders. He did what he was ordered to, though he wasn't always in agreement, and I picked him because I know he'll follow my orders with the same discipline (quoted in Nawaz 2009: 325).

Bhutto abolished the post of commander-in-chief. The three heads of the armed forces were given equal rank and seniority. The head of the army, henceforth, was to be known as the chief of army staff. His tenure was fixed at four years, later reduced to three years. The naval headquarters were moved from Karachi to Islamabad. Moreover, Bhutto began to monitor the promotion of officers; those suspected of harbouring sympathies for oppositional political parties were denied promotion. Such interference in the affairs of the powerful military earned him the resentment of many senior officers (Shafqat 1997: 175).

Civilian Rule

It was in such circumstances that the government convened the National Assembly on 14 April 1972. A consensus on lifting martial law was reached forthwith. An interim constitution, written by Federal Law Minister Mian Mahmud Ali Kasuri, was adopted on 17 April, and came into effect on 21 April. Bhutto took the oath, under it, as president. Nurul Amin, a prominent Bengali politician who had remained loyal to Pakistan, became prime minister though his post remained largely nominal; Bhutto, as president, retained the real power. The National Assembly appointed a committee of twenty-five members, under the chairmanship of Kasuri, to prepare a new constitution based on the parliamentary form of government.

War Criminals and the POW Issue

Profound resentment existed, among Bengalis, against the Pakistani POWs for the latter's alleged war crimes. Hence, sporadic clashes erupted in different parts of Bangladesh when Pakistanis were attacked – which was one reason for India's decision to move them to camps in India. On 24 December 1971, Bangladesh's Home Minister, A.H.M. Kamaruzzaman, announced that Bengali authorities had arrested thirty top Pakistani civilian officials who would soon be put on trial for genocide. This was followed by the widows of seven Bangladeshi officers, who had been killed by the Pakistanis, asking India to put some Pakistani officers on trial for war crimes. After returning home, Sheikh Mujib initiated a formal process of a war crimes trial. On 29 March 1972, the Bangladesh government announced a plan to try some 1100 Pakistani military prisoners, including General Niazi and General Rao Farman Ali, for war crimes. Initially, India agreed to hand over all military prisoners against whom Bangladesh could present 'prima facie cases' of atrocities. Later, on 14 June 1972, India decided to hand over a more restricted list of 150 POWS, later increased to 195 including Niazi, to Bangladesh for trial. Such pressure continued to grow; on 19 June – that is ten days before the Simla summit was to take place – Mujibur Rahman reaffirmed his commitment to try the Pakistanis (Ahamed 2010).

Pakistan reacted by putting many of the Bengalis living in West Pakistan into detention. According to one estimate, nearly 400,000 Bengalis were in

Pakistan at the time of the fall of Dacca. Moreover, Bhutto convinced China to veto Bangladesh's membership in the United Nations. Thus, on 25 August 1972, China cast its veto when Bangladesh applied for membership to the United Nations. Meanwhile, the issue of Pakistani POWs in Indian detention camps loomed large in Pakistani political and media discussions. India's prime minister, Indira Gandhi, was anxious not to keep the POWs for too long for different political and diplomatic reasons, even when voices were being raised to put those guilty of crimes against humanity on trial. She probably also felt that, given India's obvious position of strength and advantage, she could succeed in clinching a favourable deal with Pakistan over Kashmir. Consequently, she despatched a seasoned diplomat, D.P. Dhar, to Pakistan to invite Bhutto to a summit at the famed hill station of Simla, the former summer capital of the British. Bhutto responded with enthusiasm and the ball was set rolling (Taseer 1979: 135). Bhutto consulted a broad spectrum of Pakistani politicians; considerable attention was given to gathering the opinions of influential interests. For the Pakistani public, the release of the POWs was prime of importance.

The Army's Brief

Shuja Nawaz has brought forth very interesting information on the stand the Pakistan Army took on any negotiations with India. No doubt, the POW issue was of utmost importance to the military. The brief it prepared suggested that recognition of Bangladesh must be made conditional on the Indian and Bangladeshi governments fulfilling a number of preconditions. With regard to India, the Pakistan military insisted that Indian troops should be pulled back from the international border and ceasefire line; the POWs released; and no Pakistani military personnel put on trial for war crimes. Further, it was stressed that Pakistani POWs should be exchanged for Bengali military and civil personnel detained in Pakistan. Where Bangladesh was concerned, it was to ensure that the Biharis, and other pro-Pakistan elements in Bangladesh, were treated properly.

It is interesting to note that while demanding proper treatment for the Biharis, the military strongly opposed any idea of them being sent to Pakistan – asserting that they had a home in Bangladesh (Nawaz 2009: 328–9). On the question of Kashmir, Bhutto was advised to take a firm stand: 'We should not concede the Indian-held Kashmir to India. We should continue to insist that the Kashmiris have a right of self-determination and India must give them this right. Pakistan could, however, agree to an (sic) arbitration on the question of Kashmir' (ibid., 330). The army also wanted Bhutto to tell India that it should reduce the size of her armed forces to remove fear of aggression in Pakistan (ibid.). Nawaz has made this interesting remark:

> This was not an army that had just lost a war. It sounded more like the terms of surrender offered to a defeated enemy. The brief was aimed as much at India as convincing Bhutto that if the Indian 'threat' remained at a high level, then 'obviously we will have to maintain a proportionately higher level of standing Armed Forces. It conceded however that should India reduce its threat, the size of the Pakistan armed forces could be reviewed accordingly (ibid.).

The Simla Agreement

A large delegation, including leading journalists, accompanied Bhutto to Simla at the end of June 1972. The summit opened formally on 28 June 1972. Both sides expressed a sincere desire to end conflict and to establish a durable and lasting peace. The bottom line of Indira Gandhi's strategy was to insist on a comprehensive settlement that would cover all the issues that had arisen in the aftermath of the war between them. From the Indian point of view, that, most centrally, meant a settlement of the Kashmir dispute. Pakistan took a very different approach: the end to the occupation of Pakistani territory and the release of its POWs was emphasised as the necessary preliminary first step to pave the way for an amicable resolution of the Kashmir dispute.

Bhutto asserted that putting Pakistani military officers on trial for war crimes would not create the required conducive atmosphere for resolving the Kashmir dispute. Such an argument seemed to have convinced the Indian prime minister and her advisers who went along with it. On 2 July 1972, the Simla Agreement was signed between the two leaders. Both sides affirmed to work together towards the creation of durable peace and harmony between them, to cease carrying out hostile propaganda against each other, and to promote understanding between each other through exchanges in the fields of culture and science.

It was stated that the two countries resolved to settle their differences by peaceful means through bilateral negotiations or by any other peaceful means mutually agreed upon between them. Pending the final settlement of any of the problems between the two countries, neither side would unilaterally alter the situation and both would prevent the organisation, assistance, or encouragement of any acts detrimental to the maintenance of peaceful and harmonious relations.

It was further laid down that, in Jammu and Kashmir, the line of control resulting from the ceasefire of 17 December 1971 would be respected by both sides without prejudice to the recognized position of either side. Neither side would seek to alter it unilaterally, irrespective of mutual differences and legal interpretations. Both sides further undertook to refrain from the threat, or the use, of force in violation of this line.

It was also stated that the representatives of the two sides would meet to further discuss the modalities and arrangements for the establishment of durable peace and normalization of relations, including a final settlement of Jammu and Kashmir (Simla Agreement 1972).

Conspicuous by its absence in the Simla Agreement was any reference to a plebiscite. This was a significant departure from the hitherto UN resolutions pertaining to Kashmir.

Interpretations of the Agreement

On the whole, the Simla Agreement was a great success for Bhutto. He had pleaded Pakistan's case from a position of patent weakness. Indira Gandhi, who was in a much stronger position, could not exploit that to her advantage in procuring an overall settlement of all issues, especially on Kashmir. In one sense, the victor at Simla was the Pakistani army whose brief prevailed – albeit because of Bhutto's skills. Why Indira Gandhi gave in remains a puzzle. Reportedly, Bhutto was able to convince her that it would be impossible for him to begin negotiations to resolve the Kashmir dispute without the settling of the POW issue. Bhutto returned to Pakistan in a very carefully orchestrated public relations offensive that projected him as a great statesman and patriot. Also, apart from the absence of any reference to the UN resolutions pertaining to a plebiscite, no concessions were made to India on Kashmir. The only significant change was that the Ceasefire Line became the Line of Control.

Soon afterwards, both sides began to interpret the Simla Agreement in a manner that they deemed was advantageous to them: India insisted that the principle of bilateralism meant that the Kashmir problem was not an international issue any longer, and that the line of control had in practice become the international border; Pakistan insisted that the Simla Agreement recognised that the Kashmir problem had yet to be resolved (Taseer 1979: 141–3).

Repatriation of POWs

Just before the Simla Summit, India agreed to deliver 150 Niazi and other alleged war criminals, to Bangladesh for trial. Mujib issued a statement that Bangladesh would try them for war crimes. At Simla, both sides considered it prudent not to probe this issue too deeply (Ahamed 2010).

Back at home, Bhutto took a firm stand that recognition of Bangladesh would be subject to the release of the POWs. He strongly objected to India handing over the Pakistanis charged with war crimes to Bangladesh to be put on trial. Such positioning, in light of the fact that hundreds of thousands of Bengalis were in Pakistan who, if not detained, were not being allowed to leave for Bangladesh meant that Pakistan could exert considerable pressure on both India and Bangladesh to withdraw their plans of putting the 195 Pakistanis on trial. Consequently, the repatriation process slowly got underway (ibid.) In November 1972, Bangladesh and India decided to repatriate some 6000 family members of Pakistani POWs and, in response, Pakistan agreed to release some 10,000 Bangladeshi women and children held in Pakistan. Thereafter, more such exchanges took place. However, Bangladesh took the stand that India would not release the initial 195 Pakistani POWs but would try them, along with their local collaborators, for war crimes. Bhutto threatened that if Bangladesh carried out the trial of the 195 Pakistanis, Pakistan would also follow suit. In an interview on 27 May 1973, Bhutto remarked: 'Public opinion will demand trials [of Bangladeshis] here.... We know that Bengalis passed on information during the war. There will be specific charges. How many will be tried, I cannot say.' (quoted in Ahamed). Thereafter, 203 Bengalis stranded in Pakistan were rendered virtual hostages.

On 28 August 1973, India and Pakistan signed the Delhi Accord which allowed the release of most of the stranded Bangladeshi and Pakistanis held in Pakistan and India, respectively. Pakistan and India also agreed that the issue of the 195 accused Pakistanis would be settled between Bangladesh and Pakistan. Pakistan excluded the 203 Bangladeshis, who had been taken into custody, out of the repatriation process. Later, Pakistan proposed that if Bangladesh agreed, the 195 men could be tried in special tribunals in Pakistan. Bangladesh finally accepted Pakistan's proposal realising that its citizens would be retained in Pakistan if it went ahead with the trials. That paved the way for the complete repatriation of the Pakistani POWs in India, and the Bengalis in Pakistan, by 15 April 1974 (Ahamed 2010).

The 1973 Constitution

Meanwhile, Bhutto had invested a great deal of effort and prestige in the transition to democracy. An all-parties constitutional committee submitted its recommendations to the National Assembly in April 1973. The constitution retained the description 'Islamic Republic' for the state. The president was to only be a figurehead; real power was vested in the office of the prime minister. On 10 April 1973, the National Assembly voted by 125 votes, out of a total of 133, in favour of the draft that the Kasuri committee had prepared. Even the NAP voted in favour of it, although relations between the PPP and it had soured considerably, especially after Bhutto dismissed the NAP government in Balochistan. The constitution proposed a parliamentary democracy based, in principle, on a federal division of power between the centre and provinces; however, the centre continued to enjoy overriding powers vis-à-vis the provinces.

In ideological terms, the 1973 constitution took some further steps towards an Islamisation of the polity. Besides a reiteration of the clauses on the removal of all laws repugnant to the Quran and Sunnah, and bringing existing laws into conformity with the Quran and Sunnah, the new constitution required that not only the president – as was required of the 1956 and 1962 constitutions – but also the prime minister were to be Muslims. Moreover, they were required to take an oath affirming their belief in the finality of the prophethood of Muhammad (Ahmed 2010: 198). Consequently, the Ahmadiyya issue was debated in the National Assembly; the head of the mainstream Rabwah group, Mirza Nasir Ahmad, and his advisers presented their views to parliament. The record of those proceedings remains classified.

On 7 September 1974, the National Assembly declared the Ahmadiyya community non-Muslims.

Although the Baloch leaders Khair Bakhsh Marri and Mir Ali Ahmed Talpur did not sign the constitution, Bhutto was sworn in as the prime minister of the country on 14 August 1973, having secured 108 votes in a house of 146 members. Fazal Ilahi Chaudhry, from Punjab, was elected as the president under the new constitution. However, within four hours of the signing of the constitution, the fundamental rights proclaimed in it were suspended under the Proclamation of Emergency order that was adopted. It empowered Bhutto 'to "fix" his political opponents, have them arrested and incarcerated until they were tamed, men such as Khair Bakhsh Marri, Ghaus Bakhsh Bizenjo, Ataullah Mengal and Wali Khan', recalled veteran Pakistani columnist Ardeshir Cowasjee (*Dawn*, 10 January 2010).

The Federal Security Force

While investing in parliamentary democracy, Bhutto created a paramilitary force – the Federal Security Force (FSF) – that would be directly under civilian control. Ostensibly, it was to assist the government deal with smugglers, black marketeers, and other criminal elements but, in practice, it served as Bhutto's private army. The noted political scientist Khalid bin Sayeed has described such an urge to establish personal control over the state as Bonapartism. The Bonapartist state is one in which a political movement is set in motion that emphasizes the need for a strong centralised state ruled by a strongman. Sayeed, arguing that this tendency emerged with Ayub's ascent to power but was consummated under Bhutto, has observed: 'Bhutto was primarily motivated by animus dominandi, that is, the aggrandizement of his own power, he wanted to control every major class or interest by weakening its power base and by making it subservient to his will and power' (Sayeed 1980: 91).

In any event, some serving and retired senior police officers were hired to organise and manage the FSF – which was a 15,000-strong force, equipped with semi-automatic weapons. Many of the activities of the FSF were of a highhanded type and, in some cases, in stark violation of the law (Hussain 2010: 189–190). In one infamous case, FSF goons were involved in seriously assaulting a founder member of the PPP, J.A. Rahim, and his son. They were badly beaten up; the son suffered fractured limbs. Over time, Bhutto became surrounded by sycophants while many left-leaning and democratic-minded senior members of his party either left the cabinet or were sidelined (Chishti 1996: 84–7).

Military Action in Balochistan

Although the PPP had the majority of the seats in the National Assembly, it had won majorities in only two provinces – Punjab and Sindh. In March 1972, Bhutto reached an agreement with the NAP and the Jamiat-e-Ulema-e-Islam (JUI) – a Deobandi political party – under which a NAP–JUI coalition government was formed in the NWFP, and a NAP government in Balochistan. According to Gul Hassan Khan, Bhutto had not reached the understanding in good faith and started 'undermining the governments in the NWFP and Balochistan by intrigue and other repugnant methods, to replace them with those of his own party' (Khan 1993: 377). In any event, in February 1973, the Pakistan government claimed to have detected a cache of arms concealed in a diplomatic shipment to the Iraqi embassy in Islamabad. At that time, Baloch guerrillas were involved in skirmishes with the Pakistan Army in the Pat Feeder area – an agricultural oasis surrounded by the vast and desolate terrain of the province. Bhutto declared the capture of arms, and the armed conflict in Balochistan, as yet another conspiracy against Pakistan.

He alleged that the Baloch sardars had failed 'to take effective measures to check large scale disturbances in different parts of the province…causing a growing sense of insecurity among the inhabitants and grave menace to the peace and tranquillity of the Province' (Nawaz 2008: 333). The Balochistan government was removed from office on 12 February 1973, under the pretext that it had exceeded its constitutional authority and that it had been involved in a conspiracy to begin an armed rebellion. The Pakistan Army was ordered to go in to establish law and order, and undertake modernising measures such as the building of roads and schools and the provision of electricity. Prominent sardars who held office in the NAP government in Balochistan, or were sympathetic to it, were taken into custody, charged with treason, and later put on trial. The governor of Sindh, Mir Rasul Baksh Talpur, a Sindhi like Bhutto and considered close to him, also had to resign as his brother, Mir Ali Ahmed Talpur, was suspected of being involved in the Balochistan resistance movement. The first skirmish occurred on 18 May 1973 at Tandoori near Sibi: eight Sibi Scouts were killed; and the army moved into the Marri area on 21 May. Later, the conflict escalated as the families of the fighters shifted to Afghanistan while the men stayed behind to carry on with the armed resistance (Interview, Mir Muhammad Ali Talpur). Some young men from Punjab, inspired by Marxist ideas while studying at Cambridge University, also took part in the insurgency. The response of the Pakistan military was firm and ruthless. It launched a major military operation against the insurgents. Iran provided generous help of $200 million in emergency military and financial aid, and despatched Huey Cobra helicopters to assist the Pakistanis (Harrison 1981: 36).

On the other hand, the Baloch fighters found sanctuary in Afghanistan from where they launched surprise attacks on the army. At its height, the conflict involved more than 80,000 Pakistani troops and at least 35,000 Baloch guerrillas. According to one estimate, some 5300 Baloch were killed or wounded. There were 3300 army casualties (Khan 1983: 71). Some army sources deny that the military operation was conducted on such a large scale, or that so many Baloch took part in the armed struggle. In any event, fighting continued throughout Bhutto's stint in power. The major fallout of the military confrontation in Balochistan was that it brought the military back into politics, with direct responsibility to ensure Pakistan's territorial integrity.

Ban on the NAP and Arrest of Pakhtun Leaders

Although the NAP government in Balochistan had been dismissed, its leaders arrested, and military action ordered against the Baloch insurgents, the NAP–JUI government remained in power amid rising tensions in the NWFP. Partly, the tension was an effect of the overthrow of King Zahir Shah of Afghanistan, in 1973, in a coup engineered by his cousin, Sardar Daud Khan. Daud was known for his pro-Soviet leanings. He revived the Pakhtunistan issue and challenged the legality of the Durand Line as the border between Afghanistan and Pakistan. Pakistani intelligence sources suspected that such posturing would have destabilising repercussions on their side of the disputed border. Bhutto responded by ordering the military to take appropriate measures to counter hostile Afghan propaganda.

Those measures included support for conservative Afghan forces opposed to the new government in Kabul. As part of a long term engagement in

Afghanistan, the future legendary SSG officer, Sultan Amir Tarar alias Colonel Imam, who played a prominent role in the anti-Communist jihad of the 1980s, was sent to the United States in 1973 to receive training with the United States Army Special Forces. He told me that the decision to destabilise Afghanistan had been taken by the Bhutto regime, in the event that Daud continued with his pro-Pakhtunistan pronouncements (Interview, Colonel Imam). Moreover, Bhutto was convinced that Wali Khan and other Pakhtun nationalists were secretly in alliance with Daud. Major General Naseerullah Babar has written that Bhutto began to support anti-Daud Afghans in 1973. They were given basic infantry weapons and training to conduct guerrilla warfare under an SSG team. This was done in total secrecy – only Bhutto, Aziz Ahmed, COAS General Tikka Khan, and Major General Babar knew about it (Amin 2001).

On the other hand, Wali Khan had begun to distance himself from the legacy of his father, Abdul Ghaffar Khan, whose pro-Congress credentials and opposition to the partition of India were seen by him as a liability and, thus, a drawback to his ambitions of becoming a mainstream Pakistani nationalist. In a surprise move, the NAP–JUI government decided to use Urdu, and not Pushto, as the medium of education in NWFP. Moreover, Wali Khan embarked on a strategy of extending his support and influence in Punjab. Bhutto found such a strategy disturbing. On 23 March 1973, as Wali Khan addressed a public meeting in Rawalpindi's historic Liaquat Bagh, it was attacked by armed gunmen who opened fire resulting in the death of a dozen people and many more wounded. It was widely believed that the outrage had been carried out by the FSF. Wali Khan narrowly escaped a bullet during the attack (Mazari 2001: 296–7; Wali 2003: 2). This attack greatly infuriated the Pakhtuns who wanted to launch a huge agitation in the NWFP capital, Peshawar. However, Wali Khan decided not to court direct confrontation with the central government and stopped the agitation from taking place.

Moreover, on 21 April 1973, when the new constitution was put to the vote, Wali Khan and his party members and allies voted in favour of the constitution despite some reservations on provincial autonomy and the concentration of power in the office of the prime minister. Wali Khan, with the support of all the oppositional parties in the National Assembly, was elected the leader of the opposition. Such overtures obviated an immediate clash between their parties for the time being. When Hayat Muhammad Khan

Sherpao, the governor of NWFP and a close ally of Bhutto, was assassinated on 8 February 1975 in a bomb blast, Bhutto held Wali Khan and the NAP responsible for that crime. Wali Khan, and most of the senior leadership of the NAP, were arrested. They were put on trial before the same Hyderabad tribunal that was trying the Baloch leaders. The trials dragged on for years and were considered a farce (Newburg 2002: 146–150). The Baloch and Pakhtun leaders remained in incarceration while Bhutto was in power.

Failed Coup Attempt

Ever since he had come into power, resentment against Bhutto had been simmering among some junior and middle-ranking army and air force officers. The fact that he had retired Yahya and his close associates, but retained many senior commanders who were involved in the East Pakistan debacle including Tikka Khan, was viewed with dismay. Their dissatisfaction grew, over the months, as the reform policies unfolded. In 1972, Bhutto retired Brigadier F.B. Ali, who had taken the lead in the officers' agitation that resulted in Yahya Khan and his ilk stepping down. That added to the frustration of the brigadier's admirers in the armed forces. The creation of the FSF convinced them that Bhutto was on the way to consolidating a personal authoritarian rule and dictatorship. Consequently, they began to meet to discuss the situation, but were penetrated by military intelligence and the plot was foiled, resulting in the arrests of several officers on 30 March 1973 (Nawaz 2008: 336).

The arrested men were put on trial in Attock Fort. Bhutto selected Major General Muhammad Zia-ul-Haq to head the military tribunal to try the alleged conspirators. Zia had come to Bhutto's notice when the latter had visited Multan. Apparently, he had been impressed by Zia's modesty and lack of ambition! Also, while serving with the Jordanian Royal Army, Zia had distinguished himself by crushing the Black September Uprising of 1970. In any case, the plotters were subjected to a thorough investigation. The trial, on the whole, was fair. Those convicted were sentenced and sent out to different prisons. The government was keen to keep them dispersed and to discourage them from receiving visitors easily. As a balancing gesture, Bhutto undertook a set of measures purported to appease the military – for example, he increased their pay scale and permitted the army to expand its recruitment. Moreover, defence expenditure was increased, in nominal terms, from ₹3725 million in 1971–2 to ₹8210 million in 1976–7 (Nawaz 2008: 339–43).

Consolidating His Rule

The diverse range of activities that Bhutto initiated were augmented by a number of moves to enhance control over the civil and military oligarchy – for example, guarantees to civil servants against dismissal from office were removed. Consequently, the axe fell on some 1300 bureaucrats who were sent into retirement or dismissed on charges of corruption (Yusuf 1999: 146). On the other hand, the government tried to induct its own men into the administration through the 'lateral entry' procedure, whereby the Establishment Division headed by a Bhutto loyalist, Viqar Ahmed, could induct officers through far less vigorous recruitment procedures than those applied to the Central Superior Services examination. As a result, during 1973–77, 1374 officers were recruited through lateral entry (Burki 1980: 102). With regard to the military, the new constitution invested the prerogative to appoint the three service chiefs, as well as the COAS, in the prime minister. The constitution explicitly forbade military takeovers by describing any such move as high treason, and prescribed the death sentence for any such act. However, Bhutto was cautious as only forty-three senior officers were retired (Yusuf 1999: 144). Among those were six from the air force (Shafqat 1997: 175).

Diversification of Pakistan's External Support Base

Z.A. Bhutto was undoubtedly the architect of Pakistan's foreign policy reorientation in the 1960s – from the nearly complete dependence on the United States to the building of relationships with other major players of which China was the most important. He had spelt out such ideas in his major work, The Myth of Independence (1969). In it, he had justified the right of developing nations to exercise sovereignty and to make foreign policy decisions in light of their objective self-interest. Bhutto presented a widely shared Pakistani point of view that, in spite of India's rejection of the United States' overtures to join the western camp, the United States always meted out preferential treatment to India. Such policy adversely affected the national security of Pakistan. The US arms embargo placed on India and Pakistan in 1965 hurt Pakistan more because only Pakistan relied heavily on American arms (Bhutto 1969: 2–3). Such a decision, he asserted, whittled down the importance of the military alliance between the United States and Pakistan to a mere formality.

He prepared a strong brief for a Sino–Pakistan alliance, arguing that China – and not the Soviet Union – was going to be the main rival of the United States in the future, as Asia became increasingly more important. A strong Sino–Pakistan alliance would also be an effective counterweight to India's expansionist designs, backed by an incessant urge to isolate and weaken Pakistan and to deny it the right to Jammu and Kashmir. Therefore, Bhutto urged that Pakistan should not be lured by promises of joint business ventures and cooperation with India as long as the Kashmir dispute was not settled (ibid., 176–84).

Bhutto's emergence, as the most powerful man in Pakistani politics, was viewed with some anxiety by the White House. However, before leaving the United States having attended the US Security Council session in December 1971, Bhutto had met Nixon and senior officials. He had told the American president that Pakistan was 'completely in the debt of the United States during the recent trying months' (Kux 2001: 204), Further, he assured them that although he was called a 'Yankee hater', he wanted to establish good relations with the United States. Nixon's response was equally warm. He assured Bhutto that he would do everything within his power to help Pakistan but that, because of congressional opposition, it could not be in the form of military aid; it would be economic and development aid (ibid.). An American diplomat who met Bhutto on 7 January 1972, after he had nationalised the major heavy industries and when the atmosphere was charged with revolutionary fervour, recorded that Bhutto assured him that he was not anti-American; that the US was the greatest power his own daughter was studying in the US, and so on. He went on to say that he was neither anti-Soviet nor anti-Indian. The American noted that, some days earlier, Bhutto had told the Canadian high commissioner to Pakistan that he had been elected on a platform that called for 'confrontation with India and that he was guided accordingly' (Aijazuddin 2002: 125).

Subsequently, Bhutto toned down his radicalism, and his anti-imperialist rhetoric and utterances on the United States became more benign. In meetings with the Americans, Bhutto lauded the help that the US had rendered to Pakistan by issuing an ultimatum to India in 1971 not to attack West Pakistan (Jain 2007a: 90). The Americans noted that Bhutto's refrain continued to be one of India exploiting Pakistan's weaknesses. For their part, the Americans reiterated that they were committed to the preservation of Pakistan's integrity and sovereignty. In March 1973, Nixon released $24 million worth of military equipment that had been blocked since 1971, and reinstated the 1967 arms-supply policy that enabled Pakistan to procure spare parts and non-lethal equipment for weapons previously supplied to it (Kux 2001: 209). Bhutto also sought US help in constructing a new port at Gwadar, on the Arabian Sea coast in Balochistan, saying that the US Navy could use the facility. Nixon did not show much interest as the United States did not want to upset the Soviet Union and India. Interestingly, this idea was supported by the Chinese – when Kissinger visited China in November 1973 (ibid., 211).

Lahore Islamic Summit and Indian Nuclear Explosion

In February 1974, Bhutto invited Muslim heads of state and governments, as well as leaders of liberation movements, to Pakistan to attend an Islamic Summit in the historic city of Lahore. Almost all of them came, including the Palestine Liberation Organization (PLO) leader, Yasser Arafat. Sheikh Mujibur Rahman also attended, much to the chagrin of Indira Gandhi – but this gave the message that the separation of East Pakistan was complete and relations between Bangladesh and Pakistan could normalise. In his address to the dignitaries, Bhutto waxed eloquently when he described the 'Pakistan Army as the Army of Islam' (Hilaly 26 March 2011). Solidarity with the Palestinians, and bringing Israeli occupation of Jerusalem to an end, were declared the cornerstones of his government's policy (Beg 1974). Such flourish meant that Pakistan could take up cudgels on behalf of the universal Muslim Umma. The Islamic Summit was a grand exercise in national projection by Bhutto. It greatly exaggerated Pakistan's military capabilities, but was consistent with earlier examples of Pakistani leaders marketing their state and nation to foreign powers in the hope that such services would return dividends in the form of economic and military aid.

Pakistan's sense of insecurity was greatly accentuated when, in May 1974, India exploded a nuclear device. According to a secret State Department report dated 14 January 1972 – quoted by the Indian newspaper, The Asian Times – Nixon's tilt towards Pakistan, and the US–China liaison facilitated by Pakistan, had apparently caused concern in New Delhi; and, its decision to carry out the nuclear test was motivated by that sense of insecurity (The Asian Age, 6 December 2011).

Pakistan had, since 1956, been pursuing a peaceful nuclear programme and several facilities had been set up. Uranium deposits had also been discovered in southern Punjab. In March 1965, Bhutto was reported to have said to a British journalist, of the Manchester Guardian, that if India were to acquire nuclear capability 'then we should have to eat grass and get one, or buy one, of our own' (Nawaz 2008: 340).

President Gerald Ford – who succeeded Nixon after the latter had to resign office because of the Watergate scandal – continued with his predecessor's policy vis-à-vis Pakistan, assuring his country's support for Pakistan's integrity but without making any major effort to lift the arms embargo. This position was particularly unacceptable to Pakistan once India had carried out the nuclear test. Subsequently, the Americans were persuaded to lift the arms embargo, but this applied to both India and Pakistan. The lifting was announced on 24 February 1975 when Bhutto visited Washington. The Ford administration emphasised that the sales would be made on a case-to-case basis and that efforts would be made to avoid stimulating an arms race between the two rivals. It was noted, however, that India had been acquiring weapons, on a large scale, from the Soviet Union while Pakistan had mainly received armament from China, albeit on a relatively smaller scale (Jain 2007a: 321–2). During a press conference on 10 March, Bhutto recalled that Pakistan had two treaties with the United States – 1954 and 1959 – which obliged the United States to provide arms to Pakistan. However, the lifting of the embargo enabled Pakistan to buy weapons on a case-to-case basis only and not receive them gratis, as was laid down in the treaties (ibid., 322).

The Kahuta Nuclear Facility

The first major step towards the development of a nuclear bomb was a meeting in Multan, in January 1972, to which the government invited leading Pakistani scientists including future Nobel Laureate Abdus Salam. In his highly emotive address to them, Bhutto challenged them to build a nuclear bomb. That started the ball rolling. Pakistan sought financial support from Libya and Saudi Arabia, and possibly also Iran (Nawaz 2008: 340–41). American officials started worrying about Pakistan's nuclear ambitions, which began to be described as an 'Islamic bomb'. A State Department briefing paper dated 31 January 1975 expressed the view that Pakistan was 'trying to acquire an independent nuclear fuel cycle and the technical skills that would make the nuclear weapon explosion option feasible' (Kux 2001: 219). Pakistan, however, went ahead and signed a deal to purchase an advanced French nuclear processing plant.

Dr Abdul Qadeer Khan, a metallurgist and the so-called 'father of the Pakistani nuclear bomb', had been in contact with Bhutto for some time and returned from the Netherlands in 1975. In 1976, he joined the team that had been deputed the task of developing the nuclear weapon. The Pakistan military, initially, was not involved in the nuclear weapons programme but Zia, who had been promoted to COAS in March 1976, was told by Bhutto that the army should assist in building an enrichment plant at Kahuta near Islamabad. Zia assigned that task to Brigadier Zahid Ali Akbar. A.Q. Khan had successfully brought, with him, enrichment centrifuges from the Dutch laboratory; work on constructing the bomb began in real earnest. Apparently, there was considerable friction between A.Q. Khan and the Pakistan Atomic Energy Commission's scientists. On Brigadier Akbar's strong pleas, the matter was resolved by making the Kahuta operation autonomous; A.Q. Khan was put in charge of it. In any case, thenceforth, the army was closely involved in providing it with security and monitoring its activities (Nawaz 2008: 340–2).

Sensing that something was afoot on the nuclear front, Kissinger paid a number of visits to Pakistan to dissuade Pakistan from going ahead with the building of a nuclear bomb. Such trips bore offers of military aid – in terms of advanced aircraft and other equipment – as well as warnings that economic aid would be cut off if Pakistan persisted with its nuclear ambitions. This threat was concretized with amendments proposed by the Democratic senators John Glenn and Stuart Symington, to the US foreign assistance bill, that barred assistance to Nuclear Non-Proliferation Treaty (NPT) signatories that imported uranium-enrichment or nuclear fuel reprocessing technology. Kissinger warned that, in light of the amendment, economic aid to Pakistan could be cut off. Bhutto and his senior advisers, however, remained steadfast in their resolve not to give in to US pressure (Kux 2001: 221–6).

The Fall of Bhutto

In 1976, Bhutto began to plan a general election in 1977. According to the terms of the 1973 constitution, it was not due till 1978 but Bhutto felt confident and secure and wanted to cash in on the popularity he perceived he enjoyed. Meanwhile, the opposition had begun to close ranks to collectively challenge a government it loathed and feared. On 7 January 1977, the government announced that general elections would be held in two months' time, on 7 March. The PPP declared, in its election manifesto, that, among other things, teaching of the Quran would be a compulsory subject of basic education. Sixteen thousand plots would be allotted, gratis, to workers every year and productivity would be increased by fifty percent (Chishti 1996: 79). Immediately, the very next day, several opposition parties banded together to form the Pakistan National Alliance (PNA). Although the PNA consisted of parties of all shades, it was essentially a right-wing Islamist alliance and included major players such as the Jamaat-e-Islami, the Deobandi Jamiat Ulema-e-Islam, and the Barelvi Jamiat Ulema-e-Pakistan. They clamoured for the so-called Nizam-e-Mustafa, or Islamist state from the time of Prophet Muhammad (pbuh) and his pious successors. The former National Awami Party, banned by Bhutto, changed its name to National Democratic Party (NDP) and joined the PNA. Another important player was the Tehrik-e-Istiqlal, led by former Air Marshal Asghar Khan. Relations between Bhutto and Asghar Khan had deteriorated over the years. Although they had briefly been together during the anti-Ayub movement, they became arch rivals later. Asghar Khan always maintained that Bhutto bore a major portion of the blame for the loss of East Pakistan. On 23 January 1977, Asghar Khan said that, after coming into power, the PNA would try those responsible for the dismemberment of Pakistan (Chishti 1996: 79). Obviously, such a threat was directed not only at Yahya and his clique but also at Bhutto.

On the other hand, Bhutto was notorious for ridiculing and even using abusive language against his opponents, including Asghar Khan. Former Inspector General Police and Special Intelligence Adviser to Bhutto, Rao Abdur Rashid, has alleged that Asghar Khan also used abusive language against Bhutto, and was the first to mention that he would see to it that Bhutto was hanged (Rashid 2010: 177). In any case, the election campaign progressively degenerated into a bitter and violent confrontation. The opposition took recourse to the notorious bogey of the Pakistan movement: that 'Islam was in danger'. The PPP retaliated by describing the opposition as a collection of useless men serving vested interests.

The election results revealed that the PPP won 154 out of the 200 seats, while the PNA secured only 36 seats. Initially, the PNA claimed that rigging had taken place at fifteen seats, but later increased that figure to twenty and finally to forty, and declared that the newly-elected PPP government was illegitimate. Consequently, the PNA boycotted the provincial elections that followed on 10 March, and claimed that the PPP had resorted to bogus voting (Chishti 1996: 88). The Jamaat-e-Islami's supreme leader, Maulana Maududi, gave a call for Bhutto's overthrow, which was followed by a display of street power and violent clashes that took place in many parts of the country between the PNA, PPP supporters, and the police. The Islamists, in particular, targeted Lahore's cinemas and set many ablaze; their calls for Nizam-e-Mustafa were raised loud and shrill. The PNA seemed determined to bring the government down.

The massive demonstrations and agitations rudely shook the overconfident and triumphant Bhutto. On 21 April, the government clamped martial law on Karachi, Hyderabad, and Lahore, followed by press censorship. Apparently, the military high command had been consulted and gave Bhutto their backing. That temporarily dampened the PNA's resolve to bring the government down through agitation and strikes. However, Asghar Khan took the view that the opposition should try to lobby the support of the ruling generals; many retired military commanders, including Gul Hassan and Rahim Khan, were drafted into this role (Taseer 1979: 172–3). This was followed by the opposition calling on General Zia to present their grievances. At that stage, Bhutto also started alleging that the United States was involved in a plot to oust him. Dennis Kux has observed:

> During an emotional address in the National Assembly on April 28, 1977, the prime minister charged that the United States was financing a 'vast, colossal, huge international conspiracy' to oust him from power. Bhutto alleged that Washington was punishing him for opposing US Vietnam policy, for backing the Arab cause against Israel, and for refusing to bow to Washington's pressure on the nuclear processing issue (Kux 2001: 230).

In any event, things began to get out of control for the government. When the agitators took out a procession in Lahore, in defiance of the martial law, the military refused to intervene. It was the police that used teargas to disperse them. In some other parts of the country, as well, local military commanders refused to take determined action (Khan 2008: 93). In a state of panic, Bhutto made further concessions to demands for the enforcement of Islam. Thus, instead of Sunday, Friday was declared as the day of rest. A ban was imposed on the sale and consumption of alcohol, as well as on gambling.

Bhutto offered to hold talks with PNA leaders and went to meet Maududi at his home in Lahore. This was followed by further talks with other PNA leaders but, by 4 July, it became clear that a political impasse had taken place (Mazari 2001: 476). Finally, on 5 July 1977, the military staged a coup on the orders of General Muhammad Zia-ul-Haq. One of the key players instrumental in taking the decision to overthrow Bhutto, Lieutenant General Faiz Ali Chishti, corps commander of Rawalpindi, denied that any agreement had been reached between the government and the opposition. He justified the military takeover as imperative to saving the country from civil war:

> Had Mr Bhutto signed the peace agreement with the PNA, there would have been no coup d'ëtat....Our task was to separate the rival parties and to take the political leaders into protective custody....Gen Zia did not come to power through a conspiracy. He was sucked in by circumstances. And in the final analysis Mr Bhutto was himself responsible for bringing General Zia into power (Chishti 1996: 134).

In any case, Bhutto and members of his cabinet were arrested; senior PPP and PNA leaders were also detained. Zia announced that martial law had been imposed, the constitution suspended, all assemblies dissolved, and promised that elections would be held within 90 days. He then ordered the release of Bhutto and the other leaders. On 29 July, Bhutto was released and headed for his hometown of Larkana where he received a rousing welcome. Instead of lying low, he decided to tour across Pakistan. His meetings attracted mammoth crowds as people lined up along the railway line to welcome him. The response in Lahore, the Punjab capital, was massive. One of the witnesses at the Lahore gathering, Ahmed Faqih, remembers hearing Bhutto say that there was no reason to worry. While August and September belonged to the military government and its PNA collaborators, October would mark the return of the PPP as elections would prove that it enjoyed the trust of the people. Things came to a head when Bhutto visited Multan, in southern Punjab. The administration tried, in vain, to prevent a huge gathering. Disorder and tumult followed. Moreover, Bhutto had behaved rudely with General Zia when they met after the coup; his wife, Nusrat Bhutto, had displayed similar hostility towards him (Taseer 1979: 173–5). Bhutto was re-arrested on 3 September, this time accused of authorising the murder of a political opponent in March 1974. In the actual ambush, allegedly ordered by Bhutto, the father of the target, Ahmed Raza Kasuri, once a PPP stalwart, was killed (Khan 2008: 119). General Zia now began to describe Bhutto as a 'murderer and corrupt villain' (Taseer 1979: 173).

However, things, took a dramatic turn when, ten days later, a Lahore High Court judge, Justice Samdani, threw out the case against Bhutto on the grounds that the evidence against him was contradictory and incomplete. Three days later, Zia arrested Bhutto again on the same charges, this time under martial law. When the PPP organized demonstrations, Zia exploited the volatile situation to cancel the upcoming elections. Thereafter, a 'judicial process' followed that seemed determined to prove Bhutto guilty. Ironically, Masood Mahmood, director general of the FSF, testified against Bhutto asserting that Bhutto had ordered Kasuri's assassination and that four members of the Federal Security Force had organized the assassination on Bhutto's orders. The four alleged confessed to their role but one of them later recanted, declaring that his confession had been extracted from him under torture. The counter-evidence and arguments put forth by the defence were ignored, and not even recorded in the verdict that declared him to be the mastermind in the conspiracy to assassinate Kasuri – but which, instead, resulted in the death of his father, Nawab Muhammad Khan Kasuri.

The five judges' bench of the Lahore High Court passed a death sentence on Bhutto. An appeal in the Pakistan Supreme Court resulted in a split four-to-three majority decision upholding the death sentence. On 24 March 1979, the Supreme Court dismissed the appeal. The four judges who had found him guilty were Punjabis, while the three who wanted to acquit him were non-Punjabis. Bhutto was hanged at the Central Jail, Rawalpindi, on 4 April 1979. No great agitation or popular uprising broke out, to protest the hanging of Pakistan's only democratically-elected prime minister, partly because the martial law regime had successfully repressed the PPP by then and partly because many of his close associates had either left the party in frustration or been compelled to leave or been thrown out.

Conspiracy theories about what brought Bhutto down are legion. In his book, *If I am Assassinated* (1979) – written while in prison and smuggled out and published posthumously in India – Bhutto asserted that General Zia initially admitted to the *Newsweek*, *BBC*, and *UPI* that the prime minister 'did sincerely attempt to reach an agreement with the opposition. In fact what Mr Bhutto agreed to was probably the maximum that any politician could agree to' (Bhutto 1979: 4). Bhutto refuted the White Paper, later published by the martial law regime on 25 July 1978, alleging that a serious law and order situation had emerged, threatening the security and integrity of the country, because of a deadlock in the negotiations between his government and the opposition. Instead, he claimed that an agreement had been reached with the PNA on 4 July, and only minor points needed to be sorted out the next day, when the military staged the coup (ibid.). He went on to allege that the military had been planning the coup for quite some time; also, not only had Pakistani capitalists, but also foreign powers, funded the PNA campaign against him – and that the funds from the external sources were far greater. He obliquely alluded to American involvement – as a consequence of his defiance of the US by going ahead and acquiring the nuclear processing plant.

In fact, during the height of the PNA movement, the PPP had begun to allege that the United States was backing the opposition and millions of dollars had been brought in in sacks and distributed to the miscreants (Rashid 2010: 176–7). This impelled the US Secretary of State, Cyrus Vance, to write a letter to Bhutto dated 29 April 1977 in which he categorically refuted such charges. Among other things, he wrote, 'We have given no assistance, financial or otherwise, to any political organization or individuals in Pakistan' (Jain 2007a: 97). In any case, according to Bhutto, the key villain in the alleged conspiracy against him was Mian Tufail Muhammad of the Jamaat-e-Islami who was in close contact with General Zia (Bhutto 1979: 169–72). The rest of the book is an attempt to account for his indefatigable commitment to make Pakistan self-reliant and militarily strong.

> The weakness in the chain of arguments is that Bhutto does not explain why the military first set him free, if a conspiracy to get rid of him had existed for some time. Also, he does not explain why the military

would be party to some foreign hand's attempt to punish Bhutto for acquiring the reprocessing plant. It is more likely that the conspiracy to get rid of him began to take form only after he started to tour the country and pulled mammoth crowds to his gatherings.

11

General Zia Braces the Fortress of Islam

The military returned to the political domain after six and a half years of a hectic civilian rule that had been democratic, authoritarian, populist, and vindictive. While he had been in power, Bhutto had dominated the political arena virtually all by himself. But, the India-centric orientation of the Pakistani state remained unchanged. In fact, Bhutto had taken a number of measures to bolster the doctrine that a credible defence against the much bigger foe on the eastern front was imperative to Pakistan's survival. It is needless to emphasise that such a conviction enjoyed an upsurge after the breakup of Pakistan – which the Pakistani establishment found expedient to ascribe entirely to India's nefarious designs. However, no military confrontation took place between the two countries during Bhutto's time in office. On the contrary, the Simla Agreement and the return of the Pakistani POWs helped defuse tensions. Both Z.A. Bhutto and Indira Gandhi were constrained, by challenges to their governments from domestic opposition, to turn inwards.

Zia inherited a highly volatile Pakistan, and his immediate concern was to establish his hold over the political process. He had overthrown an elected, though beleaguered, prime minister whose popularity had plummeted during the PNA movement post-March 1977, but then displayed a dramatic surge when he was released on 29 July and remained free till he was rearrested on 3 September – on the charge of ordering a political opponent's murder. If anything, Pakistan was a profoundly polarized society and Zia had to develop tactics and a strategy that would ensure the military government's continuance. Simultaneously, more than any other ruler of Pakistan, he was committed to substantiating and consolidating the two-nation theory – not merely as an identity concern to distinguish Pakistan from India, but as an ambitious ideological enterprise in its own right. To achieve such objectives, he augmented the ideological and cultural indoctrination of the military – as an Islamic fighting force armed with armament that enhanced its defensive and offensive capabilities to deal with India. Such undertakings took place while Zia sought transformative nation and state building.

The Immediate Political Challenges

Zia began by suspending – not abrogating – the 1973 constitution. He promised to hold free and fair elections within 90 days, and hand power over to the elected representatives of the people. Martial law was imposed throughout the country. As political parties were not banned, they began to prepare for the forthcoming elections in October. However, Zia changed course and began to argue that he had discovered gross irregularities that had been committed by the PPP regime. This stand received support from the PNA, especially Asghar Khan. The dramatic revival of support for Z.A. Bhutto most probably convinced the PNA politicians that they stood no chance in a free and fair election, and so started a chorus with the refrain that those responsible for the misuse of power should be held accountable before the holding of fresh elections (Baxter 1991: 31).

On 1 March 1978, the government went a step further by banning political activities, but not political parties. Several pro-PPP newspapers were closed down. Journalists who dared write critical comments were severely punished, including obscene public whippings. Writers, poets, and intellectuals were penalized in a brutal manner (Bhutto 2010: 200–2). In any case, the government declared that general elections would be held in 1979. Several PNA parties, including the Muslim League and the Jamaat-e-Islami, permitted their members to join the cabinet.

In a BBC interview given the day his father was hanged, Murtaza Bhutto pledged to avenge his father's death; the organisation, Al-Zulfikar, was formed and its bases established in neighbouring Afghanistan. In 1981, Al-Zulfikar cadres hijacked a PIA airliner. An army officer, Major Shahid Rahim, who was on board the flight was killed before it landed at Kabul. It was then allowed to proceed to the Syrian capital, Damascus, where the Syrians allowed the hijackers to land. The drama came to an end on 15 March. Zia agreed to release fifty-four PPP men in jail, while the plane was allowed to return to Pakistan.

Several other operations, including murderous attacks on government functionaries and collaborators of Zia, were carried out in Pakistan. Some assassination attempts were also made on Zia, including the firing of a Soviet-origin SAM 7 at a PAF plane carrying Zia in February 1982. The Indian spy agency Research & Analysis Wing (R&AW), was allegedly involved in a plan (originating in London) aimed at liquidating Zia. Its ringleader and other operatives were arrested in Lahore when they arrived to take delivery of the weapons that R&AW was to provide. Pakistan alleged that Al-Zulfikar had set up training camps in India and Libya as well as Afghanistan; it was also allegedly assisted by the Soviet Union and Syria (Hussain 2010: 270–2).

Al-Zulfikar, however, failed to establish a popular base in Pakistani society and so was unable to set in motion any sort of popular resistance or revolution that would cause a major societal upheaval. Moreover, in the two provinces that had historically always had bad relations with the federal government, the martial law regime enjoyed goodwill among the Pakhtun and Baloch leaders – while Bhutto had jailed them, it was Zia who released them. Local bodies elections were held in September 1979, but on a non-party basis. That was to become a matter of principle for Zia, who believed that political parties were divisive and against the supposedly consensus-based political traditions of Islam (ibid., 273). Nevertheless, a large number of pro-PPP candidates were elected. The government responded by postponing the national and provincial assemblies' elections scheduled for 17 and 20 November 1979, once again invoking the need to maintain law and order. Additionally, parties were also banned.

Nusrat Bhutto had appealed to the Supreme Court against the proclamation of martial law. The Supreme Court ruled that the martial law regime could 'perform all such acts and promulgate legislative measure, which fell within the scope of the law of necessity, including the power to amend the Constitution' (quoted in Baxter 1991: 34). While Zia's opponents saw it as supportive of the martial law government, the Zia regime was irked as it perceived it as an attempt to decide whether a measure was or was not within the scope of the law of necessity. Consequently, Zia promulgated the Provisional Constitution Order of 1980, which removed that possibility by excluding all martial law actions from the jurisdiction of the courts. In future, laws and decrees issued by the military government could not be reviewed by any court. This assertion was overruled by the Quetta High Court. The government responded by issuing the Provincial Constitution Order of 1981, which supplemented the 1980 Order by requiring the judges of the Supreme and high courts to take an oath to 'act faithfully in accordance with the Provisional Constitution Order of 1981 and abide by it' (quoted in Baxter 1991: 34). Some judges resigned in protest but others accepted the new rules. The net result was that the subordination of the court system, to the martial law system, was fully consummated.

Although political parties had already been banned, the PPP and several smaller parties formed the Movement for the Restoration of Democracy (MRD) in February 1981. Its main mission was to work towards the ending of martial law and for holding free elections in accordance with the suspended 1973 constitution. MRD activism was, at that time, largely confined to Sindh though some agitation had also taken place in Punjab. The government retaliated with full fury. Labour unions were banned and trade union activists rounded up. In particular, suspected Al-Zulfikar activists and sympathisers were hunted down all over Pakistan. Torture was employed extensively. Consequently, the movement in Sindh, as well as elsewhere, collapsed under the full weight of state repression. Some 300 Sindhis died in the police and military operations (Kardar 1992: 313; Khan 1983: 168–70). The only parts of Sindh that remained passive were the Mohajir strongholds of Karachi and Hyderabad.

Having crushed the MRD movement, General Zia arranged a referendum in 1984 on the Islamic character of Pakistan. The people were asked to vote on whether the people endorsed the process of Islamization of laws begun by the government. The government claimed a turnout of sixty-four percent, of which ninety-six percent were reported to have voted in favour of General Zia's reforms. However, international news agencies such as Reuters and the Manchester Guardian reported the turnout to be as low as ten percent (Bhutto 2008a: 270). Next, in January 1985, Zia called for national elections. However, the candidates had to contest as private individuals. In the absence of political parties, ethnic ties such as those based on biradari (patrimonial lineages), sect, tribe, and other such particularistic differences became the basis for vote-gathering (Mehdi 1988: 31). Zia appointed, from amongst the elected members of the National Assembly, a relatively unknown Sindhi, Mohammad Khan Junejo, as prime minister.

After handing over power to Junejo, Zia lifted martial law and got the new legislature to retroactively accept all his actions of the past eight years, including his coup in 1977. More importantly, he armed himself with the constitutional authority to dominate the political system through several amendments to the constitution, most notably the Eighth Amendment. Article 58 2(b) conferred powers on the president to dissolve the lower house of parliament, the National Assembly – though not the upper house, the Senate – if, in his opinion, 'a situation has arisen in which the Government of the Federation cannot be carried on in accordance with the provisions of the Constitution and an appeal to the electorate is necessary'.

The MQM and ISI

Notwithstanding such manipulations, Zia continued to worry about the volatile Sindh province. Ethnic tensions between the indigenous Sindhis and Urdu-speaking Mohajirs had begun to emerge in the early 1970s, and a number of skirmishes between militants from both groups had occurred. A Sindhi separatist tendency had emerged soon after independence but remained marginal. The rise of the PPP, led by a Sindhi, had resulted in such separatism being further marginalised but it revived when Bhutto was overthrown and executed. The radicalisation of Sindhis propelled apprehensive Mohajirs to organise themselves along ethnic lines.

Thus, on 18 March 1984, the Mohajir Quami Movement (MQM) was founded by Altaf Hussain, the non-office-holding supreme leader of the MQM. It is now an open secret that the MQM was a creation of the ISI, and that Zia had masterminded its formation. This was confirmed by General Mirza Aslam Beg, who succeeded Zia as COAS after the latter's sudden death in an air crash (Hasan 2007: 7). Zia wanted to curb the rise of the PPP at any cost. The MQM was also allegedly supplied its arms by the ISI. The MQM was encouraged to claim that the Mohajirs were a separate nationality – thus raising the spectre of a break-up of Sindh along ethnic lines. Ironically, Zia was able to placate the main protagonist of Sindhi separatism, G.M. Syed, from whom the PPP had wrested away the mantle of Sindhi nationalism in 1972. Thus, support for the MQM and dissensions within Sindhi political factions effectively blunted Sindhi separatism and, at the same time, weakened the PPP-inspired insurgency, especially in the Mohajir-dominated key cities of Karachi and Hyderabad. Such a strategy in the political realm, however, was only a partial expression of Zia's overall agenda to consolidate military rule.

Islamising the Garrison State

Zia was also determined to implement a transformative programme of change that would affect all sectors of society. Under his patronage, the garrison state – a polity deriving its identity from perceived existentialist threats from external as well asinternal enemies – acquired incontrovertible Islamist features. Stephen Cohen has asserted that, from the beginning, the Pakistan military considered itself an Islamic fighting force. He found that 'the professional journals of the Army are filled with studies of the question of Islamization of the military, and all come back to the question of the degree to which traditional Indian Army patterns need to be altered to Islamic principles' (Cohen 1992: 37). Under Zia, the unit maulvis (clerics) were upgraded and given the rank of junior commissioned officer – on the pattern of the military chaplains in the US Army. He has also noted that heavy indoctrination into Islamism was not necessary for the armed forces because 'Islam naturally supports the idea of the military professional' (ibid., 139). Cohen's findings suggest that such a self-image varied from the moderate to the extreme, but the military retained the overall organisational structure and practices inherited from the colonial past. He does not mention that the cultivation of an Islamist army received approbation from the United States as it coincided with Pakistan's role as a frontline state in the so-called Afghan jihad.

At any rate, indoctrination was pursued with much greater zeal during Zia's term than asserted by Cohen. Such a process needs to be put in perspective, in light of the changing socio-cultural background of the officer corps when Zia came into power. The old guard, mainly comprising Sandhurst-trained officers, was gradually replaced by an indigenised Pakistani officer class. Such a process started rather early and received expansionist spurts in the aftermaths of the 1947–48, 1965, and 1971 wars with India. The new officers were from middle, and lower-middle class, backgrounds – and no longer exclusively from the select districts of northern Punjab or NWFP. The relaxed lifestyle in which music, dance bands, and alcohol were part of the social milieu prevalent in the officers' messes had already received a jolt when Bhutto opportunistically banned the consumption of alcohol. A catalyst was needed to push the military into an Islamist direction. General Zia was eminently suited to play that role.

Zia's overall transformation of the Pakistani state and society along Islamist lines envisaged the establishment of a garrison state in which the military would stand out clearly as an ideological institution. Such a weltanschauung could only be realised in practice through social engineering on a grand scale. However, as some writers have noted, in the case of Zia such conviction was tempered by a prudent assessment of what is possible rather than what should ideally exist. His fundamentalist proclivities apart, Zia was a practical and modern man. He could sense that Pakistan was too complex and diversified culturally, ethnically, and in sectarian terms. Therefore, wholesale imitation and replication of either the Iranian, or rather the Saudi, model that he admired was not possible. Nevertheless, he took determined steps to foster an Islamist garrison state that harked back to a golden age of conquest and expansion, as well as a supposedly ideal and just social order that existed at the time of the dawn of Islam.

No doubt, a commitment to make Pakistan into an ideal polity infused with Islamic ideas of justice and progress, or more fundamentalist versions of it, had been part of the official rhetoric of all governments. However, no previous government undertook the necessary and sufficient measures to construct a national identity that comprehensively reflected the ideology of an Islamist garrison state. Rather, rhetoric and ad hoc measures characterised the conduct of governments before General Zia came to power.

Hitherto, the modernist elite had been dithering between their commitment to democracy, on the one hand, and political Islam, on the other. Such ambivalence was conspicuous by its absence from Zia's single-minded commitment to a patently, anti-liberal, anti-democratic, anti-minorities, and anti-women agenda. He wanted to establish a social order 'in which all sectors of life including administration, judiciary, banking, trade, education, agriculture, industry and foreign affairs are regulated in accordance with Islamic principles' (Noman 1988: 141). Consequently, a range of 'reforms' was undertaken to realize the hegemony of an Islamist garrison state in Pakistan.

The Legal Framework Order, issued by General Yahya Khan as martial law administrator, had mentioned an 'Ideology of Pakistan' that, under Bhutto, began to acquire the trappings of Islamism; but, it was Zia who completed it in proper measure. He consulted a wide range of ulema but the ideas of the amir of the JI, Syed Abul Ala Maududi, clearly exercised the profoundest influence on him. Maududi's theory of the state was based on an unhistorical idealization of the pristine Islamic community and polity that Prophet Muhammad (PBUH) had founded and was continued by his immediate successors, especially the first two caliphs, Abu Bakr and Umar. The laws and cultural practices of that period prescribing strict segregation of men and women, and non-Muslims paying the protection tax, jizya, have been considered to be authoritatively binding on subsequent generations of Muslims (Maududi 1979a; 1979b; 1980). Equally, Maududi wrote a highly dogmatic treatise, Al-Jihad Fi-al Islam, in which he subscribed to the classic dichotomy of the world – into dar-ul-Islam (abode of peace where Islamic law prevails) and dar-ul-harb (enemy territory where non-Muslims rule) – as propounded by the early jurists of Islam. According to such disposition, peace between Islamic and non-Islamic states could be established only temporarily because such states were, in principle, at war. Resorting to circumlocutions and chicanery about jihad being justified when Islam and Islamic communities are threatened, he also justified jihad as offensive warfare when non-Muslims do not accept Islam. He had no problem in upholding outmoded practices such as slavery and concubinage – non-Muslims defeated in war who are unable to pay ransom are to be enslaved, with women entering the harem as chattel of their owners (Maududi 1981).

Maududi's theories were almost identical to the ideologue of the Muslim Brotherhood, the Egyptian Syed Qutb, and only superficially different in detail from those set forth by the Shiite ideologue Imam Khomeini. Neither Maududi, nor Qutb, nor Khomeini differ in any way from traditional Sharia law pertaining to international relations: dogmatic Sharia is incognizant of peace based on modern notions of respect for sovereignty and the territorial integrity of states as upheld by the UN Charter (1945). With regard to personal beliefs on doctrine and adherence to rites and rituals, Zia is generally believed to have subscribed to the puritanical Deobandi school of radical Islam. Some people who knew him personally say that he spent long hours at Sufi shrines, particularly at that of Ali bin Usman Al-Hajweri – popularly known as Data Sahib – in Lahore. If that is true, then he seemed to have been quite eclectic, combining radical Islam with the folksy Barelvi– Sunni Islam. The irony, of course, was that General Zia had no qualms about privately inviting Bollywood superstar Shatrughan Sinha to his home to meet his mentally challenged daughter who adored Indian film stars and especially Shatrughan

Sinha. He became a family friend and used to visit Pakistan regularly. That relationship continued even after Zia's death (*The Tribune*, 4 August 2005).

Legal Reforms

Already, in 1977, Zia announced his intention of introducing Islamic punishments for a number of offences, as prescribed in the Quran. After a period of preparation and consultation with Islamist scholars, the government, in 1979, announced the imposition of the Hudood Ordinance, i.e. punishments for the offences of adultery (death by stoning), fornication (one hundred lashes), false accusation of adultery (eighty lashes), drinking alcohol (eighty lashes), theft (cutting off of the right hand), highway robbery (when the offence is only robbery, cutting off of hands and feet; for robbery with murder, death either by the sword or crucifixion) (Munir 1980: 124–32).

A Federal Shariat Court was established in 1980 to try Hudood offences. A special bench of the Pakistan Supreme Court, called the Shariat Appellate Bench, comprising three Muslim judges was established to hear appeals against the verdicts of the Federal Shariat Court (Usmani 1990: 68–71). Although scores of people were tried for Hudood offences, and sentences were passed that prescribed stoning and amputation of limbs, the sentences were changed to prison sentences at the higher levels of appeal. Immense international pressure, as well as protests from the highly-educated liberal sections of society organised in NGOs, played an important role in creating an atmosphere that made the judiciary at the higher level change its mind. On the other hand, initially, the whipping and hanging of some culprits was meted out publicly in front of large crowds that assembled to see the macabre spectacles. However, after a while, such punishments were removed from the public sphere and were carried out in the jails. However, the military regime remained determined to institutionalise the discrimination of women and non-Muslims with the view to creating a chaste Islamic nation.

Women

In 1980, a circular was issued to all government offices prescribing a proper Muslim dress-code for female employees. The wearing of a chador (loose cloth covering the head) was made obligatory. A campaign to eliminate obscenity and pornography was also announced. It, however, took the form of a campaign against the general emancipation and equal rights of women. Leading Muslim theologians hostile to female emancipation were brought onto national television to justify the various restrictions on women. Moreover, the legal status and rights of women diminished dramatically because of the Hudood laws and their examination by the Shariat courts. For example, rape, as sexual intercourse forced upon a woman, is not recognized in the Quran, but it was acknowledged by Muslim jurists as zina bil jabr or sexual intercourse under duress. Under the Anglo-Muhammadan codes that Pakistan had inherited from the colonial system, the evidence of the victim was accepted in rape cases. Under the Zina ordinance, neither the evidence of the victim nor that of any other woman was admissible. To prove that adultery and rape has been committed, the traditional requirement of four male witnesses was instituted. Moreover, PPC Section 375, as the earlier law on rape was called, had protected girls under the age of fourteen by providing that, even with their consent, sexual intercourse with them would constitute rape. This immunity was not included in the zina ordinance (Mehdi 1994: 123). In 1984, a new Law of Evidence was adopted which reduced the evidence of a female witness to half, in worth, of a male witness – pertaining to written financial transactions – in a court of law (ibid., 231–2; Weiss 1986). The cumulative effect of such measures was, undoubtedly, that the legal and social position of women was greatly weakened.

Noted women's rights activists Asma Jahangir and Hina Jilani have demonstrated that such legislation resulted in the meting out of harsh punishments to many victims simply because they could not produce male witnesses who could give evidence that they saw the actual penetration of the vagina by the male phallus of the accused (Jahangir and Jilani 2003). The Human Rights Commission of Pakistan noted that the incidence of so-called honour killings by close relatives, or through hired killers, increased significantly in the wake of the legal and social oppression introduced by General Zia (State of Human Rights 1991–2006). As the general situation of women deteriorated, some of the educated women of the larger cities of Lahore, Karachi, and Islamabad brought out demonstrations demanding a stop to the anti-women campaign. Such agitation did little to mitigate the hardened climate against women (Mumtaz and Shaheed 1987).

Non-Muslims

With regard to the non-Muslims in Pakistan, the general atmosphere became dramatically hostile after Zia introduced the blasphemy law in 1982. It declared any insult to Prophet Muhammad (pbuh) and Islam to be a major offence. The maximum punishment prescribed for it was life imprisonment. In 1986, blasphemy was made even harsher when the death penalty was included as the maximum punishment. Section 295-C of the Penal Code declared that:

> Use of derogatory remarks etc. in respect of the Holy Prophet: Whether by words, either spoken or written, or by visible representations, or by any imputation, innuendo or insinuation, directly or indirectly, defiles the sacred name of the Holy Prophet (peace by upon him) shall be punishable with death, or imprisonment for life, and shall be liable to fine (Ahmed 2005: 203).

In subsequent years, the blasphemy law was invoked many times to punish alleged offenders; it was mostly Christians who were targeted for blasphemy. The trial procedure was deeply flawed and unsafe. Almost invariably, the lower courts would sentence the accused to severe punishment. However, protests from Pakistani human rights organizations and other NGOs, Western states, the UN, Amnesty International, and other such entities compelled the superior courts to either acquit them on some technical grounds or to allow them to seek asylum in the West. In some cases, fanatics brutally murdered individuals who they believed had blasphemed. Only two such culprits have been convicted for these extra-judicial executions. There have been many cases of churches being burnt and bombed, and of Christians, especially women, being forced to convert to Islam.

The declaration, in 1974, of the Ahmadiyya community as non-Muslims had solidified Pakistan's confessional character. In 1983–84, further restrictions were imposed on the Ahmadiyya community. It was forbidden to use Islamic nomenclature for its worship rituals, places of worship, and so on. Attacks on Ahmadi places of worship increased as a result. Over the years, the anti-Ahmadi legislation resulted in vicious attacks, resulting in hundreds of deaths of members of the Ahmadiyya community.

In 1985, separate electorates for non-Muslims were instituted. Non-Muslim voters were not to vote for general seats in the general elections;

they were to only vote for non-Muslim candidates. Zia argued that such a procedure would be more effective in enabling non-Muslims to get elected and represent their interests in the legislatures because, if they contested general seats, they stood no chance of getting elected. The reality was that the already socially alienated religious minorities were, as a consequence, politically excluded from the mainstream Muslim nation also. A Christian leader and decorated 1965 war hero, Group Captain Cecil Chaudhry of the Pakistan Air Force, expressed his disappointment over such blatant anti-minority laws in an article, 'Remembering Our Heroes', published in the Defence Journal of June 2001:

> In Pakistan our political order is based on religious apartheid through the Separate Electorate System.... The Separate Electorate System, thrust upon the nation by Zia-ul-Haq in 1985, divides the entire nation into five religious groups and does not allow any political interaction between any two of the groups. The seats of the National and the Provincial Assemblies are so divided that Muslims, Christians, Hindus, Ahmadis, and other religious minorities can only contest for and vote within their own group. This system has completely broken down social harmony thus paving the way for sectarianism strife.... A political system so deeply rooted in religion when allowed to perpetuate will most definitely cause dissensions within each group and give rise to religious extremism, even to the extent of spreading terrorism in the name of religion.... The non-Muslim citizens have proved that they do not want the Separate Electorates by very effectively boycotting the first two phases of the on-going Union Council elections.... Having said this let me state that in India the extremist Hindu is targeting the Christians mainly. I also believe this situation will not last and we can already see things improving in India.... With deep regret I have to admit that there is no comparison. India is a proven secular country and the state of religious tolerance and equality is far better than that of Pakistan.... If this government allows the present state of gross sectarianism to continue we are doomed as a nation (Amin 2001).

On a personal note, Cecil Chaudhry believed that his promotion beyond group captain was overruled by Zia because he was Christian. On the whole, it must be granted that after Zia introduced comprehensive Islamisation, the overall ideological stance and cultural milieu became manifestly biased against the religious minorities; moreover, the Islamisation measures that he introduced provided a basis for institutionalised discrimination. That trend has continued into the present times because no succeeding government has dared to repeal the laws that Zia had enacted.

Sectarian Polarization

Hitherto, not only were Sunnis of all descriptions, but also the Ithna Ashari Shias, reckoned to be Muslims. However, certain moves during his time began to expose the brittle nature of such categorisation because, doctrinally, Zia harboured the Deobandi and, politically, Jamaat-e-Islami sympathies. The other Sunni sub-sects and Shias were concerned that they would be marginalised. Not only did the Shias object, but many Sunni sub-sects also had reservations about the authority of the Deobandi scholars. In the economic field, banking reforms were introduced which ostensibly eliminated 'interest' and replaced it with 'profit' (Ahmed 1999: 231). The alms tax, zakat, was imposed on Muslim citizens. However, the Shias refused to pay zakat to the government of General Zia-ul-Haq as the government was Sunni in its orientation and, therefore, could not claim zakat from them. The government initially dismissed the Shia demand, which resulted in widespread agitation by the Shias who threatened to paralyse the government and marched to Islamabad in their thousands. The unruly protests and demonstrations that ensued in the capital resulted in open conflict with the police, and a serious law and order situation was created. However, with the theocratic regime founded by the Ayatollahs in neighbouring Iran inspiring them to resist real and imagined Sunni oppression, the agitators defied the police. Such determined resistance forced the government to change its policy: Shias were exempted from paying zakat (ibid.). In one sense, assertive Shia behaviour inadvertently helped in conferring a Sunni identity to the Pakistani state. Constitutionally, Pakistan did not distinguish between Sunnis and Shias as both were considered bona fide Muslims but, after the Shias politicized and sectarianized the zakat tax – which was meant for the use of the poor and needy – the Shia–Sunni chasm became even wider.

Such cleavages were severely compounded in the wake of the contest between Iran and Saudi Arabia to lead the Muslim world. Both, staggeringly rich because of income from oil, began to activate their sectarian affiliates all over the world. In Pakistan, such a contest erupted into a proxy war in the 1990s between militias – receiving funding and extremist propaganda via audio-cassettes and video films – from these two centres of Islamic fundamentalism (Ahmed 1998: 176–8).

Educational Reforms

A search for an 'ideological basis' of education had already started, in 1947, when Pakistan came into being. The emphasis was on Islamizing education though, at that time, it was interpreted as the promotion of a social-democratic culture and not fundamentalism. Religious education was to be given priority. The emphasis on Islam was also meant to delegitimise provincialism and linguistic nationalism. However, Islamisation did not mean fundamentalism till Zia came to power (Rahman 2004: 7–17).

During Zia's long period in office, the process of long-term and deep indoctrination of society, through the educational system, began with a concerted effort – to infuse Islamic values and culture, so as to make the pupils feel that they were part of the universal Islamic Umma, make them fully aware of the purpose for which Pakistan was created, and inculcate abiding loyalty to Islam and Pakistan (ibid., 17). Textbooks covering the whole fourteen-year period, from primary school to university, were to be Islamised along fundamentalist lines. In his pioneering work on Pakistani textbook curricula, *The Murder of History* (1993), Pakistan's premier historian, Professor K.K. Aziz, examined sixty-six textbooks dealing with history, social studies, and Pakistan studies, from the elementary to the university level, and amply demonstrated the distortion of facts and twisting of ideas. Muslim invasions and conquerors received positive emphasis while Hindus and the Hindu religion were denigrated. Moreover, great emphasis was laid on glorifying the Pakistani military. It was asserted that, in the 1965 war, India was on the verge of being beaten by Pakistan and begged the United Nations to arrange a cease-fire (ibid., 153).

About the breakup of Pakistan, the textbooks blamed the Bengalis while India was projected as the villain of the piece (ibid., 154). Moreover, General Zia's Islamisation policy was praised as an honest attempt to fulfil the promise allegedly given by Jinnah to create an Islamic system of government (ibid., 158). Aziz, using a language that very closely resembles Lasswell's understanding of a controlled citizenry, wrote:

> The goal, it seems, is to produce a generation with the following traits: docility, inability to ask questions, capacity to indulge in pleasurable illusions, pride in wearing blinkers, willingness to accept guidance from above, alacrity to like and dislike things by order, tendency to ignore gaps in one's knowledge, enjoyment of make-belief, faith in the high value of pretences (ibid., 188).

Among the core themes that Aziz has identified in the textbooks are: support for military rule; glorification of war; and hatred of India (ibid., 190–3). The bottom line in Aziz's argument is that Pakistani pupils were being indoctrinated with a perverted religio-militarist ideology of hate. He told me, in London in 1996, that he has been subjected to threats and feared that his life may be in danger. Taking their cue from Aziz, other Pakistani academics dilated upon the pernicious effects of such curricula on the formation of attitudes and values. In her essay, 'History, Social Studies and Civics and the Creation of Enemies', Rubina Saigol has particularly focused on the negative implications of the national identity cultivated in the textbooks. The history of conquests by Muslim invaders, and the rise of the separatist movement among India Muslims, primarily hinges on casting Hinduism, Hindus, and India in a bad light. She has written:

> The main source of the construction of the Pakistan Self, are Indians in general, and Hindus in particular. Since Pakistan emerged within the political paradigm of the two-nation theory, which poses Hindus and Muslims as two irreconcilable communities, most identity-forming textbooks revolve around the story of the two nations. The latter consideration allows Hindus to play the major role of the national demon' (Saigol: 2003: 163).

Continuing, she has remarked that the merger of political Islam, into the Pakistani National Self, generates an obsessive, paranoid type of mindset in which a number of internal and external enemies of Islam and Pakistan are identified. Consequently, not only India but even Western nations and Israel are included among the enemy. However, Hinduism and India remain the paramount enemies and threats to Muslims and Pakistan. The message being inculcated through such textbooks is that Pakistan cannot enter into normal relations with India under any circumstances (ibid., 166–7). She has noted that, in the post-Zia period, emphasis has shifted from a macho-type glorification of Pakistan to the inculcation of fear of India as a bigger and better-armed enemy always on the look out to harm Pakistan.

The impact of such textbook curricula has indeed been profound and lasting. Thus, for example, A.H. Nayyar and Ahmad Salim of the Islamabad think-tank, Sustainable Development Policy Institute (SDPI), published a critical report on the educational curricula in 2004 entitled, The Subtle Subversion: The State of Curricula and Textbooks in Pakistan. Their joint article, 'Glorification of War and the Military' specifically highlights the emphasis on jihad (holy war), shahadat (martyrdom), ghazi (victor in war), shaheed (martyr), and so on in the textbooks (Nayyar and Salim 2004: 79–90).

In a televised discussion, Nayyar was attacked by a number of right-wing opponents for criticising qatal (killing). One of them, Ataul Haq Qasmi, was of the view that if feelings of jihad and shahadat were not inculcated in the pupils, then there was no point in mentioning the Quran, hadith (sayings of the Prophet Muhammad [pbuh]), and Allama Iqbal (Pakistan's national poet) in such textbooks. In other words, he was of the view that readiness to take up arms was the core message of Islam. Dushka Saiyid assumed a very similar stand and argued that there was nothing wrong with teaching jihad to children. Islam was not the religion of Christ, who taught its followers to turn the other cheek. She wondered how jihad could be wrong when it is directed against the Americans. Moreover, were Pakistanis supposed to prostrate themselves in front of India? She stated that Muslim history was full of jihad; the Holy Prophet himself took part in jihad (Ahmed 2004).

A dispassionate assessment of the textbook curricula would reveal that Aziz, Saigol, Nayyar, and Saleem approached the purpose of education as a means of producing a balanced and rational frame of mind that would help pupils become good and responsible citizens of a liberal, pluralist society. On the other hand, those who had authored the textbooks aimed at using the textbooks to produce a mindset consistent with the fundamental logic underlying the two-nation theory: that Hindus and Muslims were two separate nations, and Pakistan was an ideological state wedded to confessional criteria. It had been demanded in negation of India as the homeland of all communities. The founder of Pakistan himself had laid down the foundations of a We–They mutually exclusive dichotomy between Hindus and Muslims, and followed that position relentlessly in his struggle for Pakistan. Jinnah's presidential address at the March 1940 annual session of the Muslim League in Lahore very forcefully underlined the irreconcilability between Hindus and Muslims (Speeches of Mr Jinnah 1968: 151–72). What the textbooks did was add patently militaristic overtones to such reasoning.

Islamist Military

Zia certainly realised that the Islamisation process underway in other branches of the state and society would be inadequate without the military being transformed into an Islamist institution as well. In fact, the core institution for the consolidation of the Islamist garrison state had to be the military. In this regard, a book authored by Brigadier S.K. Malik, *The Quranic Concept of War* (1979), epitomises the philosophy of war and armed conflict that the military rulers of Pakistan wanted to inculcate in their men in order to transform them into Islamist warriors. It includes a most revealing foreword by General Zia, which includes the following:

> I write these few lines to commend Brigadier Malik's book on 'The Quranic Concept of War' to both soldier and civilian alike. Jehad Fi-Sabilillah [Holy War for God] is not the exclusive domain of the professional soldier, nor is it restricted to the application of military force alone.
>
> This book brings out, with simplicity, clarity, and precision, the Quranic philosophy on the application of military force, within the context of the totality that is JEHAD. The professional soldier in a Muslim army, pursuing the goals of a Muslim state, CANNOT become a 'professional' if he does not take on 'the colour of Allah' in all his activities (Malik 1979).

The author marshalled a number of arguments to establish that war is natural in human nature and, therefore, has been a part of human societies down the ages. However, warfare for territory, national self-interest, etc. have no place in the Quranic scheme of war. Proceeding on the classic jurisprudential dichotomy of Muslim jurists, that the world was divided into dar-ul-Islam (abode of peace where Islamic law prevails) and dar-ul-Harb (abode of strife under non-Muslim rule), Malik has asserted that it is obligatory for Muslims to defeat the non-Muslim enemies. He has quoted the Quranic verse that reads as follows, 'And fight them on until there is no more tumult or oppression, and there prevail justice and faith in Allah altogether and everywhere' (1979: 28). He has conceded that peace can be temporarily established, by treaty, with pagans. However, warfare can be initiated if the treaty is violated. Moreover, even if the agreement is not explicitly violated by the pagans, but the Islamic state suspects treason from the pagans, then the treaty can be broken (ibid., 30). Jews and Christians who agree to pay jizya can be taken under the protection of the Islamic state. Warfare against hypocrites – those who convert to Islam only in name but not in the true sense – is also justified. The author has summarised the Quranic theory of war in the following words, 'To recapitulate, in the Quranic perspective, the object of war is to obtain conditions of peace, justice and faith. To do so, it is essential to destroy the forces of oppression and persecution' (Malik 1979: 35).

It is not difficult to deduce, from such convoluted reasoning, that the author considered the preconditions for 'peace, justice and faith' to be fulfilled only if the Islamic order prevails all over the world. He reviewed the Quranic 'ethics of war', and concluded that 'the checks and controls imposed by the Holy Quran on the use of force have no parallel' (ibid., 49). At another point, he examined the Quranic strategy of war in which divine help, in the form of thousands of angels, is assured if it is fought properly (ibid., 55). Referring to the famous battles fought under the leadership of Muhammad (pbuh), he observed, 'We see that, on all these occasions, when God wishes to impose His will upon His enemies, He chooses to do so by casting terror in their hearts' (ibid., 57). Consequently, according to Malik:

> The Quranic military strategy thus enjoins us to prepare ourselves for war to the utmost in order to strike terror into the hearts of the enemies, known or hidden, while guarding ourselves from being terror-stricken by the enemy....Terror struck into the hearts of the enemies is not only a means, it is the end in itself. Once a condition of terror into the opponent's heart is obtained, hardly anything is left to be achieved. It is the point where the means and the end meet and merge. Terror is not means of imposing decision upon the enemy; it is the decision we wish to impose on him (ibid., 58–9).

As the purpose of an army is to strike terror into the hearts of the enemy, therefore it is both a matter of military preparation – to have the best trained and armed troops – as well as of ideological preparation. The ideological preparation would mean imbibing a strong faith in Islam and, especially, its call to jihad. Death on the battlefield, or on some other mission for the glory of Islam, is not to be feared because Allah ensures that such individuals will be amply rewarded in Paradise. Referring to a Quranic verse, Malik has described it as a bargain that God has made with believers who fight for him (ibid., 141). The book ends with a list of all the verses related to war (ibid., 147–50).

The aim of the book seems to be to present a 'Quranic theory of just war'. The problem is that, according to it, war is conceived of as an incessant and perpetual phenomenon rather than an occasional undertaking to defeat an oppressor; warfare would only cease with Islam defeating all un-Islamic forces and establishing global peace based on justice as defined by Islamic law. He has made the significant point that the Quranic approach to war is more humane and considerate: women, children, servants, and even slaves who might accompany their masters in war, would be spared, as would 'the blind, the monks, the hermits, the old, the physically deformed and the insane or mentally deficient' (ibid., 47). Such circumlocution and sophistry runs throughout his book. It is a typical amalgam of unbending dogmatism tempered by concerns to present it as a necessary evil to defeat and eradicate the forces of evil. That it may have become obsolete in the contemporary era, because of the Geneva Conventions or the UN Charter, is not entertained at any point in the book. On the contrary, it is a resounding call to arms under the mantle of jihad.

The 'Quranic concept of war' was never formally declared as the philosophy of the Pakistan military. It was, however, on the highly recommended reading list of the Command and Staff College, Quetta and the National Defence College, Islamabad. Since Zia had, himself, endorsed the book, it must have been treated with considerable seriousness – whether out of a strong conviction or for sheer instrumental reasons is difficult to assess. It was published around the time when the Afghan jihad was about to begin, and must have been one of the factors that easily convinced the US–Saudi sponsors of that jihad to adopt the Pakistan Army as its main operational channel for the anti-Soviet military campaign. Some dissenting voices, about the Islamisation of the military, are reproduced below. The remarks of an Indian officer, who fought against Pakistan in the 1965 and 1971 war, are also given.

Major (Retd.) Agha Humayun Amin

'I joined the Pakistan Military Academy Kakul as a cadet on 3 May 1981 and was commissioned in the tank corps in 11 Cavalry on 17 March 1983. At that time, Arabic had become compulsory subject in the academy. Many of the guest speakers were known for having some extreme views on religion. Evening prayers were compulsory. However, I am told that after 1983 religious indoctrination became more pronounced and reached its height when General M. Malik was the commandant at the academy. Brigadier S.K. Malik's, The Islamic Concept of War, was part of recommended readings at Staff College Quetta. It was considered a good investment, career-wise, to pray with senior officers. Most officers did it to please their superiors. I remember some absolute free thinkers who drank heavily doing it with promotion in mind. In 1984, Nazim Us Salat campaign was ordered. It meant that most army formations were sent on tableegh campaign (convincing people to follow Islam in letter and spirit). Notwithstanding such pious tasks, in December 1984 army units were tasked to stamp Zia's referendum ballots with a yes vote. Thus we were involved in blatant election rigging.

'On the whole, the so-called 'Islamization' measures only lowered professional standards. This happened from the very onset when cadets were recruited. Zia placed military officers in key civil posts. Thus for example, Admiral Sharif was recruited as the boss of the Federal Public Service Commission. His focus during the interviews with candidates was on religion alone. He asked questions like 'do you know dua-e-qanoot?' (prayer). He pronounced a top level candidate, Zafar Bukhari, as unfit for all key administrative positions and fit only for the postal services. The reason was that he had written in his exam that the leftist Faiz Ahmed Faiz was his favourite poet.'

An army officer who wants to remain anonymous has provided the following insights into how the egalitarian and congenial atmosphere in the officers' mess was subverted by the introduction of puritanical practices:

'Prior to the dry mess created by Bhutto, the officers' messes were places where senior and junior officers could meet and talk freely, sharing jokes and repartees and having a drink. We could easily disagree with our seniors and army matters were freely discussed and debated. There used to be dance and music. It was a very lively atmosphere in which we socialized and fraternized.

Of course there were the religious type who kept away but the general rule was that it is up to the individual to choose his life style and regimentation of morals and values was frowned upon.

'All that was reduced to naught with the Islamist inputs. Now, the walls in the messes and in the corridors hung verses from the Quran and each and every individual was expected to say the correct thing in line with the reigning ideology of the High Command. As a result the spontaneity and warmth that prevailed previously was supplanted by formalism and correctness. Debate and discussion disappeared and instead one was bombarded with sermons on chaste conduct. Such measures received full appreciation from the Americans. After the so-called Afghan jihad started Zia and his advisers made it a point to exaggerate the Islamist character of the army. Zia appeared on the cover of Time and Newsweek. At that time the Americans were all too keen that the Pakistan Army should become a jihadist institution.

'The officers were expected to join the ranks during the prayers. This might sound as something radically egalitarian but it was not. Standing together by no means broke down the hierarchies of rank and status. On the contrary, the officers had to play the role of moral leaders; most of the time this resulted in hypocritical behaviour rather than genuine conversion to piety.

'Previously Pakistan Christians would seek a career in the armed forces and were considered good fighters and patriotic Pakistanis, but Islamization discouraged them from coming to the messes. Over time they stopped seeking a career with us. That further accentuated the religious identity of the army. However, even Zia did not dare go so far as to encourage the divisions between Shias and Sunnis. The Pakistan Army, however, became an Islamist fighting force. The jihad in Afghanistan proved a bonanza to the Islamist forces who then were groomed into the art of Islamic warfare – a bogus art and science but which received patronage from the Chief and his coterie of advisers.

'Anti-India rhetoric was part of the overall grooming of the Pakistan Army but after General Zia became the COAS and later martial law administrator and president such an orientation became the raison d'être for the maintenance of armed forces ready to fight for the glory of Islam. The fact is that even then troops posted on the India-Pakistan border regularly interacted with one another. Many belonged to the same colonial regiments, others sometimes turned out to be from the same villages. Sometimes the trust became so great that one could visit the other side. I remember some Indian officers wanted to visit the famed Heera Mandi of Lahore (Diamond Market or Red Light Area) and they were taken there to a mujra (dance session with a courtesan), while our officers could visit Amritsar and other places to have a drink. The same would start shooting at each other whenever tensions arose. This is the truth.'

Brigadier (Retd.) Vijai Nair

Brigadier Nair of the Indian Army confirmed this in a long interview to me. He said: 'My family originally belonged to Kunjah in Gujrat district of West Punjab. I fought against Pakistan in both the 1965 and 1971 wars. Under normal conditions contacts between the two sides were very friendly and the officers would develop good rapport and behave with one another in a courteous and respectful manner. We exchanged greetings on a regular basis and even socialized. Conduct during war was of course a call to duty and both sides fought to the best of their abilities'.

12

The Afghan Jihad

As noted already, while Pakistan's national security paradigm had always been premised on the perceived threat from India, relations with Afghanistan – about the disputed Durand Line – had also been a cause for worry all along. During the Cold War, while Pakistan had co-opted itself into the US military strategy to prevent any southward movement towards the hot waters of the Arabian Sea, the Afghan monarchy had been cultivated by the USSR – although the Afghans did not enter into any military pact with the Soviet Union. The situation in Afghanistan was destabilised on 17 July 1973 when King Muhammad Zahir Shah (1933–73) was overthrown by his cousin Sardar Muhammad Daud Khan. Daud was a proactive Pakhtun nationalist who revived the controversy over the Durand Line with Pakistan. However, his rule was unpopular with sections of his population as he employed repression against both the leftists and the conservative sections of Afghan society. In June 1975, the Jamiat-e-Islami [no direct affiliate of the Pakistan Jamaat-e-Islami] attempted an overthrow of the government, which was crushed by the Daud government but resulted in many militants taking refuge in Pakistan. At that time, Z.A. Bhutto was in power in Pakistan. He ordered support for the insurgents (Farr, 1985: 94). Already, at that stage, the American CIA and the Pakistani ISI had begun to connect in order to bolster a resistance to the Daud regime. Thus, for example, the legendary Colonel Imam (Sultan Amir Tarrar) was sent to the United States in 1973 for training in insurgency warfare (Interview, 18 December 2008).

However, Daudals fell out with the Afghan communists. Consequently, an insurgency began to take shape under the leadership of the People's Democratic Party of Afghanistan (PDPA) – which represented the Afghan communists. On 27 April 1978, pro-PDPA officers of the Afghan Army overthrew Daud and executed his family members. At that stage, the Americans were not particularly concerned about it. A close associate of General Zia, Lieutenant General (Retd.) K.M. Arif, has written that it was Zia who wrote to President Carte 'suggesting that the US might take a serious note of the strategic imbalance created in the region. Carter ignored the warning as an overreaction from a weak country' (Arif, 2001: 175). This stance of the Americans was to change dramatically later.

Nur Muhammad Taraki, Secretary-General of the PDPA, became the president and prime minister of Afghanistan, assisted by a Revolutionary Council. The PDPA was already faction-ridden: the Khalq faction led by Taraki and Hafizullah Amin, and the Parcham faction represented by Babrak Karmal (Suleri, 1990: 14–15). The two factions clashed and many Parcham members were executed while others went into exile. In any case, the Marxist government embarked upon an ambitious programme of modernisation; in particular, the position of women was greatly improved through a reform of the marriage customs. Young women were encouraged to take to modern education and to reject conservative lifestyles. Land reforms weakened the position of the traditional landowners as, besides the breaking up of large holdings, usury was abolished. Debts incurred in the past by poor farmers, to the landlords, were abolished. These and other such related reforms resulted in a backlash from the deeply conservative Afghan society.

Already, in mid-1978, a rebellion had taken place in the Nuristan region; soon afterwards, the rudiments of a civil war began to emerge. However, the first major setback to the Marxist regime was from within the Khalq faction of the PDPA. Violent internal conflict resulted in Taraki being brutally killed and Hafizullah Amin seizing power in September 1979. This resulted in further instability as Amin began to victimise his opponents in the PDPA. Many fled the country, mostly to the USSR. Amin tried to balance the Soviet influence through secret overtures to Pakistan and the United States, and toned down the secular credentials of the regime by taking on a more sympathetic position on religious rights, especially on Islam. Pakistan began providing covert military assistance to the growing Afghan resistance in late 1978 – much before the United States started doing so (Arif, 2001: 177).

Now, the Soviet Union had been providing economic and military aid to Afghanistan since the 1920s and, over the years, its influence had grown. After the April Revolution, Soviet advisers and military personnel had arrived in large numbers to assist the Afghan Communists. The Soviet Union also provided armament, including military aircraft. Such assistance was formalised through a peace treaty signed in December 1978, which allowed the Afghan government to call upon the Soviet Union for military support. After Amin took over, the influence of the Soviet Union declined; however, a rebellion by Islamists forced him to change this policy and he sought more military assistance from the Soviet Union. This was granted, but the Soviets did not trust Amin. On 27 December, he was assassinated by KGB agents and their Afghan accomplices, and denounced as a CIA agent. The same day, the Red Army began its march into Afghanistan; forces landed by air at Kabul Airport; within a short period of time, some 100,000 Soviet troops were in Afghanistan. A stunned Jimmy Carter described it as 'the greatest threat to peace since World War II' and advised Brezhnev to 'either withdraw the Soviet military or face serious consequences' (quoted by Arif from the *International Herald Tribune* of 31 December 1979, 2001: 175).

Such a huge influx of foreign troops did not help pacify the volatile situation. On the contrary, the rebellion against communist rule proliferated. As a result, the Red Army was engaged in fighting Afghan insurgencies in different parts of the country. Islamic countries condemned the Soviet intervention: foreign ministers from thirty-four Islamic nations adopted a resolution condemning it. The UN General Assembly passed, by a vote of 104:18, a resolution protesting the Soviet invasion of Afghanistan. Although US military assistance started much later, initial US involvement in Afghanistan began after Daud had captured power – when the Pakistan military sent some of its officers for training in insurgency warfare. Immediately after the Communist takeover, the US sought greater contacts with Afghan rebels. Some six months before the Soviet deployment on 3 July 1979, President Carter signed an executive order authorising the CIA to carry out covert propaganda operations against the Kabul regime. This was an ideal opportunity for the Americans to reinvigorate the notorious Great Game that had been going on in the region since the nineteenth century. The Red Army's arrival in Afghanistan greatly transformed US involvement, as it now strove to set up an effective resistance to the foreign troops. It was the opportunity the Americans had been waiting for, to conduct a proxy war against its arch rival. The humiliation suffered in Vietnam could now be avenged, irrespective of the suffering it would inflict on the natives of the region.

Pakistan Becomes a Frontline State

The Soviets committed extensive atrocities against the Afghans who mainly headed to Pakistan, but also to Iran, in search of safe havens. Whereas the Iranians strictly monitored the use of their territory for the launching of armed incursions into Afghanistan, the response of Pakistan was just the opposite. The Soviet intervention in Afghanistan resurrected Pakistan's erstwhile role as a frontline state in the US strategy to contain the spread of Communism. The military pacts between the United States and Pakistan, from the 1950s, had been dormant and the two allies had moved away from each other as already noted. Now, that alliance was resurrected – although, the immediately preceding period was one in which relations between the two had touched their lowest ebb. The Carter Administration was particularly concerned about Pakistan's refusal to forgo its nuclear weapons development. In March 1979, it had threatened to cut off economic aid under the Symington Amendment. Zia had taken the position that Pakistan's nuclear programme was as 'peaceful' as that of India's – which was considered unacceptable and a month later, in April, the United States cut off economic aid to Pakistan. Such a drastic measure particularly exercised the Pakistani government because it felt that although the Indians had introduced nuclear weapons in South Asia, the Carter Administration had rewarded the new Indian prime minister, Morarji Desai, with a warm reception in July 1977, and with a presidential visit to Delhi in early 1978. Relations between Pakistan and the US touched their nadir when it was revealed that the State Department had been considering an attack on Pakistan's nuclear facilities to terminate its nuclear infrastructure as one of their options (Abbas, 2005: 95–6).

From the Pakistani point of view, the American policy in South Asia was grossly skewed in favour of India. It was under these circumstances that, when on 21 November 1979 the news broke that some group had tried to take over the holiest shrine of Ka'aba in Makkah, Zia reportedly said that international transmissions suggested it had been inspired by the Americans. Spontaneous crowds of enraged Pakistanis – joined by students from the prestigious Quaid-i-Azam University, Islamabad, led by the Islami Jamiat Talaba, the student wing of the fundamentalist Jamaat-e-Islami – marched on the US Embassy in Islamabad. The mobs, shouting angry slogans of 'Allah-o-Akbar' (God is Great), 'Down with America', and 'Zia-ul-Haq Zindabad (Long live Zia-ul-Haq)' overpowered the Pakistani and US guards, climbed over the walls, and set fire to the buildings inside. Two Americans, and two Pakistani employees of the embassy, were killed in the raid. The Pakistan Army base was not far and soldiers could easily have arrived within half an hour. But, it took them four hours to come to the rescue of those besieged inside the embassy as the army was involved in providing Zia with security as he rode a bicycle from his residence to his office – a publicity stunt he thought would go down well with the Pakistanis, as the icons of the pristine Islamic state at Madinah – the pious caliphs – were known to have shunned all pomp and show and lived like ordinary citizens even when they were the heads of the state and government. That such a publicity stunt coincided with an attack on the American embassy was accidental, though the Americans suspected that the raid was orchestrated by someone in the government (ibid., 96).

Under the circumstances, the Soviet intervention proved to be the catalyst that would transform relations between the two countries from profoundly estranged to closest cooperation, albeit without necessarily surmounting the trust deficit that had accumulated on both sides. Rather, close cooperation was dictated by the purely instrumentalist concerns of both sides. Nevertheless, on 21 January 1980, Carter offered $400 million to Pakistan, of which $200 million would consist of military equipment on credit and $200 million of economic aid. Zia famously described it as 'peanuts' (Suleri 1990: 15). A joint statement of 3 February 1980, by Zia and by Carter's nation security adviser, Zbigniew Brzezinski, invoked the 1959 Agreement emphasizing that the United States was committed to Pakistan's independence and security (Jain, 2007a: 104). However, Pakistan was not satisfied with the limited help that the Americans were willing to offer. Also, the Carter Administration seemed reluctant to raise the stakes, and informed Pakistan that the 1959 Agreement was only an executive agreement and not a proper treaty because it had not been adopted by the US Congress through proper procedure. On 5 March 1980, Zia's foreign affairs adviser, Agha Shahi, openly expressed displeasure at what Zia had already described as 'peanuts'. In particular, the $200 million military sales credit was considered to be too insignificant to meet Pakistan's defence requirements at that critical juncture (ibid., 104–5).

However, Brzezinski – who had already masterminded an active policy to encourage dissidents to protest in the name of human rights in Eastern Europe – also organised a campaign to covertly finance the Afghan Mujahideen through the CIA and Britain's MI6. In an interview dated 13 June 1997, he made a clean breast of US strategy in Afghanistan:

> We immediately launched a twofold process when we heard that the Soviets had entered Afghanistan. The first involved direct reactions and sanctions focused on the Soviet Union, and both the State Department and the National Security Council prepared long lists of sanctions to be adopted, of steps to be taken to increase the international costs to the Soviet Union of their actions. And the second course of action led to my going to Pakistan a month or so after the Soviet invasion of Afghanistan, for the purpose of coordinating with the Pakistanis a joint response, the purpose of which would be to make the Soviets bleed for as much and as long as is possible; and we engaged in that effort in a collaborative sense with the Saudis, the Egyptians, the British, the Chinese, and we started providing weapons to the Mujaheddin, from various sources again – for example, some Soviet arms from the Egyptians and the Chinese. We even got Soviet arms from the Czechoslovak communist government, since it was obviously susceptible to material incentives; and at some point we started buying arms for the Mujaheddin from the Soviet army in Afghanistan, because that army was increasingly corrupt (Brzezinski, 2011).

Thus, while overt military aid remained modest during Carter's term in office, Brzezinski managed to circumvent official structures via the CIA. The most significant player in the new clandestine alliance was Saudi Arabia. Its vast oil wealth and a fanatical zeal to wage war on the godless Soviet Union converged into a golden opportunity to thwart the leadership challenge posed to it by its arch-rival, Iran, under the equally fanatical Imam Khomeini and his Shia clergy. As the self-styled leader of the Muslim world, Saudi Arabia did not even maintain formal diplomatic relations with the USSR. For years, it had quietly cooperated with the CIA by letting it interview pilgrims from the central Asian republics of the Soviet Union at the time of the annual Hajj (Coll, 2004: 81). British involvement was also present from the start as old Afghan hands were included among the consultants. Egypt and other smaller Islamic players also took part in the recruitment of Islamic warriors.

China

In this regard, China's often gets eclipsed but constitutes yet another deviation from the formal rules of war. Serious differences between the Soviet Union and China had emerged in the 1960s and split the international communist movement into hostile pro-Moscow and pro-Beijing configurations. The Chinese had taken the stand that Soviet social imperialism was the bigger enemy of the international proletariat and socialist revolution. In the 1970s, the US–China liaison facilitated by Pakistan had already resulted in an understanding that Soviet influence should be curtailed in Asia. Mao's successor, Deng Xiaoping, had decided to make a complete break with the socialist economy and, instead, go full-throttle for capitalism. Such a 180-degree about-turn necessitated greater cooperation with the Americans to access capital, technology, and markets. It also implied military cooperation with the once-demonised citadel of capitalism. Now, an opportunity had arisen to elevate that understanding into a working alliance of all sorts against the Soviets.

Thus, in January 1980, American officials visited Beijing where it was agreed that the two sides would cooperate to counter the Soviet invasion of Afghanistan, as well as against Vietnam – which had moved closer to the Soviet Union following the former's war with the pro-Chinese Pol Pot in Cambodia. The Americans also secretly promised to allow technology transfers. Thus began the American, Saudi, Egyptian, and Chinese aid to the Afghanistan jihad (Cooley, 2000: 66–7). This involvement was also motivated by Chinese interest in the Karakoram Highway – historically known as the Silk Road – which passed though Pakistan and China, only thirty-five miles away from the Afghan border. China used its air space, and the Karakoram Highway, to transport its own weapons as well as those of the Americans and other nations. Later, according to the beleaguered Afghan president, Najibullah, Chinese military aid exceeded $400 million. The ISI denied that the Chinese were involved in the provision of weapons (ibid., 72–80).

General Zia's Strategy for Conducting the Afghan Jihad

Pakistan had become a sanctuary for a huge influx of Afghan refugees. In spite of its meagre resources, it offered generous humanitarian help and the provision of facilities for the establishing of an Afghan resistance against

Soviet occupation. Pakistan received the sympathy and support of many Western and Islamic countries. Brzezinski paid generous compliments about Pakistan's role in the Afghan jihad, stating:

> There was a certain coolness and distance in the American–Pakistan relationship prior to the Soviet invasion of Afghanistan. After that invasion, we collaborated very closely. And I have to pay tribute to the guts of the Pakistanis: they acted with remarkable courage, and they just weren't intimidated and they did things which one would have thought a vulnerable country might not have the courage to undertake. We, I am pleased to say, supported them very actively and they had our backing, but they were there, they were the ones who were endangered, not we (Brzezinski, 2011).

One need not emphasise that it was Zia who was at the helm of affairs in Pakistan, and the risks that Pakistan was taking were a tribute to his leadership. Once Ronald Reagan assumed the presidency on 21 January 1981, attitudes in the White House, the Pentagon, and the State Department changed stridently in favour of backing the Mujahideen to the hilt. Consequently, an ambitious aid package, to the tune of $3.2 billion for the period 1982–7, was offered to Pakistan. It was divided equally between economic aid and military sales. Pakistan accepted the package without any hesitation. Speaking to newsmen on 21 April 1981, after talks with Reagan's secretary of state, Alexander Haig, Agha Shahi explained that the new package was accepted not only because it was bigger but that:

> The Carter Administration's offer did not carry the credibility of a US–Pakistan relationship nor was the package commensurate with the magnitude of the threat; the Reagan Administration had put forward a Five-Year Plan that was the difference. We believe in the determination of the new Administration to strongly support the independence of Pakistan (Jain, 2007a: 107).

The main difference was that it was not simply one player of the Carter Administration, Brzezinski, who was in favour of backing Pakistan but the whole administration was determined to convert the struggle in Afghanistan into a proxy war against the Soviet Union.

Pakistan began to be praised as a 'pivotal state', a 'frontline state', and so on (Arif, 2001: 184–5). In reward for its services, General Zia demanded a free hand in organising the resistance and the right to dispose of the funds – which was readily conceded by the US. Thus, Pakistan acquired modern armament and related technology on a massive scale, and its conventional arsenal vis-à-vis India was replenished after years of bans on procurement from the United States. Although some concerns about Pakistan's nuclear program were expressed by prominent members of the American Congress, the US government looked the other way (Haqqani, 2005: 216). Pakistan continued, clandestinely, to pursue its nuclear program (ibid., 185–6). General Zia tasked the ISI, rather than the regular military, with primary responsibility for masterminding actions against the Soviets and Afghan communists. The CIA and the ISI Directorate worked in concert, though the actual operations were managed exclusively by the ISI. Pakistan's elite SSG commandos were deeply involved in those operations (ibid., 186). A call to jihad was heralded all over the world; Muslim zealots from forty-three Muslim countries, as well as from the West, began to arrive in the Pakistani city of Peshawar. These warriors, known as Mujahideen, were trained exclusively by the ISI to use modern weapons and explosives. While foreign warriors arrived in Peshawar in the thousands, the real backbone of the liberation struggle was borne by the Afghan and Pakistani Mujahideen. Except for the communists and some left-leaning liberals, all other sections of Afghan society took part in the jihad – including the Deobandi, Wahhabi, and Sufi orders. Equally, in Pakistan, the Jamaat-e-Islami as well as the Wahhabi-oriented Ahl-e-Hadith and the Deobandi Jamiat Ulema-e-Islam were deeply involved in recruiting and indoctrinating young men for the Afghan jihad. Even Sufi-oriented Sunnis, doctrinally the same as the Barelvis, took part in the religious war (Rana, 2004; Rashid 2000).

Madrassas and Mujahideen

Besides immediate mobilisation and recruitment, long-term investment was made in these areas through the madrassas (religious schools). Zia encouraged Saudi charities to build madrassas along the Afghan border. Madrassas – where pupils were imparted education in Islamic theology, law, and beliefs – had always existed in Muslim societies, and were supported by government and private donations and endowments. Ironically, in the pre-colonial era, the pupils belonged to upper-class families. Such pupils were then qualified to serve in religious positions in mosques and other related institutions. That changed when secular schools imparting modern education came into being during the British period. The search for employment required a different kind of knowledge and training. Thereafter, it was mostly children from poor backgrounds who were sent to the madrassas where they received clothes, free board and lodging and, once trained in the basic rituals and beliefs of Islam, usually found work as prayer leaders and functionaries in Islamic institutions. In the 1970s, there were only a few hundred madrassas. After the politicisation of Islam as jihad ideology, the number of madrassas proliferated – to 12,000–15,000 by the mid-1980s – particularly along the Afghanistan–Pakistan border. It is estimated that 1.5 to 2 million pupils (Taliban) were the products of the madrassas (Ali, 2009: 15–25).

In this regard, the US role in promoting the jihad ideology is noteworthy. According to Joe Stephens and David B. Ottaway, who wrote an article entitled 'From the U.S., the ABC of Jihad' (23 March 2002), school textbooks designed by the Centre for Afghanistan Studies at the University of Nebraska-Omaha, under a USAID grant worth US$50 million, were published with a view to promoting the idea of jihad among the Mujahideen. They observed:

> In the twilight of the Cold War, the United States spent millions of dollars to supply Afghan schoolchildren with textbooks filled with violent images and militant Islamic teachings, part of covert attempts to spur resistance to the Soviet occupation.
>
> The primers, which were filled with talk of jihad and featured drawings of guns, bullets, soldiers and mines, have served since then as the Afghan school system's core curriculum. Even the Taliban used the American-produced books, though the radical movement scratched out human faces in keeping with its strict fundamentalist code (2002).

The books were mostly printed in Pakistan; during 1984–94, over thirteen million were distributed at Afghan refugee camps and Pakistani madrassas 'where students learnt basic math by counting dead Russians and Kalashnikov rifles' (Jan. 2002). Mahmood Mamdani has quoted an example given by the Pakistani physicist and political debater, Pervez Hoodbhoy, from a fourth-grade mathematics textbook published under the programme. In it was included the following exercise: 'The speed of a Kalashnikov [the ubiquitous Soviet-made semiautomatic machine gun] bullet is 800 meters per second. If a Russian is at a distance of 3200 meters from a mujahid, and that mujahid aims at the Russian's head, calculate how many seconds it will take for the bullet to strike the Russian's forehead' (Mamdani, 2004: 137). I contacted Professor Jack Schroder at Nebraska University through Dr Saleem Ali; the latter had studied madrassa education in Pakistan. Schroder denied that such material was printed in Nebraska and asserted that it was done locally in Afghanistan. He sent me a facsimile of a maths lesson in which counting dead Russians was used to teach the students to count.

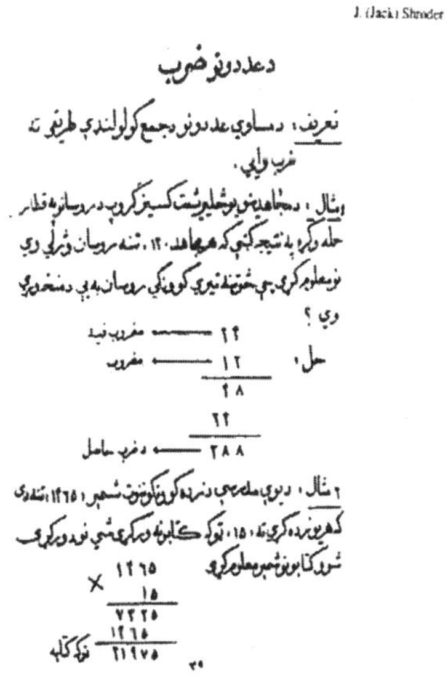

Numbers multiplication
• Description the shortest way of adding equal numbers is called multiplication.

Examples:
A group of 24 mujahid attacked the Russians. As a result each mujahid killed 12 Russians. Find out how many aggressive Russians were eliminated?
24 x 12 = 288

Example 2
A madrasa (RELIGIOUS SCHOOL) has 1465 students. Each student was given 15 books. How many books were distributed?
1465 x 15 = 21,975

Fig.: Facsimile page (in Pushto, with translation) from one of the textbooks produced by the Afghanistan Ministry of Education in Exile and printed by the UNO team in Peshawar, Pakistan, in the 1980s. The text was designed to each arithmetic skills and was commensurate with the daily lives of the Afghanistan mujahideen resistance to the Soviet invasion and their refugee children.

Although the programme was discontinued in 1994, the textbooks continued to be used in the madrassas. Steve Coll has observed that relishing the killing of as many Red Army troops as possible seemed to have been an obsession with Howard Hart, CIA's chief of station in Islamabad:

> For many in the CIA the Afghan jihad was about killing Soviets, first and last. Hart even suggested that the Pakistanis put a bounty out on Soviet soldiers: ten thousand rupees for special forces soldiers, five thousand for a conscript, and double in either case if the prisoners were brought alive. This was payback for Soviet aid to the North Vietnamese and the Vietcong, and for many CIA officers who had served in that war, it was personal (Coll, 2004: 59).

That such practices may induce a violent culture in the hundreds of thousands of Mujahideen, and one day come to haunt the Americans themselves, was not given any consideration at that stage. I have heard CIA operatives on *CNN* and *BBC* who, without any remorse, described such policy as cost-effective and imperative in the battle to defeat their arch enemy. Another negative implication of introducing monetary incentives was that corruption, bribery, an illicit arms trade, and poppy cultivation became rampant and percolated all sections of Afghan society, and indeed the Pakistan military and ISI. While Secretary of State Hillary Clinton has, on a number of occasions, acknowledged US guilt in creating such monsters, when I posed the question to former US Ambassador to Pakistan Wendy Chamberlin (July 2001–June 2002) whether she felt that the US had any responsibility in the creation of the terrorist mind-set, she retorted that General Zia sufficed in turning Pakistan into a fanatical Islamic society. The US assistant secretary of state for South and Central Asian Affairs, Robin Raphael, whose former husband Arnold Raphael was ambassador to Pakistan during the Zia period and died in the plane crash with him, emphasised that at the time it was important for Pakistan to preserve its integrity and survival against a Soviet thrust into its territories at all costs, and that the United States provided crucial support at that time.

Strategic Depth

As the Pakistani military expanded its role in Afghanistan, it also began to re-define its stature in the region. As already noted, Pakistani defence strategists had always worried about Pakistan's lack of 'strategic depth' vis-à-vis India (Cheema, 2003: 3). Consequently, ambitions to overcome such a disadvantage, combined with optimism that Islamic ideology and belief had created a strong fighting force that had defeated the Soviet Union (and precipitated its collapse), led to the evolution of a project aimed at the creation of an Islamic bloc – initially comprising Pakistan, Afghanistan, and liberated Kashmir. More ambitious plans, to bring the various central Asian Muslim republics, Iran, and Turkey, into a confederation of Islamic states, also existed. In an interview, Selig Harrison, a leading American South-Asia expert, claimed that General Zia's involvement in Afghanistan was meant to promote a pan-Islamic super-state in the region. He has also alleged that such a scheme had powerful backers in the Pakistani military establishment (Harrison, 2001). However, from the Pakistani point of view, the primary benefit accruing from the Afghan jihad was the huge inflow of arms and weapon systems, advanced technology, and fighting experience (Hasan, 1990: 92). Such gains could be used to settle scores with India; India had inflicted a humiliating defeat on it in 1971, and was occupying the predominantly Muslim-majority Kashmir.

Soviet Losses

A CIA estimate from the beginning of 1984 suggested that the Mujahideen had killed or wounded 17,000 Soviet soldiers and destroyed 350–400 Soviet aircraft, 2750 tanks and armoured carriers, and nearly 8000 trucks and other vehicles. This had been achieved in a most cost-effective manner: $300 million contributed by the US taxpayers and $200 million by Saudi Arabia. CIA Director William Casey became an ardent champion of jihad. Reagan had been re-elected, and people with even stronger conservative views now became part of the administration. They looked upon the Afghan jihad as a God-sent opportunity to defeat the 'evil empire'. Congressman Charlie Wilson became the mouthpiece of the rabid anti-Communist lobby in the United States. He developed close relations with Zia, and began to provide more money and sophisticated weapons systems into the CIA's classified Afghan budget – in particular, the Stinger missile which could be fired from a single soldier's shoulder, and proved to be the undoing of the Soviet air force as both attack helicopters and fixed-wing aircraft became easy targets and were shot down in increasing numbers.

An Islamic–Christian War against Communism

A number of devout Catholics, with strong anti-communist sympathies, were now running the covert Afghan operations. Such proclivities bound them even closer to the Islamist extremists who were conducting the actual operations against the Soviet troops (Coll, 2004: 89–93). Steve Coll has put this convergence of religious fanaticism in the following words, 'Casey saw political Islam and the Catholic Church as natural allies in the "realistic counter-insurgency" of covert action he was forging at the CIA to thwart Soviet imperialism' (ibid., 97–8). Charlie Wilson, a great champion of the jihad, was able to procure shoulder-fired Stinger missiles for the Islamic warriors. Many such weapons ended up on the illegal weapons market. As a result, there was a dramatic escalation in the funding to the Afghan jihad as well as in the military operations, including ISI operations, against military targets inside the Muslim Central Asian republics of the Soviet Union. The KGB and the Afghan KHAD had carried out sabotage and assassination missions inside Pakistan. By 1987, 90 percent of the 770 terrorist incidents recorded worldwide had taken place in Pakistan (Abbas, 2005: 122). So, it was tit-for-tat. As the casualties mounted, the Soviet Union sent a warning to both the United States and Pakistan. While the Americans denied any involvement, Zia ordered the man in charge of such operations, Brigadier Mohammad Yousaf, to go slow as they widened the scope for terrorism. Many Arab Mujahideen studied these tactics with great interest: Al-Qaeda would later turn such lessons against the Americans.

On 15 December 1986, Casey suffered a massive stroke and died a few weeks later. Thereafter, important changes took place in the attitude of the United States' policy makers. Doubts began to be expressed about a strategy that bolstered anti-American Islamists, such as Gulbadin Hekmatyar, whom Zia and the ISI considered their man among the various Afghan leaders. The CIA, however, continued to support the ISI strategy; the mission, which was still to kill Soviets. Colonel Imam (Sultan Amir Tarar, a Punjabi Jatt who spoke fluent Pashto) explained to me, in an extended interview at his residence in Rawalpindi in December 2008, that he trained and led the Afghan and Pakistani Pakhtuns in hundreds of missions aimed at killing Russians. He stated that this did not pose a problem for his conscience because he was acting for the glory of Islam. However, there was some criticism, within the Afghan resistance, about the ISI's manipulation of the Afghan jihad to serve Pakistan's interests; the critics included local commanders such as Abdul Haq, who had lost a leg during the campaign. Haq enjoyed the trust of the Americans, including American journalists covering the events.

In any event, the secretary-general of the Communist Party, Gorbachev, and his advisers had, from the beginning of 1987, begun to doubt the wisdom of a continuing Soviet presence in Afghanistan. It had caused a great loss of men, material, and prestige (Arif, 2001: 179). Gorbachev had initiated reforms in the rigid communist system and wanted to make a break with the type of state system that he had inherited from his predecessors. He and his advisers were, therefore, also willing to extricate themselves from the Afghan situation. They were amenable to a negotiated withdrawal provided power was handed over to moderate Afghan elements and not Islamists. Soviet Foreign Minister Shevardnadze communicated such an intention to his counterpart, George Shultz, while on a visit to Washington, DC. This was later discussed by the head of the KGB and the acting CIA chief, Robert Gates, in Washington DC (Coll, 2004: 168).

The Afghan communists, on the other hand, were very worried that if the Soviets withdrew they may not be able to hold on to power. Meanwhile, Babrak Karmal, who had earlier taken over power with Soviet help, had been replaced by Dr Najibullah as president of Afghanistan in November. Under Soviet instructions, the new government sought a moderate image with a multiparty system and provisions for Islamic law. But, such changes did not make any difference as the Afghan Islamists and the ISI were determined to establish a dogmatic Islamic state. On the other hand, modern educated women and liberal-minded Afghans, who had benefitted from the modernist reforms of the communists, feared an Islamist takeover by Hekmatyar.

Despite opposition from the Islamabad-based hard-line CIA officers who continued to put their trust in the ISI, in the spring of 1988 the State Department assigned Edmund McWilliams with the task of liaising with rebel Afghan leaders without the ISI being informed. The Americans were now in tacit agreement with the Soviets that the withdrawal of the Red Army should not bring an Islamic fundamentalist regime into power in Afghanistan. Because of the efforts of both the superpowers, the Geneva Accords were signed on 14 April 1988 whereby the Soviet withdrawal from Afghanistan was to begin on 5 May 1988 and be completed by 15 February 1989. The accord required Afghanistan and Pakistan to abide by the principles of non-interference and non-intervention in each other's affairs. Afghan refugees were to be facilitated to return voluntarily. The United States and the USSR became guarantors of the Geneva Accords. The Afghan rebels were party to neither the negotiations nor to the Geneva Accords, and refused to accept the terms of the agreement. As a result, the civil war continued after the completion of the Soviet withdrawal. Pakistan was obviously sidelined in these negotiations; in particular, Zia, and the new ISI chief, Hamid Gul, who the Americans erroneously assessed as being pro-West but who wanted to install a pro-Pakistan Islamist government under Hekmatyar (Coll, 2004: 174–7).

American Concerns about Pakistan Going Nuclear

Notwithstanding cooperation on Afghanistan, which started taking shape – albeit, initially, at a low level – increasingly under Brzezinski's influence, the Carter Administration kept pressurising Pakistan to give up its nuclear weapons programme. Such pressure proved futile; this was admitted in secret communications between US officials. Pakistani officials kept saying that their country had the 'unfettered right to do what it wishes' (*The United States and Pakistan's Quest for the Bomb,* 2010). In any case, because of American pressure, France backed out of a contract to supply a nuclear reprocessing plant to Pakistan on 23 August 1978. Such a decision was a setback, but the Kahuta plant had already been commissioned and Zia gave his full backing to its completion. Zahid Malik has observed that, besides security concerns, there was an ideological dimension to Zia's commitment to Pakistan's nuclear weapons programme. He has written that 'any true Pakistani who believes in the two-nation theory concept as the basis of Pakistan invariably feels that Pakistan can exist only as an antithesis of India, politically and militarily' (Malik, 1990: 78).

American pressure diminished after the Soviet Union intervened in Afghanistan. This change in approach had begun during Carter's term; Brzezinski was responsible for this change. During the Reagan years, the pressure diminished even more significantly. As an incentive not to go nuclear, the Reagan administration modified the Symington amendment and agreed to sell forty F-16 planes to Pakistan, in small batches, over a number of years. It was asserted that such advanced aircraft would not upset the balance with India, and that the United States was fully aware of India's concerns. It was also asserted that Pakistan needed the F-16s for a defensive role (Jain, 2007a: 327–8). On the whole, concerns about Pakistan's nuclear weapons were low-key. Thus, for example, on 12 September 1983, Deputy Assistant Secretary of State Marshall formulated the administration's concerns in these mild terms: 'The United States does remain concerned with certain Pakistani plans – specially any unsafeguarded operation of its new lab reprocessing plants and its continued efforts to complete construction of an unsafeguarded enrichment plant....' (ibid., 330). Formally, the Americans kept demanding that Pakistan sign the NPT. It was becoming clear, by 1987, that the Red Army would be forced to withdraw in the not-so-distant future – which resulted in the Reagan Administration changing its stance; Pakistan was pressured to sign the NPT before a new $4.02 billion aid package could be put before the US Congress for its approval (Malik 1990: 80). Zia resisted such pressure with great diplomatic skill. In his meetings with Reagan and members of Congress, Zia continued to assert that Pakistan was not interested in making nuclear weapons. However, such a strategy could not conceal the reality for too long because, according to Hassan Abbas, Dr Abdul Qadeer Khan, the so-called father of the Pakistan nuclear bomb:

> ...who was known to be chasing after money and publicity as well, opened his mouth to a leading Pakistani newspaper, and when the story appeared in newspapers in early 1987 it sent a shudder all across. In it there was Qadeer's claim that Pakistan had already succeeded in enriching uranium to weapons grade (Abbas 2005: 119).

Within three months of such revelations, three Pakistanis in the United States and two in Canada were arrested for trying to illegally export materials and equipment that could help advance Pakistan's nuclear programme. Pakistan denied any involvement, but the Americans were not impressed (ibid.).

Relations with India

The most interesting aspect of Zia's political acumen was that although he invested, with considerable consistency, his ideological convictions and political skills in conferring an unmistakable Islamist identity on Pakistan, he succeeded quite well in keeping traditional enmity towards India out of his public pronouncements. Moreover, with Pakistan's military deeply involved in Afghanistan, it was necessary that India should not create mischief on its eastern border. Zia ensured that the Americans kept that in mind; he himself, deployed a number of diplomatic overtures to keep India on the back foot. Thus, for example, he proposed that both countries sign the Nuclear Non-Proliferation Treaty. Another measure he put forth was that both should agree to joint inspections of their nuclear sites by the International Atomic Energy Agency. He also proposed a pact, between them, to terminate weapons development programmes and allow mutual inspection of each other's facilities. He also considered that, besides Pakistan and India, other South Asian countries such as Bangladesh and Sri Lanka and others could agree to jointly declare South Asia a nuclear-free zone (Malik, 1990: 81). In the international realm, Pakistan gained considerable approbation; Zia's conditional offer to sign the NPT in 1985 became 'an oft-quoted document in world forums on the subject. He offered to sign the NPT provided India does so' (ibid., 80–81). Craig Baxter has summed up Zia's nuclear diplomacy in the following words:

> India in each case either did not respond or rejected the proposals. It seems clear that Zia was looking for a means to end the Pakistan program [nuclear programme], but could only do so with some concessions from India. Ending the program would presumably save resources and would get Zia out of a serious bind with the United State, especially with many in the United States Congress. Pakistan also offered India a 'no-war pact', but this was not seriously pursued by India (Baxter 1991: 139–40).

Indian worries about a China that had already inflicted a humiliating defeat in 1962, and possessed nuclear weapons since 1964, meant that Zia's overtures were not going to be reciprocated. Moreover, Prime Minister Indira Gandhi nurtured immediate grievances against the Zia regime for its alleged covert support to the Sikh, and later Kashmiri, separatists. The idea of a separate Sikh state in the Indian Punjab – Khalistan – was born among the Sikhs settled in North America and Britain, but emerged as a serious political threat to India in the 1980s when Indira Gandhi cultivated the support of a fundamentalist Sikh preacher – Sant Jarnail Singh Bhindrawale – to challenge the leaders of the conservative Sikh party, the Akali Dal, which dominated the politics of East Punjab and was in opposition to her Congress party in that state. They were also part of the national opposition to the Congress government at the centre. India accused two of the main leaders of the Khalistan movement, Dr Jagjit Singh Chauhan and Ganga Singh Dhillon – the former based in the United Kingdom and the latter in the US – of being in contact with American members of Congress and senior Pakistani officials (White Paper on the Punjab Agitation, 1984). The Indian government and press maintained that Pakistan was providing bases, training, and other help to Sikh separatists. The greatest degree of Pakistani involvement allegedly took place during the Zia period (1977–88). Pakistan, of course, denied such accusations.

With regard to Indian-administered Kashmir, while Pakistan's involvement in its internal resistance to Indian rule began in real earnest during the post-Zia period, the basic framework for launching jihad in that disputed territory was developed during his time. In the event, the armed struggle in Indian-administered Kashmir began on 31 July 1988, when the Jammu Kashmir Liberation Front (JKLF) exploded bombs in three buildings that belonged to the Government of India in the Kashmiri capital, Srinagar (Noorani, 1991: 123). Kashmir Chief Minister Farooq Abdullah alleged that Pakistan was supporting the JKLF. This allegation was made just before Zia died in a plane crash in August 1988.

Siachen

A more specific and direct confrontation took place between India and Pakistan on the prohibitive heights of the Siachen Glacier – located in the disputed Kashmir region. The Siachen Glacier is located at a height of over 6000 metres (20,000 ft). It is a most inhospitable terrain, mostly due to the extreme cold weather and the concomitant hazards of maintaining a base in such a place. It is some 900–1000 sq miles altogether (2300 sq km). The origin of the Siachen conflict derives from the incompletely demarcated territory between India and Pakistan, known as NJ9842, denoting the Siachen glacier.

The 1972 Simla Agreement did not address the issue of who controlled the glacier but merely stated that, from the NJ9842 location, the boundary would proceed 'thence north to the glaciers'. However, after Pakistan began to grant permission to international mountaineering teams to climb some of the high peaks in the Siachen area, India became concerned that Pakistan was thus staking claim to the territory.

Consequently, the Indians began to send secret army expeditions to the Siachen Glacier. On 13 April 1984, the Indian Army and Air Force personnel went into the glacier territory and dug into the highest mountaintops. It was, therefore, India that took the initiative in establishing a military presence, on a continuous basis, in the disputed area. Pakistan made several attempts to dislodge the Indians. The most determined effort was in 1987 when a mission, led by the elite SSG commandos, failed to achieve its objective. General Pervez Musharraf, however, has expressed the view that the Indians have to suffer far more than the Pakistanis because the Indians have to cover a long trek, while the glacier is easily accessible from the Pakistani side (Musharraf, 2006: 68–70). The Siachen conflict has dragged on and remains unresolved up till now.

Overall Diplomacy vis-à-vis India

Zia visited Delhi in 1983 to take part in a NAM conference. On that occasion, he visited his alma mater, St. Stephen's College in Delhi, and interacted with Indian leaders on an apparently friendly basis. However, India's favourable remarks on the Movement for the Restoration of Democracy irked the Zia regime; at the same time, India kept alleging that Pakistan was helping the Sikhs. After Indira Gandhi's assassination in 1984, Rajiv Gandhi tried to modify the conventionally inflamed relationship. Zia reciprocated amply. As a result, an exchange of delegations, led by the foreign secretaries, took place. Direct dialling between the two countries was started. In 1985, Zia visited India on his way back from Maldives when both countries agreed, in principle, not to attack each other's nuclear installations. However, such gestures did not, in any meaningful sense, alter the mutual distrust that has always marred their relationship. As already mentioned, Pakistan blamed India for having a hand in the unrest in Sindh, while India alleged that Pakistan gave sanctuary and logistical support to the Sikh secessionists.

Indian Military Exercise Brasstacks

Throughout the post-independence period, India, from time to time, has taken steps that have accentuated Pakistan's sense of vulnerability. One such major provocation was the military exercise christened Brasstacks – from November 1986 to March 1987 – in Rajasthan, close to the Pakistan border. Nearly the whole Indian Army was mobilised. Zia looked upon Operation Brasstacks as provocation and, possibly, preparation for an invasion of Pakistan. In response, he ordered his armoured units to move to the border. India enjoyed conventional superiority and had exploded a nuclear device. There was suspicion, in security circles, that Pakistan had also acquired nuclear capability. Following the Second World War, this was the greatest concentration of troops ready to go into battle. The Indians threatened to take retaliatory action if Pakistani troops were not moved away from the border. This self-righteous threat was delivered by the Indian minister of state for foreign affairs, K. Natwar Singh, to Pakistan's high commissioner in Delhi, Dr Humayun Khan, on 23 January 1987 (Arif, 2001: 268). That Pakistan had moved its troops in response to Indian provocation seemed not to have been considered a legitimate reason by K. Natwar Singh. Hawkish elements in the Indian establishment, with the Indian Army Chief General Sunderji, at the centre of it, were undoubtedly in a bellicose mood at that time.

Zia retained his nerve and displayed considerable political acumen. He contacted Rajiv Gandhi and, as a result, both sides agreed to withdraw some of their forces from the border. Later, in February, Zia visited India on the invitation of the Indian cricket board to watch a cricket match. That further helped to defuse the tension. Slowly, things returned to 'normal' although both sides remained equally suspicious of each other. General K.M. Arif has discussed Operation Brasstacks in detail; his conclusion is that the Indian military high command exceeded its brief, and Rajiv Gandhi was not fully aware of the objectives the generals had in mind.

Some critical voices were raised in the Indian media as well against Operation Brasstacks – acknowledging that it was provocative and heightened Pakistani security concerns (Arif, 2001: 242–76). During this period, the international community was again very concerned about war between these two neighbouring states, whose potential nuclear capability worried them. It is not difficult to conclude that Brasstacks must have convinced Pakistan that it needed nuclear weapons to deter India, which enjoyed a distinct advantage over Pakistan by virtue of its superior numerical strength and greater arsenal of conventional weapons – in addition to its demonstrated nuclear weapon-making capability.

Saudi Arabia

In ideological terms, the most significant development in the external sphere during Zia's term was the close affinity that he felt with Saudi Arabia. Saudi influence in Pakistan had been growing after the 1974 Islamic Summit. Already, hundreds of thousands of Pakistanis were working in the Arab states of the Persian Gulf. The Pakistanis were culturally prone to hold all things Arab in deference and, although their treatment at the hands of Arabs was harsh and insulting, their living in that region began to impact their traditional Islamic identity – with the result that, instead of the Sufi-oriented traditions of the past, Arab Islam with its strict adherence to orthodox Islamic prayer and habits began to affect them. In fact, millions of Muslims working in Saudi Arabia and the other oil-rich states of the Persian Gulf created the rudiments of a global Islamic revival with Pakistan, in particular, becoming radicalised into a puritanical Islam – which was rather easily amenable to radical Islam.

While such changes were underway among the largely unskilled workers, shopkeepers, and even the professional middle classes, the Pakistan military too became integrated into such processes as, in 1983, some 30,000 Pakistani military personnel were posted on duty overseas, almost all in the Middle East. The bulk – some 20,000 – were stationed in Saudi Arabia, including one armoured brigade (Arif, 2001: 194). Zia, himself, had served in Jordon in the 1970s, from where he had received a very favourable reference which apparently helped Bhutto choose him as COAS. A friend of mine from the Pakistan Army told me that the Saudis had opposed Pakistani Shias being posted in Saudi Arabia, but Zia did not accept such pressure because he did not want to introduce divisions in the armed forces. Other reports suggest that no such Saudi demand was made. In any case, the Pakistani units in Saudi Arabia were removed in 1988, apparently because Pakistan continued to maintain close ties with Iran. Later, after the invasion of Kuwait by Saddam Hussein in 1991, the Pakistan Army was again stationed in Saudi Arabia and a number of other Arab states in the Persian Gulf (Baxter, 1991: 142–3). The radicalisation of the Pakistan military was facilitated by the physical presence of its personnel in the Middle East, especially in the holy land – Saudi Arabia.

The Economic Basis of Zia's Policies

Shahid Javed Burki has given a highly positive evaluation of Zia's economic policy – that he made the prudent decision not to interfere with it, recognising its crucial importance. Thus, he did not subject it to the Islamisation juggernaut that had rolled over other sectors of society. Consequently, the management of the economy was left to technocrats and some industrialists as advisers. Ghulam Ishaq Khan, chairman of the Planning Commission, was entrusted with the task of reorganising the economy along free-market principles. He moved cautiously and embarked upon a programme of gradual denationalisation. Later, in 1985, when Ghulam Ishaq was elected chairman of the Senate (of the National Assembly), the well-known World Bank economist Mahbub ul Haq was given the task of managing the economy. Relations with the World Bank were normalised, and it restored development aid to Pakistan. Burki, as a caption to their achievements, wrote that such changes produced an 'economic development record with few parallels in the Third Word'. During Ghulam Ishaq's stewardship, the size of the GNP increased by seventy-six percent, and per capita income by thirty-four percent. How much of this percolated to the poor has not been accounted for in Burki's review. However, he has asserted that, during 1975–85, Pakistan received $25 billion in remittances from Pakistani workers in the Middle East, and these helped the poor (Burki, 1991: 12–15).

Burki has not brought the role played by money from the illicit trade in weapons and narcotics, that accrued during this time, into the discussion on the economy. Ayesha Siddiqa has noted that during the same Zia era, 'the senior generals acquired the political power that allowed them to engage in predatory financial acquisition' (2007: 139). She has asserted that, during Zia's rule, new provisions were introduced to expand the military's share in the economy. Industries related to fertilisers, oil and gas, the agro-industry, and army farms all became areas where the military established its own production. Such measures benefitted the military organisationally, as well as individual officers. Moreover, secret 'regimental funds' were introduced for the commanders' utilisation. These were drawn from the defence budget for classified projects, as well as from money earned through small cooperative business and industrial ventures. Such, and other, avenues provided the higher officers with ample gains – and thus their loyalty to the regime was assured. The military also developed interests in transportation and in the construction of roads, bridges, and related areas. Land grants in rural and urban areas further bolstered the economic interests of the officer corps. As a result, the military become economically autonomous. Additionally, the army established its own elite schools, with English as the medium of instruction, inside the cantonment areas. A number of welfare foundations were established by the army, as well as by the air force and navy. In short, the military greatly expanded its presence and interests in the Pakistan economy (ibid., 139–44).

General Zia's Exit

In terms of opposition at home, Zia's main worry remained the PPP. The leadership of the party was with Z.A. Bhutto's daughter, Benazir, who, along with her mother, Nusrat Bhutto, was put under house arrest. Nusrat was allowed to travel abroad for medical treatment in November 1982. In January 1984, after six years of house arrest and imprisonment, Zia even allowed Benazir to travel abroad for medical reasons. In both cases, pressure from the US and from their friends and supporters abroad made the martial law government relent. Benazir Bhutto returned to Pakistan in August 1985 along with the dead body of her younger brother, Shahnawaz Bhutto, who had died under mysterious circumstances in his flat in Cannes (Bhutto, 2008a: 289–300).

Zia had appointed Muhammad Khan Junejo, a Sindhi politician, as prime minister just before Benazir returned to Pakistan. The two men had reached an agreement that while Zia would lift martial law, Junejo would arrange to have the National Assembly pass amendments to the constitution that would give:

> Zia and his generals blanket immunity from any manner of prosecution for all acts of commission and omission after the July 1977 coup; mention him by name as the president of the country for the next five years while concurrently holding the appointment of the chief of army staff: and give him powers to dismiss the prime minister and National Assembly (Abbas, 2005: 120).

Zia did secure the safeguards that he wanted but, soon afterwards, his relations with Junejo began to sour over a number of promotions and appointments that the prime minister considered irregular and arbitrary. Instead of being the pliant protégé, Junejo turned out to be a man of principles and integrity – which Zia found unacceptable. Such differences generated tensions in their relationship; matters came to a head when Junejo decided to sign the Geneva Peace Accord, while Zia wanted to ensure that a pro-Pakistan Islamist regime was firmly established in Afghanistan. Zia was convinced that Junejo had been used by the Americans to pre-empt his ambitions in Afghanistan. Four days before the Geneva Accords were signed, on 10 April 1988, a massive explosion took place at the Ojhri Camp – the depot where all ordnance for the Afghan jihad was stored – midway between Islamabad and its twin city of Rawalpindi. It caused havoc as bombs, missiles, and other explosives exploded; hundreds of casualties were incurred. Sabotage was suspected. Junejo wanted to institute an enquiry to determine who the perpetrators were, while Zia was keen that the Americans should replace the destroyed ammunition. On 29 May 1988, Zia dismissed Junejo and the National Assembly. This was done via a statement personally delivered by Zia on Pakistan television. The prime minister and parliamentarians were accused of failing to stamp out corruption and of their inability to enforce Islamic law (ibid., 124).

On 17 August 1988, a C-130B Hercules transport aircraft carrying Zia and several other senior generals, including the chairman joint chief of staff and head of the ISI during the Afghan jihad, General Akhtar Abdul Rahman, the US ambassador to Islamabad, Arnold Lewis Raphael, and Brigadier General Herbert Wasson, took off from Bahawalpur in southern Punjab. Just before taking-off, they, and other Pakistani officers, had witnessed the performance of the US M-1 Abrams tank. The plane crashed a few minutes after take-off, all thirty-one people on board perished. The cause of the crash has never been definitively established but it is widely believed that sabotage was the cause of the crash. The CIA, KGB, Khad, RAW, and even dissident Pakistani officers and Shia opponents of Zia's Sunni Islamism have been named in journalistic tracts. It remains a mystery. Zia's admirers believe that the Americans and Soviets had reached an understanding that an Islamist regime in Afghanistan was not in their interest and, therefore, they entered into a conspiracy to get rid of Zia as he was determined to install a pro-Pakistan Islamist regime in Kabul. That the crash could be the result of a technical fault does not seem to be the explanation that most commentators want to believe in. Zia died when he felt confident and master of the situation. According to Shahid Javed Burki, Zia told him, on 29 June 1988, that he would remain in power for a long time. That proved to be a wrong prediction!

There can be no denying that Zia's death was mourned by large sections of the public. For the Afghan Mujahideen, he was their saviour and hero. More than a million people attended Zia's funeral in Islamabad. A large number of Afghans, including leaders of all the Islamist factions, took part in the ceremony. While the liberal intellectuals abhorred the reforms that Zia had undertaken, those measures were naturally lauded by Islamists – not only in Pakistan but internationally as well. The London-based Palestinian secretary of the Islamic Council, Salem Azzam, considered by many to be Osama bin Laden's mentor, in his eulogy to Zia summed up the immense respect and admiration he enjoyed among radical Muslims:

> Zia was a Muslim leader who was genuinely committed to working for the glory of Islam. Unlike some Muslim rulers, he did not pay mere lip service to Islam.…Only Zia made a determined effort to establish an Islamic order in Pakistan and made significant progress in this direction. Had he lived longer he would have certainly pursued his mission to successful completion. I am confident that the Muslim people of Pakistan, who loved and respected Zia, will not rest until Pakistan is turned into an Islamic state in the true sense of the word. This was, after all, the raison d'être of Pakistan (Azzam 1990: xiv).

13

Civilian Governments and the Establishment

Following the death of General Zia, general elections were announced for 19 November 1988. Eleven years of the Zia regime had greatly strengthened the establishment vis-à-vis the political class. The political campaign picked up momentum quickly. It became clear that the contest would be between the PPP, led by Benazir Bhutto and the Pakistan Muslim League, led by Mian Muhammad Nawaz Sharif. Benazir Bhutto took over the leadership of the party from her mother, Nusrat Bhutto, sidelining her brother, Murtaza Bhutto, whose credentials had been sullied because of his involvement in terrorism. While in exile, Benazir had been lobbying support for herself and her party in the corridors of power of important Western nations. Particularly, she visited Washington DC to cultivate sympathy for herself with the State Department and influential senators and congressmen as a moderate and progressive leader who no longer subscribed to the anti-Americanism associated with her father. As a result, Zia had been pressured to allow her to return to Pakistan, and she received a tumultuous welcome upon her return in 1986.

Under the circumstances, Zia began looking for a counterweight to any threat that Benazir may pose to his rule. On the recommendation of the Punjab governor, Lieutenant General Jilani, Zia began to patronize Nawaz Sharif. The Sharifs were a phenomenal post-partition Muslim success story. Mian Muhammad Sharif – Nawaz's father – and his brothers had pooled their humble resources to acquire a rudimentary iron foundry in Lahore in the 1930s (Warraich, 2008: 28–9). They prospered famously in the independent Pakistan. However, Z.A. Bhutto's erratic nationalisation had hit the Sharifs severely. Under Zia's patronage, the Ittefaq Group of Industries was re-launched with liberal bank loans from the government, and the Sharifs were catapulted into the higher echelon of the entrepreneurial class of Pakistan. Moreover, Nawaz was rewarded with the post of finance minister in the Punjab government in 1981. In that role, he established a sound reputation as a business-friendly, free-market, right-of-centre politician. In 1985, he was elected chief minister of the Punjab (ibid., 61–3).

The 1988 Election

The announcement of elections animated political activists. Nawaz was supported by an alliance known as the Islami Jamhoori Ittehad (IJI). According to Benazir, the acting president, Ghulam Ishaq Khan, passed a decree to change the election laws so that several PPP candidates could be purged from the ballot; moreover, he declared that all voters must have national identity cards – knowing full well that, in the rural areas where the PPP's strength was greatest, 'only a third of the men and a mere five percent of women actually had these cards' (Bhutto, 2008b). Moreover, the ISI carried out a vicious campaign to malign Benazir. The ISI head, General Hamid Gul, and his assistant, Brigadier Imtiaz, frankly warned the Islamists that 'The ISI has intelligence that Benazir Bhutto has promised the Americans a rollback of our nuclear program. She will prevent a Mujahideen victory in Afghanistan and stop plans for jihad in Kashmir in its tracks' (quoted in Haqqani, 2005: 202).

The ISI distributed millions of rupees to her opponents to join the IJI. Years later, the former head of the ISI, Lieutenant General Asad Durrani, admitted in an affidavit submitted to the Pakistan Supreme Court that he had been given money by the government [read Ishaq Khan and COAS Aslam Beg] to distribute among the politicians and political parties. The money had been donated by the business community. The sums paid to some of the leading politicians were as follows: ₹10 million to Mir Afzal in NWFP; ₹3.5 million to Nawaz Sharif in Punjab; ₹5.6 million to Lieutenant General (Retd.) Rafaqat for a media campaign; ₹5 million to the Jamaat-e-Islami; ₹1 million to Begum Abida Hussain; in Sindh, where Benazir enjoyed broad support, several politicians were among the recipients – ₹5 million to former PPP leader Ghulam Mustafa Jatoi, ₹5 million to Jam Sadiq, ₹2.5 million to the recent prime minister, Muhammad Khan Junejo, and ₹2 million to Pir Pagara. In Balochistan, ₹1 million was given to Nadir Mengal (Kharal, 2010).

In spite of such bribery, the PPP emerged as the main winner, winning 94 of the 217 directly-elected seats in the house. That figure went up to 122 when the members from the tribal areas, minorities, and women were added. The IJI could win only fifty-five seats. According to Benazir, the ISI head, General Hamid Gul, began to plot the dismemberment of the PPP by urging some of its leaders to defect (Bhutto, 2008a: 197). Simultaneously, Ishaq Khan opened discussions with other political leaders in the hope that a coalition government could be cobbled together with the help of the minority parties and independents. That attempt foundered. Meanwhile, Benazir gave assurances to the president and the military that neither would she interfere in the appointment of senior military officers nor with Pakistan's policy on security, especially in relation to Afghanistan, India, or the nuclear weapons programme. The US ambassador, Robert Oakley, took part in behind-the-scenes negotiations with Ishaq Khan and General Beg to facilitate her being invited to form the government (Haqqani, 2005: 203).

Benazir Bhutto as Prime Minister (2 December 1988–6 August 1990)

Benazir was sworn in as Pakistan's first female prime minister on 2 December 1988. She kept the portfolio of finance minister with herself, and ignored Ishaq Khan who had been at the helm of economic planning during Zia's time and prided himself for having put the economy on a sound footing. Benazir further antagonized Ishaq Khan when she began to make appointments to different posts through the 'placement bureau'. Some 200,000 vacancies were filled on the recommendation of PPP members of parliament (Aziz, 2009: 99–101). On the other hand, she released political prisoners, ended press censorship, and undertook reforms for women – such as Ministry of Women's Development, women's studies programmes at universities, the Women's Development Bank; also, separate police stations with female staff were established in some places and were expected to be expanded. However, on the other hand, the harsh Islamic laws that Zia had introduced were left unchallenged. Her plea was that she lacked the requisite two-thirds parliamentary majority to amend the constitution.

At the fourth South Asian Association for Regional Cooperation (SAARC) Summit in Islamabad in December 1988, Benazir and the Indian prime minister, Rajiv Gandhi, seemed to have struck a friendly rapport. Benazir was of the view that Pakistan should re-orient its foreign policy towards democracy and, since India was a democracy, relations with that country should improve. During their meeting, it was agreed that the two countries would not attack each other's nuclear facilities. Some understanding also emerged on increasing trade and resolving the dispute over the Siachen Glacier. The military, as well as the IJI, were critical of such a standpoint (Shafqat, 1997: 234–5). In any case, a rumour began to circulate after the SAARC Summit that Benazir had handed over the names of the Khalistani Sikhs who had, hitherto, received sanctuary in Pakistan.

The United States revived its aid to Pakistan, which had virtually dried up once the Red Army had withdrawn from Afghanistan. Benazir has written:

> Instead, our team in Islamabad and Washington worked to get the White House and Congress to greatly increase aid to Pakistan, making the country the third-largest recipient of foreign assistance from the United States, after Israel and Egypt.…We negotiated a nuclear confidence-building measure with the United States, making 'no export of nuclear technology' part of our nuclear doctrine. We also decided not to put together a nuclear device unless the country's security was threatened (Bhutto, 2008b: 199–200).

Allegedly, in 1989, the Al-Qaeda leader, Osama bin Laden, offered money to members of parliament, including those from the PPP, to pass a no-confidence vote to make her government fall. When some of them informed her about the conspiracy, Benazir used some of them as 'Trojan horses' in the 'ISI–IJI' camp, to confuse it into believing that a majority existed against her. Benazir wrote: 'I used another group to videotape Brigadier Imtiaz Ahmed asking my members to defect because "the army" did not want me. And I worked on members of the opposition who had known my father or were disgruntled with the IJI' (ibid., 201). The no-confidence vote failed and Benazir continued in office. This assertion of Benazir's – subsequently corroborated by Brigadier Imtiaz during an inter view on *Dunya TV* – was called Operation Midnight Jackal. Imtiaz revealed that COAS General Aslam Beg wanted to replace her as her policies were deemed to be contrary to those of the army (*The Daily Times*, 28 August 2009).

When she tried to rehabilitate some pro-PPP army officers, who had deserted when her father was overthrown, the army overruled her decision. Moreover, the head of the ISI, General Hamid Gul, continued to maintain links with the IJI. In short, she was treated like a security risk (Abbas, 2005: 136–38). She tried to assert herself by using her executive prerogative to appoint pro-PPP judges and bureaucrats, and spread a wide net of partisan appointments. The head-on collision with the establishment took place when Benazir tried to take control of the ISI by removing its director-general, General Hamid Gul, and replacing him with General Shamsher Rahman Kallu. She has written:

> General Gul [Hamid] got President Ishaq Khan and General Mirza Aslam Beg, the army chief of staff, to authorize the transfer of the ISI's duties to Military Intelligence (MI)....While the ISI's ability to destabilize the government was neutralized, the military security campaign continued under the aegis of the MI (Bhutto, 2008b: 202).

Benazir was in a vulnerable position vis-à-vis the overall domestic power balance. Ethnic violence in Sindh, between the MQM and PPP and other Sindhi nationalists, caused hundreds of casualties. During the period 1 January 1990 to 31 July 1990, 1187 people were killed and 2491 injured in various incidents in Sindh; of these, 635 were killed and 1433 injured in ethnic terrorism (Aziz, 2009: 102). She sought the help of the army which insisted that, as militants were present on both sides, it needed proper legal powers to conduct an even-handed clean-up operation. Benazir was reluctant to accede to this. In Punjab, the PML won 108 out of the 240 seats and formed the government. Nawaz, who had been elected to both the National Assembly and the Punjab Assembly, decided to become the chief minister of Punjab. Consequently, confrontational politics over the distribution of funds and resources characterised the restoration of civilian rule after years of military-led dictatorship. The veteran civil servant, parliamentarian, finance and foreign minister, Sartaj Aziz, asserted that the PPP tried to oust Nawaz from the post of Punjab chief minister by trying to win over 'at least twenty-five members of the IJI government led by Nawaz Sharif' (ibid., 99), but failed. Nawaz retaliated by rejecting federal government appointments of senior officers to and from Punjab. The two rivals entered a zero-sum contest that made a mockery of responsible government. Exercising his special powers under Article 58 (2-b) of the constitution, also known as the Eighth Amendment, Ishaq Khan dismissed Benazir on 6 August 1990. He listed several reasons in the charge-sheet against her, but the crux of the argument was that public office had been abused to plunder national wealth to promote the interests of the PPP to such an extent that politics in Pakistan became synonymous with corruption.

Interim Arrangements and New Elections

A caretaker government was appointed under a dissident Sindhi PPP leader, Ghulam Mustafa Jatoi. A number of other ex-PPP leaders also joined the cabinet. Fresh elections to the national assembly were announced for 24 October 1990. As was the case previously, the contest was between the two main alliances – the People's Democratic Alliance (PDA) led by Benazir Bhutto and the rightwing IJI led by Nawaz Sharif. Nawaz denounced Benazir, not only for corruption but also because she had allegedly sold out to American imperialism, blackmail, and exploitation (Kux, 2001: 311). Benazir accused the establishment of supporting Nawaz, and the intelligence services of rigging the elections once again – even though she had won on the previous occasion. Air Marshal (Retd.) Asghar Khan has recorded that 'trucks carrying ballot papers had entered the Ittefaq Industries premises' (Khan, 2008: 409). The IJI secured 106 seats while the PDA could muster merely 44 seats in the 217-seat National Assembly. Benazir accused the ISI of conspiring to inflict a defeat on her. On the other hand, Nawaz asserted that Ishaq Khan and COAS Aslam Beg had wanted Jatoi to be prime minister and, only reluctantly, accepted him (Nawaz) as prime minister though he had won a landslide victory (Warraich, 2008: 78–9).

Nawaz Sharif as Prime Minister (6 November 1990–18 April 1993)

Nawaz turned out to be assertive and confident vis-à-vis the deep state. He ushered in free-market reforms that included the de-nationalisation of state enterprises that had been nationalised earlier by Z.A. Bhutto. In doing so, he has claimed that his government carried out liberalisation earlier than India. Nawaz also introduced easy instalment loans for unemployed youths and other such people to run duty-free imported taxis. Such measures won him praise from the World Bank and the International Monetary Fund (IMF). But, surprisingly, not from the United States which stopped economic and military aid soon after Benazir was overthrown (Abbas 2005: 144). More crucially, liberalisation and denationalisation did not please Ishaq Khan who had invested his skills in running nationalised industries efficiently. Nawaz's relations with Ishaq Khan turned into open hostility when Nawaz expressed his intention to waive parts of the Eighth Amendment that would restore the supremacy of parliament (Warraich, 2008: 78–80).

With regard to the military, Nawaz has noted that, initially, he had amiable relations with the top commanders. There was no disagreement on Afghanistan. However, his relations with General Beg quickly assumed negative features over the Iraqi invasion of Kuwait in 1990. Nawaz and Beg initially agreed to send Pakistani troops to the Persian Gulf in support of Kuwait and Saudi Arabia, against the Iraqi invasion. Afterwards, Beg changed his stance and began to oppose it (Kux, 2001: 312; Warraich, 2008: 85–8). Ishaq Khan appointed General Asif Nawaz Janjua as COAS in August 1991, overruling the man that Nawaz had wanted in that position. General Janjua felt that the prime minister was cultivating a constituency in the army by showering favours on some generals and making arbitrary appointments to senior positions. Such differences assumed political implications as the prime minister and the COAS clashed over the reasons, and responsibility, for the rampant lawlessness and ethnic violence in Sindh (Nawaz, 2008: 449–59).

Janjua and the corps commander of Karachi, Lieutenant General Naseer Akhtar, wanted to cut the MQM down to size, but Nawaz was not willing to do that as it was part of his ruling coalition at the centre. It was widely speculated, in the Pakistani newspapers, that the MQM's supreme leader, Altaf Hussain, feared some sort of action against him by the army. And so, he left for Britain in January 1992 from where he began to direct his followers via the telephone and recorded messages on video tapes. Thus, terrorism continued to rage in Sindh. At the end of May 1992, Home Minister Shujaat Hussain made a statement to the effect that India's main spy agency, the Research and Analysis Wing, was directly involved in training and funding Jiye Sindh and Al-Zulfikar cadres (Jang, 28 May). Prime Minister Nawaz Sharif reiterated the same allegations at the beginning of June, and announced that the United Nations had been intimated of such interference (*Jang*, 9 June 1992). The background to such allegations was the proliferation of roving gangs of dacoits who killed and plundered, and resorted to kidnappings and abductions. When pursued by the police, these gangs would cross into India through the vast border in the Sindh desert. General Janjua and General Akhtar wanted to carry out stern actions against both the dacoits as well as the political miscreants. Thus, Operation Clean-Up was launched in May 1992, with a very different remit from what the government had wanted.

Actual action began a few weeks later, in June, with raids by the army against the strongholds of the MQM as well as the dacoits in the interior of Sindh. The army made spectacular discoveries of MQM prisons, torture chambers, and a sizable cache of arms in the possession of the terrorists. Within the first few weeks, most of the top leaders of the MQM had been arrested (*Jang*, 21–29 June 1992). The MQM members of the Pakistan National Assembly and Sindh Assembly resigned in protest.

General Janjua died suddenly on 8 January 1993, apparently because of a heart attack, although his family suspected foul play. The post-mortem report did not confirm foul play, but his brother, Shuja Nawaz, has expressed doubts about the report (Nawaz 2008: 599–606). Asif Nawaz's successor, General Abdul Wahid Kakar, was also not Nawaz's choice. Ishaq Khan, allegedly, chose him without consulting the prime minister (ibid., 85–8).

Friendly Gestures towards the United States

Nawaz had come to power with the impression of being a strong proponent of Pakistan's independence vis-à-vis the United States. However, once in power, he softened that image. His support for the anti-Saddam coalition was an important move in that direction. He expressed a willingness to stop production of enriched uranium, but not to destroy what Pakistan already possessed. Consequently, the sanctions imposed under the Pressler Amendment were eased and Pakistan was allowed to obtain $120 million of arms sales – primarily spare parts for the F-16s. The Americans were worried that continuing sanctions would render Pakistan increasingly dependent on China. Pakistan, on the other hand, was getting increasingly worried about India's growing missile capabilities. China, the Americans suspected, began to help Pakistan with some of its missile requirements (Kux, 2001: 312–20).

The Dismissal of Nawaz Sharif

However, such moves in the international arena had no bearing on Nawaz's standing vis-à-vis the deep state. Ishaq Khan dismissed him on grounds of corruption to the tune of $20 billion (Tahir 2010). The charge sheet included accusations of extra-judicial killings, victimisation of opponents, and other such charges. His mega-construction schemes and yellow taxi initiatives had won Nawaz the honorific title of Sher Shah Suri (legendary Muslim reformer of the sixteenth century) of Pakistan from his admirers, but his critics alleged that these schemes were accompanied by kickbacks and illicit commissions. Moreover, his cooperative bank schemes had collapsed, rendering thousands of widows, orphans, and retired personnel who had deposited their savings in those ventures destitute. Most such banks were owned by members of Sharif's Muslim League. More serious was the fact that his family business, Ittefaq Industries, benefited enormously because of tariff and customs duty manipulation. The personal fortunes of the Sharif family magnified because of abuse of public office (Abbas, 2005: 146).

Nawaz, proffering a conspiracy theory about his downfall, alleged that Benazir conspired with Ishaq Khan to bring him (Nawaz) down. The alleged proof of such connivance was that when Nawaz was dismissed, Ishaq Khan took Benazir's spouse, Zardari, and other PPP leaders into his interim government (Warraich, 2008: 80). But, on the other hand, Benazir denied any involvement in the dismissal of Nawaz and accused him of undoing her social programmes – especially those related to the uplift of women – re-introducing press censorship, and denying the opposition access to the state media (Bhutto, 2008b: 203).

Another Caretaker Government and New Elections

A caretaker government was appointed under Mir Balakh Sher Mazari. However, the Supreme Court of Pakistan overturned the unseating of Nawaz six weeks later, and returned him to power on 26 May 1993. At that point, the Pakistan Army stepped in and told Nawaz to resign. He resisted; COAS

General Kakar mediated in the negotiations involving Nawaz, Ishaq Khan, and Benazir – which resulted in a compromise solution that required both Nawaz and Ishaq Khan to resign their offices. The chairman of the Senate, Wasim Sajjad, became the interim president. The establishment then invited a retired vice-president of the World Bank, Moin Qureshi, to assume the duties of prime minister until an elected government could take over after the elections scheduled for 6 October, 1993. The elections returned a more diversified National Assembly. The PPP won eighty-six seats and the PML-Nawaz (PML-N) seventy-two seats. Several small parties and independents captured the rest of the seats in the 217-seat National Assembly. Although Benazir alleged that the results had been delayed by several hours and that the intelligence agencies had again conspired against her, ultimately, the PPP won more seats than any of the other parties. And so began the negotiations with the minor parties and independents. On 14 November, Farooq Ahmed Leghari, a PPP stalwart who had served as foreign minister during the first Benazir government, was elected president.

Benazir Bhutto
(19 October 1993–5 November 1996)

Benazir's return to power, on 19 October 1993, greatly perturbed the opposition. She alleged that the ISI and Al-Qaeda had tried to assassinate her (ibid., 205). However, she was not deterred. She reinvigorated the social action plan from her previous incomplete term; development initiatives were undertaken pertaining to education, health, housing, sanitation, infrastructure, and women's rights. The stock exchange was modernised, and the State Bank computerised; 100,000 women were trained to work in health and family planning in both rural and urban areas; and 30,000 primary and secondary schools were constructed. Moreover, tax revenues were doubled and national economic growth tripled. Pakistan was being celebrated as one of the ten emerging markets of the world. The law and order situation improved. Her government came out strongly against terrorism. Crackdowns on kidnapping and hostage-taking took place. She claimed that had her government continued for the full five-year term, international terrorism would not have succeeded in finding a base in Pakistan (ibid., 206). Her return to power and her policies received appreciation from the West; in

1995, the United States gave $368 million in aid for the purchase of US military equipment.

In the political biography of Benazir Bhutto, Goodbye Shahzadi, the Indian journalist Shyam Bhatia, who studied at Oxford University with Benazir, has made some startling revelations about her involvement in the proliferation of nuclear technology. Bhatia has written that, in the off-the-record interview given to him in Dubai in 2003, Benazir claimed that while her father was the 'father of Pakistan's nuclear weapons programme', she was the 'mother of the missile programme' (Bhatia, 2010: 39). The story was that in 1993, Pakistan's nuclear research was under scrutiny from the Indian, Western, Israeli, and Russian secret services. As it was widely believed that Pakistani scientists were engaged in industrial espionage with a view to acquiring technology that would help them achieve nuclear weapons' capability, their trips abroad were strictly monitored. Benazir, who enjoyed the reputation of being a dovish prime minister with regard to the nuclear programme, was ideally suited to dupe the spy agencies in evading detection. This she did in 1993 when she visited North Korea. According to Bhatia:

> The gist of what she told me was that before leaving Islamabad she shopped for an overcoat with the 'deepest of pockets' into which she transferred CDs containing the scientific data about the uranium enrichment that the North Koreans wanted...but she implied with a glint in her eyes that she acted as a two-way courier, bringing North Korea's missile information on CDs back with her on her return journey to Pakistan (ibid., 41).

The story received considerable attention worldwide; US experts on Pakistan, such as Selig Harrison, considered Bhatia's story credible (Kessle, 2008). Not surprisingly, the Pakistan Foreign Office dismissed Bhatia's claims as unfounded and misleading.

Coup Attempt

In September 1994, the Military Intelligence (MI) uncovered a plot to overthrow Benazir's government. The masterminds of the conspiracy were Major General Zaheer-ul-Islam Abbasi, Brigadier Mustansir Billa, Colonel Azad Minhas, and some other officers. The plan was to overthrow the government, declare Pakistan a Sunni religious state, and kill the top commanders in the GHQ – the conspirators expected the rest of the army to accept it as a fait accompli. Apparently, the plotters were not in command of the troops with whose help they could have succeeded in their bid to carry out an Islamist coup d'état. As the plotters were aiming to liquidate the top generals, not only was it a conspiracy against Benazir but also against the establishment. COAS General Kakar reacted by overhauling the intelligence power structure. The new director of the ISI, Lieutenant General Javed Ashraf Qazi, was tasked with purging the ISI of Islamists – a task he carried out with determination and courage. The ringleaders and their followers were court-martialled and handed down prison sentences, others were retired (Abbas, 2005: 152–3).

Benazir's reputation continued to be tainted by rumours that she and her spouse were relentlessly looting the national treasury once again. Her niece, Fatima Bhutto, has affirmed the corruption charges in ample measure, giving many examples (Bhutto, 2010: 384–8). Benazir's appointment of twenty new judges of the Punjab High Court caused considerable controversy. Syed Sajjad Ali Shah, a Sindhi whom Benazir had chosen as chief justice of the Pakistan Supreme Court, refused to endorse her appointments, while she refused to implement the court ruling. Justice Shah sought the help of President Leghari to resolve the tangle. Leghari prevailed upon her to relent. Benazir had expected the president to rubber-stamp her decisions. Further tensions were generated between them when Benazir used her own men, in the intelligence agencies, to spy on Leghari. She also used such elements to pass information to her on some corps commanders and ISI and MI officials (Abbas, 2005: 156–7).

On 20 September 1996, Benazir's brother, Murtaza Bhutto, was gunned down in a spray of bullets. Murtaza had established a separate PPP faction. According to Benazir, Murtaza and she had reconciled their differences two months earlier. However, the intelligence agencies began spreading rumours that her husband, Zardari, had masterminded the murder. A judicial inquiry set up to investigate the crime, Benazir informs, cleared Zardari of any involvement (Bhutto, 2008b: 209). Murtaza's daughter Fatima, however, has referred to Leghari's statement on *Dunya TV* in January 2010 in which he said that Zardari had come to him, along with Benazir, and insisted that Murtaza should be eliminated. Zardari had said, 'It's either him or me' (Bhutto, 2010: 423). In any case, Benazir's second term in office was cut short when, after Murtaza's death, a terrorist attack on Shias resulted in twenty-one deaths. Leghari considered such developments to be a sign of a deteriorating law and order situation. By invoking his prerogative under the Eighth Amendment, and in consultation with General Karamat, he dismissed Benazir on 5 November 1996. The charge sheet against her was a familiar one about massive corruption and abuse of office. An investigative journalist at the *New York Times*, John F. Burns, wrote a report that mentioned that Pakistani investigators traced more than $100 million to Benazir's secret accounts in foreign banks.

A close confidant of Benazir's explained to the present author, on pledge of anonymity, that Benazir and her family had suffered great economic hardship in Pakistan, and later while living in exile. They were nearly broke when she returned to Pakistan. Therefore, Zardari and she resorted to corruption to acquire the economic means to sustain themselves politically. Shyam Bhatia, too, touts such a story while admitting that Benazir and her husband had indulged in unabashed corruption (Bhatia, 2010: 28–37).

Caretaker Government Again

The same day, veteran politician Malik Meraj Khalid (5 November 1996–17 February 1997) took over as caretaker prime minister. He introduced austerity measures, shunning unnecessary protocol and pomp and show. New elections were held on 3 February 1997. Nawaz won a landslide victory: the PML-N won 137 seats, while the PPP was routed and only won 18 seats. Benazir accused the intelligence services of massive rigging against the PPP.

Nawaz Sharif (17 October 1997–12 October 1999)

Some smaller parties and independents joined the coalition government led by Nawaz. Leghari continued as president. With 165 members supporting him, Nawaz had an unprecedented two-thirds majority in the National Assembly in support of his government. Not surprisingly, he managed to have the Thirteenth Amendment passed – which took away presidential power to dismiss the prime minister. A few months later, the Fourteenth Amendment was passed, which subjected members of parliament to very strict party discipline whereby party leaders could dismiss legislators who failed to vote as instructed. It virtually eliminated any chance of parliament throwing an incumbent prime minister out of office through a no-confidence motion. Some opposition members moved a writ petition against the Fourteenth Amendment, and the Supreme Court declared it ultra vires, much to the chagrin of Nawaz (Abbas, 2005: 159–60).

Meanwhile, Nawaz instituted the Ehtesab (accountability) Bureau. It was purported to hold politicians and holders of public office accountable, so as to prevent corruption. However, its ire was directed against political opponents and journalists. Nawaz also developed differences with the chief justice of the Supreme Court, Justice Shah. A mob of PML-N goons raided the Supreme Court premises and disrupted court proceedings. On 28 November 1997, Nawaz dismissed Sajjad Ali Shah, alleging that Justice Shah and President Leghari were conspiring to overthrow him; and, further, that like Benazir he, too, had heard that Shah was aspiring to become prime minister. He claimed that this information was provided to him by the intelligence agencies (Warraich, 2008: 108).

Afghanistan, Taliban and Kashmir Jihad

The domination of the military and some powerful bureaucrats – variously described as the establishment, oligarchy, or deep state – during the civilian governments of the 1990s was met by efforts, by both Benazir and Nawaz, to assert their authority against them. However, during the same period, policy towards Afghanistan and Indian-administered Kashmir remained virtually the exclusive preserve of the military and intelligence services, most notably the ISI. Both Benazir and Nawaz deemed it expedient to go along with, and even take the initiative on, these two subjects.

Afghanistan

When Benazir came to power in 1988, the Soviet Union's withdrawal from Afghanistan had begun; it was completed in February 1989. However, the pro-Soviet regime headed by Dr Najibullah was still in power. Benazir and the Americans were in favour of a negotiated settlement in Afghanistan, between the communist and anti-communist factions, but the ISI and Islamists favoured military means to establish a government of the Afghan Mujahideen, preferably under the fanatical Pakhtun leader, Gulbuddin Hekmatyar (Haqqani, 2005: 213). Consequently, a frontal military attack was launched on Afghan cities – which proved to be unsuccessful. The ISI even tried to set up an Afghan interim government in Peshawar, but Benazir refused to extend it recognition as long as it did not control any major Afghan territory. The JI called for recognition of the interim government, while the IJI government – headed by Nawaz in the Punjab – hosted a reception for the interim government leaders in Lahore. This was a contravention, in constitutional terms, as the holding of such receptions for foreign dignitaries is the exclusive right of the federal government; but, with the ISI backing him, constitutionalism was irrelevant. In any case, the ISI and Islamists persisted with their policy of a military campaign to oust Dr Najibullah. The American military went along with the campaign, even though American and Pakistani diplomats – notably Foreign Minister Sahibzada Yaqub Ali Khan – and Benazir were against it (Haqqani, 2005: 214–5).

The Afghan Civil War

Benazir's dismissal, and Nawaz's installation, as prime minister did not affect the ISI's and military's Afghan policy. Efforts to overthrow Najibullah continued but proved unsuccessful. He survived in office for four years without the help of Soviet troops. However, defections by some powerful warlords – such as the Uzbek leader, General Abdul Rashid Dostum, who joined an alliance led by the non-Puktun Tajik leader, Ahmed Shah Massoud – weakened Najibullah. What followed was a tussle between the Islamist Mujahideen backed by the ISI and the Dostum-Massoud forces that came to be known as the Northern Alliance. The latter were victorious. The Afghan president, who had taken refuge in the UN office in Kabul, was dragged out and pitilessly lynched.

The removal of the last relic of the short communist rule brought out, into the open, the deep ethnic and regional tensions and conflicts in the disparate Afghan population. Hitherto, the warlords had joined ranks to oust the Red Army and its Afghan hosts, but such unison was misleading and fake. What followed was several years of bloodshed and terrorism that paled the horrors of the warfare during the anti-Soviet jihad. Various ethnic and sectarian factions, led by their warlords, began an internecine butchery. Pakistan threw its weight behind the Pakhtun leader, Gulbuddin Hekmatyar, in his opposition to the government of the Tajik, Burhanuddin Rabbani, who was supported by the Dostum-Massoud forces.

However, at some point, the ISI tried to work out a broader alliance between different traditional Islamists, both Pakhtun and non-Pakhtun. Brigadier Yasub Ali Dogar was, at that time, heading the ISI operations in Afghanistan. The ISI was instrumental in establishing a broad coalition with, first, Sibgatullah Mujadid (28 April 1992–28 June 1992) and then Burhanuddin Rabbani (28 June 1992–29 September 1992). Later, Hekmatyar served as prime minister from 1993–1994, and again briefly in 1996. That greatly boosted Pakistan's prestige as a regional power. However, Hekmatyar expended his energies on intensifying violent confrontations with his ethnic rivals. Thousands of Afghans were killed, the incidents of rape and other gross excesses against women and sectarian minorities – such as the Shia Hazaras – multiplied. There was a complete breakdown of law and order during the wars of the warlords (Amin, Osinski, and DeGeorges, 2010: 25–7). It was also a period when the international supporters and backers of the different factions began to actively support them. Most notably, India cultivated the Uzbek–Tajik alliance, while Pakistan backed the southern Pakhtun forces. However, the balance of power was such that neither Hekmatyar nor the National Alliance could decisively weaken the other. The gory and destructive civil war, stalemated, adding to the already staggering amount of suffering of the Afghan people (Haqqani, 2005: 238).

The Taliban

It was under these circumstances that, from the end of 1994, the Taliban (students of Islamic madrassas) of the Pakhtun belt on both sides of the Durand Line, led by Mulla Omar, more or less spontaneously joined the contest; the civil war had resulted in total anarchy and chaos, and drug barons and other criminals reigned supreme. Unlike the Mujahideen who had fought the Soviets, most Taliban were younger and entered the bloody conflict after the Soviet Union had withdrawn. Their leaders were, of course, veterans of the anti-Soviet jihad. Apparently, besides embodying a strict Deobandi type of militant Sunni Islam, the Taliban were also supported by Pakistani transport and smuggling mafias looking for a route to the central Asian markets. Others who supported the Taliban movement were the Islamist ally of Benazir, Maulana Fazlur Rahman of the JUI, and Pakhtun military and political officers from Pakistan. In other words, it was essentially a Pakhtun movement that represented a curious blend of the religious and mundane interests of the Pakhtuns on both sides of the Durand Line.

The United States initially approved of Pakistan's efforts to bring the Taliban and other Afghan factions to the peace table. At the same time, the American oil company Unocol negotiated a gas pipeline deal that would extend from Turkmenistan to Pakistan, through Afghanistan (Haqqani, 2005: 238–40). Many other international companies were also on the look-out for a share in such possibilities. Also, the Americans were hoping that the Taliban would bring an end to terrorism, as well as narcotic trafficking; additionally as the Taliban were fanatical Sunnis, they would curb Iranian influence in the region. The regime, that the Taliban established, made Washington realize that many of its calculations were delusional (Kux, 2001: 336–7).

At any rate, the Taliban's movement towards Kabul, from Kandahar, was swift and dramatic. As they advanced, the weary and devastated locals joined them because they were perceived as pious and humble, and none of the notorious warlords was among their ranks. On the way to Kabul, the Taliban established peace and 'law and order'. They routed all others and captured Kabul in September 1996. Pakistan rejoiced over their victory because, for the first time, a friendly government had come into power in Afghanistan. Both Benazir and Nawaz welcomed the Taliban regime. Later, Benazir and her interior minister, Naseerullah Khan Babar, were to claim to have played a leading role in helping the Taliban capture power, though she regretted that Saudi Arabia had hijacked them (Khan 2005: 197). More importantly, that tall claim carried negative implications that Benazir had not counted on: it encouraged Pakistani Islamists to demand, and agitate with greater vigour and devotion, for a similar government in Pakistan. As usual, the JI was on the barricades leading the diehard Islamists.

The triumph of the Taliban was celebrated by the Pakistani military establishment and the ISI as a major strategic asset. For the first time, a government was in power that was not hostile to it. Indian influence plummeted as the National Alliance was driven out of Kabul and pushed into small pockets in the northern provinces. However, it was far from self-evident that the Taliban were merely creatures of the ISI with no will or interests of their own. Thus, for example, despite Pakistani pressure, the

Taliban never conceded that the Durand Line was the international border between Afghanistan and Pakistan (Rashid, 2008a: 186–7). Moreover, the Taliban acquired control over the trade and movement of smuggled goods that passed through Afghanistan on their way to and from the Central Asian Republics, Afghanistan, China, and Pakistan. As a result of the Taliban-controlled smuggling, the Pakistani economy lost vast amounts of custom revenues annually. Between 1992 and 1998, such losses totalled $900 million. Afghan smuggling mafias established a strong presence in the southern Pakistani province of Balochistan (ibid., 191).

In any event, the Taliban regime was initially successful in establishing peace, rooting out opium and heroin gangs, and maintaining primitive justice. Soon afterwards, it began to impose an Islamic order that, by its severity, outdid the repressive fundamentalist regimes of Iran and Saudi Arabia by a wide margin. In particular, the Taliban seemed obsessed with any modicum, even symbolic, of female emancipation. In their perception, a female's presence in the public sphere and public gaze could jeopardize the moral order and chaste conduct that Islam required of all pious Muslims. Although men who raped women and committed other indignities were publicly executed, the brunt of the Taliban's wrath was directed against women. Female teachers, doctors, and nurses were sent home. Female education was declared un-Islamic, and no woman could step out of her four walls without a male escort. In sectarian terms, the Taliban let loose a reign of terror against the Shias. Moreover, the Taliban began to impose harsh Islamic laws against alleged offenders in public places. The stoning to death of adulterers, whipping of fornicators, and chopping off of the hands of thieves were carried out with astonishing zeal. Moreover, a ban was imposed on music, cinemas, and photography. Traders and shopkeepers who kept such items were publicly flogged. Ahmed Rashid has provided detailed insight into the scourge that the Taliban visited upon the Afghan people. By the summer of 1998, the Taliban controlled ninety percent of the territory, and the Northern Alliance was a shambles. It resulted in Iran almost threatening to invade Afghanistan, and accusing Pakistan of being the main backer of the Taliban (ibid., 1–5).

The extreme monotheism that the Taliban professed acquired pathological proportions as their jihad was generalised to include all non-Muslims – who, thus, became legitimate targets (Ghazali and Ansari, 2002; Stern, 2000). Both Hindus and Sikhs had lived in Afghanistan since, at least, the time of Maharaja

Ranjit Singh. The traditional Pakhtun social code – the Pakhtunwali – had, in the past, guaranteed the security of those minorities but the Taliban began to harass them to convert to Islam or pay the Islamic protection tax, jizya – which resulted in Hindus and Sikhs, in increasing numbers, emigrating to India or the Pakistani side of the Durand Line. Consequently, not only was India, but so were the US, Israel, and in fact the whole non-Muslim world, declared enemies of Islam (Wright, 2000).

Jihad in Indian-Administered Kashmir

With the border with Afghanistan now supposedly secure because of the friendly Taliban regime, the Pakistan military, and especially the ISI, began to recruit warriors for the liberation of Kashmir from Indian control – so actualising their dream of attaining strategic depth. The triumph of the Taliban had created the belief that a greater Islamic republic or union of states – of Iran, Turkey, the Central Asian Muslim republics, Afghanistan, and Pakistan – could be formed. However, such a grand pan-Islamist state would be incomplete as long as Kashmir was not liberated from Indian rule. This was an absurd non-concept in military terms, 'unless one is referring to a hard-to-reach place where a defeated army might safely cocoon', according to the noted Pakistani scholar-activist Eqbal Ahmad (Rashid, 2008a: 187).

However, optimism that Kashmir could be liberated had increased after a popular insurgency emerged, in the late 1980s, among the Kashmiri Muslims – against Indian rule in Kashmir. Thousands of Kashmiris crossed the border into Pakistan, and then fanned out to training camps in Afghanistan and Pakistan. After the Red Army left Afghanistan, many foreign Mujahideen were drafted into the Kashmir jihad. The ISI tried to cultivate Islamist militants of the pro-Pakistan Hizbul Mujahideen, rather than the more secular JKLF, that stood for an independent Kashmir. In the 1990s, the Harkat-ul-Mujahideen (HuM), Laskhar-e-Tayyaba (LeT), and the Jaish-e-Muhammad (JeM) established themselves as Pakistan-based organizations waging jihad against India, especially in the part of Kashmir under India's control (Hussain, 2008: 24–5). The ISI and the Saudi millionaire, Osama bin Laden, a veteran of the Afghan jihad, sponsored bases for Kashmiri militants in Afghanistan.

The Pakistan military and ISI began to nurture Pakistani fundamentalist organisations that, in turn, actively recruited volunteers to fight in the Indian

Kashmir. It became standard practice that, after the weekly Friday prayers, donations were collected from the worshippers to help fund the jihad in the Indian Kashmir. The Indian government alleged, many times, that these organisations received support from the Pakistan government, and that the training camps for the militants existed in Pakistani Kashmir as well as in parts of Pakistan. The Pakistan government denied their existence; instead, it described the militants as freedom fighters (Rana 2004). In early 1990, India deployed large numbers of troops in Kashmir; Pakistan did the same. The new Indian prime minister, V.P. Singh, publicly spoke of the possibility of a war between India and Pakistan. The American ambassadors to India and Pakistan became concerned as suspicions already existed that both sides possessed nuclear weapons' capability. Deputy National Security Adviser Robert Gates visited South Asia and urged both sides to exercise restraint. He believed that India could easily inflict defeat on Pakistan, and did not accept Pakistan's position that it was not involved in the Kashmir insurgency. In any case, Gates' intervention helped defuse the tension, and confrontation between the two rivals was avoided (Kux, 2001: 306–7).

In 1992–93, the United States, under pressure from India, came close to describing Pakistan as a terrorist state. Pakistan responded by moving the militants' bases to eastern Afghanistan. Pakistan had to pay the Taliban to acquire these facilities (Rashid, 2008a: 186). Prime Minister Nawaz Sharif replaced the hardline ISI director-general, Lieutenant General Javed Nasir, with the more liberal Lieutenant General Javed Ashraf Qazi. On the other hand, Pakistani officials complained that the Mujahideen were described by the Americans as freedom fighters when they fought the Soviets, but were now being branded as terrorists when they were involved in the Kashmiris' just struggle for liberation from Indian occupation (Kux, 2001: 322–23). Pakistan's stand on Kashmir unexpectedly received great help from the American side when, on 28 October 1991, Assistant Secretary of State for South Asia Robin Raphael, told journalists:

> We view Kashmir as a disputed territory. We do not recognise and that means we do not recognise that Instrument of Accession as meaning that Kashmir is forever an integral part of India. And there were many other issues at play in that time frame as we all here know.... The people of Kashmir have got to be consulted in any kind of final settlement in

> the Kashmir dispute, because we believe at this point, there is no way that any resolution can be stable and lasting unless agreed to by the people of Kashmir (Jain, 2007a: 127–8).

Not surprisingly, while the Pakistanis were jubilant, the Indians were deeply agitated. However, Raphael held her ground and, in a hearing before the US Senate on 4 February 1994, she reiterated that stand stating that what she had said did not signal a change in the US position on Kashmir. She further elaborated:

> We look at the former princely state as a whole. What we mean by that is that not only are Indian-held portions in dispute but also portions held by Pakistan are in dispute....
>
> We also emphasise regularly on the Indian government our view that they should let international human rights organisations into Kashmir (ibid., 129).

Such statements did not allay Indian fears that the Americans were leaning towards Pakistan. Raphael tried to dispel such an impression when, on 9 February 1994 at a luncheon jointly sponsored by the Asia Society and the India Council of the State Department, she said that it was fair to stop all aid to Pakistan after the end of the Afghanistan war. She defended that decision by saying that since the world situation had changed, the US must also reformulate its policy goals based on its interests (ibid.). Her statement heightened Indian suspicions and fears about US intentions. Then, on 25 March 1994, Raphael spoke at the American Center in New Delhi where she modified her position somewhat. She told the audience that the US position (as presented by her in October 1993) had been misinterpreted and terribly distorted. The correct position was that the United States supported a negotiated settlement of the Kashmir dispute; further, that it should be resolved in accordance with the Simla Accord; human rights violations in Indian-administered Kashmir should be monitored in a credible manner; and 'we vigorously oppose outside aid to the militants and have repeatedly made that clear in capitals where it needs to be heard' (ibid., 130). This line of argument was subsequently adhered to by her, and her colleagues in the Clinton administration, while civilian governments were in office in Pakistan. In an interview with me, Raphael said that she had to suffer subsequently because her initial stand had been fiercely attacked by the Indians, and also failed to find favour with the US establishment which was turning increasingly pro-India.

The main concern of the Clinton administration remained Pakistan's nuclear weapons programme. American officials acknowledged that the economic and military sanctions were doing great harm to Pakistan but regretted that nothing could be done as long as Pakistan did not come clean on its nuclear ambitions. The Americans also strongly urged the Indians not to go nuclear, but the refrain from New Delhi was that the Chinese posed a threat to their national security and therefore they would keep 'all options open' (Talbott, 2004: 46).

Nuclear Test Explosions

Such pressure proved futile. On 11 and 13 May 1998, India carried out five nuclear test explosions. Indians took to the street, delirious as they celebrated their brute power. Joy was expressed across the political divide. In fact, the Congress government of P.V. Narasimha Rao had considered nuclear tests but, as the Hindu nationalist party, Bharatiya Janata Party (BJP), had carried them out, jingoism and chauvinism were given full expression. Not surprisingly, the sense of insecurity increased profoundly in Pakistan. The government deliberated the pros and cons of an identical Pakistani response but could not immediately agree on how to react. Benazir resorted to theatrical tactics on television, urging Nawaz to wear bangles if he did not want to act in a manly manner. The Clinton Administration, the EU, and Japan exerted extreme pressure on Pakistan to desist from conducting nuclear tests, while Saudi Arabia urged Pakistan to go ahead. Pakistan carried out nuclear test explosions on 28 and 31 May. Nawaz earned the applause of a Pakistani nation that, no doubt, felt extremely vulnerable after India's display of military might. However, once the euphoria was over and the United States and other countries imposed severe sanctions on Pakistan, its economy was nearly crippled (Warraich, 2008: 113).

The government reacted by freezing foreign bank accounts. Rumours spread that, before doing so, Nawaz and his ilk had illicitly transferred their own foreign currency out of the country. Nawaz's popularity plummeted in a tailspin. He aggravated the situation when he suspended many civil liberties, dismissed the Sindh provincial government, and set up military courts. On 8 October 1998, he moved the Shariat Bill in the National Assembly which proposed that the Quran and Sunnah be declared the supreme law. The bill was discussed by his cabinet and, after some modifications, presented to the lower house of parliament – the National Assembly. It was passed on 10 October 1998 by 151 votes to 16. However, it required approval by the upper house – the Senate.

Human rights and women's rights NGOs took out demonstrations and protest actions. The government responded angrily, by stigmatising them as agents of Western imperialism and anti-Islamic forces (Ahmed, 2002). However, the government did not have the required two-thirds support in the Senate and, therefore, the bill was defeated. But Nawaz persisted and, on 16 January 1999, Islamic law was imposed in the tribal areas along the Afghanistan-Pakistan border. Nawaz threatened to impose strict Sharia law in Pakistan as well, in spite of losing the vote in the Senate. However, before he could do anything of the sort, his government was overthrown by General Musharraf on 12 October 1999 (Abbas, 2005: 164–5).

An aide of Osama bin Laden's, Ali Mohamed, claimed that he had arranged a meeting between bin Laden and representatives of Nawaz. After the meeting, Nawaz's representatives were allegedly rewarded with $1 million for allowing the Taliban to flourish in Afghanistan as well as establishing their influence in Pakistan's NWFP (*ABC News*, 30 November 2007). Such allegations notwithstanding, Nawaz restored Sunday as the day of rest – which Z.A. Bhutto had replaced with Friday. In this case, at least, Nawaz's trader instinct trumped his Islamist orientations.

In any event, since October 1998, Nawaz had been drawn into a confrontation with COAS General Karamat over the latter's advocacy of the creation of a National Security Council. Nawaz perceived it as a conspiracy to involve the military in a more active role in Pakistani politics, and severely criticised the military chief who resigned (Warraich, 2008: 117–9). Nobody put that more bluntly than Nawaz's handpicked COAS and nemesis, General Pervez Musharraf, who wrote, 'What shocked me…was the meek manner in which General Karamat resigned. It caused great resentment in the army, as soldiers and officers felt humiliated' (Musharraf, 2006: 84) Nawaz appointed Musharraf as army chief by making him supersede other senior generals: a decision Nawaz deplored vehemently in his conversation with Warraich

(Warraich, 2008: 120). Musharraf has claimed that his relations with Nawaz were cordial initially, but not for long. When he disputed some appointments and dismissals of the prime minister, and refused his instructions to court-martial a journalist, Nawaz became a bully. Moreover, he never read anything but took orders from Abbaji (his father, Mian Sharif) in whose hands, allegedly, the real reins of power rested. Therefore, antipathy between them developed progressively (Musharraf, 2006: 113).

Peace Mission to Lahore of Atal Bihari Vajpayee

Such antipathy between Nawaz and Musharraf was manifest when the Indian prime minister, Atal Bihari Vajpayee, visited Lahore in February 1999 to talk peace. Actually, the initiative – from the Indian side – had been taken by his predecessor, Inder Kumar Gujral. Gujral and Nawaz Sharif had met in Dhaka in May 1997. As the vibes were very positive, they decided to try to bring their two nations closer to each other (Gujral, 2011: 407). Both were Punjabi refugees whose families had been forced to flee to the other side when India was partitioned. They spoke to each other in Punjabi – something Benazir tried to exploit by casting aspersions on such behaviour as inimical to Pakistan. I saw this myself on television. At any rate, Vajpayee now came across as a dove – having won laurels from his hawkish Hindu nationalist BJP for carrying out the nuclear test explosions in May 1998. When Pakistan followed suit, the Indian leadership realized that the balance of power remained constant.

Vajpayee visited the Pakistan Minaret in the historic Minto Park where, on 23 March 1940, the demand for Pakistan was first made by the Muslim League. The visit was to symbolise the acceptance, by Hindu nationalists, of the partition of India as an irreversible fact and the beginning of a new era of cooperation between the two nations (Talbott, 2004: 153). The Lahore Declaration of 21 February 1999 laid down that both sides would strive for a mutually beneficial relationship; resort to arms would be avoided; and all disputes including Kashmir would be settled through negotiations. Both sides admitted that, as nuclear weapons states, their responsibilities had increased. Vajpayee came to Lahore with a large delegation that included veterans with links to the Pakistani West Punjab; among them were the matinee idol of the 1950s and 1960s Dev Anand, the singer Mahendra Kapoor, and journalist Kuldip Nayyar. At the Wagah border, most of the delegates were driven to Lahore in buses while Vajpayee was flown to the Governor's House in a helicopter. The JI and other opponents of the reconciliation process demonstrated all along the road, and stones were thrown at the buses. Nawaz has alleged that, apart from the JI cadres, ISI functionaries were also involved in the stone-throwing (Warraich, 2008: 123–4). Dev Anand wrote about the nostalgia that gripped him when he visited his alma mater, Government College Lahore. He mentioned the crowds lined up on both sides cheering the visitors. The reception he received was very friendly, and Nawaz Sharif took him to meet his cabinet ministers. Dev Anand has not mentioned any untoward incident, perhaps not to convey any negative impression of a visit that was meant to foster good relations (2007: 364–70).

The Kargil Mini-War

A dramatic anticlimax to the peace process was the covert military operation that Musharraf and his coterie of generals launched in the Kargil mountain range on the LoC, apparently before Vajpayee had arrived in Lahore. Nawaz has pleaded complete ignorance about the Kargil operation:

> As prime minister I was not taken into confidence at all. And when after four months I was told a bit, it was said that the attack would neither cause any trouble nor result in loss of life. It was also said the army would not participate in the attack; rather it would be made by the Mujahideen exclusively. However, when the attack was made, the entire Northern Light Infantry perished; two thousand martyred and hundreds wounded; the death toll was higher than the 1965 and 1971 wars put together. When such heavy losses took place I reminded Musharraf that he had said no loss would be caused to the army, and asked what was happening. He said the Indians are carrying out carpet-bombing. I then asked whether he hadn't known that the Indians could do so. He said no, he hadn't. I was informed that our men were being killed like anything by Indian bombardment because there were no roofs over the trenches. I must tell you that when the Washington Pact was concluded, the Indian Army had got Kargil vacated. They were advancing swiftly. It was I who saved our army from dishonour and disgrace (Warraich, 2008: 126).

Nawaz goes on to say that, as a result, Pakistan lost the international community's sympathy. The biggest setback was to the Kashmir issue that Vajpayee and he had agreed should be resolved peacefully and quickly. The Pakistan Army began to be described as a rogue army in the international media. The Indian leadership felt betrayed as the Kargil operation was in complete contravention of the Lahore Declaration. Even after the dishonourable defeat that the army had sustained, the generals did not inform Nawaz that regular Pakistani troops had taken part in the operation – it was Vajpayee who told him that it had, indeed, been the Pakistan Army. Before Nawaz left for the United States, Musharraf went to him and implored him to arrange a ceasefire at all costs because, otherwise, the Indians would inflict an extremely crushing defeat on Pakistan. Nawaz praised Bill Clinton for his understanding and efforts to bring about the ceasefire. Had the Americans not helped, Pakistan would have suffered a humiliating defeat. Clinton also informed him that Pakistan had been moving its nuclear warheads from one place to another – a move that would have caused great worry to the Indians, and that such moves could have resulted in a nuclear exchange between the two rivals (ibid., 127–135).

Not surprisingly, Musharraf sets forth a diametrically opposite interpretation of the Kargil war. He makes a clean breast of the army preparing an operation at Kargil on the Indian side of the LoC from at least January 1999. The reason, according to Musharraf, was that by occupying definite posts at Siachen, the Indians had already violated the principles of the Simla Agreement and had, allegedly, been moving their positions forward on the LoC since then. Consequently, he had ordered a counter-manoeuvre to checkmate the Indians. This was done with great success as the Kashmiri Mujahideen and Pakistani volunteers surreptitiously occupied those bunkers and military posts that the Indians routinely vacated during the winters. In May 1999, when the Indians realised that the Mujahideen were there, some 500 miles in the Kargil area were already under the control of the freedom fighters. He has given the following assessment of the Kargil operation:

> Considered purely in military terms, the Kargil operations were a landmark in the history of the Pakistan Army. As few as five battalions, in support of the freedom fighter groups, were able to compel the Indians to employ more than four divisions, with the bulk of the Indian

> artillery coming from strike formations meant for operations in the southern plains. The Indians were also forced to mobilize their entire national resources, including their air force. By July 4 they did achieve some success, which I would call insignificant. Our troops were fully prepared to hold our dominating positions ahead of the watershed (Musharraf 2006: 93).

Musharraf has deplored Nawaz's capitulation before Clinton, and has claimed that Pakistan was in a very advantageous position with the freedom fighters determined to dig in. Nawaz should have demanded concessions on Kashmir before agreeing to not only a ceasefire but also an unconditional withdrawal. Musharraf has asserted that, were it not for his sense of responsibility to not let down the elected government at such a critical juncture, he would have gone public and shown how the advantage was lost because of political mishandling. He has refuted the claim that Nawaz had not been taken into confidence. According to Musharraf, the prime minister was briefed on 29 January and then again a few days later on 5 February 1999 and, on 15 March at the ISI headquarters, given detailed information about the situation inside Indian-occupied Kashmir. Later briefings followed on 17 May, 2 June, and 22 June. Musharraf has rejected, out of hand, that the Indian Air Force or ground forces stood any chance of defeating the freedom fighters (ibid., 95–6). As on several previous occasions during wars with India, the key actors laid the blame for their reverses at each other's doors. In this particular case, it seems that Musharraf's account was less reliable. Once again, it underlined that the operation as a whole lacked proper strategic planning. According to former US Deputy Secretary of State Strobe Talbott, Musharraf and his generals were hoping to achieve a different line of control that would be favourable to Pakistan (Talbott, 2004: 157).

I interviewed Brigadier Vijai Singh Nair of the Indian Army in Noida, outside Delhi, on 14 November 2010. He told me that since Pakistan had taken the absurd position that there was no involvement of Pakistani forces in the Kargil operation, and that those who participated in it were Kashmiri Mujahideen and Pakistani volunteers, there was no available procedure in the military manuals whereby India could hand over the bodies of the disowned soldiers – who had died fighting – to Pakistan. Consequently, the Indian Army buried them according to Islamic rites. This was possible because, since Indian Muslims serve in the Indian Army, the regiments have maulvis (Muslim clerics) attached to them; it was they who performed the funeral rights for the Pakistanis slain at Kargil.

US–India Develop an Understanding

Bill Clinton came out strongly in favour of the Indian position on Kargil, which was appreciated in New Delhi. This was followed by extended parleys between Talbott and the Indian defence minister, Jaswant Singh. The two men developed a close personal relationship which greatly helped bring their two nations closer (Talbott 2004). More importantly, it paved the way for significant military-to-military co-operation between their two countries. Such measures helped to reverse the impact of the severe reaction from the Clinton administration at the time of the May 1998 nuclear tests (Cohen and Dasgupta, 2010: 166). The understanding, no doubt, stemmed from their mutual concerns about China's rise as an economic and military power in Asia.

A Dramatic 12 October 1999

In the aftermath of the Kargil misadventure, differences between Nawaz and Musharraf had turned into a very strong and mutual antipathy. Nawaz has alleged that the chief architects of the Kargil operation – General Musharraf, General Aziz, and General Mahmood – began to plot to topple his government simply to cover their tracks since the Kargil fiasco was their doing. Musharraf, on the other hand, has accused Nawaz of heading a government of thugs who doled out favours to their sycophants while increasing their staggering personal wealth through rampant misuse of power.

On 12 October 1999, Nawaz removed General Musharraf as army chief. Instead, General Zia-ud-din [an ethnic Kashmiri like Nawaz] of the Engineers Corps was made COAS. Nawaz has claimed that Zia-ud-din had all the merits required for the post and had been serving as the head of the ISI at the time of his appointment as COAS. Musharraf was informed about his dismissal while he was in the air, on a Pakistan International Airlines flight back to Karachi from Colombo (Sri Lanka) where he had gone on an official visit. Nawaz has claimed that he had instructed his military secretary to tell the corps commander of Karachi, Lieutenant General Usmani, to receive him with respect and take him to his house. The decision to dismiss Musharraf was also conveyed to all the other corps commanders, including his Kargil accomplices, General Aziz and General Mahmud (Warraich, 2008: 143–6).

Musharraf has challenged that version. He has alleged that Karachi airport was sealed off to prevent the PIA airliner he was travelling on from landing. Moreover, his pilot was told to take the aircraft away from Pakistani airspace and land elsewhere. The pilot informed Musharraf that the aircraft only had enough fuel to fly for one hour; it would not be enough to take it out of Pakistani airspace. Thus, not only was Musharraf's life put in jeopardy, but also those of the other 200 people on board including a number of Pakistani school children returning from a goodwill visit to Sri Lanka. Musharraf contacted his top army generals from the air, and decided to take over the reins of power. The PIA airliner first landed at Nawabshah in Sindh and then, once Karachi Airport had been secured, it flew into Karachi. Most of the commanders remained loyal to Musharraf and the coup took place without any violent clashes with the pro-Nawaz elements. Musharraf claimed that the army had been caught completely off guard and that Nawaz had acted in complete secrecy (Musharraf, 2006: 101–40).

On taking over the government, Musharraf has claimed, he discovered that the degree to which the Nawaz government had exploited its public office to amass illicit wealth was beyond his comprehension. Except for the highway projects, all the other mega schemes were failures and the country was made to pay billions of rupees in excessive costs. He extended his criticism to cover the whole period of 1988–1999, to cover Benazir's two incomplete terms as prime minister, and argued that expenditure on useless projects, to the tune of ₹1.1 trillion, was imposed on the nation (Musharraf, 2006: 147).

Nawaz was tried by Pakistan's Anti-Terrorism Courts which, in 2000, handed down a life sentence on him for kidnapping, attempted murder, hijacking, and corruption – the hijacking charges were based on Nawaz allegedly not allowing the plane to land at Karachi. Originally, it was rumoured that the death sentence would be passed on him but since Nawaz enjoyed considerable goodwill with the Saudi royal family, who intervened on his behalf, the court passed a sentence of life imprisonment on him. Later, the military government agreed to exile him to Saudi Arabia. Nawaz has made the incredible assertion that he was willing to go to prison but, as a Muslim, being sent to the holy land in exile was a blessing he could not refuse and so he accepted that option. Nawaz reportedly gave an undertaking that he would abstain from politics for the next ten years, but he does not mention any such deal (Warraich, 2008: 156).

Lieutenant General Javed Ashraf Qazi made an interesting observation about Benazir and Nawaz during an interview with me. He said:

> In the 1990s, I was serving in the GHQ [later became chief of ISI]. The emissaries of Benazir and Nawaz used to make the rounds at the GHQ with a view to cultivating the sympathies of senior officers for themselves and against the two rivals. I would not say, who used such tactics most but it was certainly part of their strategy to win over senior officers to their side. Whenever they were in office they used the public office to confer favours on their sycophants. There was nothing inspiring about them. They made a mockery of democracy and responsible government.

Islamisation of the Armed Forces Continued

Irrespective of the political vicissitudes attendant upon the civil– military relations during the two incomplete terms of both Benazir and Nawaz, the process of Islamization of the armed forces, or rather of the army, continued unabated. An official publication – Pakistan Army Green Book: Year of the Commanding Officer 1991 – highlights that the Pakistan Army has to be an ideological fighting force, and the ideology, science, and art of war that it should follow is to be derived from the Quran (Pakistan Army Green Book, 1991). Major (Retd.) Agha Humayun Amin sent me a copy of The Army Regulations Volume II (Instructions) 1991, which states in Section 18:

> In case of stoning to death of a male convict, he will be firmly secured to an object, whereas for a female convict a hole or excavation should be dug to receive her as deep as her waist. As regards amputation of hand, foot or both, it will be, after medically examining the convict, at the discretion of the authorised medical officer to decide as to the manner in which the sentence will be executed (The Army Regulations 1991: 1080).

Sectarian Terrorism

In the 1990s, Pakistan served as the arena for a three-pronged proxy war between Iran and Saudi Arabia on the one hand, and Iran and Iraq on the other (Ahmed, 1998: 176–8). The three rentier states, whose staggering wealth was derived from a single natural gift – crude oil – poured a great deal of money and propaganda materials in through their sectarian and sub-sectarian affiliates in Pakistani society. Gun-toting armed militias committed atrocities against one another and against completely innocent people. During 1990–2002, 994 people died because of sectarian terrorism – of these, 593 were Shias and 388 Sunnis. Also killed in those terrorist incidents were forty-four individuals belonging to the police and other law-enforcing agencies (Rana, 2004: 586). The elected governments, while ritually condemning such crimes, proved to be helpless and ineffective.

Persecution of Hindus, Christians, and Ahmadis

With regard to the religious minorities – Hindus, Christians, and Ahmadis the period when civilian governments were in power saw a marked increase in terrorist attacks on temples, churches, and Ahmadiyya 'worshipping places' [as the Ahmadis are prohibited from using Islamic nomenclature for their religion and religious practices]. In 1991, the law on blasphemy was amended so that life imprisonment, as the maximum punishment, was replaced by the death penalty which became the automatic punishment for individuals 'proved' guilty of blasphemy (Ahmed, 2011: 90). As a result, several non-Muslims were booked for blasphemy – often on unreliable evidence – found guilty in the lower courts, but then had their sentences reduced at the higher level. In some cases, fanatics killed such individuals before their trials took place or if they were released. Some were granted humanitarian asylum in the West, and thus could escape with their lives. Incidents of forced conversion and abduction of Hindu and Christian girls were also reported (Ahmed, 2002: 57–89).

14

Vicissitudes of the Musharraf Regime

Pakistan was on the verge of economic insolvency when the military returned to power after eleven years. The sanctions, especially those imposed in the wake of the 1998 nuclear explosions, had bitten deep into Pakistan's fragile economic structure. Moreover, during those eleven years, any doubts whether or not the ultimate reins of power resided in the GHQ had been dispelled. There was no doubt that civilian authority had suffered considerable atrophy and diminution.

Internationally, the Kargil episode cast Pakistan in a very bad light; the major Western powers began to perceive Pakistan as a pariah state – personified by Musharraf and his top generals who were perceived as irresponsible military commanders whose roguery threatened peace in South Asia and beyond. There were hardly any takers for Musharraf's claim that the Kargil showdown had, once again, placed the Kashmir dispute squarely on the agenda of international politics. Moreover, Pakistan dissipated whatever goodwill it had hitherto enjoyed in international forums vis-à-vis Kashmir. Thus, initially, the military regime was completely isolated in relation to the western powers. In fact, the consequences of the Kargil operation were far more damaging than anything to date. The United States, and other major Western players, began to orient towards India in no uncertain terms. This became very apparent when Clinton paid a visit to South Asia in the spring of 2000: while he spent five days in India, he spent a mere five hours in Pakistan. While in Pakistan, he addressed the Pakistani nation on television, extolling the virtues of democracy and the rule of law – but refused to appear on television together with Musharraf.

The Terrorist Attacks of 11 September 2001

Since the 1990s, Al-Qaeda had been involved in a number of attacks on US targets, including the twin towers of the World Trade Center in 1993 and US embassies in two East African capitals in 1998. The Afghan jihad had given birth to a number of extremist movements dedicated to the revival of the caliphate that had existed till 1924 – when the Turkish leader Kemal Ataturk abolished the Ottoman caliphate and instead founded a secular-national republic. Internationally, the Hizb-ul-Tahir had emerged, oddly in London, as the voice of international jihad. In southwest Asia, besides the Taliban, there were the Hizb-e-Islami of Gulbadin Hekmatyar, various Tajik and Uzbek Islamist movements, Pakistani India-specific groups such as the HuM, LeT, and JeM, and Shia-specific groups such as the SSP and Lashkar-e-Jhangvi (LeJ). They formed links and networks that firmly connected the extremist politics of Afghanistan and Pakistan. Thousands of foreign warriors were living in the tribal belt. In short, Islamist extremism had become a worldwide phenomenon with various local, regional, and global agendas (Zahab and Roy, 2002).

On 11 September 2001, a number of teams of terrorists hijacked four US commercial aircraft flying to various US cities. Two of the planes were forced to crash into the World Trade Center, the third hit the Pentagon, and the fourth – apparently meant to crash into the US Congress or even the White House – crashed into fields in a rural county of Pennsylvania. An estimated 2749 US and foreign citizens were killed, thus constituting the most massive terrorist attack on US soil. The American nation was totally traumatized; leading American politicians and analysts described the outrage as a declaration of war on the United States. In a *CNN* interview, senior diplomat Richard Holbrooke emphasised that, under international law, the United States was fully justified in retaliating against those who had so brazenly breached US security and caused may hem and death on an unprecedented scale.

The United States immediately blamed Al-Qaeda. Initially, Al-Qaeda denied any involvement but, when inculpating evidence began to be unearthed and some of its operatives were arrested and confessed their involvement, Osama bin Laden decided to change tactics. In a video clip that was released by Al-Qaeda, bin Laden claimed responsibility for the attacks; he even tried to prove that, as an engineer, he had worked out the impact of the planes hitting the World Trade Center: so that it would be of sufficient intensity to bring the two towers crumbling down like a house of cards. In the Muslim world in general, and in Pakistan in particular, conspiracy theories did a roaring business as so-called experts, talk-shows pundits, and hosts wove bizarre theories of the Bush Administration, the CIA, the Israeli Mossad, international Jewry, and cunning Hindus conspiring to create grounds for a major assault on Islam and Muslims. Within the United States, too, conspiracy theories were spun that suggested a sinister insider job ordered by the Bush-Cheney-Rumsfeld trio to prepare a basis for capturing Middle Eastern oil wells. Later, Saudi Arabia admitted that, of the nineteen hijackers, fifteen were Saudi citizens. The Americans also provided detailed information on some of the terrorists who had received training at flying clubs and schools. The conspiracy theories, however, persisted and proliferated.

The US Attack on Afghanistan

On 12 September, Secretary of State Colin Powell called President Musharraf, who was in Karachi at the time. The latter has narrated:

> The next morning I was chairing an important meeting at the Governor's House when my military secretary told me that the US secretary of state, Colin Powell, was on the phone. I said I would call back later, but he insisted that I come out of the meeting and take the call. Powell was quite candid, 'You are either with us or against us.' I took this as a blatant ultimatum. ...When I was back in Islamabad the next day, our director-general of Inter Services Intelligence (General Mahmud), who happened to be in Washington, told me on the phone about his meeting with the US deputy secretary of state, Richard Armitage. In what has to be the most undiplomatic statement ever made, Armitage added to what Colin Powell had said to me and told the director-general not only that we had to decide whether we were with America or with the terrorists, but that if we chose the terrorists, then we should be prepared to be bombed back to the Stone Age. This was a shocking barefaced threat, but it was obvious that the US had decided to hit back, and hit back hard (Musharraf, 2006: 201).

Armitage confirmed that the conversation had taken place, but denied using the threat of military action. At any rate, Musharraf asserted that he made a dispassionate, 'military-style' analysis and concluded that Pakistan stood no chance – militarily, economically, or otherwise – to survive an all-out attack by the US. The next day, the US ambassador to Pakistan, Wendy Chamberlin, brought a set of seven demands. According to Musharraf (2006: 200–5), these were:

1. Stop Al-Qaeda operatives at the Pakistan border and prevent all supply of weapons and logistical support to Bin Laden.
2. Provide the US with access to Pakistani airspace to conduct military and intelligence operations.
3. Provide to the US territorial access to all allied military intelligence against the perpetrators of terrorism, including access to Pakistan's naval ports, air bases, and strategic locations on borders.
4. Provide the US immediately with intelligence, immigration information, and databases, and internal security information to prevent the terrorists from committing further such crimes.
5. Continue to publicly condemn the terrorists and curb all domestic expressions of support [for terrorism] against the US, its friends, or its allies.
6. Cut off all supply of fuels to the Taliban and prevent recruitment from Pakistan.
7. Should the evidence strongly implicate Osama bin Laden and the Al-Qaeda network in Afghanistan and the Taliban continue to harbour him and his network, Pakistan should break off diplomatic relations with the Taliban government and assist in the destruction of Osama Bin Laden and his network.

Musharraf has claimed that he rejected the second and third demands as they jeopardised Pakistani security. What was offered was a narrow flight corridor that was far from any sensitive areas. Moreover, they were granted limited access, for logistics and aircraft recovery, to only two bases – Shamsi in Balochistan and Jacobabad in Sindh. These bases could not be used to launch attacks. Therefore, no 'blanket permission' was given for anything. 'The rest of the demands we could live with. I am happy that the US government accepted our counterproposals without any fuss,' the general concluded

(Musharraf, 2006: 206).

After a meeting with his top generals the next day, on 13 September, Musharraf issued a statement in which he said, among other things:

> I wish to assure President Bush and the US government of our unstinted cooperation in the fight against terrorism.... We regard terrorism as an evil that threatens the world community.... Concerted international effort is needed to fight terrorism in all forms and manifestations.... Pakistan has been extending cooperation to international efforts to combat terrorism in the past and will continue to do so (Jain, 2007a: 167).

On 19 September, Musharraf addressed the Pakistani nation. Beginning with a condemnation of the terrorist attacks and condolences for the bereaved families, he informed the people that the Americans were greatly angered by the attacks and were going to retaliate, and that their first and foremost targets were Osama bin Laden and Al-Qaeda as well as the Taliban for giving them refuge. He also mentioned that, for a long time, the US had been demanding the extradition of Osama bin Laden and his associates, for the earlier attacks on US embassies and personnel in other parts of the world. The war on terror was going to be a protracted one. The Americans were not calling it a war on Islam or on the people of Afghanistan; it was a war on terrorists (Musharraf, 19 September 2001). Musharraf stated, further, that Pakistan had been contacted to help the campaign in three ways – with intelligence and information, permission to use Pakistani airspace, and general logistical support. The US was going to launch a concerted campaign with the help of a UN Security Council resolution; it enjoyed the support of the UN General Assembly as well. Musharraf added that many Islamic countries had supported the UN resolution. He then went on to describe the internal situation in Pakistan as having been critical, and the worse it had been since 1971 when the eastern wing seceded, further stating that a most serious threat was posed to Pakistan's strategic nuclear assets and the cause of Kashmir. Musharraf then referred to Indian designs:

> They [Indians] offered all their military facilities to the US. They have offered without hesitation all their facilities, all their bases and full logistic support. They want to enter into an alliance with the US and

> get Pakistan declared a terrorist state. They want to harm our strategic assets (nuclear assets) and the Kashmir cause (ibid.).

It is to be noted that Indian Prime Minister Vajpayee did offer full cooperation to the United States, including landing facilities and use of its airspace. Had Pakistan refused to cooperate, and India become a key player in the 'war on terror', it would have greatly jeopardized Pakistan's security. Yet, the reference to India – as the main beneficiary at the expense of Pakistan – was not enough to placate the Pakistani people who had been told, time and again, that the Taliban and Al-Qaeda were the embodiment of the spirit of jihad and Islamic valour. Consequently, Musharraf decided to embellish his address with populist rhetoric that would make cooperation with the Americans justifiable in Islamic terms. He referred to pristine Islamic history, and examples of the Prophet Muhammad (pbuh) making pragmatic compromises in the larger interest of Islam, thereby suggesting that working with the US did not constitute an act of cowardice but, rather, the best way to safeguard the security of the country from external threats and preserve the country's strategic nuclear and missile assets as well as the Kashmir cause.

On 7 October 2001, the United States, the UK, and the Afghan Northern Alliance jointly launched Operation Enduring Freedom, seeking to oust the Taliban regime and destroy Al-Qaeda. The Taliban had refused to hand the Al-Qaeda leaders over to the Americans, though they expressed a willingness to do so to an impartial court set up in a neutral country. The Americans announced that they would remove the Taliban from power and, instead, help a democratic government come to power in Afghanistan. Operation Enduring Freedom proved to be highly successful in its initial phases. The relentless aerial bombing proved too over whelming; the Taliban decamped, rather quickly, from Kabul on 13 November and the Northern Alliance took over. In December 2001, an International Security Assistance Force (ISAF) was established by the UN Security Council with a mandate to secure Kabul and its surrounding areas. Its command, on 11 August 2003, was assumed by NATO. ISAF included troops from many countries, with the NATO members providing the core of the force. American, British, and Northern Alliance troops were assigned combat roles.

Meanwhile, the United States had been applying the proverbial 'stick and carrot' strategy to Pakistan. The stick was, of course, the threat that Musharraf had talked about. The carrot was put on display at a press conference jointly presented by Musharraf and Secretary of State Colin Powell in Islamabad on 16 October. Musharraf emphasised the need to help the Afghans establish a durable peace and to provide assistance to Pakistan with the repatriation of the millions of Afghan refugees from Pakistan. For his part, Powell observed, 'President Bush has lifted a number of sanctions to allow us to resume cooperation with Pakistan. We have also helped reschedule $479 million in Pakistan's bilateral debt and voted for new IMF loans' (Jain, 2007a: 169).

Further major concessions followed in a statement by Richard Boucher, spokesman for the State Department, on 31 October 2001:

> President Bush signed into law a bill that authorizes him to waive sanctions against Pakistan through fiscal year 2003. It is the final stage in easing sanctions imposed on Islamabad after the 1999 military coup led by General Pervez Musharraf. President Bush has already exercised his authority to end prohibitions imposed under the Glenn Amendment (nuclear testing), the Pressler Amendment (possession of a nuclear device) and the Symington Amendment (uranium enrichment). (Ibid., 170–1)

Boucher further elaborated that economic assistance was going to increase dramatically. The US would provide US$1 billion. Several more billions would follow from international aid organizations. Pakistan was also going to receive help in boosting its exports. More such statements followed when Musharraf and Bush met in New York on 10 November 2001.

Developmentalism within a Neo-Liberal Market Economy Framework

On taking over power in October 1999, Musharraf had assumed the position of 'Chief Executive'. Such a description, of the highest political office, was devised by the veteran jurist Sharifuddin Pirzada who, in the past, had advised former governments on how to brow-beat calls for democracy and people's power with clever legal subterfuge. Musharraf tried to build a popular basis for his government by focusing his attention on a revival of the economy, notwithstanding the continuing constrictions imposed by the US sanctions regime. Taking his cue from Ayub and Zia, he wisely decided to hire technocrats who enjoyed a benign reputation as competent economists and bankers. He has written, in his memoir, that the basic criterion for choosing his team of economic and financial advisers was that their reputation should not be tarnished by a notoriety for corruption. Consequently, the team of technocrats chosen included an international banker, Shaukat Aziz, who was made the finance minister; the governorship of the State Bank of Pakistan was given to Ishrat Husain; Razzak Dawood, a scion of the leading industrialist Dawood family, was appointed as the commerce minister; and Tariq Ikram was appointed as the head of the Export Promotion Bureau. Musharraf has claimed that his team of experts greatly boosted economic development, especially exports.

Feeling confident that his government had received a positive response from the people, Musharraf appointed himself president of Pakistan on 20 June 2001. When this move was challenged in the courts, he responded by issuing an order requiring the judges to swear allegiance to military rule. Some refused and resigned, but others complied. The impact of the controversial self-appointment, and its validation by the Supreme Court, was rendered somewhat less brazen as the Supreme Court ordered Musharraf to hold national elections by 12 October 2002.

Civilianisation of Military Rule

In the meanwhile, pro-Musharraf politicians had been preparing the ground for the civilianization of military rule – a tradition that was also rooted in Pakistan's political history – which was achieved with the establishment of the Pakistan Muslim League-Quaid-i-Azam (PML-Q) prior to the elections of 2002. It was a right-of-centre party to which supporters of General Zia, and breakaway members of Nawaz Sharif's PML-N, flocked. PML-Q quickly became known as the King's Party. For the next step, in gaining a greater anchorage in society, the government arranged a referendum for 30 April 2002 – to seek approval, from the people, to extend Musharraf's rule for five years after the October elections. According to the government estimate, the turnout for the referendum was seventy percent; around ninety eight percent of the counted votes backed General Musharraf continuing in office. The opposition, on the other hand, claimed that not more than five percent of the electorate had bothered to vote. The Human Rights Commission of Pakistan (HRCP) reported some flagrant abuses: it alleged that, in some instances, multiple voting took place and state employees were pressurised to cast their votes. Such criticism was dismissed by the government as irrelevant, as it proclaimed that popular legitimisation of the Musharraf regime had been achieved.

To consummate the process of 'legitimisation', general elections were held in October as announced. A number of qualifications and modifications were introduced in the election system: for example, the separate electorates that Zia had instituted were abolished and the religious minorities voted as part of the general voters; seats were reserved for religious minorities and women in the legislatures – moreover, the new rules required that all political parties nominated religious minorities and women for the reserved seats; convicted people were barred from taking part in the election; the age limit for voting was lowered to eighteen years from twenty-one years; an educational bar was introduced – only candidates holding a bachelor's degree could contest elections – which directly affected some politicians who did not have a university degree. More than seventy parties took part in the elections. The two main oppositional leaders, Nawaz Sharif and Benazir Bhutto, were both living in exile at that time. Their parties took part in the elections as the Pakistan Peoples Party Parliamentarians (PPPP) and PML-N, respectively. An alliance of six religious parties, known as the Muttahida Majlis-e-Amal (MMA), and the MQM were the other major contestants.

No party won an overall majority. Not surprisingly, the PML-Q won most seats in the National Assembly – 126 in a house of 342. The PPPP secured eighty-one seats, while the PML-N – from which many of the leaders had decamped and joined the PML-Q – did badly, winning only nineteen seats. An unexpectedly large number of seats were won by the religious alliance known as Muttahida Majlis-e-Amal. It won sixty-three seats, emerging as the third largest party in the National Assembly. The MMA performed well as it cashed in on popular sentiment opposing Pakistan's partnership with the United States in the so-called, war on terror. The MMA received a clear-cut majority in NWFP, while it formed a coalition government in Balochistan. In Punjab, the PML-N formed the government, while a coalition government was formed in Sindh as no party had won a complete majority. The turnout was 41.8 percent.

On the federal level, the PML-Q formed a majority coalition with the support of the MQM and independents. However, the government was paralysed for a long time as the MMA was opposed to Pakistan's continuation in the US-led alliance, which it saw as inimical to Islam and pious Muslims. Musharraf surmounted the obstacles being created by the MMA by making a deal with them in December 2003 – if their legislators would support him to muster the two-thirds majority he required to pass the Seventeenth Amendment, which retroactively legalised his 1999 coup, he would leave the army by 21 December 2004. However, he reneged on his deal with the MMA and had a bill passed that allowed him to keep the post of president as well as of chief of army staff.

Having armed himself with constitutional provisions that rendered his position more or less unassailable, Musharraf went on to induct military personnel in ever-increasing numbers into the civil administration. This resulted in men from the armed forces manning some 300 senior posts in government and semi-government institutions. Local government reforms, popularised as devolution of power, were introduced by Lieutenant General Tanvir Naqvi, chairman of the National Reconstruction Bureau, in 2000. These reforms reduced the powers of the linchpin of the old order, the deputy commissioner. The elected nazim became the chief in the district. However, critics noted that new local elite that came into being were dependent on the federal government. Moreover, political parties suffered as a consequence, because elections were based on biradari ties and other ethnic factors rather than political ideology. In other words, devolution helped the federal government circumvent the strictures of federalism and created a class of local power-wielders who were directly dependent on it (*Devolution in Pakistan,* 2004).

In any event, the type of political leadership that emerged in the Pakistani federation was that of an overbearing president armed with a number of constitutional amendments and supported by a loyalist party, the PML-Q, who began to assert his power as a moderate Muslim leader. This did not apply to the NWFP, where the pro-Taliban MMA introduced repressive Islamic laws that prescribed segregation and imposed a ban on entertainment such as music and films. Islamist reforms were less acceptable in Balochistan where the Baloch leaders were opposed to them. On the whole, the Taliban and other extremists exploited the favourable milieu that existed in the NWFP as a result of the MMA government. This helped Al-Qaeda and the Taliban ensconce themselves firmly in the Federally Administered Tribal Areas (FATA) and, in the longer run, in the Balochistan capital, Quetta.

Pakistan–India Relations

The most dramatic change in Musharraf's political posturing was in relation to India. A super hawk, who had dared to provoke a military showdown with India that many feared could result in full-fledged war, became a peacenik willing to seek reconciliation with India and a win-win settlement of the Kashmir dispute. Such a change of heart was the result of a dispassionate military calculation that the liberation of Kashmir, through warfare, was a non-starter (Musharraf, 2006: 297). Presumably, the US also encouraged him to resume dialogue with India as it did not want any distractions in its bid to defeat Al-Qaeda and its Taliban supporters. The breakthrough came when a massive earthquake hit the Indian state of Gujarat. Musharraf rang up Vajpayee to offer his sympathy and Pakistani relief goods and other help. That broke the ice; Vajpayee invited him to Agra for talks. Musharraf went to India, visited his ancestral home in Delhi, and charmed Indian audiences with his off-the-cuff repartee and other graces. Then, both met in Agra amid great media hype about a breakthrough. I watched the events on television from afar in Stockholm, through *BBC*, *CNN*, and the Indian *Zee TV*. Musharraf has recorded:

> We began our formal dialogue on the morning of July 16, 2001. What followed was initially quite encouraging, but ended on a disappointing note. During two prolonged interactions, before and after lunch, initially one-on-one but then joined by our respective foreign ministers, we drafted a joint declaration. This declaration contained a condemnation of terrorism and recognition that the dispute over Kashmir needed resolution in order to improve bilateral relations.... The signing ceremony was scheduled for the afternoon in the Hotel J.P. Palace where Prime Minister Vajpayee was staying and where we had held our dialogue. Preparations in the hotel were complete, down to the table and two chairs where we would sit for the signing ceremony. The hotel staff and all the delegates were truly exuberant.... We were approaching the climax of our visit. Instead, it was an anticlimax, when after barely an hour my foreign minister and foreign secretary informed me that the Indians had backed out. I could not believe my ears. 'What could that be? Why?' I asked.

'The cabinet has rejected it, sir,' was the answer. 'Which cabinet?' I asked. 'There is no cabinet in Agra.' I became very angry, and my impulse was to leave for Islamabad immediately. The two diplomats cooled me down, asking for some time to try a redraft. I allowed it, and reluctantly cancelled my evening visit to Ajmer Sharif. The redrafting took another two or three hours of intense haggling over words and sentences. But ultimately my team returned, signalling success.

They showed me the new draft, which I approved. I thought it still carried the essence of what we wanted, except that now the language was different. They returned to the other hotel to make fair copies of the draft. I assured my wife, saying that the 'Agra declaration' would be the headlines the next day.

Yet this too was not to be. Just as I was about to leave for the signing ceremony I received a message that the Indians had backed down again. This was preposterous.... I sent a message to the media that I would hold a press conference at the hotel. I later found that this was disallowed. No one from the media was allowed to enter either Vajpayee's hotel or mine. So much for the freedom of expression in 'the largest democracy in the world.' (Musharraf, 2006: 298–99).

On 15 December 2008, accompanied by Colonel (Retd.) Aslam Cheema, I had a long conversation with General Pervez Musharraf at his residence. Musharraf recalled his meetings with both Vajpayee and later Manmohan Singh, noting that both the Indian prime ministers were keen to develop a friendly relationship with Pakistan but that the Indian political system severely constrained their ability to make decisions on contentious foreign policy matters, of which Kashmir was probably the most sensitive. Musharraf's observations seem reasonable as there is no doubt that hawks on the Indian side had conspired to subvert the normalisation of relations between the two rivals. Rumours were that Home Minister L.K. Advani and Information and Broadcasting Minister Sushma Swaraj, both representing the powerful right-wing of the BJP, were opposed to any concession to Pakistan that recognized that Kashmir was an international dispute.

Further Estrangement

The downhill trend that set in after Agra received further momentum when, on

1 October, a terrorist attack took place on the Kashmir Assembly in Srinagar – the capital of Indian-administered Kashmir – resulting in several fatalities. The US, the European Union, Japan and many other states condemned the attack. It was a distraction that the Americans found most annoying as they prepared for their punitive mission against the Taliban. Much worse was to follow a few weeks later when, on 13 December, armed militants tried to break into the Indian Parliament with the intention of taking some of the members hostages (Hoodbhoy, 2006: 160). Five gunmen rode into Parliament House in a car carrying 'Home Ministry' and 'Parliament' plates and credentials, got out of the vehicle, and began firing their weapons. The guards and security personnel shot back. One of the militants was shot dead while his four colleagues were captured. Five policemen, a parliament security guard, and a gardener were killed, and eighteen others were injured. No member of parliament or the government was hurt. The whole operation was seen on television screens and, thus, flashed across the world. India accused Pakistan of being behind the attacks, although the Pakistan government strongly denied any hand in the operation and strongly condemned it.

Suddenly, South Asia seemed headed for another major armed conf lict between the two rivals. India dispatched hundreds of thousands of troops to the roughly 2000 miles India–Pakistan border, including the LoC in Kashmir. Pakistan followed suit. More than a million soldiers were amassed on both sides of the border (Yusuf, 2006: 18). I remember watching General Musharraf on television, assuring the Pakistani nation that the armed forces of Pakistan were prepared to defend Pakistan by all means. In his address, he famously remarked 'Pakistan Islam ka Qila hai' (Pakistan is a fortress of Islam). Such rhetoric apart, there was no doubt that a war between India and Pakistan would carry disastrous consequences. Once again, the possibility of a nuclear exchange taking place between the two upstart neighbours, in case the conflict escalated, loomed large. As a result, international pressure increased enormously on the two states to withdraw from their standoff. However, India refused to do so as long as Pakistan supported what it described as cross-border terrorism. The standoff was eventually defused through pressure from the US, which dispatched several high-level officials to Delhi and Islamabad (Bidwai, 2006: 54). Moreover, the US exerted intense pressure on Pakistan to forgo its support of militant groups (Cohen, 2006: 91). Other major players, such as Britain, Japan, and the EU, also pressured Pakistan to change course.

Musharraf Announces Changes in Kashmir Policy

Such cumulative pressure proved too overwhelming. In an address to the Pakistani nation on 12 January 2002, Musharraf made a complete break with Kashmiri militancy and unlinked Pakistan from global fundamentalist Islam. He stated:

> The Kashmir problem needs to be resolved by dialogue and peaceful means in accordance with the wishes of the Kashmiri people and the UN resolutions. We have to find the solution of this dispute. No organization will be allowed to indulge in terrorism in the name of Kashmir. We condemn the terrorist acts of 11 September, 1 October and 13 December. Anyone found involved in any terrorist act would be dealt with sternly. Strict action will be taken against any Pakistani individual, group or organization found involved in terrorism within or outside the country. Our behaviour must always be in accordance with international norms (Jain 2007a: 174).

He informed the nation about his relentless efforts, even since he took power, to promote moderation – including a ban, imposed in June 2001, on sectarian organizations such as the militant Sunni Sipah-e-Sahaba Pakistan (SSP), Lashkar-e-Jhangvi, and their Shia adversary Sipah-e-Mohammad. But, he noted that sectarian terrorism continued to wreck the lives of innocent Pakistanis, including doctors (the SSP and Laskhar-e-Jhangvi targeted Shia doctors in particular), and emphasised that extremist organisations would be crushed. Accordingly, he extended the ban on such organisations to the two main militant organisations active in Indian-administered Kashmir and India, the JeM and the LeT (ibid., 174–5). Banning the two Kashmir-specific militant groups was a major break with the policy of his, and earlier, governments of describing militants involved in Indian-administered Kashmir as freedom fighters. For years, after Friday prayers, donations had been collected from the pious to support jihad in Kashmir. To describe such organisations as terrorist entities was, therefore, disorienting and perplexing for the people of Pakistan.

More deviations followed in the long address that had been prepared with a view to projecting Pakistan as a modern Muslim state based on a moderate, tolerant interpretation of Islam. After nearly half a century of suppression by successive governments, Jinnah's 11 August 1947 speech was resurrected; Musharraf alluded to it to assert that Pakistan was meant to be a progressive Muslim state that granted equal rights to all its citizens. Later, in an address to Muslim clerics on 18 January, he spelt out a tolerant, non-divisive approach to Islam, appealing to Islamic solidarity and compassion and debunking extremism and violence. He urged the ulema to help him disseminate a humane and tolerant image of Islam, derived from Sufi traditions (Musharraf, 18 January 2002). However, a rider to moderation was introduced in his public addresses. He dispelled speculation that Pakistan might become a secular state, and rejected suggestions by US congressmen that the law passed by the Pakistan National Assembly in 1974 expunging the Ahmadiyya community from the fold of Islam should be rescinded. Moreover, he stated categorically that the Hudood and blasphemy laws were an intrinsic part of the Pakistani constitution and would remain in force, but measures would be taken to ensure that they were not used in an arbitrary manner (Kamran, 2002).

Miscellaneous Actions

Musharraf introduced some progressive changes. The system of separate electorates was abolished. The minorities became free to contest any seat in any of the elected assemblies. Seats were reserved for non-Muslims in the national and provincial legislatures and local bodies. All the political parties, including the Islamist parties, were required to nominate non-Muslims as their candidates for the reserved seats (Ahmed, 2011a: 96). Moreover, the rape law introduced by Zia was reformed. Under the protection of the Women Act, 2006, rape was removed from the Hudood offenses and brought under the Pakistan Penal Code. What this meant was that the requirement of four male witnesses, to establish guilt, was removed. The new law permitted conviction on the basis of forensic as well as circumstantial evidence; evidence given by the victim and other females was declared admissible (Ahmed, 2011b: 115–6).

The annual SAARC summit had not been held since 1998 because of the Kargil mini-war. But, when it was finally held in January 2002 in Kathmandu, Musharraf made another effort to improve relations with India. When he met Prime Minister Atal Bihari Vajpayee at the Summit, Musharraf walked up to Vajpayee and offered his hand; Vajpayee reciprocated, but after some hesitation.

Vajpayee, then, decided to attend the next SAARC summit in Islamabad in 2004. As a result, the Islamabad Declaration was signed committing both sides to engage in a multi-faceted composite dialogue to normalise relations between their nations and usher in an era of mutually-beneficial interaction. However, the BJP suffered a surprise defeat in the Indian general elections; and so, the momentum that had gathered was dissipated and a new start had to be made. That took some time. Musharraf's interaction with Prime Minister Manmohan Singh of the Congress party proved to be equally congenial, and the Pakistani president noted that the Indian prime minister was equally keen to normalise relations with Pakistan. The two met in Delhi where Musharraf had arrived, on Singh's invitation, to attend a one-day India–Pakistan cricket match – which served as an opportunity for the two leaders to discuss the Kashmir issue. Both agreed that there was a need to find a solution 'outside the box'.

Musharraf has noted: 'The prime minister did say that he could not agree to any redrawing of borders, while I said I could not agree to accepting the Line of Control as permanent' (Musharraf, 2006: 301). Further meetings took place in New York in September 2005, when Musharraf invited Singh to visit Pakistan, which the Indian prime minister accepted. However, the visit did not take place. Musharraf believed that while Singh seemed sincere and willing to resolve the Kashmir dispute, the Indian establishment was not. He has noted, 'I think the Indian establishment – the bureaucrats, diplomats, and intelligence agencies and perhaps even the military – has gotten the better of him' (ibid., 302).

In his overall observations on a just solution of the Kashmir dispute, Musharraf presented a four-point framework. Point one identified five geographic regions constituting the historically undivided Jammu and Kashmir State. The Pakistani-administered Kashmir consisted of the Northern Areas and Azad Kashmir, and the Indian-administered Kashmir of three regions, namely Jammu, Kashmir Valley, and Ladakh. All five regions should be placed on the table for negotiations. Point two required demilitarisation of the five parts and the curbing of militancy. Point three required the introduction of genuine self-government to those five regions. The final point was a proposal for a joint management mechanism comprising Pakistanis, Indians, and Kashmiris who would oversee self-governance and deal with residual subjects (ibid., 303).

Musharraf described such ideas as personal and not official, but one can safely infer that he spoke on behalf of the Pakistani establishment – which enjoyed greater notoriety than the Indians when it came to resolving the Kashmir issue. In subsequent pronouncements, Musharraf offered further concessions. He said that Pakistan would be willing to adopt a more flexible attitude on the Line of Control in Kashmir. On the other hand, the Indians were slow in responding to the Pakistani peace overtures in equal measure. However, in 2006, Prime Minister Manmohan Singh expressed a desire to sign a 'treaty of peace, security and friendship' with Pakistan (Ahmed, 6 January 2007). During much of 2007, progress on the peace question remained suspended as political turmoil within Pakistan demanded the attention of the Pakistan government; India decided to remain aloof.

Some significant improvement took place between the two countries in trade and communications. A weekly bus service between Delhi and Lahore was inaugurated when Vajpayee paid his historic visit to Lahore in 1999. The service continued, even during the Kargil showdown, until it was suspended after the attacks on the Indian Parliament on 13 December 2001. It was revived in 2003 when bilateral relations improved; it was followed by a weekly bus service between the capitals of the two Kashmirs – Srinagar and Muzaffarabad – in April 2005, between Amritsar and Lahore in January 2006, and between Lahore and the Sikh holy shrine of Nankana Sahib in March 2006. There was a substantial increase in bilateral trade between the two nations in 2006–2007 – an increase of 88 percent to the tune of US$1.6 billion – which was envisaged to grow to $2.7 billion in 2007, but suffered a decline because of the political turmoil in Pakistan that greatly weakened Musharraf's standing. On the other hand, both sides continued to modernise and develop their missile programmes, thus acquiring greater range and accuracy in their killing power in case of war.

Action against Abdul Qadeer Khan

The United States which, by then, had begun to provide huge economic and military aid to Pakistan, pressured Musharraf to rein in A.Q. Khan and his nuclear proliferating cohorts. When, in December 2003, Libya announced that it was abandoning its nuclear weapons programme – which it admitted it had been pursuing with clandestine Pakistani assistance – the Pakistani government's persistent blanket denials of such involvement were no longer tenable. Suddenly, evidence mounted of illicit nuclear weapons technology transfers, not only to Libya but also to Iran, North Korea, and other countries. Musharraf, who was compelled to order an investigation into A.Q. Khan's activities, took the rather incredulous stance that even if there had been wrongdoing, it had occurred without the knowledge or approval of the government of Pakistan (Musharraf, 2006: 447–50). However, critics noted that virtually all A.Q. Khan's overseas travels – to Iran, Libya, North Korea, Niger, Mali, and the Middle East – were by official Pakistan government aircraft, and he was often accompanied by senior members of the Pakistani nuclear establishment.

In January 2004, A.Q. Khan was interrogated by Pakistani investigators. On 25 January 2004, the authorities reported that A.Q. Khan, and another high-ranking officer, had provided unauthorised technical assistance to Iran's nuclear weapons programme in the late 1980s and early 1990s, allegedly in exchange for tens of millions of dollars. It was also reported that ex-COAS, General Mirza Aslam Beg, was implicated in the illicit nuclear trade with Iran (John, 2007: 174). On 31 January, A.Q. Khan was dismissed from his post as the Science Adviser to the President of Pakistan. On 4 February, he appeared on national television and confessed to running a proliferation ring. The next day, Musharraf pardoned him (Musharraf 2006: 289–94). Although he was put under house arrest, US pleas to permit its experts to interrogate him were rejected.

Miscellaneous Foreign Policy Initiatives

Musharraf dared to challenge some other orthodox features of Pakistani foreign policy that incensed right-wing forces in Pakistani politics. Traditionally, Pakistan had been at the forefront in the support for the Palestinians, which had led to open hostility towards Jews and Israel. Musharraf decided to forgo such a confrontational posture because, according to him, it served no useful purpose. He issued a statement that if Israel agreed to the establishment of a Palestinian state, acceptable to the Palestinians, Pakistan could consider recognising Israel. That pronouncement received a positive response from the American Jews who had invited Musharraf to address the American Jewish Congress in New York. Before that happened, the Pakistan foreign minister had met his Israeli counterpart in Istanbul on 1 September 2005. A few days later, on 17 September, Musharraf addressed the American Jewish Congress. His speech was well-received as it presented a strong case for the two-state solution that would entail recognition of Israel by the Muslim nations (ibid., 305). Domestically, such statements did not register well because Musharraf was also seen on television screens going forward to shake hands with Israeli Prime Minister Ariel Sharon, a man held in great contempt for conniving at the massacre of Palestinians by Christian militias in the refugee camps of Sabra and Shatila in Lebanon in 1982.

The Advent of Terrorist Attacks in Pakistan

For the Islamists, super hawks, and ultra-nationalists, Musharraf had forfeited his claim to be a patriot the day he meekly joined hands with George W. Bush to wage war against Al-Qaeda and the Taliban – ironically, Musharraf had disparaged Nawaz Sharif in a similar manner when the latter had relented, without any resistance, to Bill Clinton's advice that the Kargil conflict end and Pakistan vacate territory on the Indian side of the LoC. This time round, Musharraf was perceived as a traitor to not only Pakistan but also to Islam and the Muslim Umma. As already noted, Taliban and Al-Qaeda leaders and cadres had taken refuge in the tribal areas, known as the Federally Administered Tribal Areas, and, from their inaccessible hideouts in the difficult mountainous terrain, they began to undertake terrorist missions in Pakistan. Moreover, the Islamists had served in the Pakistani state apparatuses as well, especially the intelligence and armed services. Despite attempts to weed them out, they continued to escape detention; those who had retired continued to be part of the networks that were sympathetic to the extremists. And so, a fairly widespread clandestine support base existed that assisted terrorists commit crimes in Pakistan. Terrorism on Pakistani soil raised its ugly head soon after 9/11. Nevertheless, Musharraf continued to enjoy the loyalty of the armed forces or, rather, the key corps commanders without whose help a successful coup could not be mounted. Equally, in spite of the rogue elements, the ISI and other intelligence services, as well as the PML-Q and his other allies, continued to provide him with the necessary support to maintain him in power. It was within such a complicated framework of opposition and support that the scourge of terrorism visited Pakistan.

The Beheading Of Daniel Pearl

In December 2001, the *Wall Street Journal's* Daniel Pearl and his wife, Marianne, arrived in Pakistan to inter view a religious figure in connection with a failed attempt by Richard Reed – a British citizen who had recently converted to Islam, to carry out a mid-flight explosion while flying to the United States from Britain, having hidden the explosive device in his shoes. Apparently, Daniel Pearl was investigating another story as well. While in Karachi, he was kidnapped, tortured, and executed. His horrific execution was displayed on the internet – he was seen confessing about his Jewish origins before he was beheaded. The story immediately made headlines all over the world. Investigations by the Pakistani authorities found that the kidnappers included time-tested terrorists, such as Omar Sheikh, who had been involved in several atrocities in India since 1994. Sheikh, along with the leader of the JeM, Maulana Masood Azhar, had been arrested and imprisoned in India. But, both were released in 1999 in exchange for the release of an Indian airplane that had been hijacked and taken to Kandhar, Afghanistan. According to Musharraf, Omar Sheikh confessed to his involvement in the kidnapping but denied any part in the decision to behead Daniel Pearl. It was the Al-Qaeda senior operative, Khaled Sheikh Muhammad, Amjad Faruqi, and several others who were involved in the plot to kidnap Pearl. They were probably also involved in the actual execution of Pearl. Khaled Sheikh Muhammad was handed over to the United States. In May 2002, Fazal Karim, an operative of the rabid anti-Shia Lashkar-e-Jhang vi, was captured. During his interrogation, he confessed, without any remorse, to his participation too in the beheading of Pearl; he helped the police find Pearl's body which had been hacked into ten pieces (Musharraf, 2006: 225-8). On the other hand, Omar Sheikh was sent to a prison in Pakistan to stand trial.

Terrorism Wreaks Havoc on Pakistanis

While the horrific story of Daniel Pearl shocked the world, and Israeli Prime Minister Ariel Sharon promised to avenge his gruesome murder – a declaration that was rejected by Daniel's father who did not want his son's death to be exploited politically – the terrorists unleashed a wave of attacks against miscellaneous domestic targets. Unlike the terrorism of the 1990s, which was primarily directed against religious and ethnic minorities, this time round no person or institution was beyond the reach of the crazed jihadists who were hell-bent on imposing their worldview, and the concomitant social and political orders, in Pakistan by all means. On 17 March 2002, hand grenades were hurled at the congregation of worshippers in a Protestant church in Islamabad's diplomatic enclave. Six people were killed and forty-two injured, including the Sri Lankan ambassador. The terrorist had apparently blown himself up; the authorities could not identify the perpetrators of that atrocity. Thus, the phenomenon of suicide bombings arrived in Pakistan in a big way in March 2002.

Another terrorist assault, involving foreigners, was launched in the port city of Karachi on 8 May. A car driven by a suicide bomber rammed into a bus of the Pakistan Navy, as it left the hotel in the morning. The bus was carrying French engineers and technicians who were working on a French submarine that Pakistan had purchased. Eleven Frenchmen and two Pakistanis were killed. Twenty-four people were injured. The visiting New Zealand cricket team, which was going to play a match a little later that day, decided to call their tour off and left the country. Once again, Pakistan was in the global media for all the wrong reasons. Investigations led to the Harkat-ul-Mujahideen al-Alami, the international wing of the organisation HUM which had been one of the pioneers in fomenting terrorism in Indian-administered Kashmir being behind the attack on the bus.

A few months later, on 5 August, a Christian school was the object of another terrorist atrocity. The guard, very courageously, obstructed their entry. Although he was killed by them, the alarm bell had been rung and, thus, the culprits could not harm anyone else. They were pursued by a junior commissioned officer of the Pakistan Army, but all three blew themselves up. Four days later, the terrorists struck again, this time at the church inside a Christian hospital in Taxila, just outside Islamabad. Four women were killed and twenty were injured. One of the terrorists, Kamran Mir, died as a grenade exploded in his hand, while his accomplices escaped. The police raided Mir's home and found vital clues that helped them trace the other conspirators. On interrogation, it was learnt that the attacks on the Christians were part of a much bigger conspiracy that included JeM's leader, Masood Azhar, and others belonging to the anti-Shia LeJ. Referring to the ringleader of the attacks on the Christians, Saif-ur-Rahman Saifi, Musharraf remarked:

> Saifi was a highly indoctrinated person. Once he was arrested in Multan on August 15, 2002, he confessed that he also had links with Lashkar-e-Jhangvi, the militant wing of the Sunni sectarian Sipah-e-Sahaba, and also to al Qaeda. Thus did the nexus of al Qaeda and our local extremist organizations become clear: al Qaeda provided the money, weapons, and equipment, and the local organizations provided the manpower and motivation to actually execute the attacks (ibid., 231).

The first wave of terrorist attacks subsided for a while as the police and intelligence services uncovered some of the ringleaders and operatives. Information extracted during the interrogations had led to the arrest of some of them. However, terrorist cells and nexuses were too widely spread in Pakistan, and they had devised such effective methods and techniques of indoctrination, that Pakistan would be made to pay a very heavy price for its government's decision to cooperate with the Americans and other perceived enemies of Islam and Muslims. Stakes were raised to the highest levels when, on 14 December 2003, a powerful bomb went off minutes after Musharraf's convoy crossed a bridge in Rawalpindi. Apparently, a jamming device in the vehicle prevented the remote-controlled explosives from blowing up the bridge as the convoy passed over it (*The Daily Times*, 15 December 2003). Colonel (Retd.) Aslam Cheema, who was travelling with him in the car, described the whole incident to me in detail. Musharraf had kept his nerve and directed the chauffer to continue driving to the COAS residence where he lived. The tires had burst and the car was limping on one side but it made its way to his residence.

Another attempt to kill Musharraf, on the heels of the first one, took place eleven days later when, on 25 December, two suicide bombers unsuccessfully tried to assassinate him. It was found that some junior personnel from the SSG commandos, to which Musharraf himself belonged, were involved in the conspiracy to assassinate him (Musharraf, 2006: 252). Amjad Faruqi, who had also been involved in the murder of Daniel Pearl, was identified as the mastermind of the assassination attempt as his mobile phone calls were picked up by the security and intelligence services. After a massive manhunt, he was finally shot dead by the Pakistani forces in September 2004 (ibid., 254–7).

In any case, the terrorists extended their targets to other top officials of the Musharraf regime. On 10 June 2004, a hail of bullets was fired at the car in which Karachi's corps commander, Lieutenant General Ahsan Saleem Hayat, was on the way to his office. The gunshots were fired because the bomb that had been planted on the road, to blow the car up, luckily did not explode as the phone call that was being used as the remote control did not function. The general's driver and other staff were killed. All seven men in the military jeep that was following him were also killed, as were two bystanders. The general survived. The cell phone was found as the assassins ran away in panic. Investigations led to the discovery of another rabidly anti-Shia group, the Jandullah, which was particularly active in the Iranian Baluchistan. I was later to see, with my own eyes on YouTube, Jandullah fanatics beheading their victims who were lying on the ground and writhing in excruciating pain as their heads were being severed from their necks. Later, the heads were waved around, the same way butchers do with severed sheep and goat heads. On 30 July 2004, an attempt was made on the life of Prime Minister Shaukat Aziz while he was on a by-election campaign contesting the seat from Attock, about sixty miles north of Islamabad. While Aziz survived, several people were killed including those travelling with him.

The government reacted by capturing several Al-Qaeda operatives. Many were handed over to the United States. It was the transit routes for the United States and its allied forces, the provision of bases in Pakistan, and the sharing of intelligence with the Americans, which enabled them to target Al-Qaeda enclaves, which earned Musharraf the wrath of the Taliban. Musharraf has devoted at least two chapters of his book to elucidate the services his men rendered in the fight against terrorism. In 2006, Musharraf wrote:

> We have captured 689 and handed over 369 to the United States. We have earned bounties totalling millions of dollars. Those who habitually accuse us of 'not doing enough' in the war on terror should simply ask the CIA how much prize money it has paid to the government of Pakistan (ibid., 237).

Those surrendered to the Americans were mainly Al-Qaeda operatives and belonged to Arab and other nationalities. However, while such conduct might have endeared Musharraf and his generals to the Americans, it greatly angered the Islamists in Pakistan. Terrorism by extremist groups, and sectarian militias, continued to menace Pakistani society during 2004–6.

The US–India Nuclear Deal

In spite of Pakistan joining the war on terror, US policy of moving closer to India in a 'strategic partnership', initiated by Bill Clinton, received a great boost under his successor, George W. Bush. Preceded by years of preparation on both sides, a process was initiated when Bush visited India in March 2006 whereby the restrictions that had previously existed on supplying nuclear technology to India could be removed. Neither India nor Pakistan had signed the Comprehensive Test Ban Treaty (CTBT) or the NPT, despite intense pressure from the United States; hence, its ban on the export of nuclear technology to both. The Americans, impressed by India's impressive economic growth and the resilience of its democracy, were keen to exploit the Indian market. Nuclear technology was to be included among the US exports, provided procedures could be agreed on to use it for civilian purposes. Suffice it to note that the US-India nuclear deal had taken several years to negotiate. There was considerable opposition to it in India, from the left-wing parties and the BJP, as the Manmohan Singh government was perceived to be compromising Indian sovereignty by agreeing to place its civilian reactors under the International Atomic Energy Agency (IAEA) – even though the reactors it used for military purposes were to be exempted. This US–India deal took more than three years to finally be consummated on 20 October 2008 (Sikri, 2009: 175–84).

The Americans used their clout to ensure that no international opposition to such a deal, especially by China – a member of the coveted five-member nuclear club – stood in the way. India, thus, became the only known country with nuclear weapons which, though not a party to the NPT, is still allowed to carry out nuclear commerce with the rest of the world. Pakistan protested and urged that it, too, should be extended the same treatment but the Americans remained unmoved. It has had to remain content with being described, earlier in 2004, as America's major 'non-NATO ally'.

Conflict in Balochistan

Disappointment in the international arena compounded the difficulties that plagued Pakistan at home. Besides the spate of terrorism being carried out by the Islamists, the Musharraf regime ran into trouble with the Baloch nationalists as well. That vast, but desolate, province had always had grievances against the central government. Jamil Ahmad, who served in Balochistan for years as a civil servant and retired as chief secretary of Balochistan, told me that the Pakistan military was guilty of excessive use of power against the Baloch, and that that part of the country had always felt alienated from the rest of the country, especially the Punjabi-dominated centre.

In the early twenty-first century, trouble and armed conflict again emerged in Balochistan, between the Baloch nationalists and the forces representing the government in Islamabad. The background to this included the accumulated grievances from the past about the exploitation of natural gas and other minerals, as well as new grievances about the development of Gwadar as a port city on the Balochistan coast – without the Baloch being given a proper share in those ventures. Baloch grievances were also directed at the Chinese who had been granted mining rights in the province and were a major player in the development of Gwadar. With regards to mining, the Saindak copper-gold project worth $297 million, run by a Chinese contractor on a ten-year lease, was the most important. It had been running for three years without any independent monitoring. In May 2009, the Saindak Metal Limited released figures that 7,746 tons of gold, 86,013 tons of copper, 11.046 tons of silver, and 14,482 tons of magnetite concentrate (iron) worth $633.573 million were produced during 2004–8. Neither the Baloch in general, nor the locals in district Chagai where the mines are located, benefited from such wealth. According to the contract, the Chinese keep most of the profits, Pakistan receives $500,000 monthly for the next 10 years, while Balochistan is to receive only $0.7 million per year as royalty. The environmental damage the mining is causing to Balochistan has been completely ignored (Talpur, 5 December 2009).

However, it is the port which is the most important project for the Chinese. Once the Karakoram Highway is completed, Gwadar would serve as the hub for Chinese goods en route to markets in central and western Asia. It will also serve as a naval base for Chinese submarines, according to a noted Pakistani defence analyst, Ahmad Faruqui (2008: 2). As the economic importance of Gwadar, as a major outlet for trade as well as a strategic naval base to monitor the Arabian Sea, has grown, the Pakistan military has built a number of military bases and garrisons in Balochistan. In 2005, the Baloch leaders, Nawab Akbar Bugti and Mir Balach Marri, presented a fifteen-point agenda to the Pakistan government. The key thrust of the agenda was a demand for greater control of the province's resources and a moratorium on the construction of military bases (*The New York Times*, 2 April 2006). As had happened in the past, such demands were unacceptable to the centre. The Baloch decided to put up an armed resistance to what they believed was renewed exploitation of their resources by a Punjabi-dominated military regime in Islamabad. As a result, armed encounters and skirmishes began to take place.

On 15 December 2005, Inspector-General of the Frontier Corps Major General Shujaat Zamir Dar and his deputy, Brigadier Salim Nawaz, were wounded after shots were fired at their helicopter in Balochistan. The helicopter landed safely. That was followed by the Pakistan Army launching a hunt for the ringleaders of the resistance movement, and culminated in Akbar Bugti being killed on 26 August 2006 (*The New York Times*, 28 August 2006). The Pakistan government later claimed that he was behind a series of bomb blasts, including a rocket attack on Musharraf. It was also alleged that at least sixty Pakistani soldiers and seven officers were killed by Baloch fighters. Moreover, Pakistan alleged that India was supporting the Baloch rebels. The Baloch, on the other hand, accused the Musharraf regime of carrying out a vicious military campaign against their people that had resulted in hundreds of deaths.

The Pakistan Taliban

An interesting development during that period was the emergence of an autonomous Taliban movement on the Pakistani side of the Durand Line. It was led by a new generation of fighters, among whom Baitullah Mehsud was the most prominent. The story of Mehsud's evolution, as a fanatical Islamist, was not very different from that of thousands of other young men from the tribal areas who were inducted into jihadist activities at a tender age. He was probably recruited after the Soviet Red Army withdrew from Afghanistan in 1989, because Mehsud (born in 1974) was only fifteen at that time. Mehsud attended a madrassa in the tribal areas for a few months, and was converted to a world view that made any individual or group a legitimate target for liquidation if they did not adhere to the severe and militant version of Islam that he and his followers subscribed to. He swore allegiance to the Afghan leader Mulla Omar, who had headed the Taliban regime in Afghanistan.

While Omar continued to lead the Afghan Taliban, by early 2005, Mehsud had consolidated his position as the leader of the Taliban in Pakistan. The Taliban carried out punishments, such as chopping the hands off of alleged thieves and stoning adulterers to death, in the areas under their control in Pakistan. There is some evidence to suggest that the Afghan and Pakistani Taliban did not always see eye to eye, and Omar's overall leadership of the entire Taliban was more symbolic than real. During 2005–6, the Taliban and their sectarian allies in other parts of Pakistan targeted Shias, Christians, Ahmadis, and foreigners, inflicting death and injury on hundreds. As that brought terrorism deep into Pakistani towns and cities outside the tribal belt, the Musharraf regime intensified its military operations against Taliban and Al-Qaeda enclaves in the tribal areas.

Clash and Truce with the Taliban

President George W. Bush visited South Asia in March 2006. Although India, understandably, received most attention from the Americans, this time there was no question of ostracising or humiliating Pakistan as had happened in the aftermath of the Kargil conflict when Bill Clinton had paid a visit to South Asia. The striking of a 'strategic partnership' with India, no doubt, was uppermost in Bush's mind, but he made it a point to emphasize a special relationship with Pakistan when he met President Musharraf in Islamabad on 4 March 2006 and expressed solidarity with Pakistan for fighting terrorism. He said:

> Mr President and I reaffirmed our shared commitment to a broad and lasting strategic partnership. And that partnership begins with close cooperation in the war on terror. President Musharraf made a bold decision for his people and for peace, after September the 11th, when Pakistan chose to fight the terrorists. The American people appreciate your leadership, Mr President, and so do I (Bush, Whitehouse archives 2006).

The extremists responded with pro-Taliban tribesmen in Mir Ali, a small hamlet in North Waziristan, opening fire on vehicles carrying paramilitary forces. Pakistan's army retaliated with helicopter gunships and artillery fire. At least forty-nine people were killed in the fighting, a spokesman said. The background to the clash was dated a few days earlier: when a military strike took place on a suspected Al-Qaeda camp in the nearby village of Saidgi. Although Pakistan had deployed about 80,000 troops along the Afghan frontier, the fighters were able to move across the border, between Afghanistan and Pakistan, without any great difficulty. The fighting spread to the main town of North Waziristan, Miran Shah, where about 500 tribesmen traded fire with paramilitary forces in the bazaar and, according to security officials, occupied some government buildings. Both sides could be seen firing mortars and assault rifles. Some mortar shells hit closed shops.

According to the ISPR spokesman, Major General Shaukat Sultan, a local cleric named Maulvi Abdul Khaliq had called for a jihad against the Pakistan Army. He stated that twenty-one militants were killed in Mir Ali, and twenty-five in Miran Shah, but added that the toll could be higher. Three government troops had also died, and about ten were wounded, he said. The army spokesman said that the tribesmen had started firing rockets at a Frontiers Corps base in Miran Shah, and the army had responded with artillery fire. Officials said helicopter gunships also targeted the tribal fighters' positions. According to security and intelligence officials who spoke on condition of anonymity, the actual number of deaths of pro-Taliban tribesmen was eighty. Moreover, the army reportedly destroyed a hotel in Miran Shah bazaar that the tribal militants had used as a position for firing their rockets.

Tension, with intermittent firing from both sides, continued to drag on for months. Finally, a truce was reached in September 2006. However, clashes again broke out when Pakistan ordered air strikes on a madrassa in Damdola village on 30 October 2006, in which eighty people, most teenagers, were killed. The military alleged that the madrassa, which it had successfully targeted, was being used as a terrorist camp. However, it was later learnt that an American drone (unmanned aerial vehicle) had been used to fire missiles to kill the madrassa students. In retaliation, on 8 November 2006, a suicide bomber killed forty-two soldiers and injured another twenty in Dargai (Raman 2006). Drone attacks had begun in 2004. Although operated from as far as Creech Air Force Base in Nevada, USA, it was later learnt that they took off from Shamsi Airfield in Balochistan (interview Christine Fair). Such operations were indicative of the close covert cooperation between the US and Pakistan militaries. Publically, however, the Pakistan military could not admit to that as the drone attacks claimed many innocent lives and, as such, were acts of extra-judicial killing.

Escalation and Proliferation of Terrorism

The new wave of attacks was characterized by the emergence of the dreadful phenomenon of suicide bombing. In 2007, at least 56 suicide bombings took place, resulting in 419 security officials and 217 civilians being slain. The significance of such an escalation can be grasped from the fact that, in the previous year, only six suicide bombings had been directed at the military. Despite this tenfold increase in suicide bombings, the regime failed to track down a single culprit (Rashid 2008: 379). From the beginning of 2007, almost daily reports of attacks on police and security personnel began to pour in from the tribal areas along the Afghanistan border in Waziristan. On 26 January, two persons – the suicide bomber and a security guard – were killed in a blast at the prestigious Marriott Hotel in Islamabad. A meeting, to celebrate India's Republic Day, was to take place at the hotel; Indian diplomats were scheduled to attend it. The blast was, undoubtedly, planned for that reception but went off earlier (*The Daily Times*, 27 January 2007). The garrison-type security arrangements in the Islamabad–Rawalpindi area were further challenged when an insurgency, headed by hardcore fundamentalists, began to surface in the Pakistani capital in March 2007.

The Lal Masjid Showdown

The Lal Masjid, or Red Mosque, was a hotbed of Islamism in Islamabad, right under the nose of the Musharraf regime. Founded by Abdullah Ghazi – a veteran of the Afghan jihad and a great admirer of Osama bin Laden – his sons, Abdul Aziz Ghazi and Abdul Rashid Ghazi, made no bones about their intention of imposing a Taliban-type of Islam on Pakistan (Hussain, 2010: 105–111). On 28 March, niqab-wearing armed women of the women's section at Lal Masjid, the Jamia Hafsa – described by someone as the Lal Brigade – raided the premises of a madam who allegedly ran a brothel, arrested her and her family, and forced a confession that she was guilty of running a sex trade (*The News International*, 29 March 2007). The same day, several bomb blasts and rocket and mor tar attacks on security forces and government installations, by tribal militants, took place in the Tank district of NWFP. Twenty-five people, including a soldier of the paramilitary Frontier Constabulary, were killed (ibid.). On 6 April, the Islamists set up a Sharia

Court inside the mosque. The most senior cleric, Maulana Abdul Aziz, vowed to launch thousands of suicide attacks if the government interfered in the activities of the court. On 9 April, the Sharia Court handed down a fatwa (edict) against Punjab Tourism Minister Nilofer Bakhtiar, accusing her of committing a sin when she was shown, in newspaper photographs, embracing her paragliding instructor following a charity jump in France (Ahmed, 16 July 2007). The situation deteriorated further when, on 28 April, there was an assassination attempt on the then interior minister, Aftab Ahmad Khan Sherpao, in Charsadda, NWFP. He survived but twenty-eight people were killed (*The News International*, 29 April 2007). On 23 June, the Lal Brigade cadres raided a Chinese massage parlour in Islamabad and abducted the Chinese couple who owned it, and the five Chinese and two Pakistani girls who worked there. They released the Chinese couple and girls later.

Such attacks on the nationals of Pakistan's all-weather friend were very embarrassing for Musharraf. The rise of extremism and terrorism among China's Uyghur Muslims, of Xinjiang province, had been a cause for concern for the Chinese government. Musharraf had taken several measures to curb the Chinese Mujahideen's presence in Pakistan, and had himself gone and spoken to them about Islam being a religion of peace and the need for them to remain loyal citizens of China. However, Uyghur militants had continued to receive training in camps set up by jihadist organisations – something the Chinese government had strong objections to (Faruqui, 2008: 1–3). In a rare display of concern about events in Pakistan, the Chinese minister for public security, Zhou Yongang, told visiting Pakistani Interior Minister Sherpao, 'We hope Pakistan will look into the terrorist attacks aiming at Chinese people and organizations as soon as possible and severely punish the criminals' (*Shanghai Daily*, 27 June 2007). Things came to a head when, on 8 July, unidentified gunmen killed three Chinese workers and wounded another near Peshawar, in what Pakistani officials said was a reprisal attack linked to the ongoing siege of militants in the Lal Masjid (*The News International*, 9 July 2007). The same day, in Islamabad, a senior military officer, Lieutenant Colonel Haroon Islam, who was stationed outside the Lal Masjid, was gunned down by the militants inside (ibid.).

Musharraf felt compelled to act firmly and ruthlessly. The security forces were ordered to carry out Operation Sunrise in full force. Initially, it had been named Operation Silence (*Dawn*, 12 July 2007). Perhaps the government was hoping to carry out a relatively small-scale assault but the resistance inside the mosque made that impossible. Thus, when Operation Sunrise was launched, it bore the hallmarks of a major military action. While many inside the mosque panicked and surrendered or tried to escape, several hundred diehards decided to go down fighting. The major assault was launched on 10 July. A total of 150 people were reported killed, of which 10 were army personnel, including an officer. However, some people challenge the government figures and claim that many more inside the mosque lost their lives.

The attack on the Lal Masjid was supported by the US, while Al-Qaeda's second in command, Ayman al-Zawahiri, issued a video message calling for Pakistanis to join the jihad against Musharraf to avenge the deaths of the Islamists (ibid.). Retaliation followed soon when, on 15 July, there was a suicide attack and car bombs exploded in many parts of the NWFP. At least forty-nine people were killed and hundreds wounded. Among them were eleven security personnel (*The News International*, 16 July 2007). Further attacks followed on 19 July in Hub, Hangu, and Kohat in the NWFP; another fifty-two persons lost their lives and 127 were injured. Chinese engineers working in that area were the intended targets but, instead of them, security personnel and other ordinary people including women and children suffered (*The News International*, 20 July 2007).

Terrorist Attacks Continue Unabated

On 2 August, the police in Sargodha shot dead a suspected suicide bomber after the man failed to detonate the explosives he was wearing. He had entered a police training centre and killed a policeman before being gunned down. On 4 September, at least twenty-five people were killed and sixty-six injured in two suicide bomb attacks in Rawalpindi cantonment. Among the dead were uniformed officials, as well as civilians, who had been in a bus carrying them to their workplace (*The News International*, 5 September 2007). On 13 September, at least twenty off-duty commandos were killed and eleven injured in an apparent suicide blast at an army mess near the Tarbela Dam, NWFP. Among the targeted men were commandos from the SSG Karar Company, apparently because they were believed to have taken part in the assault on the Lal Masjid (*The News International*, 14 September 2007).

The First Attack on Benazir Bhutto

Meanwhile, the United States had, behind the scenes, been brokering a deal between Musharraf and Benazir Bhutto – that Benazir would be allowed to return to Pakistan, corruption charges would be dropped against her and her spouse, elections would be held, and the results would be engineered to enable Benazir to form the government while Musharraf would continue as president. The negotiations that ensued – including their meeting in Dubai – proceeded smoothly, but Musharraf warned Benazir not to come to Pakistan because he feared that there was a threat to her life. She ignored the warning, pinning her hopes on the Americans to ensure that her safety would be guaranteed by Musharraf. She arrived in Karachi, where a mammoth crowd had gathered to welcome her, on 18 October. The procession from the airport to the mausoleum of Jinnah dragged on for hours. Shortly after midnight, utter savagery and mayhem was let loose on the convoy carrying her and other PPP leaders – probably by two suicide bombers. Initial reports suggested that 125 people died and more than 500 were injured, though Benazir and the other leaders, who were in a bomb-proof truck, were saved (*The News International*, October 2007). Later, Benazir put the number of dead at 179, including 50 youth from her party who had volunteered to protect her life (Bhutto, 2008b: 12). It was the single-most deadly act of terrorism in Pakistan. Benazir revealed, in a statement that I myself saw on television, that she had written to Musharraf that she feared an assassination attempt would be made on her life, and that sympathisers in his government and administration were involved in a conspiracy to kill her.

There was no let-up in the terrorism. On 30 October, a suicide bomber struck a police checkpost in a high-security zone of Rawalpindi, less than a mile from General Musharraf's camp office (*The News International*, 31 October 2007). I was attending a conference in Islamabad when it happened. On 1 November, another suicide bomber blew himself up, along with seven officers of the Pakistan Air Force and three civilians, at Sargodha – where the Pakistan Air Force has its regional headquarters (*The News International*, 2 November 2007). On 24 November, two separate attacks targeting military personnel and installations in Rawalpindi resulted in thirty-two deaths. This time it was the personnel of the ISI that were particularly targeted (*The News International*, 25 November 2007). Further attacks followed on 9 December, when ten people including three policemen and seven civilians – including two children – perished in a car bombing near Matta, Swat district. The next day, a suicide attack took place on a school bus carrying the children of air force employees during the morning rush hour in Sargodha (*The News International*, 11 December 2007). On 13 December, suicide bombings near an army checkpoint in Quetta killed seven people, including three personnel of the Pakistan Army (*The News International*, 14 December 2007).

At Nowshera, NWFP, on 15 December, a suicide bomber rammed his explosives-laden bicycle into a military checkpoint, killing five people and injuring eleven others (*The News International*, 16 December 2007). On 17 December, twelve security personnel were killed, and five wounded, in a suicide attack in Kohat, NWFP; the victims were members of the army's local football team (*The News International*, 18 December 2007). On 21 December, a suicide bomb blast again targeted Aftab Ahmad Khan Sherpao, killing at least fifty-seven and injuring over one hundred at Jamia Masjid in Charsadda district. Sherpao survived the blast, but his younger son, Mustafa Khan Sherpao, was injured (*The News International*, 22 December 2007). On 23 December, at least thirteen people, including four security personnel, were killed and another twenty-three wounded as a suicide bomber targeted an army convoy near Mingora, Swat district (*The News International*, 24 December 2007).

This spiralling violence took place in the background of the formation of the Tehrik-e-Taliban Pakistan (TTP) in December 2007. About thirteen groups of the Taliban, on the Pakistani side of the Durand Line, united under the leadership of Baitullah Mehsud with the objective of organising resistance to the Pakistani state, enforcing the Sharia as interpreted by them, and offering the United States and other NATO forces stiff resistance in Afghanistan. Non-state actors became the bearers of the terrorist scourge.

The Lawyers Movement against Musharraf

While the Islamists intensified their attacks on the Musharraf regime, especially on the military as it was involved in ongoing operations against the Taliban and Al-Qaeda, a popular and peaceful movement for the restoration of civilian democratic rule gained momentum in March 2007. According to the largely suspended and heavily amended Pakistan Constitution of 1973, general elections had to be held every five years. After overthrowing Nawaz Sharif in October 1999, Musharraf had assumed the position of chief executive. On 20 June 2001, he appointed himself the president of Pakistan. This was followed by a number of other steps to acquire the semblance of legitimacy. Among them, the most important was the general election held in October 2002. All tactics, including the rigging of elections, gerrymandering, and intimidation, were employed to ensure that a majority of the seats in parliament were won by the pro-Musharraf Pakistan Muslim League-Quaid-i-Azam (PML-Q). EU election observers described the election process as flawed (The *Daily Times*, 13 October 2002). The PML-Q formed a majority coalition with the help of some right-wing parties and independents. As already noted, Musharraf had, over the years, tried to establish the reputation of a moderate and progressive Muslim leader for himself. Moreover, several reputable international economic and financial agencies had noted that while Pakistan's financial standing had improved substantially, inflation, unemployment, and abject poverty continued to ravage the lives of nearly one-fourth of the Pakistani population who were officially categorised as living below the poverty line (Ahmed, 1 December 2007).

In any case, new elections were due in 2007 and, from the beginning of the year, voices began to be raised for free and fair elections. Many liberals and secularists who had, with some reservations, been backing Musharraf as a counterweight to the Islamists, turned against him in the spring of 2007 – when he declared Chief Justice Iftikhar Mohammad Chaudhry of the Pakistan Supreme Court non-functional (a novel term meaning 'practically removed from his office') on allegations of misuse of office. It was widely believed that Justice Chaudhry had told Musharraf that the latter could not contest elections while remaining in uniform, and that the election for the presidency had to be carried out before the end of 2007. Moreover, Justice Chaudhry took up several habeas corpus cases of Pakistani citizens, mainly journalists critical of the Musharraf regime and political activists abducted by the security forces, ordering that the detained individuals be produced in court (*The News International*, 17 March 2007).

Justice Chaudhry's removal resulted in protest marches and demonstrations, mainly by lawyers and the political cadres (Ahmed et al. 2007; Zaidi, 2008). The demonstrations and protest actions continued, in the courts' premises, despite violent assaults by the police and security agencies. In the absence of a political leadership, civil society took the lead in protesting against dictatorship. International support and messages of solidarity helped the struggle to continue. Subsequently, Chaudhry was reinstated by a Supreme Court bench on 10 July. However, that did not mean that the stand-off between Musharraf and him had ended; rather, Chaudhry embarked upon judicial activism that clearly sought confrontation with Musharraf. Meanwhile, civil society actors, as well as the opposition, began to give calls for Musharraf to step down and for a caretaker government to hold free and fair elections. In a bid to pre-empt any move that would threaten his presidency, Musharraf had himself elected president by the outgoing members of the national and provincial assemblies, who were mostly his supporters, on 6 October. In any event, the Pakistan Election Commission announced 8 January 2008 as the date for the general elections.

The crisis deepened when Nawaz Sharif was allowed to return to Pakistan, under intense pressure from the US and Saudi Arabia, on 27 November. A couple of months earlier, in September, when he and his brother, Shahbaz Sharif, had tried to return to Pakistan they had been told that they were unwelcome. Benazir's and Nawaz's presence set in motion popular rallies as the election campaign picked up momentum. Meanwhile, Musharraf resigned as chief of army staff on 28 November, and General Ashfaq Pervez Kayani became the new military chief. General Kayani had, earlier, held the key posts of corps commander of Rawalpindi and director-general of the powerful ISI. Media descriptions of him generally projected the image of a quiet, professional soldier who shunned publicity – in sharp contrast to his predecessor who thrived on it.

Directives Issued by General Kayani

Among the earliest decisions taken by Kayani was a directive instructing army officers not to maintain contact with politicians. They were told that they had no role to play in politics, and emphasised that soldiers should pay heed to their professional responsibilities. Elaborating on this theme, General Kayani told them not to summon any politician to the General Headquarters. Those who violated the directive would have to explain their conduct, as was also stressed in his communication to the officers (*The News International*, 14 January 2008). An even more significant decision, taken by

General Kayani on 11 February 2008, was to recall all officers serving in civil departments. The military spokesperson, Director of the Inter-Services Public Relations Major-General Athar Abbas, told the press, 'More than 300 army officers are presently working in various civil departments and the majority of them have been asked to report to the General Headquarters immediately.' (*Dawn*, 12 February 2008)

The decision had been agreed on at the corps commanders' conference on 7 February 2008, presided over by General Kayani. More importantly, it was asserted that General Kayani did not support President Musharraf's clumsy handling of the conflict with Justice Chaudhry. General Kayani was not known to have abused his office to help his relatives or for personal gain (Yusufzai, 28 November 2007). Other less charitable representations stressed his past as the head of the ISI, suggesting that he must have taken part in the political manoeuvrings that the ISI was notorious for. Moreover, he must have had to interact with the Taliban and Punjabi extremist organisations, such as the LeT and JeM, and, therefore, was not likely to take a firm stand against them.

In any event, not only had resentment against the military been growing among the politicians, but also among the civil servants. Initially, the civil servants, with the assistance of the military, had constituted the oligarchy that called the shots, while the politicians were reduced to being mere pawns in its hands. That relationship had been reversed under Zia, and the military had been appropriating more and more power as a result. Akbar S. Ahmed, himself a civil servant before he became an academic, vividly described in an interview to this author the way in which the military started sidelining the better-educated civil servants in the 1980s. He asserted that such intrusions partly explained why the general standard of administration deteriorated over the years – because military officers had no experience or training in managing civilian affairs. The former Punjab governor, Shahid Hamid, told me that, from the time of Zia onwards, the president and COAS have been at the de facto apex of the power structure and decision-making process in Pakistan. Prime ministers and other ministers have not been relevant. For example, on the question of defence spending, it is the president and COAS who have made the most decisions while the defence ministers have played no important role and could be ignored.

Grievances against the military's involvement in civilian affairs had been growing in the key province of Punjab as well where, in the past, the men in uniform had enjoyed great popularity. Thus, the traditional support for the military had been declining in the major cities of the Punjab – from where the civil service officers mainly hailed. In contrast, the social background of military officers is predominantly of rural Punjab, or from the smaller towns of northern Punjab. This author was able to assess the resentment in the Punjab by talking to a cross section of Punjabi elite during several visits in 2000–2009. Given such developments, the military badly needed to improve its standing in society. Therefore, General Kayani's decision to recall serving officers from the civilian departments was an imperative and long overdue measure.

The Assassination of Benazir Bhutto

While terrorist assaults on security and military personnel continued unabated, Benazir Bhutto carried out a round of meetings to solicit votes for the general elections announced for 8 January 2008. On 27 December, having just addressed one such huge public meeting, she was assassinated (*The News International*, 28 December 2007). Some twenty other people, including five PPP volunteers, were also killed in the bomb blast. A bitter controversy, laced with conspiracy theories, broke out with regard to her killers and whether she had died of gunshots fired by the assassin(s) or the bomb blast that took place concurrently.

The government claimed to have intercepted a telephone conversation between the Al-Qaeda leader, Baitullah Mahsud, and a cleric in which both congratulated each other on her death and praised the men who participated in it (Ahmed, 31 December 2007). Benazir Bhutto had committed herself to working closely with the US in the war on terror, and even to allowing the Americans to interrogate A.Q. Khan – a national hero who is fondly referred to as the father of the Islamic or Pakistani atomic bomb. An Al-Qaeda statement described her death as the end of 'America's most precious asset in Pakistan'. However, a spokesperson for Mehsud denied that the Al-Qaeda leader had anything to do with the murder (Ahmed, 31 December 2007). Efforts to establish who, exactly, were involved in the bomb blasts and gunshots that took place at the time of her death were frustrated because of the many irregularities that had followed her assassination. The Zardari-

Gilani PPP-led government that took office in March 2008 sought help from Scotland Yard, whose team arrived and investigated the circumstances of her violent death. It concluded that she probably died from the impact – falling violently and hitting her head on the roof of the car – resulting in her skull cracking. They could not ascertain whether she died because of her fall when she was shot at or because of the shockwaves caused by the bomb blasts – not least because no post-mortem was conducted on her dead body: her husband Asif Ali Zardari had overruled a post-mortem! A UN Commission of Inquiry found many suspicious circumstances, including a lapse in security, the threat from the Taliban, and the named odd behaviour of some of the officials and even PPP stalwarts; but, it did not categorically establish who could have been involved in the conspiracy to kill her. It noted, however, that the police deliberately failed to effectively investigate the causes of her death (UN Commission of Inquiry, 2010).

The Commission noted that Al-Qaeda had strong motives to order her assassination, because of her support for western-type democracy, pro-US leanings, and her opposition to jihad and terrorism. Such a hostile disposition was shared by the Taliban, who found a woman with modernist ideas an anathema to their deeply misogynist worldview. The Pakistan establishment was also identified, in the report, to have a motive for her elimination: she had been castigating the ISI in her writings and had pledged to bring the military and intelligence services under the control of her civilian government. She had named the super-hawk, General Hamid Gul, and Brigadier Ejaz Shah, the former head of the Intelligence Bureau (IB) and also an ISI officer, as individuals who, though retired, could activate their links with extremists to have her killed (UN Commission of Inquiry 2010: 45–53). An interesting twist to the Commission's findings was that, given the salience of the Sunni jihadist groups in Pakistan, a sectarian motive for the heinous crime was also possible. It noted that as both Benazir's mother and husband were Shias, she was also suspected of being a Shia (ibid., 49–50).

In the buzzing Pakistani market of conspiracies, this was significant because both Benazir (2008b: 54) and her niece, Fatima Bhutto (2010: 50–2), categorically stated in their books that their paternal lineage was solidly Sunni. In a long discussion that I had in 2010 with Syeda Abida Hussain, a veteran politician and close confidant of Benazir Bhutto, and belonging to one of the most prominent Shia families of Punjab, she told me that Benazir had confided in her that she was a Sunni. Abida Hussain also told me that, while in Dubai, Benazir had begun to regularly attend a Sunni mosque and took her children along with her. Whatever the truth, it was strongly indicative of the sectarian polarization that had taken place in Pakistan. Previously, two heads of state, both unelected, were Shias – Iskander Mirza and General Yahya Khan. Shias had been serving as ministers, as well as in very senior positions in both the military and civil bureaucracies.

15

Transition to Democracy and Proliferation in Terrorism

The election of 2008 was held in a highly-charged and volatile atmosphere; the situation in Sindh was explosive. There was rioting in interior Sindh as Mohajir shops and businesses were attacked and some casualties took place. The military issued shoot-to-kill orders. Zardari, appealing for calm, condemned the attacks on innocent people in Sindh and regretted the violence that had erupted. For his part, General Kayani decided not to interfere in the election process. Since General Zia's time, at least, the ISI had been involved in election manipulation and, as a result, its reputation as a 'state within the state' had become part of the popular Pakistani political parlance. Kayani declared that holding a free and fair election was the sole responsibility of the Election Commission, and that the 'army will meet only its constitutional obligations and help the civil administration maintain law and order, as and when required' (*Dawn* 12 February 2008). Had Benazir Bhutto not been assassinated on 27 December 2007, a US-sponsored power-sharing deal between Benazir and Musharraf would have achieved two objectives: through elections, the Muslim League-Quaid and the continuingly popular Pakistan Peoples Party would have gained the most seats, and Musharraf would have continued as president. Benazir wanted the Americans to ensure that she was provided with proper security when she visited Pakistan, and to be absolved of all the corruption charges against her (Suskind, 2008: 262–66).

In any event, the general elections on 18 February 2008 proved to be free and fair in spite of some vote rigging by local strongmen and a complicit administration. The result turned out to be a massive protest vote against authoritarianism. The PPP and the Pakistan Muslim League-Nawaz (PML-N) emerged as the main winners, securing 120 and 90 seats, respectively, in the 342-member National Assembly. In the provincial assemblies, too, they did very well in places where their influence was known to exist. The Islamist parties were wiped out in the strategic NWFP, on the Afghan border where the Taliban and Al-Qaeda extremists had their strongholds. The main winner was the Awami National Party (ANP), a secular-nationalist party that had always, historically, enjoyed significant support in the province. The main pro-Musharraf party, the PML-Q, suffered a major loss, winning only fifty-one seats in the National Assembly. Its support in the provincial assemblies plummeted sharply as well. The exception was Balochistan, where Musharraf's earlier military action had resulted in many casualties, including the killing of the powerful tribal leader, Akbar Bugti, in 2006. Consequently, the Baloch nationalists had boycotted the election and the seats were captured by the PML-Q.

The PPP and PML-N, both bitter rivals in the past, decided to form a broad-based coalition government which included the ANP as well as the pro-Musharraf MQM and the Jamiat Ulema-e-Islam. After several weeks of intense political manoeuvring, Yousaf Raza Gilani was nominated as the PPP candidate for prime minister on 22 March. He was elected on 24 March, having secured 264 votes while the pro-Musharraf PML-Q candidate, Chaudhry Pervaiz Elahi, received only 42 votes. Gilani was sworn in by Musharraf on 25 March but Zardari, Sharif, and several other leaders did not attend the ceremony, presumably to protest against Musharraf's continuation as president (*The News International*, 26 March 2008).

Among the first orders that Gilani issued, after being elected prime minister, was the removal of all hindrances on the movement of the deposed chief justice of Pakistan, Iftikhar Mohammad Chaudhry, and the other judges of the Pakistan Supreme Court who had been kept in detention. In his maiden speech as prime minister, Gilani announced that his government would continue to combat terrorism but that the conflict could not be solved through military means only. Efforts would be made to find a political solution that would establish peace and order in Pakistan (*The News International*, 30 March 2008). However, talks between the PPP and PML-N, about the re-instatement of the judiciary, ended in deadlock. Both had agreed, in the Bhurban Declaration of 9 March 2008, that the judges would be reinstated, through a resolution, within thirty days of the formation of government. That did not transpire and Nawaz Sharif decided to pull his party's nine ministers out of the twenty-four-minister federal cabinet. The coalition government continued in office while the PML-N decided to sit in the opposition.

Terrorism in 2008

The spate of terrorist attacks that caused hundreds of deaths and injuries during 2007 emanated from the FATA where the Afghan Taliban and Al-Qaeda leaders were suspected to have taken refuge. They received help and protection from extremist organizations such as the Haqqani group led by the Afghan Maulvi Jalaluddin Haqqani and his son Sirajuddin Haqqani who the Americans suspected enjoyed sanctuary in North Waziristan with the connivance of the ISI. FATA had not been properly integrated into the Pakistani mainstream, though it had been granted representation in the National Assembly and the Senate. Its societal affairs were still regulated by Pakhtunwali, the traditional code of interaction. Extreme poverty, deprivation, and lack of education and economic opportunities, coupled with a traditional arms-bearing culture, rendered FATA prone to extremist and violent ideas and practices (Dogar, 2009).

At any rate, the restoration of democracy in the rest of Pakistan did not carry any benign fallout for peace. Terrorist attacks by suicide bombers, mainly against government personnel and premises, continued to take place in 2008. On 10 January, a suicide attack outside the Lahore High Court, before a lawyer's protest march was scheduled to begin, resulted in twenty-four deaths and injury to sevnty-three people; the police were the main targets of the attack (*The News*, 11 January 2008). On 4 February, students and officials of the Army Medical College near Military Headquarters in Rawalpindi were the victims of another attack when a suicide bomber crashed his bike into the bus carrying them; ten died and twenty-seven were injured (*The News*, 5 February 2008). In the NWFP, bomb blasts took place at the election rallies of the PPP and the ANP, as did attacks on the police and military, during February. On 25 February, the head of the medical corps, Lieutenant General Mushtaq Baig, was killed along with his driver and security guard, when a suicide bomber attacked their vehicle. Again, the terrorists launched an attack in Lahore when two suicide bombers blew themselves up at the Pakistan Navy War College. Eight people were killed and twenty-four others injured (*The News International*, 26 February 2008).

Another gory attack took place in Lahore on 11 March when two suicide bombers carried out separate missions. In the first attack, the Federal Investigation Agency (FIA) office on Temple Road, in the centre of the city, was ripped apart and thirty people were killed, including sixteen policemen. The target was the office of the personnel being trained in counter-terrorism operations by the Americans. The second attack was on the office of an advertising agency in the posh area of Model Town near Bilawal House – the latter owned by the late Benazir Bhutto and her husband, Asif Ali Zardari. Three people lost their lives in that assault (*The News*, 12 March 2008).

However, once the new government had been sworn in, there was a respite in the bombing campaign for a while – probably in the hope that Musharraf would be forced to step down as president, and then Pakistan would withdraw from the war on terror and stop helping the Americans. As that did not happen, another wave of terrorism swept over Pakistan from July onwards.

A Bloody July

On Sunday 6 July 2008, a suicide bomber blew himself up near the Lal Masjid (Red Mosque) in the Pakistani capital, Islamabad. He succeeded in killing at least twenty-one, including fifteen policemen. The mayhem the blasts caused was a shocking reminder of the fact that terrorist networks that had been dormant for some time were back in the killing business. The government claimed to have made proper security arrangements to prevent terrorist attacks. Three thousand policemen were reportedly stationed in Islamabad during the commemorative conference being held by the Islamists to mark the attack on the Lal Masjid. The Pakistani media reported that several speakers at the conference whipped up passions, describing the dead leaders and cadres of the Lal Masjid as martyrs in the cause of Islam. Not surprisingly, such suggestions placed the Pakistan military in the role of killers and aggressors. Whatever the preparations and calculations, letting the extremists commemorate the Lal Masjid carnage proved to be a myopic decision. On 7 July, six crude bombs exploded in different parts of Karachi, causing grievous injury to 25 people. Pakistan blamed Baitullah Mehsud for the attacks – the Tehrik-e-Taliban-e-Pakistan was suspected of establishing its hold over some Pakhtun-majority areas of Karachi, which had brought the Taliban into conflict with the MQM (Hussain, 2008).

Attack on the Indian Embassy in Kabul

On 7 July 2008, the Indian embassy in Kabul was the object of a major terrorist assault. The terrorists were able to successfully penetrate the heavily guarded and fortified locality, where many Afghan ministries were located, and explode multiple bombs outside the gate of the embassy. Fifty-nine people, including four members of the Indian diplomatic staff, were slain. The Afghans immediately alleged that the attack had been masterminded by an intelligence agency of a neighbouring country. Given the strained relations between Afghanistan and Pakistan, it was not difficult to apprehend that the Afghans were pointing their finger at Pakistan. A few days later, India made similar accusations. President Hamid Karzai of Afghanistan went on to claim that his government had convincing evidence that implicated the Pakistani intelligence. Although the American secretary of defense, Robert Gates, initially stated that he had not seen any evidence of Pakistani involvement, the United States' position changed soon afterwards when the Afghans and Indians presented the evidence they had collected to the Bush administration (Ahmed, 11 July 2008).

President George Bush, as well as presidential candidates John McCain and Barrack Obama, and other leaders whom Gilani met urged him to do much more to root out extremism and terrorism. The American media raised the same concerns. When Bush warned Gilani that the United States would take serious action, Gilani agreed to investigate. But, the Pakistan Foreign Office dismissed the accusation, that the ISI was involved, as rubbish. Notwithstanding the very negative image that marred Gilani's visit to the United States, the US Congress voted in favour of a US$15 billion aid package to Pakistan, of which the major portion would be spent on economic development. Such a peculiar discrepancy in US behaviour towards Pakistan was indicative of the extent to which the Americans were dependent on the latter for the realisation of their long-term goals in Afghanistan, and in South Asia in general.

On 26 July, the Pakistan government announced that the ISI had been placed under the Interior Ministry. However, the same evening, the Press Information Department (PID) issued a clarification that both the agencies were still under the prime minister. Later, it was announced that the ISI had been placed under the defence ministry again (*The News*, 6 August 2008). In another move, the government declared, on 25 August 2008, that the TTP had been banned, its bank accounts and assets frozen, and that it was barred from media appearances. This measure was undertaken because the TTP had been terrorising people in different parts of the NWFP and, increasingly, attacking government functionaries and destroying government buildings and installations.

Embarrassment for Gilani in Colombo

Soon afterwards, Gilani attended the SAARC summit in Colombo, Sri Lanka (27 July–3 August). There, too, instead of show-casing his democratically-elected government, he had to spend most of the time assuring his South Asian counterparts that his government was determined to fight terrorism. In an interview with a Sri Lankan newspaper, he rubbished all accusations that the ISI was involved in the Kabul bombing, asserting that it took orders from him and reported to him in accordance with requirements laid down in the Pakistan constitution. In any case, in a forty-five-minute long meeting with Indian Prime Minister Manmohan Singh, Gilani pointed out that Pakistan, too, was a victim of terrorism and that both Pakistan and India should work together to fight that evil. In a separate meeting with President Karzai, he promised to carry out an investigation to ascertain whether there was any ISI involvement in the Kabul bombing – thus contradicting his earlier categorical denial to the Sri Lankan newspaper.

Gilani was making a technically correct statement when he said that, constitutionally speaking, the ISI was under his jurisdiction and reported to him. But, for all practical purposes, it is the chief of army staff to whom the ISI reports and takes its orders from. In the past, whenever a civilian government had tried to establish its control over the ISI by appointing a general it trusted, but who was unacceptable to the military establishment, the establishment trumped it by appointing its own men to strategic positions dealing with intelligence on internal politics. Thus, the ISI continued to maintain a watch on the activities of the civilian government too (Ahmed, 15 August 2008).

In any case, Gilani received support from President Musharraf who described the ISI as 'Pakistan's first line of defence' (*The News*, 6 August 2008). In a statement issued by the Pakistan government, the United States was criticised for blaming Pakistan for the recent terrorist activities. It was pointed out that, on 24 May 2008, Pakistan had provided the Americans with the exact location and movement of Baitullah Mehsud, who had driven to a remote South Waziristan mountain-post in his Toyota Land Cruiser to address the press, but that he returned to his abode safely. The statement went on to say that the United States military has the capacity to direct a missile to a precise location at very short notice, as it had done close to twenty times in the last few years to hit Al-Qaeda targets inside Pakistan. However, no action was taken against Mehsud. This attitude was described by, Pakistan, as intriguing and confusing. Pakistan also alleged an Indian hand in the trouble in Balochistan, and that the Afghanistan government was protecting Baloch secessionists.

Musharraf Exits

The strong defence of the ISI was the last significant, but controversial, statement that Musharraf made because, on 18 August 2008, he finally resigned. In his resignation speech, Musharraf insisted that he was acting in the best interests of Pakistan, by stepping down to avoid a protracted power struggle and political uncertainty. Musharraf's two indispensable backers – Pakistan's military and the United States – were apparently no longer interested in supporting him. His support in the domestic sphere had declined drastically; for example, the provincial assemblies of Punjab, Sindh, NWFP, and Balochistan had tabled motions, with overwhelming support, demanding Musharraf seek a vote of confidence – which he knew he would lose badly (Jetly, 25 August 2008).

Zardari as President

The election for the new president took place within three weeks of Musharraf's resignation. Zardari surprised many when he announced that he would contest the presidential election. He was endorsed by the PPP and the MQM. The PML-N nominated Justice (Retd.) Saeed-uz-Zaman Siddiqui, and the PML-Q nominated Mushahid Hussain Syed. Zardari got 481 out of the 702 votes of the electoral college – which comprise the two houses of the federal parliament and the provincial assemblies. At the inauguration ceremony on 9 September 2008, Afghan President Hamid Karzai was the guest of honour. In his address, Zardari pledged to combat terrorism and strengthen democracy in Pakistan and peace in South Asia. However, differences between Zardari and the military establishment surfaced quite quickly over relations with India. Indian newspapers referred to an interview, given by Zardari to the *Wall Street Journal*, in which he referred to the militants active in Indian-Kashmir as terrorists. He also stated that India did not pose a threat to Pakistan (*The Hindustan Times*, 5 October 2008; *The Hindu* 6 October 2008). That news was not highlighted in the Pakistani media but, on 7 October, Lahore's *Daily Times* reported that such an announcement had been denounced by the leader of the JeT, Hafiz Muhammad Saeed. Another controversial statement followed in which Zardari said that Pakistan would not resort to a nuclear strike first in case of war with India (*The Times of India*, 22 November 2008). It seems reasonable to presume that Zardari was making such unorthodox pronouncements because he enjoyed the support and backing of the United States, and may have been encouraged to make them by the Americans. Obviously, none of these three positions corresponded to those held by the military. This was confirmed when the whistle-blowing website WikiLeaks released a US diplomatic cable reporting that General Kayani did not subscribe to the position of not striking first with nuclear weapons (*The Times of India*, 6 May 2011).

Although military spokespersons alluded to the Taliban as the imminent threat to Pakistan's security on a number of occasions, there was no fundamental reconsideration of India remaining the main and constant threat to Pakistan's security. In fact, the military, and even civilian ministers, alleged that the Indian consulates in the border towns of Afghanistan were being used to spy on Pakistan, and that India was involved in helping the separatist insurgency in Balochistan.

In April 2011, the *Dawn* reported a statement by the former British foreign secretary, David Miliband, that Zardari and Manmohan Singh had agreed on a deal over Kashmir but General Kayani had been reluctant to endorse it (*Dawn*, 4 April 2011). A breakthrough on Kashmir has been in the offing for a long time and, on a number of occasions, a settlement seems to have been reached only to be subverted at the last moment by the conservatives on both sides.

Attack on the Marriott Islamabad

On 20 September 2008, a dump truck filled with explosives crashed past the guards at Islamabad's prestigious Marriott Hotel – located close to the diplomatic enclave – and detonated. At least 54 people were killed and 255 injured. Although most of the casualties were Pakistanis, at least five foreign nationals were killed and fifteen injured. The bomb explosion took place soon after Zardari had delivered his first address to the Pakistan parliament. Once again, Pakistan's reputation as the epicentre of terrorism reverberated loud and clear all over the world. The elected government seemed helpless, and the military and intelligence services unable, to stem the continuing spate of terrorist activities.

The Mumbai Terrorist Outrage

Stakes were raised to a critical level when, on 26 November 2008, a series of terrorist attacks were launched on India's megalopolis and financial capital, Mumbai, by suspected members of the Pakistan-based jihadist organization, the Lashkar-e-Tayyaba (LeT). The phenomenon of non-state actors, emanating from Pakistan, spearheading terrorist attacks on foreign soil greatly traumatised the Indian nation and was treated with revulsion by the international community. While earlier attacks, such as the July 2006 Mumbai commuter train bombings, had caused 209 deaths, the Mumbai attacks attracted greater worldwide attention. Not only had the culprits placed the bombs stealthily, but they had also carried out their operation in a very public manner. For some sixty hours, the Indian security forces battled with the terrorists. Finally, only one, Ajmal Amir Kasab, was captured alive. The Indian authorities claimed to have found the bodies of nine alleged terrorists. The attackers had apparently taken the sea route from Pakistan's port city of Karachi, and landed by boat at Mumbai. Indian coastal defence and intelligence apparatuses completely failed to detect them. Some writers described the Mumbai attacks as India's 9/11 because the culprits had deliberately targeted symbols of Indian affluence and grandeur, such as the Taj Mahal and Oberoi Trident hotels and places where westerners gathered such as the Leopold Café. Targeting the Jewish centre at Nariman House was certainly meant to create maximum effect and capture international attention.

A group calling itself the 'Deccan Mujahideen' claimed to have carried out the attacks. Such a label suggested that it was the doing of Indian Muslims having roots or affiliations with Hyderabad Deccan in southern India, but the Indian authorities dismissed it as a fake name and a diversion. Indian Muslims, in general, protested against the terrorist attacks. They refused to give a proper Islamic burial to the terrorists and refused permission to bury their bodies in Muslim graveyards.

On the other hand, Pakistani and foreign journalists and TV channels visited Kasab's village, Faridkot, in southern Punjab and interviewed his parents, friends, and neighbours who admitted that the man shown on Indian television was indeed Kasab. That created a furore in India. The Indians believed that such evidence sufficed to incriminate him. The Pakistani authorities imposing restrictions on any journalists visiting Faridkot.

I arrived in Pakistan on 29 November 2008. The trip had been planned months ahead, as part of my research on the role of the military in Pakistan for the Institute of South Asian Studies. Eliciting the views of senior Pakistani military officers and other public figures, on how they explained the role of the military, was my main concern. I also wanted to probe the Indian perceptions of the Pakistani military. There was no doubt that relations between India and Pakistan had turned dangerously tense. Whoever masterminded the Mumbai attacks had succeeded in bringing the two countries to the brink of war. Within hours of the attacks, Indian Prime Minister Manmohan Singh alluded to Pakistani involvement. Other spokespersons also emphasized such a connection. The initial response from Pakistan was conciliatory and sympathetic, and it offered its cooperation. Newly-elected President Asif Ali Zardari and Prime Minister Gilani denied that their government had ordered the attacks. Foreign Minister Shah Mehmood Qureshi promised full cooperation in investigating the incident. Prime Minister Gilani even agreed, on India's request, to send the director-general of the ISI, Lieutenant General Ahmed Shuja Pasha, to India to examine the evidence the Indians claimed they had gathered to prove that the attacks had been carried out by Pakistanis. Later, however, the Pakistan government retracted the offer, presumably under pressure from the military; no one from the ISI was sent to India.

In any event, international diplomacy went into action to defuse the situation forthwith. The international community, including key players such as the United States and the United Kingdom, expressed sympathy for India and condemned terrorism. United States Secretary of State Condoleezza Rice and Britain's Prime Minister Gordon Brown, were among those who paid visits. As an escalating armed encounter between the two South Asian rivals would spell disaster, not only for the region but for the world as well, the international concerns were understandable.

There is little doubt that the Mumbai attacks reinforced Pakistan's already sullied reputation as 'a rogue state', 'the epicentre of terrorism', and so on. Former United States Secretary of State Madeline Albright succinctly captured the apprehensions being felt in the United States about Pakistan, in the context of the Mumbai attacks, when she said, 'Pakistan has everything that gives you an international migraine. It has nuclear weapons, it has terrorism, extremists, corruption, very poor and it's in a location that's really, really important to us.' In the same statement, Madeleine Albright emphasised that President Asif Ali Zardari was trying very hard to deal with the situation. She was expressing a view widely shared by the Bush administration, and even India, that it was not the elected Pakistani government that had ordered the attacks. But, on the other hand, the role of the military and intelligence agencies remained a matter of speculation. India rejected the official Pakistani position that the attacks had been carried out by non-state or independent actors. This position was stressed by no less than the Indian president, Pratibha Patil, in her address on the eve of India's Republic Day anniversary. Without naming Pakistan, she said, 'Arguments that terrorism is being perpetuated by independent actors are self-defeating and cannot be accepted. Countries must own up their responsibilities as must the international community in defeating terrorism.'

Her reiteration of the accusation, made earlier by other Indian leaders, reflected the frustration Indians felt about the denial mode Pakistan had been operating in after the government's calm and reasonable statements initially. Such frustration was partly the product of the so-called 'media war' between India and Pakistan. Some Indian commentators demanded an all-out military attack on Pakistan, while others advocated surgical strikes on the offices and training camps of the LeT – Indian anger had manifestly assumed jingoistic overtones. Pakistani warmongers warned India of dire consequences in case of any military adventure because Pakistan, after all, was a nuclear weapon state. Some went on to suggest that the Indian intelligence agencies had masterminded the whole operation with a view to tarnishing Pakistan's image and exploiting this to order a military offensive. Agitated Indian commentators began to sound even more belligerent, while so-called experts counted the troops and weapons on both sides and concluded that India had a definite upper hand.

In reaction, the direction of Pakistani media discussions changed from explaining a possible Pakistani connection to projecting an imminent threat posed by a belligerent India. Responding to the growing sense of insecurity, Prime Minister Gilani invited all the political parties to a national discussion on the perceived Indian threat. A resolution was adopted which expressed condolences for the loss of lives, but the main thrust was on all the parties pledging support for the government in case of war. Even the Pakistan Taliban, who were engaged in a daily violent conflict with government troops, announced that they would fight shoulder-to-shoulder with the Pakistan Army if war broke out.

As the days passed, the Indian leaders increased the pressure on Pakistan by demanding that Pakistanis suspected of involvement in the attacks should be handed over to stand trial in India. As no extradition treaty existed between the two states, Pakistan refused to comply with such a demand. However, it kept assuring India that if evidence was provided that proved the guilt of any Pakistanis, they would then be punished severely through the due process of law. International pressure mounted on Pakistan as the United Nations declared the Jama'at-ud-Da'wah, a charitable front organization representing the LeT (which had formally been banned by Pakistan in 2002), a terrorist organisation. Pakistan followed suit. Some of the LeT's top leaders were put under house arrest and its offices sealed.

Moreover, India supplied both the United States Federal Bureau of Investigation (FBI) and Pakistan with material it claimed incontrovertibly established the Pakistani origin of Kasab and the other men. The FBI declared the Indian evidence reliable and authentic, and declared that its own independent investigations clearly established a link with the LeT. The Indians again began to demand that Pakistan hand over culprits involved in terrorism in India; the names of the LeT's chief, Hafiz Muhammad Saeed, and of Jaish-e-Muhammad's Maulana Masud Azhar, among others, were on the list. Later, the Indian authorities asserted that, during interrogations, Kasab had named Zaki-ur-Rahman Lakhvi as his immediate mentor and the person who had ordered him to carry out the killings in Mumbai. He, as well as another leader of the LeT, Yousaf Muzzamil, were named as directly responsible for masterminding the Mumbai attacks. On 7 January 2009, the Pakistan government admitted that Kasab could be of Pakistani origin (Ahmed, 30 January 2009).

Views of Pakistani Military Officers on Mumbai Attacks

I talked to several retired senior officers during my visit to Pakistan in 2008. COAS General Jehangir Karamat and former ISI director-general, Lieutenant General Javed Ashraf Qazi, asserted that the Islamists had been purged from the military and intelligence services. They conceded, however, that retired Islamists could still wield influence as they were part of different networks. Most of the senior officers that I talked to were of the opinion that India was largely to blame for continuing to provide the jihadists with an axe to grind by refusing to solve the Kashmir issue. This was notwithstanding the fact that General Musharraf had gone out of his way to placate Indian fears by announcing that Pakistan no longer insisted on the implementation of the UNSC's resolutions pertaining to Kashmir, and was willing to consider any solution that could reasonably satisfy India, Pakistan, and the Kashmiri people. Since that opportunity had been missed, the jihadis were again up in arms.

General Pervez Musharraf, who made a clean breast of the Pakistan military's and ISI's culpability in creating the Islamist monster that was now striking terror within Pakistan, told me:

> The Americans wanted us to produce Islamic warriors that could be deployed in the Afghanistan jihad. We obliged without thinking out the consequences such brainwashing would carry for our own society. We trained them to become jihadists. We trained them to kill. We sent

> them into Afghanistan and in the Indian-administered Kashmir. Now, they have unleashed their terror on our own people. They are killing our soldiers and will stop at nothing to impose their brutal ideology on us. I recently saw a video in which the throat of a man was being split open with a long knife, while some bearded men in the background were shouting 'Allah-o-Akbar'.

Lieutenant General (Retd.) Nasir Akhtar – who as corps commander of Karachi in the early 1990s had considerable experience of dealing with terrorism fomented by the Mohajir Qaumi Movement and Sindhi nationalists – was of the opinion that the Mumbai attacks bore the signature of Al-Qaeda, and that huge amounts of money from Arab patrons must have gone into its preparation. He was of the view that the Kashmir dispute needed an early resolution, and converting the Line of Control into some sort of porous border was the only thing the Indians were likely to agree to. He, too, stressed that the Indian leadership had missed a very good opportunity when General Musharraf's overtures on Kashmir were not given a proper response.

A senior officer, who until recently held key portfolios in the ISI and was directly responsible for planning national security, confided in me – on the assurance that his identity would not be disclosed – that had India proceeded with military strikes on Pakistan, it would have resulted in very extensive loss and damage. He believed that the Indians had gained a lot by behaving as a responsible regional power. He lamented that Islamism and extremism had been imposed on Pakistan because of the Afghanistan jihad, and dismissed suggestions that someone currently serving in the military or the ISI may have ordered the terrorist attacks of 26 November 2008. According to him, Pakistan did not stand to gain anything from such a misadventure but had much to lose. India derived maximum advantage, as a responsible and peace-loving state, by not resorting to force while Pakistan was being demonised in the world as a rogue state. He believed that the Pakistani Taliban and Al-Qaeda had co-operated to carry out the attacks in Mumbai, and was of the view that the extremists had no problem in getting hold of funds to finance their jihad. Huge amounts of money from the drugs trade, and donations from Arab patrons in Saudi Arabia and the United Arab Emirates, furnished abundant resources and incentives to promote extremism and terrorism.

The well-known Islamist and ex-ISI chief, Hamid Gul, dismissed all suggestions that Pakistan, or any Pakistan-based group, had carried out the attacks. He asserted that the ISI was wrongly blamed for placing a bomb on the Samjhauta Express in February 2007. Later, it was established by Indian investigators that Hindu terrorists, including some from the Indian military – such as Colonel Shrikant Purohit – were responsible for it. He was emphatic that the Mumbai attacks, too, were an inside job masterminded by Hindu extremists. On reports that he had been placed on a terrorist list by the United States, General Gul observed,

> I have been told that after the Mumbai attacks I have been placed on a terrorist list by the Americans. What hypocrisy! When they needed us to fight in Afghanistan, they described us as freedom fighters; now we are terrorists. I am not worried about such a label being put on me. In fact it is an honour to be declared a terrorist by a government that is guilty of unforgivable crimes against humanity by invading Iraq and Afghanistan. The fact is that socialism failed some years ago. Capitalism is now in tatters. The United States is a power in irreversible decline. The future belongs to Islam.

Brigadier (Retd.) Yasub Ali Dogar drew my attention to a theory held by some Pakistani military and defence analysts that the Taliban's degree of sophistication in their armed conflict with Pakistani forces was indicative of the foreign help being rendered to them. Besides drug money and Arab donors, it was suspected that Indian intelligence was actively involved in strengthening the Taliban. India had established several consulates near the Pakistan border in Afghanistan which served as sources for the supply of money and materials, through clandestine networks, to the Taliban. The conflict with the Taliban has been bleeding the Pakistan military in the same way as Pakistani militants, such as LeT, despatched into Indian-administered Kashmir have been bleeding the Indian military through ambush and sabotage. Quite simply, tit-for-tat.

Indian Views

During my brief visit to India, I was able to interview Lieutenant General (Retd.) Dr B.S. Malik, former chief of western command. He was of the view that, since Pakistan lacked strong democratic institutions, it was not surprising that the most efficient organisation in the country, the military, began to call the shots from quite early on. He did not believe that the military had ordered the Mumbai attacks but observed that the situation in Pakistan was out of control. Besides the LeT, any set of conspirators could have been involved in the Mumbai attacks. In meetings with the South Asian Cluster at the Indian Defence Studies and Analysis (IDSA), and the Indian Centre for Land Warfare Studies, it became clear that India had been rudely shaken by the Mumbai attacks. While the experts were aware of the grave dangers that a war between the two rivals could pose, they expressed strong scepticism about the normalisation of relations between the two countries unless Pakistan came clean and co-operated sincerely in the investigation, and the culprits were properly punished.

Change of Guard in the White House

In November 2008, the Democratic Party's candidate, Barack Hussein Obama, was elected the first African-American and forty-fourth president of the United States. Obama had emphasised, while campaigning, that he would continue with the war on terror but would adopt a strategy requiring Pakistan to deliver more effectively in lieu of the aid it receives from the United States. The term 'AfPak' was coined by Richard Holbrooke in 2008, to designate Afghanistan and Pakistan as a single theatre of military operations. Holbrooke was appointed the US special representative to Afghanistan and Pakistan by the Obama administration. Holbrooke described the AfPak concept in the following terms:

> It is an attempt to indicate…the fact that there is one theatre of war, straddling an ill-defined border, the Durand Line, and that on the western side of that border, NATO and other forces are able to operate. On the eastern side, it's the sovereign territory of Pakistan. But it is on the eastern side of this ill-defined border that the international terrorist movement is located (World Wide Words 2009).

Pakistan reacted with dismay at the neologism 'AfPak', which bracketed it with Afghanistan. In its self-esteem, Pakistan considered itself qualified to be bracketed with India. Afghanistan, on the other hand, it considered a loose confederacy of tribes and warlords, with the government at Kabul representing only a rudimentary type of state authority. Initially, Holbrooke and some other experts had suggested that, in order to convince Pakistan to take part whole-heartedly in the war on terror, it was necessary that it be assured that the United States was sympathetic to the resolution of Kashmir. Moreover, Pakistan had serious reservations about India's prominent presence in Afghanistan. Consequently, the Obama administration did obliquely allude to the inclusion of India in a broader South Asian concentric arena of multifaceted policy initiatives, but the neologism – AfPakInd – was never formally proposed. India reacted angrily to such a suggestion, asserting that the Americans were not welcome to any mediatory role in Kashmir. The Americans quickly retreated and AfPak made no further reference to India.

The scourge of terrorism continued to spiral out of control, exposing the Pakistani establishment's limitations on its capacity to bolster the 'fortress of Islam' with impunity. The TTP and its affiliates continued their concerted and sustained terrorist campaign within Pakistan. In early 2009, the centre of gravity of terrorism shifted to the Swat Valley.

An Islamic Emirate in the Swat Valley

Since 1989, Sufi Muhammad – a veteran of the Afghan jihad – had actively been promoting militant Wahabism in the idyllic Swat Valley. Unlike other parts of the NWFP, although the people of Swat were mainly Pakhtuns, they had no tradition of bearing arms. Rather, its record of a peaceful existence extended to the distant past when a Buddhist civilization flourished there. At the time of the partition of India, many Hindus from the NWFP shifted to Swat because its ruler, the Wali, was known for his tolerant rule. Although the Wali decided to accede to Pakistan, Swat was not amalgamated into the NWFP until

1969. Sufi Muhammad's Tehrik-e-Nifaz-e-Shariat-e-Muhammadi (TNSM) began to undermine the old order. What supplanted it was the all-too-familiar obscurantist and brutal way of life and arbitrary government that thrives on summary executions of sex offenders and criminals. The TNSM emerged as an affiliate of the TTP, albeit with its own local autonomy and doctrinal peculiarities deriving from its Wahabi orientation – in distinction to the largely Deobandi Taliban. In terms of politics, there was hardly any difference. In fact, the TNSM's zeal in destroying girls' schools, and modern education for both boys and girls in general, exceeded that of the Taliban. Peace deals between the TNSM and the Pakistan government in 2007 and in 2008 allowed the TNSM to impose Sharia law in areas under its control; in return, they were required to acknowledge the writ of the state and abstain from terrorist activities. Neither the TTP nor the TNSM was keen to honour the pledge it had made. The United States considered such peace deals to be capitulation, and a betrayal by Pakistan of its pledge to sincerely and unequivocally take part in the war on terror. Pakistan, however, continued to insist that the imposition of Sharia law, in limited areas, did not contradict its commitment to fighting terrorism.

In January 2009, reports began to emanate of a major offensive launched by the TNSM to convert Swat into an Islamic emirate. The TNSM had previously blown up schools and government buildings in Bajaur and Mohmand agency, and now the Swat Valley was subjected to the same treatment. The hallmark of such an emirate was the destruction of hundreds of girl schools, and was part of a wider campaign that included public amputations, floggings, and stoning of alleged sexual offenders and other criminals. The military had previously made deals with Sufi Muhammad which had stipulated that while the TNSM was allowed to impose harsh Islamic laws, it acknowledged the overall sovereignty of the Pakistani state. Those deals foundered quickly as the TNSM continued to violate its terms and continued the intimidation of the people and harassment of government troops. That latest deal was made on 5 February 2009 and allowed the imposition of Sharia laws and the establishment of Sharia courts, but under the government's supervision through a Shariat appellate bench of the Supreme Court in the Malakand region. That was interpreted as carte blanche by the TNSM – to brutalise the people of Swat. Besides destroying girl schools, the TNSM ruled that, in future, girls could at most attend school up to the fifth class. When President Zardari asserted that appeals against the verdict of the Shariat courts could be moved before the Pakistan Supreme Court, this was rejected by the TNSM, which intensified its terror campaign.

In another part of NWFP – the Orakzai Agency – the TTP intensified its reign of terror by demanding that the Sikh minority pay the poll-tax, jizya, or flee or face the sword. Hitherto, Sikhs and Hindus in the tribal areas had lived in peace among the Pakhtuns, in accordance with the values and practices of Pakhtunwali. Under the circumstances, thousands of people belonging to the Hindu, Sikh, and Christian communities began to flee from the tribal areas.

Attack on the Sri Lanka Cricket Team

Brutalization of the tribal areas and the plains of the NWFP had become endemic since the 1980s; sectarian terrorism had been wrecking lives in the Punjab since the end of the 1980s; but, in March, the long hand of militant extremism did not even spare sport. On 3 March 2009, the centre of gravity of terrorism shifted to Lahore, the capital of the dominant Punjab province. As the bus carrying the Sri Lankan cricket team neared the Qaddafi Stadium, it was attacked with bullets, grenades, bombs, and rocket launchers. Since the target was a fast-moving one, not all the deadly ammunition hit the target. Eight Sri Lankan players were injured, none critically, while five Pakistani security personnel died defending them. Two other Pakistanis were also reported killed in the attack. One could see, on television, the twelve terrorists moving around with great ease and confidence, shooting at will and showing no signs of nervousness or hurry. Not surprisingly, a senior minister in the Punjab cabinet, Raja Riaz, unequivocally drew parallels between the attack and the Mumbai atrocity, alleging that the same forces were involved in the Lahore attack. Because of the proliferation of terrorism, other countries had refused to play in Pakistan; only the Sri Lankans had agreed. This attack proved to be the catalyst that was needed to make the Pakistani media highlight the imminent danger that home-grown terrorism posed to Pakistan. However, conspiracy theories continued to circulate about a sinister Indian-Afghan government hand behind the assault.

Nawaz Sharif Announces Long March

While the public was still coming to terms with the shock of a friendly country's cricket team being attacked by fanatics, Nawaz Sharif exacerbated the volatile milieu by announcing, in the second week of March 2009, his intention of joining the so-called 'long march' that the lawyers had announced to protest against the continuing deposition of Justice Chaudhry and his colleagues. Partly, the impetus to join the long march was decided by the verdict of a three-judge bench of the Lahore High Court that had declared his brother, Shahbaz Sharif, and him ineligible to hold public office. It was feared that PML-N and PPP supporters could be drawn into street power manifestations that, in turn, could result in violent clashes between them. Undeterred by such a prospect, Nawaz Sharif threatened to bring hundreds of thousands of protestors to the capital, Islamabad. He claimed that he was willing to risk his life to resituate the honourable judges to their rightful places on the Supreme Court benches; such enthusiasm probably reflected an attempt, on his part, to rehabilitate his tarnished reputation following his goons' raid on the Supreme Court during his second government. The JI, and the charismatic leader of the Tehrik-e-Insaaf (TeI), cricket idol Imran Khan, also announced their intention to join the march.

Prime Minister Gilani responded by imposing Section 144, which prohibited groups of more than five people assembling in one place. The police clashed with demonstrators in Karachi, Lahore, Islamabad, and other places. Hundreds of protestors were arrested. However, the government realised that, without the excessive use of force, the long march could not be prevented. The PPP-MQM coalition government in Sindh, as well as the governments in the North-West Frontier Province and Baluchistan, played a responsible role by informing the PPP leadership that, in the event that the long march took place, the people of their provinces were likely to join it. Alarm bells began to ring in Washington DC. The United States did not want Pakistan to be destabilised. Secretary of State Hilary Clinton called both President Zardari and Nawaz Sharif urging restraint. The United States ambassador to Pakistan, Anne Petterson, and other officials also conducted hectic diplomatic activities to defuse the conflict. Nawaz Sharif, reportedly, informed the Americans that he would not budge from his stand and that the long march would go ahead if the PPP continued with its authoritarian policies.

As the prospects of a showdown loomed large, with Nawaz Sharif planning to start his long march on 16 March 2009, the first signs of major disagreements within the PPP leadership became public in a dramatic manner. Information and Broadcasting Minister Sherry Rehman resigned when the transmissions of the popular private television channel, *Geo News*, were stopped without her being consulted. Earlier, Mian Raza Rabbani resigned as federal minister for inter-provincial coordination to protest against the appointment of President Zardari's personal lawyer, Farooq Naik, as chairman of the Senate. Unlike

Rabbani, Naik was not even a member of the Senate. The Punjab police, also, refused to use further violence and repression against the people. All this clearly demonstrated that, in the key province of Punjab, the PPP would not be able to prevail in a showdown with the PML-N. During his visit to the United States in late February 2009, Kayani had told the Americans that the Pakistan Army would stay out of politics. However, with Pakistan headed towards another major showdown between the politicians, he decided to exercise the clout the military undoubtedly enjoyed. He reportedly advised the government not to resort to force. The military realised that the people supported the restoration of Justice Chaudhry and his colleagues. Under the circumstances, the government was forced to give in.

Consequently, just as the long march was about to begin, Prime Minister Gilani announced, 'My countrymen, in accordance with my commitment and the commitment made by the president of Pakistan, I declare reinstatement of Mr Iftikhar Muhammad Chaudhry and all other deposed judges to their positions'. At the same time, Gilani announced that the government would appeal against the debarring of the Sharif brothers by the Lahore High Court because the public sentiment against that verdict was very strong.

American Pressure Builds

Events in Pakistan were naturally causing anxiety in faraway Washington DC. The Americans had invested heavily, in terms of money and material, in Pakistan in the hope that its military could be persuaded to go after the terrorist enclaves and networks in Pakistan. Internal instability, that verged on the breakdown of law and order, was hardly the type of milieu it wanted to prevail in Pakistan. With the advent of AfPak – a description that Pakistan resented and which the Americans prudently started using less frequently without compromising its policy content – visits by senior US officials increased rapidly. It seems the Americans had decided that constant and frequent trips to Pakistan were essential to make it stay the course in the fight against Al-Qaeda and the hard-core Taliban. Consequently, a set rhetorical pattern began to take shape. While some prominent US official would express doubts about the military's determination to fight the terrorists – the Pakistani officialdom reacted angrily and rebuffed such allegations – another would say a few words praising Pakistan's contribution to the war on terror. This new pattern stabilised after General Kayani became COAS. Musharraf was associated with the Bush era while Kayani represented change – notwithstanding the continuing convoluted paternalism of the military.

In particular, Admiral Mike Mullen, the US chairman of joint chiefs of staff, paid several visits to Islamabad in 2008 and 2009. In April 2009, Richard Holbrooke, the new US special envoy to Afghanistan and Pakistan, and he first visited Afghanistan and then Pakistan. Talking informally to some prominent Pakistanis at a dinner hosted by US Ambassador Anne Patterson, they both emphasised that Pakistan lay at the core of America's strategic concerns. The Afghans had apparently told them that Afghanistan's problems lay exclusively in Pakistan and that the ISI was the villain of the piece; Holbrooke repeated these misgivings. This criticism of the ISI created a diplomatic row as the military expressed its displeasure over it. Mullen then tried to mitigate the negative fallout by describing Kayani as a straight-talking general with whom he could work with mutual trust and benefit at the tactical and strategic levels. However, Mullen and Holbrooke left no doubt in anyone's mind that the economic and military aid to Pakistan would be linked to Pakistan's concrete support in the war against Al-Qaeda, adding that America respected Pakistan's sovereignty and there was no chance of American 'boots on ground' in the Pakistani tribal areas (*Daily Times* 7 April 2009).

Hillary Clinton alleged that Pakistan had abdicated to the Taliban by agreeing to the imposition of Islamic law in a part of the country, and that nuclear-armed Pakistan poses a 'moral threat' to world security. In an interview with CNN soon after Mrs Clinton's remarks, Pakistan's ambassador to the US, Husain Haqqani, refuted the threat of Talibanisation in Pakistan. He found suggestions made by the US media, that the Taliban were steadily extending their influence and power in Pakistan and that their writ prevailed less than sixty miles from the Pakistani capital, Islamabad, gross exaggerations (*The News International* 23 April 2009).

Such denials, however, singularly belied the harsh facts on the ground in Pakistan. A YouTube clip showed Taliban brutes flogging a girl for appearing in public without a legally-correct male escort. As always, the right-wing media began to circulate stories suggesting that it was a fake. A spokesman for the Taliban also tried to rebuff the flogging allegation. Simultaneously, the Taliban continued to make almost daily announcements that they were going to enforce Sharia laws all over Pakistan; in one of their statements, they threatened the legal community with dire consequences for functioning within the non-Sharia legal system inherited from the heathen British. Interior Minister Rehman Malik tried another tactic: he sought to divert attention, from mainstream politics, to a joint Indian and Russian plot aimed at supporting the insurgency mounted by the Balochistan Liberation Army to realise its secessionist ambitions. Malik urged India to stop interfering in Balochistan, and upped the ante by describing India as 'an open enemy of Pakistan'. Such assertions were made in parliament. Some senators from Balochistan challenged his accusations, but he stood his ground (*News* 23 April 2009).

Military Decides to Launch Offensive Against the TNSM

Throughout the early months of 2009, daily stories of Taliban atrocities figured in the Pakistani print media and on television talk shows; some experts deplored the primitive methods of the jihadists. Alarm bells had begun to ring in Islamabad from early April as the TNSM destroyed government offices, civil and military personnel fled in panic, and an exodus of hundreds of thousands of ordinary people took place. On Friday 24 April 2009, General Kayani condemned the Taliban in the strongest terms. 'The army will not allow the militants to dictate terms to the government or impose their way of life on the civil society of Pakistan', (*Daily Times* 25 April 2009) he said, referring to the strict Sharia codes imposed by the Taliban in the areas of their domination. General Kayani admitted that doubts were being voiced about the intent and the capability of the army to defeat the Taliban. He went on to say that the 'Pakistan Army never has and never will hesitate to sacrifice whatever it may take, to ensure safety and well-being of the people of Pakistan and the country's territorial integrity.' He went on to say that 'The victory against terror and militancy will be achieved at all costs' (*Daily Times* 25 April 2009). The COAS condemned statements from a number of countries expressing concerns about the future of Pakistan, and said that 'a country of 170 million resilient people under a democratic dispensation and strongly supported by the army' was capable of handling any crisis that it might confront (*Daily Times* 25 April 2009).

Operation Black Thunderstorm

On 26 April 2009, Operation Black Thunderstorm was launched in several areas adjoining the Swat valley. Beginning with heavy artillery and aerial bombardment, followed by infantry incursions that cleared the way, it was followed by Sub-Operation Rah-e-Rast (the right path) that included airborne troops storming Taliban strongholds in the Swat valley. After a few weeks, the Taliban were dislodged from the urban areas. Pakistani soldiers engaged the Taliban in street fighting, and there were hundreds of casualties on both sides. On 30 May, the Pakistani military informed that, barring some pockets of resistance, it had regained control of the main city of Mingora. Prior to the fighting, Mingora had a population of 200,000 people. Most of them fled to safety outside Swat. As the fighting was extended to other parts of Swat, there was a veritable exodus of people from the valley. More than two million abandoned hearth and home.

Kayani inspected the operation area in Swat from the air. Chief Marshal Rao Qamar Suleman, who accompanied him, said the army and air force were united in ending the curse of terrorism (*Daily Times* 16 June 2009). Fighting continued during June and July. The military claimed success all along. One of the leaders of the Swat Taliban, Sufi Muhammad, was captured in June. The more fanatical Fazlullah was reportedly hit during air strikes but not captured. The military claimed to have established a complete hold over the Swat valley. By 22 August, 1.6 million of the 2.2 million returned home.

Operation Rah-e-Njiat (Path to Salvation) in South Waziristan

Success in Swat encouraged the Pakistan military to pursue the TTP in their stronghold of South Waziristan. Operation Rah-e-Njiat (Path to Salvation) started on 19 June 2009. On 5 August 2009, Baitullah Mehsud was killed by missiles fired by a US drone. It was indicative of the close cooperation between the American and Pakistani intelligence and military functionaries. An unsuccessful assassination attempt on Federal Minister for Religious Affairs Hamid Saeed Kazmi took place on 2 September. The immediate reason for the attack was that Kazmi had arranged a meeting of ulema and mashaikh (spiritual guides or Sufi masters) who had condemned terrorism and issued a fatwa against it. I met the minister at a conference in Islamabad in May

2009 when he told me that Barelvi mosques were being taken over, not only in the NWFP but also in Punjab, including Islamabad, by pro-Taliban maulvis, but the government felt helpless.

In any event, in early September, Kayani inaugurated a rehabilitation centre for men whom the Taliban had indoctrinated and trained in terrorism and suicide bombing. He emphasised that the military had broken the terrorists' backs and Operation Rah-e-Rast would continue as long as the last terrorist was not eliminated. He told a gathering of local leaders and soldiers that the terrorist network had been dismantled and peace restored to the Swat valley. He also discussed issues of rehabilitating and resettling the internally displaced population of the area. The local elders assured him of their complete support for the army (*Daily Times* 5 September 2009). On 11 September 2009, the army arrested some top leaders of the Swat Taliban. The army announced that, in all, 1800 Taliban were slain during the Swat operation alone.

Kerry–Lugar Bill

The determined and effective military operations by the Pakistan Army received immediate applause from the Americans. On 24 September 2009 the US Senate, and on 30 September the House of Representatives, approved the 'Enhanced Partnership with Pakistan Act of 2009' – popularly known as the Kerry-Lugar bill but more correctly the Kerry-Lugar-Berman bill, after its three sponsors, Senator John Kerry (Democrat) and Senator Richard Lugar (Republican) and Representative Howard Berman (Democrat). It provided economic and military aid worth more than $7.5 billion to Pakistan over a period of five years. The bill primarily sought to extract optimal output from the Pakistani civil and military elites in the fight against Al-Qaeda and the Taliban. However, it was also designed as a political engineering project that would facilitate civilian supremacy over the military in the interest of democracy. Moreover, it introduced specific rules and standards for monitoring the use of the money so that corruption and embezzlement at the Pakistani end could be kept to a minimum (The Kerry-Lugar Bill 2009).

A huge ruckus was created by the right-wing Pakistani print media, while populist intellectuals and Islamists railed against the bill and let loose conspiracy theories about a devious American plot to subvert Pakistani sovereignty. In the past, these forces had had no qualms of conscience about receiving money from the Americans to launch jihad in Afghanistan. Now, when the Obama administration was trying to change course and return to the pristine UN Charter of creating a world order anchored in collective security, Pakistan's reactionary politicians were greatly exercised by Pakistan's sovereignty allegedly being compromised. It was alleged that the Kerry–Lugar bill was a sinister plot to, step-by-step, gain economic, political, and military control over Pakistan. One of the main author's of the bill, Senator John Kerry, as well as President Obama's special adviser on Afghanistan and Pakistan, Richard Holbrooke, visited Pakistan to allay Pakistani concerns about the bill (*Daily Times,* 20 October 2009). They both asserted that the bill did not, in any way, impose preconditions on, or compromise, Pakistani sovereignty. There was, of course, a critique of the same bill from another quarter in Pakistan: the military. The Kerry–Lugar bill provided amply for it to be trained and equipped to fight terrorism, but it also included clauses requiring the dismantling of terrorist outfits such as the LeT and JeM as well as the liquidation of Al-Qaeda and Taliban.

The ISPR issued a statement that, in a meeting of the top commanders with General Kayani in the chair held at the GHQ, 'The forum expressed serious concerns regarding clauses impacting national security'. Kayani was reported as saying, 'Pakistan is a sovereign state and has all the rights to analyse and respond to the threat in accordance with her own national interests'. However, it was observed that in the military commander's considered view, 'it is parliament that represents the will of the people of Pakistan, which would deliberate on the issue, enabling the government to develop a national response'. In his concluding remarks, Kayani reiterated that Pakistan stands committed to global and regional peace and wishes to live in harmony with its neighbours (*The News International,* 8 October 2009).

The military's response was partly a reflection of its anxiety about a new balance of power coming about in Pakistan, in which civilian institutions may gain greater clout and prestige at its expense – it was probably a manifestation of Ayesha Siddiqa's thesis of an institutional interest, in the broader sense, explaining the response of the military. The catch was, of course, that Pakistan could reject the Kerry–Lugar bill. However, given the endemic economic and military dependence that the military had cultivated over the years – a relationship that helped maintain its own vantage position in the Pakistani power equation – there was little chance that the establishment would reject the bill. President Obama signed the bill on 15 October 2009, and it became the basis for future US–Pakistan cooperation in the fight against terrorism.

Attack on GHQ

The Taliban upped the ante when, on Saturday 10 October 2009, Taliban militants donning military attire drove into the compound of the Pakistan Army's General Headquarters in Rawalpindi. When the security guards challenged them, they began to shoot and throw grenades at them. The security personnel returned fire and, in the shootout that ensued, six security guards and four terrorists lost their lives. Some of the Taliban, however, managed to enter the GHQ premises and took dozens of people hostage. Sporadic shooting continued through the night. By early morning, Pakistani commandos from the elite SSG had succeeded in freeing most of the hostages; four more terrorists were killed and one, believed to be their ringleader – Aqeel, also known as Dr Usman – was captured. Among the Pakistan Army personnel who lost their lives were a brigadier and a lieutenant-colonel. Eight security personnel, nine terrorists, and three civilians – altogether, twenty people – were killed. Media reports suggest that the conspiracy to attack the GHQ may even have links to Punjab where, in the southern-most districts, fanatical Islamists have been growing by the day. A new outfit, The Punjabi Taliban, began to circulate in the media and on the internet.

It was, undoubtedly, the most audacious and daring assault by the Taliban–Al-Qaeda nexus. Questions were asked about any intelligence lapse that may have occurred, because the security arrangements around GHQ are most stringent and impregnable. It is difficult to believe that complete outsiders plotted the attack; help and assistance from rogue elements, either serving or retired or a combination of both, must have played some role in it.

The assault on the GHQ was preceded by two other vicious attacks in the same week. On Monday 5 October, a suicide bomber dressed in the Frontier Constabulary uniform succeeded in entering the premises of the UN Food Programme Office and blew himself up. Five people were killed, including a UN diplomat and three female employees. The culprit was able to deceive more than twenty security guards who were on duty at that time. Then, on Friday 9 October, another suicide bomber blew himself up in Soekarno Square, a very busy and central part of the capital of the North-West Frontier Province, Peshawar. Many school children, who were on a passing bus, were among them; more than fifty fatalities and one hundred injuries occurred.

Hillary Clinton visits Pakistan

US pressure on Pakistan continued to mount but with the usual mixture of carrot and stick. Hillary Clinton visited Pakistan from 28–30 October. Her visit took place at a critical juncture: the Taliban–Al-Qaeda forces had sharply accelerated their terrorist campaign against Pakistan; serious doubts had been expressed, within Pakistani political circles and sections of the power elite, about US commitment to Pakistan's security and sovereignty; simultaneously, the Americans continued to be sceptical about Pakistan's approach to the Taliban–Al-Qaeda nexus.

During Clinton's visit, the Pakistani media highlighted the alleged presence and activities of a large number of Blackwater security personnel in Pakistan. The security firm had gained considerable notoriety for its criminal behaviour in occupied Iraq – which had resulted in several deaths and incidents of torture and humiliation of Iraqi detainees. The Pakistani media alleged that Blackwater operatives were an extension of the CIA and were involved in activities aimed at getting hold of Pakistan's nuclear assets, as well as an even more nefarious conspiracy to subvert Pakistani sovereignty. The Pakistani Washington DC-based Pakistani analyst, Shuja Nawaz, deplored that the Americans were not providing the required weaponry to Pakistan to fight the Taliban in rugged and difficult territories such as Waziristan (Nawaz 2009). Moreover, according to other Pakistan sources, when the military launched Operation Rah-e-Nijat and entered South Waziristan, instead of sealing all entry and exit routes into Waziristan the Americans did just the opposite: they removed scores of security checkpoints on the Afghanistan side of the Pak–Afghan border (*Daily Times*, 20 October 2009).

Such a decision allegedly helped the Taliban infiltrate from Afghanistan into South Waziristan, as well as escape from there into Afghanistan. General Kayani took up this issue with the top US commander in Afghanistan, General McChrystal, and urged him to seal the border. On the other hand, the Americans expressed concern and criticism about Pakistani actions. They alleged that Pakistan was restricting its military operation to South Waziristan, where the Pakistani Taliban (TTP) who had been attacking Pakistani targets were entrenched, but showed no inclination in going after the Taliban in northern Waziristan or in the capital of Baluchistan, Quetta, where the pro-Pakistan, Afghan Taliban and Al-Qaeda leadership were hiding, according to the US. US analysts floated the idea that Pakistan distinguished between good Taliban (Afghan Taliban) and bad Taliban (TTP and its Pakistani affiliates). Pakistan vehemently rejected such accusations. Just before she left Washington DC, a correspondent for Pakistan's leading newspaper, *Dawn*, interviewed Clinton. When asked to comment whether the United States' demand was fair, that a Pakistani military unit using a certain weapon on the Afghan border should leave that weapon behind when it's transferred to another location, she responded by saying that 'A lot of military equipment is 'fungible' and mobile and can be used in different places' (*Dawn*, 28 October 2009). The Pakistani media interpreted this as a move to accommodate Indian concerns about Pakistan acquiring modern weapons.

Consequently, when Clinton addressed Pakistani newspaper editors in Lahore on 29 October and asserted that the Al-Qaeda leadership was hiding in Pakistan, many Pakistanis were greatly disturbed, but she insisted that her accusations were based on information she had at her disposal. She remarked, 'I find it hard to believe that nobody in your government knows where they are and couldn't get them if they really wanted to. Maybe that's the case; maybe they're not gettable. I don't know.... As far as we know, they are in Pakistan' (*Daily Times*, 30 October 2009). In terms of diplomatic praxis, it was perhaps too blunt an accusation to be made publicly by a visiting high-ranking diplomat of a country allied to a host country in an ongoing major violent conflict, but Clinton only expressed an opinion that had, for quite some time, been aired by US think-tanks and State Department functionaries. I had been told this repeatedly by several US analysts when I visited Washington DC in July 2009.

In any event, the overall thrust of Clinton's interactions with the public, as well as the government and military, was that fighting terrorism and defeating the Taliban–Al-Qaeda duo was in the best interests of Pakistan; that the United States would fight terrorism side by side with Pakistan; and, therefore, there was no reasonable ground to suspect bad faith from her country. She, particularly, committed US help and assistance in bolstering

Pakistan's counter-insurgency capabilities, and went on to propose a set of practical measures to improve Pakistan's fiscal and economic performance, urging Pakistan to expand its tax base and to modernise its taxation system. She also announced funding for several educational and developmental projects, including help in solving Pakistan's serious problem of a shortage of energy.

She also urged a resumption of the India–Pakistan dialogue which had remained more or less suspended after the Mumbai terrorist attacks of November 2008. India had become a strategic partner of the United States and, following the nuclear deal that was agreed between them in 2009; it enjoyed a special relationship with the latter. The Obama presidency was viewed with some anxiety in India, but both Obama and Hillary Clinton assured the Indians that the US would not interfere in the relationship between the two South Asian rivals and both must resolve their disputes through bilateral negotiations.

In any case, the American Congress passed a special bill that required 'efforts to track where US military hardware sent to Pakistan ends up, as well as a warning that the aid must not upset "the balance of power in the region" – a reference to tensions between Pakistan and India' (*Daily Times,* 24 October 2009). President Obama put his signature to the bill and it became law. On the whole, the chasm between US and Pakistani perceptions about each other's intentions and objectives laid bare the fact that the actors formally allied to each other, and involved in fighting terrorism, did not share deep mutual trust and confidence.

Pakistan's Nuclear Assets

A raid on the so-called state-within-a-state – the supposedly ubiquitous office of the ISI – in Peshawar on Friday 13 November 2009 left at least twenty people dead, including ten ISI officials. It was yet more proof that the establishment's vain efforts to establish a 'fortress of Islam', through a proliferation of fanatical jihadists, were egregiously flawed. The Taliban–Al-Qaeda nexus, once again, demonstrated its capability of hitting the supposedly most well-guarded targets representing the power and authority of the state. On the other hand, the media reported that some terrorists had tried to enter the restricted area where the nuclear facilities were located but were unable to infiltrate it, having been stopped at the outer security ring. The

American journalist Seymour Hersh suggested that the United States was seeking a greater role in the protection of Pakistan's nuclear weapons from terrorists. He referred to President Barack Obama's positive response to a question, by a journalist, about the safety of those weapons.

Hersh considered a number of scenarios that could plunge regional and world peace into jeopardy. The most serious was the possibility of a mutiny within the military stationed at Pakistan's nuclear weapon sites. This was based on the assumption that support for radical Islam, and sympathy for the Taliban–Al-Qaeda ideology, could exist among the soldiers and officers stationed in locations where the weapons were kept. Hersh has stated that when he probed that possibility with military officers he talked to, they rejected such a turn of events and told him that the personnel working at such locations were thoroughly scrutinised; those whose ideological orientation or mindset was suspect were screened out. Moreover, he was told that the nuclear devices were kept in deep tunnels that could not be detected by spy satellites. Even more importantly, the procedure adopted to make the nuclear weapons operational was exceedingly complex. The different elements and parts of a nuclear bomb were kept separate from one another. In order to use them, they needed to be assembled at one place. The procedure had been streamlined and, in case of war or some threat to national security, a select group of military personnel could quickly make them operational (*The New Yorker*, 10 November 2009).

The chairman joint chiefs of staff committee, Lieutenant General Tariq Majid, dismissed Hersh's worst-case scenario of a mutiny by the army stationed at the nuclear weapon sites as sensational and mischievous. Instead, he emphasised that a strict security regime had complete control over the weapons. He remarked:

> We have operationalised a very effective nuclear security regime, which incorporates very stringent custodial and access controls. As overall custodian of the development of strategic programme, I reiterate in very unambiguous terms that there is absolutely no question of sharing or allowing any foreign individual, entity or a state, any access to sensitive information about our nuclear assets (*The News International*, 10 November 2009).

Arrest of Headley and Rana

Media attention was once again drawn to the Mumbai terrorist attacks of November 2008 when two US citizens of Pakistani origin, David Coleman Headley (Daood Gilani) and Tahawwur Hussain Rana, were arrested in the US for complicity in the Mumbai attacks. In Pakistan, the authorities arrested a retired major for allegedly having had links with both Headley and Rana (*Daily Times*, 26 November 2009). Such happenings corrected the impression that the LeT was a purely Pakistani–Punjabi territorial entity, and thus its linkages with regional and global networks were brought into sharp relief.

Later, some newspapers reported that Headley was actually a CIA plant who had been recruited to infiltrate the LeT. However, he had double-crossed the CIA and transferred his loyalties to the LeT. The CIA was aware of his trips to India, and that he had played a pivotal role in the realization of the attacks in Mumbai, but had kept quiet. The Indian authorities demanded an opportunity to interrogate him, but the media reported that the Americans were reluctant to cooperate.

Retired Senior Indian and Pakistani Officials, Reflections on the Pakistan–India Relationship

During my three-year stint (2007–2010) at the Institute of South Asian Studies (ISAS), Singapore, I met a number of Indian and Pakistani researchers and senior officials. Extended discussions with them about current and future India–Pakistan relations provided me with many useful insights. Two specimens are presented below:

Rajiv Sikri, who retired as secretary of India's ministry of external affairs, spoke to me on 25 May 2009 about his book, *Challenge and Strategy: Rethinking India's Foreign Policy* (2009), in Singapore when we were both at the ISAS. My impression was that he was cautiously optimistic about the rigid zero-sum culture that pervaded Pakistan–India interaction, provided both sides made a sincere effort. He was, however, of the opinion that as long as the military called the shots in Pakistan, and did not curb terrorism against India, it would be difficult to change course. I told him that the Pakistan military was the most important and powerful institution in Pakistan. Therefore, any future settlement with Pakistan would require it to be on board, and that that was not impossible. He agreed.

In his book, he has expressed the view that India, in the twenty-first century, should strive to become a major power. It should try to work for a greater understanding between South Asian nations, and seek to revitalize SAARC as the framework for greater cooperation among the peoples and nations of the region on the basis of a common history and shared culture that permeates all religious communities. He urged India to work hard to convince its smaller neighbours that it is not a big brother or bully, and to support democracy and democratic movements in the region. He described Pakistan as India's 'most difficult neighbour', and that bad relations became worse after the Mumbai terrorist attacks. However, he took cognition of Pakistan adopting a flexible position on Kashmir and noted that, as far as the people of the two nations were concerned, whenever they have met during cricket matches, their warmth towards each other has been an embarrassment for the hawks.

The author observed that because the jihadists had even started targeting personnel of the Pakistan armed forces, both countries had an interest in weakening them. He also urged that India should encourage greater trade between the two nations – as a means of developing mutually beneficial interests. He also emphasized the need for India to establish a good rapport with the elected government of Zardari and Gilani. At the same time, he noted that it would be impossible for India to agree to a change to its borders (Sikri 2009: 16–45). But, he hoped that, one day, there would be South Asian regional integration within an EU-type framework, and asserted, 'It may come about when the younger generation of South Asians, which does not carry bitter memories of old feuds and antagonisms, begins to wield political power' (ibid., 37). He considered the 1960 Indus Waters Treaty unfavourable to India, and urged the need to renegotiate it. He stressed that while India, as the upper riparian, enjoyed an advantage over Pakistan which, if needed, it could exploit, a mutually agreed negotiated settlement of the water question with regard to Kashmir would be preferential (ibid., 47–52). On Afghanistan, he remarked: 'Improbable as it may sound, India will have to work with Pakistan in Afghanistan if there is to be any hope for lasting peace and stability there' (ibid., 289).

My experience of talking to senior Indian military officers and diplomats has been that they, by and large, share the point of view that Sikri expressed to me and elaborated in his book. They concede that, in the long run, cooperation and non-confrontation were in the best interests of both countries and their peoples.

Former Pakistan Finance Minister's Reflections on the Pakistan–India Relationship

I used the opportunity also to probe the views of another colleague, a fellow Pakistani, Shahid Javed Burki, former World Bank vice-president for Latin America and briefly Pakistan's finance minister during the interim government of Moin Qureshi. Burki, while presenting Pakistan's experience of dealing with India, asserted that the erstwhile Indian leadership was not reconciled to the creation of Pakistan. It hoped that Pakistan would fail to take-off as a viable state and would, therefore, return to the Indian fold.

Burki, subsequently, presented his thoughts in a book in which he assessed the past relationship as well as made recommendations for the future to rectify the relationship. In it, he has written that three major problems cropped up in the immediate period after Pakistan came into being. First, was that the Indian government was not willing to pay Pakistan its share of the money that the British had left behind as common assets. Financial wherewithal was needed to buy even the most rudimentary equipment to run the state as everything had to be started from scratch. Prime Minister Liaquat Ali Khan and Finance Minister Ghulam Mohammad Khan had to go to Delhi personally to plead their case before the money was released (Burki 2011: 70). As already pointed out, the Indian government had withheld Pakistan's share on the grounds that it would be spent to buy arms to conduct hostilities in Kashmir. It was only Gandhi's fast-unto-death that made the Indian government relent.

The second problem, according to Burki, was over the distribution of the waters of the rivers that flowed in the territories of both India and Pakistan. A standstill agreement was reached in 1948 to maintain the status quo. However, during 1949 and 1950, Pakistan felt that India was violating the agreement. For a very short while, the Indian government stopped the flow of water to Lahore and its adjoining areas. The famous waving of his fist by Liaquat Ali Khan – threatening war with India – was a reaction to the perceived breach of the standstill agreement. The third crisis in India-Pakistan relations occurred in 1949 when Pakistan refused to devalue its currency although all the other members of the British Commonwealth did so in relation to the US dollar. This decision changed the rate of exchange, between the Indian and Pakistan rupee, to the disadvantage of India. The Indian deputy prime minister, Sardar Patel, reacted angrily and imposed a trade blockade on Pakistan. Burki asserted that while such measures created a deep sense of insecurity in Pakistan, they also helped it to develop its economy independent of India's – giving priority to industrialisation. He has noted that, before the trade war, more than half of Pakistan's exports went to India, and India was the source of about the same proportion of imports; afterwards, both exports to, and imports from, India were reduced to a mere trickle' (Burki 2011: 70–72).

The main thrust of his book is that the burden of history must be set aside and forward-looking pragmatism be adopted by both countries. Basing his argument on strong economic rationale, he has asserted that Pakistan and India stand to gain a great deal through co-operation, especially mutually-beneficial trade (ibid., 145–61).

These two standpoints are useful illustrations of the alternative ways of thinking that are prevalent on both sides. The notorious zero-sum postures that often prevail are not without their critics and sceptics among the influential individuals who have had a close association with policy-making in their respective societies. An argument to convert South Asia into a region of peace and prosperity through the SAARC project has been advanced by a host of researchers at ISAS (Muni 2010).

16

The United States Prepares for Exit

President Obama had begun to consider a withdrawal from Afghanistan after it became clear that the war was unwinnable and most of his European allies were not keen to prolong their participation in the war. Indeed, public opinion in the NATO countries was largely apathetic to the war – even in the United States support for it had been declining as more and more people began to doubt that the Taliban could be defeated militarily. When President Obama met his NATO allies in Portugal in November 2009, it was agreed that they would withdraw their troops from Afghanistan by the end of 2014. By that time, the training of an effective Afghan military would be completed.

The top US commander in Afghanistan, General Stanley McChrystal, had been requesting a surge in US troops – up to 50,000 – for months, but Obama was prevaricating. Finally, on 30 November while addressing cadets at the West Point Military Academy, he announced a surge of 30,000 troops to Afghanistan. However, the surge was to be accompanied by plans to begin the withdrawal of the reinforcements in eighteen months. The Republicans welcomed the surge, but expressed doubts about the announcement of a firm date for the withdrawal as they believed that it would embolden the Taliban and Al-Qaeda.

US Complaints and Misgivings Persist

On 15 December, Admiral Mullen reiterated concerns about the Taliban and Al-Qaeda terrorist groups taking refuge across the border in Pakistan. While visiting Kabul, to discuss the upcoming build-up and training of Afghanistan's security forces, he told reporters that he would discuss the issue with Pakistani authorities during their talks in Islamabad later. Meanwhile, the *Los Angeles Times* claimed that senior US officials, including some military leaders, were pushing to expand drone strikes into Quetta in an attempt to pressure the Pakistan government into pursuing the Taliban in Balochistan's provincial capital. 'Proponents...argue that attacking the Taliban in Quetta – or at least threatening to do so – is critical to the success of the revised war strategy' (*Los Angeles Times*, 16 November 2009). Increasing American involvement in Pakistan's politics followed, with Clinton calling for a resumption in Indo–Pak talks on Kashmir, warning that the terrorists would try to provoke a conflict between the two countries if that issue was not resolved.

General David Petraeus chipped in by praising Pakistan's gains in Waziristan and asserting that he did not believe that the Pakistan Army had any desire to endanger civilian rule. Dilating upon the new US policy on Afghanistan, he stated that President Obama would increase US troops by 30,000 and that all the stakeholders would be engaged ahead of the start of the troop withdrawals in July 2011 – a process that would be completed by the end of 2014. Such a statement generated considerable anxiety in some quarters. India expressed concern; voices of concern were raised in Afghanistan and Pakistan too. During that time, Afghans were to be trained to take charge. Meanwhile, rumours that drone attacks could be extended to Balochistan were refuted by Petraeus, who quoted a statement by Defence Secretary Robert Gates denying such a plan. Some further clues, to future US policy in Afghanistan, were provided by him when he said that the US would work with those Taliban who renounced violence but that, thus far, only low and middle level Taliban leaders had responded positively to the US policy of establishing dialogue with them.

Terrorism within Pakistan

In December, controversy about whether foreign powers were orchestrating terrorism in Pakistan surfaced again in the Pakistani media. Interior Minister Rehman Malik ruled out the presence of any US-sponsored terrorists in Pakistan. 'There is no presence of Blackwater in Pakistan. Unfortunately, all the terrorists in the country are Pakistani nationals.' He further stated that seventy-four terrorists had been apprehended (*Daily Times*, 11 December 2009). Malik had been insisting, for several months, that he had conclusive and incontrovertible proof of Indian involvement in terrorism, as well as in secessionism in Balochistan. He challenged India's defence minister, A.K. Antony, to come to Pakistan to see the evidence for himself. Antony ignored the invitation and rejected his accusations. Apparently, the proof of Indian involvement was sent to the foreign ministry by the interior ministry. However, Foreign Minister Qureshi expressed his doubts about the material he had received. The proof probably comprised disturbing snapshots of naked, dead, uncircumcised men.

In any case, a horrendous assault in Karachi on 28 December 2009 – the main Shia day of mourning: the 10th of Muharram – claimed at least 43 lives and inflicted injuries on hundreds of others. It was accompanied by more than 2000 shops and businesses being vandalized or set ablaze. The damage was estimated to be to the tune of ₹30–50 billion. The authorities claimed that the rioting was not a spontaneous expression of anger by a crowd gone berserk, but well-planned and organised. During 2009, the highest number of fatalities, as a result of terrorism, took place in Pakistan. The announcement of a definite date, for the beginning of the withdrawal of US and NATO troops, was received, understandably, with mixed reactions from the different stakeholders. The Taliban and its affiliates and sympathisers celebrated it as further proof of the decline of US power and global hegemony, and its inevitable defeat in Afghanistan and Pakistan. Pakistan officially expressed concern over a US exit without a viable peace deal having been put into place that would keep arch-rival India at bay in Afghanistan. The Pakistan military expected recognition of its competence and capacity, as an effective fighting force, because it had dealt severe blows to the Taliban in Swat and South Waziristan. In political terms, this meant that Pakistan had to be recognised as the paramount power in southwest Asia. The Indian reaction was one of alarm. It perceived the withdrawal of western troops, without the Taliban having been defeated, as an invitation for trouble as it could embolden the Taliban to embark on another jihad campaign, especially in Kashmir. Iran offered its good offices to help the political process. It had been providing monetary aid to the Afghan government, and had also taken care of refugees during the Soviet occupation. It also exercised some influence through the Shia Hazaras (Ahmed 2010).

For quite some time, the key player – the Karzai government – had been discussing, with the British, the possibility of a deal with the Taliban. An idea was put forth that if the Taliban accepted the Afghan constitution, which in principle stood for democracy and gender equality of sorts, they could be accommodated into the state structure including the government. Some analysts began arguing that the Taliban were a regional entity, uneducated, crude, and limited to their immediate surroundings in their ambitions. Moreover, it was asserted that the Taliban comprised a plethora of groups on both sides of the border. There were those who had a good standing with the Pakistani establishment – who considered them to be a strategic asset in terms of the power game in Afghanistan; however, the Taliban led by the TTP were loathed by the Pakistani establishment. Then, there were those who were linked to Russia and Iran (in spite of rabid aversion to Shiaism). Taliban groups were also involved in drug trafficking in a massive way – with some collaboration from even American and other Western elements. Then, there was the Punjabi Taliban which included Punjabis who had relocated themselves in the tribal belt; it also enjoyed a stronghold in southern Pakistan (Amin, Osinski, and DeGeorges 2010).

From the American point of view, Al-Qaeda and those groups among the Taliban and their other affiliates that constituted nexuses directed against US interests had to be dealt with effectively. The problem, of course, was that Al-Qaeda was no longer simply a physical entity consisting of Arab, and other veterans of the Afghan jihad hiding in Afghanistan and Pakistan. After Bush had extended the war on terror to an invasion of Iraq, the radicalisation of Muslims proliferated dramatically and Al-Qaeda-inspired groups had come into being all over the world. Nevertheless, the pursuit and destruction of the erstwhile Al-Qaeda leadership – especially the iconic Osama bin Laden who symbolised international terrorism – was imperative. Such an objective had to be achieved to assuage the American public and remind the world at large that those who threaten US security would not receive any quarter anywhere in the world. The Americans were acutely aware of the fact that the hunt for the Al-Qaeda leaders required Pakistani cooperation. On the other hand, their military and intelligence experts were convinced that Al-Qaeda and Taliban leaders, involved in aiding and abetting terrorism against US and NATO forces, were hiding in FATA, especially in North Waziristan, and in Quetta, the capital of Balochistan in southern Pakistan. Furthermore, the Americans suspected that Al-Qaeda, and top Afghan Taliban, leaders enjoyed the protection of powerful elements in the Pakistani establishment –

necessitating a multifaceted strategy including covert activities. That strategy was encapsulated in the Kerry–Lugar bill which committed the United States to a generous five-year commitment, including a range of developmental inputs, but stipulated that Pakistan had to go after the strongholds of the fugitive leaders in North Waziristan and the local networks that supported them, especially the Haqqani group. On the other hand, during Clinton's visit in October 2009, the Pakistan media had published reports of the presence of hundreds of undercover Americans – particularly the Blackwater security firm – in Pakistan.

McChrystal visited Pakistan in early January 2010. Talking to journalists at the US embassy, he stated that a trust deficit was the main issue between the United States and Pakistan, as well as between Pakistan and Afghanistan. He said, 'The best we can do is build trust' to achieve the desired results in the war against terror. As usual, he had some words of appreciation for the Pakistan Army's recent operations against the Pakistan Taliban, but he also demanded more action against the Haqqani group in North Waziristan (*Daily Times*, 5 January 2010).

International Conference at Lancaster House

It was against the backdrop of such concerns and objectives that were emerging in US strategic thinking that the UK prime minister, Gordon Brown, invited a host of countries to a conference at Lancaster House, London. Some key players, such as China, Turkey, Iran, and Russia, had met in Istanbul, preparatory to the conference, to discuss the conference's concept and to promote consensus on it. On 28–29 January, some 70 countries as well as the United Nations backed a US$500 million drive by the Afghan government to tempt fighters to give up their weapons in exchange for jobs and other incentives. A conspicuous feature of the conference was that Pakistan's position, as the key player in any peace deal in Afghanistan, was affirmed. On the other hand, India was not invited to the Istanbul contact group meeting (Ahmed 2010). At the conference, it became clear that US and NATO troops would begin a drawback beginning July 2011, which would be completed by the end of 2014. Fairly large numbers of Afghan military and security forces were to be trained to take over the main responsibility of maintaining the peace. The conference was a setback to India, which had been insisting that the Taliban, as a whole, had to be defeated because they were committed to an ideology that was rabidly militaristic and expansionist, and any concession to them would gravely threaten India's security.

The Lancaster House conference met with early disappointment: an invitation from President Karzai, to Taliban leaders to attend the traditional consultative assembly – the Loya Jirga, was not responded to by them. On the other hand, Kayani made some interesting observations. He said, 'Pakistan doesn't want a "talibanised" Afghanistan'. Elaborating on the point, he said that Pakistan did not want for Afghanistan what it did not want for itself. Further, that his country had no intention of controlling Afghanistan. He offered Pakistan's assistance and help in training the Afghanistan military. He also made the important point that Pakistan's geostrategic location continues to be relevant in the post-Cold War and post–9/11 periods, and urged NATO to fully appreciate that objective reality (*Daily Times,* 2 February 2010). A few days earlier, the Pakistan Army spokesperson, Major General Athar Abbas, announced that there would be no major offensive for the next 6–12 months. The Pakistan military could bask in the glory that an elected government remained in power and that the military had helped the political process take its natural course in Pakistan (*Dawn,* 22 January 2010).

Indian Two-Front Doctrine and US Advice on Cooperation in South Asia

Meanwhile, during a closed-door seminar in Simla, the Indian Army Chief, General Deepak Kapoor, remarked that the Indian Army was preparing to take Pakistan and China on simultaneously in case of a future war. He said that the Indian forces would 'have to substantially enhance their strategic reach and out-of-area capabilities to protect India's geopolitical interests stretching from the [Persian] Gulf to Malacca Strait' and 'to protect our island territories' and assist 'the littoral states in the Indian Ocean Region' (Blumenthal 1 December 2011).

Earlier, on 3 January 2010, Indian External Affairs Minister S.M. Krishna, in an interview, emphasised that China's continued supply of weapons to Pakistan, as well as the activities of Chinese companies in Azad Kashmir, were a matter of concern and that India was talking to China about all these issues. Explaining why India saw the activities in Azad Kashmir as 'illegal',

Krishna said, 'Jammu and Kashmir is an integral part of the country; neither Pakistan nor China has a locus standi there (*The Indian Express*, 2 January 2010).' The reaction from Pakistan, to Kapoor's doctrine, was one of ridicule. The chairman of the joint chief of staff committee, General Tariq Majid, expressed doubts whether General Kapoor had devised any such doctrine – but that, if he had, then, 'Leave alone China, General Deepak Kapoor knows very well what the Indian armed forces cannot and Pakistan armed forces can pull of militarily' (*The Times of India* 2 January 2010).

Amid such jingoistic rhetoric from both sides, Defence Secretary Robert Gates visited South Asia. While in Delhi, he warned that Al-Qaeda's 'syndicate' – which includes the TTP and the Taliban in Afghanistan, as well as Lashkar-e-Tayyaba – posed a danger to the region as a whole. It was trying 'to destabilise not just Afghanistan, not just Pakistan, but potentially the whole region by provoking a conflict perhaps between India and Pakistan through some provocative act', Gates said. Further, it would be 'very dangerous' to single out any one group of the syndicate as a target as all of them needed to be combated together. He added that it was important for all the countries concerned to 'remain engaged and eliminate the terror groups'. Suggesting transparent Indian and Pakistani operations in Afghanistan, the US defence secretary denied the idea that India would be given any military role in such operations. He said that India's support in the development of Kabul, to the tune of $1.3 billion, was ideal and significant. Then he remarked:

> Let us be honest with one another, there is real suspicion in Pakistan to what India is doing in Afghanistan. And so I think focusing on development, humanitarian assistance, probably in some limited areas of training but with full transparency towards each other is what will help allay these suspicions and create opportunities of greater help for the Afghan government,' he added (*Daily Times* 21 January 2010).

General Kayani on Pakistan's Sacrifices in the War on Terror

In late January, Kayani visited NATO headquarters in Brussels where he explained Pakistan's role in the war on terror and its defence priorities. Upon his return, he briefed senior Pakistani journalists, and told them that Pakistan could not close its eyes to the Indian 'Cold Start Strategy' – as aired by his Indian counterpart. Responding to US accusations that Pakistan was playing a double game, he asserted that the Pakistani nation had offered unprecedented sacrifices in terms of lives and property. Whereas the NATO and allied forces' casualties in the war on terror stood at 1582 – over the eight years – 2273 officers and jawans (soldiers) of the Pakistan Army had been martyred; 6512 had sustained injuries during one year alone. Seventy-three Pakistani intelligence officers were martyred, compared with eleven intelligence officers of the allied forces, in Afghanistan. He said, 'Our martyrs include one three-star general, one two-star general and five brigadiers'. He went on to say, 'We have made it clear to US that it will have to keep in view interests of Pakistan before taking any decision with reference to Afghanistan'. He added that, given the bad track record because of India–Pakistan relations, vigilance and preparation to face Indian threats could not be slackened, describing India's military and war preparations as Pakistan-specific (*Nation* 4 February 2010).

Earlier, in the wake of Gates' visit, India had offered to resume talks with Pakistan. Immediately, the leader of the Hizbul Mujahideen and chairman of the sixteen-party Jihad Council, Syed Salahuddin, remarked in Muzaffarabad, 'The Kashmir issue cannot be resolved through dialogue. Jihad (holy war) is the only way to free Kashmir from Indian rule.... I want to tell my brothers across the border that we will remain with you until India quits Kashmir.' A statement issued after the meeting declared, 'Jihad will continue until India ends its occupation of Kashmir. If Pakistan cannot offer material support, it should extend its political and moral support to the Kashmir movement' (*The Daily Times,* 5 February 2010).

US Military Personnel Killed in Pakistan, Prominent Taliban Leaders Captured

On 10 February, *The Daily Times* reported that three US soldiers and four female students were among nine killed when a blast targeted a military-led convoy in Lower Dir, near Swat. The US soldiers were travelling in a convoy with local troops, journalists, and officials to the opening of a girls' school. At least 115 people – including 95 schoolgirls – were injured in the attack. According to a statement by the US embassy in Islamabad, the US troops killed in the attack were training Frontier Constabulary soldiers on a request by the Pakistani government. The police gave a figure of nine fatalities – including four schoolgirls and 'three foreigners'.

Some excitement was caused when the Taliban military commander and, a close ally of Mullah Omar, Mullah Abdul Ghani Baradar, was captured from Karachi. The *BBC* reported that it was the result of a joint US-Pakistan operation (*BBC*,17 February 2010). Some other senior Taliban were arrested in NWFP. Later, the Pakistan media reported the arrest, from Karachi, of two more aides of Mullah Omar's and of the slain TTP leader Baitullah Mehsud (*The Daily Times,* 1 March 2010).

Shuja Nawaz's Testimony on Islamic Militancy

Shuja Nawaz, director of the South Asia Center at the Atlantic Council, Washington DC, testified before the House Foreign Relations Committee subcommittee on the Middle East and South Asia on 11 March 2011. He provided information and analysis on the growing militancy in Pakistan. He acknowledged that the LeT, set up to assist the Kashmir freedom movement, had permutated into 'a powerful Sunni Punjabi movement with an agenda that appears to have taken on a broader regional role'. He went on to say:

> Successive civil and military leaders of Pakistan supported the movement as a strategic asset to counter a powerful India to the East and to force it to negotiate for a settlement of the disputed territory by waging a war of 'a thousand cuts'.
>
> Over time, however, the sponsored organization took on a life of its own, finding the socially disadvantaged area of Central and Southern Punjab to be a fertile territory for recruitment of Jihadi warriors.... LeT spread its wings nationwide, using its contacts to raise funds from the public and gradually attained autarkic status. Collection boxes for the Kashmiri jihad in shops, at mosques, and around the festivals of Eid al Fitr and Eid al Adha gave it a steady source of income. It spun off a social welfare organization, the Jamaat ud Dawa, that served to proselytize on behalf of the LeT while providing much needed social services. In doing this, the LeT was playing to the weakness of the corrupt political system of Pakistan that failed to recognize and meet the basic needs of its population at large while catering to the elites....

The Inter-Services Intelligence started becoming less controlling as the LeT became more self-sufficient. But the realization that the LeT had become autonomous was slow in being understood or accepted in the ISI and in the military leadership of Pakistan under General Pervez Musharraf. His ambivalence about the LeT even in 2002 was evident in his confusion during an interview with Australian Broadcasting Corporation when he challenged the interviewer who stated that the LeT had been banned. Musharraf thought only the Jaish-e-Mohammed had been banned, referring to another surrogate of the ISI in Kashmir. Today, LeT is banned. But the Jamaat ud Dawa remains a functioning entity.

General Musharraf made an effort to lower the political temperature in Kashmir and began distancing the state from the LeT. However, the process was not handled as well as it could have been…the LeT was cut loose without a comprehensive plan to disarm, re-train, and gainfully employ the fighters. A dangerous corollary was the induction into the militancy of some former members of the military who had trained and guided them in their war in Kashmir…

Enough evidence exists now to link the Sipah-e-Sahaba and Jaish-e-Mohammed with Al-Qaeda and the Taliban. The LeT's emerging role as a trans regional force that has broadened its aim to include India and perhaps even Afghanistan, by linking with the Students Islamic Movement of India or SIMI and the Harkat ul Jihad al Islami or HUJI of Bangladesh. It poses a serious threat to regional stability. Another Mumbai-type attack might bring India and Pakistan close to a conflict, a prospect that should keep us awake at night. In Pakistan, both the civil and the military now appear to recognize the existential threat from home grown militancy. The army appears to have dislocated the Tehreek-e-Taliban of Pakistan. Yet, it faces a huge threat in the hinterland, in the form of the LeT.

My own research into the recruitment of the Pakistan army over 1970 to 2005 indicates that the army is now recruiting heavily in the same area. Unless we change the underlying social and economic conditions, the Islamist militancy that appears to be taking root there will start seeping into the military' (Nawaz Congressional testimony, 11 March 2010).

Such a frank appraisal of the Pakistan situation obviously also reflected the thinking and information that was prevalent among the Washington-based security analysts. Earlier, when I visited Washington DC in July 2009, I spoke to Shuja Nawaz at length and sought several clarifications about his book, *Crossed Swords*. I also interviewed Syed Mowahid Hussain Shah, a former member of the Punjab cabinet, about the troubled Pakistan-US relations. He told me that he was present at the White House, at President Obama AfPak policy briefing. He was of the view that the Americans were determined to go after Al-Qaeda and would focus on such an objective. The executive director of the Pakistani American Leadership Center, Taha Gaya, and Amjad and Noreen Babar also shared their views with me on the US–Pakistan relationship. They were of the opinion that both sides needed to build their relations on honesty and not on a purely instrumentalist basis.

I also spoke to a cross-section of the American security community; Walter Andersen; Christine Fair; Ambassador Wendy Chamberlin; Director South Asia at the Woodrow Wilson Center Robert Hathaway; Professor Selig Harrison; Dr Teresita Schaffer. They all lay considerable stress on the trust deficit that was prevalent in the Pakistan–US alliance against terrorism. On the other hand, Ambassador Richard Boucher and Ambassador Robin Raphael, while recognizing the problem of mutual mistrust, expressed a greater understanding of the difficulties surrounding Pakistan and recognized that it had rendered important service in the struggle against terrorism. In a meeting with Akbar S. Ahmed, I was able to get useful insights into the post-9/11 situation of Muslims in the United States.

Pakistan Submits Wish List to the United States

Nevertheless, the month of March saw several high-powered Pakistani officials, including Foreign Minister Shah Mahmood Qureshi and General Kayani, visiting the United States with the aim of soliciting more economic and military aid. The fifty-six-page document, submitted to the Americans, included requests for pilotless drones and helicopters as well as economic and other aid. Pakistan also wanted a civilian nuclear arrangement with Washington DC, similar to that agreed between the United States and India. Pakistani officials also expressed concerns about India's growing role in Afghanistan. Pakistan's ambassador to the United States, Husain Haqqani, stated that Islamabad wanted to be certain that its own security concerns were addressed in the region. Kayani met senior US defence officials, to discuss ways and means of deepening cooperation between the two countries (*The Daily Times*, 24 March 2010).

Talking Peace at Thimpu

In late April, Yousaf Raza Gilani and Manmohan Singh met in the Bhutanese capital, Thimpu, when they attended the sixteenth SAARC Summit. Both vowed not to allow their soil to be used against the other. Gilani assured Singh that the perpetrators of the Mumbai attacks would be brought to justice. Both agreed that there was a trust deficit between them. Among the topics that came up for discussion were Kashmir, Siachen, and Sir Creek. Indian Foreign Secretary Nirupama Rao remarked that Gilani was serious about India's concerns on terrorism and had assured a speedy trial of the Mumbai attacks suspects. She said, 'We need to understand each other' (*The Hindu*, 30 April 2010). Meanwhile, the US media reported that Pakistan had moved 100,000 troops, from the Indian border to the border with Afghanistan. This was quickly denied by Pakistan. Major General Athar Abbas observed:

> Our armed forces are conducting operation against the terrorists on the western borders. We are facing threat of conventional war from the eastern borders, therefore, the troops deployed on the eastern borders alongside India have not been thinned out and nor will this strength be scaled down.... The number of troops required to be deployed on the eastern border is still there and any question to relocate them to the western border stands ruled out.

Some well-informed contacts in Pakistan, however, told me that a thinning of troops on the border with India had taken place but making such an admission was not politically correct, especially from the point of view of the establishment. The India-threat factor was intrinsic to the national security paradigm upon which the army's institutional interests hinged.

The Execution of a Former ISI Agent

On 30 April, a former ISI agent, Khalid Khawaja, was brutally executed by a hitherto unknown group called the Asian Tigers. He was found dead in

Miranshah, North Waziristan – a month after being kidnapped by the Asian Tigers. He had gone there along with the legendary Colonel Imam – Sultan Amir Tarar – and a UK journalist of Pakistani origin, Saad Qureshi. Khalid Khawaja's body was found riddled with bullets. A note left by the executioners stated that this would be the fate of all agents of the United States. Khalid Khawaja had been a squadron leader in the Pakistan Air Force before he changed career to become an ISI officer. He claimed to having been close to Osama bin Laden. Apparently, he was dismissed from the ISI for his outspoken views on jihad and his support of Al-Qaeda (*The Daily Times*, 1 May 2010).

Some years earlier, I had seen Khalid Khawaja on an international television network telling the interviewer something like this: 'You [the West] value life, we consider worldly existence a transition so how can you fight with us?' The message he wanted to convey was precisely that jihad was a natural duty for all Muslims and that 'martyrdom' was an exalted and coveted station to attain. On that occasion, I could not help but notice the irony in Khalid Khawaja's derision of life on earth: he had himself succeeded in growing to middle-age and some grey hairs could be seen in his beard. He had not volunteered to become a suicide bomber, but had probably been very successful in convincing others to do so. As a result, many lives had been destroyed while he lived to pontificate the virtues of death during jihad. His execution, by some group who found him to have been not only a CIA agent but also a Qadiyani (i.e. member of the despised Ahmadiyya community), as some media reports suggested, was the ultimate irony and tragedy of the self-righteous terrorism that is prevalent in Pakistan.

Faisal Shahzad

Khalid Khawaja's execution set in motion a spate of conspiracy theories about who betrayed him and how he was captured – exposing intricate networks and rivalries within the intelligence services, notably the ISI, Islamists cells and nexuses, journalists, and talk-show charlatans. However, such news generated excitement and sensationalism in the domestic sphere only. On 1 May, an incident in faraway New York once again put Pakistan in the spotlight as the epicentre of terrorism. Faisal Shahzad, thirty-one years old, married, of Pakhtun ancestry, the son of a retired Pakist ani air vice-marshal, and a naturalised US citizen, was apprehended for an attempted car bombing in

Times Square. A vigilant passer-by reported something suspicious about a car that was parked there. The authorities managed to defuse the explosive material just in time, and a major terrorist incident was prevented. Shahzad was taken into custody at John F. Kennedy International Airport on 3 May after he had boarded an Emirates Airline flight bound for Islamabad.

Faisal did not fit the bill of the usual suicide bomber, having been born and brought up in privileged circumstances. It turned out that he had been recruited by Islamists in Karachi while visiting Pakistan. Faisal confessed to ten counts related to the bombing attempt. The US media reported that he had admitted to training in bomb-making at a terrorist camp run by a militant Islamist faction in Waziristan. His arrest elicited angry reactions in the United States, and there were some suggestions that another terrorist attack on American soil, by Pakistan-based operatives, would be met with a severe punitive response. That it could entail the deployment of ground troops in Pakistan was a possibility that became relevant. The Pakistan government and media complained that Faisal was a US citizen and, therefore, Pakistan could not be blamed for his actions. The point, valid as it was, did not detract from the fact that too many things in Faisal's terroristic behaviour had a Pakistani linkage. On 5 October 2010, Shahzad was sentenced to life imprisonment without the possibility of parole.

A few days earlier, on 23 September, another US citizen of Pakistani origin, Dr Aafiya Siddiqui, a neuroscientist, had been sentenced to an eighty-six-year prison term having been found guilty on two counts of attempted murder, armed assault, using and carrying a firearm, and three counts of assault on US officers and other US employees. She had been arrested in 2008 from Afghanistan. The Americans believed she was a dangerous Al-Qaeda fanatic. Her arrest had evoked angry responses from different sections of Pakistani society. Prime Minister Gilani had gone out of his way and committed his government to footing her defence lawyers' bill. For Pakistani Islamists, Aafiya became the epitome of continuing US aggression against Islam and Muslims.

The American president and his administration worried the most about a future terrorist attack, with nuclear weapons, in the United States. So, he wanted to concentrate on Al-Qaeda rather than the Taliban movement as a whole. Moreover, he began to plan the US withdrawal, beginning July 2011, from Afghanistan. Obama told Bob Woodward of *The Washington Post* that he would tell the Afghans that the United States was committed to the long-term security and stability of their country, but that 'it's time for us to start thinking in terms of how you guys are going to be able to stand on your own two feet' (Woodward 2010: 377).

Attack on Ahmadis in Lahore

Meanwhile, the jihad offensive continued within Pakistan. On, 28 May, twin suicide bombing attacks took place on congregations of Ahmadi worshippers at the time of Friday prayers. More than 100 people lost their lives. Security officials suggested a link to the southern Punjab as TTP's networking was rapidly spreading beyond the NWFP. The new crop of terrorists belonged to banned organizations such as the LeJ, JeM, and SSP – all Deobandi affiliates of the TTP and Al-Qaeda. Interior Minister Rehman Malik remarked that 'militants who were hiding in southern Punjab are now surfacing'. He went on to state that there were more than 20,000 madrassas in the country, of which forty-four percent were in Punjab. The government banned 29 organisations and put 1764 people on the wanted lists – of those, 729 were from southern Punjab. A security official believed that the headquarters of Jaish-e-Muhammad, in Bahawalpur, was involved in recruiting volunteers for the Taliban (*The Daily Times*, 31 May 2010).

Floods Devastate Pakistan, Military Budget Increases, and Americans Demand Action

The summer of 2010 witnessed the worst monsoon rains in living memory in Pakistan, which led to floods that caused unprecedented destruction and devastation. Some twenty million people were badly affected, of which some eight million were rendered homeless. International help took some time in coming to the aid of the Pakistani people, but the United Nations did put a mechanism in place to deliver the help. President Zardari, who was travelling in Europe, allegedly to take care of his vast properties and financial assets, decided not to return immediately. He said that the prime minister and his cabinet were there to help the nation. Such a callous decision received scathing criticism both in the domestic and international media. The government did organise a relief effort after some time, but it was the Islamist organisations – known for their extremist agendas and involvement in terrorist activities –

who stepped in with their existing networks and rendered succour to the people, thus creating a nightmare for the United States and other Western nations who dreaded that it would help the extremists expand their support base among the people. The Americans provided the most aid; their military took part in the relief effort in a prominent way. A redeeming factor was that India made an offer of $4 million in aid, which it later increased to $20 million. Foreign Minister Qureshi accepted it, for which he received scathing criticism from a leading right-wing newspaper (*Nawa-i-Waqt*, 15 August 2010). Consequently, India was advised, by Pakistan, that it should channel its aid through the United Nations.

On 1 September, the United States designated the TTP as a foreign terrorist organization. Baitullah Mehsud's successor, Hakimullah Mehsud, and his close associate, Wali ur-Rehman, were designated global terrorists; the State Department issued a $5 million reward for information on the location of the two individuals. The designation of the TTP as a foreign terrorist organisation made it a crime to provide support for it or to do business with it. Anyone found to be aiding the TTP would have their financial assets frozen. Conspiracy theories in Pakistan portrayed the TTP as a hostile and treacherous organization. It is noteworthy that the US took a long time in banning the TPP which had been causing death and destruction in Pakistan for many years. That had created suspicions, among the Pakistanis, that the TTP was a clandestine protégé of some foreign powers.

At any rate, even as the United States offered considerable aid and assistance to Pakistan and its military personal took a leading part in the relief effort, Clinton and Holbrooke emphasised that Pakistan had to make its own efforts to cover the total cost of rehabilitation. They suggested that the rich in Pakistan be taxed to raise the revenues needed for such a task. Simultaneously, Holbrooke, who was visiting Islamabad, stated that his country would not accept any 'slackness', on the part of the Pakistan Army in the fight against the Taliban, due to their engagement in the flood relief efforts. 'Neither the security situation has changed fundamentally, nor the Taliban threat has receded and with the Americans placed in a difficult situation in Afghanistan, we certainly will not like to see slackness on the part of the Pakistan Army in the war on terror' (*The Daily Times*, 18 September 2010). Such blunt demands clearly showed that the Americans felt that Pakistan had to render some services in the war on terror in lieu of the various types of aid America gave Pakistan.

The response of the democratically-elected government was rather peculiar. It decided to severely cut funding to the seventy-one public sector universities, which impelled the vice-chancellors to resign en bloc. In sharp contrast, parliament approved a dramatic increase in the projected defence expenditure: from $5.14 billion to $6.41 billion in the 2010–11 budget, an increase of 30 percent (Ahmed, 12 October 2010). It is to be noted that the increase in the defence expenditure took place in response to a twelve percent hike in Indian spending on defence announced earlier in the year. The vicious circle that attended India–Pakistan relations made no exceptions to the unprecedented difficulties that Pakistan was facing.

Musharraf's Admissions

At this stage, the now retired General Pervez Musharraf made some startling admissions about Pakistan's complicity in promoting terrorism in Indian-administered Kashmir. Asked why Pakistan trained militant underground groups to fight India in Kashmir, the former president said that Nawaz Sharif's apathy to the Kashmir issue was one of the reasons, as was the fact that the world had turned a blind eye to the dispute (*The Times of India*, 5 October 2010). He said that he had no regrets about the Kargil intrusion that he had ordered, which had led to an armed conflict with India in 1999, and asserted that each country had the right to promote its national interest. He condemned the international community for courting India with a view to making strategic deals, while treating Pakistan as a rogue state. He asserted that the worst blunder of the United States would be to quit Afghanistan without winning. He further observed, 'Then militancy will prevail not only in Pakistan, India and Kashmir, but perhaps also in Europe, the United Kingdom and in the United States. That's my belief' (ibid.).

Stunned by Musharraf's admission that Pakistan had trained militant groups to fight in Kashmir, the Pakistan Foreign Office rubbished the former military ruler's statement as 'baseless'. Foreign Office Spokesman Abdul Basit said, 'I do not know really what prompted him (Musharraf) to say this because he is not in Pakistan and I would not really know as to the purpose of saying this'. Further, he said, 'But as far as government of Pakistan is concerned, I strongly refute these baseless suggestions.' He also stated that Pakistan supported the Kashmiri people's struggle which he said was 'purely indigenous and legitimate in accordance with UN charter and in accordance with international law' (*The Times of India*, 5 October 2010).

The *Dawn*, on 18 October 2010, reported that US federal officials had acknowledged that David Coleman Headley, who had confessed to his involvement in the Mumbai terror attacks, had been a mole of American intelligence agencies in the Lashkar-i-Tayyaba and other terrorist outfits. In court papers submitted by the FBI, US federal authorities said that they hoped to reach top Al-Qaeda leaders through him, but Headley went rogue and slipped out of their hands. The LeT, however, succeeded in brainwashing Headley, who then started leaking only selective information to his American bosses.

US–Pakistan 'Strategic Dialogue'

Soon afterwards, a United States–Pakistan strategic dialogue took place in Washington DC against the backdrop of deep-rooted suspicion and unease. The Obama administration approved $2 billion in military aid for the purchase of US-made arms and accessories – specifically for counter-insurgency purposes. The aid was subject to approval by Congress which, if granted, would be available from 2012 to 2016. A powerful editorial in Lahore's *The Daily Times*, dated 24 October 2010, observed that the United States had experienced an unreliable partner in the Pakistani military: during Musharraf's time, US military aid was used to amass weapons that had nothing to do with counter-insurgency but had everything to do with stockpiling against India. And that, this time round, the Pakistani military could be sure that the aid, if approved, would be subject to extremely close scrutiny and audit. Efforts to bolster Pakistan's counter-insurgency capabilities were intended to nudge the Pakistan military towards an all-out offensive in North Waziristan where safe havens existed, not just for the Haqqani network but also for the Pakistani Taliban (TTP) and, allegedly, Al-Qaeda. Pakistan was clearly seen to be dragging its feet, saying that if and when it conducted an operation in North Waziristan it would be in the light of its 'national interest'. Such a standpoint was seen, by the Americans, as a strategy to keep the Afghan Taliban intact until the last US soldier left Afghanistan. The writer then made the following comment:

> 'The US has not backtracked during this session on its insistence on an offensive in North Waziristan. It does not seem likely that Pakistan will abandon its Afghan cohorts whom it may like to have represented in a post-US withdrawal Afghan dispensation. The Pakistani military has staked too much on strategic depth in Afghanistan and if the US tries to keep Pakistan out of any Afghan talks, the Pakistani military is likely to use its leverage through the Afghan Taliban, irrespective of diplomacy and dialogue.'

The US is aware of the fact that in this war on terror, Pakistan has been flexing its muscles to beat back the TTP. The US's real enemy, however, is still operational and the US is not happy. That is why the superpower continues to use its policy of sweet-talking and coddling with occasional threats thrown in for good measure. This cat and mouse game cannot go on forever. If the present minuet breaks down, a conflict could occur between the two allies, one that Pakistan may end up on the losing side of.

The usual pies were thrown in the sky, namely Kashmir and our civil nuclear designs. In both cases, the US's preference for India can be seen with the Obama administration siding with its strategic partner over its tactical one. Resolving Kashmir was Obama's election pledge; it is now an issue that the US does not want to "mediate" on. Our expecting to be treated like India when it comes to a civil nuclear pact is naïve since Pakistan stands accused of nuclear proliferation in the past and has been described as the epicentre of the region's troubles. We have no choice therefore but to rely on China, a reliable friend and one that will not backtrack on Washington's insistence.

All in all, the dialogue is bridging the gulf of mistrust to some extent but the same doubts and legacies remain, "process" and $2 billi on notwithstanding'.

In November, President George W. Bush published his memoirs, Decision Points, in which he shed light on how his administration became gradually sceptical of, and disillusioned with, Pakistan's motivations for joining the war against terrorism. He had become convinced that Pakistan would not act determinedly against extremist militants. He acknowledged that Pakistan had 'paid a high price for taking on extremists' and that its forces were successful for several years in targeting Al-Qaeda militants crossing the porous border with Afghanistan. But, he added, 'Over time, it became clear that Musharraf either would not or could not fulfil all of his promises.' Further, 'Some in the

Pakistani intelligence service, the ISI, retained close ties to Taliban officials. Others wanted an insurance policy in case America abandoned Afghanistan and India tried to gain influence there.' He recalled a meeting with US Special Forces returning from Afghanistan in which someone pleaded with him, 'We need permission to go kick some ass inside Pakistan.' He noted that the Predator – an unmanned predator drone – 'was capable of conducting video surveillance and firing laser-guided bombs.' He admitted, 'I authorised the intelligence community to turn up the pressure on the extremists. Many of the details of our actions remain classified. But soon after I gave the order, the press started reporting more Predator strikes'. Bush said that Pakistan's cooperation was impeded by its 'obsession' with India. 'In almost every conversation we had, Musharraf accused India of wrongdoing', Bush wrote (*Dawn,* 10 November 2010).

Drone Attacks

In this context, it is important that the drone attacks – which the Pakistani media always condemned – had also been claiming innocent lives. Pakistan had been insisting that the requisite technology and equipment to launch drone attacks should be transferred to it but the Americans had not acceded to such requests. The drone attacks increased under President Obama and contributed to his unpopularity, especially among the ultra-nationalists, right-wing media, and Islamists. From the American point of view, it was an effective way to target and kill Taliban and Al-Qaeda leaders without risking US troops. However, the Pakistan government's and military's public postures – protesting against the drone attacks, denouncing them as violations of Pakistan's sovereignty, and that were killing its civilians and risked worsening anti-US sentiment – were rather deceptive. As noted already close collaboration between the US and Pakistan militaries and their intelligence agencies became public with the liquidation of the TTP leader, Baitullah Mehsud, in August 2009 as a result of a US drone attack in which Pakistan had provided intelligence about his location (Ahmed 2009).

Escalating Violence in Balochistan

While violence emanating from Islamist sources had become endemic in

Pakistan's mainstream politics, the situation in Balochistan had continued to be highly volatile and explosive. The main armed encounters were between the security forces and Baloch nationalists, but vicious attacks on the Hazara Shia minority by Sunni fanatics and attacks on Punjabi settlers by Baloch ethno-nationalists also claimed hundreds of lives. Besides such recurring patterns of violence, the Americans continued to claim that Afghan Taliban leaders were hiding in the province. Balochistan had a large Pakhtun population, and the Taliban had found sanctuary among them. The Taliban had allegedly been launching raids on NATO oil tankers and containers, while they were in transit from Karachi to Kandahar, for years. Balochistan had become the stronghold of smugglers, dacoits, kidnappers, and other such criminal nexuses. Many Baloch sardars ran their own private armies and jails and were involved in criminal activities. But, the main conflict in the province was political violence – between the federal government and the Baloch nationalists – that escalated after the murder of Akbar Bugti. The Baloch complained that hundreds of Baloch were missing as a result of abduction by the security forces; many were later found brutally killed or continued to be missing ('Conflict and Insecurity in Balochistan' 2010; Talpur, 3 April 2011). The Pakistan government continued to reiterate that foreign powers, especially India, were behind the Baloch insurgency.

Mid-term Defeat for Democrats and Obama's Visit to India

President Obama visited India in November, soon after his Democratic Party suffered a heavy defeat in the US mid-term elections. The rival Republican Party gained control of the US House of Representatives while the Democrats managed to maintain their slight lead in the Senate. The voters were mainly concerned about the poor state of the US economy. National security issues, including foreign wars and homeland security, were hardly mentioned by either the voters or the candidates. Consequently, not only were its NATO allies facing a lack of support in their national constituencies but the main protagonist leading the military campaign in the war on terror in the AfPak region was also facing diminishing support for the engagement. The idea that the war could not be won was gaining strength, much to the chagrin of those determined to annihilate Al-Qaeda and its diehard Taliban allies.

According to Chindanand Rajghatta of *The Times of India* (29 September

2010), preparatory to his visit to India, Obama began to formulate a strategy that stipulated that India must solve the Kashmir issue if it wanted a permanent seat at the UN Security Council. Thus, notwithstanding India's categorical objections to the Kashmir issue being connected to AfPak, the Americans wanted to make such a connection obliquely. In the US perception, that would create a stable Pakistan which could then be persuaded to whole-heartedly commit its military to eradicating Al-Qaeda and Taliban from its territory and thus facilitate the exit of US forces from that theatre. This line of argument was reportedly developed by Bruce Riedel, the reputed architect of the AfPak strategy. However, Riedel and other US policy makers recognised that the biggest hurdle to a settlement with India would be the hard-line Pakistani military. They expected the civilian leadership in Pakistan to embrace the deal but doubted if the army chief, General Kayani, would come on board. Except for Admiral Mullen, most other top US officials believed that Kayani was a hardliner intent on perpetuating hostile relations with India. Kayani reportedly said, during a meeting with US officials, 'I'll be the first to admit it, I'm India-centric' (Rajghatta 29 September 2010).

The Indian government and media, however, expressed displeasure at this initiative. Most opposition parties also opposed the American attempt to broker a deal between India and Pakistan. Having suffered a major defeat in the mid-term elections, Obama's ability to assert himself was no doubt dented. As a result, he prudently avoided broaching the Kashmir issue during his three-day visit to India. At a special session of the Indian Parliament, Obama spoke of US–India ties as an 'indispensable and defining relationship of the twenty-first century.' He acknowledged India's contributions to science and backed India's demand for a permanent seat on the United Nations Security Council. For his part, Manmohan Singh expressed great satisfaction at the growing trust and confidence between the two countries. Such an exchange of compliments was viewed with concern in Pakistan where the government and media complained about the Americans' discriminatory treatment – in spite of the huge sacrifices Pakistan had made in human lives and material wealth to participate in the war against terrorism. The market for conspiracy theories was again abuzz with fantastic scenarios of a forthcoming assault on Pakistani sovereignty and integrity, and its nuclear arsenal, by the Christian West and Hindu India.

Attack on Shrines

Terrorism within Pakistan continued to find new targets: this time round it was the shrines of Sufis venerated by mainstream Barelvi-Sunnis. Some of the famous shrines that were attacked by suicide bombers included that of Data Sahib in Lahore (1 July 2010), Abdullah Shah Ghazi in Karachi (7 October 2010), Baba Fariduddin Ganjshakar at Pakpattan in eastern Punjab (25 October 2010), and Sakhi Sarwar at Dera Ghazi Khan in southern Punjab (3 April 2011). Hundreds of devotees have been killed in the mayhem. Attacks on lesser-known shrines also took place. The Taliban and their affiliates were behind these atrocities and claimed responsibility. However, one can argue that extremism flourished because the state had patronised militant organisations that had probably begun to act on their own and were out of control. Such attacks were, undoubtedly, carried out to wipe out all traces of deviation from the fanatical monotheism that the Taliban and Al-Qaeda uphold as the true Islam. Ironically, in Pakistani textbooks on history and Pakistan Studies, the advent of Islam in the subcontinent is attributed to the peaceful efforts of the Sufis. The nihilism that the Taliban represented seemed determined to put that line of argument into doubt (Ahmed, 2011).

Chinese Premier's Visit to India and Pakistan

In December 2010, the Chinese prime minister, Wen Jiabao, visited India and Pakistan. The Pakistani media gave a lot of attention to the visit; friendship with China tends to be referred to in hyperbolic terms – as higher than the mountains, deeper than the oceans, and so on. Understandably, the Pakistani leaders were concerned as to how such a friend could relate to a country that Pakistan had had constant enmity with. The Chinese and Indian leaders agreed to increase their trade to $100 billion by 2015. The Chinese also promised to rectify the trade imbalance between them; China exported much more to, than it imported from, India. The Chinese premier said that there was room for both India and China to grow and, therefore, there was no need to go down the path of confrontation. He did not, however, make concessions on their border disputes. The Chinese were reticent about India's ambitions to become a permanent member of the UN Security Council.

Later, when in Pakistan, Jiabao announced that Pakistan would benefit from Chinese investments to the tune of $25 billion. He also assured Pakistan that his country would always be a reliable friend and would not let Pakistan down. The Chinese probably wanted to keep the pressure on India in case India got too cosy with the Americans. While in India, the Chinese also did not agree to refer to a Pakistani hand in the Mumbai terrorist attacks of 26 November 2008. However, more significant was that China advised India and Pakistan to resolve the Kashmir dispute through negotiations. On the other hand, it must be remembered that China was no less worried than India about Pakistan becoming a springboard for a Taliban-type of jihad that could entail the destabilization of the Muslim-majority province of Xinjiang (Ahmed, 4 January 2011).

American Pressure on Pakistan to Act in North Waziristan

In mid-December, a number of top US officials, the US ambassador to Pakistan, Ambassador Cameron, and Defence Secretary Robert Gates demanded that Pakistan should dismantle the terrorist bases in North Waziristan, and stated that Pakistan would continue to be the epicentre of terrorism and a threat to US security and interests as long as that did not happen. Such statements were mixed with expressions of under-standing that Pakistan could not conduct the operation immediately – partly because of winter and partly other factors – but that it must do so in order to fulfil its responsibilities as an ally in the war on terrorism. Such pronouncements were made in the context of a five-page unclassified summary of the effects of the surge in Afghanistan. It was claimed that the allies had made 'notable operational gains' in Afghanistan, but that progress in Pakistan was uneven. The latter's border areas were perceived to be the main obstacle to the success of Obama's strategy because it allowed a free flow of militants into Afghanistan (*Dawn,* 17 December 2010).

Already, during Clinton's visit in October 2009, the Pakistani media had published reports of the presence of hundreds of undercover Americans in Pakistan – the Blackwater security firm had been singled out.

Assassination of Governor Salman Taseer

In November 2010, a judge of a lower court in Sheikhupura, Punjab, sentenced a poor Christian farmhand and a mother of four children, Aasia

Bibi, to death by hanging, and a fine of an equivalent of $1100 for allegedly blaspheming against Prophet Muhammad (pbuh). This was the first time that a woman had been sentenced to death for blasphemy. Understandably, the news made headlines all over the world. While appeals for mercy began to be made from many quarters of the world, including the Pope, it generated unprecedented hysterical manifestations of fanaticism within Pakistan and exposed deep chasms within the ruling PPP federal government. Punjab Governor Salman Taseer, a stalwart of the PPP, criticised the death sentence. He wanted the blasphemy law to be rescinded, or radically amended, to prevent it being used arbitrarily. He met Aasia Bibi in jail, when she denied having said a word against the Prophet. She asserted that, because she had drunk water from the same cup as some Muslim women, they had objected to it. This had resulted in an altercation with the result that they falsely accused her of blasphemy. Taseer believed her story and expressed solidarity with her. He urged President Zardari to grant her a pardon, which he did. On the other hand, Prime Minister Gilani, Home Minister Rehman Malik, and Law Minister Babar Awan issued statements that they were opposed to the blasphemy law being interfered with. The Lahore High Court stayed the order. Lawyers who had recently brought down Musharraf, and had been celebrated as harbingers of democracy, now began to spearhead the call for Aasia Bibi's execution. District bars, one after the other, passed resolutions to that effect. Such a witch-hunt by the legal fraternity was reflective of the limits of democracy in a confessional state. Meanwhile, leaders of all the Sunni and Shia religious parties and organisations formed a committee to defend, what they called, the honour and sanctity of the Prophet (*News*, 12 December 2010). Salman Taseer began to be demonized as a renegade from Islam who had taken up cudgels on behalf of Aasia Bibi in order to please the West. Calls were given for his assassination (Ahmed, 2011).

On 4 January 2011, Salman Taseer was slain by his official bodyguard, Malik Mumtaz Hussain Qadri, a police commando, while his other bodyguards looked on. Later, Qadri proudly admitted his guilt on television, and then in court, saying that Taseer deserved to die because he had described the blasphemy law as draconian. When his death was announced, hundreds of leading clerics issued fatwas (religious rulings) that Taseer should not be given an Islamic burial. Munawwar Hasan, the head of the leading fundamentalist party, the Jama'at-e-Islami, blamed Taseer for provoking pious sensibilities by describing the blasphemy law in an uncharitable manner. The Islamists insisted that Qadri should be honourably released because he had not committed a crime but had done his duty, as required under Islamic law, to defend the honour of the Prophet. Qadri proudly claimed, in the court, that he was proud of having killed Taseer and that it was the duty of all Muslims, who must punish those who commit sacrilege against the Prophet of Islam. The court, however, charged him with murder. The presiding judge took the position that laws on blasphemy were available in the legal system – which precluded the private execution of alleged blasphemers. The assassination of the governor put the degree to which extremism has pervaded the security and police apparatuses into sharp relief. Also, the mass hysteria that the clerics were able to generate is indicative of the fact that violent behaviour has become intrinsic in the wider society. Later, the anti-terrorism court found Qadri guilty of murdering Taseer and sentenced him to death (*The Daily Times,* 2 October 2011). However, immediately afterwards, the presiding judge, Pervez Ali Shah, went on a visit to Muslim holy places and has remained abroad. Aasia Bibi remains in prison thus far.

Execution of the Legendary Colonel Imam

On 24 January, the Nation reported that Sultan Amir Tarrar, known as Colonel Imam, had been killed by his abductors in North Waziristan. It may be recalled that the colonel had gone there in the spring of 2010 – along with former ISI agent Khalid Khawaja and a British journalist of Pakistani descent, Asad Qureshi. On 30 April 2010, former ISI agent Khalid Khawaja was brutally executed by their captors who had described Khalid Khawaja as an American agent. Asad Qureshi was released (presumably after paying a heavy ransom). Colonel Imam was famous for having played a key role in the Afghan jihad, and was also known as the mentor of Taliban leader Mullah Omar. Before his execution, video footage – apparently recorded in July 2010 – was released by the abductors in which he was shown saying that his life was in danger and urging the government to fulfil his kidnappers' demand of freeing a number of prisoners held for terror activities (Youtube, khalifaconcepts, 22 January 2011).

On his execution, the TTP released video footage showing Colonel Imam being shot to death in the presence of the TTP chief, Hakimullah Mehsud.

Amid the raising of slogans chanting the glory of Islam, a man shot Colonel Imam several times. Just before being killed, the colonel could be seen on his knees in a humiliating posture. The real reason for his execution was that the ransom money demanded by his kidnappers had not been paid (*Nation* 24 January 2011).

Assassination of Minister for Minority Affairs Shahbaz Bhatti

Terrorising religious minorities had become endemic in Pakistani society. In 2009, hordes of fanatics attacked Christians in a village near Gojra, in Punjab, on the grounds that they had burnt the Quran – a charge that the Christians denied but to no avail. According to established practice, the raiders were given theological cover by clerics who described death for non-Muslims who committed such crimes as the bounden duty of all Muslims. The Christians' houses were set ablaze, and at least eight people died. Many more were injured; the whole village was subjected to a rampage as the delirious extremists went around seeking targets to vent their wrath on. On that occasion, the government acted with some determination. Prime Minister Gilani personally visited the spot, and economic compensation was announced for the victims. He ordered the minister for minority affairs, Shahbaz Bhatti, to stay on and provide relief to the beleaguered and traumatized villagers. Shahbaz Bhatti, a Roman Catholic, described the police response and later investigation as ineffective – following which he began to receive death threats. Some months later, when Aasia Bibi was charged with blasphemy, Bhatti was very outspoken in his opposition to the continuation of the blasphemy law. After Taseer's murder, he alone among the ministers kept insisting that the blasphemy law should be repealed.

In Islamabad, on 2 March 2011, armed men on motorcycles stopped the vehicle in which Bhatti was returning after visiting his mother. They fired a hail of bullets, sparing the driver but aiming at Bhatti who succumbed quickly. Apparently, he had not been provided maximum security in spite of daily death threats being issued to him. Home Minister Rehman Malik blamed the deceased for being negligent on his frequent visits to his mother – in other words, that Bhatti had not demanded high security. After Taseer's death, it was doubtful whether the security forces were reliable anymore but even Malik had been remiss in placing his colleague (Salman Taseer) in the category of highest security. Bhatti's death was bewailed by the Christian minority. Not a single Muslim cleric condemned the murder. On the other hand, his fellow ministers and the prime minister took part in the funeral rites and expressed sympathy and condolences for the deceased.

17

The Gory End of Osama bin Laden

The United States had designated the TTP as a terrorist organization in September 2010, and two of its top leaders as global terrorists. On 20 January 2011, another TTP leader, Qazi Hussain, was placed on the terrorist list for allegedly playing a leading role in the recruitment and training of terrorists. The same day, the United Kingdom banned the TTP on its soil. However, such measures did not suffice to dispel the conspiracy theory that the TTP was a protégé of the CIA and R&AW.

On 26 January, this theory received a great boost when Raymond Allen Davis, a former US soldier who was a private security firm employee (Blackwater) and contractor with the CIA, killed two armed men in Lahore. There were some suggestions, in the media, that Raymond Davis was not his real name. In any case, after shooting the two men, Davis got out of his car and filmed the two men on his mobile phone as they lay in a pool of blood – with firearms on their persons. It was evident that he was not panic-stricken and that he had executed them with deadly accuracy – suggesting that he was a professional gunman. Davis, in police custody, claimed that he shot them in self-defence. The media reported that the two men had earlier robbed someone in the same neighboured and were criminals. Immediately afterwards, a third Pakistani was also killed when a car, apparently despatched by the US consulate in Lahore to rescue Davis, sped down the wrong side of a road and killed a passer-by. The driver of that vehicle mysteriously disappeared. Davis claimed diplomatic immunity and demanded that he be released. The United States forthwith backed his claim and pressed for his immediate release. In an almost unprecedented move, both Clinton as well as President Obama made direct appeals on television for his release. On 6

February, Shumaila Kanwal, the widow of one of the men slain by Davis, committed suicide with an overdose of pills, suspecting that Davis would be released without trial. She demanded that he should not be released and that she wanted blood for blood: Davis should be killed in the same way as he had killed her husband (*Dunya News*, 8 February 2011).

A video clip showed that while Davis was being interrogated at the police station, he was secretly recording the proceedings with a camera. In the initial enquiry, he can be seen claiming that he was posted at the US consulate general in Lahore, and that he had given his passport to the first police officer to arrive at the scene of the shooting. The TV commentator then asks Naseer Wagah – presumably a journalist working for *Dunya News* – to give more details. Wagah asserts that Davis cannot be a diplomat by any stretch of the imagination and that he is a spy: a professional who killed the two men with deadly accuracy and, having shot them through the windscreen of his vehicle and hit them in their heads, then got out of the car, photographed them, and then calmly waited in his car until the police arrived. Wagah comments that Davis had a variety of guns in his car, as well as more than 100 rounds of ammunition and, both, still and video cameras (*Dunya News*, 9 February 2011). In another clip, dated 15 February 2011, Davis can be seen claiming to be a diplomat and refusing to answer questions during police interrogation. When the interrogator tells him that he is not a diplomat, Davis retorts by saying that he is not going to answer any further questions and gets up from his chair waving his hand at the interrogator in a dismissive manner (*Dunya News*, 15 February 2011).

While such bizarre events were taking place in Pakistan, the United States issued a threat that it would break off contact with Pakistan, expel the Pakistan ambassador, Husain Haqqani, and cut off aid (*Dawn*, 9 February 2011). A meeting scheduled between Clinton and Foreign Minister Shah Mehmood Qureshi was cancelled. Later, the Obama administration refuted that any of these moves were contemplated. There was no doubt that the Americans were resorting to blatantly crude methods to extract compliance from the Pakistan government. Given Pakistan's chronic economic and military dependence on the United States and other foreign powers, for which it had been renting out its services to them, it was equally clear that the issue would not be decided on the basis of international law and diplomatic praxis. A weak elected government, that itself was dependent on US support, and a military that had endemically cultivated American patronage meant that the Americans would prevail.

The problem was the fierce reaction of the Pakistani people towards Davis' cowboy bravado. Right-wing and ultra-nationalist media and religious parties demanded that Davis be tried in court for double murder. With few exceptions, even liberals raised their brows over American arrogance and flagrant disrespect for Pakistan's sovereignty. Columnists wondered how a foreigner could go around Pakistan's most famous city bearing firearms, shooting Pakistani citizens dead on a busy road, and then calmly taking photographs of the dying men.

The government's response was inconsistent and contradictory. While the powerful home ministry headed by Rehman Malik affirmed that Davis carried a diplomatic passport, Foreign Minister Qureshi denied that Davis enjoyed any such status – for which he was penalized immediately: a cabinet reshuffle took place, the portfolio of foreign minister was taken away from him, and he was offered another ministry which he refused. Left in the wilderness, Qureshi retaliated by criticising the government for not standing up to the Americans. He stated that Clinton had tried to force him to confirm that Davis enjoyed diplomatic immunity but he had refused (*The Daily Times,* 13 February). The PPP machinery went into action; Qureshi was subjected to a severe reprimand by Zardari and Gilani loyalists. Kayani and some other top generals expressed displeasure that the United States had planted hundreds of agents in Pakistan, who were gathering intelligence without informing the Pakistani authorities. The line taken by the civilian government was that the issue would be decided in a court of law in accordance with Pakistani laws and legal procedure.

Senator John Kerry, the former Democratic presidential candidate and the architect of the Kerry–Lugar bill, arrived in Pakistan. He gave a press conference in Lahore on 15 February where he emphasized the importance of the US–Pakistan relationship. He regretted the loss of lives and expressed his sympathies to the families of the men. However, his main thrust was that Davis was a diplomat and, since Pakistan had signed the Geneva Convention of 1961, he enjoyed diplomatic immunity according to Article 31 of that instrument of international law (YouTube). Kerry also met the main opposition leader, Mian Nawaz Sharif, who also took the line that the issue would be decided in accordance with Pakistani law. The Jamaat-e-Islami's amir, Munawwar Hassan, denounced all suggestions that Davis enjoyed diplomatic immunity. In an extraordinary move, President Obama issued a statement from the White House that Davis was a diplomat and should be released because he enjoyed immunity. The TTP warned Pakistan not to release Davis, describing him as a spy (*Dawn,* 16 February 2011).

US security expert Stephen Cohen took part in a Pakistani talk-show, on *NDTV*, in which he argued that it was obvious that Davis was not an ordinary diplomat as diplomats did not normally carry guns and shoot people. The lack of awareness of his presence and activities was also indicative of the Pakistani intelligence services' failures. He asserted, however, that such drastic measures were presumably being taken because Pakistan was unable to curb and control the terrorism that was striking at US and NATO targets in Afghanistan, and generally creating insecurity in the AfPak and the wider South Asian region (*NDTV,* 23 Februar y, 2011). Such a line of argument obliquely confirmed the suspicion that the CIA had been organizing its own intelligence gathering, and Davis' shooting of the two Pakistanis exposed the ongoing war among the agencies that had been going on for quite some time in Pakistan. From the American point of view, Pakistan had been procrastinating for too long by not striking at the Haqqani and other terrorist networks despite receiving huge amounts of US aid.

In any event, the story of why he had shot the two men changed. Instead of their being armed robbers, the media reported that they were ISI operatives who were shadowing Davis to keep track of his unlawful movements. He was accused of being involved in a sinister conspiracy to destabilise Pakistan. Such clandestine activities included funding the TTP and its affiliates in Punjab which, it was widely believed, were behind the suicide bombings and other acts of terrorism in Pakistan. The ultimate aim of the destabilisation conspiracy was to get hold of Pakistan's nuclear arsenal, and thus render it militarily ineffective and weak. In other words, it was alleged that Davis was the key protagonist in a plot to break-up Pakistan.

Even US officials revealed that Davis was a contractor working for the CIA. An unnamed ISI official stated that Davis had contacts in FATA and knew both the men he had shot dead (*The Daily Times* 9 February 2011). The *Dunya News* TV channel showed a clip of photographs taken by Davis, of sensitive areas in and around Lahore close to the India–Pakistan border. It was also shown that of the men he had killed, one could be seen carrying a gun in his hand, suggesting that Davis had shot him in self-defence The media reported that data had been retrieved from Davis' phones and from the sophisticated Global Positing System or satellite phone device he had in his vehicle (YouTube, 11 February). Such satellite technology helped him determine locations with accuracy. Davis had been to Islamabad, Lahore, Peshawar, and the tribal areas and was involved in the drone attacks that had been taking place in the region.

It is interesting to note that the drone attacks were disrupted after Davis' arrest. Damage limitation activities had started immediately after his arrest. At that point, media discussions also started on Davis paying 'blood money' – as is permitted under the prevalent Islamic law – to the victims in order to secure his release. Such a procedure has been criticised by human rights NGOs as it can be manipulated to free culprits through monetary inducements; and, in the case of honour killings, by the family pardoning the culprits. Some clerics argued that the Islamic law of qisas and diyat did not apply in Davis' case. The government prudently maintained the 'principled' position, that the issue would be decided according to legal procedure. On 16 March, a Pakistani court ordered Davis to be released after the relatives of the dead men attended the court – convened in a prison in Lahore – and received blood money.

The compensation, reportedly some $2.3 million, was sufficiently attractive. The lawyers representing the families of the victims later revealed that the Pakistani authorities excluded them from the negotiations and that the deal was closed in utter secrecy. American pressure had prevailed, notwithstanding the rage that was evident at demonstrations and protest marches all over Pakistan. Clinton denied that the US government had paid any blood money (*The News International,* 17 March 2011). It appears that it was arranged behind-the-scenes, ostensibly through non-official channels. There was a hue and a cry about Pakistan having bartered away its sovereignty and national honour. But, the fuss could not conceal the fact that the relationship between the United States and Pakistan, since a very long time, had been one of dependence – where America's vital interests were concerned, it could extract compliance from the latter.

Drone Attacks Resumed, Pressure on Pakistan Intensifies

The day after Davis was released, a drone attack took place in North Waziristan, killing forty people – apparently civilians – who had gathered to discuss some routine matters. The incident greatly embarrassed the Pakistani establishment as it manifested an utter disregard by the Americans for public sentiments which, at that particular moment in time, were highly inflamed against the United States. The ISPR announced that General Kayani strongly condemned the drone attack as it had caused the death of innocent Pakistani citizens. He reportedly stated that such attacks would not be acceptable (17 March 2011). Ambassador Munter was summoned to the Foreign Office to receive a strongly worded protest. Ostensibly, the Pakistan Air Force was ordered to prepare for action in case Pakistani airspace was violated again. Drone attacks had been taking place since 2004, and it was widely known that they took off from the Shamsi Air Force Base in Balochistan.

It is doubtful if each drone flight was approved by the Pakistani authorities. In this particular case, the attack must have taken place without any consultation with the Pakistanis. Given the highly inflamed public opinion in Pakistan, it is very unlikely that the military had acquiesced to the attack. However, as usual, some conciliatory utterances were made in Washington DC, only to be followed by a concerted chorus of top officials questioning Pakistan's intentions and objectives in not going all out to eliminate terrorist enclaves in North Waziristan and elsewhere.

Typical of such tactics was the press conference Admiral Mullen gave in Washington DC, at which he remarked that it was 'hugely important' that Pakistani forces take action against militants in North Waziristan. He praised Pakistan's willingness to fight insurgents elsewhere but noted that the campaign needed to move to North Waziristan where members of the Al-Qaeda and Haqqani networks were based. It was reported that he said: 'They have lost thousands of soldiers and thousands of civilians in a very impressive counter insurgency campaign to clear Swat valley and the other areas.' Then, he went on to express an understanding for Pakistan's concerns about preserving its influence in neighbouring Afghanistan – so that the latter did not become a proxy for India and remained friendly with Pakistan (*Dawn*, 18 March 2011).

Some Regional Peace Initiatives

Cricket diplomacy between Pakistan and India was in action once again when Prime Minister Gilani accepted his counterpart Manmohan Singh's invitation and visited Mohali, in the Indian Punjab, to attend the semi-final between their two countries' teams in the Cricket World Cup Tournament 2011. Thousands of Pakistanis were granted visas to attend the match. As before, they were received with warmth and generosity – just as Pakistanis had played host to Indians on similar occasions in the past. Both leaders pledged to take the peace process forward, and agreed to set up a hotline on terrorism so that both sides could share intelligence. The Foreign Service bureaucracies were, thus, to be set in motion again in search of the normalisation of relations and peace (*The Daily Times*, 31 March 2011).

General Pasha Visits CIA Headquarters

With regard to Pakistan–US relations, DG ISI General Pasha and his delegation met the CIA head, Leon Panetta, and his men at CIA headquarters in Virginia on 11 April. Given the fierce reaction that took place when Davis was released, Pasha took an ostensibly tough line threatening that greater control would be exercised on CIA covert activities in Pakistan in the future. The Americans were told that a serious breach of trust had occurred, and a 'clear code of conduct' needed to be devised. Pasha asked the CIA for a complete list of its employees and contractors in Pakistan, and made it clear that some may be asked to leave. From the American point of view, this could entail restrictions on drone attacks taking off from the Pakistani bases. The CIA carried out 118 drone strikes in Pakistan in 2010 – more than in all the previous years of the programme combined – according to independent estimates (*The Daily Times*, 13 April 2011). The CIA confirmed that it had 300 men in Pakistan training the Pakistanis on counter-terrorism (*The Daily Times*, 14 April 2011). That, of course, referred to those whose presence in Pakistan had been approved through the proper channels.

A High-Powered Delegation Visits Kabul

In mid-April, a high-powered delegation consisting of Prime Minister Gilani,

COAS General Kayani, and Director General ISI Lieutenant General Pasha visited Kabul in mid-April. As a result of the talks that were held, it was agreed that a joint commission would carry forward the reconciliation process, with the approval of the United States, following the withdrawal of foreign troops from Afghanistan. The Afghan president, Hamid Karzai, hoped that the commission would find a way of reaching a peace deal with the Taliban (*The Daily Times,* 17 April 2011).

Scathing Criticism of ISI

Such diverse moves did not mean that the US had relented in its aim of compelling Pakistan to take decisive action against terrorist networks it believed were inimical to its vital interests. In fact, the ante was upped. According to a long report – 'Mullen launches diatribe against the ISI' – filed by *Dawn*'s Baqir Sajjad Syed following an interview with Admiral Michael Mullen in Islamabad, the latter stated that the ISI was protecting the Haqqani and other terrorist networks in North Waziristan and elsewhere, and that such a relationship was at the core of 'Pakistan's problematic relationship with the United States'. He noted that the ISI's relationship with the Haqqani group was unacceptable to the United States. He indicated that the CIA would continue to monitor the situation in Pakistan through a strong physical presence, and that drone attacks on the Haqqani group in North Waziristan would continue until the ISI dissociated itself from the Haqqanis. He reportedly said: 'I have a sacred obligation to do all I can to make sure that the network is no longer able to support insurgents in Afghanistan.' He depicted a destabilising scenario in which several terror groups would become increasingly interlinked, and said, 'What I worry about all these organisations, whether it is Haqqani network, Al-Qaeda, JuD, LeT…there is a syndication which has occurred in the region here over the course of last three years, which is more and more worrisome and increasingly so TTP, under [Hakimullah] Mehsud, has espoused aspirations outside the region'.

Mullen reiterated that such prospects led to no conclusions except that 'this area…the border area between Pakistan and Afghanistan is the epicentre of terrorism in the world'. During his interview, on more than one occasion, he suggested a close collaboration between India, Afghanistan, and Pakistan to deal with the terror threat emanating from the tribal areas. Some mitigating remarks were also made praising Pakistan's counter-terrorism efforts elsewhere. He stressed that, despite the challenges in bilateral ties, 'the military-to-military relations between the US and Pakistan had remained strong' (*Dawn*, 21 April 2011).

For his part, General Kayani rebuffed such categorical accusations by the United States' top soldier. He vehemently rejected the negative propaganda that Pakistan was not doing enough and that the Pakistani Army lacked clarity on the way forward. He asserted that the 'army's ongoing operations are a testimony of our national resolve to defeat terrorism' (*Dawn*, 21 April 2011). Another drone attack took place in North Waziristan the next day, killing at least twenty-one people including children. The Americans, it seemed, were determined to continue with their independent efforts to knock terrorist bases out (*Dawn*, 22 April 2011). More embarrassing material surfaced a few days later when a US military classified document was published by the *New York Times* in which the ISI was described, in 2007, as 'a terrorist support entity' (*Dawn*, 25 April 2011). On 26 April, terrorists attacked Pakistan Navy buses carrying personnel. Four people were killed and fifty-six injured. The TTP claimed responsibility and said that such attacks would continue as long as Pakistan's armed forces killed their own people at the behest of the Americans (*The Daily Times* 27 April 2011).

The Obama administration submitted its biannual report on the situation in Afghanistan and Pakistan to Congress, grimly stating that there is 'no clear path toward defeating the insurgency in Pakistan, despite the unprecedented and sustained deployment of over 147,000 [Pakistani] forces' (Landay: 5 April 2011). The report expressed concern about Pakistan's failure to sustain counterinsurgency operations against militants in the country's northwest, noting that Pakistani forces had conducted three major operations in the Mohmand agency in the last two years – though the unclassified report made no explicit calls for further operations, especially in troubled North Waziristan. The report also called Pakistan's worsening economic situation 'the greatest threat to Pakistan's stability over the medium term' (*New York Times*).

Operation Geronimo

In the early hours of 2 May 2011, the United States finally found Osama bin Laden's hideout in Pakistan's garrison town of Abbottabad. US Special Forces flew into the compound of the large building and, within forty minutes, killed the iconic head of Al-Qaeda. His dead body, along with those of his Pakistani protectors, were loaded onto a US helicopter and flown out of Pakistani territory. The hunt had begun even before 9/11 as Al-Qaeda had hit US targets in both the United States and globally. However, following the slaughter of thousands of its citizens in the September 2001 attacks, the search for Osama bin Laden became a top security priority for the world's leading superpower. His followers had created a mystique around him – as the great hero of Islam who would restore the glory of Islam through armed struggle. Bin Laden successfully eluded his pursuers until he was traced by US Special Forces – who had been rehearsing for such a raid for several weeks in a prototype construction at a US base.

The first public announcement about the raid was made on television by President Barack Obama. In a long and carefully prepared speech, he announced that, shortly after taking office, he had directed the CIA director, Leon Panetta, to make 'the killing or capture of bin Laden the top priority of our war against al Qaeda, even as we continued our broader efforts to disrupt, dismantle, and defeat his network'. He went on to say, among other things:

> Then, last August, after years of painstaking work by our intelligence community, I was briefed on a possible lead to bin Laden. It was far from certain, and it took many months to run this thread to ground. I met repeatedly with my national security team as we developed more information about the possibility that we had located bin Laden hiding within a compound deep inside of Pakistan. And finally, last week, I determined that we had enough intelligence to take action, and authorized an operation to get Osama bin Laden and bring him to justice.
>
> Today, at my direction, the United States launched a targeted operation against that compound in Abbottabad, Pakistan. A small team of Americans carried out the operation with extraordinary courage and capability. No Americans were harmed. They took care to avoid civilian casualties. After a fire fight, they killed Osama bin Laden and took custody of his body...
>
> Over the years, I've repeatedly made clear that we would take action within Pakistan if we knew where bin Laden was. That is what we've done. But it's important to note that our counterterrorism cooperation with Pakistan helped lead us to bin Laden and the compound where

> he was hiding. Indeed, bin Laden had declared war against Pakistan as well, and ordered attacks against the Pakistani people.

The very next morning, Pakistani experts on the various television channels discussed the assassination of bin Laden. The majority were of the opinion that it was not possible, under any circumstances, to carry out such a mission without the cooperation of the Pakistani authorities. The day dragged on but neither the prime minister nor the president addressed the nation, to take it into confidence about the official standpoint. After some time, however, the Pakistan Foreign Office made a brief statement that the operation had been conducted exclusively by the Americans, suggesting that Pakistan had played no part in it (*Dunya News,* 2 May 2011; *Dawn,* 3 May 2011).

The idea that the Americans stood no chance of bringing their men into Pakistan in helicopters without Pakistani involvement was dispelled some time later in the day. A live transmission of a press conference given by Deputy National Security Advisor on Security to the White House John Brennan provided other details about the operation. He categorically denied that the Pakistanis had been informed about the covert operation. It was an exclusive US commando raid on the compound in which bin Laden was suspected of hiding. The US Special Forces men – American Navy Seals – had flown in from Afghanistan in two helicopters. They were joined by two more US aircraft already stationed in Pakistan. He stated that leads to bin Laden's hideout were found when US analysts and agents located one of the Al-Qaeda leader's couriers in Abbottabad.

The courier had previously been a detainee at the Guantanamo detention facility. Thereafter, sustained surveillance of his movements – on the basis that bin Laden needed to communicate with his comrades elsewhere – led to cumulative circumstantial evidence that bin Laden was, in all probability, hiding inside the compound. Brennan said that it was inconceivable that bin Laden did not have a support system in the country, and suggested that he had been living there for the last five or six years. He, however, did not elaborate on whether, by that, he meant support from the government or, more specifically, the military and ISI. Besides bin Laden, three other men and a woman were killed, including the courier and his brother, a son of bin Laden, and one of his wives.

Bin Laden had apparently been living in the building with two of his wives and six of his children. There were other children there too. Brennan said that the whole operation took just forty minutes and that it was followed, minute-by-minute, by Obama and his close advisers who were privy to the operation. The US aircraft had left Pakistani air space before the Pakistanis could react. Although one helicopter was lost, as its rotors had struck the wall of the compound, Brennan asserted that no US troops were lost and everybody returned to base safely. Moreover, they collected whatever documents were available on the premises.

Brennan's explanation was a corrective of the initial statement by Obama in which he had suggested cooperation with Pakistan in the search for bin Laden. Brennan informed the audience that bin Laden's body was flown out to Afghanistan, and then to a US ship in the Arabian Sea, where, after Islamic rites, he was consigned to the sea (BBC live news broadcast (YouTube, 2 May 2011).

In Pakistan, sinister conspiracy theories were pedalled in talk-shows. The fact that the Americans had not shown bin Laden's dead body was interpreted as proof that someone else had been killed or that nothing had happened and the whole drama was a charade. So-called security experts, such as Zaid Hamid, Orriya Maqbool Jan, and Piracha, were of the opinion that the façade had been masterminded to enable Obama to win the elections in 2011. As expected, they vehemently asserted that the real plot against Pakistan was only just beginning to unfold – the penultimate objective was to capture Pakistan's nuclear assets; the ultimate goal was to break up Pakistan. Party to the grand conspiracy against Pakistan were not just the Americans and their NATO minions, but also India's R&AW and Israel's Mossad. Former Ambassador Zafar Hilaly, however, described the denial of Osama's death as delusional (*Dunya News*, 3 May 2011).

The Indian reaction was expectedly harsh against Pakistan. The official position was put forth by the Home Ministry: 'This fact [bin Laden's presence in Pakistan] underlines our concern that terrorists belonging to different organizations find sanctuary in Pakistan. We believe that the perpetrators of the Mumbai terror attack, including the controllers and handlers of the terrorists who actually carried out the attack, continue to be sheltered in Pakistan' (Times of India 2 May 2011).

CIA Director Leon Panetta presented further clarification of why Pakistan had not been taken into confidence before the raid on Osama bin Laden's compound was carried out. He stated candidly that they feared that their Pakistani counterparts might alert the Al-Qaeda chief. Some further details of the plan were revealed by him. He stated that the options presented to President Barack Obama included bombing the compound with B-2 bombers or firing a 'direct shot' with cruise missiles. Air strikes were ruled out because of the risk of a high degree of collateral damage in the form of civilian casualties. He further said that there was no foolproof evidence, such as satellite photographs of bin Laden, available to the Obama team that had masterminded the raid (*The News International,* 3 May 2011).

The ISI, on the other hand, came up with the explanation that the largish house where bin Laden had been staying was checked in 2003 but nothing suspicious was found. Thereafter, no further checks were carried out. However, on 3 May, the *BBC*'s correspondent, Aleem Maqbool, was seen on television talking to a young man who said that the security services checked the ID cards of people in the neighbourhood of bin Laden's hideout on a daily basis, especially in the evenings. More details surfaced when other foreign correspondents spoke to the neighbours. One said that a goat was delivered to the house in a red car every day. Also, the children who played cricket in the area, and sometimes hit their ball into the compound, were never returned the ball but were given a generous sum of money. That all this had happened without the Pakistan military knowing anything about the occupants of the building became increasingly incredible.

Former DG ISI Lieutenant General Asad Durrani, and the well-known commentator, Professor Akbar S. Ahmed, were interviewed by the *BBC*. Both ruled out the possibility that the authorities would have had no knowledge about bin Laden's presence in Abbottabad. General Durrani even argued that the actual operation by the American Navy Seals must have received some ground support from Pakistan. He explained that Pakistan could not possibly own up to its participation in the operation because that could inflame public opinion in Pakistan. Pretending that the Americans carried out the raid without any prior notice to Pakistan was more acceptable, than admission of complicity.

However, the Obama administration consistently maintained that Pakistan had not been informed about the raid at all. Widespread frustration and anger was expressed in the US media, and even by leading Democrats and Republicans, about Pakistan harbouring a terrorist. South Florida Congressman

Allen West expressed the view that the government of Pakistan may have aided and abetted Osama bin Laden's lengthy hideout from US forces. He insisted that, unless the United States got a clear explanation of what Pakistani officials knew about bin Laden's whereabouts, all aid to the country should be stopped. He went on to say that Pakistan may have actually helped bin Laden elude capture, to keep the $20 billion of aid flowing since the 9/11 attacks (*The Daily Times,* 5 May 2011). Further information provided by the Americans indicated that bin Laden did not put up a resistance. That set in motion a discussion on whether killing him constituted an unlawful act under international law. The US attorney-general asserted that, by ordering a terrorist attack on the United States, bin Laden had committed an act of war and, therefore, was a legitimate target for elimination.

Further twists to the incident occurred: the Americans decided not to show bin Laden's body on television, on the grounds that it had been disfigured because of the gunshots; they claimed that, after he had been given a proper Islamic funeral, his body had been consigned to the sea – instead of buried on land – to prevent his admirers making his burial site a place of pilgrimage (*The Daily Times,* 3 May 2011). Not surprisingly, the rumour mills in Pakistan began to churn out conspiracy theories, including: bin Laden had died a long time ago and the United States had carried out the charade as a face-saving measure to hide the fact that it had been roundly defeated in Afghanistan and Pakistan; bin Laden had been taken captive and was alive. Later, the Americans released video clips showing him in his hideout – in which he looked much older than in his previous photographs. Some time later, Al-Qaeda confirmed that bin Laden had indeed been killed in the raid carried out by the US Navy Seals on Abbottabad. Hard-core Islamists held funeral prayers all over Pakistan, followed by protest marches and slogans threatening to avenge his assassination (*Dawn,* 7 May 2011).

Meanwhile, in a belated response to the raid on bin Laden's hideout in Abbottabad, the Pakistan Foreign Office expressed displeasure that Pakistani sovereignty had been breached and that such acts did not constitute acceptable behaviour. Prime Minister Gilani, on a visit to France, took the position that Pakistan's failure to know about bin Laden's whereabouts was a failure of the international community as well – to gather reliable intelligence (*The Daily Times,* 5 May 2011).

On the other hand, one can argue that the Pakistan government had facilitated the search for bin Laden and other terrorists by issuing hundreds of visas to CIA agents and other elements. Those people moved around more or less freely and conducted their covert activities in total secrecy. This was amply illustrated by the Raymond Davis incident that took place earlier in the year. What is more likely is that Zardari and Gilani, and other ministers in the federal government including Interior Minister Malik, had been kept in the dark. It is to be remembered that protecting bin Laden began long before the PPP government came to power.

Later, the Pakistani military and ISI chiefs appeared before Pakistan's National Assembly where they were quizzed about how the Americans could violate Pakistani sovereignty with such ease. The National Assembly passed a resolution condemning the US raid on Abbottabad as a violation of Pakistani territory. It was regretted that while 30,000 Pakistan citizens – men, women, and children – and more than 5000 military personnel have lost their lives since Pakistan joined the war on terror, those unique sacrifices were ignored by the world (*The News International*, 14 May 2011). Just two days later, the US launched two missile strikes killing seven people in North Waziristan. Meanwhile, General Pasha warned India not to contemplate emulating the US' raid on Abbottabad because it would be met with retaliation in equal measure (*The Hindustan Times* 15 May 2011). In a surprising deviation from the standard response of the military and security forces, of directing their wrath against India, the opposition leader, Nawaz Sharif, urged Pakistanis not to treat India as their 'biggest enemy'. He called for a reappraisal of relations with India 'if we want to go forward and progress' and stated that if Pakistan did that, the government could reduce its expenditure by fifty percent (*Dawn*, 17 May 2011).

More surprises were in store. A top Pakistani air force commander told the Pakistani media that the Shamsi airfield was under the control of the United Arab Emirates, and was used by Arabs coming to Pakistan for falconry – this I first learnt from Christine Fair in July 2009. That, however, did not detract from the fact that the Americans had been using it since 2001, and had used it on multiple occasions to launch drone attacks (*Dawn*, 19 May 2011). The *Dawn* of 20 May published some very embarrassing US cables, that it acquired exclusively from WikiLeaks, which suggested that General Kayani had, contrary to his public posture, been urging the Americans for more drone attacks. Such requests could be traced as far back as 2008.

The next day, more cables were revealed which indicated that the US had obtained considerable latitude in carrying out undercover activities in Pakistan. Ambassador Patterson dated such concessions from early 2009. They included 'intelligence fusion centres' comprising Pakistani and American functionaries in different parts of Pakistan, and joint operations launched by those fusion centres (*Dawn,* 21 May 2011). The Pakistan Army, forthwith, refuted such allegations as groundless. This was followed by some US military trainers being asked to leave Pakistan.

Taliban Retaliation

After the killing of Osama bin Laden, fears that revenge attacks would follow were proven correct as a number of vicious assaults took place in the FATA region and elsewhere, but the full impact of such a fury was felt on Sunday 22 May when terrorists attacked a Pakistan naval base, PNS *Mehran*. They destroyed two naval surveillance aircraft, ten security personnel were killed, including one naval officer, three navy commandos, three naval firemen, a sailor, and two paramilitary soldiers; fifteen others were wounded. At the time, US 'contractors' and some Chinese engineers were also present at the site (*Dawn,* 23 May 2011). The TTP claimed responsibility for the attack and threatened more.

The attack on the naval base sent shivers down the spines of defence analysts in the West and India, as questions were raised about whether Pakistan's nuclear arsenal was in safe hands. The *BBC*'s defence and diplomatic correspondent, Jonathan Marcus, reported that it was suspected that Pakistan possessed seventy to eighty nuclear bombs which, if they were to fall into the hands of the Taliban, could spell unimaginable disaster (Marcus, 23 May 2011). Hillary Clinton told the Pakistanis that anti-Americanism and conspiracy theories would not help them, and she urged greater cooperation as it was in the interest of both countries (*Dawn,* 27 May 2011). The month of May ended with the shocking news that the body of a gifted forty-year old Pakistani journalist, Saleem Shahzad, was found near Islamabad. He had been abducted some days earlier and his body bore marks of torture. It was later revealed that Shahzad had found evidence that an Al-Qaeda cell in the Pakistan Navy had facilitated the attack on the Mehran naval base. Apparently, the ISI had issued him a warning for one of his reports that Pakistan had released Mullah Baradar, an associate of Taliban leader Mullah Omar (Syed, 3 June 2011). Later, the authorities arrested a serving brigadier and three majors for allegedly having links with the Hizbul Tahrir – an organization banned in Pakistan (*BBC News*, 23 June 2011).

Obama Announces Troop Withdrawal from Afghanistan

Although the United States had announced a phased withdrawal of troops from Afghanistan – to begin in July 2011 and be completed by the end of 2014 – a statement on how it would begin had not been made. In the aftermath of the successful raid on the compound in Abbottabad where Osama bin Laden had been hiding, and with the death of the most hated man in America, President Obama found the opportunity to make known his plans for the withdrawal. On 23 May, he addressed the American people and told them that, beginning in July, 10,000 US troops would return by the end of the year and 33,000 by the next summer. Afghan security forces would take over, and the US mission in Afghanistan would change from a combat one to a support one. The transition would be completed by 2014, when the Afghans would be responsible for their own security. Obama said that the United States was ready to carry out more assaults against any safe havens harbouring terrorists, and added that no other country was more endangered by violent extremists than Pakistan (*The Daily Times,* 24 June 2011).

Pressure on Pakistan Continued

Amid all this, standard practices continued: the United States warning Pakistan to participate seriously and sincerely in the war against terror; Pakistan complaining against such callous and apathetic behaviour of the Americans; then some US top official stating that Pakistan was indispensible to the war on terror and had rendered meritorious services and suffered great loss of life as a result. The ISI arrested five Pakistani informants who had allegedly been feeding information to the CIA before the raid that killed bin Laden. One of the detainees was reported to be a Pakistani army major whom officials said copied licence plates of cars visiting bin Laden's hideout in Abbottabad. The Pakistan Army, however, denied that a major was among those arrested (*The Daily Times,* 16 June 2011). Relations further deteriorated when Pakistan decided to send some military trainers back to the US, while a top US official alleged that the ISI was involved in the murder of Saleem Shahzad.

Nevertheless, as paymaster, the Americans expected Pakistan to deliver on Al-Qaeda. Thus, US Secretary of Defence Leon Panetta told the Pakistanis that they must go after bin Laden's successor, Al Zawahiri (*The Daily Times,* 10 July 2011). The next day, the Obama administration announced that one-third of the annual $2 billion military aid – $800 million – was being withheld because of differences that had arisen between the two governments over how to conduct the war on terror. Pakistan retorted by saying that it had previously requested the United States to direct money to non-military projects; later, an official statement was issued stating that it did need American money to fight terrorism. Some experts immediately warned that Pakistan may move closer to the Chinese – something the Americans have always been concerned about as they need to maintain consistent pressure on Pakistan to realise their goals beyond the extermination of Osama bin Laden.

Despite the apparently deteriorating relations, US drones fired a barrage of missiles over several days killing forty-eight people in North and South Waziristan (*The Daily Times,* 13 July 2011). Thus, there was no let-up in the American resolve to go after the terrorists they suspected of carrying out raids on their troops in Afghanistan. However, when the Pakistan Supreme Court released the LeJ's Malik Ishaq – accused of masterminding the attack on the Sri Lankan cricket team in March 2009 – on bail, the action once again underlined the argument that people accused of serious terrorist crimes are able to receive a sympathetic treatment in the country. The credibility of the Pakistani political and legal systems, therefore, remains a matter of concern to the international community (*The Daily Times* 15 July 2011).

On 7 August 2011, R.J. Hillhouse, a well-connected American who has specialized on the 'outsourcing of the war on terror' – i.e. hiring specialized firms such as Blackwater to carry out some tasks related to combating terrorism – published a story on her blog entitled 'Bin Laden turned in by Informant – Courier was Cover Story'. In it, she has claimed that the United States obtained the vital information about bin Laden from a Pakistani intelligence officer who came forward to collect the $25 million prize as well as the right to settle in the United States with his family. Allegedly, that officer told the Americans that Saudi Arabia had been paying the Pakistanis to shelter and keep Osama bin Laden under house arrest in Abbottabad (*The Spy who Billed Me*, 7 August 2011).

On 8 August 2011, *The New Yorker* published a detailed report by Nicholas Schimdle, 'Getting bin Laden: What happened that night in Abbottabad?' in which he argued that Pakistan's air defences and radars were all fixed eastwards towards India and, therefore, were disadvantaged in picking up any signals from the US helicopters entering Pakistani airspace from Afghanistan. According to Schimdle, bin Laden was unarmed; the decision had already been taken that he should be killed.

Nawaz Sharif's Address at SAFMA Conference

On 13 August 2011, Nawaz Sharif, made a complete break with orthodox Pakistani foreign policy thinking when, while speaking to Indian journalists and intellectuals who were in Lahore to attend a conference arranged by the South Asian Media Association (SAFMA), he said that the people of Pakistan and India were the same in all essential senses – culture, food, habits, sensibilities, and aesthetics. He deplored the fact that his efforts, as prime minister, to improve relations with India were subverted by Pervez Musharraf who had started the Kargil misadventure. He praised the Indian leaders, especially Atal Bihari Vajpayee, for sincerely wanting good relations with Pakistan. He said that Pakistan and India would gain enormously through trade and commerce, and the solution to the Kashmir problem would be found in an overall improvement of relations between the two nations. He winded up his speech by pointing out that the concept of God, given in the Quran, was that He was the blesser of all human beings and not just Muslims. Therefore, it was the duty of Pakistan to wish its immediate neighbour, India, the best. He believed that people on the other side also nurtured similar sentiments (SAFMA, Youtube 13 August 2011).

The Scourge of Terrorism

Pakistan's involvement in the so-called 'war on terror' has been devastating in terms of loss of life, destruction of property worth billions of dollars, and the proliferation of terrorism within Pakistan. Pakistan has been the major victim of extremism and terrorism. This has not been fully realised and appreciated by the foreign powers that focus on how it affects their interests. That is understandable, but it is important to put, into perspective, the great harm such activities have done to the Pakistanis. According to the Islamabad-based Pakistan Institute for Peace Studies (PIPS), between 2 May and 22 July 2011 alone, in the aftermath of Osama bin Laden's death, 102 terrorist attacks have taken place in Pakistan. As a result, 489 people have been killed and 698 injured. Terrorism has been afflicting Pakistan since the late 1980s, originally as sectarian clashes, raids, and attacks on non-Muslims but, after 9/11, government personnel and installations began to be targeted as well. Such activities continued to grow until they gained momentum in 2005, and spiralled from 2007 onwards, as disgruntled Islamists rallied around the TTP.

Several organisations and 'sleeping cells' came into being over time, thus generating the nightmare of decentralised terrorism which is almost impossible for a state, even one with garrison capabilities, to control. Such activities have been accompanied by reckless parallel propaganda, by not only militant organisations (*Understanding Militants' Media in Pakistan*, 2010), but also ostensibly by parliamentary parties such as the Jamaat-e-Islami which maintains a most disciplined publication section and churns out views and opinions that maintain an environment of intolerance and anti-Western and anti-Indian nationalism (Grare, 2001). Ultra-nationalist talk-show charlatans reproduce, on a daily basis, a culture of fear and hatred. It is not surprising that the impact of such inputs is inevitably nihilistic.

The PIPS Security Report for 2006 (2007: 2), mentions that as many as 657 terrorist attacks, including sectarian attacks and clashes, took place in 2006. As a result, 907 persons lost their lives and 1543 were wounded. The economic cost of such destruction ran into billions of rupees. In 2007, there were 1442 terrorist assaults altogether. The Taliban, Pakistani jihadists, sectarian groups, and Baloch nationalist insurgents were involved in them. There were 3448 fatalities and 5353 injuries – a sharp increase of 127 percent and 491.7 percent, perspectively as compared to 2006 and 2005. This included the assassination of Benazir Bhutto (PIPS Security Report for 2007, 2008: 2). During 2008, a total of 2148 terrorist, insurgent, and sectarian attacks took place, killing 2267 persons and injuring 4558. There was an astronomical increase, of 746 percent, in terrorist attacks since 2005 (PIPS Security Report for 2008, 2009: 4). Such crimes against human beings peaked in 2009 when a total of 2586 terrorist attacks took place that claimed the lives of 3021 people and 7334 were wounded. The highest number of attacks took place in NWFP (1137), followed by Balochistan (792) and FATA (559). As many as forty-six took place in Punjab, thirty in Sindh, twelve in Islamabad, and five each in the Pakistan-administered Kashmir and Gilgit-Baltistan (PIPS Security Report for 2009, 2010: 3). During 2010, there was an 11 percent decrease in terrorist attacks – the total for such attacks was 2113, including insurgent and sectarian-related attacks. 2913 persons were killed, while 5824 sustained injuries. The highest number of attacks took place in Balochistan (737), followed by FATA (720), Khyber-Pakhtunkhwa (459), Sindh (111), Punjab (62), Gilgit-Baltistan (13), Islamabad (6), and Pakistani Azad Kashmir (5) (PIPS Security Report for 2010, 2011: 2). At the beginning of 2011, Punjab Governor Salman Taseer and Federal Minister for Minorities Shahbaz Bhatti were mercilessly gunned down in Islamabad. How significant the decline in terrorist attacks in 2010 can, therefore, be discussed. The trend that seems to have emerged is that jihadists willing to spill blood have infiltrated the most sensitive areas of state security. 237 terrorist attacks have taken place altogether until 22 July 2011, claiming 613 lives and injuring 541. From 2007, when such activities escalated, till 22 July 2011, there have been 11,726 fatalities and 23,037 injuries (Pakistan Institute for Peace Studies, 2011).

In the Aftermath of Osama bin Laden's Liquidation

In the weeks and months after Operation Geronimo had resulted in the death of bin Laden, relations between Pakistan and US continued to plummet to levels never reached hitherto. US pressure on Pakistan – to act decisively against the Haqqani network, Mullah Omar, and other such individuals – now became brazenly emphatic without any pretence at diplomatic restraint. In this connection, some of the statements by top US officials are noteworthy. For example, on 22 September, outgoing US Chairman of Joint Chiefs of Staff Admiral Mike Mullen, asserted in a US Senate hearing that the Haqqani network in Pakistan's North Waziristan was a 'veritable arm of the ISI'. This statement was made in the wake of an assault on the US embassy in Kabul a week earlier. Mullen went on to say that Pakistan was exporting violent extremism to Afghanistan, and warned of US action to protect American troops. He remarked: 'If they keep killing our troops that would not be something we would just sit idly by and watch'. Defence Secretary Leon Panetta, who was present at the hearing, also expressed frustration and reiterated that the United States would safeguard its troops (*Dawn*, 22 September 2011).

The next day, White House spokesman Jay Carney said: 'It is critical that the government of Pakistan breaks any links they have and take strong and immediate action against this [Haqqani] network' (ibid., 24 September 2011). This strong-worded statement was made while Pakistani Foreign Minister Hina Rabbani Khar was in New York. She expressed her feelings in the following words: 'Anything which is said about an ally, about a partner, publicly to recriminate, to humiliate, is not acceptable' (*The Straits Times*, 24 September 2011). Pakistan's top soldier, General Kayani, termed Mullen's remarks as 'very unfortunate and not based on facts'. He went on to say that such remarks did not help create a climate for a 'constructive and meaningful engagement for a stable and peaceful Afghanistan, an objective to which Pakistan is fully committed' (*The Daily Times*, 24 September 2011). It was followed by a statement by a Pakistani official that Pakistan had no plans to immediately go after the Haqqani Group (*Dawn*, 26 September 2011).

Apparently, such a standpoint indicated that Pakistan was willing to defy the US when it came to its vital interest of maintaining the Haqqani group as an asset in Afghan politics – to contain Indian influence and clout in Kabul. A couple of days later, the United States modified its stance by saying that the White House did not categorically endorse Admiral Mullen's claims. White House spokesman Jay Carney put the concerns of his government in the following words: 'It is not the language I would use. I think the fact that there are links that exist between the Pakistan government and the Haqqani network – the nature of those can be assessed and is complicated. But there is no question that they have safe havens in Pakistan' (ibid., 29 September 2011).

Such toning down did not mean that the US had altered its basic stance – that a close relationship existed between Pakistan and the Haqqani group. On 4 October, Afghanistan and India announced their agreement on a 'strategic partnership'. With regard to 'political and security cooperation', they explicitly stated that such a partnership included cooperation on security, including the combating of terrorism, and India training and capacity-building the Afghan National Forces (*Dawn*, 5 October 2011). Not surprisingly, concerns were expressed in Pakistan over it.

The Memogate Scandal

On 10 October, an American businessman of Pakistani-descent, Mansoor Ijaz, in an op-ed published in *The Financial Times*, he, accused Pakistan's ambassador to the US, Husain Haqqani, of approaching him to pass a secret memo on to Admiral Mullen, in which Haqqani purportedly urged the US to intervene and help reform Pakistan's military and intelligence agencies. The 'disclosure' became a hot topic in the Pakistani media and Mansoor Ijaz, on 17 November, reiterated his allegations. This resulted in General Kayani calling upon President Zardari; their photograph, released to the Pakistan media, suggested that the army had taken strong notice of it. Haqqani denied any wrong-doing but was summoned forthwith to Islamabad. The matter ended with him submitting his resignation.

In the meanwhile, the *BBC* aired a documentary that purported to prove that the ISI and the Pakistan military were complicit to a long-standing conspiracy to support the Afghan Taliban in carrying out terrorist attacks in Afghanistan. Pakistan's response, expectedly, was a fierce denial of any such linkage or backing of terrorism.

However, the Memogate scandal continued to hold centre-stage in the Pakistani media. Mansoor Ijaz claimed that he had met the ISI head, General Pasha, in London – at the latter's request – on 22 October and apprised him of the contents of his article, published in *The Financial Times*, in which he had presented his evidence against Haqqani. Pasha later confirmed that he had met him, and that he was satisfied with what Mansoor had told him (*The News* 16 December 2011). Apparently, the memo had been initiated because Zardari wanted the US to help prevent a coup that the military had, allegedly, been planning against the civilian government for quite some time (*The Washington Times* 21 December 2011). The British daily, *The Independent*, quoted Mansoor Ijaz as saying that soon after the death of Osama bin Laden, the ISI head, General Pasha, toured several Arab countries – most notably Saudi Arabia – seeking their support for the overthrow of the Zardari–Gilani government! (*The Independent,* 14 December 2011). As expected, the ISPR dismissed the allegation as baseless and mischievous propaganda (*Dawn,* 22 December 2011).

US–Pakistan Relations and Miscellaneous

Amid such accusations and denials, Pakistan-US relations turned from bad to worse when, on 26 November, NATO aircraft from Afghanistan opened fire on Pakistani outposts, killing twenty-four soldiers and injuring many more (*The Daily Times*, 27 November 2011). It created an uproar in Pakistan. An immediate halt was imposed on the movement of NATO supplies through Pakistan; hundreds of tonnes of supplies were stopped on their way to Afghanistan. Some fifty percent of NATO supplies were normally routed through Pakistan. Moreover, the Americans were ordered to vacate the Shamsi base from where they had been flying their drones – in spite of Pakistan's official denials hitherto – within fifteen days, i.e. by 11 December. Apologies by the US and NATO, and pledges to order an immediate inquiry, failed to placate the Pakistanis. China and Russia joined in by condemning the violation of Pakistani sovereignty (*The Daily Times* 29 November 2011). Moreover, the fierce response culminated in Pakistan deciding to boycott the Second Bonn Conference, scheduled to begin on 5 December 2011. Germany had earlier played host to a conference in 2001, after the 9/11 terrorist attacks.

The Second Bonn Conference was a follow-up to work out an understanding between the US, NATO, and the regional actors, including Russia, on maintaining peace and stability in Afghanistan after the US–NATO withdrawal in 2014 (Second International Bonn Conference, 2011). Pakistan was urged to reconsider its decision by US Secretary of State Clinton and German Chancellor Angela Merkel who described Pakistan's decision not to participate in the Bonn Conference as unfortunate. This time round, however, the Pakistani power elite remained firm and steadfast and did not yield to such supplications (*Dawn*, 30 November 2011). The Pakistani decision opened the way for speculation about Pakistan's intentions with regard to Afghanistan. Later, Pakistan also declined a NATO invitation to participate in a joint inquiry on the 26 November incident. It is worth noting that an agreement existed between the US and Afghan governments that, even after the formal withdrawal in 2014, a sizeable number of US troops would remain in Afghanistan until such time that the Afghans had established stable civilian rule and an effective military and security regime. The future direction of Afghan politics, therefore, remains unclear.

On the other hand, some improvement in Pakistan–India relations was noted after Hina Rabbani Khar visited India in July, where she was warmly received. She, and her Indian counterpart, S.M. Krishna, expressed the hope that relations between the two countries would improve significantly. She also called on Manmohan Singh – to convey her government's greetings as well as a message of goodwill. Once again, brisk diplomatic activities began between the two estranged nations. In October, Khar announced that Pakistan had, in principle, agreed to grant Most Favoured Nation (MFN) status to India (*Dawn,* 12 October 2011) – something the latter had granted to Pakistan years earlier. She issued a statement that the Pakistan military was on board with regard to the granting of the MFN status to India (*The Nation,* 6 November 2011). However, Prime Minister Gilani later issued a statement that while MFN status was being considered for India, a decision had not been taken as yet (*The Hindu* 17 November 2011). It seems that final clearance on MFN status for India has been put on hold for the time being.

On the domestic front, temperatures again began to rise as the rift between the ruling PPP government and the main opposition, PML-N, grew and they locked horns. The latter demanded that Zardari and Gilani should resign or get ready to face the public's wrath (*Dawn,* 29 October 2011). Former cricketer Imran Khan's Pakistan Tehrik-e-Insaf, which for years had failed to win mass appeal surprisingly pulled a huge crowd at a public rally in Lahore on 30 October 2011. In his address to the hundreds of thousands of people who had come to listen to him, Khan demanded an end to corruption and tax evasion and warned the politicians that he would start a countrywide civil disobedience movement if they did not publicly declare their assets (*The Daily Times* 31 October 2011). I was in Lahore during 10–17 November and witnessed the typical trend of prominent politicians, one after the other, decamping from the mainstream parties to join the PTI.

Zardari and Haqqani had Prior Knowledge about 2 May US Raid on Abbottabad On 3 December, Mansoor Ijaz – the man involved in the so-called 'Memogate' scandal – made the sensational claim, in an article published in the *Newsweek* magazine, that not only had Husain Haqqani had prior knowledge about the 2 May US attack on Osama bin Laden's Abbottabad hideout, but so had President Zardari (*Dawn,* 3 December 2011).

Haqqani immediately denied such an allegation and retorted:

> In the strongest terms possible, I categorically reject as reckless, baseless and false the allegations levied against me by Mr Mansoor Ijaz about

> prior knowledge of US plans for a raid in Abbottabad in violation of Pakistani sovereignty to eliminate Osama bin Laden as well as his earlier charges about my role in a memo he wrote and sent to the US Chairman Joint Chiefs." (*Dawn* 3 December 2011).

Haqqani threatened to initiate legal action against the magazine unless the article, written by Mansoor Ijaz, was retracted. On the other hand, Nawaz Sharif filed a petition in the Supreme Court requesting a probe of the Memogate scandal. It was admitted after some resistance from the Registrar of the Supreme Court. It is interesting to note that when the Court ordered the Ministry of Defence to submit a written reply in the issue of the memo scandal case, the Ministry of Defence, in its written reply, stated that it has no control over the operations of the Army/ISI (*The News*, 21 December 201) On the other hand, in a rejoinder submitted to the Supreme Court over the Memogate affair, General Kayani opined that the memo was a reality and was meant to demoralise the military (*The Daily Times*, 22 December 2011).

Prime Minister Gilani's Outburst Against the Military

The Ministry of Defence's statement, that it had no control over the activities of the military and ISI, elicited a most unusual tirade against the army by the prime minister. Although, only a few days earlier, he had said that there was no conflict between the government and the military, Prime Minister Gilani deplored the fact that conspirators were plotting to bring down his government. Without naming the military directly, he left no doubt that he considered the military to be acting like the state within the state. In his scathing observations, he asserted that while the government had stood by the security services over the storm of American pressure in regards to the 2008 attacks on Mumbai, Osama bin Laden's killing in May, and the 26 November 2011 NATO attack, yet the military–ISI nexus had been acting as the state within the state. In his other scathing remarks he said, among other things:

> If they say that they are not under the ministry of defence, then we should get out of this slavery, then this parliament has no importance, this system has no importance, then you are not sovereign.... They are being paid from the State Exchequer, from your revenue and from your taxes...if somebody thinks that they are not under the government, they

> are mistaken. They are under the government and they shall remain under the government, because we are the elected representatives of the people of Pakistan.... In the worst circumstances we doubled their salaries. They have to be accountable to parliament.... We are being asked by the judicial commission [examining the 2 May US raid that killed bin Laden raid and how the al Qaeda leader lived in Pakistan undetected] about issuance of visas [to Americans].... But I want to ask how was [bin Laden] living here for the past six years? On what type of visa was he living here? Why was security not taken care of, if he entered in [sic] Pakistan without a visa? (*Dawn* 22 December 2011).

General Kayani responded forthwith that the military was not planning to overthrow the government and democracy would not be derailed. It was followed by Gilani saying that he had full trust in Kayani and the head of the ISI, General Pasha, and that the government would complete its term. Chief Justice Iftikhar Chaudhry issued a statement that, unlike in the past when military takeovers had been validated under the so-called Doctrine of Necessity, this time there would be no such support forthcoming from the highest court of the country (*Dawn,* 24 December 2011). 2011 ended with Gilani announcing that there would be no early general election and that relations between Zardari and Kayani were good (*Daily Times* 31 December 2011).

US–Pak relations at the End of 2011

Meanwhile, the Americans tightened the screws on Pakistan – the US Congress voted to freeze $700 million in aid until Pakistan gave convincing assurances that it was serious about fighting against terrorism. Pakistan expressed regret over such a decision (*Daily Times* 13 December 2011). Later, the US Congress did vote to put a freeze on the aid (*The News* 17 December 2011); the bill was sent to the US president for further action according to procedure. The State Department issued a statement that the Congress had only passed a bill to withhold the $700 million, and that it was not law yet. If, however, the bill did become law, then the government would look into how it could fulfil its requirements. It was suggested that the civilian aid would not be cut.

Pakistani officials announced that US and NATO supplies via Pakistan would not be resumed immediately. Emphasis was also laid on zero tolerance for the violation of Pakistani territory and attacks on Pakistani troops. It was also reported that US troops had vacated the Shamsi air base by 11 December. On the other hand, the NATO military chief contacted General Kayani to discuss the resumption of normal relations with Pakistan. Defence Secretary Leon Panetta issued a statement that stable ties with Pakistan were critical to success in the war against terrorism in Afghanistan (*The Daily Times*, 14 December). Moreover, Pakistan was expected, in 2012, to be the third biggest recipient of aid at $ 2965 million; Israel and Afghanistan receive more (*Dawn*, 14 December 2011). Furthermore, the Pentagon made some mitigating gestures when it expressed regret over the 26 November attack on the Pakistani checkpoint that killed twenty-four Pakistani soldiers, and blamed inadequate coordination for the unfortunate incident (*Dawn*, 22 December 2011). Such conciliatory gestures, after expressions of exasperation and disgust, were the typical pattern expressing Pakistan–US relations. In other words, the basic donor-recipient relationship that has existed between the United States and Pakistan could be expected to continue.

Consequently, at the end of 2011, the situation in Pakistan and in its environs remained highly volatile and uncertain. The Pakistan military's de facto powers remained unchallenged. In fact, its premium may have risen sharply in light of the 'Memogate' scandal and the confrontational approach it has assumed towards the US after the 26 November NATO attack on Pakistani checkpoints. Whether this is a passing phase, a deception, or a genuine attempt by Pakistan to break away from US dependence remains to be seen. The hard facts are: Pakistan's economic and military dependence on the US remains considerable; the Americans have been involved in Pakistani domestic affairs since a long time; their military and intelligence connections and linkages with Pakistani counterparts are of long standing; and, above all, the US, as a superpower, still enjoys military and technological superiority – as witnessed most dramatically during the raid on bin Laden's hideout in Abbottabad. Hence, Pakistan cannot easily withdraw from its commitment to fighting terrorism. The Americans interpret this commitment as Pakistan's duty to go after the Haqqani group and other anti-US networks in the region. Suffice it to say that the hallmarks of a post-colonial garrison state remain manifest and steadfast in the Pakistani political dispensation.

18

Analysis and Conclusion

Historical Legacy

The claim that the Muslims of South Asia constituted a nation by virtue of their religious faith and were, therefore, entitled to a separate, independent state required a break-up of India. Initially, this claim was not looked upon favourably by the three main victorious powers of the Second World War, though for different reasons. While Britain was hoping to remain the paramount power in South Asia, even after its withdrawal, it believed that it had more to gain from an undivided India as a united India would be stronger both economically and militarily – and thus, in a better position to prevent the Soviet Union from gaining a foothold in the subcontinent. However, that calculation was revised in the spring of 1947, and the creation of Pakistan was deemed advantageous to their interests should India be divided. Later, once the British accepted the demand for Pakistan, they tried to limit the damage to their interests by ensuring that both India and Pakistan remained in the British Commonwealth and thus, presumably, continued to make their resources and help available to the metropolitan country. At that time, the British did not foresee that their role in world politics would diminish dramatically once they had pulled out of India.

The United States was a champion of Indian freedom and put pressure on Britain, during the war, to grant self-rule to its colony during the war, but was apathetic towards the concept of Pakistan – even till the last days before the British handed over power to the Muslim League leaders. The Muslim League's charm offensive, in marketing itself as a dependable ally against the spread of Communism, did not impress the Americans at that time. This was especially true of the Roosevelt administration which wanted to cultivate the friendship of the Soviet Union in favour of collective security, peace, and democracy. The Soviet Union, too, was sceptical about the division of India but seemed to have been convinced, just before the end of British rule, that it was the legitimate demand of the oppressed Muslim minority – liberation from the domination of Hindu moneylenders and capitalists. It, therefore, came around to the idea of Pakistan but remained wary about the consequences of a divided subcontinent.

The most critical aspect of the division of India was the question of the Indian Army. For the British, it was a matter of the utmost strategic importance. They were hoping to retain control over South Asia, even after the transfer of power to the Indians, and were convinced that the Indian Army was pivotal to the maintenance of that control and to ward off any invasion by Soviet Russia. Therefore, they favoured a united army – even if India was partitioned. However, the Muslim League insisted that it would only accept power in Pakistan if a separate army, navy, and air force were created through the division of the joint Indian armed forces. At that stage, the British establishment made another assessment: that Pakistan would be more easily amenable to their quest for bases and other facilities to safeguard their interests in the Persian Gulf and against Communism.

The 3 June 1947 Partition Plan formalised the division of India as well as of the Indian Army, the Royal Indian Navy, and the Royal Indian Air Force. The process, set in motion to bring about the division of the armed forces and their assets, was not an easy affair as both Congress and the Muslim League raised objections on some matters. That the Congress and Sikh leader, Baldev Singh, were not forthcoming in giving Pakistan its due share became apparent even before the actual division of assets was completed. On the other hand, contrary to popular perception in Pakistan, evidence suggests that, until 1 August 1947, Mountbatten – who remained governor-general of undivided India till 14 August – wanted to be fair in distributing the assets of the Indian armed forces to Pakistan. Later, as governor-general of only India, he represented Indian interests.

The Dialectics of Geography

Pakistan, as it appeared on the world map, possessed almost unique geographical features. Its two wings were separated by some 1000 miles. In between, lay a bigger and more powerful and resourceful neighbour. Such difficulties were compounded by the close proximity of its major urban centres to the Indian border, coupled with an unfriendly neighbour – Afghanistan – on its western border. Pakistan was, therefore, a national security nightmare long before the United States propounded the national security doctrine to prepare for the Cold War. On the other hand, Pakistan could market its sui generis geostrategic location to convince the Americans that it could be useful in the containment of communism, not only in South Asia but also in the Middle East and Southeast Asia. Contrary to popular perception, the idea of wooing the Americans originated with the founder of Pakistan, and not with the military, though it is possible he was advised on this matter by military experts. Those experts could have been both British and Pakistani. In any event, the Pakistani power elite relentlessly lobbied the Pentagon and State Department for years about their state's potential as a frontline state against communism, and succeeded in obtaining both economic and military aid.

The Threat from India

Pakistan's defence and security doctrines and foreign policy, from the very outset, acquired India-specific, India-driven, and Kashmir-focused properties. Such core issues have remained beyond the purview of Pakistani public opinion. This is not to deny that the nascent Pakistan was beset with a veritable struggle for survival. Some actions of the erstwhile Indian leadership suggested that they expected Pakistan to fail and return to the Indian union. The Pakistani list of grievances and apprehensions is long: the Kashmir dispute; threatening large-scale military exercises by the Indian armed forces along the Pakistani borders in the 1950s and again thereafter; military intervention in East Pakistan in 1971 resulting in the break-up of Pakistan; India's nuclear test in 1974; and the Brasstacks exercises in the late 1980s. The Indians, surely, have their own catalogue of grievances but that is beside the point. It is the Pakistani perception that is the subject of this study.

However, belief in Indian intentions to not allow Pakistan to survive needs to be put into perspective – against the puzzling fact that Pakistan initiated four of the five armed conflicts, including three wars, with India. Since 1

January 1949, when a UN Security Council-brokered ceasefire came into operation, Pakistan has roughly one-third of Kashmir in its possession while the rest is with India. The fear that the Maharaja was secretly contemplating acceding to India, as asserted by Major General Shahid Hamid, has not been established conclusively. It is correct, however, that if that were to happen, the Indian border would come dangerously close to the GHQ of the Pakistan Army. Nevertheless, in the last sixty-six years, the only dramatic change that has taken place is that the 1949 ceasefire line has been converted into the LoC – in 1972 as part of the Simla Agreement.

The second military showdown was at the Rann of Kutch in the spring of 1965. Apparently, the Pakistanis performed well but deployed Patton tanks and other advanced US weapons in contravention of the agreement with the United States. This created a false sense of superiority amongst the Pakistani military and the hawks in the Foreign Office. Their complacency goaded them into another bid to annexe Kashmir, by sending infiltrators in under the garb of freedom fighters or Mujahideen. This time round, the Indians did not hesitate to escalate the conflict by crossing the international border at Lahore. The full-fledged war that broke out on 6 September 1965 lasted for seventeen days. Field Marshal Ayub Khan and his more hawkish foreign minister, Z.A. Bhutto, were shocked into realising that the Indians were putting up tough resistance and, in some theatres, out-manoeuvring the Pakistanis. The attrition cost became unbearable within days. Yet, the propaganda machinery – masterminded by Information Secretary Altaf Gauhar – perpetuated the myth of superior Pakistani fighters and glorious victories on land, in the air, and at sea. One myth persisted: that Akhtar Malik was about to capture Akhnur and so block any Indian advance towards Kashmir but was let down by his superiors who ordered a change of command. The crucial date of 4 September is mentioned as the time when the Pakistani initiative was frittered away because of a suspension of activities during the change of command – which, allegedly, enabled the Indians to regroup and re-organise, and thus prevent the capture of Akhnur. In this study, different points of view have been presented on this controversial incident. The significance of the one-day delay, as a result of the change of command, cannot be denied. However it is doubtful if it was enough to change the course of history. Suffice it to say that there were many chinks in Akhtar

Malik's armour. As noted already, movement towards Akhnur was not his immediate priority. Therefore, the myth that Kashmir was somehow within the grasp of the Pakistan military must be discarded. Actually, the Indians came to the battlefield better prepared and executed their order of battle with greater coherence and cohesion.

The third war took place when the Indian Army intervened in East Pakistan in November 1971, to help the Bengalis seeking separation from Pakistan. The reason for the outbreak of the civil war was that the military was not willing to hand over power to the Awami League, even though it enjoyed a parliamentary majority. This war resulted in the break-up of Pakistan. While it has been explained away as Hindu India's incessant hostility to the existence of Pakistan, it has never been properly acknowledged that the West Pakistani power elite may have provided such an opportunity to India. The evidence is overwhelming that was the case. On the other hand, all evidence suggests that Indira Gandhi and her generals had a clear plan, which they executed efficaciously.

Z.A. Bhutto, who came to power as prime minister of the truncated Pakistan, climbed down from his previous hawkish stance vis-à-vis India. But, after India tested a nuclear device, he made the famous pledge to make Pakistanis eat grass if that was the price they would have to pay to make Pakistan's own nuclear bomb. In that sense, Indian provocations continued to inform Pakistani security fears. In the 1980s, Pakistan and India were again involved in a vain attempt to trump the other over the Siachen Glacier. That conflict originated with the Indians establishing permanent posts on the glacier. India had earlier accentuated Pakistan's sense of vulnerability by conducting the Brasstacks military exercises near the Pakistani border in the late 1980s. The May 1998 nuclear test explosions by India and Pakistan raised the stakes between them to unprecedented levels of mutually assured destruction. The Kargil mini-war was, once again, the result of infiltrators being sent – by General Musharraf and his clique of generals – to occupy posts that the Indians were in the habit of vacating during the winters. Not only did that mini-war prove to be a disaster, but it also rendered Pakistan, especially the military, a rogue entity in the eyes of the world's leaders. India was the main gainer because, thereafter, whatever goodwill Pakistan had previously enjoyed over Kashmir in international forums was severely depleted. No war has taken place between the two but they continue to play zero-sum games. However, both sides have directed huge amounts of their budgets to brace their defence capabilities.

As Barry Buzan has argued, such spending has not ensured a greater sense of security: on the contrar y, the arms race has effectively subverted development agendas and heightened insecurities – and has sustained the vested interests, on both sides, who draw economic and other benefits from such a state of confrontation. Machiavelli's thesis – that the freedom of nations is essentially dependent on the existence of powerful military forces – has been exploited thoroughly. However, instead of just realism informing military expenditure, a fair amount of manipulation of the fear of aggression has resulted in a cynical exploitation of it – to claim vast resources of national wealth by the two military establishments. In the case of Pakistan, this is all too obvious while the Indians can always point at the even bigger threat from China.

With regard to the so-called nuclear assets possessed by both sides, it is important to stress that the absence of war does not mean peace. In a perverted manner, terrorism seems to have thrived in the context of an all-out war becoming less likely. It has served as a catalyst to delusional ideas about getting away with impunity, even with major terrorist outrages such as the one carried out in Mumbai in November 2008. On the other hand, some improvements in the Pakistan-India relationship can be discerned nevertheless. Both sides have taken steps to minimise the chances of accidental nuclear war. They annually exchange information about their nuclear installations, terrorism, and other related matters for cooperation; a hotline has also been set up. The situation can hopefully begin to improve.

In between, both sides have made several peaceful gestures but nothing happened to change the essentially hostile relationship between the two states. In this regard, Musharraf's efforts to reach a settlement on the Kashmir dispute were a serious attempt to change the equation. Vajpayee and Manmohan Singh reciprocated in a similar vein. On the whole, the Indians have been less forthcoming on the Kashmir issue and hope to maintain the status quo at all costs. Some sort of non-territorial solution to the Kashmir dispute, with tangible win-win outcomes for India, Pakistan, and the Kashmiris, is imperative to close this vain contest.

Afghanistan

Afghanistan opposed Pakistan's membership of the United Nations, thus initiating a long period of mutual antipathy. The sticking point was the Durand Line which the Afghan government did not accept as the international border. In the wake of the Communist takeover of power in Kabul in April 1978, followed by the Soviet Union sending its troops in the thousands to help the communists consolidate power, an Afghan resistance evolved that resulted in bloodshed – thousands were killed, and hundreds of thousands sought refuge in Pakistan. The US–Saudi jihad against Soviet occupation was conducted through Pakistan. As a result, Pakistan gained a prominent physical presence in Afghanistan and its military commanders began to believe that strategic depth may now be possible – some sort of confederation with Afghanistan, extending westwards and into Central Asia as well. For a while, Pakistan suffered a setback as the Northern Alliance triumphed over the Pakistan-backed Pakhtun Islamists. This was a time when India gained the greater influence as an ally of the Northern Alliance.

However, after the Taliban captured power in 1996, Pakistan's clout was restored in Afghanistan and that of India marginalised. Pakistan became the main patron of the Taliban regime and, other than Saudi Arabia and the United Arab Emirates, the only state to recognise the Taliban. The Taliban let loose a reign of terror on its own people, which the Pakistani hawks and Islamists celebrated as an ideal Islamic state. However, even in such a circumstance, the Taliban did not accept the Durand Line as the international border: indicating the limits of Pakistani leverage over the Taliban. The fall of the Taliban, in November 2001, and the subsequent coming into power of Hamid Karzai put Pakistan on the back foot once again. The rest of the story is too well-known, and adequately narrated in the preceding chapters.

Alliance Building

The story of Pakistan lobbying the United States, offering to help it against the Soviet Union, predated the creation of the state itself; once it came into being, the political and military leadership of Pakistan launched a major diplomatic offensive that they pursued relentlessly. The United States remained unmoved for several years as it did not consider South Asia to be significant at that point in time, and concentrated on building an alliance to contain the Soviet Union in Europe. That perception changed gradually. Harry Truman's national security doctrine, the onslaught of McCarthyism, and the Cold War greatly facilitated Pakistan's candidature as a frontline state. In 1951, the first package of economic and military aid to Pakistan arrived. Later, Eisenhower and his secretary of state, John Foster Dulles, became enamoured by the Pakistanis' monotheistic religiosity and, in 1954 and again in 1959, signed military agreements that enabled Pakistan to acquire more arms and economic aid.

However, the halcyon days of Pakistan–US courtship were of a short duration. By the late 1950s, the Americans were clear that the Pakistanis had essentially entered into a military alliance with them to acquire weapons to assert themselves vis-à-vis India. However, since Pakistan was providing facilities to the United States for aerial surveillance over the central Asian Soviet Republics, and other such services, it was considered a useful arrangement.

In any case, US economic aid served Pakistan well and enabled it to achieve impressive industrial development based on the import-substitution strategy. This created jobs and wealth, but they were not shared equitably between East and West Pakistan. The Americans were keen that their allies follow free market principles, and serve as examples of the superiority of the capitalist system over all forms of socialism and state capitalism. Pakistan was a precursor of the type of free market economy models that lifted South Korea and Taiwan out of poverty and backwardness. That the Pakistanis, instead, decided to provoke armed confrontation with India and, as a result, invested in war rather than economic development must be blamed on the Pakistani leadership.

The Americans were alarmed when Pakistan deployed the Patton tank and other advanced US military equipment in the Rann of Kutch skirmish with India – something they did in contravention of clear American pronouncements that US arms were not to be used in a war with India. For their part, the Pakistanis seem to have first begun to realise, during the 1962 Sino–Indian border showdown, that the Americans prioritized the unity of India and would render it all help against China and other powers that may want to harm it. The increase in economic and military aid to India, which was not an ally like Pakistan, deeply exercised Ayub Khan. Yet, the

Pakistanis did not seem to have got the message. Thus, when the United States imposed an arms embargo on both India and Pakistan during the 1965 war, Z.A. Bhutto angrily protested that India was the aggressor. In any event, the Pakistan–US alliance cooled off in the aftermath of the 1965 war, but it was American warnings to India, in late 1971, that dissuaded it from an invasion of West Pakistan – something that Indira Gandhi may have wanted to do. In any case, the Pakistan–US equation warmed up once again after the Soviet Union, in 1979, sent its soldiers into Afghanistan to help the Communist regime. The Pakistan–US equation was entirely based on real-politik calculations on both sides.

With regard to the domestic sphere, it is possible that the Americans were in the loop about the military coup in 1958, but there is no evidence to suggest that they instigated it. During General Zia-ul-Haq's long dictatorship, the Americans prudently remained aloof from Pakistan's domestic politics – when the dictator brutalised the people of Pakistan through Islamization. As noted already, the American strategy of cultivating and patronizing extremist Islam, via its client state of Saudi Arabia, emerged in the 1950s and was formalized in organizational terms in 1960. Moreover, as Nelson-Pallmeyer has noted, using religion to boost dictatorships was part of the so-called national security paradigm under which the Americans turned a blind eye to the military juntas in Latin America – juntas that could indulge in massive human rights violations with impunity.

When civilian government was revived, and Benazir Bhutto and Nawaz Sharif formed governments based on democratic elections, the prestige and power of the prime minister's office had, in practice, suffered considerable diminution. Instead, the military – or rather, the army – and some powerful civil servants had acquired real power in the Pakistani political dispensation. During that period, the United States' involvement and influence in Pakistani domestic politics – as troubles-shooter and broker – became quite prominent. Needless to say, there were limits to its influence in the domestic sphere as well as to its role as a facilitator of the Pakistan-India dialogue. The Americans stepped back after General Musharraf's Kargil misadventure. After he overthrew Nawaz, and established military rule, the US disapprobation became pronounced. On the other hand, cultivation of India as a strategic ally began to be pursued relentlessly by the United States; the Indians reciprocated in equal measure.

However, a reinvigorated US–Pakistan alliance emerged after 9/11, but it was purely instrumentalist in nature in spite of all the rhetoric and hypocrisy that the leaders from both sides expressed about the scourge of terrorism and each other's importance and commitment to defeating it. The Americans were willing to pay the Pakistani military for delivering on Al-Qaeda and Taliban leaders and cadres. The Pakistanis were willing to render such a service on a selective basis, as some Afghan Taliban were calculated to be valuable to Pakistan's interests in Afghanistan in the post-US period.

In any case, the unequal nature of the relationship – between a superpower and a post-colonial middle-range power – became apparent because the Americans were able to exert immense pressure on Pakistan to grant hundreds of visas to US undercover agents who, mistrusting Pakistan, conducted their own search for bin Laden. The dramatic exposure of such covert operations took place, by chance, when an undercover agent, Raymond Davis, was apprehended after he killed two Pakistanis who were trailing his vehicle on a motorcycle. Nothing epitomised such a lack of trust more dramatically than Operation Geronimo which culminated in US Navy Seals, on 2 May 2011, hunting down and killing Osama bin Laden in his hideout in the garrison town of Abbottabad.

However, a number of secret communications between the US and Pakistani military functionaries, revealed by Wikileaks, have shown that the US drone attacks in FATA were not only assisted by the Pakistani military but, in fact, requested by them. Yet, there is no denying that, after Operation Geronimo, relations between Pakistan and the United States have continued to deteriorate – the 26 November 2011 NATO aircraft fire on a Pakistani checkpoint epitomises the almost total distrust on both sides. Nevertheless, Pakistan's dependence on the Americans is enormous and although a bigger armed confrontation between the two states cannot be overruled, it is most unlikely. Most probably, behind-the-scenes moves will restore some sort of working relationship. However, it is very clear that, in this battle of nerves, the Americans are not going to give up easily on Pakistan reining in the Haqqani group, Mullah Omar, and other stalwarts of the Afghan Taliban. The United States' ability to wield the infamous carrot-and-stick policy – that major powers and superpowers are able to exercise – remains considerable. On the other hand, Pakistan is a major power in southwest Asia. Its military prowess, including its nuclear assets, cannot be ignored. The Americans cannot but take that into account as they relate to the AfPak region and in the larger context to South Asia.

China

The Pakistan–China liaison has been a down-to-earth, balance-of-power, my-enemy's-enemy-is-my-friend type of calculation. However, although China began to supply MiG aircraft and other hardware to Pakistan, this did not mean that it was willing to risk its own security by invading India on Pakistan's behalf in 1965 or 1971. However, when India tested a nuclear device, the Chinese allegedly helped Pakistan attain nuclear weapon capability. This was consistent with Chinese policy to keep India pinned down on its western border with Pakistan. China and Pakistan were part of the Afghan jihad as well but, after 9/11, a complication and tension began to arise. While China expanded its role in the construction of the Gwadar port on the coast of southern Pakistan, and acquired mining rights for gold and other precious minerals in Balochistan, the Islamist movement of the Uyghur people of China's north-western province of Xinxiang was networking with Pakistani jihadist organisations. Some of them went back and fomented unrest and resistance to Chinese rule. Chinese protests resulted in harsh treatment from the Pakistani government.

Saudi Arabia

The third major patron that Pakistan managed to obtain was Saudi Arabia. Linkages between the Wahabi regime and its admirers in Pakistan were established in the 1960s, when an ideological network was established with the connivance of the Americans who backed Islamism to counter the left-leaning nationalist regime of Gamel Abdul Nasser of Egypt. Z.A. Bhutto's Islamic Summit at Lahore probably helped market Pakistan to the Saudis because, thereafter, thousands of Pakistani workers found work in the Persian Gulf. However, it was General Zia's coup against Bhutto, the 1978 Afghan Communist coup, the rise of Shiite Iran under Khomeini in February 1979, and the December 1979 Soviet intervention in Afghanistan that furnished the Saudis with a leading role in Pakistani politics, both internal and external.

The Iranian clerics demonstrated the power of political Islam as an ideology that could be used to capture power and establish a medieval tyranny with the trappings of modern practices and institutions, such as elections and a parliament – albeit both distorted to return a government dominated by Shite clerics. That message reverberated throughout the Muslim world, but the arithmetic of sectarian numbers favoured Sunni leadership. That role was taken over by the Saudis who found the regime of General Zia, and the Soviet intervention in Afghanistan, opportunities that could be exploited to their advantage. The Iranian-Saudi proxy war, in the context of Pakistan, meant sectarian terrorism between Pakistani Shias and Sunnis. The depth of the vitiating impact of Saudi influence is not yet fully fathomed but it would not be an exaggeration to say that the brutalisation of the sensibilities of Pakistani society, at all levels, has taken place because of it.

Thousands of Pakistani military personnel have being posted to Saudi Arabia and made fortunes, big and small, because of the lucrative salaries available to them. Therefore, an 'institutional interest' in maintaining the Saudi connection is rooted in the officer corps of the Pakistan military. Moreover, hundreds of thousands of Pakistanis who work in Saudi Arabia are exposed to a form of Islam which is very different from their own syncretic traditions. It is puzzling that, despite being comprehensively treated with contempt by the Saudi state and society, many return to Pakistan immersed in a culture of extremism and intolerance. Terrorism and extremism now pervade all sections of society; the Taliban and other extremist organisations thrive in such a milieu.

The Rise of the Military in the Internal Domain

The induction of the military into politics was largely an outcome of the failure of politics. The assassination of Liaquat Ali Khan in 1951, of Dr Khan Sahib in May 1958, and of the deputy speaker of the East Pakistan Assembly, Shahid Ali, later the same year, compounded by a sluggish economy and a food crisis, created mass disenchantment with such governments which, from the beginning, had been formed without general elections being held to lend them legitimacy. It was under these circumstances that the military began to assume a role in politics. On 27 October 1958, Ayub Khan carried out the first military coup. The second coup took place when senior commanders forced Ayub Khan to hand over power to General Yahya Khan in March 1969. LePorte, who has described Pakistan as a garrison state, interpreted this as proof of the military, as an institution, possessing the power of the final arbiter in Pakistani politics.

The third coup was carried out by General Zia, in July 1977, when he ousted Z.A. Bhutto's increasingly erratic regime, which had been facing mounting resistance from the political opposition for his high-handed polices against political opponents. General Zia-ul-Haq ruled Pakistan with an iron hand and did not even try to acquire the trappings of a civilian ruler. The ascendency of the military, over the politicians, was completed. The elected governments that followed, under Benazir Bhutto and Nawaz Sharif, were quite powerless while the military and some powerful bureaucrats practically enjoyed the power of veto. The Pakistani establishment began to be described as the deep state. Nawaz Sharif tried to revive the Islamisation project that had been in abeyance, when he made a bid to get the Sharia declared as the supreme law of the country.

Musharraf overthrew Nawaz Sharif and established the fourth military government in 1999. During his rule, the trend to transfer military personnel to the civil sector greatly accelerated. His fall from power, and the restoration of elected civilian government in 2008, did not detract from the fact that the de facto veto powers have remained with the military. General Kayani let the politicians manage the political process but has intervened on critical occasions to ensure that Pakistan is not destabilised again because of the perennial power tussles between the government and the opposition. At present, this formula seems to be working. At the same time, the military's involvement in Balochistan has been controversial, notwithstanding the fact that powerful secessionist challenges have emanated from that province.

From the time General Zia came to power, there have been no doubts as to who has formulated Pakistan's foreign policy in relation to India and Afghanistan, as well as its defence policy – especially related to nuclear armament. President Zardari has been overruled by the military on a number of occasions when he has expressed some unorthodox opinions: about those involved in terrorism in Indian-administered Kashmir; over Pakistan's policy of not using a nuclear bomb first; and when Prime Minister Gilani and he expressed a willingness to cooperate with India in the investigation into the plotters of the Mumbai terrorist attacks of 26 November 2008. That situation has remained largely unchanged although, towards the end of 2011, it seems that some breakthrough is possible as Pakistan is considering offering MFN status to India. However, one cannot read too much into this important change in policy till such time as it is finalized and implemented.

Needless to say, the rise of the military has been concurrent with the ISI and other intelligence services expanding their roles far beyond their formal remits. Backing ethnic parties, such as the MQM as well Kashmir-centric organizations such as HuM, JeM, and LeT, indicates that the specialists on violence have enjoyed far greater power and clout than is permissible to the intelligence-gathering agencies of a state. However, this study also shows that there are dissenting voices within the military. The military is not a monolith. There are hard-line Islamists as well as pragmatic, secularly-inclined officers and generals. There is also evidence to suggest that the intelligence agencies do not always cooperate or agree, and a competition takes place between them. None of these discoveries is surprising because it is quite normal that people who work in such large organisations and institutions tend to subscribe to different points of view on contentious matters. The notion of an establishment or a deep state is, nevertheless, valid because organisations and institutions do represent collective interest over and above the interests of their functionaries. Anyhow, there is no reason to doubt that the Pakistani military, with the army at the centre, enjoys de facto veto rights over not only foreign and defence policy but also domestic politics. It is, so to say, the state within the state, with the ISI in particular playing an extra ordinarily important role in sustaining the 'fortress of Islam' myth. However, theories that assume that the military was, from the beginning, seeking to overthrow the civil government and establish its hold over the state have to be discarded because there is no empirical evidence to confirm them. Alavi's structuralism takes that for granted: structural explanations are typically backed up by poor empirical evidence since it is in the nature of the structure that society will behave in a particular way. This inquiry shows that the military takeovers were the result of the failure of the political process and a lack of clarity on ideology and societal objectives.

Mazhar Aziz has suggested that the first military coup established a precedent – it was followed by more coups, thus creating a pattern because military interventions weakened the politicians' positions and undermined the prestige of the representative institutions. That argument is true but Aziz seemed to assume that path-dependency means a cyclical movement of civil and military governments, one after the other, as if such a phenomenon has a life of its own. The evidence provided in this investigation suggests that, cumulatively, the volatility and violence that such a political pattern has acquired has become quite difficult to control and, if such a situation persists, can result in systemic collapse. Also, stability continues to be conspicuous by its absence at the level of parliamentary practice. The showdown between Gilani and Kayani, in the last weeks of 2011, indicated that one cannot assume military dominance to be immutable or absolute. The premium of the Pakistani military, with the United States, is currently low. While one can assume that the Pakistani civilian government stands to gain from this, one must also wonder whether the gain will be enough to bring about a decisive shift in the balance of power. At present, Pakistan is far from a normal chain of command that would institutionalise civilian supremacy over the military and bureaucracy. There are other problems as well. The current federal and provincial governments came to power in 2008 and their term would end in 2013, but the opposition parties are again on the warpath, threatening to resort to mass power to bring down the government. Under the circumstances, the fragility and vulnerability of Pakistan's fledgling democracy remains a persistent problem.

The Politics of Identity

Complications in Pakistan's political travails have also emanated from its peculiar preoccupation with national identity. All states have to cull out a national identity that distinguishes them from other states. Pragmatic states can work their way towards a national identity with relative ease because they do not take on, for themselves, more duties than the maintenance of national security, reproduction of the economic means to sustain their populations, maintenance of law and order, maintenance of basic services, and welfare and related auxiliary tasks. On the other hand, ideological states are committed to the realization of a grand ideal that requires social engineering. If the ideological state professes extra-secular objectives, such as ensuring the salvation of its citizens in the hereafter, as one of its primary objectives, then it encroaches on the autonomy of individuals in a more comprehensive manner. The Objectives Resolution of 7 March 1949 proclaimed the sovereignty of God rather than the Pakistani Parliament. That provided the ideational basis for the incremental expansion of religious features to the constitution. Such features, cumulatively, established the supremacy of Islamic law in the formula that all laws in Pakistan would be brought in consonance with the Quran and Sunnah. Later, comprehensive Islamisation during General Zia's rule consummated that process. As a result, the institutionalisation of discrimination through the legal process against women and religious minorities took place. An unintended consequence of such policies was that the Sunni–Shia cleavage deepened during this period, and relations between different Sunni sub-sects' divisions also resulted in tension and conflict.

Centre–Province Relations

A strong centre, dominated by the military, was a reflection not only of the imbalance between the powerful military and civil bureaucratic apparatuses of the state and the relative weakness of representative institutions and elected governments, but also an indirect product of the constant use of executive power to overrule parliamentary practice within the federal systems. It emanated from the dismissal of the Dr Khan Sahib ministry in the NWFP, and was followed by similar steps later, most notably the declaration of Urdu as the sole national language of Pakistan – which provoked mass protests by the Bengali majority in the former East Pakistan. The grievances of the Baloch, as well as Sindhi resentment against the allotment of agricultural land to the military and Punjabis in Sindh, kept tensions high within the internal domain – which, in turn, required the military to always maintain a strong presence in the centrifugal areas. Military action in East Pakistan culminated in the break-up of Pakistan and the establishment of Bangladesh. In Balochistan, the centre-province tension has continued to persist and has, from time to time, reached alarming proportions. Military solutions to political issues are, usually, not the wisest way to resolve the issues.

Terrorism within Pakistan

In the aftermath of the 11 September 2001 terrorist attacks on the United States, ordered by Al-Qaeda, the jihad philosophy has clashed directly with the interests of that very same superpower which, along with Saudi Arabia, had sponsored it. General Musharraf's decision to join the war on terror exposed Pakistan to terrorism that has been perpetrated by the TTP and its affiliates. The havoc wreaked has not given quarter to anyone. It is widely believed that such acts of terrorism have taken place with the help of rogue elements – however few – within the military and intelligence services. At least 35,000 Pakistanis have lost their lives, and even more badly wounded, because of the violence-prone political culture that pervades Pakistan. Among these are military and ISI functionaries, as well as Punjab Governor Salman Taseer and Federal Minister for Minority Affairs Shahbaz Bhatti. Fanatical jihadist groups and cells seem to be present at all levels of state and society. Unless it is brought under control and dismantled, home-grown terrorism can set processes of implosion in motion that can, in the long run, pose a veritable existentialist threat to Pakistan.

Terrorism in the External Domain

The catalogue of terrorist crimes, allegedly committed by Pakistan-based groups outside Pakistan, is long. It includes attacks in India and the Indian-administered Kashmir by the HuM, JeM, and LeT. Pakistan-origin US and UK citizens have been involved in several terrorist attempts. In one atrocity at least – the carnage in Mumbai on 26 November 2008 – enough evidence has been provided to implicate LeT operatives.

The United States has many grievances about Afghan Taliban and Al-Qaeda operatives hiding in Pakistan and carrying out terrorist acts against their troops in Afghanistan. The Haqqani group, ensconced in North Waziristan, has repeatedly been named; as have the names of Mullah Omar and other Afghan Taliban featured in the American list of individuals they want arrested or eliminated.

The Americans, of course, bear a great responsibility for sponsoring extremism among Islamic warriors. Without losing a single soldier of their own, they were able to drive the Russians out of Afghanistan and, thus, precipitate the collapse of communism in eastern Europe. But, in doing so, they left behind a political legacy soaked in blood and armed with vile ideas about killing and destroying anyone considered to be an enemy of Islam. This legacy exposes the poverty of the Realism School of International Relations in proffering a formula of peace and stability, except one which is precariously maintained through weapons, weapons of mass destruction, and unscrupulous military alliances. It is up to moral philosophers and historians to assess what harm the United States did to the world by harnessing the fierce energy of fanatical Islam to maintain its status as the champion of the liberal-capitalist word during the Cold War. That its long shadows continue to haunt the world need not be overemphasised.

The Post-Colonial Garrison State

Tan Tai Yong has argued that a major portion of the colonial Indian Army was inherited by Pakistan. Stephen Cohen has asserted that recruitment of the Pakistan Army continued to be largely from the same narrow regional base representing some nine percent of the total population of Pakistan. More recently, Shuja Nawaz has asserted that the recruitment base has broadened, though only just; the officer corps continues, largely, to be from the traditional recruiting districts; moreover, the 'Zia-bharti', or Zia recruits, hail from the conservative areas of central Punjab and from the radicalised southern Punjab. He suspects that such an army, especially the officer class, would be prone to an esprit de corps laced with Islamist jihadist values. That such a military has acquired a significant stake in the Pakistani economy has been demonstrated by Ayesha Siddiqa. Moreover, Pakistan faltered badly by not taking advantage of the economy of growth that US aid and the World Bank provided in the 1960s. Instead, its leaders frittered away that head start by the 1965 misadventure in Kashmir that resulted in war with India. Since then, Pakistan's economy has done well from time to time but terrorism, corruption, and mismanagement have taken a big toll on it. As a result, educated young men continue to seek career opportunities in the armed forces. Consequently, social, ideological, and economic factors converge to render the Pakistan military a coveted institution. Harold Lasswell has emphasized that the specialists on violence would constitute the core element in a garrison state, and the Pakistani version of it clearly bears those hallmarks.

Lasswell's main argument, however, was that the garrison state grows out of a perpetual fear of foreign aggression – a fear the specialists on violence invoke to establish their political and ideological hold over state and society. That has been demonstrated abundantly in this inquiry. He also feared that the development of a militaristic culture and esprit de corps inevitably claims democracy as its main casualty. Democracy, even if it is retained, is reduced to a ritual. Instead, a culture of fear grows which is manipulated to grow out of proportion; in the process, a docile citizenry comes into being, always looking up towards the specialists on violence for their security and existence. With regard to Pakistan, that has indeed been very true.

However, a modifying thesis with regard to the issue of democracy in Pakistan has been advanced in this study. It has been argued that the prospects for democracy in Pakistan were never strong from the onset. The lack of competent politicians and of a grassroots mass political party, compounded by the death of Jinnah and the assassination of Liaquat Ali Khan, created conditions that were not conducive to democracy. The powerful landowning class of West Pakistan and the West Pakistan-based national bourgeoisie needed the state to establish itself and grow. This furnished the social base for Alavi's 'overdeveloped state'. Additionally, and perhaps more importantly, an ambiguity existed from the beginning about the purpose for which Pakistan had been created. As the special state created for the Muslim nation of the subcontinent, the relationship between Islam and the state could not remain ambiguous once the state came into being. Jinnah's heroic effort to delink that relationship in his oft-quoted 11 August 1947 speech did not convince even his closest associates. On 7 March 1949, the Objectives Resolution established the format for defining the relationship between Islam, the state, and its citizens. That it progressively incorporated Islamist features was not inevitable, but it was very likely because of all the negative factors, mentioned above, that converged against democracy.

An authoritarian type of state emerged at a very early stage. Powerful civil servants, such as Ghulam Mohammad and Iskander Mirza, demeaned the role of the prime minister while another civil servant, Chaudhri Muhammad Ali, formulated a constitution that described Pakistan as an Islamic republic premised on the supremacy of the will of God. The military coup of 1958 completed the process of authoritarianism. Authoritarianism has been modernistic under Ayub Khan, fundamentalist under Zia, and 'moderate' under Musharraf. Democracy under Zulfikar Ali Bhutto was compromised by his personal dictatorship and high-handed politics. In the later years, the balance of power tilted inconvertibly in favour of the military vis-à-vis the civilians.

The fear of foreign aggression, as the leitmotif of the garrison state idea, received equally strongly support from the politicians and the military establishment. It was Jinnah who invited the Americans to use Pakistan as a frontline state against Communism. Ayub Khan aug-mented such a strategy with additional arguments and relentless lobbying of US administrations. Therefore, the fear of external aggression – real and contrived – existed from the outset because of the perceived threat from India, compounded by bad relations with Afghanistan. Given the exigencies of the Cold War, and the lack of order and a concomitant unified chain of command in the international system, the anarchy which existed was exploited by the Pakistani power elite to solicit American patronage. The arms that were acquired generated a false sense of superiority in Pakistan, and led to a number of military misadventures. Max Weber's observation that the warrior class and its ethics came to characterise the structure of power in early Muslim societies added historical authenticity to the culture of militarism, which reached apogee during Zia's rule.

Participation in the so-called Afghan jihad greatly enhanced the power and prestige of the military and ISI in Pakistani politics which, in turn, helped the Pakistani garrison state, acquire pronounced features of the national security state that Nelson-Pallmeyer deplores. Pakistan acquired nuclear weapons which the Pakistan military made its exclusive preserve. Chinese and Saudi patronage furnished additional resources to overcome the problems of underdevelopment, lack of industrial infrastructure, and meagre indigenous economic resources. All such developments greatly strengthened the military and helped the top commanders exercise virtually de facto veto powers in Pakistani politics. Thus, the impediments posed by the absence of an advanced industrial infrastructure were surmounted by a peculiar mixture of alliance building, realpolitik, and ideological manipulation to bring about and perpetuate the post-colonial garrison state model symbolised by the notion of a 'fortress of Islam'.

Some Futuristic Reflections

In light of the above discussion, we can now make some projections about future developments that can be relevant for Pakistan.

1. Threat from India

The perceived threat from India cannot be wished away. It is a constant. As long as mutual trust is found to be wanting, India's military superiority will always pose a threat that the Pakistan military will have to be prepared to meet with some credible deterrent. On the other hand, it is doubtful if the search for 'strategic depth' is the right response to it. Any so-called strategic depth cannot alter the fact that Lahore and other major towns and cities in Punjab will always be where they are: in close proximity to the Indian border. One must discard any hope of transcending such negative objective geographical reality. An expansion into India through conquest is out of the question, as is a military annexation of the Indian-administrated Kashmir. Also, wild ambitions to expand into central Asia, through some arrangement with Afghanistan, must be discounted.

Pakistan has the capability to deter India from any misadventure against it. The nuclear bomb and missile technology cannot assure Pakistan victory over India, but most certainly mutually assured destruction. However, having a strong and powerful neighbour does not in itself constitute a threat. Canada has an overwhelmingly powerful United States next to it; so do the smaller nations of Europe, such as Ireland, Belgium, and the Netherlands. Britain and France are nuclear weapon states with the narrow English Channel separating them. They have a long history of wars between them. Yet, now, they are the closest of allies and much more. If Pakistan and India sort out their differences and resolve their disputes by abandoning the zero-sum attitudes that prevail in the corridors of power on both sides, the danger posed by their nuclear weapons can diminish.

There is no denying that, even if India did not the initiate armed conflicts with Pakistan, the military exercises close to the Pakistan border, its rapid armament policy after the 1962 war with China, and the testing of a nuclear weapon in 1974 constantly produced tensions and accentuated Pakistan's sense of vulnerability. That such actions were motivated by the perception of a Chinese threat to India does not help remove Pakistani concerns about Indian intentions and designs. The military intervention of 1971 led to the break-up of Pakistan, and the self-fulfilling prophecy shared by Pakistan's power elite was confirmed. The trauma it caused left deep scars in the Pakistani national psyche, notwithstanding the fact that the crisis in East Pakistan was the result of the failure of Pakistani politicians and the military to agree on the rules of democracy and the right to form the government.

On the other hand, it is true that the Pakistani power elite has thrived on the threat-from-India standpoint. It is interesting that before Pakistan received its first cache of US weapons in 1951 when, theoretically, it was at its weakest in relation to India, the latter did not take advantage of the situation and invade Pakistan. Equally, at least since 2009 when the Pakistan Army started its operations in Swat and South Waziristan, there has been a thinning of troops on the eastern border – notwithstanding denials by the Foreign Office. Thousands of troops are now stationed in FATA, Swat, and other sensitive areas along the border with Afghanistan – again, India does not seem to have taken advantage of this. Therefore, the whole notion of the Indian threat needs to be put into perspective. The distinction between a threat and a threat-perception is significant in terms of making sense of perceived Indian designs. Threat perception can easily lend itself to exaggeration – resulting in the military claiming an unreasonably large portion of national resources.

Eisenhower warned about the US military-industrial complex acquiring too much power and influence; in Pakistan, that power and influence is not a matter for suspicion. In practical terms, however, it is a huge drain on development; development that Pakistan urgently needs. Not only does it cause an appalling neglect of basic needs and rights such as food, education, and health, but also a huge dearth of electricity and other sources of energy that have led to frustration and despair among the middle and lower-middle classes.

The Pakistani and Indian establishments have lacked the vision and courage to take the steps that would reduce tensions in a substantive way. The bus service between Amritsar and Lahore, and Srinagar and Muzaffargarh, are good and useful steps but more good will and courage is needed to transcend the acrimony of the past 65 years. Both sides stand to gain a lot, in terms of men and material, by resolving the Siachen Glacier imbroglio. It is, at present, probably the most wasteful confrontation between any two states.

Current and future realities of South Asia call for a concept of security that is not narrowly defined in terms of national security. Regional security and human security need to be added to it. Environ-mental degradation, which now plagues the whole world, particularly portends dire consequences for South Asia. Unless Pakistan and India, and other states in this region, learn to cooperate to solve the water problem, population explosion, and many other egregious challenges that industrialisation and economic growth have created, South Asia may face great devastation and destruction.

There is a lot of goodwill on both sides. The only thing needed is the courage and conviction to accept good neighbourly relations as the best remedy to all the ills that afflict their relationship. The Kashmir dispute is not the malady; it is the symptom of a confrontation that effectively claims, and wastes, scarce resources for military competition. It can also symbolise hope and optimism. After all, the most durable example of pragmatism and mutual accommodation is the Indus Waters Treaty that continues to define the sharing of water between India and Pakistan. In recent years, it has resulted in a number of disputes but both sides have wisely submitted to international arbitration and accepted its ruling. The Kashmir dispute is, in essence, a hydro-political problem. There is no way of resolving it; it is a case of maintaining the status quo while making adjustments and concessions that bring benefit to both Pakistan and India.

One can argue that the current spirit of reconciliation in India– Pakistan relations can help provide the threshold to cross over from a zero-sum games situation to a win-win formula. The LoC can become the international border, but one that would be rendered merely symbolic if it is porous and Kashmiris on both sides – Hindus, Muslims, Buddhists, Sikhs, and others – are able to enjoy substantive autonomy and freedom. The global economy is rendering the notion of international borders as impassable barriers, for the movement of goods, capital, and even people, as an anachronism. The SAARC framework exists to facilitate mutually beneficial trade that can generate wealth and prosperity, and now is the time to take that opportunity seriously. Since the 2004 Islamabad SAARC Summit, India–Pakistan relations have been moving in the direction of a constructive engagement – notwithstanding the Mumbai terrorist attack of 26 November 2008. There is absolutely no doubt that the people of South Asia are hardworking, industrious, enterprising, and with enough cultural variation and wisdom, bequeathed by history, to be able to establish good neighbourly relations and cultivate ties of friendship and solidarity. The Pakistani and Indian leadership must show courage to make a determined and decisive break with the past in the interests of their people. If India and Pakistan can establish a trade regime that ensures mutual benefit, the dividends can be enormous. Bangladesh and India have recently agreed to establish joint industrial ventures, most notably in the jute industry. Similar enterprises can be established between India and Pakistan, ensuring a fair share to Pakistan.

2. *Afghanistan*

The most dramatic change that is going to take place imminently in South Asia is the withdrawal of US and NATO forces from Afghanistan. The withdrawal will be completed by the end of 2014 – at least, that is the declared policy of President Obama. However, it is doubtful whether the Americans will abandon this region in the way they abruptly did in 1989. This time round, they will try to ensure that they enjoy enough clout in Kabul to ensure that the Taliban do not return to power. However, such planning cannot guarantee success, and the post-US–NATO situation in Afghanistan remains highly ambiguous and volatile. In case a pro-Western government in Kabul collapses, civil war could break out again – in which case, both Pakistan and India would be drawn into the conflict. But, if they abandon the zero-sum strategies that have hitherto marked their behaviour in Afghanistan, they can play a constructive role in helping the Afghans establish a moderate government.

In such a situation, Pakistan can legitimately demand that the Durand Line be recognized as the international border between Afghanistan and Pakistan. It could be a basis for negotiations between Pakistan and Afghanistan – to remove territorial ambiguities with regard to the formal demarcation of their borders. In this regard, the United States, along with India, can play a very important role in convincing the Afghans that converting the Durand Line into the de jure international border would not, in any practical way, jeopardise the existing arrangements which permit easy movement of the native tribes on both sides. Rather, Afghanistan would gain the most – as a result of expanding trade between south and central Asia. This would be possible if the borders could become mere symbols of state authority while the people on both sides of these borders could make use of their historical affinities – derived from their ethnicity and shared culture. In other words, normalisation and peace in the so-called AfPak region will be determined, to a large extent, by normalisation and peace between Pakistan and India.

3. *Dependence on External Patrons*

Although the final word on Pakistan's dependence is yet to be spoken, on the whole, patronage from the United States, China, and Saudi Arabia cannot be taken for granted. One can even argue that it is not desirable. After the fall of the Soviet Union, Pakistan's frontline status has become redundant and the current relationship is brittle and precarious and not likely to last longer than the United States needs to use Pakistan to destroy whatever threat Al-Qaeda and its affiliates pose to its security. Current American backing is conditional and limited, and it involves penalties as well. Moreover, the United States, and the West in general, are always going to be concerned about Pakistan's nuclear assets. A Taliban-type takeover, or some mad generals declaring an intention to use nuclear weapons, will almost certainly be met with determined pre-emptive action from the West. It is important that Pakistan curbs extremism and terrorism at home and abides by the norms and standards of international law to dispel, or at least keep at bay, real or contrived conspiracies by the enemies of Islam and Pakistan. On the other hand, it will be in Pakistan's interest to maintain good and friendly relations with the United States. US economic and educational cooperation will still be needed to modernize and develop as a progressive South Asian nation.

The Chinese connection will continue to thrive provided we curb Islamism, and as long as the containment of India remains a paramount concern of Chinese defence and foreign policy. On the other hand, if China and India improve their relations, it need not mean that Pakistan will lose Chinese favour. On the contrary, Pakistan can serve as a bridge between them. China will probably always back Pakistan to keep a handle on India, but is not likely to back Pakistani military misadventures in Kashmir or elsewhere.

The Saudi influence has been very pervasive ideologically, and has included an economic dimension – lucrative appointments in Saudi Arabia and other Arab emirates in the Persian Gulf. On the whole, such a connection has seriously harmed the modicum of democratic modernity that existed in Pakistan, and that connection will continue to impact in the future. The Arab Spring of 2011 has kindled hopes of a democratic development in the Muslim world but, as long as the rentier states of Iran and Saudi Arabia can leverage their enormous wealth and claims to self-styled sectarian leadership of the Muslim world, the struggle for democracy will always face the threat of sub-version through their client terrorist militias and an inflow of extremist propaganda.

4. The Role of the Military

The direction Pakistan takes in the coming months and years will depend on the role the military plays. It remains the most powerful institution in the country and, for any break with the past to materialise, it must begin with serious introspection and self-criticism. There is no doubt that, in traditional terms, security means national security and state security; that role can, and must, only be played by the military. As argued earlier, the problem is not that democracy has been subverted in Pakistan because of military coups. The political class has been seriously wanting in its commitment to democracy – that, in contemporary terms, means the prerogative of elected civilians to make important decisions on behalf of the nation that conform to contemporary standards of democracy: which means not only majority rules and minority rights, but also inalienable human rights of individuals, equality between the sexes, and non-discriminatory, inclusive citizenship. That has not been the basis on which even formal democracy has been practised by the politicians in Pakistan. Equally, the military's notion of democracy has meant a strong executive with quasi-dictatorial powers vested in the general turned president. Under the circumstances, a thorough discussion on democracy, deradicalization, and the rule of law needs to be conducted, and the search for a constitutional formula that is practical, enlightened, and compatible with the rule of law and international law must be found and instituted.

The most egregious problems that Pakistan faces are rampant corruption, an economy that is in very bad shape, and massive social and economic inequalities that sprawl throughout the country. The ruling class, especially the landowners, do not pay taxes. Moreover, defence expenditure remains too high for a poor nation to bear without compromising its developmental commitments. Poverty afflicts large sections of Pakistani society. In such circumstances, it is not surprising that poor youths are lured by jihadist organizations. Most of the suicide bombers come from the most impoverished sections of society. It is not surprising that most of them have hailed from the tribal areas of Khyber-Pakhtunkhwa; southern Punjab is also a recruiting ground for terrorist organisations. Pakistan will have to give priority to economic and social development if it is ever to extricate itself successfully from the quagmire in which it has been gradually been sinking for at least the last thirty years.

Conclusion

This study demonstrates that Pakistan's travails as a post-colonial garrison state, and its more colourful representation as the 'fortress of Islam', have been the product of highly complicated historical, geo-graphical, political, ideological, and military-security factors. Such factors impinged upon Pakistan's political evolution as a Muslim-majority state in the context of the Cold War, the anarchic international political system, the tension-ridden South Asian region, and the endemically chequered domestic arena replete with ideological excesses. Under the circumstances, the state that Pakistan managed to build acquired the attributes of the garrison state that Harold Lasswell had propounded in the early 1940s. However, instead of such a garrison coming into being as a result of a combination of an advanced industrial development that provided the scope for control over large-scale production and control over the economy but facing existentialist threats from an external enemy, the Pakistani power elite, comprising both politicians and the military, successfully transcended the problems of underdevelopment through alignment with powerful and resourceful foreign donors willing to provide it with armament and training to create a large class of specialists on violence. Thus, the obstacles that industrial backwardness imposed were successfully circumvented and Pakistan could evolve as a garrison state. So, Pakistan became a post-colonial garrison state, with its hawkish leaders and supporters romanticising it as the 'fortress of Islam'.

However – and even when the Pakistani power elite made good use of the contradictions and room for manoeuvre in the international system of big and small, and powerful and weak states to graduate from a poorly endowed polity to a middle-range power armed with nuclear weapons – its vulnerability to pressure from its powerful donors compromised its sovereignty in very many different ways. There is no doubt that the movement towards an Islamic state was largely internal-driven, but foreign economic and military aid played a very significant role in its growth and consolidation. Consequently, abject poverty and illiteracy continued to afflict large sections of its population.

The state seems to have lost control in the internal domain as fanatics have been able to hit targets almost at will. Pakistan's reputation as the epicentre of global terrorism and a rogue state is there to stay for quite some time. Another major terrorist attack outside Pakistan can create a dangerous situation for the security and existence of Pakistan. It is, therefore, imperative that the stakeholders in the Pakistan power equation – especially the military – work out a long-term policy and strategy that can create stability, peace, and prosperity within Pakistan as well as help normalise relations with its neighbours – provided they, too, nurture similar aspirations.

Notes

CHAPTER 1

Abbas, Hassan, 2005, *Pakistan's Drift into Extremism: Allah, the Army, and America's War on Terror*, New Delhi: Pentagon Press.

Ahmed, Ishtiaq, 1987, *The Concept of an Islamic State: An Analysis of the Ideological Controversy in Pakistan*, London: Frances Pinter.

Alavi, Hamza, 1972, 'The State in Post-Colonial Societies: Pakistan and Bangladesh', New Left Review, 1/74 July–August.

Aziz, Mazhar, 2008, *Military Control in Pakistan*, London and New York: Routledge.

Bhaskar, C. Uday, 18–23 October 2008, 'Revisiting civil-military relations: The ever supplicant "fauj" in India', Lahore: *The Friday Times*

Buzan, Barry, 1991, *Peoples, States and Fears*, New York, London: Harvester Wheatsheaf.

Cheema, Pervaiz Iqbal, 1990, *Pakistan's Defence Policy*, 1947–58, London: Macmillan Press.

Cohen, Stephen, 1998, *The Pakistan Army*, Oxford: Oxford University Press.

Eisenhower, Dwight D., 1961, Eisenhower's Farwell Address to the Nation, HYPERLINK http://mcadams/http://mcadams. posc.mu.edu/ike.htm (accessed on 23–04–2008), (17 January 1961).

Faruqui, Ahmad, 2003, *Rethinking the National Security of Pakistan: The Price of Strategic Myopia*, Hampshire: Ashgate.

Finer, S.E., 1976, *The Man on the Horseback: The Military in Politics*, Harmondswoth, Middlesex: Penguin Books.

Ganguly, Sumit, 2010, 'The Genesis of Nonalignment', in Ganguly, Sumit (ed.), India's Foreign Policy: Retrospect and Prospect, New Delhi: Oxford University Press.

Global Fire Power, 2011, India, HYPERLINK http://www.globalfirepower.com/country-military-http://www.globalfirepower.com/country-military-strength-detail.asp?country_id=India (accessed on 6 May 2011).

Global Fire Power, 2011, Pakistan, HYPERLINK http://www.globalfirepower.com/country-military-http://www.globalfirepower.com/country-military-strength-detail.

asp?country_id=Pakistan (accessed on 6 May 2011).

Haqqani, Husain, 2005, *Pakistan between Mosque and Military*, Washington DC: Carnegie Endowment for International Peace.

Huntington, Samuel P., 1962, *Changing Pattern of Military Politics,* New York: Free Press of Glencoe.

Hussain, Zahid, 2008, *Frontline Pakistan: The Path to Catastrophe and the Killing of Benazir Bhutto*, London: I.B. Tauris and Co Ltd.

Jalal, Ayesha, 1990, *The State of Martial Law: The Origins of Pakistan's Political Economy of Defence*, Cambridge: Cambridge University Press.

Jha, Lalit K., 2009, 'India and Pakistan very casual in talking nuking of each other: Bill Clinton', *Indian Express*, 30 September 2009.

Khan, Fazal Muqeem, 1973, *Pakistan's Crisis in Leadership, Islamabad*: National Book Foundation.

Khan, M. Asghar, 2005, *We've Learnt Nothing from History, Pakistan: Politics and Military Power,* Karachi: Oxford University Press.

Khan, M. Asghar, 2008, *My Political Struggle*, Karachi: Oxford University Press.

Khan, Mohammad Ayub, 2006, *Friends not Masters: A Political Autobiography*, Islamabad: Mr Books.

Khan, Raja Muhammad, 2011 (6 June), 'Pakistan: Inside the Military Budget', Opinion Maker: Islamabad, HYPERLINK http://www.opinion-maker.org/2011/06/pakistan-inside-the-http://www.opinion-maker.org/2011/06/pakistan-inside-the-military-budget/ (accessed on 1 January 2012).

Khan, Zulfikar Ali, 1988, *Pakistan's Security: The Challenge and the Response*, Lahore: Progressive Publishers.

Kux, Dennis, 2001, *The United States and Pakistan 1947–2000: Disenchanted Allies*, New York: Oxford University Press.

LaPorte, Jr., Robert, 1969, 'Succession in Pakistan: Continuity and Change in a Garrison State', *Asian Survey*, Vol. 9, No. 11, (November 1969).

Lasswell, Harold, 1997, *Essays on the Garrison State*, New Brunswick, New Jersey: Transaction Publishers.

Machiavelli, Niccolo, 1982, *The Prince and Other Political Writings*, London: Everyman's Library.

Morgenthau, Hans J., 1948, *Politics among Nations: The Struggle for Power and Peace*, New York: Alfred Knopf.

Nawaz, Shuja, 2008, Crossed Swords: *Pakistan, Its Army, and the Wars Within*, Karachi: Oxford University Press.

Nelson-Pallmeyer, Jack, 1993, *Brave New World Order: Can we pledge allegiance*, Maryknoll, New York: Orbis Books.

Oldenburg, Philip 2010, *India, Pakistan and Democracy: Solving the Puzzle of Divergent Paths*, London: Routledge.

Rashid, Ahmed, 2009, Descent into Chaos: *The World's Most Unstable Region and the Threat to Global Security*, London: Penguin Books.

Rizvi, Hasan-Askari, 2000, *The Military and Politics in Pakistan 1947–1997*, Lahore; Sang-e-Meel Publications.

Rizvi, Hasan-Askari, 2003, *Military, State and Society in Pakistan*, Lahore: Sang-e-Meel Publications.

Schwartz, Howell H., 2005, *Fear and the Garrison State*, Washington DC: Rand Corporation, 26 Apri HYPERLINK http://www.rand.org/commentary/2005/04/26/UPI.html) l 2005, (htHYPERLINK http://www.rand.org/commentary/2005/04/26/UPI.html) tp://www.rand.org/commentary/2005/04/26/UPI.html) (accessed on 6 May 2011).

Siddiqa, Ayesha, 2007, *Military Inc. Inside Pakistan's Military Economy*, Karachi: Oxford University Press.

Siddiqi, A.R. (Brigadier, Retd.), 1996, *The Military in Pakistan: Image and Reality*, Lahore, Vanguard.

SIPRI, 2011, '14 March 2011: India world's largest arms importer according to new SIPRI data on international arms transfers', HYPERLINK http://www.sipri.org/media/pressreleases/2011/http://www.sipri.org/media/pressreleases/2011/ armstransfers, (accessed on 6 February 2012), Stockholm: SIPRI.

Stanley, Jay, 1997, 'Introduction: An Invitation to Revisit Lasswell's Garrison State', in Lasswell, Harold, Essays on the Garrison State, New Brunswick, New Jersey: Transaction Publishers.

Stanley, Jay and Segal, David R., 1997, 'Conclusion, Landmarks in Defense Literature', in Lasswell, Harold, Essays on the Garrison State, New Brunswick, New Jersey: Transaction Publishers.

Visual Economics, 2010, 'How Countries Spend their Money', HYPERLINK "http://www.visualeconomics"http://www.visualeconomics. com/how-countries-spend-their-money.

Walt, Stephen M., 1987, *The Origins of Alliances*, Ithaca: Cornell University Press.

Waltz, Kenneth N., 1979, *Theory of International Politics*, New York: McGraw Hill.

Waseem, Muhammad, 2009, 'Civil-Military Relations in Pakistan', in Jetly, Rajshree (ed.), Pakistan in Regional and Global Politics, New Delhi: Routledge.

Weber, Max, 1993, *The Sociology of Religion*, Boston: Beacon Press.

Wink, Andre, 1997, *Al-Hind: the Making of the Indo-Islamic World*, volume 2, Leiden, New York, Koln: Brill.

Yong, Tan Tai, 2005, *The Garrison State, The Military, Government and Society in Colonial Punjab*, 1849–1947, New Delhi: Sage Publications Ltd.

Autonomous Report

IPP's Third Annual Report 2010, 2010, Lahore: Institute of Public Policy, Beaconhouse University.

Interviews

Pakistan

General Mirza Aslam Beg, 31 October 2007, Rawalpindi

Lieutenant General (Retd.) Nasir Akhtar, former Corps Commander Karachi, 7 December 2008, Lahore

Brigadier (Retd.) Yasub Ali Dogar, 25 January 2008, Singapore

Lieutenant General (Retd.) Muhammad Asad Durrani, 31 October, Rawalpindi

Colonel (Retd.) Aslam Cheema, 12 December 2008, Rawalpindi

Major General (Retd.) Sarfraz Iqbal, 14 December 2008, Rawalpindi

Lieutenant General (Retd.) Hamid Gul, 17 December 2008, Rawalpindi

Lieutenant General (Retd.) Javed Ashraf Qazi, 19 December 2008, Rawalpindi

General Jehangir Karamat, 22 December 2008, Lahore

Lieutenant General (Retd.) Nishat Ahmed, 22 December 2008, Lahore

Major General (Retd.) Mahmud Ali Durrani, 20 March 2009, Singapore

Major (Retd.) Agha Humayun Amin, 10 November 2011, Lahore

India

Lieutenant General (Retd.) Kuldip Singh Khajuria, 10 November 2010, Noida, outside Delhi

Major General (Retd.) Afsir Karim, 10 November 2010, Noida, outside Delhi

Brigadier (Retd.) Vijai Nair, 10 November 2010, Noida, outside Delhi

Commodore (Retd.), C. Uday Bhaskar, 29 November 2011, via email from New Delhi

CHAPTER 2

Adhikari, G., 1944, *Pakistan and National Unity*, Bombay: People's Publishing House. Ahmed, Ishtiaq, 1998, State, Nation and Ethnicity in Contemporary South Asia, London: Pinter.

Ahmed, Ishtiaq, 1999, 'The 1947 Partition of Punjab: Arguments put forth before the Punjab Boundary Commission by the Parties Involved', in Talbot, Ian and Singh, Gurharpal (eds.), *Region and Partition: Bengal, Punjab and the Partition of the Subcontinent*, Karachi: Oxford University Press.

Ahmed, Ishtiaq, 2009, 'The Spectre of Islamic Fundamentalism over Pakistan

1947–2007', in Jetly, Rajshree (ed.), *Pakistan in Regional and Global Politics*, New Delhi: Routledge.

Ahmed, Ishtiaq, 2012, *The Punjab Bloodied, Partition and Cleansed: Unravelling the 1947 Tragedy through Secret British Reports and First Person Accounts*, New Delhi: Rupa Publications.

Antonova, K., Bongard-Levin, G., and Kotovsky, G.G., 1979, *A History of India, Book 1*, Moscow: Progress Publishers.

Carter, Lionel, 2006, *Punjab Politics, 1 January 1944–3 March 1947: Last Years of the Ministries, Governors' Fortnightly Reports and other Key Documents*, New Delhi: Manohar.

Chatterji, Joya, 1999, 'The Making of a Borderline: The Radcliffe Award for Bengal', in Talbot, Ian and Singh, Gurharpal (eds.), *Region and Partition: Bengal, Punjab and the Partition of the Subcontinent*, Karachi: Oxford University Press.

French, Patrick, 1997, *Liberty or Death: India's Journey to Independence and Division*, London: HarperCollins Publishers.

Horowitz, David, 1967, *From Yalta to Vietnam*, Harmondsworth, Middlesex: Penguin Books.

Jalal, Ayesha, 1985, *The Sole Spokesman*, Cambridge: Cambridge University Press.

Jansson, Erland, 1981, *India, Pakistan or Pakhtunistan?*, Uppsala: Act a Universitatis Upsaliensis.

Khan, Wali, 1987, *Facts are Facts: The Untold Story of India's Partition*, New Delhi: Vikas Publishing House Pvt Ltd.

Kux, Dennis, 2001, *The United States and Pakistan 1947–2000*: Disenchanted Allies, New York: Oxford University Press.

Lenin, Vladimir, I., 1970, *Imperialism, the Highest Stage of Capitalism*, Moscow: Progress Publishers.

Moore, R.J., 1983, 'Jinnah and the Pakistan Demand', Modern Asian Studies, Vol. XVII, No. 4, pp. 529–561, Cambridge: Cambridge University Press.

Qureshi, M. Naeem, 1999, *Pan-Islam in British Indian Politics: a Study of the Khilafat Movement 1918–1924*, Leiden: Brill.

Ray, Aswini K., 2004, *Western Realism and International Relations: a Non-Western View*, New Delhi: Foundation books.

Reitz, Dietrich, 1995, *Hijrat: The Flight of the Faithful, a British File on the Exodus of Muslim Peasants from the North India to Afghanistan 1920*, Berlin: Verlag Das Arabische Buch.

Sarila, Narendra Singh, 2005, *The Shadow of the Great Game: The Untold Story of India's Partition*, New Delhi: HarperCollins Publishers India and The India Today Group.

Seervai, H.M. 1989, *Partition of India: Legend and Reality, Bombay*: Emmanem Publications.

Talbot, Ian, 1996, Khizr Tiwana: *The Punjab Unionist Party and the Partition of India*, Richmond, Surrey: Curzon.

Tuker, Sir Francis, 1951, *While Memory Serves, London, Toronto, Melbourne, Sydney*, Wellington: Cassell and Company Ltd.

Wolpert, Stanley, 1984, *Jinnah of Pakistan, New York*: Oxford University Press.

Official Documents

Constituent *Assembly of Pakistan Debates, Vol.* 5, 1949, Karachi: Government of Pakistan Press.

Mansergh, Nicholas and Lumby, E.W.R., (eds.), 1970, *The Transfer of Power, Volume 1, The Cripps Mission, January–April 1942*, London: Her Majesty's Stationery Office.

Mansergh, Nicholas and Moon, Penderel (eds.), 1977, *The Transfer of Power, Volume VII, The Cabinet Mission 23 March–29 June 1946*, London: Her Majesty's Stationery Office.Mansergh, Nicholas and Moon, Penderel (eds.), 1979, *The Transfer of Power, Volume VIII, The Cabinet Mission 3 July–1 November*, London: Her Majesty's Stationery Office.

Mansergh, Nicholas and Moon, Penderel, (eds.), 1976, *The Transfer of Power, Volume VII, The Post-War Phase: New Moves by the Labour Government, 1 August 1945–22 March 1946*, London: Her Majesty's Stationery Office.

Mansergh, Nicholas and Moon, Penderel, (eds.), 1980, *The Transfer of Power 1942–1947, Volume IX, The fixing of a time limit, 4 November 1946–22 March 1947*, London: Her Majesty's Stationery Office.

Mansergh, Nicholas and Moon, Penderel, (eds.), 1981, T*he Transfer of Power 1942–1947, Volume X, The Mountbatten Viceroyalty, Formulation of a Plan, 23 March–30 May 1947*, London: Her Majesty's Stationery Office.

Mansergh, Nicholas and Moon, Penderel, (eds.), 1982, *The Transfer of Power 1942–1947, Volume XI, The Mountbatten Viceroyalty, Announcement and Reception of the 3 June Plan, 31 May–7 July 1947*, London: Her Majesty's Stationery Office.

Interviews with Pakistani Communists

C.R. Aslam, 17 December 2000, Lahore
Mian Minatullah, 19 December 2000, Lahore
Abdullah Malik, 17 April 2003, Lahore
Tahira Mazhar Ali Khan 25 April 2003, Lahore
Khawaja Masud Ahmed, 12 December 2004, Islamabad

CHAPTER 3

Ahmed, Ishtiaq, 1987, *the Concept of an Islamic State: An Analysis of the Ideological Controversy in Pakistan*, London: Frances Pinter.

Ahmed, Ishtiaq, 1999, 'The 1947 Partition of Punjab: Arguments put Forth before the Punjab Boundary Commission by the Parties Involved', in Ian Talbot and Gurharpal Singh (eds.), *Region and Partition: Bengal, Punjab and the Partition of the Subcontinen*t, Karachi: Oxford University Press.

Ahmed, Ishtiaq, 2002, 'The 1947 Partition of India: A Paradigm for Pathological Politics in India and Pakistan', in *Asian Ethnicity*, Volume 3, Number 1, Newburg, California: Sage Publications.

Ahmed, Ishtiaq, 2009, 'The Spectre of Islamic Fundamentalism over Pakistan (1947–2007)', in Rajshree Jetly (ed.), *Pakistan in Regional and Global Politics*, New Delhi: Routledge.

Ahmed, Ishtiaq, 2012, 'The Punjab Bloodied, Partitioned and Cleansed: Unravelling the 1947 Tragedy through Secret British Reports and First-Person Accounts, Karachi: Oxford University Press.

Alavi, Hamza, 2002, 'Misreading Partition Road Signs', *Economic and Political Weekly*, 2–9 November, Mumbai.

Ali, Imran, 1989, T*he Punjab under Imperialism 1885–1947*, Karachi: Oxford University Press.

Allen, Charles, 2006, *God's Terrorists: The Wahabi Cult and the Hidden Roots of Modern Jihad*, London: Little Brown.

Amin, Agha Humayun, 1999, *The Pakistan Army till 1965*, Arlington, VA: Strategicus and Tacticus.

Cohen, Stephen, 1998, *The Pakistan Army (1998 Edition)*, Karachi: Oxford University Press.

Dalrymple, William, 2006, *The Last Mughal: The Fall of a Dynasty*, Delhi, 1857, London: Bloomsbury Publishing Inc.

Faruki, Kemal A., 1971, *The Evolution of Islamic Constitutional Theory and Practice*, Karachi: National Publishing House.

Haq, Noor-ul, 1993, *Making Pakistan: The Military Perspective*, Islamabad: National Institute of Historical and Cultural Research.

Hamid, Shahid (Major-General retd.), 1986, *Disastrous Twilight*, London: Leo Cooper in association with Seckler & Warburg.

Husain, Noor A. (Brigadier retd.), 'The Role of [sic] Muslims Martial Races of Today's Pakistan in British-Indian Army in World War II', Defence Journal, Karachi, http:// HYPERLINK http://www.defencejournal.com/sept99/martial-races.htm www.defencejournal.com/sept99/martial-races.htm (accessed on 15 December 2009).

Jafar, Mohammed, Rehman, I.A., and Jafar, Ghani, 1977, *Jinnah: As a Parliamentarian*, Lahore: Azfar Associates.

Khan, Mohammad Ayub, 2006, *Friends not Masters: A Political Biography*, Islamabad: Mr Books.

Marston, Daniel P., 2009, 'The Indian Army, Partition, and the Punjab Boundary Force, 1945–1947', War in History, No. 16, Volume 4, Newbury Park, California: Sage Publications.

Nath, Ashok, 2009, Izzat: *Historical Records and Iconography of Indian Cavalry Regiments 1750–2007*, Centre for Armed Forces Historical Research.

Nehru, Jawaharlal, 1955, *An Autobiography*, London: The Bodley Head.

Qureshi, Naeem A., 1999, *Pan-Islam in British Indian Politics: A Study of the Khilafat Movement 1918–1924*, Leiden: Brill.

Riza, Shaukat (Major General retd.), 1989, *The Pakistan Army 1947–1949*, Lahore: Service Book Club.

Yong, Tan, Tai, 2005, *The Garrison State: The Military, Government and Society in Colonial Punjab, 1849–1947*, New Delhi, Thousand Oaks, London: Sage Publications.

Official Documents

Mansergh, Nicholas and Moon, Penderel, 1981, *The Transfer of Power 1942–1947, Volume X, The Mountbatten Viceroyalty, Formulation of a Plan, 23 March–30 May 1947*, London: Her Majesty's Stationery Office.

Mansergh, Nicholas and Moon, Penderel, 1982, *The Transfer of Power 1942–1947, Volume XI, The Mountbatten Viceroyalty: Announcement and Reception of the 3 June Plan, 31 May–7 July 1947*, London: Her Majesty's Stationery Office.

Mansergh, Nicholas and Moon, Penderel, 1983, *The Transfer of Power 1942–1947, Volume XII, The Mountbatten Viceroyalty, Princes, Partition and Independence, 8 July–15 August 1947*, London: Her Majesty's Stationery Office.

CHAPTER 4

Ahmed, Ishtiaq, 1998, *State, Nation and Ethnicity in Contemporary South Asia*, London and New York: Pinter Publishers.

Ahmed, Ishtiaq, 2010, 'Gandhi and the Politics of Religion', *Daily Times*, Lahore, 16 November 2010.

Ahmed, Ishtiaq, 2012, *The Punjab Bloodied, Partitioned and Cleansed: Unravelling the 1947 Tragedy through Secret British Reports and First-Person Accounts*, Karachi: Oxford University Press.

Amin, Agha Humayun, 1999, *The Pakistan Army till 1965*, Arlington, VA: Strategicus and Tacticus.

Banu, R.A., 1991, 'Ethnic Conflict, Autonomy, Democracy and National Integration: The Case of Chittagong Hill Tracts in Bangladesh', in Lindgren, G.L., Nordquist, K., and Wallensteen, P. (eds.), *Peace Processes in the Third World*, Uppsala: Department of Peace and Conflict Research.

Burki, Shahid Javed, 1991, *Pakistan: The Continuing Search for Nationhood, Boulder*, Colorado: Westview Press.

Cheema, Pervaiz Iqbal, 2003, *The Armed Forces of Pakistan*, Karachi: Oxford University Press.

Choudhary, S., 1991, *What is the Kashmir Problem?*, Luton: Jammu Kashmir Liberation Front.

Cloughley, Brian, 2000, *A History of the Pakistan Army: Wars and Insurrection*, Karachi: Oxford University Press.

Cohen, Stephen, 1998, *The Pakistan Army*, Karachi: Oxford University Press.

Fyzee, A.A.A., 1991, 'Accession of Kashmir is not Final', in Engineer, Asghar (ed.), *Secular Crown on Fire: The Kashmir Problem*, Delhi: Ajanta Publications.

Gankovsky, Y.V., and Gordon-Polonskaya, L.R., 1972, *A History of Pakistan (1947–1958)*, Lahore: People's Publishing House.

Hamid, Shahid, 1986, *Disastrous Twilight: A Personal Record of the Partition of India*, London: Leo Cooper in association with Secker and Warburg.

Haque, M., 1992, 'U.S. Role in the Kashmir Dispute: A Survey', *Regional Studies*, Vol. X, No. 4, Islamabad: Institute of Regional Studies.

Harrison, S.S., 1981, *In Afghanistan's Shadow: Baluch Nationalism and Soviet Temptations*, Washington DC: Carnegie Endowment for International Peace.

Jain, Rashmi (ed.), 2007a, *The United States and Pakistan 1947–2006: A Documentary Study*, New Delhi: Radiant Books.

Jalal, Ayesha, 1990, *The State of Martial Law: The Origins of Pakistan's Political Economy of Defence*, Cambridge: Cambridge University Press.

Jansson, Erland, 1981, *India, Pakistan or Pakhtunistan?*, Uppsala: Acta Universitatis Upsaliensis.

Khan, Muhammad Akbar, 1992, *Raiders in Kashmir*, Lahore: Jang Publishers.

Navlakha, Gautam, 1991, 'Bharat's Kashmir War', *Economic and Political Weekly*, vol. XXVI, no. 51, 21 December.

Nor val, Mitchell, 1968, *Sir George Cunningham: A Memoir, Edinburgh*, London: Blackwood.

Osborn, Robert B., 1994, *Field Marshal Sir Claude Auchinleck: The Indian Army and the Partition of India*, Ann Arbor, Michigan: UMI.

Riza, Shaukat (Major-General, retd.) 1989, *The Pakistan Army 1947–1949*, Lahore: Service Book Club.

Schaffer, Howard B., 2009, *The Limits of Influence: America's Role in Kashmir*, Washington Dc: Brookings Institute.

Siddiqi, A.R. (Brigadier, retd.), 1996, *The Military in Pakistan: Image and Reality*, Lahore, Vanguard.

Subrahmanyam, K., 1990, *'Kashmir', Strategic Analysis*, May 1990, Vol. XIII No. II, Delhi: Institute for Defence Studies and Analyses.

Teng, M.K. 1990, *Kashmir Article 370*, New Delhi: Anmol Publications.

US Library of Congress, http://lc wcb2.lo c.gov/cgi-bin/qucr y/r?f rd/c3tdy:@f icld (DOCID+in0189), (accessed on 21 July 2011)

Young, John W., 1993, *The Longman Companion to Cold War and Détente 1941–91*, London and New York: Longman.

Official Documents

Mansergh, N. and Moon, P., (eds.), 1976, T*he Transfer of Power, vol. vii, The Post-War Phase: New Moves by the Labour Government, 1 August 1945–22 March 1946*, London: Her Majesty's Stationery Office.

Interview

Lt. General (Retd.) Kudip Singh Khajuria, 10 November 2010, Noida, outside Delhi.

CHAPTER 5

Ahmed, Ishtiaq, 1987, *The Concept of an Islamic State: An Analysis of the Ideological Controversy in Pakistan*, London: Frances Pinter.

Ahmed, Ishtiaq, 1998, *State, Nation and Ethnicity in Contemporary South Asia*, London and New York: Pinter Publishers.

Alavi, Hamza, 1972, 'The State in Post-Colonial Societies: Pakistan and Bangladesh', *New Left Review*, 1/74 July–August.

Amin, Agha Humayun, 1999, *The Pakistan Army till 1965, Arlington*, VA: Strategicus and Tacticus.

Banu, R.A., 1991, 'Ethnic Conflict, Autonomy, Democracy and National Integration: The Case of Chittagong Hill Tracts in Bangladesh', in Lindgren, G.L., Nordquist, K., and Wallensteen, P. (eds.), *Peace Processes in the Third World*, Uppsala: Department of Peace and Conflict Research.

Bourke-White, Margaret, 1949, *Halfway to Freedom*, New York, Simon and Schuster.

Buhle, Paul, and Wagner, David, 2003, *Hide in Plain Sight: The Hollywood Blacklistees in Film and Television*, 1950–2002, Palgrave Macmillan, New York.

Burki, Shahid Javed, 1991, *Pakistan: The Continuing Search for Nationhood*, Boulder, Colorado: Westview Press.

Callard, Keith, 1957, *Pakistan: A Political Study*, London: Allen and Unwin.

Callard, Keith, 1959, *Political Forces in Pakistan 1947–1958*, New York: Institute of Pacific Relations.

Caroe, Sir Olaf, 1951, *Wells of Power*, London: Macmillan.

Cheema, Pervaiz Iqbal, 1990, *Pakistan's Defence Policy*, 1947–58, London: Macmillan Press.

Choudhary, S., 1991, *What is the Kashmir Problem?*, Luton: Jammu Kashmir Liberation Front.

Cloughley, Brian, 2000, *A History of the Pakistan Army: Wars and Insurrection*, Karachi: Oxford University Press.

Dreyfuss, Robert, 2005, *Devil's Game: How the United States Helped Unleash Fundamentalist Islam*, New York: Metropolitan Books/Henry Holt and Company.

Gankovsky, Y.V., and Gordon-Polonskaya, L.R., 1972, *A History of Pakistan (1947–1958)*, Lahore: People's Publishing House.

Harrison, S.S., 1981, *In Afghanistan's Shadow: Baluch Nationalism and Soviet Temptations*, Washington DC: Carnegie Endowment for International Peace.

Horowitz, David, 1967, *From Yalta to Vietnam, Harmondsworth*, Middlesex: Penguin Books.

Jain, Rashmi (ed.), 2007a, *The United States and Pakistan 1947–2006: A Documentary Study*, New Delhi: Radiant Books.

Jain, Rashmi (ed.), 2007b, *The United States and India 1947–2006: A Documentary Study*, New Delhi: Radiant Books.

Jalal, Ayesha, 1990, *The State of Martial Law: The Origins of Pakistan's Political Economy of Defence*, Cambridge: Cambridge University Press.

Jones, K.W., 1989, *The New Cambridge History of India: Socio-Religious Reform Movements in British India*, Cambridge: Cambridge University Press.

Khan, Ghulam Jilani (Lt Col, Retd.), 2004, SSG *Tarikh ke Aine Main, Cherat:* Headquarters SSG.

Khan, Mohammad Ayub, 2006, *Friends not Masters*, Islamabad: Mr Books.

Khan, Muhammad Akbar, 1992, *Raiders in Kashmir*, Lahore: Jang Publishers.

Khan, M. Asghar, 2005, *My Political Struggle*, Karachi: Oxford University Press.

Kux, Dennis, 1992, *India and the United States: Estranged Democracies*, Washington DC: National Defense University Press.

Kux, Dennis, 2001, *The United States and Pakistan 1947–2000: Disenchanted Allies*, New York: Oxford University Press.

Mitha, Major General A.O., 2003, *Unlikely Beginnings: A Soldier's Life*, Karachi: Oxford University Press.

Nawaz, Shuja, 2008, Crossed Swords: *Pakistan, its Army, and the Wars Within*, Karachi: Oxford University Press.

Nor val, Mitchell, 1968, Sir George Cunningham: *A Memoir, Edinburgh*, London Blackwood.

Osborn, Robert B., 1994, *Field Marshal Sir Claude Auchinleck: The Indian Army and the Partition of India*, Ann Arbor, Michigan: UMI.

Ray, Aswini K., 2004, *Western Realism and International Relations: a Non-Western View*, New Delhi: Foundation Books.

Report of the Court of Inquiry constituted under Punjab Act II of 1954 to enquire into the Punjab Disturbances of 1953, 1954, Lahore: Government Printing Press.

Riza, Shaukat (Major-General, Retd.), 1989, *The Pakistan Army 1947–1949*, Lahore: Service Book Club.

Siddiqi, A.R. (Brigadier, Retd.), 1996, *The Military in Pakistan: Image and Reality*, Lahore: Vanguard.

Sohail, Massarat, 1991, *Partition and Anglo-Pakistan Relations, 1947–51*, Lahore: Vanguard.

Speeches and Writings of Mr Jinnah, vol. II, 1976. Lahore: Sh. Muhammad Ashraf.

Young, John W., 1993, *The Longman Companion to Cold War and Détente 1941–91*, London and New York: Longman.

Official Documents

Constitution of the Islamic Republic of Pakistan, Karachi: Government Printing Press, 1956.

The Pakistan Constituent Assembly Debates, Volume V, Karachi: Government Printing Press, 1949.

Government Commission Report

Report of the Court of Inquiry constituted under Punjab Act II of 1954 to enquire into the Punjab Disturbances of 1953, 1954, Lahore: Government Printing Press.

CHAPTER 6

Aijazuddin, Fakir Syed, 2002, *The White House and Pakistan: Secret Declassified Documents*, 1969–1974, Karachi: Oxford University Press.

Bhutto, Zulfikar Ali, 1966, *The Quest for Peace*, Karachi: The Pakistan Institute of International Affairs.

Bhutto, Zulfikar Ali, 1969, *The Myth of Independence*, London: Oxford University Press.

Gauhar, Altaf, 1998, Ayub Khan: *Pakistan's First Military Ruler*, Lahore: Sang-e-Meel Publications.

Huntington, Samuel P., 1962, *Changing Pattern of Military Politics,* New York: Free Press of Glencoe.

Jain, Rashmi (ed.), 2007a, *The United States and Pakistan 1947–2006: A Documentary Study*, New Delhi: Radiant Books.

Jain, Rashmi (ed.), 2007b, *The United States and India 1947–2006: A Documentary Study*, New Delhi: Radiant Studies.

Jalal, Ayesha, 1991, *The State of Martial Law Rule: The Origins of Pakistan's Political Economy of Defence*, Cambridge: Cambridge University Press.

Khan, Mohammad Asghar, 2005, *We've Learnt Nothing from History*, Pakistan: Politics and Military Power, Karachi: Oxford University Press.

Khan, Mohammad Ayub, 2006, *Friends not Master: A Political Autobiography*, Islamabad: Mr Books.

Kux, Dennis, 2006, *The United States and Pakistan 1947–2000: Disenchanted Allies*, New York: Oxford University Press.

Malik, Bashir A., 2005, *Indus Waters Treaty in Retrospect*, Lahore: Brite Books.

Maxwell, Neville, 1970, *India's China War*, New York: Pantheon Books.

Nawaz, Shuja, 2008, *Crossed Swords: Pakistan, Its Army, and the Wars Within*, Karachi: Oxford University Press.

Nyrop, Richard F., 1984, *Pakistan: A Country Study*, Washington DC: The American University.

Ray, Aswini K., 2004, *Western Realism and International Relations: a Non-Western View*, New Delhi: Foundation books.

Rizvi, Hasan-Askari, 2009, T*he Military and Politics in Pakistan 1947–1997*, Lahore: Sang-e-Meel Publications.

Schofield, Julian, 2007, *Militarization and War*, Houndsmill, Basingstoke, Hampshire: Palgrave Macmillan.

Siddiqa, Ayesha, 2007, *Military Inc. Inside Pakistan's Military Economy*, Karachi: Oxford University Press.

Singleton, George, 2010 (8 May), 'Remembering Gary Powers' U2 flight from Peshawar in 1960', Lahore: *Daily Times*.

Tahir-Kheli, Shirin, R., 1997, *India, Pakistan and the United States: Breaking with the Past*, New York: Council on Foreign Relations Press.

Ziring, Lawrence, 1971, *The Ayub Khan Era: Politics in Pakistan 1958–1969*, Syracuse: Syracuse University Press.

CHAPTER 7

Abbas, Hassan, 2005, *Pakistan's Drift into Extremism: Allah, the Army, and America's War on Terror*, New Delhi: Pentagon Press.

Amin, Agha Humayun, 1999, *The Pakistan Army till 1965, Arlington*, VA: Strategicus and Tacticus.

Cloughley, Brian, 2000, *A History of the Pakistan Army: Wars and Insurrections*, Karachi: Oxford University Press.

Gauhar, Altaf, 1998, *Ayub Khan: Pakistan's First Military Ruler*, Lahore: Sang-e-Meel Publications.

Husain, Syed Wajahat, 2010, *Memoirs of a Soldier: 1947 Before*, During, After, Lahore: Ferozsons (Pvt) Ltd.

Jain, Rashmi (ed.), 2007a, *The United States and Pakistan 1947–2006: A Documentary Study*, New Delhi: Radiant Books.

Jain, Rashmi (ed.), 2007b, *The United States and India 1947–2006: A Documentary Study*, New Delhi: Radiant Studies.

Khan, Gohar Ayub, 2007, *Glimpses into the Corridors of Power*, Karachi: Oxford University Press.

Khan, Gul Hassan, 1993, *Memoirs of Lt. Gen. Gul Hassan Khan*, Karachi: Oxford University Press.

Khan, M. Asghar, 2004, *My Political Struggle*, Karachi: Oxford University Press.

Khan, Nur, 2005, 'Nur Khan reminisces '65 war', *Dawn*, Karachi, HYPERLINK "http://www.dawn" http://www.dawn. com/2005/09/06/nat2.htm, (accessed on 3 May 2010).

Khan, Sultan Muhammad, 1997, *Memories and Reflections of a Pakistani Diplomat*, Karachi: Paramount Publishing Enterprise.

Kux, Dennis, *The United States and Pakistan 1947–2000: Disenchanted Allies*, New York: Oxford University Press.

LaPorte, Jr., Robert, 1969, 'Succession in Pakistan, continuity and change in a garrison state', *Asian Survey*, 9, 11 November 1969.

Nawaz, Shuja, 2009, *Crossed Swords: Pakistan, its Army*, and the Wars Within, Karachi: Oxford University Press.

Schofield, Julian, 2007, *Militarization and War*, Houndsmill, Basingstoke, Hampshire: Palgrave Macmillan.

Siddiqi, A.R. (Brigadier, Retd.), 1996, *The Military in Pakistan: Image and Reality*, Lahore: Vanguard.

Singleton, George, 2010 (8 May), 'Remembering Gary Powers' U2 flight from Peshawar in 1960', Lahore: *Daily Times*.

US Library of Congress, http://l c web2.l oc.gov/cg i-b in/query/r?frd/cs tdy:@ field(DOCID+in0189) (accessed on 21 July 2011).

Ziring, Lawrence, 1971, *The Ayub Khan Era: Politics in Pakistan 1958–1969, Syracuse*: Syracuse University Press.

Interviews

Pakistani Officers

Brigadier (Retd.) Yasub Ali Dogar, from Lahore through several emails and internet interview during March–May 2010

Colonel (Retd.) Aslam Cheema, 12 December 2008, Rawalpindi Major (Retd.) Saeed

Akhtar Malik, 17 December 2008, Rawalpindi Major (Retd.), Agha Humayun Amin, 10 November 2011, Lahore

Indian Officers

Lt. Gen. Kuldip Singh Khajuria, 12 November 2010, New Delhi Major General Afsir Karim, 12 November 2010, New Delhi Brigadier Vijai K. Nair, 12 November 2010, New Delhi

US–Pakistan Experts

Christine Fair, 6 July 2009, Washington DC Walter Andersen, 8 July 2009, Washington DC Selig Harrison, 17 July 2009, Washington DC Marvin Weinbaum, 19 July 2009, Washington DC

CHAPTER 8

Ahmed, Feroz, 1973, 'The Structural Matrix of the Struggle in Bangladesh', in Gough, K. and Sharma, H.P. (eds.), *Imperialism and Revolution in South Asia*, New York: Monthly Review Press.

Ahmed, Ishtiaq, 1998, State, *Nation and Ethnicity in Contemporary South Asia*, London and New York: Pinter Publishers.

Aijazuddin, Fakir Syed, 2002, *The White House and Pakistan: Secret Declassified Documents 1969–1974*, Karachi: Oxford University Press.

Alam, S.M. Shamsul, 1995, *The State, Class Formation, and Development in Bangladesh*, Lanham: University Press of America.

Ali, Nadir (Colonel, Retd.), 2010, 'A Khaki Dissident on 1971', *Viewpoint*, Online Issue No. 31, 17 December 2010, HYPERLINK http://www.viewpointonline.net/a-khaki-dissident-on-1971 http://www.viewpointonline.net/a-khaki-dissident-on-1971.html (accessed on 17 December 2010).

Ali, Syed Shafaat, 2007, *The Soldier: A Memoir of Colonel (Retd.) Syed Shafaat Ali*, Karachi: Royal Book Company.

Baxter, Craig, 1997, *Bangladesh, from a Nation to a State*, Boulder: Westview Press.

Callard, Keith, 1957, *Pakistan: A Political Study*, London: Allen and Unwin.

Chowdhury, Iftekhar Ahmed, 2009, *The Roots of Bangladeshi National Identity: Their Impact on State Behavior*, Singapore: Institute of South Asian Studies.

Cloughley, Brian, 2000, *A History of the Pakistan Army: Wars and Insurrection*, Karachi: Oxford University Press.

Deora, M.S. (ed.), *India and the Freedom Struggle of Bangladesh*, New Delhi: Discovery of Publishing House.

Gankovsky, Y.V., and Gordon-Polonskaya, L.R., 1972, *A History of Pakistan (1947–1958)*, Lahore: People's Publishing House.

Jackson, Robert, 1975, *South Asian Crisis: India–Pakistan–Bangladesh*, London: Chatto and Windus.

Khan, Ayub, Mohammad, 2006, *Friends not Masters*, Islamabad: Mr Books.

Khan, Fazal Muqeem (Major General, Retd.), 1973, *Pakistan's Crisis in Leadership*, Islamabad: National Book Foundation.

Khan, Mohammad Asghar, 2005, *We've Learnt Nothing from History*, Pakistan: Politics and Military Power, Karachi: Oxford University Press.

Khan, Sultan Muhammad, 2006, *Memories & Reflections of a Pakistani Diplomat (second edition)*, Karachi: Paramount Books.

Kux, Dennis, 2001, *The United States and Pakistan 1947–2000: Disenchanted Allies*, Karachi: Oxford University Press.

Mitha, A.O. (Major General, Retd.), 2003, *Unlikely Beginnings: A Soldier's Life*, Karachi: Oxford University Press.

Nawaz, Shuja, 2008, Crossed Swords: *Pakistan, Its Army, and the Wars Within*, Karachi: Oxford University Press.

Niazi, Amir Abdullah Khan, 1999, *The Betrayal of East Pakistan*, Karachi: Oxford University Press.

Qureshi, Major General Hakeem Arshad, 2002, *The 1971 Indo-Pak War: A Soldier's Narrative*, Karachi: Oxford University Press.

Siddiqi, A.R. (Brigadier, Retd.), 2004, *East Pakistan, The Endgame: An Onlooker's Journal 1969–1971*, Karachi: Oxford University Press.

Sisson, Richard and Rose, Leo E., 1991, *War and Secession: Pakistan, India, and the Creation of Bangladesh*, Berkeley, Los Angeles, Oxford: University of California.

Story of Pakistan, HYPERLINK http://www.storyofpakistan.com/articletext.asp?artid=A115 http://www.storyofpakistan.com/articletext.asp?artid=A115 (accessed on 3 May 2010).

The Bangladesh Papers, no date given, Lahore: Vanguard.

Zaheer, Hasan, 1995, *The Separation of East Pakistan: The Rise and Realization of Bengali Muslim Nationalism*, Karachi: Oxford University Press.

Ziring, Lawrence, 1971, *The Ayub Khan Era: Politics in Pakistan 1958-1969*, Syracuse: Syracuse University Press.

Government Report

The Report of the Hamoodur Rehman Commission of Inquiry into the 1971 War: As Declassified by the Government of Pakistan, 2001, Lahore: Vanguard.

Interview

Juned Chowdhury, 19 April 2010, Singapore.

CHAPTER 9

Ahmed, Feroz, 1973, 'The Structural Matrix of the Struggle in Bangladesh' in Gough, K. and Sharma, H.P. (eds.), Imperialism and Revolution in South Asia, New York: Monthly Review Press.

Ahmed, Ishtiaq, 1998, State, *Nation and Ethnicity in Contemporary South Asia*, London and New York: Pinter Publishers.

Aijazuddin, Fakir Syed, 2002, *The White House and Pakistan: Secret Declassified Documents 1969–1974*, Karachi: Oxford University Press.

Alam, S.M. Shamsul, 1995, *The State, Class Formation, and Development in Bangladesh*, Lanham: University Press of America.

Ali, Nadir (Colonel, Retd.), 2010, 'A Khaki Dissident on 1971', Viewpoint, Online Issue No. 31, 17 December 2010, HYPERLINK http://www.viewpointonline.net/a-khaki-dissident-on-1971 http://www.viewpointonline.net/a-khaki-dissident-on-1971.html (accessed on 17 December 2010).

Ali, Syed Shafaat, 2007, *The Soldier: A Memoir of Colonel (Retd.) Syed Shafaat Ali*, Karachi: Royal Book Company.

Baxter, Craig, 1997, *Bangladesh, from a Nation to a State*, Boulder: Westview Press.

Callard, Keith, 1957, *Pakistan: A Political Study*, London: Allen and Unwin.

Cloughley, Brian, 2000, *A History of the Pakistan Army: Wars and Insurrection*, Karachi: Oxford University Press.

Deora, M.S. (ed.), *India and the Freedom Struggle of Bangladesh*, New Delhi: Discovery of Publishing House.

Jackson, Robert, 1975, *South Asian Crisis: India–Pakistan–Bangladesh*, London: Chatto and Windus.

Khan, Ayub, Mohammad, 2006, *Friends not Masters*, Islamabad: Mr Books.

Khan, Fazal Muqeem (Major General, Retd.), 1973, *Pakistan's Crisis in Leadership*, Islamabad: National Book Foundation.

Khan, Mohammad Asghar, 2005, *We've Learnt Nothing from History*, Pakistan: Politics and Military Power, Karachi: Oxford University Press.

Khan, Sultan Muhammad, 2006, *Memories & Reflections of a Pakistani Diplomat (second edition)*, Karachi: Paramount Books.

Kux, Dennis, 2001, *The United States and Pakistan 1947–2000: Disenchanted Allies*, Karachi: Oxford University Press.

Mitha, A.O. (Major General, Retd.), 2003, *Unlikely Beginnings: A Soldier's Life*, Karachi: Oxford University Press.

Nawaz, Shuja, 2008, *Crossed Swords: Pakistan, Its Army, and the Wars Within*, Karachi: Oxford University Press.

Niazi, Amir Abdullah Khan, 1999, *The Betrayal of East Pakistan*, Karachi: Oxford University Press.

Qureshi, Major General Hakeem Arshad, 2002, *The 1971 Indo-Pak War: A Soldier's Narrative*, Karachi: Oxford University Press.

Siddiqi, A.R., 2004, East Pakistan, *The Endgame: An Onlooker's Journal 1969–1971*, Karachi: Oxford University Press.

Sisson, Richard and Rose, Leo E., 1991, *War and Secession: Pakistan, India, and the Creation of Bangladesh, Berkeley*, Los Angeles, Oxford: University of California.

Story of Pakistan, HYPERLINK http://www.storyofpakistan.com/articletext.asp?artid=A115 http://www.storyofpakistan.com/articletext.asp?artid=A115 (accessed on 3 May 2010).

The Bangladesh Papers, no date given, Lahore: Vanguard.

The Report of the Hamoodur Rehman Commission of Inquiry into the 1971 War: As Declassified by the Government of Pakistan, 2001, Lahore: Vanguard.

Zaheer, Hasan, 1995, *The Separation of East Pakistan: The Rise and Realization of Bengali Muslim Nationalism*, Karachi: Oxford University Press

Interviews

Lieutenant General (Retd.) Javed Ashraf Qazi, 19 December 2008, Islamabad Brigadier (Retd.) Yasub Ali Dogar, 27 April 2010, via email from Lahore Iftekhar Ahmed Chowdhury, 28 April 2010, Singapore

Colonel (Retd.), Riaz Jafri, 17 December 2011, via email from Rawalpindi

CHAPTER 10

Ahamed, Syeed, 2010 (May), 'The Curious Case of the 195 War Criminals', in *Forum* (a monthly publication of the Daily Star, 5 May 2010) HYPERLINK http://www.thedailystar.net/ (http://www.thedailystar.net/ forum/2010/may/curious.htm (accessed on 29 September 2010).

Ahmed, Ishtiaq, 2010, 'The Pakistan Islamic State Project: A Secular Critique', in Michael Heng Siam-Heng and Ten Chin Liew (eds.), *State and Secularism: Perspectives from Asia*, Singapore: World Scientific Publishers Co. Pte. Ltd.

Ahmed, Viqar and Amjad, Rashid, 1984, *The Management of Pakistan's Economy 1947–82*, Karachi: Oxford University Press.

Aijazuddin, Fakir Syed, 2002, *The White House and Pakistan: Secret Declassified Documents 1969–1974*, Karachi: Oxford University Press.

Amin, Agha Humayun, 2001, 'Remembering our Heroes: Group Captain (Retd.) Cecil Chaudhry, *Defence Journal*, 4, No. 11, June 2001, Karachi.

Beg, Aziz, 1974, *Story of Islamic Summit in Lahore*, Lahore: Babur and Amer Publications.

Bhutto, Zulfikar Ali, 1969, *The Myth of Independence*, London: Oxford University Press.

Bhutto, Zulfikar Ali, 1979, *If I am Assassinated*, New Delhi: Vikas Publishing House Pvt Ltd.

Burki, Shahid Javed, 1980, *Pakistan Under Bhutto*, 1971–1977, London: The Macmillan Press.

Chishti, Faiz Ali, 1996, *Betrayals of another Kind: Islam*, Democracy and the Army in Pakistan, Lahore: Jang Publishers.

Harrison, Selig S., 1981, *In Afghanistan's Shadow: Baluch Nationalism and Soviet Temptations*, Washington DC: Carnegie Endowment for International Peace.

Hilaly, Zafar, 2011 (26 March), 'Nayyar need not worry', *The News*, Karachi.

Hussain, Syed Shabbir, 2010, *Ayub, Bhutto and Zia*, Lahore: Sang-e-Meel Publications.

Jain, Rashmi (ed.), 2007a, *The United States and Pakistan 1947–2006: A Documentary Study*, New Delhi: Radiant Books.

Khan, Gul Hassan, 1993, Memoirs of Lt. Gen. Gul Hassan Khan, Karachi: Oxford University Press.

Khan, M. Asghar, 2008, *My Political Struggle*, Karachi: Oxford University Press.

Khan, M. Asghar, 1983, *Generals in Politics: Pakistan 1958–82*, New Delhi: Vikas Publishing House Pvt Ltd.

Kux, Dennis, 2001, *The United States and Pakistan 1947–2000: Disenchanted Allies*, New York: Oxford University Press.

Mahmud, Khalid, 1987, *Pakistan Mein Mazdoor Therik (The Labour Movement in Pakistan)*, Lahore: Maktab-e-Fikr-o-Danish.

Mazari, Sherbaz Khan, 2001, *Pakistan: A Journey to Disillusionment*, Karachi: Oxford University Press.

Nawaz, Shuja, 2008, *Crossed Swords: Pakistan, its Army, and the Wars Within*, Karachi: Oxford University Press.

Newburg, Paula, 2002, *Judging the State: Courts and Constitutional Politics in Pakistan*, Cambridge: Cambridge University Press.

Rashid, Rao, 2010, Jo Meiney Dekha: *Pakistani Syasat aur Hukumrani ki Haqiqat (What I Saw: The Inside Story of Pakistani Politics and Governance)*, Lahore: Jamhoori Publications.

Saeed, Shahid, 2010 (22 September), 'Much ado about feudalism', Lahore: *Daily Times*.

Sayeed, Khalid Bin, 1980, *Politics in Pakistan: The Nature and Direction of Change*, New York: Praeger.

Shafqat, Saeed, 1997, Civil-Military Relations in Pakistan: From *Zulfikar Ali Bhutto to Benazir Bhutto*, Boulder, Colorado: Westview Press.

Taseer, Salman, 1979, *Bhutto: A Political Biography*, London: Ithaca Press.
Wali, Asfandyar, 2003 (26 August), 'More autonomy to the provinces', Karachi: Dawn, HYPERLINK http://www.dawn.com/2003/08/26/fea.htm#2 http://www.dawn.com/2003/08/26/fea.htm#2 (accessed on 20 October 2010).
Yusuf, Hamid, 1999, Pakistan: *A Study of Political Developments 1947–97*, Lahore: Sang-e-Meel Publications.

Newspapers

Dawn, 10 January 2010, Karachi.
The Asian Age, 6 December 2011, New Delhi

Interviews

Dr Ghulam Husain (former PPP general secretary and federal minister), 26 September 2010, Stockholm
Ahmed Faqih (PPP activist from Lahore), 26 September 2010, Stockholm
Mir Muhammad Ali Talpur, from Hyderabad, Sindh, 26 October 2010, via email

CHAPTER 11

Ahmad, Jamil-ud-Din (ed.), 1968, Speeches and Writings of Mr Jinnah, Vol. I, Lahore: Sh. Muhammad Ashraf
Ahmed, Ishtiaq, 1987, The Concept of An Islamic State: An Analysis of the Ideological Controversy in Pakistan, London: Frances Pinter; New York: St. Martin's Press.
Ahmed, Ishtiaq, 1998, State, Nation and Ethnicity in Contemporary South Asia, London/ New York: Pinter.
Ahmed, Ishtiaq, 1999, 'South Asia', in David Westerlund and Ingvar Svanberg (eds.), Islam Outside the Arab World, Richmond: Curzon Press.
Ahmed, Ishtiaq, 2005, 'The Politics of Group Rights in India and Pakistan', in Ishtiaq
Ahmed (ed.), The Politics of Group Rights: The State and Multiculturalism, Lanham, Maryland: University Press of America.
Ahmed, Khaled, 2004 (16 April), 'Debate on textbooks, Pakistani style', Friday Times, Lahore.
Amin, Agha Humayun, 2001, 'Remembering our Heroes: Group Captain (Retd.) Cecil Chaudhry, Defence Journal, 4, No. 11, June 2001, Karachi.
Aziz, K.K., 1993, The Murder of History: A Critique of History Textbooks used in Pakistan, Lahore: Vanguard Books. Baxter, Craig, 1991, 'Restructuring the Pakistan Political System' in Burki, Shahid Javed and Craig, Baxter (eds.), Pakistan Under the Military: Eleven Years of Zia ul-Haq, Bounder, Colorada: Westview Press.

Bhutto, Benazir, 2008a, Daughter of the East: An Autobiography, London: Pocket Books.

Bhutto, Fatima, 2010, Songs of Blood and Sword: A Daughter's Memoir, New Delhi: Viking.

Chaudhry, Cecil (Group Captain), 2001, 'Remembering our Heroes', Defence Journal, 4, No. 11, June 2001, Karachi.

Cohen, Stephen P., 1992, The Pakistan Army, Karachi: Oxford University Press.

Hasan, Khalid, 2007 (27 May), 'Zia formed the MQM: General Aslam Beg', *Daily Times*, Lahore.

Hussain, Syed Shabbir, 2010, Ayub, Bhutto and Zia: How they fell Victim to their own Plans, Lahore: Sang-e-Meel Publications.

Jahangir, Asma and Jilani, Hina, 2003, The Hudood Ordinances: A Divine Sanction? Lahore: Sang-e-Meel Publications.

Kardar, Shahid, 1992, 'Polarizations in the Regions and Prospects for Integration' in Zaidi, S.A. (ed.), Regional Imbalances & The National Question in Pakistan, Lahore: Vanguard.

Khan, M.A. 1983, Generals in Politics: Pakistan 1958–1982, New Delhi: Vikas Publishing House Pvt Ltd.

Malik, S.K., 1979, The Quranic Concept of War, Lahore: Wajidalis.

Maududi, Syed Abul Ala, 1979a, Islami Riyasat, Lahore: Islamic Publications Ltd.

Maududi, Syed Abul Ala, 1979b, Khilafat-o-Malukiat, Lahore: Idara Tarjuman-ul-Quran.

Maududi, Syed Abul Ala, 1980, The Islamic Law and Constitution, Lahore: Islamic Publications Ltd.

Maududi, Syed Abul Ala, 1981, Al-Jihad Fi Al-Islam, Lahore: Idara Tarjuman-ul-Quran.

Mehdi, S., 1988, Politics without Parties: A Report on the 1985 Partyless Election in Pakistan, Lahore: A SAHE Publication.

Mumtaz, Khawar and Shaheed, Farida, 1987, Women of Pakistan, Lahore: Vanguard.

Munir, Muhammad, 1980, From Jinnah to Zia, Lahore: Vanguard.

Nayyar, A.H. and Salim, Ahmad, 2004, The Subtle Subversion: The State of Curricula and Textbooks in Pakistan, Islamabad: SDPI.

Noman, Omar, 1988, The Political Economy of Pakistan 1947–85, London: Kegan Paul International.

Rahman, Tariq, 2004, Denizens of Alien Worlds: A Study of Education, Inequality and Polarization in Pakistan, Karachi: Oxford University Press.

Saigol, Rubina, 2003, 'History, Social Sciences and Civics and the Creation of Enemies', in Zaidi, Akbar S., Social Sciences in Pakistan in the 1990, Islamabad: Council of the Social Sciences.

Usmani, Muhammad Taqi, 1990, 'Islamization of Laws in Pakistan', Shaheed-ul Islam Muhammad Zia ul-Haq, London: Indus Thames Publishers.

Weiss, Anita M. (ed.), 1986, The Application of Islamic Law in a Modern State, Syracuse: Syracuse University Press.

Newspapers

The Tribune, 4 August 2005, Chandigarh.

Interviews

Major (Retd.) Agha Humayun Amin, 19 December 2010, via email from Lahore
Brigadier (Retd.), Vijai Nair, 21 February 2011, Noida, outside Delhi

CHAPTER 12

Abbas, Hassan, 2005, *Pakistan's Drift into Extremism: Allah, the Army, and America's War on Terror*, New Delhi: Pentagon Press.

Ali, Saleem H., 2009, *Islam and Education: Conf lict and Conformity in Pakistan's Madrassahs*, Karachi: Oxford University Press.

Arif, General Khalid Mahmud, 2001, *Khaki Shadows: Pakistan 1947–1997*, Karachi: Oxford University Press.

Azzam, Salem, 1990, 'Foreword by Salem Azzam, Secretary General, Islamic Council, London', *Shaheed-ul Islam Muhammad Zia ul-Haq*, London: Indus Thames Publishers.

Baxter, Craig, 1991, 'Pakistan Becomes Prominent in the International Arena' in Burki, *Shahid Javed and Baxter, Craig (eds.), Pakistan Under the Military: Eleven Years of Zia ul-Haq*, Boulder, Colorado: Westview Press.

Bhutto, Benazir, 2008a, *Daughter of the East: An Autobiography*, London: Pocket Books.

Bhutto, Fatima, 2010, *Songs of Blood and Sword: A Daughter's Memoir*, New Delhi: Viking.

Brzezinski, Zbigniew, 2011, 'Inter view', HYPERLINK http://www.gwu.edu/%7Ensarchiv/coldwar/http://www.g wu.edu/~nsarchiv/coldwar/ interviews/episode-17/brzezinski2.html, The National Security Archive: The George Washington University, (accessed on 7 January 2011).

Burki, Shahid Javed, 1991, 'Zia's Eleven Years', in Burki, Shahid Javed and Baxter, Craig (eds.), *Pakistan Under the Military: Eleven Years of Zia ul-Haq*, Boulder, Colorado: Westview Press.

Chaudhry, Cecil (Group Captain), 2001, '*Remembering our Heroes*', *Defence Journal*, 4, No. 11 (Karachi) (June 2001).

Cheema, Pervaiz Iqbal, 2003, *Pakistan's Defence Policy*, 1947–8, Karachi: Oxford University Press.

Cohen, Stephen P., 1992, *The Pakistan Army*, Karachi: Oxford University Press.

Coll, Steve, 2004, *Ghost Wars: The Secret History of the CIA, Afghanistan, From the Soviet Invasion to September 10, 2001*, New York: Penguin Books.

Cooley, John K., 2000, *Unholy Wars: Afghanistan, America and International Terrorism*, London: Pluto Press.

Farr, Grant M., 1985, *'The Effect of the Afghan Refugees on Pakistan' in Craig Baxter (ed.), Zia's Pakistan: Politics of Stability in a Frontline State*, Lahore: Vanguard.

Haqqani, Husain, 2005, *Pakistan: Between Mosque and Military*, Washington DC: Carnegie Endowment for International Peace.

Harrison, Selig, 2001, '*CIA Worked in Tandem with Pak to Create Taliban*', *in Times of India*, New Delhi (8 March 2001).

Hasan, Ibn-ul, 1990, '*Zia-ul-Haq – A Defence Planner*', *Shaheed-ul Islam Muhammad Zia ul-Haq*, London: Indus Thames Publishers.

Jain, Rashmi (ed.), 2007a, *The United States and Pakistan 1947–2006: A Documentary Study*, New Delhi: Radiant Books.

Jan, Abid Ullah, 2002, 'Target: Jihad, madrassa or Islam?', Muslim Uzbekistan, http,// archive.muslimuzbekistan.com/eng/islam/2002/09/ a09092002.html (accessed on 3 January 2010), (9 September 2002).

Malik, Zahid, 1990, '*Pakistan's Atomic Programme and General Zia-ul-Haq*', *in Shaheed-ul Islam Muhammad Zia ul-Haq*, London: Indus Thames Publishers.

Mamdani, Mahmood, 2004, *Good Muslim, Bad Muslim*, New York: Pantheon Books.

Musharraf, Pervez, 2006, *In the Line of Fire*, London: Simon and Schuster.

Noorani, A.G., 1991, 'Benazir's Surrender to Generals' in Engineer, A. (ed.), *Secular Crown on Fire: The Kashmir Problem*, Delhi: Ajanta Publications.

Rana, Muhammad Amir, 2004, *A to Z of Jehadi Organizations in Pakistan (translated into English by Saba Ansari)*, Lahore: Mashal Books.

Rashid, Ahmed, 2000, *Taliban, Militant Islam, Oil and Fundamentalism in Central Asia*, New Haven: Yale University Press.

Siddiqa, Ayesha, 2007, *Military Inc.: Inside Pakistan's Military Economy*, Karachi: Oxford University Press.

Stephens, Joe and Ottaway, David B., 2002, 'From the U.S., ABC of Jihad', *The Washington Post*, HYPERLINK http://www.washingtonpost.com/ac2/wp-dyn/ A5339%E2%80%932002Mar22?language http://www.washingtonpost.com/ac2/ wp-dyn/A5339-2002Mar22?language=printer, (23 March 2002), (accessed on 3 January 2010).

Suleri, Z.A., 1990, 'A Leader of Humanity, Faith and Vision', Shaheed-ul Islam Muhammad Zia ul-Haq, London: Indus Thames Publishers.

The United States and Pakistan's Quest for the Bomb, HYPERLINK http://www.gwu.edu/%7Ensarchiv/ http://www.gwu.edu/~nsarchiv/ nukevault/ebb333/index.htm, The National Security Archive: The George Washington University, (accessed on 7 January 2011).

White Paper on the Punjab Agitation, 10 July, 1984, New Delhi: Government of India.

Interviews

Lt. Gen. (Retd.) Hamid Gul, 17, December, 2008, Rawalpindi

Colonel (Retd.) Imam, a.k.a. Sultan Amir Tarar, 18 December 2008, Rawalpindi

Ambassador Wendy Chamberlin, 8 July 2009

Ambassador Robin Raphael, 16 July 2009, Washington DC

Shahid Javed Burki, 27 May 2010, Singapore

CHAPTER 13

Abbas, Hassan, 2005, *Pakistan's Drift into Extremism: Allah, the Army, and America's War on Terror*, New Delhi: Pentagon Press.

ABC News, 30 November 2007, HYPERLINK http://blogs.abcnews.com/theblotter/2007/11/musharraf-http://blogs.abcnews.com/theblotter/2007/11/musharraf-rival.html (accessed on 13 February 2011).

Ahmed, Ishtiaq, 1998, *State, Nation, and Ethnicity in Contemporary South Asia*, London and New York: Pinter Publishers.

Ahmed, Ishtiaq, 2002, 'Globalisation and Human Rights in Pakistan', *International Journal of Punjab Studies*, Vol. 9, No. 1, pp. 57–89, January–June 2002.

Ahmed, Ishtiaq, 2011, 'Religious nationalism and minorities in Pakistan: The Constitutional and Legal Bases of Discrimination', in Ahmed, Ishtiaq (ed.), *The Politics of Religion in South and Southeast Asia*, London: Routledge.

Amin, Agha Humayun, Osinski, David J., and DeGeorges, Paul Andre, 2010, *The Development of Taliban Factions in Afghanistan and Pakistan: A Geographical Account*, February 2010, New York: The Edwin Mellen Press Ltd.

Anand, Dev, 2007, *Romancing with Life*, New Delhi: Viking/Penguin.

Aziz, Sartaj, 2009, *Between Dreams and Realities: Some Milestones in Pakistan's History*, Karachi: Oxford University Press.

Bhatia, Shyam, 2010, Goodbye *Shahzadi: A Political Biography of Benazir Bhutto*, New Delhi: Lotus Collection, Roli Books.

Bhutto, Benazir, 2008b, *Reconciliation: Islam, Democracy, and the West*, New York: HarperCollins Publishers.

Bhutto, Fatima, 2010, *Songs of Blood and Sword: A Daughter's Memoir*, New Delhi: Viking.

Burns, John F., 1998, 'House of Graft: Tracing the Benazir Millions – A special report; Benazir Clan Leaves Trail of Corruption', *The New York Times*, (8 January 1998), http:// HYPERLINK http://www.nytimes.com/1998/01/09/world/house-graft-tracing-Benazir-millions-special- www.nytimes.com/1998/01/09/world/house-graft-tracing-Benazir-millions-special-report-Benazir-clan-leaves-trail.html (accessed on 26 January 2011).

Cohen, Stephen P. and Dasgupta, Sunil, 2010, *Arming without Aiming: India's Military Modernization*, New Delhi: Penguin, Viking.

Ghazali, Naziha and Ansari, Massoud, 2002 (June), 'School of Salvation?', *Newsline*, Karachi.

Gujral, Inder Kumar, 2011, *Matters of Discretion – an Autobiography*, New Delhi: Hay House.

Haqqani, Husain, 2005, *Pakistan between Mosque and Military*, Washington DC: Carnegie Endowment for International Peace.

Hussain, Zahid, 2008, *Frontline Pakistan: The Path to Catastrophe and the Killing of Benazir Bhutto*, London: I.B. Tauris and Co Ltd.

Jain, Rashmi (ed.), 2007a, *The United States and Pakistan 1947–2006: A Documentary Study*, New Delhi: Radiant Books.

Kessler, Glen, 2008, 'Bhutto Dealt Nuclear Secrets to N. Korea, Book Says', *Washington Post*, 1 J un e 2008, HYPERLINK http://www.washingtonpost.com/wp-dyn/content/ h t t p://w w w.washingtonpost .com/wp-dyn/content/ article/2008/05/31/AR2008053102122.html (accessed on 9 February 2011).

Khan, Asghar, 2005, *We've Learnt Nothing from History*, Karachi: Oxford University Press.

Khan, Asghar, 2008, *My Political Struggle*, Karachi: Oxford University Press.

Kharal, Asad, 2010, 'Pending case against ISI a blotch on the judiciary', *Daily Times*, Lahore, 31 March 2010. HYPERLINK http://www.dailytimes.com.pk/default.asp?page=201031 http://www.dailytimes.com.pk/default.asp?page=2010\03\31\story_31-3-2010_pg7_31 (accessed on 5 February 2011).

Kux, Dennis, 2001, *The United States and Pakistan 1947–2000: Disenchanted Allies*, New York: Oxford University Press.

Musharraf, Pervez (General), 2006, *In the Line of Fire: A Memoir*, London: Simon & Schuster, 2006.

Nawaz, Shuja, 2008, *Crossed Swords: Pakistan, its Army*, and the Wars Within, Karachi: Oxford University Press.

Pakistan Army Green Book: Year of the Commanding Officer 1991, 1991, Rawalpindi: General Headquarters.

Rana, Muhammad Amir, 2004, *A to Z of Jehadi Organizations in Pakistan*, Lahore: Mashal Books.

Rashid, Ahmed, 2008a, *Taliban, Militant Islam, Oil and Fundamentalism in Central Asia*, London: I.B. Tauris.

Shafqat, Saeed, 1997, *Civil-Military Relations in Pakistan: From Zulfikar Ali Bhutto to Benazir Bhutto*, Boulder, Colorado: Westview Press.

Stern, Jessica, 2000, 'Pakistan's Jihad Culture', *Foreign Affairs*, vol. 79, No. 6, New York.

Tahir, 2010 (3 May), 'Mian Muhammad Nawaz Sharif: Opposition Leader of Pakistan',

Paki Mag, online HYPERLINK http://www.pakimag.com/people/mian-muhammad-nawaz-sharif-,http://www.pakimag.com/people/mian-muhammad-nawaz-sharif-opposition-leader-of-pakistan.html, (accessed on 26 January 2011).

Talbott, Strobe, 2004, *Engaging India: Diplomacy, Democracy and the Bomb*, New Delhi: Penguin Books.

The Army Regulations, Volume II (Instructions) 1991, 1991, Rawalpindi: General Headquarters.

Warraich, Suhail, 2008, *The Traitor Within: The Nawaz Sharif Story in his own words*, Lahore: Sagar Publishers.

Wright, Robin, 2000 (28 December), 'The Chilling Goal of Islam's New Warriors Religion, in Pakistan, Today's Militant Faithful See the Entire World as the Battlefield for Their Holy War', in *Los Angeles Times*.

Newspapers

Daily Times, Lahore,
Jang (Urdu-language daily), Karachi

Interviews

Lieutenant General (Retd.) Javed Ashraf Qazi, 19 December 2008, Rawalpindi
Brigadier (Retd.) Vijai Singh Nair, 10 November 2010, Noida, outside Delhi

CHAPTER 14

Ahmed, Ishtiaq, 2007, 'Election Prospects in Pakistan', *ISAS Insights No. 22, 19 July*, Singapore: Institute of South Asian Studies.

Ahmed, Ishtiaq, (6 January 2007), 'A year for South Asian peace', *The News International*, Karachi.

Ahmed, Ishtiaq, (1 December 2007), 'All the glitter and the gold', *The News International*, Karachi.

Ahmed, Ishtiaq, 2007 (31 December), 'The Assassination of Ms Bhutto', *The News*, Karachi.

Ahmed, Ishtiaq, 2008, 'The Pakistan elections – a political analysis', *ISAS Brief No. 55, 22 February*, Singapore: Institute of South Asian Studies.

Ahmed, Ishtiaq, 2011a, 'Religious nationalism and minorities in Pakistan: constitutionalism and legal bases of discrimination', in Ahmed, Ishtiaq (ed.), *The Politics of Religion in South and Southeast Asia*, London, New York: Routledge.

Ahmed, Ishtiaq, 2011b, 'Women under Islamic law in Pakistan', in Ahmed, Ishtiaq (ed.), *The Politics of Religion in South and Southeast Asia*, London, New York: Routledge.

Ahmed, Ishtiaq, Rajshree Jetly, and Iftikhar Ahmad Lodhi, 2007, 'Pakistan, *the road ahead*', *ISAS Insights No. 24*, Singapore: Institute of South Asian Studies.

Bhutto, Benazir, 2008b, *Reconciliation, Islam, Democracy and the West*, New York: HarperCollins Publisher.

Bhutto, Fatima, 2010, *Songs of Blood and Sword*, New Delhi: Penguin.

Bidwai, Praful, 2006, 'Chasing the mirage of nuclear stabilisation', in Alam, Imtiaz (ed.), Sapana, *South Asian Studies, vol. VII*, Lahore: South Asia Policy Analysis Network Cohen, Stephen, 2006, The Idea of Pakistan, New Delhi: Oxford University Press.

Devolution in Pakistan: Reform or Regression, 2004 (22 March), http://www.crisisgroup.org/en/publication-type/media-releases/2004/asia/devolution-in-pakistan-reform-or-regression.aspx, Islamabad/Brussels: International Crisis Group, (accessed on 8 February 2012).

Faruqui, Ahmad, 2008, *Musharraf's Pakistan, Bush's America and the Middle East*, Lahore: Vanguard.

Hoodbhoy, Pervez, 2006, 'Nuclear flashpoint, quest for safety', in Alam, Imtiaz (ed.), Sapana, *South Asian Studies, vol. VII*, Lahore: South Asia Policy Analysis Network.

Hussain, Zahid, 2010, *The Scorpion's Trail*, New York, London: Free Press.

Jain, Rashmi (ed.), 2007a, *The United States and Pakistan 1947–2006: A Documentary Study*, New Delhi: Radiant Books.

John, Wilson, 2007, *The General and Jihad*, New Delhi: Pentagon Press.

Kamran, Mohammad, 2002 (25 May), 'Blasphemy Law, Hudood Order to stay', *Daily Times*, Lahore.

Muni, S.D., 2008, 'India 2007: Achievements and anxieties', *South Asian Journal, January– March 2008*.

Musharraf, Pervez, 2001, Address to People of Pakistan, 19 September, http//www.americanrhetoric.com/speeches/pakistanpresident.htm (accessed on 24 April 2008).

Musharraf, Pervez, 2002, Address to the Ulema and Mashaikh, 18 January, http://www. pak.gov.pk/public/President_address.htm (accessed on 9 February 2002).

Musharraf, Pervez, 2006, *In the Line of Fire*, London: Simon and Schuster.

President George W. Bush, T*he White House*, Washington DC, 2006, http://georgewbush-whitehouse.archives.gov/infocus/india-pakistan/ (accessed on 14 September 2011).

Raman. B., 2006, 'Dargai and Chenagai, waiting to hear Zawahiri's version', *International Terrorism Monitor, Paper No. 152 (also designated as Paper 2022), 13 November*, South Asia Analysis Group. http://www.south asiaanalysis.org/%5Cpapers21%5Cpaper2022.html (02–04–2008).

Rashid, Ahmed, 2008a, *Taliban, Militant Islam, Oil and Fundamentalism in Central Asia*, London: IB. Tauris.

Rashid, Ahmed, 2008b, *Descent into Chaos*, London: Penguin Books.

Sikri, Rajiv, 2009, *Challenge and Strategy: Rethinking India's Foreign Policy*, New Delhi: Sage.

Yusuf, Moeed, 2006, 'Persevering towards nuclear stability', in Alam Imtiaz (ed.), Sapana, *South Asian Studies, vol. VII*, Lahore: South Asia Policy Analysis Network.

Talpur, Mir Mohammad Ali, 2009 (5 December), 'The Saindak Saga', *Daily Times*, Lahore

Yusufzai, Rahimullah, 2007, 'General Kayani's rise from humble beginnings', *The News International*, Karachi.

Zahab, Mariam Abou and Roy, Oliver, 2002, Islamist Networks: *The Afghan-Pakistan Connection*, London: Hurst and Company.

Zaidi, S. Akbar, 2008 (9 January), 'The Political Economy of Military Rule in Pakistan: The Musharraf regime', *ISAS Working Paper No. 31*, Singapore: Institute of South Asian Studies.

Interviews

Christine Fair, 6 July 2009, Washington DC
Colonel Aslam Cheema, 15 December 2008, Rawalpindi
Dr Akbar S. Ahmed, 17 July 2009, Washington DC
General Pervez Musharraf, 15 December 2008, Rawalpindi
Jamil Ahmad, former Chief Secretary, Balochistan, 16 December 2008, Islamabad
Shahid Hamid, 9 December 2008, Lahore
Syeda Abida Hussain, 30 November 2010, Lahore

UN Report

Report of the United Nations Commission of Inquiry into the facts and circumstances of the assassination of former Pakistani Prime Minister Mohtarma Benazir Bhutto, 2010 (30 March) http://www.stateofpakistan.org/wp content/uploads/2010/04/un_bhutto_report_15april2010.pdf (accessed on 24 July 2011).

Newspapers

Shanghai Daily
The Daily Times, Lahore
The News International, Karachi-Islamabad-Lahore
The New York Times
The Washington Post

CHAPTER 15

Ahmed, Ishtiaq, 2008 (27 February), 'Now for the Hard Part', Singapore: Straits Times.

Ahmed, Ishtiaq, 2008 (11 July), 'Terrorist on a Killing Spree', *ISAS Brief No. 74*, Singapore: Institute of South Asian Studies.

Ahmed, Ishtiaq, 2008 (15 August), 'The Pakistan Inter-Services Intelligence', *ISAS Insights No. 35*, Singapore: Institute of South Asian Studies.

Ahmed, Ishtiaq, 2009 (30 January), 'The Mumbai Terrorist Attacks: An Assessment of Possible Motives', *ISAS Insights No. 47*, Singapore: Institute of South Asian Studies.

Ahmed, Ishtiaq, 2009 (18 September), 'The Pakistan Military: Change and Continuity under General Ashfaq Pervez Kayani', *ISAS Working Paper No. 90*, Singapore: Institute of South Asian Studies.

Burki, Shahid Javed, 2011, *South Asia in the New World Order: The Role of Regional Cooperation*, London: Routledge.

Dogar, Yasub Ali (Brigadier, Retd.), 2009, 'The Talibanisation of Pakistan's Western Region', I*SAS Working Paper No. 98*, 24 November, Singapore: Institute of South Asian Studies.

Hussain, Zahid, 2008, *Frontline Pakistan: The Path to Catastrophe and the Killing of Benazir Bhutto*, London: I.B. Tauris.

Jetly, Rajshree, 2008 (25 August), 'Musharraf 's Resignation: A Cause for Celebration and Concern for Pakistan', *ISAS Brief No. 79*, Singapore: Institute of South Asian Studies. Kerry–Lugar Bill, 'Full-Text', Forum Pakistan, v 2009, http://www.forumpakistan.com/ full-text-of-the-kerry-lugar-bill-details-and-conditions-t36999.html. (accessed on 1 December 2011).

Muni, S.D. (ed.), 2010, *The Emerging Dimensions of SAARC*, New Delhi: Cambridge University Press.

Nawaz, Shuja, 2009, 'How to Help Pakistan Win This Fight', *Foreign Policy*, Washington DC: http://www.foreignpolicy.com/articles/2009/10/20/how_to_help_pakistan_win_this_fight (accessed 24 February 2011).

Sikri, Rajiv, 2009, *Challenge and Strategy: Rethinking India's Foreign Policy*, New Delhi: Sage.

Suskind, Ron, 2008, *The Way of the World: A Story of Truth and Hope in an Age of Extremism*, London: Simon and Schuster.

Interview

Pakistan

Brigadier (Retd.) Yasub Ali Dogar, 25 January 2008, Singapore; via emails and Skype during March–May 2011 from Lahore

Major (Retd.) Saeed Akhtar Malik, 17 November 2008, Rawalpindi Lieutenant General

(Retd.) Nasir Akhtar, 7 December 2008, Lahore Major General (Retd.) Ghulam Umar, 7 December 2008, Karachi 2008
Rear Admiral (Retd.) M.I. Arshad, 7 December 2008, Karachi
Lt. General Khalid Nawaz, 12 December 2008, Rawalpindi
Brigadier (Retd.) Rafi Uz Zaman Khan, 12 December 2008, Rawalpindi
Brigadier (Retd.) Ghazanfar Ali, 12 December 2008, Rawalpindi
Brigadier (Retd.) Tughral Yamin, 12 December 2008, Rawalpindi
Major General (Retd.) Sarfraz Iqbal, 14 December 2008, Rawalpindi
General (Retd.) Pervez Musharraf, 15 December 2008, Rawalpindi
Brigadier (Retd) Saeed Malik, 16 December 2008, Islamabad
Lieutenant General (Retd.) Hamid Gul, 17, December 2008, Rawalpindi
Colonel (Retd.) Aslam Cheema, 12–18 December 2008, Rawalpindi.
Lieutenant General (Retd.) Javed Ashraf Qazi, 19 December 2008, Rawalpindi.
General (Retd.) Jehangir Karamat, 22 December 2008, Lahore
Lieutenant General (Retd.) Nishat Ahmed, 22 December 2008, Lahore
Major General (Retd.) Mahmud Ali Durrani, 20 March 2009, Singapore

India

Lt. General (Retd.) Dr B.S. Malik, former Chief of Western Command, 4 January 2009, New Delhi
Brigadier (Retd.) Gurmeet Kanwal, New Delhi
Brigadier (Retd.) S.K. Saini, New Delhi
Wing Commander Krishnappa, New Delhi
Commodore Om Prakash Jha, New Delhi
Colonel Arvind Dutta, New Delhi
Dr Arvind Kumar Gupta, Indian Foreign Service, New Delhi
Dr N. Manoharan, New Delhi
Dr Ashok Kumar Behuria, New Delhi
Dr M. Mahtab Alam Rizvi, New Delhi
Dr Shah Alam, New Delhi
Dr Ravi Prashad Narayanan, New Delhi
Dr Udal Bhanu Singh, New Delhi
Ms Sumita, New Delhi
Mr Vishal Chandra, New Delhi
Mr Nihar Nayak, New Delhi
Mr Vinod Kumar, New Delhi
Ms Sewonti Ray Dadwal, New Delhi
Discussions on 5 January 2009 with Indian Military and Security Experts

Singapore

Rajiv Sikri, 25 May 2009, Singapore
Shahid Javed Burki, 27 May 2010, Singapore

Newspapers

Dawn, Karachi
The Daily Times, Lahore
The News International, Karachi
Hindu, Delhi
Hindustan Times, Delhi
The Indian Express, Delhi
The Times of India, Delhi

CHAPTER 16

Ahmed, Ishtiaq, 2009 (11 August), *Taleban Leader Baitullah Mehsud Dead: Is it the Beginning of the End of Terrorism? ISAS Brief No. 122*, Singapore: Institute of South Asian Studies.

Ahmed, Ishtiaq, 2010, 'The Task Ahead', *Daily Times*, 12 October 2010.

Ahmed, Ishtiaq, 2011, 'China, India and Pakistan', *Daily Times*, 4 January 2011.

Amin, Agha H., Osinski, David J., and DeGeorges, Paul Andre, 2010, *The Development of Taliban Factions in Afghanistan and Pakistan: A Geographical Account*, New York: The Edwin Mellen Press.

BBC News, 17 February 2010, (http://news.bbc.co.uk/2/hi/8517693.stm), (accessed on 4 May 2011).

BBC News: South Asia, 2011, 'Brigadier Ali Khan: Pakistan's dissenting army officer', http://www.bbc.co.uk/news/world-south-asia–13873188 (accessed on 10 July 2011), (23 June 2011).

Blumenthal, Dan, 'India Prepares for a Two-Front War', Foreign and Defense Policy – Regional – Asia, Washington DC: American Enterprise Institute, (http://www.aei.org/ article/foreign-and-defense-policy/regional/asia/india-prepares-for-a-two-front-war/ (accessed on 1 December 2011).

Bush, George W., 2010, Decision Points, *New York*: Crown Publishers.

Daily Times editorial, 'Talking through their Teeth', *Daily Times*, 24 October 2010.

Khalifaconcepts, 2011 (22 January), http://www.youtube.com/watch?v=Cc0BLv1gnf8 (accessed on 24 May 2012).

Rajghatta, Chindanand, 2010, 'Obama's pitch: Fix Kashmir for UN Security Council seat', *The Times of India*, 29 September 2010.

The Nation, 2010, 'Pakistan sacrifices unprecedented, says Kayani', 4 February 2010, http://www.nation.com.pk/pakistan-news-newspaper-daily-english-online/Politics/04-Feb-2010/Pak-sacrifices-unprecedented-says-Kayani (accessed on 4 May 2011).

Woodward, Bob, 2010, *Obama's Wars: The Inside Story*, London: Simon and Schuster.

PIP Report

'Conflict and Insecurity in Balochistan: Assessing Strategic Policy Options for Peace and Harmony', *in Conflict Analysis–1, Conflict and Peace Studies, Volume 3*, October-December 2010, Number 4, Islamabad: PIPS.

Interviews

Christine Fair, 6 July 2009, Washington DC
Terisita Schaffer, 7 July 2009, Washington DC
Walter Andersen, 8 July 2009, Washington DC
Wendy Chamberlin, 8 July 2009, Washington DC
Taha Gaya, 10 July 2009, Washington DC
Syed Mowahid Hussain Shah, 11 July 2009, Washington DC
Amjad Babar, 13 July 2009, Washington DC
Noreen Babar, 13 July 2009, Washington DC
Robert Hathaway, 13 July 2009, Washington DC
Shuja Nawaz, 13 July 2009, Washington DC
Richard Boucher, 16 July 2009, Washington DC
Robin Raphael, 16 July 2009, Washington DC
Selig Harrison, 17 July 2009, Washington DC
Akbar S. Ahmed, 17 July, 2009, Washington DC
Marvin Weinbaum, 19 July 2009, Washington DC

Newspapers

Dawn, Karachi
Nawa-e-Waqt, 2010 (15 August), Lahore
The Daily Times, Lahore
The Indian Express, New Delhi
The Nation, Lahore
Times of India, New Delhi

CHAPTER 17

BBC News, 17 February 2010, (http://news.bbc.co.uk/2/hi/8517693.stm), (accessed on 4 May 2011).

BBC News: South Asia, 23 June 2011, 2011, 'Brigadier Ali Khan: Pakistan's dissenting army officer', http://www.bbc.co.uk/news/world-south-asia-13873188 (accessed on 10 July 2011),

Colonel Imam's appeal to Pakistan government, (ARYnews, 23 January 2011, http:// www. youtube.com/watch?v=Mh3l-Gio-) (accessed on 1 May 2011).

Colonel Imam's execution by TTP, footage released on 21 February 2011, by TTP, (http:// www.youtube.com/watch?v=xSnjbi0k5-Q&feature=related) (accessed on 1 May 2011).

Dunya News, 2011, 'Go America Go', 6 May 2011, http://www.youtub e.com/ watch?v=X3EO3fuCHXM (access 15 May 2011).

Dunya News, 2011, Live talk show, (http://www.dunyanews.tv/newsite/live_stream/ new1_live_tv.php) (accessed on 3 May 2011).

Dunya News, 2011, Live talk show, http://www.dunyanews.tv/newsite/live_stream/ new1_live_tv.php (accessed 2 May 2011).

Dunya News, 2011, live talk show, http://www.youtube.com/watch?v=4i5zZWYq5Pw&fe ature=relmfu) (accessed on 3 May 2011).

Dunya News, 9 February 2011, http://www.youtube.com/watch?v=mQxLwLLoBMA).

Dunya News, Programme Khhari Baat (Frank Truth) 11 February 2011, (http://www. youtube.com/watch?v=S2-B8hfCjCY), (accessed 30 April 2011).

Grare, Frederic, 2001, *Political Islam in the Indian Subcontinent: The Jamaat-i-Islami*, New Delhi: Manohar. Hillhouse, R.J., 2011, 'Bin Laden turned in by Informant – Courier was Cover Story', The Spy Who Billed Me: Outsourcing the War on Terror, http://www.thespywhobilledme.com/the_spy_who_billed_me/2011/08/ bin-laden-turned-in-by-informant-courier-was-cover-story.html (accessed on 16 September 2011).

ISPR statement on Gen. Kayani's condemnation of drone attack, Rawalpindi, 17 March 2011, (17 March, 2011, http://www.allvoices.com/contributed-news/8520289/ video/75566823-general-ashfaq-parvez-kayani-condemns-drone-attacks-in-north-waziristan-agency) (accessed on 1 May 2011).

Kerry, John, Press Conference in Lahore, 15 February 2011 (http://www.youtube.com/ wa tch?v=hngwG0teYCo&feature=related) (accessed on 30 April 2011).

Landay, S. Jonathan, 2011 (5 April), 'White House: Pakistan is failing to defeat militants', Washington DC: McClatchy Newspapers, http://www.mcclatchydc. com/2011/04/05/v-print/111592/white-house-pakistan-is-failing.html, (accessed on 25 May 2012).

Marcus, Jonathan, 2011, 'After Karachi: Is Pakistan's Nuclear Arsenal Safe?', BBC News: South Asia, http://www.bbc.co.uk/news/world-south-asia-13507767 (accessed on 10 July 2011), 23 May 2011.

Raymond Davis during police interrogation, 15 February http://www.youtube.com/watc h?v=3hye2lLBZfI&feature=related), (accessed on 1 May 2011).

Schmidle, Nicholas, 2011, 'What happened that night in Abbottabad?' The New Yorker, 8 August 2011.

Second International Bonn Conference, 2011, https://www.cimicweb.org/Pages/Bonn_Conference_2011.aspx, (accessed on 25 May 2012).

Sharif, Mian Muhammad Nawaz, 2011, Building Bridges in the Sub-continent, Lahore: SAFMA Meeting 13 August 2011, http://www.youtube.com/watch?v=KF0O1BS42fU&NR=1 (downloaded 18 September 2011).

Shumaila message (*Dunya News* released 8 February 2011) (http://www.youtube.com/wa tch?v=tTxsb3PFtus&feature=related (accessed on 1 May 2011).

Stephen Cohen in NDTV talk show released 23 February 2011, NDTV, 23 February 2011) (http://www.youtube.com/watch?v=jUM8A-AUv0o&feature=fvwrel) (accessed on 1 May 2011).

Syed, Wajid Al, 2011, 'On the murder – and silencing – Pakistani journalist Syed Saleem Shahzad', CNN, http://inthearena.blogs.cnn.com/2011/06/03/wajid-ali-syed-on-the-murder-and-silencing-of-pakistani-journalist-syed-saleem-shahzad/ (accessed on 10 July 2011), (3 June 2011).

Understanding the Militants' Media in Pakistan: Outreach and Impact, 2010, Islamabad: Pakistan Institute of Peace Studies (PIPS).

PIPS Reports

PIPS Security Report for 2006, Islamabad: PIPS, 2007.

PIPS Security Report for 2007, Islamabad: PIPS, 2008

PIPS Security Report for 2008, Islamabad: PIPS, 2009

PIPS Security Report for 2009, Islamabad: PIPS, 2010

PIPS Security Report for 2010, Islamabad: PIPS, 2011

The Pakistan Institute for Peace Studies, Islamabad, 2011, http://san-pips.com/index.php?action=reports&id=main, (accessed on 22 July 2011). Understanding the Militants' Media in Pakistan: Outreach and Impact, Islamabad: PIPS, 2010.

Newspapers

Dawn, Karachi

New York Times

The Daily Times, Lahore

The Financial Times, New York, London
The Hindu, Chennai
The Nation, Lahore
The News International, Karachi
The Straits Times, Singapore
The Washington Times, Washington DC
Times of India, New Delhi

Abbreviations

AfPak Afghanistan-Pakistan
AfPakInd Afghanistan-Pakistan-India
AIML All-India Muslim League
ANP Awami National Party

BJP Bharatiya Janata Party

CENTO Central Treaty Organization
CIA Central Intelligence Agency
CPI Communist Party of India
COP Combined Opposition Parties
CTBT Comprehensive Test Ban Treaty

EBDO Elective Bodies (Disqualified) Order
EBR East Bengal Regiment
EEIC English East India Company
EPR East Pakistan Rifles
ETA Euskadi Ta Askatasuna
EU European Union

FATA Federally Administered Tribal Areas
FBI Federal Bureau of Investigation
FIA Federal Investigation Agency
FSF federal Security Force

GDP Gross Domestic Product
GHQ General Headquarters

HRCP	Human Rights Commission of Pakistan
HuM	Harkat-ul-Mujahideen
IB	Intelligence Bureau
IAEA	International Atomic Energy Agency
IDSA	Indian Defence Studies and Analysis
IJI	Islami Jamhoori Ittehad
IMF	International Monetary Fund
INA	Indian National Army
INC	Indian National Congress
IRA	Irish Republican Army
ISAF	International Security Assistance Force
ISAS	Institute of South Asian Studies
ISI	Inter-Services Intelligence
ISPR	Inter-Services Public Relations
JDC	Joint Defence Council
JeM	Jaish-e-Muhammad
JI	Jamaat-e-Islami
JKLF	Jammu & Kashmir Liberation Front
JUI	Jamiat-e-Ulema-Islam
LeJ	lashkar-e-Jhanghvi
LeT	Lashkar-e-Tayyaba
LFO	Legal Framework Order
LoC	Line of Control
MFN	Most Favoured Nation
MI	Military Intelligence
MMA	Muttahida Majlis-e-Amal
MQM	Mohajir Quami Movement
MRD	Movement for the Restoration of Democracy
NAM	Non Aligned Movement
NAP	National Awami Party
NATO	North Atlantic Treaty Organization

NDP	National Democratic Party
NPT	Nuclear Non-Proliferation Treaty
NWFP	North West Frontier Province
PAF	Pakistan Air Force
PDA	People's DemocraticAlliance
PDPA	People's Democratic Party of Afghanistan
PID	Press Information Department
PIPS	Pakistan Institute for Peace Studies
PIU	Produce Index Unit
PLO	Palestine Liberation Organization
PML-N	Pakistan Muslim League-Nawaz
PML(Q)	Pakistan Muslim League – Quaid-i-Azam
PNA	Pakistan National Alliance
PODO	Public Office (Disqualification) Order
POW	Prisoners Of War
PPP	Pakistan Peoples Party
PPPP	Pakistan Peoples Party Parliamentarians
PTI	Pakistan Tehrik-e-Insaaf
R&AW	Research & Analysis Wing
SAARC	South Asian Association for Regional Cooperation
SAFMA	South Asian Media Association
SDPI	Sustainable Development Policy Institute
SEATO	South East Asian Treaty Organization
SIPRI	Stockholm International Research Institute
SSG	Special Services Group
SSP	Sunni Sipah-e-Mohammad
TNSM	Tehrik-e-Nifaz-e-Shariat-e-Muhammad
TTP	Tehrik-e-Taliban Pakistan
UNSC	United Nations Security Council
USMAAG	United States Military Aid and Advisory Group

Bibliography

Books

Abbas, Hassan, 2005, *Pakistan's Drift into Extremism: Allah, the Army, and America's War on Terror*, New Delhi: Pentagon Press.

Adhikari, G., 1944, *Pakistan and National Unity*, Bombay: People's Publishing House.

Ahmed, Ishtiaq, 1987, *The Concept of an Islamic State: An Analysis of the Ideological Controversy in Pakistan*, London: Frances Pinter; New York: St Martin's Press.

Ahmed, Ishtiaq, 1998, *State, Nation and Ethnicity in Contemporary South Asia*, London: Pinter.

Ahmed, Ishtiaq, 1999, 'South Asia', in David Westerlund and Ingvar Svanberg (eds.), *Islam Outside the Arab World*, Richmond: Curzon Press.

Ahmed, Ishtiaq, 2002, 'Globalisation and Human Rights in Pakistan' in *International Journal of Punjab Studies*, Vol. 9, No. 1, pp. 57–89, January–June 2002.

Ahmed, Ishtiaq, 2005, *The Politics of Group Rights: The State and Multiculturalism*, Lanham, Maryland: University Press of America.

Ahmed, Ishtiaq, 2010, 'The Pakistan Islamic State Project: A Secular Critique', in Michael Heng Siam-Heng and Ten Chin Liew (eds.), *State and Secularism: Perspectives from Asia*, Singapore: World Scientific Publishers Co. Pte. Ltd.

Ahmed, Ishtiaq, (ed.), 2011 (ed.), *The Politics of Religion in South and Southeast Asia*, London: Routledge.

Ahmed, Ishtiaq, 2012, *The Punjab Bloodied, Partition and Cleansed: Unravelling the 1947 Tragedy through Secret British Reports and First Person Accounts*, Karachi: Oxford University Press.

Ahmed, Viqar and Amjad, Rashid, 1984, *The Management of Pakistan's Economy 1947-82*, Karachi: Oxford University Press.

Aijazuddin, Fakir Syed, 2002, *The White House and Pakistan: Secret Declassified Documents, 1969–1974*, Karachi: Oxford University Press.

Alam, S.M. Shamsul, 1995, *The State, Class Formation, and Development in Bangladesh*, Lanham: University Press of America.

Ali, Saleem H., 2009, *Islam and Education: Conflict and Conformity in Pakistan's Madrassahs*, Karachi: Oxford University Press.

Ali, Syed Shafaat, 2007, *The Soldier: A Memoir of Colonel (Retd.) Syed Shafaat Ali*, Karachi: Royal Book Company.

Allen, Charles, 2006, *God's Terrorists: The Wahhabi Cult and the Hidden Roots of Modern Jihad*, London: Little Brown.

Amin, Agha Humayun, 1999, *The Pakistan Army till 1965*, Arlington, VA: Strategicus and Tacticus.

Ali, Imran, 1989, *The Punjab under Imperialism 1885–1947*, Karachi: Oxford University Press.

Amin, Agha Humayun, Osinski, David J. and DeGeorges, Paul Andre, 2010, *The Development of Taliban Factions in Afghanistan and Pakistan: A Geographical Account, February 2010*, New York: The Edwin Mellen Press Ltd.

Anand, Dev, 2007, *Romancing with Life*, New Delhi: Viking/Penguin.

Antonova, K., Bongard-Levin, G., and Kotovsky, G.G., 1979, *A History of India, Book 1*, Moscow: Progress.

Arif, General Khalid Mahmud, 2001, *Khaki Shadows: Pakistan 1947–1997*, Karachi: Oxford University Press.

Aziz, Mazhar, 2007, *Military Control in Pakistan*, London and New York: Routledge.

Aziz, Sartaj, 2009, *Between Dreams and Realities: Some Milestones in Pakistan's History*, Karachi: Oxford University Press.

Baxter, Craig (ed.), 1985, *Zia's Pakistan: Politics of Stability in a Frontline State*, Lahore: Vanguard.

Baxter, Craig, 1997, *Bangladesh, from a Nation to a State*, Boulder: Westview Press.

Bhatia, Shyam, 2010, *Goodbye Shahzadi: A Political Biography of Benazir Bhutto*, New Delhi: Lotus Collection, Roli Books.

Bhutto, Benazir, 2008a, Daughter of the East, London: Pocket Books.

Bhutto, Benazir, 2008b, *Reconciliation: Islam, Democracy, and the West*, New York: HarperCollins Publishers.

Bhutto, Fatima, 2010, *Songs of Blood and Sword: A Daughter's Memoir*, New Delhi: Viking.

Bhutto, Zulfikar Ali, 1966, *The Quest for Peace*, Karachi: The Pakistan Institute of International Affairs.

Bhutto, Zulfikar Ali, 1969, *The Myth of Independence*, London: Oxford University Press.

Bhutto, Zulfikar Ali, 1979, *If I am Assassinated*, New Delhi: Vikas Publishing House Pvt Ltd.

Beg, Aziz, 1974, *Story of Islamic Summit in Lahore*, Lahore: Babur and Amer Publications.

Bourke-White, Margaret, 1949, *Halfway to Freedom*, New York: Simon and Schuster.

Buhle, Paul, and Wagner, David, 2003, *Hide in Plain Sight: The Hollywood Blacklistees in Film and Television, 1950–2002*, Palgrave Macmillan, New York.

Burki, Shahid Javed, 1980, *Pakistan Under Bhutto*, 1971-1977, London: The Macmillan Press.

Burki, Shahid Javed, 1991, *Pakistan: The Continuing Search for Nationhood*, Boulder, Colorado: Westview Press.

Burki, Shahid Javed, 2011, *South Asia in the New World Order: The Role of Regional Cooperation*, London: Routledge.

Burki, Shahid Javed and Craig, Baxter (eds.), 1991, *Pakistan Under the Military: Eleven Years of Zia ul-Haq*, Bounder, Colorada: Westview Press.

Buzan, Barry, 1991, *Peoples, States and Fears*, New York, London: Harvester Wheatsheaf.

Callard, Keith, 1957, *Pakistan: A Political Study*, London: Allen and Unwin.

Callard, Keith, 1959, *Political Forces in Pakistan 1947 1958*, New York: Institute of Pacific Relations.

Caroe, Olaf, 1951, *Wells of Power: The Oilfields of South-Western Asia, A Regional and Global Study*, London: Macmillan & Co. Ltd.

Cheema, Pervaiz Iqbal, 1990, *Pakistan's Defence Policy, 1947–58*, London: Macmillan Press.

Cheema, Pervaiz Iqbal, 2003, *The Armed Forces of Pakistan*, Karachi: Oxford University Press.

Chishti, Faiz Ali, 1996, *Betrayals of another Kind: Islam, Democracy and the Army in Pakistan*, Lahore: Jang Publishers.

Choudhary, S., 1991, *What is the Kashmir Problem*?, Luton: Jammu Kashmir Liberation Front.

Cloughley, Brian, 2000, *A History of the Pakistan Army: Wars and Insurrections*, Karachi: Oxford University Press.

Cohen, Stephen, 1998, *The Pakistan Army*, Karachi: Oxford University Press.

Cohen, Stephen, 2006, *The Idea of Pakistan*, New Delhi: Oxford University Press.

Cohen, Stephen P. and Dasgupta, Sunil, 2010, *Arming without Aiming: India's Military Modernization*, New Delhi: Penguin, Viking.

Coll, Steve, 2004, *Ghost Wars*, New York: Penguin Books.

Cooley, John K., 2000, *Unholy Wars: Afghanistan, America and International Terrorism*, London: Pluto Press.

Dalrymple, William, 2006, *The Last Mughal: The Fall of a Dynasty, Delhi, 1857*, London: Bloomsbury Publishing Inc.

Deora, M.S. (ed.), *India and the Freedom Struggle of Bangladesh*, New Delhi: Discovery of Publishing House.

Dreyfuss, Robert, 2005, *Devil's Game: How the United States Helped Unleash Fundamentalist Islam*, New York: Metropolitan Books/Henry Holt and Company

Faruki, Kemal A., 1971, *The Evolution of Islamic Constitutional Theory and Practice*, Karachi: National Publishing House.

Faruqui, Ahmad, 2003, *Rethinking the National Security of Pakistan: The Price of Strategic Myopia*, Hampshire: Ashgate.

Faruqui, Ahmad, 2008, *Musharraf's Pakistan, Bush's America and the Middle East*, Lahore: Vanguard.

Finer, S.E., 1975, *The Man on the Horseback: The Military in Politics*, Harmondswoth, Middlesex: Penguin Books.

French, Patrick, 1997, *Liberty or Death: India's Journey to Independence and Division*, London: HarperCollins Publishers.

Gankovsky, Y.V., and Gordon-Polonskaya, L.R., 1972, *A History of Pakistan (1947–1958)*, Lahore: People's Publishing House.

Ganguly, Sumit (ed.), *India's Foreign Policy: Retrospect and Prospect*, New Delhi: Oxford University Press.

Gauhar, Altaf, 1998, *Ayub Khan: Pakistan's First Military Ruler*, Lahore: Sang-e-Meel Publications.

Gough, K. and Sharma, H.P. (eds.), 1973, *Imperialism and Revolution in South Asia*, New York: Monthly Review Press.

Grare, Frederic, 2001, *Political Islam in the Indian Subcontinent: The Jamaat-i-Islami*, New Delhi: Manohar.

Gujral, Inder Kumar, 2011, *Matters of Discretion—an Autobiography*, New Delhi: Hay House.

Haqqani, Husain, 2005, *Pakistan between Mosque and Military*, Washington DC: Carnegie Endowment for International Peace.

Hamid, Shahid, 1986, *Disastrous Twilight: A Personal Record of the Partition of India*, London: Leo Cooper in association with Secker and Warburg.

Harrison, S.S., 1981, *In Afghanistan's Shadow: Baluch Nationalism and Soviet Temptations*, Washington DC: Carnegie Endowment for International Peace.

Hogan, Michael J.A., 2000, *Cross of Iron: Harry S. Truman and the Origins of the National Security State, 1945-1954*, New York: Cambridge University Press.

Horowitz, David, 1967, *From Yalta to Vietnam*, Harmondsworth, Middlesex: Penguin Books.

Huntington, Samuel P., 1962, *Changing Pattern of Military Politics*, New York: Free Press of Glencoe.

Husain, Syed Wajahat, 2010, *Memoirs of a Soldier: 1947 Before, During, After*, Lahore: Ferozsons (Pvt) Ltd.

Hussain, Syed Shabbir, 2010, *Ayub, Bhutto and Zia*, Lahore: Sang-e-Meel Publications.

Hussain, Zahid, 2008, *Frontline Pakistan: The Path to Catastrophe and the Killing of Benazir Bhutto*, London: I.B. Tauris and Co Ltd.

Hussain, Zahid, 2010, *The Scorpion's Trail*, New York, London: Free Press.

Jackson, Robert, 1975, *South Asian Crisis: India – Pakistan – Bangladesh*, London: Chatto and Windus.

Jafar, Mohammed, Rehman, I.A., and Jafar, Ghani, 1977, *Jinnah: As a Parliamentarian*, Lahore: Azfar Associates.

Jahangir, Asma and Jilani, Hina, 2003, *The Hudood Ordinances: A Divine Sanction?*, Lahore: Sang-e-Meel Publications.

Jalal, Ayesha, 1985, *The Sole Spokesman*, Cambridge: Cambridge University Press.

Jalal, Ayesha, 1990, *The State of Martial Law: The Origins of Pakistan's Political Economy of Defence*, Cambridge: Cambridge University Press.

Jansson, Erland, 1981, *India, Pakistan or Pakhtunistan?*, Uppsala: Acta UniversitatisUpsaliensis.

Jetly, Rajshree (ed.), 2009, *Pakistan in Regional and Global Politics*, New Delhi: Routledge.

John, Wilson, 2007, *The General and Jihad*, New Delhi: Pentagon Press.

Khan, Muhammad Akbar, 1992, *Raiders in Kashmir*, Lahore: Jang Publishers.

Khan, Fazal Muqeem 1973, *Pakistan's Crisis in Leadership*, Islamabad: National Book Foundation.

Khan, Gohar Ayub, 2007, *Glimpses into the Corridors of Power*, Karachi: Oxford University Press.

Khan, Gul Hassan, 1993, *Memoirs of Lt. Gen. Gul Hassan Khan*, Karachi: Oxford University Press.

Khan, Mohammad Asghar, 1983, *Generals in Politics: Pakistan 1958–82*, New Delhi: Vikas Publishing House Pvt Ltd.

Khan, Mohammad Asghar, 2005, *We've Learnt Nothing from History, Pakistan: Politics and Military Power*, Karachi: Oxford University Press.

Khan, Mohammad Asghar, 2008, *My Political Struggle*, Karachi: Oxford University Press.

Khan, Mohammad Ayub, 2006, *Friends not Masters: A Political Autobiography*,Islamabad: Mr Books.

Khan, Mohammad Ayub, 2008, *Diaries of Field Marshal Mohammad Ayub Khan 1966–1972*, Karachi: Oxford University Press.

Khan, Sultan Muhammad, 1997, *Memories and Reflections of a Pakistani Diplomat*, Karachi: Paramount Publishing Enterprise.

Khan, Wali, 1987, *Facts are Facts: The Untold Story of India's Partition*, New Delhi: Vikas Publishing House Pvt Ltd.

Khan, Zulfikar Ali, 1988, *Pakistan's Security: The Challenge and the Response*, Lahore: Progressive Publishers.

Kux, Dennis, 1992, *India and the United States: Estranged Democracies*, Washington DC: National Defense University Press.

Kux, Dennis, 2001, *The United States and Pakistan 1947-2000: Disenchanted Allies*, New York: Oxford University.

Lasswell, Harold, 1997, *Essays on the Garrison State*, New Brunswick, New Jersey: Transaction Publishers.

Lenin, Vladimir, I., 1970, *Imperialism, the Highest Stage of Capitalism*, Moscow: Progress Publishers.

Machiavelli, Niccolo, 1982, *The Prince and Other Political Writings*, London: Everyman's Library.

Mahmud, Khalid, 1987, *Pakistan Mein Mazdoor Therik* (The Labour Movement in Pakistan), Lahore: Maktab-e-Fikr-o-Danish.

Malik, Bashir A., 2005, *Indus Waters Treaty in Retrospect*, Lahore: Brite Books.

Malik, S.K., 1979, *The Quranic Concept of War*, Lahore: Wajidalis.

Maududi, Syed Abul Ala, 1979a, *Islami Riyasat*, Lahore: Islamic Publications Ltd.

Maududi, Syed Abul Ala, 1979b, *Khilafat-o-Malukiat*, Lahore: Idara Tarjuman-ul-Quran.

Maududi, Syed Abul Ala, 1980, *The Islamic Law and Constitution*, Lahore: Islamic Publications Ltd.

Maududi, Syed Abul Ala, 1981, *Al-Jihad Fi Al-Islam*, Lahore: Idara Tarjuman-ul-Quran.

Maxwell, Neville, 1970, *India's China War*, New York: Pantheon Books.

Mazari, Sherbaz Khan, 2001, *Pakistan: A Journey to Disillusionment*, Karachi: Oxford University Press.

Mehdi, S., 1988, *Politics without Parties: A Report on the 1985 Partyless Election in Pakistan*, Lahore: A SAHE Publication.

Mitha, Abubakr Osman, 2003, *Unlikely Beginnings: A Soldier's Life*, Karachi: Oxford University Press.

Moore, R.J., '*Jinnah and the Pakistan Demand*', *Modern Asian Studies*, Vol. XVII, No. 4, pp. 529–561, Cambridge: Cambridge University Press, (1983).

Morgenthau, Hans J., 1948, *Politics among Nations: The Struggle for Power and Peace*, New York: Alfred Knopf.

Mumtaz, Khawar and Shaheed, Farida, 1987, *Women of Pakistan*, Lahore: Vanguard.

Muni, S. D. (ed.), 2010, *The Emerging Dimensions of SAARC*, New Delhi: Cambridge University Press.

Munir, Muhammad, 1980, *From Jinnah to Zia*, Lahore: Vanguard.

Musharraf, Pervez, 2006, *In the Line of Fire*, London: Simon and Schuster.

Nath, Ashok, 2009, *Izzat: Historical Records and Iconography of Indian Cavalry Regiments 1750–2007*, New Delhi: Centre for Armed Forces Historical Research.

Nawaz, Shuja, 2008, *Crossed Swords: Pakistan, Its Army, and the Wars Within*, Karachi: Oxford University Press.

Nayyar, A.H. and Salim, Ahmad, 2004, *The Subtle Subversion: The State of Curricula and Textbooks in Pakistan*, Islamabad: SDPI.

Nelson-Pallmeyer, Jack, 1993, *Brave New World Order: Can we pledge allegiance*, Maryknoll, New York: Orbis Books.

Nehru, Jawaharlal, 1955, *An Autobiography*, London: The Bodley Head.

Newburg, Paula, 2002, *Judging the State: Courts and Constitutional Politics in Pakistan*, Cambridge: Cambridge University Press.

Niazi, Amir Abdullah Khan, 1999, *The Betrayal of East Pakistan*, Karachi: Oxford University Press.

Noman, Omar, 1988, *The Political Economy of Pakistan 1947–85*, London: Kegan Paul International.

Norval, Mitchell, 1968, *Sir George Cunningham: A Memoir*, Edinburgh, London: Blackwood.

Nyrop, Richard F., 1984, *Pakistan: A Country Study*, Washington DC: The American University.

Oldenburg, Philip 2010, *India, Pakistan and Democracy: Solving the Puzzle of Divergent Paths*, London: Routledge.

Osborn, Robert B., 1994, *Field Marshal Sir Claude Auchinleck: The Indian Army and the Partition of India*, Ann Arbor, Michigan: UMI.

Qureshi, Naeem A., 1999, *Pan-Islam in British Indian Politics: a Study of the Khilafat Movement 1918–1924*, Leiden: Brill.

Pakistan Army Green Book: Year of the Commanding Officer 1991, 1991, Rawalpindi: General Headquarters.

Rahman, Tariq, 2004, *Denizens of Alien Worlds: A Study of Education, Inequality and Polarization in Pakistan*, Karachi: Oxford University Press.

Rashid, Ahmed, 2000, *Taliban, Militant Islam, Oil and Fundamentalism in Central Asia*, New Haven: Yale University Press.

Rashid, Ahmed, 2008, *Descent into Chaos: The World's most Unstable Region and the Threat to Global Security*, London: Penguin Books.

Rashid, Rao, 2010, *Jo Meiney Dekha: Pakistani Syasat aur Hukumrani ki Haqiqat* (What I Saw: The Inside Story of Pakistani Politics and Governance), Lahore: Jamhoori Publications.

Rana, Muhammad Amir, 2004, *A to Z of Jehadi Organizations in Pakistan* (translated into English by Saba Ansari). Lahore: Mashal Books.

Ray, Aswini K., 2004, *Western Realism and International Relations: a Non-Western View*, New Delhi: Foundation books.

Reitz, Dietrich, 1995, *Hijrat: The Flight of the Faithful, a British File on the Exodus of Muslim Peasants from the North India to Afghanistan 1920*, Berlin: Verlag Das Arabische Buch.

Riza, Shaukat 1989, *The Pakistan Army 1947–1949*, Lahore: Service Book Club.

Rizvi, Hasan-Askari, 2000, *The Military and Politics in Pakistan 1947-1997*, Lahore; Sang-e-Meel Publications.

Rizvi, Hasan-Askari, 2003, *Military, State and Society in Pakistan*, Lahore: Sang-e-Meel Publications.

Sarila, Narendra Singh, 2005, *The Shadow of the Great Game: The Untold Story of India's Partition*, New Delhi: HarperCollins Publishers India and The India Today Group.

Sayeed, Khalid Bin, 1980, *Politics in Pakistan: The Nature and Direction of Change*, New York: Praeger.

Schaffer, Howard B., 2009, *The Limits of Influence: America's Role in Kashmir*, Washington DC: Brookings Institute.

Schofield, Julian, 2007, *Militarization and War*, Houndsmill, Basingstoke, Hampshire: Palgrave Macmillan.

Seervai, H. M. 1989, *Partition of India: Legend and Reality*, Bombay: Emmanem Publications.

Shafqat, Saeed, 1997, *Civil-Military Relations in Pakistan: From Zulfikar Ali Bhutto to Benazir Bhutto*, Boulder, Colorado: Westview Press.

Shaheed-ul Islam Muhammad Zia ul-Haq, 1990, London: Indus Thames Publishers.

Siddiqa, Ayesha, 2007, *Military Inc. Inside Pakistan's Military Economy*, Karachi: Oxford University Press.

Siddiqi, A.R. (Brigadier, Retd.), 1996, *The Military in Pakistan: Image and Reality*, Lahore, Vanguard.

Siddiqi, A.R., 2004, *East Pakistan, The Endgame: An Onlooker's Journal 1969–1971*, Karachi: Oxford University Press.

Sikri, Rajiv, 2009, *Challenge and Strategy: Rethinking India's Foreign Policy*, New Delhi: Sage.

Sisson, Richard and Rose, Leo E., 1991, *War and Secession: Pakistan, India, and the Creation of Bangladesh*, Berkeley, Los Angeles, Oxford: University of California.

Sohail, Massarat, 1991, *Partition and Anglo-Pakistan Relations, 1947–51*, Lahore: Vanguard.

Speeches and Writings of Mr. Jinnah, vol. I, 1968, Lahore: Sh. Muhammad Ashraf.

Speeches and Writings of Mr. Jinnah, vol. II, 1976, Lahore: Sh. Muhammad Ashraf.

Suskind, Ron, 2008, *The Way of the World: A Story of Truth and Hope in an Age of Extremism*, London: Simon and Schuster.

Tahir-Kheli, Shirin, R., 1997, *India, Pakistan and the United States: Breaking with the Past*, New York: Council on Foreign Relations Press.

Talbot, Ian, 1996, *Khizr Tiwana: The Punjab Unionist Party and the Partition of India*, Richmond, Surrey: Curzon.

Talbott, Strobe, 2004, *Engaging India: Diplomacy, Democracy and the Bomb*, New Delhi: Penguin Books.

The Army Regulations, Volume II (Instructions) 1991, 1991, Rawalpindi: General Headquarters.

Tan, Tai Yong, 2005, *The Garrison State, The Military, Government and Society in Colonial Punjab, 1849–1947*, New Delhi: Sage Publications Ltd.

Taseer, Salman, 1979, *Bhutto: A Political Biography*, London: Ithaca Press.

The Bangladesh Papers, no date given, Lahore: Vanguard.

Tuker, Sir Francis, 1951, *While Memory Serves*, London, Toronto, Melbourne, Sydney, Wellington: Cassell and Company Ltd.

Walt, Stephen M., 1987, *The Origins of Alliances*, Ithaca: Cornell University Press.

Waltz, Kenneth N., 1979, *Theory of International Politics*, New York: McGraw Hill.

Warraich, Suhail, 2008, *The Traitor Within: The Nawaz Sharif Story in his own words*, Lahore: Sagar Publishers.

Weber, Max, 1993, *The Sociology of Religion*, Boston: Beacon Press.

Weiss, Anita M. (ed.), 1986, *The Application of Islamic Law in a Modern State*, Syracuse: Syracuse University Press.

Wink, Andre, 1997, *Al-Hind: the Making of the Indo-Islamic World*, volume 2, Leiden, New York, Koln: Brill.

Wolpert, Stanley, 1984, *Jinnah of Pakistan*, New York: Oxford University Press.

Woodward, Bob, 2010, *Obama's Wars: The Inside Story*, London: Simon and Schuster.

Young, John W., 1993, *The Longman Companion to Cold War and Détente 1941–91*, London and New York: Longman.

Yusuf, Hamid, 1999, *Pakistan: A Study of Political Developments 1947–97*, Lahore: Sang-e-Meel Publications.

Zaheer, Hasan, 1995, *The Separation of East Pakistan: The Rise and Realization of Bengali Muslim Nationalism*, Karachi: Oxford University Press.

Zahab, Mariam Abou and Roy, Oliver, 2002, *Islamist Networks: The Afghan Pakistan Connection*, London: Hurst and Company.

Zaidi, S.Akbar (ed.), 1992, *Regional Imbalances & The National Question in Pakistan*, Lahore: Vanguard.

Zaidi, S. Akbar (ed.), 2003, *Social Sciences in Pakistan in the 1990*, Islamabad: Council of the Social Sciences.

Ziring, Lawrence, 1971, *The Ayub Khan Era: Politics in Pakistan 1958-1969*, Syracuse: Syracuse University Press.

Official documents

Carter, Lionel, 2006, *Punjab Politics, 1 January 1944–3 March 1947: Last Years of the Ministries, Governors' Fortnightly Reports and other Key Documents*, New Delhi: Manohar.*Constitution of the Islamic Republic of Pakistan*, 1956, Karachi: Government Printing Press.

Jain, Rashmi (ed.), 2007a, *The United States and Pakistan 1947–2006: A Documentary Study*, New Delhi: Radiant Books.

Jain, Rashmi (ed.), 2007b, *The United States and India 1947–2006: A Documentary Study*, New Delhi: Radiant Books.

Mansergh, Nicholas and Lumby, E.W.R., (eds.), 1970, *The Transfer of Power vol. 1, The Cripps Mission, January—April 1942*, London: Her Majesty's Stationery Office.

Mansergh. N. and Moon, P., (eds), 1976, *The Transfer of Power, vol. VII, The Post-War Phase: New Moves by the Labour Government, 1 August 1945-22 March 1946*, London: Her Majesty's Stationery Office.

Mansergh, Nicholas and Moon, Penderel (eds.), 1977, *The Transfer of Power vol. VII, The Cabinet Mission 23 March—29 June 1946*, London: Her Majesty's Stationery Office.

Mansergh, Nicholas and Moon, Penderel (eds.), 1979, *The Transfer of Power vol. VIII, The Cabinet Mission 3 July—1 November*, London: Her Majesty's Stationery Office.

Mansergh, Nicholas and Moon, Penderel, 1980, *The Transfer of Power 1942–1947, Volume IX, The fixing of a time limit, 4 November 1946—22 March 1947*, London: Her Majesty's Stationery Office.

Mansergh, Nicholas and Moon, Penderel, 1981, *The Transfer of Power 1942–1947, Volume X, The Mountbatten Viceroyalty, Formulation of a Plan, 23 March–30 May 1947*, London: Her Majesty's Stationery Office.

Mansergh, Nicholas and Moon, Penderel, 1982, *The Transfer of Power 1942–1947, Volume XI, The Mountbatten Viceroyalty, Announcement and Reception of the 3 June Plan, 31 May–7 July 1947*, London: Her Majesty's Stationery Office.

Mansergh, Nicholas and Moon, Penderel, 1983, *The Transfer of Power 1942–1947, Volume XII, The Mountbatten Viceroyalty, Princes, Partition and Independence 8 July–15 August 1947*, London: Her Majesty's Stationery Office.

The Constituent Assembly of Pakistan Debates, Vol. 5, 1949, Karachi: Government of Pakistan Press. *White Paper on the Punjab Agitation, 10 July, 1984*, New Delhi: Government of India.

Official Commission Reports

The Report of the Hamoodur Rehman Commission of Inquiry into the 1971 War: As Declassified by the Government of Pakistan, 2001, Lahore: Vanguard.

Report of the Court of Inquiry constituted under Punjab Act II of 1954 to enquire into the Punjab Disturbances of 1953, 1954, Lahore: Government Printing Press.

Report of the United Nations Commission of Inquiry into the facts and circumstances of the assassination of former Pakistani Prime Minister Mohtarma Benazir Bhutto, 2010 (30 March) http://www.stateofpakistan.org/wp-content/uploads/2010/04/un_bhutto_report_15april2010.pdf (accessed on 24 July 2011).

Newspapers

Daily Times, Lahore
Dawn, Karachi
Hindustan Times, Delhi
Jang (Urdu language daily), Karachi
Shanghai Daily, Shanghai
The Asian Age, New Delhi
The Hindu, Chennai-Delhi
The News International, Karachi
The Nation, Lahore
The Indian Express, Delhi
The Financial Times, New York, London
The New York Time, New York
The Straits Times, Singapore
The Times of India, Delhi
The Tribune, Chandigarh
The Washington Post, Washington DC
The Washington Times, Washington DC

Articles in Journals

Alavi, Hamza, 1972, 'The State in Post-Colonial Societies: Pakistan and Bangladesh', *New Left Review, 1/74* July–August.
Alavi, Hamza, 2002, 'Misreading Partition Road Signs', *Economic and Political Weekly*, 2–9 November, Mumbai.
Bidwai, Praful, 2006, 'Chasing the mirage of nuclear stabilisation', in Imtiaz Alam (ed.), *Sapana, South Asian Studies*, vol. VII, Lahore: South Asia Policy Analysis Network.
Chaudhry, Cecil (Group Captain), 2001, 'Remembering our Heroes', *Defence Journal*, 4, No. 11, June 2001, Karachi.
Khan, Raja Muhammad, 2011 (6 June), 'Pakistan: Inside the Military Budget', Defence Journal, http://www.defence.pk/forums/general-defence/112938-pakistan-inside-military-budget.html, Karachi, (1 January 2012).
LaPorte, Jr., Robert, 1969, 'Succession in Pakistan: Continuity and Change in a Garrison State', *Asian Survey*, Vol. 9, No. 11, (November 1969).
Muni, S.D., 2008, 'India 2007: Achievements and anxieties', *South Asian Journal*, January–March 2008.
Marston, Daniel P., 2009, 'The Indian Army, Partition, and the Punjab Boundary Force,

1945–1947', *War in History*, 2009 No. 16, Volume 4, Newbury Park, California: Sage Publications.

Yusuf, Moeed, 2006, 'Persevering towards nuclear stability', in Imtiaz Alam (ed.), *Sapana, South Asian Studies*, vol. VII. Lahore: South Asia Policy Analysis Network.

Reports of research institutes

Ahmed, Ishtiaq, 2007, 'Election Prospects in Pakistan', ISAS Insights No. 22, 19 July, Singapore: Institute of South Asian Studies.

Ahmed, Ishtiaq, 2008, 'The Pakistan elections—a political analysis', *ISAS Brief No. 55*, 22 February, Singapore: Institute of South Asian Studies.

Ahmed, Ishtiaq, 2008 (11 July), 'Terrorist on a Killing Spree', *ISAS Brief No. 74*, Singapore: Institute of South Asian Studies.

Ahmed, Ishtiaq, 2008 (15 August), 'The Pakistan Inter-Services Intelligence', *ISAS Insights No. 35*, Singapore: Institute of South Asian Studies.

Ahmed, Ishtiaq, 2009 (30 January), 'The Mumbai Terrorist Attacks: An Assessment of Possible Motives', *ISAS Insights No. 47*, Singapore: Institute of South Asian Studies.

Ahmed, Ishtiaq, 2009 (18 September), 'The Pakistan Military: Change and Continuity under General Ashfaq Pervez Kayani', *ISAS Working Paper No. 90*, Singapore: Institute of South Asian Studies.

Ahmed, Ishtiaq, Rajshree Jetly, and Iftikhar Ahmad Lodhi, 2007, 'Pakistan, the road ahead', ISAS Insights No. 24, Singapore: Institute of South Asian Studies.

Chowdhury, Iftekhar Ahmed, 2009, *The Roots of Bangladeshi National Identity: Their Impact on State Behavior*, Singapore: Institute of South Asian Studies.

'Conflict and Insecurity in Balochistan: Assessing Strategic Policy Options for Peace and Harmony', in *Conflict Analysis–1, Conflict and Peace Studies*, Volume 3, October-December 2010, Number 4, Islamabad: PIPS.

Dogar, Yasub Ali (Retd., Brigadier), 2009, 'The Talibanisation of Pakistan's Western Region', *ISAS working Paper No. 98*, 24 November, Singapore: Institute of South Asian Studies.

IPP's Third Annual Report 2010, 2010, Lahore: Institute of Public Policy, Beaconhouse University.

Jetly, Rajshree, 2008, 'Musharraf's Resignation: A Cause for Celebration and Concern for Pakistan', *ISAS Brief No. 79*, Singapore: Institute of South Asian Studies, 25 August.

PIPS Security Report for 2006, Islamabad: PIPS, 2007.

PIPS Security Report for 2007, Islamabad: PIPS, 2008

PIPS Security Report for 2008, Islamabad: PIPS, 2009

PIPS Security Report for 2009, Islamabad: PIPS, 2010

PIPS Security Report for 2010, Islamabad: PIPS, 2011

SIPRI, 2011, '14 March 2011: India world's largest arms importer according to new SIPRI data on international arms transfers', http://www.sipri.org/media/pressreleases/2011/armstransfers, (accessed on 6 February 2012), Stockholm: SIPRI.

Zaidi, S. Akbar 2008 (9 January), 'The political economy of military rule in Pakistan: The Musharraf regime', *ISAS Working Paper No. 31*, Singapore: ISAS.

Selection of documents cited from Internet sources

Ahamed, Syeed, 2010 (May), 'The Curious Case of the 195 War Criminals', in *Forum* (a monthly publication of the *Daily Star*, 5 May 2010) (http://www.thedailystar.net/forum/2010/may/curious.htm (accessed on 29 September 2010).

Ali, Nadir (Colonel, retd.), 2010, 'A Khaki Dissident on 1971', *Viewpoint*, Online Issue No. 31, 17 December 2010, http://www.viewpointonline.net/a-khaki-dissident-on-1971.html (accessed on 17 December 2010).

Brzezinski, Zbigniew, 1997 (13 June), Interview, http://www.gwu.edu/~nsarchiv/coldwar/interviews/episode–17/brzezinski2.html, The National Security Archive: The George Washington University, (accessed on 7 January 2011).

Devolution in Pakistan: Reform or Regression, 2004 (22 March), http://www.crisisgroup.org/en/publication-type/media-releases/2004/asia/devolution-in-pakistan-reform-or-regression.aspx, Islamabad/Brussels: International Crisis Group, (accessed on 8 February 2012).

Eisenhower, Dwight D., 1961, *Eisenhower's Farwell Address to the Nation*, http,//mcadams.posc.mu.edu/ike.htm (accessed on 23-04-2008), (17 January 1961).

Global Fire Power, India, http://www.globalfirepower.com/country-military-strength-detail.asp?country_id=India (accessed on 6 May 2011).

Global Fire Power, 2011, Pakistan, http://www.globalfirepower.com/country-military-strength-detail.asp?country_id=Pakistan (accessed on 6 May 2011).

Jan, Abid Ullah, 2002 (9 September), 'Target: Jihad, madrassa or Islam?', *Muslim Uzbekistan*, http,//archive.muslimuzbekistan.com/eng/islam/2002/09/ a09092002.html (accessed on 3 January 2010).

Kerry-Lugar Bill, 'Full-Text', *Forum Pakistan*, v 2009, http://www.forumpakistan.com/full-text-of-the-kerry-lugar-bill-details-and-conditions-t36999.html. (accessed on 1 December 2011).

Husain, Noor A. (Brigadier retd.), 1999, 'The Role of [sic] Muslims Martial Races of Today's Pakistan in British-Indian Army in World War II', *Defence Journal*, Karachi, http://www.defencejournal.com/sept99/martial-races.htm (accessed on 15 December 2009).

Raman. B., 2006, 'Dargai and Chenagai, waiting to hear Zawahiri's version', *International*

Terrorism Monitor, Paper No. 152 (also designated as Paper 2022), 13 November, South Asia Analysis Group. http,//www.south asiaanalysis.org/%5Cpapers21%5Cpaper2022.html (Accessed on 2 April 2008).

Schwartz, Howell H., 2005, *Fear and the Garrison State*, Washington DC: Rand Corporation, 26 April 2005, (http://www.rand.org/commentary/2005/04/26/UPI.html) (accessed on 6 May 2011).

Sharif, Mian Muhammad Nawaz, 2011, Building Bridges in the Sub-continent, Lahore: SAFMA Meeting 13 August 2011, http://www.youtube.com/watch?v=KF0O1BS42fU&NR=1 (downloaded 18 September 2011).

Stephens, Joe and Ottaway, David B., 2002 (23 March), 'From the U.S., ABC of Jihad', *The Washington Post*, http://www.washingtonpost.com/ac2/wp-dyn/A5339–2002Mar22?language=printer (accessed on 3 January 2010).

Visual Economics, 2010, 'How Countries Spend their Money', http://www.visualeconomics.com/how-countries-spend-their-money, (accessed on 1 January 2012).

INTERVIEWS

PAKISTAN

Military

General (Redt.) Mirza Aslam Beg, 31 October 2007, Rawalpindi

General (Redt.) Pervez Musharraf, 15 December 2008, Rawalpindi

General (Redt.) Jehangir Karamat, 22 December 2008, Lahore

Lieutenant General (Retd.) Muhammad Asad Durrani, 31 October, 2007, Rawalpindi

Lieutenant General (Retd.) Nasir Akhtar, 7 December 2008, Lahore

Lt. General (Retd) Khalid Nawaz, 12 December 2008, Rawalpindi

Lieutenant General (Retd.) Hamid Gul, 17, December, 2008, Rawalpindi

Lieutenant General (Retd.) Javed Ashraf Qazi, 19 December, 2008, Rawalpindi.

Lieutenant General (Retd.) Nishat Ahmed, 22 December 2008, Lahore

Major General (Retd.) Ghulam Umar, 7 December 2008, Karachi 2008

Major General (Retd.) Sarfraz Iqbal, 14 December 2008, Rawalpindi

Major General (Retd.) Mahmud Ali Durrani, 20 March 2009, Singapore

Rear Admiral (Retd.) M. I. Arshad, 7 December 2008, Karachi

Brigadier (Retd.) Yasub Ali Dogar, 25 January 2008, Singapore; via emails and Skype during March–May 2011 from Lahore

Brigadier (Retd) Rafi Uz Zaman Khan, 12 December 2008, Rawalpindi
Brigadier (Retd) Ghazanfar Ali, 12 December 2008, Rawalpindi
Brigadier (Retd) Tughral Yamin, 12 December 2008, Rawalpindi

Brigadier (Retd) Saeed Malik, 16 December 2008, Islamabad
Colonel (Retd.) Aslam Cheema, 12-18 December 2008, Rawalpindi.
Colonel (Retd.), Riaz Jafri, via email on 17 December 2011 from Rawalpindi.
Major (Retd.) Saeed Akhtar Malik, 17 November 2008, Rawalpindi
Major (Retd.) Agha Humayun Amin, via email on 19 December 2010; on 10 November 2011, Lahore

Civil servants, politicians, and political activists

C.R. Aslam, 17 December 2000, Lahore
Mian Minatullah, 19 December 2000, Lahore
Abdullah Malik, 17 April 2003, Lahore
Tahira Mazhar Ali Khan 25 April 2003, Lahore
Khawaja Masud Ahmed, 12 December 2004, Islamabad
Shahid Hamid, former Governor of Punjab, 9 December 2008, Lahore
Jamil Ahmad, former Chief Secretary, Balochistan, 16 December 2008, Islamabad
Mir Muhammad Ali Talpur via email on 26 October 2010, from Hyderabad, Sindh

INDIA

Military

Lt. General (Retd) Dr B. S. Malik, former Chief of Western Command, 4 January 2009, New Delhi
Lieutenant General (Retd.) Kuldip Singh Khajuria, 10 November 2010, Noida, outside Delhi
Major General (Retd.) Afsir Karim, 10 November 2010, Noida, outside Delhi
Brigadier (Retd.) Vijai Nair, 10 November 2010, Noida, outside Delhi
Commodore (Retd.), C. Uday Bhaskar, 29 November 2011, via email from New Delhi
Discussions on 4-5 January 2009 with Indian military and Security Experts
Brigadier (Retd) Gurmeet Kanwal, New Delhi
Brigadier (Retd) S. K. Saini, New Delhi
Wing Commander Krishnappa, New Delhi
Commodore Om Prakash Jha, New Delhi

Colonel Arvind Dutta, New Delhi
Dr Arvind Kumar Gupta, Indian Foreign Service, New Delhi
Dr N. Manoharan, New Delhi
Dr Ashok Kumar Behuria, New Delhi
Dr M. Mahtab Alam Rizvi, New Delhi
Dr Shah Alam, New Delhi
Dr Ravi Prashad Narayanan, New Delhi
Dr Udal Bhanu Singh, New Delhi
Ms Sumita, New Delhi
Mr Vishal Chandra, New Delhi
Mr Nihar Nayak, New Delhi
Mr. Vinod Kumar, New Delhi
Ms Sewonti Ray Dadwal, New Delhi

SINGAPORE

Professor Stephen Cohen, 2 April, 2008
Rajiv Sikri, former Secretary Ministry of Indian Foreign Affairs Ministry, 25 May 2009
Juned Chowdhury, Singapore, 18 April 2010
Dr Iftekhar Ahmed Chowdhury, former Bangladesh foreign affairs adviser, 28 April 2010
Shahid Javed Burki, Former finance minister of Pakistan, 27 May 2010

STOCKHOLM

Dr Ghulam Husain, former PPP general secretary and federal minister, 26 September 2010, Stockholm
Ahmed Faqih (PPP activist from Lahore), 26 September 2010, Stockholm

UNITED STATES

Christine Fair, 6 July 2009, Washington DC
Ambassador Teresita Schaffer, 7 July 2009, Washington DC
Dr Walter Andersen, 8 July 2009, Washington DC
Ambassador Wendy Chamberlin, 8 July 2009, Washington DC
Taha Gaya, 10 July 2009, Washington DC
Ahmed Sheikh, 11 July 2009, Washington DC
Syed Mowahid Hussain Shah, 11 July 2009, Washington DC
Safir Rammah, 13 July 2009, Washington DC

Amjad Babar, 13 July 2009, Washington DC
Noreen Babar, 13 July 2009, Washington DC
Robert Hathaway, 13 July 2009, Washington DC
Shuja Nawaz, 13 July 2009, Washington DC
Ambassador Richard Boucher, 16 July 2009, Washington DC
Ambassador Robin Raphael, 16 July 2009, Washington DC
Selig Harrison, 17 July 2009, Washington DC
Dr Akbar S. Ahmed, 17 July, 2009, Washington DC
Dr Marvin Weinbaum, 19 July 2009, Washington DC

Acknowledgements

I would like to begin by dedicating this book to the Institute of South Asian Studies (ISAS), an autonomous think-tank at the National University of Singapore, where I spent three years (June 2007–June 2010) initially as a visiting senior fellow and then as research professor. Those three years have been the most productive in my academic life. I researched topics and themes that have a direct bearing on contemporary South Asia. It was a unique opportunity to interact with gifted researchers, distinguished visitors, and dedicated staff. Thanks must go, first of all, to ISAS Chairman Ambassador Gopinath Pillai whose abiding interest in the well-being of South Asia has been vital to developing links with Southeast Asia. ISAS Director Professor Tan Tai Yong is a distinguished scholar of both South Asia and Southeast Asia. He very kindly invited me to ISAS—agreeing to wait for a whole year so that I could wind up my commitments and responsibilities at the Department of Political Science, Stockholm University.

With regard to the research for this book at the ISAS, I especially remember my long talks with Shahid Javed Burki, Dr Iftekhar Ahmed Chowdhury, Dr S. Narayan, Ambassador See Chak Mun, Ambassador Rajiv Sikri, Ambassador Dr Dayan Jayatilleka, Professor S.D. Muni, Professor Sumit Ganguly, Professor Robin Jeffrey, Professor John Harriss, Dr Rajshree Jetly, Dr Shanthie Mariet D'Souza, Dr Sinderpal Singh, Iftikhar Ahmad Lodhi, Tridivesh Singh Maini, and Shahidul Islam Sasidharan Gopalan and Sithara Doriasamy. This is also an occasion to thank the three successive associate directors at ISAS to whom I have been in debt for their kind help and friendship: Hernaikh Singh, Dr Amitendu Palit, and Johnson Paul. To the administrative staff, a very heartfelt thanks. The list is too long to mention all the good folk at ISAS.

This book is also dedicated to a remarkable Pakistani army officer:

Brigadier (Retd.) Yasub Ali Dogar. He read all my chapters and made extensive comments on several drafts of the book. In doing so, he did not hesitate to disagree with me on many of my assertions but, as a true gentleman, he understood and graciously respected that I, as the author, had the last word on what I wrote and argued for. He also greatly helped me with key interviews with retired army officers. Each visit to Pakistan has meant getting to know him and his family ever more.

I am in great debt to two more officers. Colonel (Retd.) Aslam Cheema is the younger brother of my best friend in Stockholm, Riaz Cheema. Over the years, I have met Colonel Cheema whenever he visited Stockholm and, in 2008, I enjoyed his hospitality when I came to Rawalpindi to conduct interviews with military personnel. Those interviews have been vital to this study. Major (Retd.) Agha Humayun Amin and I became friends through my weekly columns in the Pakistani print media. He has also gone out of his way with great help whenever needed. I have also drawn on his research on the Pakistan Army.

I am also greatly in debt to my colleague and dear friend, Associate Professor Kjell Engelbrekt at the Swedish National Defence College, Stockholm, and the Department of Political Science, Stockholm University. He is a gifted scholar of international relations as well as security issues. He read the theoretical argument I had set forth in the first chapter and suggested improvements. I have incorporated them in the text with great joy.

My very sincere thanks to all those retired Pakistani military officers and civil servants who kindly granted me interviews. Such a study would be impossible without their cooperation. I found many of them men of great charm and grace and holders of quite diverse views. In this regard, I must especially mention former COAS General Jehangir Karamat, Lieutenant General (Retd.) Naseer Akhtar, Lieutenant General (Retd.) Asad Durrani, and Major General (Retd.) Mahmud Ali Durrani. I got to know them on a personal level and, with some of them, I communicated from time to time via email as well.

Thanks are also due to Indian military officers and security and defence experts who very willingly agreed to talk to me. I am especially grateful to Brigadier (Retd.) Vijai Nair who arranged some key interviews for me. Equally, during July 2009, I spent several weeks in Washington DC where I could talk to leading American experts on Pakistan and South Asia. Some of them wanted to remain anonymous. The Pakistani community in Washington DC was very helpful indeed. I especially acknowledge the kind favours of Ahmed Sheikh, Syed Mowahid Hussain Shah, Safir Rammah, Babar and Noreen Amjad, and Wajid Ali Syed, Salim Mehwar, Malik Hafeez Ahmad, and Khawar Rizvi. In Lahore, thanks are due to Haroon and Shireen Shah, and Dr Hassan Amir Shah and Rukhsana Shah I acknowledge, with thanks, permission given by Shuja Nawaz to use pictures of Pakistani generals who became rulers of Pakistan from his book, Crossed Swords (2008). He, in turn, borrowed the pictures from the Pakistan Army's Inter-Services Public Relations (ISPR).

During all these years, Meliha and our boys, Sahir and Selim, have gracefully accepted that by devoting my time to research I have not neglected them too much, and that my love for them remains my greatest joy and asset.

Index